The
Making
of a Story

The
Making
of a Story

A NORTON GUIDE TO CREATIVE WRITING

Alice LaPlante

W. W. Norton & Company
New York • London

For information about permission to reproduce selections
from this book, write to Permissions,
W. W. Norton & Company, Inc., 500 Fifth Avenue,
New York, NY 10110

Manufacturing by R.R. Donnelley, Bloomsburg Division
Book design by Charlotte Staub
Production manager: Julia Druskin

Library of Congress Cataloging-in-Publication Data

LaPlante, Alice, 1958–
The making of a story : a Norton guide to creative writing / Alice
LaPlante. — 1st ed.
p. cm.
Includes bibliographical references and index.
ISBN 978-0-393-06164-2 (hardcover)
1. English language—Rhetoric—Handbooks, manuals, etc.
2. English language—Style—Handbooks, manuals, etc.
3. Creative writing—Handbooks, manuals, etc.
4. Report writing—Handbooks, manuals, etc. I. Title.
PE1408.L31887 2007
808'.042—dc22
2007008030

W. W. Norton & Company, Inc.
500 Fifth Avenue, New York, N.Y. 10110
www.wwnorton.com

W. W. Norton & Company Ltd.
Castle House, 75/76 Wells Street, London W1T 3QT

1 2 3 4 5 6 7 8 9 0

Though this be madness,
yet there is method in't.

—*Hamlet* (Act 2, Scene 2)

For Sarah,
who continues to teach me
everything I need to know

Contents

CHAPTER

6. Who's Telling This Story, Anyway? 258

CHAPTER
9. The Plot Thickens 375

CHAPTER
10. Recognizable People 418

CHAPTER

13. Learning to Fail Better 542

Acknowledgments

It would be impossible to thank everyone who has helped in the making of this book, but special thanks go to Sarah Seidner, David Renton, Rich Seidner, Lovinda Beale, Mary Petrosky, Liza Julian, Christie Cochrell, Teresa Heger, Jan Ellison, Ann Packer, Susan Weinberg, Clare LaPlante, Maxine Chernoff, Michelle Carter, and all the faculty in the Creative Writing Department at San Francisco State University, the faculty and staff at Stanford University's Creative Writing Department, especially Nancy Huddleston Packer and John L'Heureux, and all my students who have so graced me with their presence over the years. I am, as always, eternally grateful to my agent, Arielle Eckstut, and her boss, James Levine, of the Levine-Greenberg Literary Agency. And this book could never have come into being without the incomparable editorial team at W. W. Norton, including Jill Bialosky, Nancy Rodwan, and Evan Carver.

The
Making
of a Story

CHAPTER ONE

What Is This Thing Called Creative Writing?

And how do you get started without feeling overwhelmed?

Part 1: THE BASICS

Getting Started

So you want to write. Perhaps you want to try short stories, or have a dream to write a novel or to generate personal essays about your family. Perhaps you have some ideas; perhaps you merely have an inexplicable urge to write *something*. You must have a certain amount of motivation, because you've acquired this book, or are enrolled in a class, or are participating in a writers' group. You're *here*, after all. But you don't know where to start, and you may not even be certain whether you want to write fiction or nonfiction. You may worry that you don't have enough experience. You don't know what a short story is, can't imagine starting a novel, or feel you lack the skills to embark on writing a piece of creative nonfiction.

This book is designed to help. In it, you'll be walked through all aspects of the creative process, from generating the kind of exciting ideas that spark the beginnings of novels, short stories, and personal essays; to learning and practicing all aspects of craft; to acquiring revision techniques to use once you have finished the first draft of a story, chapter, or essay.

In Part 1 of this chapter we'll talk about the basic definitions of fiction and nonfiction, and provide insight into some of the key characteristics that make up compelling creative writing. Part 2 will give you some exercises to prompt fresh and original work that may be the germs of good ideas for stories or essays. Included here (and in similar sections throughout the book) are student samples, so you can get ideas on how to complete the exercises. Part 3 gives you a contemporary story and an essay to read that underscore all we've talked about in this chapter.

Reconciling the Method with the Madness

The first question that we have to address in this book is a very basic one: Can writing be taught? With all the creative writing instruction going on in classes and books, are we producing better writers? Doing a good job of helping writers come into their own? The answer is both yes and no.

It's important to understand that there are two aspects to creating truly compelling writing. As the book's epigraph (from William Shakespeare's *Hamlet*) states, what's needed is both method *and* madness. The method is what can be learned in an academically rigorous, systematic manner. In many ways, writing is a craft, like woodworking, say, or painting, and craft can be acquired, practiced, mastered. Just as artists learn how to work with the human form or experiment with color, beginning writers can learn about imagery, dialogue, narrative, and scene-building. You can master how to characterize people (real or imagined) on the page. You can take apart story structure, learn how to build a solid personal essay.

But then there's the madness part—what is more frequently called the inspiration. "The chief enemy of creativity is good sense," said the painter Pablo Picasso, and that leaves us, as writers, in a quandary. How can we simultaneously be creative—wild, free, chaotic—and yet have sufficient presence of mind to shape all the lovely raw messy material that bubbles inside us into something coherent? How do we reconcile the method with the madness?

Many students of writing simply don't. At one end of the spectrum are those writers who work hard at mastering craft, and turn out exquisitely crafted stories or essays—which are utterly dead and boring. At the other end of the spectrum are the writers who generate exciting and profound initial drafts—but have no control, no way of shaping them into something that can speak to others.

A contemporary way of talking about this dichotomy between craft and inspiration is by referring to right-brain and left-brain capabilities. According to this theory of how the brain works, its two different sides control two different modes of thinking. Left brain: logical, sequential, rational. Right brain: random, intuitive, holistic. In today's creative writing workshops (which are currently how creative writing is taught in most colleges and universities) we are largely using our left-brain, analytical skills to read and take apart a story or poem or creative essay while trying to figure out why it does or doesn't work. We're being trained to favor our left brains over our right brains, something that can be deadly in the creative process—especially when trying to generate new material.

Of course, some people have no trouble getting the left brain and right brain to work together harmoniously. But one very common thing that happens after you have begun to acquire some craft knowledge (and the vocabulary that goes with it) is that you find it hard to turn your analytical "editor" (the one that lives in your left brain) off when you are trying to generate new material. The sad fact of the matter is, the more you know, the more likely you are to censor yourself at the very time that you should be giving yourself the most creative leeway. Unfortunately, the workshop method of teaching creative writing has no way of helping people access their deepest and most profound material.

So, what to do about this? Can the ability to tune into our private material be taught? Well, not taught exactly. But certainly nurtured. And within a classroom setting, no less. Writing teachers have known for decades that certain exercises, prompts, and "constraints" seem to take beginning writers out of themselves and push them toward writing truly inspired things. The exercises at the end of each chapter of this book are designed to help you put aside your "logical" sense and immerse yourself in the intuitive creative process. That you may then take these raw, early pieces and shape them into something meaningful is part of the craft process. So the whole thing comes full circle. Craft and creativity. Method and madness.

Are some people more talented than others? Sure. Does it come easier to some than to others? You bet. But in my years of teaching I have seen creative breakthroughs time and again that have astounded and humbled me. Perseverance, dedication, and just plain obstinacy count for more than you can possibly imagine. I happen to believe that everyone has *something* within them to express; it's just a question of helping them discover what that is by giving them the *process* tools to discover it, and the *craft* tools to express it coherently.

Some Basic Definitions

The word "fiction" comes from the Latin *fictio*, the act of fashioning, and from Latin *fingere*, to shape, fashion, "feign." *Merriam-Webster's Collegiate Dictionary* says it is "something invented by the imagination"; to "assert as if true" something that is created from the imagination.

So fiction is something made up—not factual. We *assert as if true* something that is not factually real in order to *make* it true. "Poetry lies its way to the truth," said John Ciardi, the American poet. Similarly, Picasso (who is one of the keenest commentators on the creative process) said, "Art is a lie that makes us realize the truth."

So if you want to write fiction, you are someone who thinks that you can speak the truth primarily through lying. Good. Then the purpose of this book is to teach you how to be the best liar you can be.

Notice that we are not talking about conflict–crisis–resolution, or epiphanies, character changing, or other so-called "requirements" that make a story a story or a novel a novel. We are simply rendering on the page something we are asserting to be true, even if it isn't.

Creative Nonfiction: A Working Definition

Nonfiction should be easy to define, you might think. As the opposite of fiction, the implication is that you are writing from facts, you are not making anything up—or embellishing, or embroidering, or lying in any way. *Creative* nonfiction is generally agreed to be nonfiction that is rendered using fictional techniques: dialogue, and narrative, and imagery, and other elements that are leveraged to evoke a certain emotional response. Indeed, much creative nonfiction reads like fiction. Peruse *This Boy's Life* by Tobias Wolff, or *The Liar's Club* by Mary Karr, or *Patrimony* by Philip Roth, and it's like reading a good novel. Likewise, the long articles in *The New Yorker* often read like stories, with narrative threads running through them that can be followed the way plots of stories are followed (some people call this literary journalism).

And increasingly there is a blurred line between fiction and creative nonfiction. You might wonder yourself, if you write from personal experiences, at what point does the minor embellishment or exaggeration that you do because it makes the story "better" turn your piece from memoir to fiction? At what point, when re-creating conversations that you couldn't possibly remember word for word, are you beginning to make things up whole cloth? We even have books that are called "autobiographical fiction," or books that writers say are "emotionally" autobiographical even if not factually true. (As Flaubert said about the character in his most famous book, "*Madame Bovary, ç'est moi.*" Or, "Madame Bovary is me.")

Of course, some of the best stories written are inspired by true events: events in a writer's life, stories they've heard, something they've read in a newspaper. So why is this fiction, if its source is (at some level) factual? Some would argue that every time you change a story slightly to make it a "better story," every time you make up a little white lie in order to avoid embarrassing or exposing your mother or your partner, you are creating a fiction. Others would say that the very act of writing something down transforms it—in other words, that every experience gets fictionalized simply through the transformation that naturally takes place during the creative process.

For now, we won't worry about any of that. Instead, beginning in Chapter 2, you're first going to simply discover what kind of material is inside you. You can later decide how to use it, and whether to call it fiction or creative nonfiction.

Writing That Is Surprising Yet Convincing

Okay, so we've made a valiant attempt to define fiction and creative nonfiction. So what is *good* fiction and creative nonfiction writing? Or, to ask a less difficult question, what makes something worth reading? One answer—an answer we will turn to time and time again in this book—is to paraphrase E. M. Forster, from his landmark book *Aspects of the Novel*, and say that a characteristic of good writing is that it is *surprising yet convincing*.

Notice the coupling of these two words: *surprising*—something happens that surprises us in some way, impresses us with its unexpectedness or freshness. Equally important, we are *convinced* by the surprise: it is not gratuitously startling; we get a jolt, and then a sense of the rightness of it all.

This is true of all great or even very good literature. To demonstrate this quality of being surprising yet convincing, here's a poem by Elizabeth Bishop, "Letter to NY (for Louise Crane)":

> In your next letter I wish you'd say
> where you are going and what you are doing;
> how are the plays, and after the plays
> what other pleasures you're pursuing:

This first stanza starts out innocuously enough—someone is writing a letter to a loved one asking how the trip is going.

> taking cabs in the middle of the night,
> driving as if to save your soul
> where the road goes round and round the park
> and the meter glares like a moral owl,

Now here things get a little odd. We're surprised by some of the declarations that come up in this second stanza. The writer of the letter starts imagining the things that are happening to the traveler, and they seem rather . . . well . . . not pleasant. Driving as if to save your soul? The meter glaring like a moral owl? So the letter writer isn't just missing the person, or eager for news; there's a sense of judgment—or perhaps of wishing to believe that the traveler is not necessarily having a carefree good time. The poem continues in this vein:

> and the trees look so queer and green
>   standing alone in big black caves
> and suddenly you're in a different place
> where everything seems to happen in waves,
>
> and most of the jokes you just can't catch,
>   like dirty words rubbed off a slate,
> and the songs are loud but somehow dim
>   and it gets so terribly late,
>
> and coming out of the brownstone house
>   to the gray sidewalk, the watered street,
> one side of the buildings rises with the sun
>   like a glistening field of wheat.
>
>   —Wheat, not oats, dear. I'm afraid
> if it's wheat it's none of your sowing,
>   nevertheless I'd like to know
> what you are doing and where you are going.

The odd, distressing images then fade into the calming imagery of the morning (a brief calm) before the final, almost shocking stanza, with its patronizing accusation that sowing wild oats would be none of "your" doing. And we realize that this is *not* a typical letter to a loved one, but almost a taunt, with hints of cruelty (that "dear" in the last stanza stings) and barely suppressed rancor.

So, far from having a typical letter from a loved one, we get something filled with strange emotions and undercurrents that are unsettling, even alarming. The poem keeps surprising us—yet we are also convinced by this rendering. We believe (very much) in these two women, and in the emotionally intense but ambivalent relationship that they have with each other.

Resisting Paraphrase

Flannery O'Connor said that a good story "resisted paraphrase," by which she meant that a simple summary of a plot or story line would not have the same emotional impact as the whole story. We'll add creative nonfiction to this, too. To understand what she means, think about trying to paraphrase, or describe, a Chopin sonata without actually playing any music. It simply cannot be done. The music stands for itself. Nothing can substitute for it with the same effect—not the notes on the page, not a verbal description of the melody and harmony, not even a playing of a simplified version of the main theme. This is also true of the kind of fiction and creative nonfiction we are trying to write: simply stating what the piece "is about" should not be able to convey the complexity and subtlety of the piece as a whole. Some essential mystery, or emotional subtlety, will be lost in the paraphrase.

Take the example of the poem we just read: How could you paraphrase that? It would be impossible. A letter to a loved one? Not exactly. A letter to a scorned one? No, not that either.

Here are some examples of passages from stories that resist paraphrase:

> "Well," Jewel says, "you can quit now, if you got a-plenty."
>
> Inside the barn Jewel slides running to the ground before the horse stops. The horse enters the stall, Jewel following. Without looking back the horse kicks at him, slamming a single hoof into the wall with a pistol-like report. Jewel kicks him in the stomach; the horse arches his neck back, crop-toothed; Jewel strikes him across the face with his fist and slides on to the trough and mounts upon it. Clinging to the hay-rack he lowers his head and peers out across the stall tops and through the doorway. The path is empty; from here he cannot even hear Cash sawing. He reaches up and drags down hay in hurried armsful and crams it into the rack.
>
> "Eat," he says. "Get the goddamn stuff out of sight while you got a chance, you pussel-gutted bastard. You sweet son of a bitch," he says.

How does this (from *As I Lay Dying* by William Faulkner) resist paraphrase? It's not *just* a boy being cruel to a horse. Yes, he is cruel, even sadistic—we get the impression that the violence to the horse is gratuitous, not necessary to keep the horse in line—but then he feeds the horse, apparently against the will of the caretaker, and calls him a "sweet" son of a bitch. Affection and violence are married together in a surprising yet convincing way.

> The summer before, I pegged Ysrael with a rock and the way it bounced off his back, I knew I'd clocked a shoulderblade.
>
> You did it! You fucking did it! the other boys yelled.
>
> He'd been running from us and he arched in pain and one of the other boys nearly caught him but he recovered and took off. He's faster than a mongoose, someone said, but in truth he was faster even than that. We

laughed and went back to our baseball game and forgot him until he came to town again and then we dropped what we were doing and chased him, howling. Show us your face. Let's see it just once.

Again, in "Ysrael" by Junot Díaz, it is more than just a group of children being cruel to a disfigured boy; they also admire him ("but in truth he was even faster than that") and they are fascinated by him (they "dropped what we were doing") enough to make him the center of attention when he shows up.

> In December Ennis married Alma Beers and had her pregnant by mid-January. He picked up a few short-lived ranch jobs, then settled in as a wrangler on the old Elwood Hi-Top place north of Lost Cabin in Washakie County. He was still working there in September when Alma Jr., as he called his daughter, was born and their bedroom was full of the smell of old blood and milk and baby shit, and the sounds were of squalling and sucking and Alma's sleepy groans, all reassuring of fecundity and life's continuance to one who worked with livestock.

This passage, from Annie Proulx's "Brokeback Mountain," captures the ambiguous emotions a man experiences as he settles down and starts a family with someone who is most definitely not the love of his life. Nevertheless, we see how these events center him around the things of this earth. Could you paraphrase this and get the same effect? What would you say: "A man settles down"? "A cowboy has his first child"? Neither of these summaries—or any other—can do it justice. The passage stands for itself.

Creative Nonfiction: Capturing What Has Eluded Capture

In creative nonfiction the same precepts apply. We always want to try to render on the page those things—true, in this case—that elude easy summation, or paraphrase. Just read the following passage (from "Redneck Secrets" by William Kittredge) to see this beautifully dramatized:

> Back in the late '40s, when I was getting close to graduating from high school, they used to stage Saturday night prizefights down in the Veterans Auditorium. Not boring matches but prizefights, a name which rings in the ear something like *cockfight*. One night the two main-event fighters, always heavyweights, were some hulking Indian and a white farmer from a little dairy-farm community.
> The Indian, I recall, had the word "Mother" carved on his hairless chest. Not tattooed, but carved in the flesh with a blade, so the scar tissue spelled out the word in livid welts. The white farmer looked soft and his body was alabaster, pure white, except for his wrists and neck, which were dark, burned-in-

the-fields red, burnished red. While they hammered at each other we hooted from the stands like gibbons, rooting for our favorites on strictly territorial and racial grounds, and in the end were all disappointed. The white farmer went down like thunder about three times, blood snorting from his nose in a delicate spray and decorating his whiteness like in, say, the movies. The Indian simply retreated to his corner and refused to go on. It didn't make sense.

We screeched and stomped, but the Indian just stood there looking at the bleeding white man, and the white man cleared his head and looked at the Indian, and then they both shook their heads at one another, as if acknowledging some private news they had just learned to share. They both climbed out of the ring and together made their way up the aisle. Walked away.

In this passage, just as in the fiction excerpts, the writing resists paraphrase. "Boxing is cruel"? No, that doesn't catch it. "Victims pull together"? No, that doesn't do it either. The true meaning of the passage can only be grasped by reading the passage. No weak substitution summarizing the actual words will do. Just because the events depicted are true doesn't change this most basic requirement of good writing.

On Sentiment and Sentimentality

By being both surprising and convincing, and by choosing to render things that resist easy summary, we may, if we're lucky, avoid those twin hobgoblins of creative writers: sentimentality and melodrama. Now, these words are bandied about frequently in writing classes and workshops, so let's first define our terms precisely so we know what we are talking about when we use them.

MELODRAMATIC: When a work is characterized by extravagant theatricality, and by the predominance of plot and physical action over characterization. In other words, the reader's emotions are evoked through the sensational nature of events and/or actions making up the plot rather than through more subtle elements, such as characterization. The word "melodrama" comes from early dramatic pantomimes, when action was staged to music, usually without any dialogue at all; naturally, in such cases, subtlety of character was often lost in favor of dramatic physicality.

SENTIMENTAL: Falsely emotional in a maudlin way. Extravagant or affected feeling or emotion. When a work exhibits an *excess* of emotion that doesn't feel "earned" by the piece. When a piece is imbued with sentiment (feeling) *independent of a meaningful context.*

That is, the writer is depending on a reader's stock emotional response derived from *general* cultural or human experience, rather than creating an exact and believable context for that response within the world of the story.

We tend to associate the word "sentimental" with things that are precious, mawkish: squishy, "soft" subjects such as babies and kittens and whatnot. But that's only a small part of what can be sentimental. Something is sentimental if it attempts to induce an emotional response in a reader that exceeds what the situation warrants. And this can happen with so-called "hard" subjects like war or death as much as with ruminations on love and ducklings and flowers.

The best way to describe "sentimental" is by use of example, and the best examples come from advertisements—certainly print, but especially television. These advertisements are trying, deliberately, to push our buttons, to provoke an emotional response with a thirty- or sixty-second video clip. Advertisements for camera equipment fall into this category, for example, by tapping into our fear that life is passing us by and that we need to capture precious moments on film (or, increasingly, in electronic form) in order to remember them. Telephone companies mine our fears similarly with ads of grown children calling their aged mothers or "reaching out and touching someone." What these advertisements *don't* want is complexity: they don't want us to think that many moments of family life can be painful or tedious or frustrating; they don't want us to think that we can have conflicting feelings about calling our mothers—that they can impose guilt on us, that we can sense their loneliness which brings out our own fears of mortality, etc. These advertisements are after the knee-jerk responses that are already fully prepared in our minds.

> NOTE: Sentiment is not bad. Sentiment is variously defined as "refined feeling"; "delicate sensing of emotion"; "an idea colored by emotion." If we don't strive for true sentiment, we will never achieve truly moving work. But if a piece is *sentimental*, this basic "good" thing has been overextended or misapplied.

As I. M. Richards says in *Practical Criticism*:

> A response is sentimental when, either through the over-persistence of tendencies or through the interaction of sentiments, *it is inappropriate to the situation that calls it forth* [emphasis mine]. What is bad in these sentimental responses is their confinement to one stereotyped, unrepresentative aspect of the prompting situation . . .

In other words, marriages and births are always happy, funerals are sad, old people are lonely and waiting at home for phone calls. These are stereotyped and *unrepresentative* depictions in that they do not represent the range of emotion and feeling and complexity that such situations frequently, if not always, evoke. We all know of births and deaths that conjure up more ambiguous emotions for people: people reluctant, in their hearts, to become parents, people who are in certain ways relieved that someone has finally died.

Sentimental writing tends to trigger what Richards calls "stock responses" in the reader. As he goes on to say:

> [Stock responses] have their opportunity whenever a poem invokes views and emotions already fully prepared in the reader's mind, *so that what happens is more of the reader's doing than the poet's* [emphasis mine]. The button is pressed, and then the author's work is done, for immediately the record starts playing in quasi- (or total) independence of the poem which is supposed to be its origin or instrument.

William Shakespeare was a master of avoiding the sentimental. Here, in one of his sonnets, he actually thumbs his nose at sentimental notions of love and beauty:

> My mistress' eyes are nothing like the sun;
>   Coral is far more red than her lips' red;
> If snow be white, why then her breasts are dun;
> If hairs be wires, black wires grow on her head.
>   I have seen roses damask'd, red and white,
>   But no such roses see I in her cheeks,
> And in some perfumes is there more delight
> Than in the breath that from my mistress reeks.
>   I love to hear her speak, yet well I know
> That music hath a far more pleasing sound;
>   I grant I never saw a goddess go,
> My mistress when she walks treads on the ground.
>   And yet, by heaven, I think my love as rare
>   As any she belied with false compare.

This poem contradicts our stock responses. That is, the piece doesn't let us fall back on sentimental or simplistic or prepackaged notions of love or romance; rather, it says that his love for his mistress confounds all the usual expectations. We are adamantly pushed away from any sentimental interpretation of this love song by its bold declarations of all the "negative" qualities of the beloved.

And sentimentality can infest the opposite end of the spectrum from treacly sweetness. Rather than trying to make everything too "nice," it can also be found in writing that represents things as stereotypically bleak or sordid. Again from I. M. Richards's *Practical Criticism*:

> The man, in reaction to the commoner naive forms of sentimentality, prides himself upon his hard-headedness and hard-heartedness, his hard-boiledness generally, and who seeks out or invents aspects with a bitter or squalid character, for no better reason than this, is only displaying a more sophisticated form of sentimentality . . .

So the student who decides "No sentimentality for me!" and puts her characters in a trailer park, shouting at each other, drinking whiskey and generally living a life of degradation and emotional ruin, can be making exactly the same mistake as the student who writes chirpily about his pet cat: it is still narrow, nonrepresentative, stereotypical, and lacking complexity.

Some writers are so afraid of being called sentimental that they fail to take emotional risks with their pieces—they shut them down and fail to push them to the limit. Yet to avoid real emotion is to avoid the reason that most of us write to begin with: to put some complex, urgent emotion down on the page.

Here's a passage that risks sentimentality because it deals with death; it's a deathbed scene, in fact, between a mother and her two sons. See how Larry McMurty, in *Terms of Endearment*, handles it:

> "First of all, troops, you both need a haircut," Emma said. "Don't let your bangs get so long. You have beautiful eyes and very nice faces and I want people to see them. I don't care how long it gets in back, just keep it out of your eyes, please."
>
> "That's not important, that's just a matter of opinion," Tommy said. "Are you getting well?"
>
> "No," Emma said. "I have a million cancers. I can't get well."
>
> "Oh, I don't know what to do," Teddy said.
>
> "Well, both of you better make some friends," Emma said. "I'm sorry about this, but I can't help it. I can't talk to you too much longer either, or I'll get too upset. Fortunately we had ten or twelve years and we did a lot of talking, and that's more than a lot of people get. Make some friends and be good to them. Don't be afraid of girls, either."
>
> "We're not afraid of girls," Tommy said. "What makes you think that?"
>
> "You might get to be later," Emma said.
>
> "I doubt it," Tommy said, very tense.
>
> When they came to hug her, Teddy fell apart and Tommy remained stiff.
>
> "Tommy, be sweet," Emma said. "Be sweet, please. Don't keep pretending you dislike me. That's silly."
>
> "I *like* you," Tommy said, shrugging tightly.

"I know that, but for the last year or two you've been pretending you hate me," Emma said. "I know I love you more than anybody in the world except your brother and sister, and I'm not going to be around long enough to change my mind about you. But you're going to live a long time, and in a year or two when I'm not around to irritate you you're going to change your mind and remember that I read you a lot of stories and made you a lot of milkshakes and allowed you to goof off a lot when I could have been forcing you to mow the lawn."

Both boys looked away, shocked that their mother was saying these things.

"In other words, you're going to remember that you love me," Emma said. "I imagine you'll wish you could tell me that you've changed your mind, but you won't be able to, so I'm telling you now I already know you love me, just so you won't be in doubt about that later. Okay?"

"Okay," Tommy said quickly, a little gratefully.

Talk about a situation rife with pitfalls of sentimentality! A dying mother on her deathbed, talking to her sons for the last time. Yet McMurty avoids giving us any "expected" or overly familiar dialogue. He grounds us thoroughly in the world of the story, in the characters and their relationships, and we pull through this difficult moment relieved—and infinitely moved.

Our First Job as Writers: To Notice

How do we manage to write things that are neither melodramatic nor sentimental? Simple. By noticing things. *Really* noticing things. That is our first job.

Whether you realize it or not, you've always noticed. There have always been things that caught your attention, piqued your interest, or otherwise caused you to pay closer attention to something than perhaps someone else would. Indeed, the very individual nature of noticing is your greatest strength as a writer.

If you took a walk around your town with a friend, you would have, in effect, two different experiences. You'd remember different things about the walk, about what you saw, what you talked about, what happened. One of you might comment on the cold while the other might note the homeless person on the corner of your block. One of you might have been looking at the gardens of the houses you walked past, or at the merchandise in the shop windows, while the other scrutinized people's faces. There's no right or wrong, no "correct" thing to have noticed, you're just making observations based on your individual experience of the walk.

Now, notice what you noticed. No, go further: tell yourself the audacious thing that because you noticed it, it matters. That man you noticed on the corner of 5th and Vine? The one with the black umbrella and navy overcoat? You noticed him. You noticed the way he was standing, the expression on his face—sad? no, wistful—and the remarkable orderliness of his dress. Okay, so you noticed that. It's a beginning.

Because here's the important thing: creative work comes from noticing. You are being given a warning, an intimation of something, and that something is the creative urge, sometimes buried quite deep in your subconscious, telling you that something matters, there's information and *intelligence* there to be considered, material to uncover there, memories and associations to explore.

Here is a passage that illustrates this point wonderfully well. In "Good bye to Berlin," Christopher Isherwood talks about his neighborhood in prewar Berlin, and about *noticing*:

> From my window, the deep solemn massive street. Cellar-shops where the lamps burn all day, under the shadow of top-heavy balconied façades, dirty plaster frontages embossed with scroll-work and heraldic devices. The whole district is like this: street leading into street of houses like shabby monumental safes crammed with the tarnished valuables and second-hand furniture of a bankrupt middle class.
>
> I am a camera with its shutter open, quite passive, recording, not thinking. Recording the man shaving at the window opposite and the woman in the kimono washing her hair. Some day, all this will have to be developed, carefully printed, fixed.

Your first job then, is to turn your "camera" on, to notice as you walk. As the passage states, you can worry about "developing" it later. All that matters is that the camera is on.

Avoiding the "Writerly" Voice

Something happens sometimes when we sit down to write. We want what we write to be Important, we want it to Matter, and so we can get pompous. We can sound like we're making proclamations instead of observations. Or, we can try so hard to make the language sound sophisticated that it comes off flowery and overwrought. I've often scrawled on students' early papers: "This feels too 'written.'"

What do I mean by that? Consider the following as an example of what *not* to do, from a letter that Anton Chekhov wrote to the novelist Maxim Gorki:

It is intelligible when I write, "The man sat down on the grass"; it is intelligible because it is clear and does not impede the reader's attention. Conversely, I will be unintelligible and tax the reader's brain if I write: "The tall, narrow-chested man of average build, who had a short, red beard, sat down on the green grass, already trampled by passersby; sat down noiselessly, timidly, and fearfully glancing around him." One's brain cannot grasp this at once, yet fiction must be grasped at once, on the spot.

One of the things that can be hardest for beginning fiction writers to grasp is that they must develop a voice that is unique, and natural to them. One of your main jobs, throughout your writing life (it doesn't necessarily come easy, or soon, or ever stop changing) is to discover and/or develop that voice. It might not be the same as your speaking voice. It is the unique way you have of expressing yourself in the written word, and the more straightforward and honest you are in the words and sentences you put on the page, the more your voice will shine through. For the most part, this means forgetting about using big words, complex sentence structures, ornate language, *unless that comes naturally to you*. You may be a natural user of metaphor, or have a strong sense of imagery. Good. Great. Use your gifts. But one of the operative words is "honest." We try to be honest not just in what we say (even if we are lying through fiction) but in *how* we say it.

The goal is to find *your* voice, the voice that isn't like everyone else's. And this is a very difficult thing to do, for the plain reason that we have mostly spent our lives trying to fit in. Mostly, we don't want to be noticed because we're different. We want to make sure that we dress appropriately, speak appropriately, act appropriately. Well, creative writing is the one area where you don't want to be "appropriate." Appropriate is for dinner parties. This is the place where the things that make you weird, the things about yourself that you *know* are different and even difficult, count the most.

In the following lovely passage from Muriel Spark's novel *A Far Cry from Kensington*, the narrator gives some very wise advice about writing.

"You are writing a letter to a friend," was the sort of thing I used to say. "And this is a dear and close friend, real—or better—invented in your mind like a fixation. Write privately, not publicly; without fear or timidity, right to the end of the letter, as if it was never going to be published, so that your true friend will read it over and over, and then want more enchanting letters from you. Now, you are not writing about the relationship between your friend and yourself; you take that for granted. You are only confiding an experience that you think only he will enjoy reading. What you have to say will come out more spontaneously and honestly than if you are thinking of numerous readers. Before starting the letter rehearse in your mind what you are going to tell; something interesting, your story. But don't rehearse too much, the story will develop as you go along, especially if you write to a special friend, man or woman, to make them smile or laugh or cry, or anything you like so long as you know it will interest. Remember not to think of the reading public, it will put you off."

Part 2: EXERCISES

The following exercises are meant to be used to supplement the text and readings so that you can practice the underlying concepts presented in this chapter. These exercises can be done in the classroom, assigned as homework, or performed independently of a formal class.

Especially designed to help you "let go" and stop thinking logically, these prompts should open things up emotionally for you as a natural part of the process.

Exercise 1: "I Don't Know Why I Remember ..."

Goal: To pinpoint some previously unexplored material that remains "hot" for you in some important emotional way.

What to do: 1. "Scan" back over your life and think of things that have stuck in your mind, but for no obvious reason. (No births or deaths or other "important" moments, please. Go for the small ones.)

2. Render them precisely on the page using concrete details, beginning each one with the phrase, "I don't know why I remember."

3. Don't try to explain why they stuck with you, or interpret the meaning of them. Just put your reader *there*.

Here's an example of how to do this exercise from student Steven Thomas:

I don't know why I remember going fishing with my father. He'd come over to the apartment where my mother and I were living since the divorce, bringing a cup of coffee sweetened to the point of making me choke when I sipped it. Dawn would still be an hour or so away, but he insisted on getting started early because that's when the fish would bite, he said. We'd drive from the grimy streets of Oakland out through the lush rolling hills of Alamo and Walnut Creek, and into the dry dusty Sacramento valley where there existed a man-made reservoir. The water was a dull grey reflecting the dirty earth that rose, raw and bleak, from its edges. We'd join the band of early fishermen who were always there, standing on the edge of the gravelly beach, waiting patiently with their lines in the water. Most of them were drinking beer even though it was so early, crushing the cans and throwing them into a pile when they were emptied. My dad would drink two beers during the four hours we would fish, never more, never less. We never caught anything. As far as I remember, no one did. But we stood there, in wordless camaraderie, Saturday after Saturday, for the two long years until my father moved to Arizona without me.

Exercise 2: I Am a Camera

Goal: To notice what you notice—and to render it without trying to explain or interpret it.

What to do: 1. In the manner of Christopher Isherwood's famous passage (see page 36), turn on your "camera" (the part of your brain that notices things).

2. Take a walk or go someplace where you can have a rich sensory experience—preferably someplace with other people.

3. Record everything precisely on the page, using as many senses as possible.

4. Don't try to interpret it, or tell us what it means; everything will get "developed" and "fixed" later. For now, just record.

Student Janis Turin turned out the following prose in response to this exercise:

As the No. 17 bus passes by the corner of Mission and 17th, an elderly man carrying a brown paper bag filled with groceries trips. A tattooed young man with pink hair rushes over to help. The food of babies: Cheerios, rice cereal, tiny jars of apricot and pears and fruits. The sky grows dim as the bus heaves its way down the crowded street. Opposite me is one of the most beautiful girls I have ever seen. Her heavy hair, dyed a dead black, hangs in braids down her shoulders. She has white skin and the most luminous neck I have ever seen. She is carrying nothing: not a backpack, purse, briefcase. She is dressed casually except for her high heels, absurdly high stiletto heels.

The following response was written by student Christie Cochrell:

The hospital. The dirty carpet in the hospital elevator. The whole institution stank of soap and urine and looked overly clean and shabby at the same

time, and I don't know why that little bit of mud on the orange carpet bothered me so much. But it did. Every day, every day I'd go to the fifth floor, riding with all of the happy grandmas and aunties and new daddies carrying
stuffed toys and pink or blue flower bouquets and when they would get off
on the third floor maternity wing I would be left alone—alone or with one or
two other silent souls who were making the longer and darker and ever so
much heavier journey with me to the fifth floor—and every day I'd look
down and notice in the few moments between third and fifth, between the
level of birth and the floor of departure—every day I'd notice those same
damn mud stains made by some visitor's shoes long ago. I would think of
the mud those shoes had walked through in some past wet season, mud that
had been rain-soaked and probably cold, and I thought of how the person
who wore those shoes must have greeted and hugged and encouraged the
patient at the end of this elevator's ride. I thought of the mud on those shoes
and the murky, brown trail it left behind, and I wondered if that was all that
was left, all that was left to remember of that day, of that owner of dirty
shoes or his love for the one whom he had come to visit. I thought of the
ashes-to-ashes, dust-to-dust of that damn dried mud stain and I wondered
why no one ever cleaned out that germ-infested metal cage, that moving
basket of human contagion.

I wondered about that and other things as the little cell moved up and
then the doors would slide open. I'd walk off the elevator platform onto the
relative terra firma of the fifth floor and then I would forget the mud and the
dirt and the bacteria. I would step off of the elevator and be confronted with
all of the other things that I really don't want to remember, like *how much
longer* and *no extreme measures* and *how can I ever go on after this?*

Part 3: READING AS A WRITER

On Keeping a Notebook

JOAN DIDION

"'That woman Estelle,'" the note reads, "'is partly the reason why
George Sharp and I are separated today.' *Dirty crepe-de-Chine wrapper, hotel
bar, Wilmington RR, 9:45 a.m. August Monday morning.*"

Since the note is in my notebook, it presumably has some meaning to
me. I study it for a long while. At first I have only the most general notion
of what I was doing on an August Monday morning in the bar of the hotel
across from the Pennsylvania Railroad station in Wilmington, Delaware
(waiting for a train? missing one? 1960? 1961? why Wilmington?), but I do
remember being there. The woman in the dirty crepe-de-Chine wrapper

had come down from her room for a beer, and the bartender had heard before the reason why George Sharp and she were separated today. "Sure," he said, and went on mopping the floor. "You told me." At the other end of the bar is a girl. She is talking, pointedly, not to the man beside her but to a cat lying in the triangle of sunlight cast through the open door. She is wearing a plaid silk dress from Peck & Peck, and the hem is coming down.

Here is what it is: the girl has been on the Eastern Shore, and now she is going back to the city, leaving the man beside her, and all she can see ahead are the viscous summer sidewalks and the 3 a.m. long-distance calls that will make her lie awake and then sleep drugged through all the steaming mornings left in August (1960? 1961?). Because she must go directly from the train to lunch in New York, she wishes that she had a safety pin for the hem of the plaid silk dress, and she also wishes that she could forget about the hem and the lunch and stay in the cool bar that smells of disinfectant and malt and make friends with the woman in the crepe-de-Chine wrapper. She is afflicted by a little self-pity, and she wants to compare Estelles. That is what that was all about.

Why did I write it down? In order to remember, of course, but exactly what was it I wanted to remember? How much of it actually happened? Did any of it? Why do I keep a notebook at all? It is easy to deceive oneself on all those scores. The impulse to write things down is a peculiarly compulsive one, inexplicable to those who do not share it, useful only accidentally, only secondarily, in the way that any compulsion tries to justify itself. I suppose that it begins or does not begin in the cradle. Although I have felt compelled to write things down since I was five years old, I doubt that my daughter ever will, for she is a singularly blessed and accepting child, delighted with life exactly as life presents itself to her, unafraid to go to sleep and unafraid to wake up. Keepers of private notebooks are a different breed altogether, lonely and resistant rearrangers of things, anxious malcontents, children afflicted apparently at birth with some presentiment of loss.

My first notebook was a Big Five tablet, given to me by my mother with the sensible suggestion that I stop whining and learn to amuse myself by writing down my thoughts. She returned the tablet to me a few years ago; the first entry is an account of a woman who believed herself to be freezing to death in the Arctic night, only to find, when day broke, that she had stumbled onto the Sahara Desert, where she would die of the heat before lunch. I have no idea what turn of a five-year-old's mind could have prompted so insistently "ironic" and exotic a story, but it does reveal a certain predilection for the extreme which has dogged me into adult life; perhaps if I were analytically inclined I would find it a truer story than any I might have told about Donald Johnson's birthday party or the day my cousin Brenda put Kitty Litter in the aquarium.

So the point of my keeping a notebook has never been, nor is it now, to have an accurate factual record of what I have been doing or thinking. That would be a different impulse entirely, an instinct for reality which I sometimes envy but do not possess. At no point have I ever been able successfully to keep a diary; my approach to daily life ranges from the grossly negligent to the merely absent, and on those few occasions when I have tried dutifully to record a day's events, boredom has so overcome me that the results are mysterious at best. What is this business about "shopping, typing piece, dinner with E, depressed"? Shopping for what? Typing what piece? Who is E? Was this "E" depressed, or was I depressed? Who cares?

In fact I have abandoned altogether that kind of pointless entry; instead I tell what some would call lies. "That's simply not true," the members of my family frequently tell me when they come up against my memory of a shared event. "The party was *not* for you, the spider was *not* a black widow, *it wasn't that way at all*." Very likely they are right, for not only have I always had trouble distinguishing between what happened and what merely might have happened, but I remain unconvinced that the distinction, for my purposes, matters. The cracked crab that I recall having for lunch the day my father came home from Detroit in 1945 must certainly be embroidery, worked into the day's pattern to lend verisimilitude; I was ten years old and would not now remember the cracked crab. The day's events did not turn on cracked crab. And yet it is precisely that fictitious crab that makes me see the afternoon all over again, a home movie run all too often, the father bearing gifts, the child weeping, an exercise in family love and guilt. Or that is what it was to me. Similarly, perhaps it never did snow that August in Vermont; perhaps there never were flurries in the night wind, and maybe no one else felt the ground hardening and summer already dead even as we pretended to bask in it, but that was how it felt to me, and it might as well have snowed, could have snowed, did snow.

How it felt to me: that is getting closer to the truth about a notebook. I sometimes delude myself about why I keep a notebook, imagine that some thrifty virtue derives from preserving everything observed. See enough and write it down, I tell myself, and then some morning when the world seems drained of wonder, some day when I am only going through the motions of doing what I am supposed to do, which is write—on that bankrupt morning I will simply open my notebook and there it will all be, a forgotten account with accumulated interest, paid passage back to the world out there: dialogue overheard in hotels and elevators and at the hat-check counter in Pavillon (one middle-aged man shows his hat check to another and says, "That's my old football number"); impressions of Bettina Aptheker and Benjamin Sonnenberg and Teddy ("Mr. Acapulco") Stauffer; careful *aperçus* about tennis bums and failed fashion models and Greek shipping heiresses, one of whom taught me a significant lesson (a lesson I could have learned from F. Scott Fitzgerald, but perhaps we all must meet the very rich for ourselves) by asking, when I arrived to interview her in her orchid-filled sitting room on the second day of a paralyzing New York blizzard, whether it was snowing outside.

I imagine, in other words, that the notebook is about other people. But of course it is not. I have no real business with what one stranger said to another at the hat-check counter in Pavillon; in fact I suspect that the line "That's my old football number" touched not my own imagination at all, but merely some memory of something once read, probably "The Eighty-Yard Run." Nor is my concern with a woman in a dirty crepe-de-Chine wrapper in a Wilmington bar. My stake is always, of course, in the unmentioned girl in the plaid silk dress. *Remember what it was to be me*: that is always the point.

It is a difficult point to admit. We are brought up in the ethic that others, any others, all others, are by definition more interesting than ourselves; taught to be diffident, just this side of self-effacing. ("You're the least important person in the room and don't forget it," Jessica Mitford's governess would hiss in her ear on the advent of any social occasion; I copied that into my notebook because it is only recently that I have been able to enter a room without hearing some such phrase in my inner ear.) Only the very young and the very old may recount their dreams at breakfast, dwell upon self, interrupt with memories of beach picnics and favorite Liberty lawn dresses and the rainbow trout in a creek near Colorado Springs. The rest of us are expected, rightly, to affect absorption in other people's favorite dresses, other people's trout.

And so we do. But our notebooks give us away, for however dutifully we record what we see around us, the common denominator of all we see is always, transparently, shamelessly, the implacable "I." We are not talking here about the kind of notebook that is patently for public consumption, a structural conceit for binding together a series of graceful *pensées*;

we are talking about something private, about bits of the mind's string too short to use, an indiscriminate and erratic assemblage with meaning only for its maker.

And sometimes even the maker has difficulty with the meaning. There does not seem to be, for example, any point in my knowing for the rest of my life that, during 1964, 720 tons of soot fell on every square mile of New York City, yet there it is in my notebook, labeled "FACT." Nor do I really need to remember that Ambrose Bierce liked to spell Leland Stanford's name "£eland $tanford" or that "smart women almost always wear black in Cuba," a fashion hint without much potential for practical application. And does not the relevance of these notes seem marginal at best?:

In the basement museum of the Inyo County Courthouse in Independence, California, sign pinned to a mandarin coat: "This MANDARIN COAT was often worn by Mrs. Minnie S. Brooks when giving lectures on her TEAPOT COLLECTION."

Redhead getting out of car in front of Beverly Wilshire Hotel, chinchilla stole, Vuitton bags with tags reading:

MRS LOU FOX

HOTEL SAHARA

VEGAS

Well, perhaps not entirely marginal. As a matter of fact, Mrs. Minnie S. Brooks and her MANDARIN COAT pull me back into my own childhood, for although I never knew Mrs. Brooks and did not visit Inyo County until I was thirty, I grew up in just such a world, in houses cluttered with Indian relics and bits of gold ore and ambergris and the souvenirs my Aunt Mercy Farnsworth brought back from the Orient. It is a long way from that world to Mrs. Lou Fox's world, where we all live now, and is it not just as well to remember that? Might not Mrs. Minnie S. Brooks help me to remember what I am? Might not Mrs. Lou Fox help me to remember what I am not?

But sometimes the point is harder to discern. What exactly did I have in mind when I noted down that it cost the father of someone I know $650 a month to light the place on the Hudson in which he lived before the Crash? What use was I planning to make of this line by Jimmy Hoffa: "I may have my faults, but being wrong ain't one of them"? And although I think it interesting to know where the girls who travel with the Syndicate have their hair done when they find themselves on the West Coast, will I ever make suitable use of it? Might I not be better off just passing it on to John O'Hara? What is a recipe for sauerkraut doing in my notebook? What kind of magpie keeps this notebook? *"He was born the night the Titanic went down."* That seems a nice enough line, and I even recall who said it, but is it not really a better line in life than it could ever be in fiction?

But of course that is exactly it: not that I should ever use the line, but that I should remember the woman who said it and the afternoon I heard it. We were on her terrace by the sea, and we were finishing the wine left from lunch, trying to get what sun there was, a California winter sun. The woman whose husband was born the night the *Titanic* went down wanted to rent her house, wanted to go back to her children in Paris. I remember wishing that I could afford the house, which cost $1,000 a month. "Someday you will," she said lazily. "Someday it all comes." There in the sun on her terrace it seemed easy to believe in someday, but later I had a low-grade afternoon hangover and ran over a black snake on the way to the supermarket and was flooded with inexplicable fear when I heard the checkout clerk explaining to the man ahead of me why she was finally divorcing her husband. "He left me no choice," she said over and over as she punched the register. "He has a little seven-month-old baby by her, he left me no choice." I would like to believe that my dread then was for the human condition, but of course it was for me, because I wanted a baby and did not then have one and because I wanted to own the house that cost $1,000 a month to rent and because I had a hangover.

It all comes back. Perhaps it is difficult to see the value in having one's self back in that kind of mood, but I do see it; I think we are well advised to keep on nodding terms with the people we used to be, whether we find them attractive company or not. Otherwise they turn up unannounced and surprise us, come hammering on the mind's door at 4 a.m. of a bad night and demand to know who deserted them, who betrayed them, who is going to make amends. We forget all too soon the things we thought we could never forget. We forget the loves and the betrayals alike, forget what we whispered and what we screamed, forget who we were. I have already lost touch with a couple of people I used to be; one of them, a seventeen-year-old, presents little threat, although it would be of some interest to me to know again what it feels like to sit on a river levee drinking vodka-and-orange-juice and listening to Les Paul and Mary Ford and their echoes sing "How High the Moon" on the car radio. (You see I still have the scenes, but I no longer perceive myself among those present, no longer could even improvise the dialogue.) The other one, a twenty-three-year-old, bothers me more. She was always a good deal of trouble, and I suspect she will reappear when I least want to see her, skirts too long, shy to the point of aggravation, always the injured party, full of recriminations and little hurts and stories I do not want to hear again, at once saddening me and angering me with her vulnerability and ignorance, an apparition all the more insistent for being so long banished.

It is a good idea, then, to keep in touch, and I suppose that keeping in touch is what notebooks are all about. And we are all on our own when it comes to keeping those lines open to ourselves: your notebook will never help me, nor mine you. *So what's new in the whiskey business?* What could that possibly mean to you? To me it means a blonde in a Pucci bathing suit sitting with a couple of fat men by the pool at the Beverly Hills Hotel. Another man approaches, and they all regard one another in silence for a while. "So what's new in the whiskey business?" one of the fat men finally says by way of welcome, and the blonde stands up, arches one foot and dips it in the pool, looking all the while at the cabaña where Baby Pignatari is talking on the telephone. That is all there is to that, except that several years later I saw the blonde coming out of Saks Fifth Avenue in New York with her California complexion and a voluminous mink coat. In the harsh wind that day she looked old and irrevocably tired to me, and even the skins in the mink coat were not worked the way they were doing them that year, not the way she would have wanted them done, and there is the point of the story. For a while after that I did not like to look in the mirror, and my eyes would skim the newspapers and pick out only the deaths, the cancer victims, the premature coronaries, the suicides, and I stopped riding the Lexington Avenue IRT because I noticed for the first time that all the strangers I had seen for years—the man with the seeing-eye dog, the spinster who read the classified pages every day, the fat girl who always got off with me at Grand Central—looked older than they once had.

It all comes back. Even that recipe for sauerkraut: even that brings it back. I was on Fire Island when I first made that sauerkraut, and it was raining, and we drank a lot of bourbon and ate the sauerkraut and went to bed at ten, and I listened to the rain and the Atlantic and felt safe. I made the sauerkraut again last night and it did not make me feel any safer, but that is, as they say, another story.

1. What do you think about Didion's reasons for keeping a notebook? Do you agree with them? Why or why not?

2. What devices have you found best for generating notebook entries? Do you keep a traditional journal? Or do you find yourself jotting down odd notes, à la Didion?

3. Have you ever "mined" a journal or a notebook for fiction or nonfiction ideas? If so, how has that worked?

4. Do you agree with Didion that jotting down notes on what is happening around you is always, ultimately, about yourself? Why or why not?

Emergency

DENIS JOHNSON

I'd been working in the emergency room for about three weeks, I guess. This was in 1973, before the summer ended. With nothing to do on the overnight shift but batch the insurance reports from the daytime shifts, I just started wandering around, over to the coronary-care unit, down to the cafeteria, et cetera, looking for Georgie, the orderly, a pretty good friend of mine. He often stole pills from the cabinets.

He was running over the tiled floor of the operating room with a mop. "Are you still doing that?" I said.

"Jesus, there's a lot of blood here," he complained.

"Where?" The floor looked clean enough to me.

"What the hell were they doing in here?" he asked me.

"They were performing surgery, Georgie," I told him.

"There's so much goop inside of us, man," he said, "and it all wants to get out." He leaned his mop against a cabinet.

"What are you crying for?" I didn't understand.

He stood still, raised both arms slowly behind his head, and tightened his ponytail. Then he grabbed the mop and started making broad random arcs with it, trembling and weeping and moving all around the place really fast.

"What am I *crying* for?" he said. "Jesus. Wow, oh boy, perfect."

I was hanging out in the E.R. with fat, quivering Nurse. One of the Family Service doctors that nobody liked came in looking for Georgie to wipe up after him. "Where's Georgie?" this guy asked.

"Georgie's in O.R.," Nurse said.

"Again?"

"No," Nurse said. "Still."

"Still? Doing what?"

"Cleaning the floor."

"Again?"

"No," Nurse said again. "Still."

Back in O.R., Georgie dropped his mop and bent over in the posture of child soiling its diapers. He stared down with his mouth open in terror.

He said, "What am I going to do about these fucking *shoes*, man?"

"Whatever you stole," I said, "I guess you already ate it all, right?"

"Listen to how they squish," he said, walking around carefully on his heels.

"Let me check your pockets, man."

He stood still a minute, and I found his stash. I left him two of each, whatever they were. "Shift is about half over," I told him.

"Good. Because I really, really, really need a drink," he said. "Will you please help me get this blood mopped up?"

Around 3:30 a.m. a guy with a knife in his eye came in, led by Georgie.

"I hope *you* didn't do that to him," Nurse said.

"Me?" Georgie said. "No. He was like this."

"My wife did it," the man said. The blade was buried to the hilt in the outside corner of his left eye. It was a hunting knife kind of thing.

"Who brought you in?" Nurse said.

"Nobody. I just walked down. It's only three blocks," the man said.

Nurse peered at him. "We'd better get you lying down."

"Okay, I'm certainly ready for something like that," the man said.

She peered a bit longer into his face.

"Is your other eye," she said, "a glass eye?"

"It's plastic, or something artificial like that," he said.

"And you can see out of *this* eye?" she asked, meaning the wounded one.

"I can see. But I can't make a fist out of my left hand because this knife is doing something to my brain."

"My God," Nurse said.

"I guess I'd better get the doctor," I said.

"There you go," Nurse agreed.

They got him lying down, and Georgie says to the patient, "Name?"

"Terrence Weber."

"Your face is dark. I can't see what you're saying."

"Georgie," I said.

"What are you saying, man? I can't see."

Nurse came over, and Georgie said to her, "His face is dark."

She leaned over the patient. "How long ago did this happen, Terry?" she shouted down into his face.

"Just a while ago. My wife did it. I was asleep," the patient said.

"Do you want the police?"

He thought about it and finally said, "Not unless I die."

Nurse went to the wall intercom and buzzed the doctor on duty, the Family Service person. "Got a surprise for you," she said over the intercom. He took his time getting down the hall to her, because he knew she hated Family Service and her happy tone of voice could only mean something beyond his competence and potentially humiliating.

He peeked into the trauma room and saw the situation: the clerk—that is, me—standing next to the orderly, Georgie, both of us on drugs, looking down at a patient with a knife sticking up out of his face.

"What seems to be the trouble?" he said.

The doctor gathered the three of us around him in the office and said, "Here's the situation. We've got to get a team here, an entire team. I want a good eye man. A great eye man. The best eye man. I want a brain surgeon. And I want a really good gas man, get me a genius. I'm not touching that head. I'm just going to watch this one. I know my limits. We'll just get him prepped and sit tight. Orderly!"

"Do you mean me?" Georgie said. "Should I get him prepped?"

"Is this a hospital?" the doctor asked. "Is this the emergency room? Is that a patient? Are you the orderly?"

I dialled the hospital operator and told her to get me the eye man and the brain and the gas man.

Georgie could be heard across the hall, washing his hands and singing a Neil Young song that went "Hello, cowgirl in the sand. Is this place at your command?"

"That person is not right, not at all, not one bit," the doctor said.

"As long as my instructions are audible to him it doesn't concern me," Nurse insisted, spooning stuff up out of a little Dixie cup. "I've got my own life and the protection of my family to think of."

"Well, okay, okay. Don't chew my head off," the doctor said.

The eye man was on vacation or something. While the hospital's operator called around to find someone else just as good, the other specialists were hurrying through the night to join us. I stood around looking at charts and chewing up more of Georgie's pills. Some of them tasted the way urine smells, some of them burned, some of them tasted like chalk. Various nurses, and two physicians who'd been tending somebody in I.C.U., were hanging out down here with us now.

Everybody had a different idea about exactly how to approach the problem of removing the knife from Terrence Weber's brain. But when Georgie came in from prepping the patient—from shaving the patient's eyebrow and disinfecting the area around the wound, and so on—he seemed to be holding the hunting knife in his left hand.

The talk just dropped off a cliff.

"Where," the doctor asked finally, "did you get that?"

Nobody said one thing more, not for quite a long time.

After a while, one of the I.C.U. nurses said, "Your shoelace is untied." Georgie laid the knife on a chart and bent down to fix his shoe.

There were twenty more minutes left to get through.

"How's the guy doing?" I asked.

"Who?" Georgie said.

It turned out that Terrence Weber still had excellent vision in the one good eye, and acceptable motor and reflex, despite his earlier motor complaint. "His vitals are normal," Nurse said. "There's nothing wrong with the guy. It's one of those things."

After a while you forget it's summer. You don't remember what the morning is. I'd worked two doubles with eight hours off in between, which I'd spent sleeping on a gurney in the nurse's station. Georgie's pills were making me feel like a giant helium-filled balloon, but I was wide awake. Georgie and I went out to the lot, to his orange pickup.

We lay down on a stretch of dusty plywood in the back of the truck with the daylight knocking against our eyelids and the fragrance of alfalfa thickening on our tongues.

"I want to go to church," Georgie said.

"Let's go to the county fair."

"I'd like to worship. I would."

"They have these injured hawks and eagles there. From the Humane Society," I said.

"I need a quiet chapel about now."

Georgie and I had a terrific time driving around. For a while the day was clear and peaceful. It was one of the moments you stay in, to hell with all the troubles of before and after. The sky is blue and the dead are coming back. Later in the afternoon, with sad resignation, the county fair bares its breasts. A champion of the drug LSD, a very famous guru of the love generation, is being interviewed amid a TV crew off to the left of the poultry cages. His eyeballs look like he bought them in a joke shop. It doesn't occur to me, as I pity this extraterrestrial, that in my life I've taken as much as he has.

After that, we got lost. We drove for hours, literally hours, but we couldn't find the road back to town.

Georgie started to complain. "That was the worst fair I've been to. Where were the rides?"

"They had rides," I said.

"I didn't see one ride."

A jackrabbit scurried out in front of us, and we hit it.

"There was a merry-go-round, a Ferris wheel, and a thing called the Hammer that people were bent over vomiting from after they got off," I said. "Are you completely blind?"

"What was that?"

"A rabbit."

"Something thumped."

"You hit him. *He* thumped."

Georgie stood on the brake pedal. "Rabbit stew."

He threw the truck in reverse and zigzagged back toward the rabbit. "Where's my hunting knife?" He almost ran over the poor animal a second time.

"We'll camp in the wilderness," he said. "In the morning we'll breakfast on its haunches." He was waving Terrence Weber's hunting knife around in what I was sure was a dangerous way.

In a minute he was standing at the edge of the fields, cutting the scrawny little thing up, tossing away its organs. "I should have been a doctor," he cried.

A family in a big Dodge, the only car we'd seen for a long time, slowed down and gawked out the windows as they passed by. The father said, "What is it, a snake?"

"No, it's not a snake," Georgie said. "It's a rabbit with babies inside it."

"Babies!" the mother said, and the father sped the car forward, over the protests of several little kids in the back.

Georgie came back to my side of the truck with his shirtfront stretched out in front of him as if he were carrying apples in it, or some such, but they were, in fact, slimy miniature bunnies. "No way I'm eating those things," I told him.

"Take them, take them. I gotta drive, take them," he said, dumping them in my lap and getting in on his side of the truck. He started driving along faster and faster, with a look of glory on his face. "We killed the mother and saved the children," he said.

"It's getting late," I said. "Let's get back to town."

"You bet." Sixty, seventy, eighty-five, just topping ninety.

"These rabbits better be kept warm." One at a time I slid the little things in between my shirt buttons and nestled them against my belly. "They're hardly moving," I told Georgie.

"We'll get some milk and sugar and all that, and we'll raise them up ourselves. They'll get as big as gorillas."

The road we were lost on cut straight through the middle of the world. It was still daytime, but the sun had no more power than an ornament or a sponge. In this light the truck's hood, which had been bright orange, had turned a deep blue.

Georgie let us drift to the shoulder of the road, slowly, slowly, as if he'd fallen asleep or given up trying to find his way.

"What is it?"

"We can't go on. I don't have any headlights," Georgie said.

We parked under a strange sky with a faint image of a quarter-moon superimposed on it.

There was a little woods beside us. This day had been dry and hot, the buck pines and whatall simmering patiently, but as we sat there smoking cigarettes it started to get very cold.

"The summer's over," I said.

That was the year when arctic clouds moved down over the Midwest and we had two weeks of winter in September.

"Do you realize it's going to snow?" Georgie asked me.

He was right, a gun-blue storm was shaping up. We got out and walked around idiotically. The beautiful chill! That sudden crispness, and the tang of evergreen stabbing us!

The gusts of snow twisted themselves around our heads while the night fell. I couldn't find the truck. We just kept getting more and more lost. I kept calling, "Georgie, can you see?" and he kept saying, "See what? See what?"

The only light visible was a streak of sunset flickering below the hem of the clouds. We headed that way.

We bumped softly down a hill toward an open field that seemed to be a military graveyard, filled with rows and rows of austere, identical markers over soldiers' graves. I'd never before come across this cemetery. On the farther side of the field, just beyond the curtains of snow, the sky was torn away and the angels were descending out of a brilliant blue summer, their huge faces streaked with light and full of pity. The sight of them cut through my heart and down the knuckles of my spine, and if there'd been anything in my bowels I would have messed my pants from fear.

Georgie opened his arms and cried out, "It's the drive-in, man!"

"The drive-in . . ." I wasn't sure what these words meant.

"They're showing movies in a fucking blizzard!" Georgie screamed.

"I see. I thought it was something else," I said.

We walked carefully down there and climbed through the busted fence and stood in the very back. The speakers, which I'd mistaken for grave markers, muttered in unison. Then there was tinkly music, of which I could very nearly make out the tune. Famous movie stars rode bicycles beside a river, laughing out of their gigantic, lovely mouths. If anybody had come to see this show, they'd left when the weather started. Not one car remained, not even a broken-down one from last week, or one left here because it was out of gas. In a couple of minutes, in the middle of a whirling square dance, the screen turned black, the cinematic summer ended, the snow went dark, there was nothing but my breath.

"I'm starting to get my eyes back," Georgie said in another minute.

A general greyness was giving birth to various shapes, it was true. "But which ones are close and which ones are far off?" I begged him to tell me.

By trial and error, with a lot of walking back and forth in wet shoes, we found the truck and sat inside it shivering.

"Let's get out of here," I said.

"We can't go anywhere without headlights."

"We've gotta get back. We're a long way from home."

"No, we're not."

"We must have come three hundred miles."

"We're right outside town, Fuckhead. We've just been driving around and around."

"This is no place to camp. I hear the Interstate over there."

"We'll just stay here till it gets late. We can drive home late. We'll be invisible."

We listened to the big rigs going from San Francisco to Pennsylvania along the Interstate, like shudders down a long hacksaw blade, while the snow buried us.

Eventually Georgie said, "We better get some milk for those bunnies."

"We don't have *milk*," I said.

"We'll mix sugar up with it."

"Will you forget about this milk all of a sudden?"

"They're mammals, man."

"Forget about those rabbits."

"Where are they, anyway?"

"You're not listening to me. I said, 'Forget the rabbits.'"

"Where are they?"

The truth was I'd forgotten all about them, and they were dead.

"They slid around behind me and got squashed," I said tearfully.

"They slid around *behind?*"

He watched while I pried them out from behind my back.

I picked them out one at a time and held them in my hands and we looked at them. There were eight. They weren't any bigger than my fingers, but everything was there.

Little feet! Eyelids! Even whiskers! "Deceased," I said.

Georgie asked, "Does everything you touch turn to shit? Does this happen to you every time?"

"No wonder they call me Fuckhead."

"It's a name that's going to stick."

"I realize that."

"'Fuckhead' is gonna ride you to your grave."

"I just said so. I agreed with you in advance," I said.

Or maybe that wasn't the time it snowed. Maybe it was the time we slept in the truck and I rolled over on the bunnies and flattened them. It doesn't matter. What's important for me to remember now is that early the next morning the snow was melted off the windshield and the daylight woke me up. A mist covered everything and, with the sunshine, was beginning to grow sharp and strange. The bunnies weren't a problem yet, or they'd already been a problem and were already forgotten, and there was nothing on my mind. I felt the beauty of the morning. I could understand how a drowning man might suddenly feel a deep thirst being quenched. Or how the slave might become a friend to his master. Georgie slept with his face right on the steering wheel.

I saw bits of snow resembling an abundance of blossoms on the stems of the drive-in speakers—no, revealing the blossoms that were always there. A bull elk stood still in the pasture beyond the fence, giving off an air of authority and stupidity. And a coyote jogged across the pasture and faded away among the saplings.

That afternoon we got back to work in time to resume everything as if it had never stopped happening and we'd never been anywhere else.

"The Lord," the intercom said, "is my shepherd." It did that each evening because this was a Catholic hospital. "Our Father, who art in Heaven," and so on.

"Yeah, yeah," Nurse said.

The man with the knife in his head, Terrence Weber, was released around suppertime. They'd kept him overnight and given him an eye-patch—all for no reason, really.

He stopped off at E.R. to say goodbye. "Well, those pills they gave me make everything taste terrible," he said.

"It could have been worse," Nurse said.

"Even my tongue."

"It's just a miracle you didn't end up sightless or at least dead," she reminded him.

The patient recognized me. He acknowledged me with a smile. "I was peeping on the lady next door while she was out there sunbathing," he said. "My wife decided to blind me."

He shook Georgie's hand. Georgie didn't know him. "Who are you supposed to be?" he asked Terrence Weber.

Some hours before that, Georgie had said something that had suddenly and completely explained the difference between us. We'd been driving back toward town, along the Old Highway, through the flatness. We picked up a hitchhiker, a boy I knew. We stopped the truck and the boy climbed slowly up out of the fields as out of the mouth of a volcano. His name was Hardee. He looked even worse than we probably did.

"We got messed up and slept in the truck all night," I told Hardee.

"I had a feeling," Hardee said. "Either that or, you know, driving a thousand miles."

"That too," I said.

"Or you're sick or diseased or something."

"Who's this guy?" Georgie asked.

"This is Hardee. He lived with me last summer. I found him on the doorstep. What happened to your dog?" I asked Hardee.

"He's still down there."

"Yeah, I heard you went to Texas."

"I was working on a bee farm," Hardee said.

"Wow. Do those things sting you?"

"Not like you'd think," Hardee said. "You're part of their daily drill. It's all part of a harmony."

Outside, the same identical stretch of grass repeatedly rolled past our faces. The day was cloudless, blinding. But Georgie said, "Look at that," pointing straight ahead of us.

One star was so hot it showed, bright and blue in the empty sky.

"I recognized you right away," I told Hardee. "But what happened to your hair? Who chopped it off?"

"I hate to say."

"Don't tell me."

"They drafted me."

"Oh no."

"Oh yeah. I'm AWOL. I'm bad AWOL. I got to get to Canada."

"Oh, that's terrible," I said to Hardee.

"Don't worry," Georgie said. "We'll get you there."

"How?"

"Somehow. I think I know some people. Don't worry. You're on your way to Canada."

That world! These days it's all been erased and they've rolled it up like a scroll and put it away somewhere. Yes, I can touch it with my fingers. But where is it?

After a while Hardee asked Georgie, "What do you do for a job," and Georgie said, "I save lives."

1. What is this story ultimately about? (It's about more than just getting messed up on drugs.) What is the general *feeling* you take away from the story?
2. What purpose does Georgie play in the story? How would it be a completely different story if he weren't in it?
3. Can you point out the ways that Johnson keeps surprising us? How does he play with our expectations and deliver something that feels fresh and urgent?

CHAPTER TWO

The Splendid Gift
of Not Knowing

Part 1: WRITING AS DISCOVERY

Getting Started

"I don't have any good ideas." So goes one of the most common fears expressed by beginning writing students. It can come accompanied by "I don't have anything to write about" and "Nothing interesting has ever happened to me." And although older or more experienced writers might not say these things publicly, many of the most accomplished authors in the world openly acknowledge the uncertainty, anxiety, and dread that can arise when facing a blank piece of paper or, more recently, the blinking cursor on the computer screen.

Indeed, one of the most difficult lessons a writer must learn is that uncertainty—sometimes quite painful uncertainty—is an integral part of the writing process. It does not go away with age, experience, or praise, although all of these things—particularly critical success—can provide a writer with sufficient confidence in his or her abilities to endure the discomfort (sometimes extreme discomfort) of uncertainty with relative equanimity.

Yet, as frightening as it is, *not* knowing what to write about is often a creative advantage. Not having any "ideas" can be an excellent beginning to generating creative work that is truly fresh and original and exciting precisely because the writer has ventured out of familiar (and comfortable) territory. He or she is exploring, not retelling an old tale. He or she is learning, not teaching. And the things that make exploration and encountering the new so riveting to the writer can, under the best of circumstances, carry over to the reader. As Robert Frost so famously wrote, "No tears in the writer, no tears in the reader."

In Part 1 of this chapter, we'll explore ways writers can harness the inherent doubt and uncertainty of the creative process in order to begin discovering their own voices and material. In Part 2, carefully targeted writing exercises give you a chance to practice some of the techniques discussed. And in Part 3, an essay and a classic of contemporary short fiction effectively dramatize how the best creative work consistently engages and surprises us—and how difficult it is, even in retrospect, to summarize or paraphrase the experience we've just read our way through.

What Do You Know?

"Write about what you know" is the first solid piece of writing advice most of us are told, and we usually hear it at a fairly early age. If your primary school teacher didn't tell you this, then almost certainly you encountered it before enrolling in a college-level writing class. And it can be excellent advice for children, or for beginning writers who lack the confidence to believe that anything they know would be of interest to others. It's less helpful for older or more sophisticated students, for reasons that will be explained later in this chapter. But for now, let's accept it as a basic truth that we should write about the things we know.

Why is this good advice? Because it simultaneously grounds you in the concrete sensory world that is all around you, and discourages you from clichéd rumination on abstract topics. By emphasizing that there can be infinite value, and beauty, and meaning in the ordinary, this advice helps beginning writers avoid the trap of writing about "love" or "despair" and heroic, exotic, or sensational topics that reflect popular culture (or the desire to impress) more than honest human experience. To write a coming-of-age story about a native of Bora-Bora might seem like a great idea in theory, but when you sit down to actually write it, you'll probably find that your lack of understanding of the everyday things in the world of a thirteen-year-old Bora-Bora girl might hamper you from producing the thrilling results you'd hoped for.

This is not to say that you must avoid large or meaningful (to you) topics; neither should this be an admonition to limit use of the imagination or stick solely to a realistic rendering of the world—what a sad and lean literary heritage we would have if this were so! Rather, one of the first difficult lessons any writer must learn is how to trust his or her own personal insight and unique skills of observation, even when these conflict with accepted wisdom and the mass-produced images that bombard all of us daily.

To illustrate how you can take an ordinary moment, and through brutally honest insight transform it into the extraordinary, here is a poem by Sharon Olds:

Forty-One, Alone, No Gerbil

In the strange quiet, I realize
there's no one else in the house. No bucktooth
mouth pulls at a stainless-steel teat, no
hairy mammal runs on a treadmill—
Charlie is dead, the last of our children's half-children.
When our daughter found him lying in the shavings, transmogrified
        backward from a living body
into a bolt of rodent bread
she turned her back on early motherhood
and went on single, with nothing. Crackers,
Fluffy, Pretzel, Biscuit, Charlie,
buried on the old farm we bought where she could know nature. Well,
        now she knows it
and it sucks. Creatures she loved, mobile and
needy, have gone down stiff and indifferent,
she will not adopt again though she cannot
have children yet, her body like a blueprint
of the understructure for a woman's body,
so now everything stops for a while,
now I must wait many years
to hear in this house again the faint
powerful call of a young animal.

Even the title pushes us away from any expectations of anything "poetic" or "meaningful"—two hobgoblins of the beginning writer's psyche; the use of slang and informal diction reinforces the impression of spontaneously musing on what is, for parents of young children, a familiar scene. Yet Olds takes us beyond the seemingly trivial scene and folds us into an extraordinarily powerful moment of personal grief and longing. The concrete details anchor us in the specific moment at the same time that the images evoke deep, visceral, and—arguably—universal emotion.

It is precisely because complex and ambiguous emotions like this can only be rendered and sustained by specific concrete details that "Write about what you know" advice can still be considered valid.

In their eagerness to transcend experiences they perceive as mundane, young writers often rush to depict exotic locales or extreme circumstances they consider more interesting and worthy of treatment than their own worlds. But because they usually lack sufficient grounding on a sensory level—about the workings of a Colombian drug deal, for example, or the inner life of a taxi driver or prostitute—beginning writers end up depending on stock images, characters, and situations from movies or television. The result is predictability, or lack of authenticity, or both.

To put it another way, there is no "news" here that we haven't heard from a multitude of other sources. This is how Raymond Carver thinks about it when he gives advice to other writers in his book *Fires*: he starts out by saying that talent is commonplace—that he doesn't know many writers who are without it. What *does* distinguish certain writers as being above the crowd is a "unique and exact way of looking at things," as well as a way of expressing that way of looking. In Carver's own words:

> *The World According to Garp* is, of course, the marvelous world according to John Irving. There is another world according to Flannery O'Connor, and others according to William Faulkner and Ernest Hemingway. There are worlds according to Cheever, Updike, Singer, Stanley Elkin, Ann Beattie, Cynthia Ozick, Donald Barthelme. [. . .] Every great or even every very good writer makes the world over according to his own specifications.

Later in the essay, Carver talks about the need to "carry news" from your world to that of your readers. So what do you know? What "news"— about events, people, emotions, thoughts—within your personal experience is worth exploring creatively, and telling others about?

But wait a minute. Aren't we back to our starting point: that you might simply have not lived that exciting of a life to begin writing—yet? That you should perhaps accumulate some "experience" before trying?

Absolutely not. The kind of experience worth writing about is not necessarily a matter of what you've done (or had done to you), but the depth and breadth of what you've noticed—and your emotional response to what you've taken note of. "Experience is not a matter of having actually swum the Hellespont, or danced with the dervishes, or slept in a doss-house," Aldous Huxley reminds us. "It is a matter of sensibility and intuition, of seeing and hearing the significant things, of paying attention at the right moments, of understanding and coordinating. Experience is not what happens to a man; it is what a man does with what happens to him."

Children only three or four years old have experienced intense joys, seething hatred, and deep bereavement. They might not have the means to communicate these emotions to us, but they have experienced them. Likewise, the most timid, naive, and protected adolescent has felt terror, known exploitation and betrayal. Because the events that call forth these emotions are not necessarily dramatic, we dismiss the intensity of these emotional experiences as inauthentic, or overwrought. We do not think we have the right to claim these emotions. Yet we do. And what's more, our ability to write truly moving fiction and creative nonfiction ultimately derives from our ability to transform these very deep and very true experiences into language that effectively arouses deep, true emotions in others.

"I am the lie that always speaks the truth," the French filmmaker Jean Cocteau said about how even his most surrealistic work was based on emotional reality that audiences could recognize as true.

Creative Nonfiction: Making the Ordinary Extraordinary

The following passages, excerpts from the journals of the writer Leonard Michaels, prove how even the most trivial events can resonate with emotion when rendered carefully by someone who truly notices:

The Trip, 1976

I stopped at a roadside grocery near the Oregon border. A huge fellow with the face of a powerful dullard stood behind the counter. He turned for items on the shelf and I saw that his pants had slipped below his hips where he was chopped sheer from lower back to legs. No ass to hold up his pants. His bulk pushed forward and heaved up into his chest. He had a hanging mouth and little eyes with a birdlike shine. I bought salami and oranges from him.

Drove from Des Moines to Kansas City where the amazing beauty lives. She wore baggy pants, a man's sweater, no makeup. She had violent opinions about everything as if to show, despite her exceedingly beautiful face and body, she damn well had a mind. Then I drove west through Missouri and felt sick with regret at having met her, ready to forgive every fault, half in love with a woman I'll never see again.

A farmer came into the diner. He wore a baseball cap with a long bill. He was very tanned and dusty, and moved ponderously with the pain of this long day. His hands were much bigger than the coffee cup in front of him. He stared at it. In his eyes, no ideas, just questions. "What's this?" A coffee cup. "What do you do with it?" Pick it up. Between the first and second question, no words. No words even in the questions.

You can see how the most mundane things about the world of the writer—sitting in a local diner and watching the very ordinary inhabitants, recording his impressions of a small town—can be made quite extraordinary when in the hands of someone who is paying attention to the truth of things (as well as to the facts).

Writing Down What You Don't Know (About What You Know)

Now that we've explained how writing about what you know can be helpful advice, we need to talk about the ways it can be limiting, and even detrimental to your creative efforts.

Eudora Welty had it right: "Write about what you *don't* know about what you know," she advised. And with this, we can begin to put together a basic understanding of what we, as creative writers, are trying to accomplish.

What Welty is saying, in effect, is that yes, it can make sense to work with material that you feel closest to (both emotionally and physically). Yet there must be a sense of mystery in the material. We don't just write about contemporary urban family life because we're familiar with it. We write about it because it *interests* us, because despite its familiarity there are aspects of it that remain mysterious, unknowable, *worth exploring further*. We're interested in what we *don't* know about very familiar and (to us) ordinary scenes. So just possessing knowledge about a particular topic, or place, or person isn't going to take you very far, creatively. You won't really claim this material, the way Sherwood Anderson claimed small town Ohio life, for instance. Not unless there are things that you don't know about this topic, place, or person, and unless you are interested to the point of obsession in finding out more.

Jane Kenyon put it this way:

> Why do we want to write? What is behind this crazy impulse? The wish to connect with others, on a deep level, about inward things. The pressure of emotion, which many people prefer to ignore, but which, for you, is the very substance of your work, your *clay*. There's the need to make sense of life behind the impulse to write.

As an example of using not-knowing as the basis for creative exploration, let's look at a poem by Czeslaw Milosz, translated from the Polish by the author and poet Robert Hass. Titled "In the Parish," the poem begins with the narrator's spontaneous visit to a cemetery:

> Were I not frail and half broken inside,
> I wouldn't be thinking of them, who are, like me, half broken inside.
> I would not climb the cemetery hill by the church
> To get rid of my self-pity.

Milosz goes on to comment on the fragility of the physical remains, coupled with our notions of what happens after death:

> And eternity close by. Improper. Indecent.
> Like a doll house crushed by wheels, like
> An elephant trampling a beetle, an ocean drowning an island.
> Our stupidity and childishness do nothing to fit us
> For the sobriety of last things.

He is not lecturing so much as talking out his feelings—there is rage and sorrow, and the sense that these thoughts and emotions are only now being grasped, and processed. The poem takes us along with him as he continues to explore what isn't known but begs to be understood within this utterly unremarkable small parish cemetery.

> They had no time to grasp anything
> Of their individual lives,
> Any *principium individuationis.*
> Nor do I grasp it, yet what can I do?
> Enclosed all my life in a nutshell,
> Trying in vain to become something
> Completely different from what I was.

From there he returns to the inward introspection that began the poem—what he calls "self-pity," which he hoped to eradicate by this walk. Instead, we see how he has deepened his misery and frustration with his place in the world.

The poem has another stanza, but this is enough to show the movement in the poem—how it is not a set of static statements about the world, but an obviously painful effort to push through bitterness and fear to a more comfortable state—better understanding, perhaps, or acceptance of mortality.

On Rendering, Not Solving, the Mysteries That Surround Us

"It is the business of fiction to embody mystery through manners, and mystery is a great embarrassment to the modern mind," Flannery O'Connor told a group of college students (the text of the speech can be found in *Mystery and Manners*, a collection of her essays on writing).

The mystery O'Connor is referring to is "the mystery of our position on earth," she says. What does that mean? Just that in every hour in every day, we are confronted by mysteries: by things we don't know, by things we don't understand. Yes, we're in the middle of our own life, our own worlds: the banal (or so we think) and utterly predictable world of Cleveland, Ohio, or Palo Alto, California. Yet even so, there are mysteries, O'Connor is telling us.

Although O'Connor herself viewed the world (and wrote about it) through the prism of a deep religious faith, her point is also valid from a secular perspective. The "mystery" in that case would encompass all the things in the world that we don't fully understand—not just large philosophical issues, but such questions as: why was your mother so irritable at dinner? Or, what motivated your girlfriend to suddenly drop out of school?

We are surrounded by such mysteries, large and small, and, as we discussed in the previous chapter, our very first responsibility as writers is simply to *notice* them. Everything follows from that.

All this, of course, is simply another way to say that we should write about what we *don't* know about what we know. Without using this sense of not-knowingness, or mystery, as a starting point, anything we write will be lifeless and predictable.

The following piece by Tobias Wolff illustrates this point. It was written as an essay for an anthology of "short short fiction," and was Wolff's attempt to define this hybrid genre of writing that falls somewhere between short fiction and poetry.

> I was on a bus to Washington, D.C. Two days I'd been traveling and I was tired, tired, tired. The woman sitting next to me, a German with a ticket good for anywhere, never stopped yakking. I understood little of what she said but what I did understand led me to believe that she was utterly deranged.
>
> She finally took a breather when we hit Richmond. It was late at night. The bus threaded its way through dismal streets toward the bus station. We rounded a corner and there beneath a street light stood a white man and a black woman. The woman wore a yellow dress and held a baby. Her head was thrown back in laughter. The man was red-haired, rough-looking, naked to the waist. His skin seemed luminous. He was grinning at the woman, who watched him closely even as she laughed. Broken glass glittered at their feet.
>
> There is something between them, something in the instant itself, that makes me sit up and stare. What is it, what's going on here? Why can't I ever forget them?
>
> Tell me, for God's sake, but make it snappy—I'm tired, and the bus is picking up speed, and the lunatic beside me is getting ready to say something.

Another point O'Connor stresses, which Wolff also touches on, is the question of *what next*? Okay, you've identified a mystery, a gap in your knowledge of a certain situation that you feel is worth exploring. What then?

Here's what *not* to do: Don't try to solve these mysteries. As writers, we're not looking to provide a lesson, or a moral; we're not therapists looking to cure our characters of pain or neurosis. Our job, as writers, is simply to render what *is* using precise, concrete detail.

Don't tell us *why* something is, show us *how* it is.

Don't give us easy answers. Rather, help us understand the precise nature of the questions.

This notion of rendering mysteries that are then deliberately left unresolved can be a difficult thing for beginning writers to accept, especially those people who are uncomfortable with ambiguity and who seek neat emotional resolutions and tidily wrapped-up plot lines. "For such people, fiction can be very disturbing, for the fiction writer is concerned with mystery that is lived," wrote O'Connor. (And so, we might add, is creative nonfiction.)

Moving from "Triggering" to Real Subject

We've now covered the single most important step a writer must take when generating new work: to identify potential material—whether fiction or nonfiction—by paying attention to surrounding mysteries and seeking out those mysteries that resonate loudest for him or her.

What then?

The most articulate explanation of the next stage in the creative process can be found in Chapter 1 of Richard Hugo's book *The Triggering Town*. Called "Writing Off the Subject," this chapter first underscores the notion that a poem is a process of discovery, not an archive of resolved emotion. Hugo has named this process of discovery as moving from the "triggering" subject to the "real" subject. Here is an excerpt from that text:

> A poem can be said to have two subjects, the initiating or triggering subject, which starts the poem or "causes" the poem to be written, and the real or generated subject, which the poem comes to say or mean, and which is generated or discovered in the poem during the writing. That's not quite right because it suggests that the poet recognizes the real subject. The poet may not be aware of what the real subject is but only have some instinctive feeling that the poem is done.
>
> Young poets find it difficult to free themselves from the initiating subject. The poet puts down the title: "Autumn Rain." He finds two or three good lines about Autumn Rain. Then things start to break down. He cannot find

anything more to say about Autumn Rain so he starts making up things, he strains, he goes abstract, he starts telling us the meaning of what he has already said. The mistake he is making, of course, is that he feels obligated to go on talking about Autumn Rain, because that, he feels, is the subject. Well, it isn't the subject. You don't know what the subject is, and the moment you run out of things to say about Autumn Rain start talking about something else. In fact, it's a good idea to talk about something else before you run out of things to say about Autumn Rain.

Hugo is saying that the very uncertainty we began this chapter discussing—the uncertainty that is arguably the most difficult aspect of the creative process for all writers, no matter what skill or experience level—is the driving force behind a creative work. That, rather than attempting to avoid uncertainty, the writer needs to embrace it—even to the point of changing the "subject" from one line to another. Because it is the writer's imagination that is choosing the next topic, because there must be some connection in the writer's brain (conscious or unconscious) that leads from one subject to another, then the sequence must be meaningful.

Although Hugo is talking specifically about poetry, the *process* he is discussing is equally true when writing prose—whether fiction or creative nonfiction. We are always on a path of discovery—if not, the result will be absolute dullness for the reader.

We'll be practicing some of these concepts in the exercises to come in Part 2. Here's a poem by Frank O'Hara that dramatizes this notion of a triggering subject that leads to a real subject.

Why I Am Not a Painter

I am not a painter, I am a poet
Why? I think I would rather be
a painter, but I am not. Well,

for instance, Mike Goldberg
is starting a painting. I drop in.
"Sit down and have a drink" he
says. I drink; we drink. I look
up. "You have SARDINES in it."
"Yes, it needed something there."

"Oh." I go and the days go by
and I drop in again. The painting
is going on, and I go, and the days
go by. I drop in. The painting is
finished. "Where's SARDINES?"

All that's left is just
letters. "It was too much," Mike says.
But me? One day I am thinking of
a color: orange. I write a line
about orange. Pretty soon it is a
whole page of words, not lines.
Then another page. There should be
so much more, not of orange, of

words, of how terrible orange is
and life. Days go by. It is even in
prose, I am a real poet. My poem
is finished and I haven't mentioned
orange yet. It's twelve poems, I call
it ORANGES. And one day in a gallery
I see Mike's painting, called SARDINES.

Surprise Yourself, Interest Others

"Bad books are about things the writer already knew before he wrote them," the Mexican writer Carlos Fuentes says. What does he mean by this? Simply that without a sense of discovery, a creative piece will lack urgency and interest. To paraphrase Margaret, the heroine of E. M. Forster's great novel *Howards End*, How do you know what you think until you read what you've written? Even B. F. Skinner, the father of what we know as behavioral psychology, subscribed to this theory. In an essay titled "How to Discover What You Have to Say: A Talk to Students," Skinner asserts that writing is a much more complex act than simply transcribing existing thoughts into words as accurately as possible. If this were the case, the writer would be doing little more than serving as a "reporter" of past thoughts and experiences already processed by the brain. Instead, Skinner argues that the physical act of writing is the cause, not the effect, of new and original thought, and that any creative work that is not a journey of discovery for the writer will, in turn, bore readers. "It's like driving a car at night," said novelist Robert Stone about how he copes with this uncertainty when writing longer pieces, "you can only see as far ahead as your headlights, but you can make the entire journey that way."

Beginning writers find it difficult and painful to tolerate this state of not-knowing. Yet accepting it, embracing it even, represents an important step in a writer's creative development. Good creative writing is almost always conceived in doubt, and is fueled by an urgent desire to understand something that eludes understanding. Thus the best writing is less about dispelling than acquiring wisdom, less about explaining the point of a given experience to others than about exploring and learning about it oneself.

Obsession as a Creative Virtue

But it's not enough just not to know or understand something. You have to be *interested*. If possible, you should go beyond interest to obsession, as the poet Phillip Larkin says in his essay "The Pleasure Principle."

A successful creative work has three distinct phases, according to Larkin, as follows:

1. A person becomes obsessed with something to the degree that he is "compelled to do something about it," i.e., write.
2. The person writes down words (a "verbal device") that attempt to reproduce the original emotion in "anyone who cares to read it."
3. Other people, who can be from all places and all walks of life, read the words and "set off" a device that re-creates what the writer originally felt and/or thought.

Notice how Larkin distinguishes inspiration (Step 1) from craft (Step 2). It doesn't matter how inspired or obsessed you are if you do not possess the skills that allow you to get your emotional experience down on paper. On the other hand, all the skill in the world won't help you produce a truly moving story if you just weren't all that interested in the idea to begin with. And the whole effort has failed if there is no successful reading by an intelligent and interested reader.

As Larkin says:

> If there has been no preliminary feeling, the device has nothing to reproduce and the reader will experience nothing. If the second stage has not been well done, the device will not deliver the goods, or will deliver only a few goods to a few people, or will stop delivering them after an absurdly short while. And if there is no third stage, no successful reading, the [creative work] can hardly be said to exist in a practical sense at all.

Finally, to end this chapter, here is what Rick Bass wrote about how an oilman feels about "getting oil." The excitement and even danger that he writes about is precisely what happens when, as the Greeks put it, "the muse descends."

> Finding oil is sometimes like the feeling you get driving a little over the recommended speed limit on that sharp turn on the interstate outside Baton Rouge en route to Lafayette, when you come around that climbing corner pulling Gs and truck blast a little too fast and then after that whip of a turn

find yourself looking up at that space-age takeoff ramp they call a bridge that spans, after the vertical climb, the Mississippi River. You've been driving along all morning on this pretty but bland interstate, humming along into predictability and all of a sudden there are all these surprise marks on the landscape: intense abruptions, challenges to the spirit. You find yourself almost racing up that bridge even before you've fully acknowledged its existence. You look down and see water. It makes the backs of your hamstrings, and a wide zone across your chest, tingle. That is what finding oil is like.

[from "An Oilman's Notebook" by Rick Bass]

Part 2: EXERCISES

So what does one do with this information, that not-knowing and paying attention to personal mysteries leads to good creative writing? First, one learns how to recognize mystery. Learn to understand when you don't understand. Take note of it—if possible, literally, by carrying a notebook with you. So when you see that guy at the coffee shop stare into his cup for ten minutes as if the secret of the universe lay within, or when you see that old woman totter across the street, look alarmed, and totter back again, you can realize you have some potential material in front of you. The next stage is, of course, learning how to mine that material.

Exercise 1: Things I Was Taught / Things I Was Not Taught

> Goal: To elicit fresh and surprising insights into your relationship to family, friends, and community, and the world.

What to do: 1. Choose an individual who has been enormously influential in your life (usually a parent, sometimes a sibling or a friend).
2. Create a list of the things that person has taught you. The list should be entitled: 'Things That X Taught Me."
3. Create a list of the things that same person did *not* teach you. The list should be entitled, "Things That X Did Not Teach Me."

The following piece was written as a response to this exercise by Clare Dornan:

Things my father taught me

• How if you're sick, it's your special day. Your mother makes tea with lemon and a dash of the whiskey that she hides in her bedroom closet, and your father unplugs the small black-and-white television he keeps in his workroom and allows you to watch cartoons in bed.

- How to walk in the woods after a rain and think of nothing but the smell of eucalyptus and pine.

- How to let the mud dry on your shoes so you can knock it off with a stick the next day.

- That you're allowed to make an absolute pigsty of your car, and throw coffee cups, candy wrappers, half-eaten apples on the floor with abandon. When it gets too disgusting, you take it to the car wash and pay extra for the attendants to haul away the garbage and deodorize the moldy carpet.

- How to drive to Half Moon Bay and choose the best live crabs and lobsters from the tank. You let them crawl around on the back seat, because they don't have long to live, and must be allowed to enjoy the little time left to them. You listen to them scream when you throw them into boiling salted water, then you crack them open and eat them with melted butter and lemon, but only when your father is out of town, because why go to all that trouble for something so tasteless? You must have Hostess Hohos washed down with milk for dessert after you eat a freshly killed lobster.

Things my father didn't teach me

- When it's best to ignore that your wife is deeply unhappy; when you should bring her a glass of water, but be careful not to touch her; how to sit in the same room as her, but not so she has to look directly at you; that you shouldn't notice tears, or muffled phone conversations at 3 a.m., or whether the other side of the bed has been slept in when you wake up in the morning.

- When it's appropriate to continue to embrace your wife even though she struggles at first; when you should not allow her to watch David Letterman because she gets too depressed at how heartily the audience laughs when he mocks his guests; when it's okay to get in the car next to her and let her drive 100 miles north, then 75 miles east before turning the car toward home, all without saying a word.

- How to stop drinking before you have to spend the night on the couch of people you barely know and who don't like you.

- How to keep spare light bulbs around the house so when one goes out you can replace it immediately.

- How to wash your infant son's genitals in the bathtub without feeling ashamed.

- How to cheer with just the right balance of enthusiasm and irony from the bleachers at Wrigley Field when Ernie Banks hits a homer.

Exercise 2: I Want to Know Why

Goal: To identify interesting gaps in your understanding or knowledge in order to generate raw material for short stories.

What to do: 1. Create a list of at least ten items that fit into the category of things not known: "I want to know why." Important: impose constraints to avoid abstraction or otherwise "large" topics. For example, you might want to limit the things not known to the events of that week, or to family encounters.

2. Do a freewrite based on one of them.

The following exercise was written by John Sark:

I want to know why:

- I always see the same elderly woman at the bus stop but I've never seen her actually get on a bus.
- Sometimes I just have to have curry for breakfast!
- When my mother calls, she sounds angry even if she isn't.
- My roommate buys milk by the gallon, but it always goes sour before it is even halfway gone.
- That man who works at the coffeehouse never smiles.
- I never seem to win anything—never.
- None of the girls I really like will go out with me.
- My English instructor always looks right at me when asking for comments about whatever it is we're reading.
- Whenever I need to go someplace, I'm out of gas.
- Whenever I want to cook something, I don't have the right ingredients.

Whenever I want to cook something, I don't have the right ingredients. Take last night. Mary was over, and it was a chance to impress her, to show her that I wasn't the usual kind of guy that lives in the undergraduate dorms, that in addition to living in a *real apartment* I was mature enough, etc. to cook for myself, and even for others. Anyway, I had intended to cook some chicken and some corn on the cob, and I thought I had everything I needed, but realized when the chicken was in the oven and the corn was in the boiling water that I was completely out of salt. Corn on the cob without salt! Then of course, I checked, and I didn't have any butter, either. Not a slice. More mortifying, I went to the bathroom and discovered I was out of toilet paper. Some impressive guy I was turning out to be: fulfilling all the usual stereotypes.

Part 3: READING AS A WRITER

Where Are You Going, Where Have You Been?

JOYCE CAROL OATES

For Bob Dylan

Her name was Connie. She was fifteen and she had a quick nervous giggling habit of craning her neck to glance into mirrors, or checking other people's faces to make sure her own was all right. Her mother, who noticed everything and knew everything and who hadn't much reason any longer to look at her own face, always scolded Connie about it. "Stop gawking at yourself, who are you? You think you're so pretty?" she would say. Connie would raise her eyebrows at these familiar complaints and look right through her mother, into a shadowy vision of herself as she was right at that moment: she knew she was pretty and that was everything. Her mother had been pretty once too, if you could believe those old snap-shots in the album, but now her looks were gone and that was why she was always after Connie.

"Why don't you keep your room clean like your sister? How've you got your hair fixed—what the hell stinks? Hair spray? You don't see your sister using that junk."

Her sister June was twenty-four and still lived at home. She was a sec-retary in the high school Connie attended, and if that wasn't bad enough—with her in the same building—she was so plain and chunky and steady that Connie had to hear her praised all the time by her mother and her mother's sisters. June did this, June did that, she saved money and helped clean the house and cooked and Connie couldn't do a thing, her mind was all filled with trashy daydreams. Their father was away at work most of the time and when he came home he wanted supper and he read the news-paper at supper and after supper he went to bed. He didn't bother talking much to them, but around his bent head Connie's mother kept picking at her until Connie wished her mother was dead and she herself was dead and it was all over. "She makes me want to throw up sometimes," she com-plained to her friends. She had a high, breathless, amused voice which made everything she said a little forced, whether it was sincere or not.

There was one good thing: June went places with girl friends of hers, girls who were just as plain and steady as she, and so when Connie wanted to do that her mother had no objections. The father of Connie's best girl friend drove the girls the three miles to town and left them off at a shopping plaza, so that they could walk through the stores or go to a movie, and when he came to pick them up again at eleven he never bothered to ask what they had done.

They must have been familiar sights, walking around that shopping plaza in their shorts and flat ballerina slippers that always scuffed the sidewalk, with charm bracelets jingling on their thin wrists; they would lean together to whisper and laugh secretly if someone passed by who amused or interested them. Connie had long dark blond hair that drew anyone's eye to it, and she wore part of it pulled up on her head and puffed out and the rest of it she let fall down her back. She wore a pullover jersey blouse that looked one way when she was at home and another way when she was away from home. Everything about her had two sides to it, one for home and one for anywhere that was not home: her walk that could be childlike and bobbing, or languid enough to make anyone think she was hearing music in her head, her mouth which was pale and smirking most of the time, but bright and pink on these evenings out, her laugh which was cynical and drawling at home—"Ha, ha, very funny"—but high-pitched and nervous anywhere else, like the jingling of the charms on her bracelet.

Sometimes they did go shopping or to a movie, but sometimes they went across the highway, ducking fast across the busy road, to a drive-in restaurant where older kids hung out. The restaurant was shaped like a big bottle, though squatter than a real bottle, and on its cap was a revolving figure of a grinning boy who held a hamburger aloft. One night in midsummer they ran across, breathless with daring, and right away someone leaned out a car window and invited them over, but it was just a boy from high school they didn't like. It made them feel good to be able to ignore him. They went up through the maze of parked and cruising cars to the bright-lit, fly-infested restaurant, their faces pleased and expectant as if they were entering a sacred building that loomed out of the night to give them what haven and what blessing they yearned for. They sat at the counter and crossed their legs at the ankles, their thin shoulders rigid with excitement and listened to the music that made everything so good: the music was always in the background like music at a church service, it was something to depend upon.

A boy named Eddie came in to talk with them. He sat backwards on his stool, turning himself jerkily around in semicircles and then stopping and turning again, and after a while he asked Connie if she would like something to eat. She said she did and so she tapped her friend's arm on her way out—her friend pulled her face up into a brave droll look—and

Connie said she would meet her at eleven, across the way. "I just hate to leave her like that," Connie said earnestly, but the boy said that she wouldn't be alone for long. So they went out to his car and on the way Connie couldn't help but let her eyes wander over the windshields and faces all around her, her face gleaming with the joy that had nothing to do with Eddie or even this place; it might have been the music. She drew her shoulders up and sucked in her breath with the pure pleasure of being alive, and just at that moment she happened to glance at a face just a few feet from hers. It was a boy with shaggy black hair, in a convertible jalopy painted gold. He stared at her and then his lips widened into a grin. Connie slit her eyes at him and turned away, but she couldn't help glancing back and there he was still watching her. He wagged a finger and laughed and said, "Gonna get you, baby," and Connie turned away again without Eddie noticing anything.

She spent three hours with him, at the restaurant where they ate hamburgers and drank Cokes in wax cups that were always sweating, and then down an alley a mile or so away, and when he left her off at five to eleven only the movie house was still open at the plaza. Her girl friend was there, talking with a boy. When Connie came up the two girls smiled at each other and Connie said, "How was the movie?" and the girl said, "*You* should know." They rode off with the girl's father, sleepy and pleased, and Connie couldn't help but look at the darkened shopping plaza with its big empty parking lot and its signs that were faded and ghostly now, and over at the drive-in restaurant where cars were still circling tirelessly. She couldn't hear the music at this distance.

Next morning June asked her how the movie was and Connie said, "So-so."

She and that girl and occasionally another girl went out several times a week that way, and the rest of the time Connie spent around the house—it was summer vacation—getting in her mother's way and thinking, dreaming, about the boys she met. But all the boys fell back and dissolved into a single face that was not even a face, but an idea, a feeling, mixed up with the urgent insistent pounding of the music and the humid night air of July. Connie's mother kept dragging her back to the daylight by finding things for her to do or saying suddenly, "What's this about the Pettinger girl?"

And Connie would say nervously, "Oh, her. That dope." She always drew thick clear lines between herself and such girls, and her mother was simple and kindly enough to believe her. Her mother was so simple, Connie thought, that it was maybe cruel to fool her so much. Her mother went scuffling around the house in old bedroom slippers and complained over the telephone to one sister about the other, then the other called up and the two of them complained about the third one. If June's name was mentioned her mother's tone was approving, and if Connie's name was mentioned it was disapproving. This did not really mean she disliked Connie and actually Connie thought that her mother preferred her to June because she was prettier, but the two of them kept up a pretense of exasperation, a sense that they were tugging and struggling over something of little value to either of them. Sometimes, over coffee, they were almost friends, but something would come up—some vexation that was like a fly buzzing suddenly around their heads—and their faces went hard with contempt.

One Sunday Connie got up at eleven—none of them bothered with church—and washed her hair so that it could dry all day long, in the sun. Her parents and sister were going to a barbecue at an aunt's house and Connie said no, she wasn't interested, rolling her eyes, to let her mother know just what she thought of it. "Stay home alone then," her mother said sharply. Connie sat out back in a lawn chair and watched them drive away, her father quiet and bald, hunched around so that he could back the car out, her mother with a look that was still angry and not at all softened through the windshield, and in the back seat poor old June all dressed up as if she didn't know what a barbecue was, with all the running yelling kids and the flies. Connie sat with her eyes closed in the sun, dreaming and dazed with the warmth about her as if this were a kind of love, the caresses of love, and her mind slipped over onto thoughts of the boy she had been with the night before and how nice he had been, how sweet it always was, not the way someone like June would suppose but sweet, gentle, the way it was in movies and promised in songs; and when she opened her eyes she hardly knew where she was, the back yard ran off into weeds and a fenceline of trees and behind it the sky was perfectly blue and still. The asbestos "ranch house" that was now three years old startled her—it looked small. She shook her head as if to get awake.

It was too hot. She went inside the house and turned on the radio to drown out the quiet. She sat on the edge of her bed, barefoot, and listened for an hour and a half to a program called XYZ Sunday Jamboree, record after record of hard, fast, shrieking songs she sang along with, interspersed by exclamations from "Bobby King": "An' look here you girls at Napoleon's—Son and Charley want you to pay real close attention to this song coming up!"

And Connie paid close attention herself, bathed in a glow of slow-pulsed joy that seemed to rise mysteriously out of the music itself and lay languidly about the airless little room, breathed in and breathed out with each gentle rise and fall of her chest.

After a while she heard a car coming up the drive. She sat up at once, startled, because it couldn't be her father so soon. The gravel kept crunching all the way in from the road—the driveway was long—and Connie ran to the window. It was a car she didn't know. It was an open jalopy, painted a bright gold that caught the sun opaquely. Her heart began to pound and her fingers snatched at her hair, checking it, and she whispered "Christ. Christ," wondering how bad she looked. The car came to a stop at the side door and the horn sounded four short taps as if this were a signal Connie knew.

She went into the kitchen and approached the door slowly, then hung out the screen door, her bare toes curling down off the step. There were two boys in the car and now she recognized the driver: he had shaggy, shabby black hair that looked crazy as a wig and he was grinning at her.

"I ain't late, am I?" he said.

"Who the hell do you think you are?" Connie said.

"Toldja I'd be out, didn't I?"

"I don't even know who you are."

She spoke sullenly, careful to show no interest or pleasure, and he spoke in a fast bright monotone. Connie looked past him to the other boy, taking her time. He had fair brown hair, with a lock that fell onto his forehead. His sideburns gave him a fierce, embarrassed look, but so far he hadn't even bothered to glance at her. Both boys wore sunglasses. The driver's glasses were metallic and mirrored everything in miniature.

"You wanta come for a ride?" he said.

Connie smirked and let her hair fall loose over one shoulder.

"Don'tcha like my car? New paint job," he said. "Hey."

"What?"

"You're cute."

She pretended to fidget, chasing flies away from the door.

"Don'tcha believe me, or what?" he said.

"Look, I don't even know who you are," Connie said in disgust.

"Hey, Ellie's got a radio, see. Mine's broke down." He lifted his friend's arm and showed her the little transistor the boy was holding, and now Connie began to hear the music. It was the same program that was playing inside the house.

"Bobby King?" she said.

"I listen to him all the time. I think he's great."

"He's kind of great," Connie said reluctantly.

"Listen, that guy's *great*. He knows where the action is."

Connie blushed a little, because the glasses made it impossible for her to see just what this boy was looking at. She couldn't decide if she liked him or if he was just a jerk, and so she dawdled in the doorway and wouldn't come down or go back inside. She said, "What's all that stuff painted on your car?"

"Can'tcha read it?" He opened the door very carefully, as if he was afraid it might fall off. He slid out just as carefully, planting his feet firmly on the ground, the tiny metallic world in his glasses slowing down like gelatine hardening and in the midst of it Connie's bright green blouse. "This here is my name, to begin with," he said. ARNOLD FRIEND was written in tar-like black letters on the side, with a drawing of a round grinning face that reminded Connie of a pumpkin, except it wore sunglasses. "I wanta introduce myself, I'm Arnold Friend and that's my real name and I'm gonna be your friend, honey, and inside the car's Ellie Oscar, he's kinda shy." Ellie brought his transistor up to his shoulder and balanced it there. "Now these numbers are a secret code, honey," Arnold Friend explained. He read off the numbers 33, 19, 17 and raised his eyebrows at her to see what she thought of that, but she didn't think much of it. The left rear fender had been smashed and around it was written on the gleaming gold background: DONE BY CRAZY WOMAN DRIVER. Connie had to laugh at that. Arnold Friend was pleased at her laughter and looked up at her. "Around the other side's a lot more—you wanta come and see them?"

"No."

"Why not?"

"Why should I?"

"Don'tcha wanta see what's on the car? Don'tcha wanta go for a ride?"

"I don't know."

"Why not?"

"I got things to do."

"Like what?"

"Things."

He laughed as if she had said something funny. He slapped his thighs. He was standing in a strange way, leaning back against the car as if he were balancing himself. He wasn't tall, only an inch or so taller than she would be if she came down to him. Connie liked the way he was dressed, which was the way all of them dressed: tight faded jeans stuffed into black, scuffed boots, a belt that pulled his waist in and showed how lean he was, and a white pullover shirt that was a little soiled and showed the hard small muscles of his arms and shoulders. He looked as if he probably did hard work, lifting and carrying things. Even his neck looked muscular. And his face was a familiar face, somehow: the jaw and chin and cheeks slightly darkened, because he hadn't shaved for a day or two, and the nose long and hawk-like, sniffing as if she were a treat he was going to gobble up and it was all a joke.

"Connie, you ain't telling the truth. This is your day set aside for a ride with me and you know it," he said, still laughing. The way he straightened and recovered from his fit of laughing showed that it had been all fake.

"How do you know what my name is?" she said suspiciously.

"It's Connie."

"Maybe and maybe not."

"I know my Connie," he said, wagging his finger. Now she remembered him even better, back at the restaurant, and her cheeks warmed at the thought of how she sucked in her breath just at the moment she passed him—how she must have looked to him. And he had remembered her. "Ellie and I come out here especially for you," he said. "Ellie can sit in back. How about it?"

"Where?"

"Where what?"

"Where're we going?"

He looked at her. He took off the sunglasses and she saw how pale the skin around his eyes was, like holes that were not in shadow but instead in light. His eyes were like chips of broken glass that catch the light in an amiable way. He smiled. It was as if the idea of going for a ride somewhere, to some place, was a new idea to him.

"Just for a ride, Connie sweetheart."

"I never said my name was Connie," she said.

"But I know what it is. I know your name and all about you, lots of things," Arnold Friend said. He had not moved yet but stood still leaning back against the side of his jalopy. "I took a special interest in you, such a pretty girl, and found out all about you like I know your parents and sister are gone somewheres and I know where and how long they're going to be gone, and I know who you were with last night, and your best friend's name is Betty. Right?"

He spoke in a simple lilting voice, exactly as if he were reciting the words to a song. His smile assured her that everything was fine. In the car Ellie turned up the volume on his radio and did not bother to look around at them.

"Ellie can sit in the back seat," Arnold Friend said. He indicated his friend with a casual jerk of his chin, as if Ellie did not count and she could not bother with him.

"How'd you find out all that stuff?" Connie said.

"Listen: Betty Schultz and Tony Fitch and Jimmy Pettinger and Nancy Pettinger," he said, in a chant. "Raymond Stanley and Bob Hutter—"

"Do you know all those kids?"

"I know everybody."

"Look, you're kidding. You're not from around here."

"Sure."

"But—how come we never saw you before?"

"Sure you saw me before," he said. He looked down at his boots, as if he were a little offended. "You just don't remember."

"I guess I'd remember you," Connie said.

"Yeah?" He looked up at this, beaming. He was pleased. He began to mark time with the music from Ellie's radio, tapping his fists lightly together. Connie looked away from his smile to the car, which was painted so bright it almost hurt her eyes to look at it. She looked at that name, ARNOLD FRIEND. And up at the front fender was an expression that was familiar—MAN THE FLYING SAUCERS. It was an expression kids had used the year before, but didn't use this year. She looked at it for a while as if the words meant something to her that she did not yet know.

"What're you thinking about? Huh?" Arnold Friend demanded. "Not worried about your hair blowing around in the car, are you?"

"No."

"Think I maybe can't drive good?"

"How do I know?"

"You're a hard girl to handle. How come?" he said. "Don't you know I'm your friend? Didn't you see me put my sign in the air when you walked by?"

"What sign?"

"My sign." And he drew an X in the air, leaning out toward her. They were maybe ten feet apart. After his hand fell back to his side the X was still in the air, almost visible. Connie let the screen door close and stood perfectly still inside it, listening to the music from her radio and the boy's blend together. She stared at Arnold Friend. He stood there so stiffly relaxed, pretending to be relaxed, with one hand idly on the door handle as if he were keeping himself up that way and had no intention of ever moving again. She recognized most things about him, the tight jeans that showed his thighs and buttocks and the greasy leather boots and the tight shirt, and even that slippery friendly smile of his, that sleepy dreamy smile that all the boys used to get across ideas they didn't want to put into words. She recognized all this and also the singsong way he talked, slightly mocking, kidding, but serious and a little melancholy, and she recognized the way he tapped one fist against the other in homage to the perpetual music behind him. But all these things did not come together.

She said suddenly, "Hey, how old are you?"

His smile faded. She could see then that he wasn't a kid, he was much older—thirty, maybe more. At this knowledge her heart began to pound faster.

"That's a crazy thing to ask. Can'tcha see I'm your own age?"

"Like hell you are."

"Or maybe a coupla years older, I'm eighteen."

"Eighteen?" she said doubtfully.

He grinned to reassure her and lines appeared at the corners of his mouth. His teeth were big and white. He grinned so broadly his eyes became slits and she saw how thick the lashes were, thick and black as if painted with a black tar-like material. Then he seemed to become embarrassed, abruptly, and looked over his shoulder at Ellie. "*Him*, he's crazy," he said. "Ain't he a riot, he's a nut, a real character." Ellie was still listening to the music. His sunglasses told nothing about what he was thinking. He wore a bright orange shirt unbuttoned halfway to show his chest, which was a pale, bluish chest and not muscular like Arnold Friend's. His shirt collar was turned up all around and the very tips of the collar pointed out past his chin as if they were protecting him. He was pressing the transistor radio up against his ear and sat there in a kind of daze, right in the sun.

"He's kinda strange," Connie said.

"Hey, she says you're kinda strange! Kinda strange!" Arnold Friend cried. He pounded on the car to get Ellie's attention. Ellie turned for the first time and Connie saw with shock that he wasn't a kid either—he had a fair, hairless face, cheeks reddened slightly as if the veins grew too close to the surface of his skin, the face of a forty-year-old baby. Connie felt a wave of dizziness rise in her at this sight and she stared at him as if waiting for something to change the shock of the moment, make it all right again. Ellie's lips kept shaping words, mumbling along with the words blasting his ear.

"Maybe you two better go away," Connie said faintly.

"What? How come?" Arnold Friend cried. "We come out here to take you for a ride. It's Sunday." He had the voice of the man on the radio now. It was the same voice, Connie thought. "Don'tcha know it's Sunday all day and honey, no matter who you were with last night today you're with Arnold Friend and don't you forget it!—Maybe you better step out here," he said, and this last was in a different voice. It was a little flatter, as if the heat was finally getting to him.

"No. I got things to do."

"Hey."

"You two better leave."

"We ain't leaving until you come with us."

"Like hell I am—"

"Connie, don't fool around with me. I mean—I mean, don't fool *around*," he said, shaking his head. He laughed incredulously. He placed his sunglasses on top of his head, carefully, as if he were indeed wearing a wig, and brought the stems down behind his ears. Connie stared at him, another wave of dizziness and fear rising in her so that for a moment he wasn't even in focus but was just a blur, standing z there against his gold car, and she had the idea that he had driven up the driveway all right but had come from nowhere before that and belonged nowhere and that everything about him and even the music that was so familiar to her was only half real.

"If my father comes and sees you—"

"He ain't coming. He's at a barbecue."

"How do you know that?"

"Aunt Tillie's. Right now they're—uh—they're drinking. Sitting around," he said vaguely, squinting as if he were staring all the way to town and over to Aunt Tillie's back yard. Then the vision seemed to clear and he nodded energetically. "Yeah. Sitting around. There's your sister in a blue dress, huh? And high heels, the poor sad bitch—nothing like you, sweetheart! And your mother's helping some fat woman with the corn, they're cleaning the corn—husking the corn—"

"What fat woman?" Connie cried.

"How do I know what fat woman. I don't know every goddamn fat woman in the world!" Arnold Friend laughed.

"Oh, that's Mrs. Hornby . . . Who invited her?" Connie said. She felt a little light-headed. Her breath was coming quickly.

"She's too fat. I don't like them fat. I like them the way you are, honey," he said, smiling sleepily at her. They stared at each other for a while, through the screen door. He said softly, "Now what you're going to do is this: you're going to come out that door. You're going to sit up front with me and Ellie's going to sit in the back, the hell with Ellie, right? This isn't Ellie's date. You're my date. I'm your lover, honey."

"What? You're crazy—"

"Yes, I'm your lover. You don't know what that is but you will," he said. "I know that too. I know all about you. But look: it's real nice and you couldn't ask for nobody better than me, or more polite. I always keep my word. I'll tell you how it is, I'm always nice at first, the first time. I'll hold you so tight you won't think you have to try to get away or pretend anything because you'll know you can't. And I'll come inside you where it's all secret and you'll give in to me and you'll love me—"

"Shut up! You're crazy!" Connie said. She backed away from the door. She put her hands against her ears as if she'd heard something terrible, something not meant for her. "People don't talk like that, you're crazy," she muttered. Her heart was almost too big now for her chest and its pumping made sweat break out all over her. She looked out to see Arnold Friend pause and then take a step toward the porch lurching. He almost fell. But, like a clever drunken man, he managed to catch his balance. He wobbled in his high boots and grabbed hold of one of the porch posts.

"Honey?" he said. "You still listening?"

"Get the hell out of here!"

"Be nice, honey. Listen."

"I'm going to call the police—"

He wobbled again and out of the side of his mouth came a fast spat curse, an aside not meant for her to hear. But even this "Christ!" sounded forced. Then he began to smile again. She watched this smile come, awkward as if he were smiling from inside a mask. His whole face was a mask, she thought wildly, tanned down onto his throat but then running out as if he had plastered makeup on his face but had forgotten about his throat.

"Honey—? Listen, here's how it is. I always tell the truth and I promise you this: I ain't coming in that house after you."

"You better not! I'm going to call the police if you—if you don't—"

"Honey," he said, talking right through her voice, "honey, I'm not coming in there but you are coming out here. You know why?"

She was panting. The kitchen looked like a place she had never seen before, some room she had run inside but which wasn't good enough, wasn't going to help her. The kitchen window had never had a curtain, after three years, and there were dishes in the sink for her to do—probably—and if you ran your hand across the table you'd probably feel something sticky there.

"You listening, honey? Hey?"

"—going to call the police—"

"Soon as you touch the phone I don't need to keep my promise and can come inside. You won't want that."

She rushed forward and tried to lock the door. Her fingers were shaking. "But why lock it," Arnold Friend said gently, talking right into her face. "It's just a screen door. It's just nothing." One of his boots was at a strange angle, as if his foot wasn't in it. It pointed out to the left, bent at the ankle. "I mean, anybody can break through a screen door and glass and wood and iron or anything else if he needs to, anybody at all and specially Arnold Friend. If the place got lit up with a fire, honey, you'd come runnin' out into my arms, right into my arms an' safe at home—like you knew I was your lover and'd stopped fooling around, I don't mind a nice shy girl but I don't like no fooling around." Part of those words were spoken with a slight rhythmic lilt, and Connie somehow recognized them—the echo of a song from last year, about a girl rushing into her boy friend's arms and coming home again—

Connie stood barefoot on the linoleum floor, staring at him. "What do you want?" she whispered.

"I want you," he said.

"What?"

"Seen you that night and thought, that's the one, yes sir. I never needed to look any more."

"But my father's coming back. He's coming to get me. I had to wash my hair first—" She spoke in a dry, rapid voice, hardly raising it for him to hear.

"No, your daddy is not coming and yes, you had to wash your hair and you washed it for me. It's nice and shining and all for me. I thank you, sweetheart," he said, with a mock bow, but again he almost lost his balance. He had to bend and adjust his boots. Evidently his feet did not go all the way down; the boots must have been stuffed with something so that he would seem taller. Connie stared out at him and behind him at Ellie in the car, who seemed to be looking off toward Connie's right, into nothing. Then Ellie said, pulling the words out of the air one after another as if he were just discovering them, "You want me to pull out the phone?"

"Shut your mouth and keep it shut," Arnold Friend said, his face red from bending over or maybe from embarrassment because Connie had seen his boots. "This ain't none of your business."

"What—what are you doing? What do you want?" Connie said. "If I call the police they'll get you, they'll arrest you—"

"Promise was not to come in unless you touch that phone, and I'll keep that promise," he said. He resumed his erect position and tried to force his shoulders back. He sounded like a hero in a movie, declaring something important. He spoke too loudly and it was as if he were speaking to someone behind Connie. "I ain't made plans for coming in that house where I don't belong but just for you to come out to me, the way you should. Don't you know who I am?"

"You're crazy," she whispered. She backed away from the door but did not want to go into another part of the house, as if this would give him permission to come through the door. "What do you . . . You're crazy, you . . ."

"Huh? What're you saying, honey?"

Her eyes darted everywhere in the kitchen. She could not remember what it was, this room.

"This is how it is, honey: you come out and we'll drive away, have a nice ride. But if you don't come out we're gonna wait till your people come home and then they're all going to get it."

"You want that telephone pulled out?" Ellie said. He held the radio away from his ear and grimaced, as if without the radio the air was too much for him.

"I toldja shut up, Ellie," Arnold Friend said, "you're deaf, get a hearing aid, right? Fix yourself up. This little girl's no trouble and's gonna be nice to me, so Ellie keep to yourself, this ain't your date—right? Don't hem in on me, don't hog, don't crush, don't bird dog, don't trail me," he said in a rapid, meaningless voice, as if he were running through all the expressions he'd learned but was no longer sure which one of them was in style, then rushing on to new ones, making them up with his eyes closed. "Don't crawl under my fence, don't squeeze in my chipmunk hole, don't sniff my glue, suck my Popsicle, keep your own greasy fingers on yourself!" He shaded his eyes and peered in at Connie, who was backed against the kitchen table. "Don't mind him, honey, he's just a creep. He's a dope. Right? I'm the boy for you and like I said, you come out here nice like a lady and give me your hand, and nobody else gets hurt, I mean, your nice old bald-headed daddy and your mummy and your sister in her high heels. Because listen: why bring them in this?"

"Leave me alone," Connie whispered.

"Hey, you know that old woman down the road, the one with the chickens and stuff—you know her?"

"She's dead!"

"Dead? What? You know her?" Arnold Friend said.

"She's dead—"

"Don't you like her?"

"She's dead—she's—she isn't here any more—"

"But don't you like her, I mean, you got something against her? Some grudge or something?" Then his voice dipped as if he were conscious of rudeness. He touched the sunglasses on top of his head as if to make sure they were still there. "Now you be a good girl."

"What are you going to do?"

"Just two things, or maybe three," Arnold Friend said. "But I promise it won't last long and you'll like me that way you get to like people you're close to. You will. It's all over for you here, so come on out. You don't want your people in any trouble, do you?"

She turned and bumped against a chair or something, hurting her leg, but she ran into the back room and picked up the telephone. Something roared in her ear, a tiny roaring, and she was so sick with fear that she could do nothing but listen to it—the telephone was clammy and very heavy and her fingers groped down to the dial but were too weak to touch it. She began to scream into the phone, into the roaring. She cried out, she cried for her mother, she felt her breath start jerking back and forth in her lungs as if it were something Arnold Friend was stabbing her with again and again with no tenderness. A noisy sorrowful wailing rose all about her and she was locked inside it the way she was locked inside this house.

After a while she could hear again. She was sitting on the floor, with her wet back against the wall.

Arnold Friend was saying from the door, "That's a good girl. Put the phone back."

She kicked the phone away from her.

"No, honey. Pick it up. Put it back right."

She picked it up and put it back. The dial tone stopped.

"That's a good girl. Now you come outside."

She was hollow with what had been fear but what was now just an emptiness. All that screaming had blasted it out of her. She sat, one leg cramped under her, and deep inside her brain was something like a pin-point of light that kept going and would not let her relax. She thought, I'm not going to see my mother again. She thought, I'm not going to sleep in my bed again. Her bright green blouse was all wet.

Arnold Friend said, in a gentle-loud voice that was like a stage voice, "The place where you came from ain't there any more, and where you had in mind to go is cancelled out. This place you are now—inside your daddy's house—is nothing but a cardboard box I can knock down any time. You know that and always did know it. You hear me?"

She thought, I have got to think. I have got to know what to do.

"We'll go out to a nice field, out in the country here where it smells so nice and it's sunny," Arnold Friend said. "I'll have my arms tight around you so you won't need to try to get away and I'll show you what love is like, what it does. The hell with this house! It looks solid all right," he said. He ran a fingernail down the screen and the noise did not make Connie shiver, as it would have the day before. "Now put your hand on your heart, honey. Feel that? That feels solid too but we know better. Be nice to me, be sweet like you can because what else is there for a girl like you but to be sweet and pretty and give in?—and get away before her people get back?"

She felt her pounding heart. Her hand seemed to enclose it. She thought for the first time in her life that it was nothing that was hers, that belonged to her, but just a pounding, living thing inside this body that wasn't really hers either.

"You don't want them to get hurt," Arnold Friend went on. "Now get up, honey. Get up all by yourself."

She stood.

"Now turn this way. That's right. Come over to me—Ellie, put that away, didn't I tell you? You dope. You miserable creepy dope," Arnold Friend said. His words were not angry but only part of an incantation. The incantation was kindly. "Now come out through the kitchen to me honey and let's see a smile, try it, you're a brave sweet little girl and now they're eating corn and hotdogs cooked to bursting over an outdoor fire, and they don't know one thing about you and never did and honey you're better than them because not a one of them would have done this for you."

Connie felt the linoleum under her feet; it was cool. She brushed her hair back out of her eyes. Arnold Friend let go of the post tentatively and opened his arms for her, his elbows pointing in toward each other and his wrists limp, to show that this was an embarrassed embrace and a little mocking, he didn't want to make her self-conscious.

She put out her hand against the screen. She watched herself push the door slowly open as if she were back safe somewhere in the other door-way, watching this body and this head of long hair moving out into the sunlight where Arnold Friend waited.

"My sweet little blue-eyed girl," he said in a half-sung sigh that had nothing to do with her brown eyes but was taken up just the same by the vast sunlit reaches of the land behind him and on all sides of him—so much land that Connie had never seen before and did not recognize except to know that she was going to it.

1. How does Oates define Connie's character?
2. How would you characterize the relationship between Connie and her

mother? Is it one-dimensional? Or is there something that keeps it from being flat and overly familiar?

3. How does Oates create tension in the piece? What aspects of the piece are the most suspenseful, and why?

Welcome to Cancerland

BARBARA EHRENREICH

I was thinking of it as one of those drive-by mammograms, one stop in a series of mundane missions including post office, supermarket, and gym, but I began to lose my nerve in the changing room, and not only because of the kinky necessity of baring my breasts and affixing tiny x-ray opaque stars to the tip of each nipple. I had been in this place only four months earlier, but that visit was just part of the routine cancer surveillance all good citizens of HMOs or health plans are expected to submit to once they reach the age of fifty, and I hadn't really been paying attention then. The results of that earlier session had aroused some "concern" on the part of the radiologist and her confederate, the gynecologist, so I am back now in the role of a suspect, eager to clear my name, alert to medical missteps and unfair allegations. But the changing room, really just a closet off the stark windowless space that houses the mammogram machine, contains something far worse, I notice for the first time now—an assumption about who I am, where I am going, and what I will need when I get there. Almost all of the eye-level space has been filled with photocopied bits of cuteness and sentimentality: pink ribbons, a cartoon about a woman with iatrogenically flattened breasts, an "Ode to a Mammogram," a list of the "Top Ten Things Only Women Understand" ("Fat Clothes" and "Eyelash Curlers" among them), and, inescapably, right next to the door, the poem "I Said a Prayer for You Today," illustrated with pink roses.

It goes on and on, this mother of all mammograms, cutting into gym time, dinnertime, and lifetime generally. Sometimes the machine doesn't work, and I get squished into position to no purpose at all. More often, the x-ray is successful but apparently alarming to the invisible radiologist, off in some remote office, who calls the shots and never has the courtesy to show her face with an apology or an explanation. I try pleading with the technician: I have no known risk factors, no breast cancer in the family, had my babies relatively young and nursed them both. I eat right, drink sparingly, work out, and doesn't that count for something? But she just gets this tight little professional smile on her face, either out of guilt for the torture she's inflicting or because she already knows something that I am going to be sorry to find out for myself. For an hour and a half the procedure is repeated: the squishing, the snapshot, the technician bustling off to consult the radiologist and returning with a demand for new angles and more definitive images. In the intervals while she's off with the doctor I read the *New York Times* right down to the personally irrelevant sections like theater and real estate, eschewing the stack of women's magazines provided for me, much as I ordinarily enjoy a quick read about sweat-proof eyeliners and "fabulous sex tonight," because I have picked up this warning vibe in the changing room, which, in my increasingly anxious state, translates into: femininity is death. Finally there is nothing left to read but one of the free local weekly newspapers, where I find, buried deep in the classifieds, something even more unsettling than the growing prospect of major disease—a classified ad for a "breast cancer teddy bear" with a pink ribbon stitched to its chest.

Yes, atheists pray in their foxholes—in this case, with a yearning new to me and sharp as lust, for a clean and honorable death by shark bite, lightning strike, sniper fire, car crash. Let me be hacked to death by a madman, is my silent supplication—anything but suffocation by the pink sticky sentiment embodied in that bear and oozing from the walls of the changing room.

My official induction into breast cancer comes about ten days later with the biopsy, which, for reasons I cannot ferret out of the surgeon, has to be a surgical one, performed on an outpatient basis but under general anesthesia, from which I awake to find him standing perpendicular to me, at the far end of the gurney, down near my feet, stating gravely, "Unfortunately, there is a cancer." It takes me all the rest of that drug-addled day to decide that the most heinous thing about that sentence is not the presence of cancer but the absence of me—for I, Barbara, do not enter into it even as a location, a geographical reference point. Where I once was—not a commanding presence perhaps, but nonetheless a standard assemblage of flesh and words and gesture—"there is a cancer." I have been replaced by it, is the surgeon's implication. This is what I am now, medically speaking.

In my last act of dignified self-assertion, I request to see the pathology slides myself. This is not difficult to arrange in our small-town hospital, where the pathologist turns out to be a friend of a friend, and my rusty PhD in cell biology (Rockefeller University, 1968) probably helps. He's a jolly fellow, the pathologist, who calls me "hon" and sits me down at one end of the dual-head microscope while he mans the other and moves a pointer through the field. These are the cancer cells, he says, showing up blue because of their overactive DNA. Most of them are arranged in staid semicircular arrays, like suburban houses squeezed into a cul-de-sac, but I also see what I know enough to know I do not want to see: the characteristic "Indian files" of cells on the march. The "enemy," I am supposed to think—an image to save up for future exercises in "visualization" of their violent deaths at the hands of the body's killer cells, the lymphocytes and macrophages. But I am impressed, against all rational self-interest, by the energy of these cellular conga lines, their determination to move on out from the backwater of the breast to colonize lymph nodes, bone marrow, lungs, and brain. These are, after all, the fanatics of Barbaraness, the rebel cells that have realized that the genome they carry, the genetic essence of me, has no further chance of normal reproduction in the postmenopausal body we share, so why not just start multiplying like bunnies and hope for a chance to break out?

It has happened, after all; some genomes have achieved immortality through cancer. When I was a graduate student, I once asked about the strain of tissue-culture cells labeled "HeLa" in the heavy-doored room maintained at body temperature. "HeLa," it turns out, refers to one Henrietta Lacks, whose tumor was the progenitor of all HeLa cells. She died; they live, and will go on living until someone gets tired of them or forgets to change their tissue-culture medium and leaves them to starve. Maybe this is what my rebel cells have in mind, and I try beaming them a solemn warning: The chances of your surviving me in tissue culture are nil. Keep up this selfish rampage and you go down, every last one of you, along with the entire Barbara enterprise. But what kind of a role model am I, or are multicellular human organisms generally, for putting the common good above mad anarchistic individual ambition? There is a reason, it occurs to me, why cancer is our metaphor for so many runaway social processes, like corruption and "moral decay": we are no less out of control ourselves.

After the visit to the pathologist, my biological curiosity drops to a lifetime nadir. I know women who followed up their diagnoses with weeks or months of self-study, mastering their options, interviewing doctor after doctor, assessing the damage to be expected from the available treatments. But I can tell from a few hours of investigation that the career of a breast-cancer patient has been pretty well mapped out in advance for me: You may get to negotiate the choice between lumpectomy and mastectomy, but lumpectomy is commonly followed by weeks of radiation, and in either case if the lymph nodes turn out, upon dissection, to be invaded—or "involved," as it's less threateningly put—you're doomed to chemotherapy, meaning baldness, nausea, mouth sores, immunosuppression, and possible anemia. These interventions do not constitute a "cure" or anything close, which is why the death rate from breast cancer has changed very little since the 1930s, when mastectomy was the only treatment available. Chemotherapy, which became a routine part of breast-cancer treatment in the eighties, does not confer anywhere near as decisive an advantage as patients are often led to believe, especially in postmenopausal women like myself—a two or three percentage point difference in ten-year survival rates,[*] according to America's best-known breast-cancer surgeon, Dr. Susan Love.

I know these bleak facts, or sort of know them, but in the fog of anesthesia that hangs over those first few weeks, I seem to lose my capacity for self-defense. The pressure is on, from doctors and loved ones, to do something right away—kill it, get it out now. The endless exams, the bone scan to check for metastases, the high-tech heart test to see if I'm strong enough to withstand chemotherapy—all these blur the line between selfhood and thinghood anyway, organic and inorganic, me and it. As my cancer career unfolds, I will, the helpful pamphlets explain, become a composite of the living and the dead—an implant to replace the breast, a wig to replace the hair. And then what will I mean when I use the word "I"? I fall into a state of unreasoning passive aggressivity: They diagnosed this, so it's their baby. They found it, let them fix it.

I could take my chances with "alternative" treatments, of course, like punk novelist Kathy Acker, who succumbed to breast cancer in 1997 after a course of alternative therapies in Mexico, or actress and ThighMaster promoter Suzanne Somers, who made tabloid headlines last spring by injecting herself with mistletoe brew. Or I could choose to do nothing at all beyond mentally exhorting my immune system to exterminate the traitorous cellular faction. But I have never admired the "natural" or believed in the "wisdom of the body." Death is as "natural" as anything gets, and the body has always seemed to me like a retarded Siamese twin dragging along behind me, a hysteric really, dangerously overreacting, in my case, to everyday allergens and minute ingestions of sugar. I will put my faith in science, even if this means that the dumb old body is about to be transmogrified into an evil clown—puking, trembling, swelling, surrendering

---

* In the United States, one in eight women will be diagnosed with breast cancer at some point. The chances of her surviving for five years are 86.8 percent. For a black woman this falls to 72 percent; and for a woman of any race whose cancer has spread to the lymph nodes, to 77.7 percent.

significant parts, and oozing postsurgical fluids. The surgeon—a more genial and forthcoming one this time—can fit me in; the oncologist will see me. Welcome to Cancerland.

Fortunately, no one has to go through this alone. Thirty years ago, before Betty Ford, Rose Kushner, Betty Rollin, and other pioneer patients spoke out, breast cancer was a dread secret, endured in silence and euphemized in obituaries as a "long illness." Something about the conjuncture of "breast," signifying sexuality and nurturance, and that other word, suggesting the claws of a devouring crustacean, spooked almost everyone. Today, however, it's the biggest disease on the cultural map, bigger than AIDS, cystic fibrosis, or spinal injury, bigger even than those more prolific killers of women—heart disease, lung cancer, and stroke. There are roughly hundreds of Web sites devoted to it, not to mention newsletters, support groups, a whole genre of first-person breast-cancer books, even a glossy, upper-middle-brow monthly magazine, *Mamm*. There are four major national breast-cancer organizations, of which the mightiest, in financial terms, is the Susan G. Komen Foundation, headed by breast-cancer veteran and Bush's nominee for ambassador to Hungary Nancy Brinker. Komen organizes the annual Race for the Cure©, which attracts about a million people—mostly survivors, friends, and family members. Its Web site provides a microcosm of the new breast-cancer culture, offering news of the races, message boards for accounts of individuals' struggles with the disease, and a "marketplace" of breast-cancer-related products to buy.

More so than in the case of any other disease, breast-cancer organizations and events feed on a generous flow of corporate support. Nancy Brinker relates how her early attempts to attract corporate interest in promoting breast-cancer "awareness" were met with rebuff. A bra manufacturer, importuned to affix a mammogram-reminder tag to his product, more or less wrinkled his nose. Now breast cancer has blossomed from wallflower to the most popular girl at the corporate charity prom. While AIDS goes begging and low-rent diseases like tuberculosis have no friends at all, breast cancer has been able to count on Revlon, Avon, Ford, Tiffany, Pier 1, Estée Lauder, Ralph Lauren, Lee Jeans, Saks Fifth Avenue, JC Penney, Boston Market, Wilson athletic gear—and I apologize to those I've omitted. You can "shop for the cure" during the week when Saks donates 2 percent of sales to a breast-cancer fund; "wear denim for the cure" during Lee National Denim Day, when for a five-dollar donation you get to wear blue jeans to work. You can even "invest for the cure," in the Kinetics Assets Management's new no-load Medical Fund, which specializes entirely in businesses involved in cancer research.

If you can't run, bike, or climb a mountain for the cure—all of which endeavors are routine beneficiaries of corporate sponsorship—you can always purchase one of the many products with a breast-cancer theme. There are 2.2 million American women in various stages of their breast-cancer careers, who, along with anxious relatives, make up a significant market for all things breast-cancer-related. Bears, for example: I have identified four distinct lines, or species, of these creatures, including "Carol," the Remembrance Bear; "Hope," the Breast Cancer Research Bear, which wears a pink turban as if to conceal chemotherapy-induced baldness; the "Susan Bear," named for Nancy Brinker's deceased sister, Susan; and the new Nick & Nora Wish Upon a Star Bear, available, along with the Susan Bear, at the Komen Foundation Web site's "marketplace."

And bears are only the tip, so to speak, of the cornucopia of pink-ribbon-themed breast-cancer products. You can dress in pink-beribboned sweatshirts, denim shirts, pajamas, lingerie, aprons, loungewear, shoelaces, and socks; accessorize with pink rhinestone brooches, angel pins, scarves, caps, earrings, and bracelets; brighten up your home with breast-cancer candles, stained-glass pink-ribbon candleholders, coffee mugs, pendants, wind chimes, and night-lights; pay your bills with special BreastChecks or a separate line of Checks for the Cure. "Awareness" beats secrecy and stigma, of course, but I can't help noticing that the existential space in which a friend has earnestly advised me to "confront [my] mortality" bears a striking resemblance to the mall.

This is not, I should point out, a case of cynical merchants exploiting the sick. Some of the breast-cancer tchotchkes and accessories are made by breast-cancer survivors themselves, such as "Janice," creator of the "Daisy Awareness Necklace," among other things, and in most cases a portion of the sales goes to breast-cancer research. Virginia Davis of Aurora, Colorado, was inspired to create the "Remembrance Bear" by a friend's double mastectomy and sees her work as more of a "crusade" than a business. This year she expects to ship ten thousand of these teddies, which are manufactured in China, and send part of the money to the Race for the Cure. If the bears are infantilizing—as I try ever so tactfully to suggest is how they may, in rare cases, be perceived—so far no one has complained. "I just get love letters," she tells me, "from people who say, 'God bless you for thinking of us.'"

The ultrafeminine theme of the breast-cancer "marketplace"—the prominence, for example, of cosmetics and jewelry—could be understood as a response to the treatments' disastrous effects on one's looks. But the infantilizing trope is a little harder to account for, and teddy bears are not its only manifestation. A tote bag distributed to breast-cancer patients by the Libby Ross Foundation (through places such as the Columbia Presbyterian Medical Center) contains, among other items, a tube of Estée Lauder Perfumed Body Crème, a hot-pink satin pillowcase, an audiotape "Meditation to Help You with Chemotherapy," a small tin of peppermint pastilles, a set of three small inexpensive rhinestone bracelets, a pink-striped "journal and sketch book," and—somewhat jarringly—a small box of crayons. Maria Willner, one of the founders of the Libby Ross Foundation, told me that the crayons "go with the journal for people to express different moods, different thoughts," though she admitted she has never tried to write with crayons herself. Possibly the idea is that regression to a state of childlike dependency puts one in the best frame of mind with which to endure the prolonged and toxic treatments. Or it may be that, in some versions of the prevailing gender ideology, femininity is by its nature incompatible with full adulthood—a state of arrested development. Certainly men diagnosed with prostate cancer do not receive gifts of Matchbox cars.

But I, no less than the bear huggers, need whatever help I can get, and start wading out into the Web in search of practical tips on hair loss, lumpectomy versus mastectomy, how to select a chemotherapy regimen, what to wear after surgery and eat when the scent of food sucks. There is, I soon find, far more than I can usefully absorb, for thousands of the afflicted have posted their stories, beginning with the lump or bad mammogram, proceeding through the agony of the treatments; pausing to mention the sustaining forces of family, humor, and religion; and ending, in almost all cases, with warm words of encouragement for the neophyte. Some of these are no more than a paragraph long—brief waves from sister sufferers; others offer almost hour-by-hour logs of breast-deprived, chemotherapized lives:

Tuesday, August 15, 2000: Well, I survived my 4th chemo. Very, very dizzy today. Very nauseated, but no barfing! It's a first . . . I break out in a cold sweat and my heart pounds if I stay up longer than 5 minutes.

Friday, August 18, 2000: . . . By dinner time, I was full out nauseated. I took some meds and ate a rice and vegetable bowl from Trader Joe's. It smelled and tasted awful to me, but I ate it anyway . . . Rick brought home some Kern's nectars and I'm drinking that. Seems to have settled my stomach a little bit.

I can't seem to get enough of these tales, reading on with panicky fascina-
tion about everything that can go wrong—septicemia, ruptured implants,
startling recurrences a few years after the completion of treatments, "mets"
(metastases) to vital organs, and—what scares me most in the short term—
"chemo-brain," or the cognitive deterioration that sometimes accompanies
chemotherapy. I compare myself with everyone, selfishly impatient with
those whose conditions are less menacing, shivering over those who have
reached Stage IV ("There is no Stage V," as the main character in *Wit*, who
has ovarian cancer, explains), constantly assessing my chances.

Feminism helped make the spreading breast-cancer sisterhood possible,
and this realization gives me a faint feeling of belonging. Thirty years ago,
when the disease went hidden behind euphemism and prostheses, medicine was a solid patriarchy, women's bodies its passive objects of labor.
The Women's Health Movement, in which I was an activist in the seventies and eighties, legitimized self-help and mutual support and encouraged women to network directly, sharing their stories, questioning the
doctors, banding together. It is hard now to recall how revolutionary these
activities once seemed, and probably few participants in breast-cancer
chat rooms and message boards realize that when postmastectomy
patients first proposed meeting in support groups in the mid-1970s, the
American Cancer Society responded with a firm and fatherly "no." Now
no one leaves the hospital without a brochure directing her to local support groups and, at least in my case, a follow-up call from a social worker
to see whether I am safely ensconced in one. This cheers me briefly, until I
realize that if support groups have won the stamp of medical approval,
this may be because they are no longer perceived as seditious.

    In fact, aside from the dilute sisterhood of the cyber (and actual) sup-
port groups, there is nothing very feminist—in an ideological or activist
sense—about the mainstream of breast-cancer culture today. Let me pause
to qualify: you can, if you look hard enough, find plenty of genuine, self-
identified feminists within the vast pink sea of the breast-cancer crusade,
women who are militantly determined to "beat the epidemic" and insistent on more user-friendly approaches to treatment. It was feminist health
activists who led the campaign, in the seventies and eighties, against the
most savage form of breast-cancer surgery—the Halsted radical mastectomy, which removed chest muscle and lymph nodes as well as breast tissue and left women permanently disabled. It was the Women's Health
Movement that put a halt to the surgical practice, common in the seventies, of proceeding directly from biopsy to mastectomy without ever rous-

ing the patient from anesthesia. More recently, feminist advocacy groups such as the San Francisco–based Breast Cancer Action and the Cambridge-based Women's Community Cancer Project helped blow the whistle on "high-dose chemotherapy," in which the bone marrow was removed prior to otherwise lethal doses of chemotherapy and later replaced—to no good effect, as it turned out.

Like everyone else in the breast-cancer world, the feminists want a cure, but they even more ardently demand to know the cause or causes of the disease without which we will never have any means of prevention. "Bad" genes of the inherited variety are thought to account for fewer than 10 percent of breast cancers, and only 30 percent of women diagnosed with breast cancer have any known risk factor (such as delaying child-bearing or the late onset of menopause) at all. Bad lifestyle choices like a fatty diet have, after brief popularity with the medical profession, been largely ruled out. Hence suspicion should focus on environmental carcinogens, the feminists argue, such as plastics, pesticides (DDT and PCBs, for example, though banned in this country, are still used in many Third World sources of the produce we eat), and the industrial runoff in our ground water. No carcinogen has been linked definitely to human breast cancer yet, but many have been found to cause the disease in mice, and the inexorable increase of the disease in industrialized nations—about 1 percent a year between the 1950s and the 1990s—further hints at environmental factors, as does the fact that women migrants to industrialized countries quickly develop the same breast-cancer rates as those who are native-born. Their emphasis on possible ecological factors, which is not shared by groups such as Komen and the American Cancer Society, puts the feminist breast-cancer activists in league with other, frequently rambunctious, social movements—environmental and anti-corporate.

But today theirs are discordant voices in a general chorus of sentimentality and good cheer; after all, breast cancer would hardly be the darling of corporate America if its complexion changed from pink to green. It is the very blandness of breast cancer, at least in mainstream perceptions, that makes it an attractive object of corporate charity and a way for companies to brand themselves friends of the middle-aged female market. With breast cancer, "there was no concern that you might actually turn off your audience because of the life style or sexual connotations that AIDS has," Amy Langer, director of the National Alliance of Breast Cancer Organizations, told the *New York Times* in 1996. "That gives corporations a certain freedom and a certain relief in supporting the cause." Or as Cindy Pearson, director of the National Women's Health Network, the organizational progeny of the Women's Health Movement, puts it more caustically: "Breast cancer provides a way of doing something for women, without being feminist."

In the mainstream of breast-cancer culture, one finds very little anger, no mention of possible environmental causes, few complaints about the fact that, in all but the more advanced, metastasized cases, it is the "treatments," not the disease, that cause illness and pain. The stance toward existing treatments is occasionally critical—in *Mamm*, for example—but more commonly grateful; the overall tone almost universally upbeat. The Breast Friends Web site, for example, features a series of inspirational quotes: "Don't Cry Over Anything that Can't Cry Over You," "I Can't Stop the Birds of Sorrow from Circling My Head, but I Can Stop Them from Building a Nest in My Hair," "When Life Hands Out Lemons, Squeeze Out a Smile," "Don't wait for your ship to come in . . . Swim out to meet it," and much more of that ilk. Even in the relatively sophisticated *Mamm*, a columnist bemoans not cancer or chemotherapy but the end of chemotherapy, and humorously proposes to deal with her separation anxiety by pitching a tent outside her oncologist's office. So pervasive is the perkiness of the breast-cancer world that unhappiness requires a kind of apology, as when "Lucy," whose "long term prognosis is not good," starts her personal narrative on breastcancertalk.org by telling us that her story "is not the usual one, full of sweetness and hope, but true nevertheless."

There is, I discover, no single noun to describe a woman with breast cancer. As in the AIDS movement, upon which breast-cancer activism is partly modeled, the words "patient" and "victim," with their aura of self-pity and passivity, have been ruled un-PC. Instead, we get verbs: those who are in the midst of their treatments are described as "battling" or "fighting," sometimes intensified with "bravely" or "fiercely"—language suggestive of Katharine Hepburn with her face to the wind. Once the treatments are over, one achieves the status of "survivor," which is how the women in my local support group identify themselves, AA style, as we convene to share war stories and rejoice in our "survivorhood": "Hi, I'm Kathy and I'm a three-year survivor." For those who cease to be survivors and join the more than forty thousand American women who succumb to breast cancer each year—again, no noun applies. They are said to have "lost their battle" and may be memorialized by photographs carried at races for the cure—our lost, brave sisters, our fallen soldiers. But in the overwhelmingly Darwinian culture that has grown up around breast cancer, martyrs count for little; it is the "survivors" who merit constant honor and acclaim. They, after all, offer living proof that expensive and painful treatments may in some cases actually work.

Scared and medically weakened women can hardly be expected to transform their support groups into bands of activists and rush out into the streets, but the equanimity of breast-cancer culture goes beyond mere absence of anger to what looks, all too often, like a positive embrace of the disease. As "Mary" reports, on the Bosom Buds message board:

> I really believe I am a much more sensitive and thoughtful person now. It might sound funny but I was a real worrier before. Now I don't want to waste my energy on worrying. I enjoy life so much more now and in a lot of aspects I am much happier now.

Or this from "Andee":

> This was the hardest year of my life but also in many ways the most rewarding. I got rid of the baggage, made peace with my family, met many amazing people, learned to take very good care of my body so it will take care of me, and reprioritized my life.

Cindy Cherry, quoted in the *Washington Post*, goes further:

> If I had to do it over, would I want breast cancer? Absolutely. I'm not the same person I was, and I'm glad I'm not. Money doesn't matter anymore. I've met the most phenomenal people in my life through this. Your friends and family are what matter now.

The First Year of the Rest of Your Life, a collection of brief narratives with a foreword by Nancy Brinker and a share of the royalties going to the Komen Foundation, is filled with such testimonies to the redemptive powers of the disease: "I can honestly say I am happier now than I have ever been in my life—even before the breast cancer." "For me, breast cancer has provided a good kick in the rear to get me started rethinking my life." "I have come out stronger, with a new sense of priorities." Never a complaint about lost time, shattered sexual confidence, or the long-term weakening of the arms caused by lymph-node dissection and radiation. What does not destroy you, to paraphrase Nietzsche, makes you a spunkier, more evolved sort of person.

The effect of this relentless brightsiding is to transform breast cancer into a rite of passage—not an injustice or a tragedy to rail against, but a normal marker in the life cycle, like menopause or graying hair. Everything in mainstream breast-cancer culture serves, no doubt inadvertently, to tame and normalize the disease: the diagnosis may be disastrous, but there are those cunning pink rhinestone angel pins to buy and races to train for. Even the heavy traffic in personal narratives and practical tips, which I found so useful, bears an implicit acceptance of the disease and the current barbarous approaches to its treatment: you can get so busy comparing attractive head scarves that you forget to question a form of treatment that temporarily renders you both bald and immuno-incompetent. Understood as a rite of passage, breast cancer resembles the initiation rites so exhaustively studied by Mircea Eliade: First there is the selection of the initiates—by age in the tribal situation, by mammogram or palpation here. Then come the requisite ordeals—scarification or circumcision within traditional cultures, surgery and chemotherapy for the cancer patient. Finally, the initiate emerges into a new and higher status—an adult and a warrior—or in the case of breast cancer, a "survivor."

And in our implacably optimistic breast-cancer culture, the disease offers more than the intangible benefits of spiritual upward mobility. You can defy the inevitable disfigurements and come out, on the survivor side, actually prettier, sexier, more femme. In the lore of the disease—shared with me by oncology nurses as well as by survivors—chemotherapy smoothes and tightens the skin, helps you lose weight; and, when your hair comes back, it will be fuller, softer, easier to control, and perhaps a surprising new color. These may be myths, but for those willing to get with the prevailing program, opportunities for self-improvement abound. The American Cancer Society offers the "Look Good . . . Feel Better" program, "dedicated to teaching women cancer patients beauty techniques to help restore their appearance and self-image during cancer treatment." Thirty thousand women participate a year, each copping a free makeover and bag of makeup donated by the Cosmetic, Toiletry, and Fragrance Association, the trade association of the cosmetics industry. As for that lost breast: after reconstruction, why not bring the other one up to speed? Of the more than fifty thousand mastectomy patients who opt for reconstruction each year, 17 percent go on, often at the urging of their plastic surgeons, to get additional surgery so that the remaining breast will "match" the more erect and perhaps larger new structure on the other side.

Not everyone goes for cosmetic deceptions, and the question of wigs versus baldness, reconstruction versus undisguised scar, defines one of the few real disagreements in breast-cancer culture. On the more avant-garde, upper-middle-class side, *Mamm* magazine—which features literary critic Eve Kosofsky Sedgwick as a columnist—tends to favor the "natural" look. Here, mastectomy scars can be "sexy" and baldness something to celebrate. The January 2001 cover story features women who "looked upon their baldness not just as a loss, but also as an opportunity: to indulge their playful sides . . . to come in contact, in new ways, with their truest selves." One decorates her scalp with temporary tattoos of peace signs, panthers, and frogs; another expresses herself with a shocking purple wig; a third reports that unadorned baldness makes her feel "sensual, powerful, able to recreate myself with every new day." But no hard feelings toward those who choose to hide their condition under wigs or scarves; it's just a matter, *Mamm* tells us, of "different aesthetics." Some go for pink ribbons; others will prefer the Ralph Lauren Pink Pony breast-cancer motif. But everyone agrees that breast cancer is a chance for creative self-transformation—a makeover opportunity, in fact.

Now, cheerfulness, up to and including delusion and false hope, has a recognized place in medicine. There is plenty of evidence that depressed and socially isolated people are more prone to succumb to diseases, cancer included, and a diagnosis of cancer is probably capable of precipitating serious depression all by itself. To be told by authoritative figures that you have a deadly disease, for which no real cure exists, is to enter a liminal state fraught with perils that go well beyond the disease itself. Consider the phenomenon of "voodoo death"—described by ethnographers among, for example, Australian aborigines—in which a person who has been condemned by a suitably potent curse obligingly shuts down and dies within a day or two. Cancer diagnoses could, and in some cases probably do, have the same kind of fatally dispiriting effect. So, it could be argued, the collectively pumped-up optimism of breast-cancer culture may be just what the doctor ordered. Shop for the Cure, dress in pink-ribbon regalia, organize a run or hike—whatever gets you through the night.

But in the seamless world of breast-cancer culture, where one Web site links to another—from personal narratives and grassroots endeavors to the glitzy level of corporate sponsors and celebrity spokespeople—cheerfulness is more or less mandatory, dissent a kind of treason. Within this tightly knit world, attitudes are subtly adjusted, doubters gently brought back to the fold. In *The First Year of the Rest of Your Life,* for example, each personal narrative is followed by a study question or tip designed to counter the slightest hint of negativity—and they are very slight hints indeed, since the collection includes no harridans, whiners, or feminist militants:

Have you given yourself permission to acknowledge you have some anxiety or "blues" and to ask for help for your emotional well-being?

Is there an area in your life of unresolved internal conflict? Is there an area where you think you might want to do some "healthy mourning"?

Try keeping a list of the things you find "good about today."

As an experiment, I post a statement on the Komen.org message board, under the subject line "angry," briefly listing my own heartfelt complaints about debilitating treatments, recalcitrant insurance companies, environmental carcinogens, and, most daringly, "sappy pink ribbons." I receive a few words of encouragement in my fight with the insurance company, which has taken the position that my biopsy was a kind of optional indulgence, but mostly a chorus of rebukes. "Suzy" writes to say, "I really dislike saying you have a bad attitude towards all of this, but you do, and it's not going to help you in the least." "Mary" is a bit more tolerant, writing, "Barb, at this time in your life, it's so important to put all your energies toward a peaceful, if not happy, existence. Cancer is a rotten thing to have happen and there are no answers for any of us as to why. But to live your life, whether you have one more year or 51, in anger and bitterness is such a waste . . . I hope you can find some peace. You deserve it. We all do. God bless you and keep you in His loving care. Your sister, Mary."

"Kitty," however, thinks I've gone around the bend: "You need to run, not walk, to some counseling . . . Please, get yourself some help and I ask everyone on this site to pray for you so you can enjoy life to the fullest."

I do get some reinforcement from "Gerri," who has been through all the treatments and now finds herself in terminal condition: "I am also angry. All the money that is raised, all the smiling faces of survivors who make it sound like it is o.k. to have breast cancer. IT IS NOT O.K.!" But Gerri's message, like the others on the message board, is posted under the mocking heading "What does it mean to be a breast cancer survivor?"

"Culture" is too weak a word to describe all this. What has grown up around breast cancer in just the past fifteen years more nearly resembles a cult—or, given that it numbers more than two million women, their families, and friends—perhaps we should say a full-fledged religion. The products—teddy bears, pink-ribbon brooches, and so forth—serve as amulets and talismans, comforting the sufferer and providing visible evidence of faith. The personal narratives serve as testimonials and follow the same general arc as the confessional autobiographies required of seventeenth-century Puritans: first there is a crisis, often involving a sudden apprehension of mortality (the diagnosis or, in the old Puritan case, a stern word from on high); then comes a prolonged ordeal (the treatment or, in the religious case, internal struggle with the devil); and finally, the blessed certainty of salvation, or its breast-cancer equivalent, survivorhood. And like most recognized religions, breast cancer has its great epideictic events, its pilgrimages and mass gatherings where the faithful convene and draw strength from their numbers. These are the annual races for a cure, attracting a total of about a million people at more than eighty sites—seventy thousand of them at the largest event, in Washington, D.C., which in recent years has been attended by Dan and Marilyn Quayle and Al and Tipper Gore. Everything comes together at the races: celebrities and corporate sponsors are showcased; products are hawked; talents, like those of the "Swinging, Singing Survivors" from Syracuse, New York, are displayed. It is at the races, too, that the elect confirm their special status. As one participant wrote in the *Washington Post*:

> I have taken my "battle scarred" breasts to the Mall, donned the pink shirt, visor, pink shoelaces, etc. and walked proudly among my fellow veterans of the breast cancer war. In 1995, at the age of 44, I was diagnosed and treated for Stage II breast cancer. The experience continues to redefine my life.

Feminist breast-cancer activists, who in the early nineties were organizing their own mass outdoor events—demonstrations, not races—to demand increased federal funding for research, tend to keep their distance from these huge, corporate-sponsored, pink gatherings. Ellen Leopold, for example—a member of the Women's Community Cancer Project in Cambridge and author of *A Darker Ribbon: Breast Cancer, Women, and Their Doctors in the Twentieth Century*—has criticized the races as an inefficient way of raising money. She points out that the Avon Breast Cancer Crusade, which sponsors three-day, sixty-mile walks, spends more than a third of the money raised on overhead and advertising, and Komen may similarly fritter away up to 25 percent of its gross. At least one corporate-charity insider agrees. "It would be much easier and more productive," says Rob Wilson, an organizer of charitable races for corporate clients, "if people, instead of running or riding, would write out a check to the charity."

To true believers, such criticisms miss the point, which is always, ultimately, "awareness." Whatever you do to publicize the disease—wear a pink ribbon, buy a teddy, attend a race—reminds other women to come forward for their mammograms. Hence, too, they would argue, the cult of the "survivor": if women neglect their annual screenings, it must be because they are afraid that a diagnosis amounts to a death sentence. Beaming survivors, proudly displaying their athletic prowess, are the best possible advertisement for routine screening mammograms, early detection, and the ensuing round of treatments. Yes, miscellaneous businesses—from tiny distributors of breast-cancer wind chimes and note cards to major corporations seeking a woman-friendly image—benefit in the process, not to mention the breast-cancer industry itself, the estimated $12-billion- to $16-billion-a-year business in surgery, "breast health centers," chemotherapy "infusion suites," radiation treatment centers, mammograms, and drugs ranging from anti-emetics (to help you survive the nausea of chemotherapy) to tamoxifen (the hormonal treatment for women with estrogen-sensitive tumors). But what's to complain about? Seen through pink-tinted lenses, the entire breast-cancer enterprise—from grassroots support groups and Web sites to the corporate providers of therapies and sponsors of races—looks like a beautiful example of synergy at work: cult activities, paraphernalia, and testimonies encourage women to undergo the diagnostic procedures, and since a fraction of these diagnoses will be positive, this means more members for the cult as well as more customers for the corporations, both those that provide medical products and services and those that offer charitable sponsorships.

But this view of a life-giving synergy is only as sound as the science of current detection and treatment modalities, and, tragically, that science is fraught with doubt, dissension, and what sometimes looks very much like denial. Routine screening mammograms, for example, are the major goal of "awareness," as when Rosie O'Donnell exhorts us to go out and "get squished." But not all breast-cancer experts are as enthusiastic. At best the evidence for the salutary effects of routine mammograms—as opposed to breast self-examination—is equivocal, with many respectable large-scale studies showing a vanishingly small impact on overall breast-cancer mortality. For one thing, there are an estimated two to four false positives for every cancer detected, leading thousands of healthy women to go through unnecessary biopsies and anxiety. And even if mammograms were 100 percent accurate, the admirable goal of "early" detection is more elusive than the current breast-cancer dogma admits. A small tumor, detectable only by mammogram, is not necessarily young and innocuous; if it has not spread to the lymph nodes, which is the only form of spreading detected in the common surgical procedure of lymph-node dissection, it may have already moved on to colonize other organs via the bloodstream. David Plotkin, director of the Memorial Cancer Research Foundation of Southern California, concludes that the benefits of routine mammography "are not well established; if they do exist, they are not as great as many women hope." Alan Spievack, a surgeon recently retired from the Harvard Medical School, goes further, concluding from his analysis of dozens of studies that routine screening mammography is, in the words of famous British surgeon Dr. Michael Baum, "one of the greatest deceptions perpetrated on the women of the Western world."

Even if foolproof methods for early detection existed,* they would, at the present time, serve only as portals to treatments offering dubious protection and considerable collateral damage. Some women diagnosed with breast cancer will live long enough to die of something else, and some of these lucky ones will indeed owe their longevity to a combination of surgery, chemotherapy, radiation, and/or anti-estrogen drugs such as tamoxifen. Others, though, would have lived untreated or with surgical excision alone, either because their cancers were slow-growing or because their bodies' own defenses were successful. Still others will die of the disease no matter what heroic, cell-destroying therapies are applied. The trouble is, we do not have the means to distinguish between these three groups. So for many of the thousands of women who are diagnosed each year, Plotkin notes, "the sole effect of early detection has been to stretch out the time in which the woman bears the knowledge of her condition." These women do not live longer than they might have without any medical intervention, but more of the time they do live is overshadowed with the threat of death and wasted in debilitating treatments.

To the extent that current methods of detection and treatment fail or fall short, America's breast-cancer cult can be judged as an outbreak of mass delusion, celebrating survivorhood by downplaying mortality and promoting obedience to medical protocols known to have limited efficacy. And although we may imagine ourselves to be well past the era of patriarchal medicine, obedience is the message behind the infantilizing theme in breast-cancer culture, as represented by the teddy bears, the crayons, and the prevailing pinkness. You are encouraged to regress to a little-girl state, to suspend critical judgment, and to accept whatever measures the doctors, as parent surrogates, choose to impose.

Worse, by ignoring or underemphasizing the vexing issue of environmental causes, the breast-cancer cult turns women into dupes of what could be called the Cancer Industrial Complex: the multinational corporate enterprise that with the one hand doles out carcinogens and disease and, with the other, offers expensive, semi-toxic pharmaceutical treatments. Breast Cancer Awareness Month, for example, is sponsored by AstraZeneca (the manufacturer of tamoxifen), which, until a corporate reorganization in 2000, was a leading producer of pesticides, including acetochlor, classified by the EPA as a "probable human carcinogen." This particularly nasty conjuncture of interests led the environmentally ori-

---

* Some improved prognostic tools, involving measuring a tumor's growth rate and the extent to which it is supplied with blood vessels, are being developed but are not yet in use.

ented Cancer Prevention Coalition (CPC) to condemn Breast Cancer Awareness Month as "a public relations invention by a major polluter which puts women in the position of being unwitting allies of the very people who make them sick." Although AstraZeneca no longer manufactures pesticides, CPC has continued to criticize the breast-cancer crusade—and the American Cancer Society—for its unquestioning faith in screening mammograms and careful avoidance of environmental issues. In a June 12, 2001, press release, CPC chairman Samuel S. Epstein, MD, and the well-known physician activist Quentin Young castigated the American Cancer Society for its "longstanding track record of indifference and even hostility to cancer prevention . . . Recent examples include issuing a joint statement with the Chlorine Institute justifying the continued global use of persistent organochlorine pesticides, and also supporting the industry in trivializing dietary pesticide residues as avoidable risks of childhood cancer. ACS policies are further exemplified by allocating under 0.1 percent of its $700 million annual budget to environmental and occupational causes of cancer."

In the harshest judgment, the breast-cancer cult serves as an accomplice in global poisoning—normalizing cancer, prettying it up, even presenting it, perversely, as a positive and enviable experience.

When, my three months of chemotherapy completed, the oncology nurse calls to congratulate me on my "excellent blood work results," I modestly demur. I didn't do anything, I tell her, anything but endure—marking the days off on the calendar, living on Protein Revolution canned vanilla health shakes, escaping into novels and work. Courtesy restrains me from mentioning the fact that the tumor markers she's tested for have little prognostic value, that there's no way to know how many rebel cells survived chemotherapy and may be carving out new colonies right now. She insists I should be proud; I'm a survivor now and entitled to recognition at the Relay for Life being held that very evening in town.

So I show up at the middle school track where the relay's going on just in time for the Survivors' March: about a hundred people, including a few men, since the funds raised will go to cancer research in general, are marching around the track eight to twelve abreast while a loudspeaker announces their names and survival times and a thin line of observers, mostly people staffing the raffle and food booths, applauds. It could be almost any kind of festivity, except for the distinctive stacks of cellophane-wrapped pink Hope Bears for sale in some of the booths. I cannot help but like the funky small-town gemütlichkeit of the event, especially when the audio system strikes up that universal anthem of solidarity, "We Are Family," and a few people of various ages start twisting to the music on the jury-rigged stage. But the money raised is going far away, to the American Cancer Society, which will not be asking us for our advice on how to spend it.

I approach a woman I know from other settings, one of our local intellectuals, as it happens, decked out here in a pink-and-yellow survivor T-shirt and with an American Cancer Society "survivor medal" suspended on a purple ribbon around her neck. "When do you date your survivorship from?" I ask her, since the announced time, five and a half years, seems longer than I recall. "From diagnosis or the completion of your treatments?" The question seems to annoy or confuse her, so I do not press on to what I really want to ask: at what point, in a downwardly sloping breast-cancer career, does one put aside one's survivor regalia and admit to being in fact a die-er? For the dead are with us even here, though in much diminished form. A series of paper bags, each about the right size for a junior burger and fries, lines the track. On them are the names of the dead, and inside each is a candle that will be lit later, after dark, when the actual relay race begins.

My friend introduces me to a knot of other women in survivor gear, breast-cancer victims all, I learn, though of course I would not use the V-word here. "Does anyone else have trouble with the term 'survivor'?" I ask, and, surprisingly, two or three speak up. It could be "unlucky," one tells me; it "tempts fate," says another, shuddering slightly. After all, the cancer can recur at any time, either in the breast or in some more strategic site. No one brings up my own objection to the term, though: that the mindless triumphalism of "survivorhood" denigrates the dead and the dying. Did we who live "fight" harder than those who've died? Can we claim to be "braver," better people than the dead? And why is there no room in this cult for some gracious acceptance of death, when the time comes, which it surely will, through cancer or some other misfortune?

No, this is not my sisterhood. For me at least, breast cancer will never be a source of identity or pride. As my dying correspondent Gerri wrote: "IT IS NOT O.K.!" What it is, along with cancer generally or any slow and painful way of dying, is an abomination, and, to the extent that it's man-made, also a crime. This is the one great truth that I bring out of the breast-cancer experience, which did not, I can now report, make me prettier or stronger, more feminine or spiritual—only more deeply angry. What sustained me through the "treatments" is a purifying rage, a resolve, framed in the sleepless nights of chemotherapy, to see the last polluter, along with, say, the last smug health-insurance operative, strangled with the last pink ribbon. Cancer or no cancer, I will not live that long, of course. But I know this much right now for sure: I will not go into that last good night with a teddy bear tucked under my arm.

1. How does the writer avoid melodrama in this piece, which is about facing death?
2. Isn't this a piece about fighting a sentimental attitude toward disease? In what ways is Ehrenreich saying the same things we read about in this chapter?

CHAPTER THREE

Details, Details

Part 1: CONCRETE DETAILS AS THE BASIC BUILDING BLOCKS OF GOOD CREATIVE WRITING

Getting Started

Details are the lifeblood of good writing—for both fiction and creative nonfiction. And not just any details, but *concrete* details, or details that are grounded in the five senses. By first and foremost relying on what we see, feel, hear, touch, and taste when we render our thoughts and emotions on the page, we are ensuring that we immerse our readers in a concrete sensory world of our own making.

We've all heard the truism that "you can't see the forest for the trees" as a way of warning against too much attention to detail—the implication being that you can get lost in the particulars and not see the big picture. Well, in riveting fiction and creative nonfiction the opposite is true: you won't see the forest unless you see *this* tree and *that* tree and *that* tree. Unless you focus on the details with great specificity.

Of course, we have to be selective. That's what being a writer is all about: making choices. You can't show the entire video of your summer vacation, you have to be discriminating—that is, if you want anyone to be interested. Choosing your trees—and rendering them precisely—is at the heart of all good writing.

And among other things, attention to details keeps us honest. As Virginia Woolf wrote, "Let a man get up and say, 'Behold, this is the truth,' and instantly I perceive a sandy cat filching a piece of fish in the background. Look, you have forgotten the cat, I say."

In Part 1 of this chapter, we first define what an image is, and discover the ways to build effective imagery in our creative work. Part 2 gives us a chance to practice our control of details with exercises designed specifically to address the need for beginning writers to think with specificity. Finally, Part 3 gives us some masterpieces of fiction to read and learn from.

On Thinking Small

In Chapter 2, we heard about triggering and real subjects: how you often start out in one place when writing only to end up in another place—and only after you've arrived being able (perhaps) to discover what you're really writing about.

Richard Hugo, in *The Triggering Town*, also stresses the need to "think small":

> Often, if the triggering subject is too big (love, death, faith) rather than localized and finite, the mind tends to shrink. Sir Alexander Fleming observed some mold, and a few years later we had a cure for gonorrhea. But what if the British government had told him to find a cure for gonorrhea? He might have worried so much he would not have noticed the mold. Think small. If you have a big mind, that will show itself. If you can't think small, try philosophy or social criticism.

In this chapter, we will be advocating starting off your writing career based on smallness and specificity—eschewing grand ideas in favor of thinking particularly. As Flannery O'Connor put it:

> The fact is that the materials of the fiction writer are the humblest. Fiction is about everything human and we are made out of dust, and if you scorn getting yourself dusty, then you shouldn't try to write fiction. It's not a grand enough job for you.

What both these writers are talking about is the difference between abstraction and specificity, about the difference between generalizations and attention to detail. "We are made out of dust" is Flannery O'Connor's way of saying that we belong to this sensory world, with its noise and dirt and various tastes and textures, and it's in this sensory world that we have to spend most of our time as writers. And, of course, what she says applies equally to creative nonfiction as to fiction.

First, some definitions:

SPECIFIC: Limiting or limited. Precise. Peculiar to, or characteristic of, something. Exclusive or special.

CONCRETE: Characterized by things or events that can be perceived by the senses. Real. Actual. Referring to a particular. Specific, not general or abstract. The reproduction, using descriptions embodying the five senses, of a place, person, or thing.

ABSTRACT: Dissociated from any specific instance. Expressing a quality apart from an object. The reverse of a concrete detail: something that is specifically *not* about a particular person, place, or object.

GENERALIZATION: To emphasize the general character rather than the specific details of something. To make vague or indefinite.

One of the problems beginning writers have is that they start out with the abstract, or the general. They want to write about love. Or family life. Or war. Or divorce. They start above the fray, rather than in it. To paraphrase O'Connor, they want to forget that we are made of dust. And things, as a result, never get off the proverbial ground.

Let's look at some examples of the difference between the specific and the general/abstract:

GENERAL/ABSTRACT: She was sad.

SPECIFIC: She sat in her favorite rocking chair in her room, knitting a gray scarf and weeping into the unfinished woolen stitches.

GENERAL/ABSTRACT: My father hated noise.

SPECIFIC: The neighbors became accustomed to my father throwing open the windows of our living room and dumping a bucket of cold water on neighborhood children who were playing too loudly near the front porch.

GENERAL/ABSTRACT: She had a drinking problem.

SPECIFIC: Three times a week she opened a bottle of white wine, not even chilled, and drank it from a coffee cup until it was dry. She brought the cup into the bathroom and would continue sipping even as she brushed her teeth.

Notice how, in each of these examples, we've moved from something indefinite to something definite; from something that we can understand in theory, to something we can actually *see* and, hopefully, experience.

Defining "Image" within a Literary Context

When you hear the word "image" you probably think of something visual. *She was the image of her mother.* (She looked just like her mother.) Yet *Merriam-Webster's Collegiate Dictionary* defines "image" as "a reproduction or imitation of the form of a person or thing; *especially* [emphasis mine] an imitation in solid form."

In other words, an image involves more than simply the visual—it includes something in "solid form" that presumably can be touched, heard, tasted, and smelled in addition to being seen.

And this is what we do with words: we try to reproduce a person, place or thing *in as solid a form as we can*. Which means it's not just visual: it's reproducing something that is alive in all our senses. Notice the words: person, place, or thing. An object that exists in this world. Not an abstraction, or an idea, but something with *form*, something that can be perceived with the senses.

As Robert Hass wrote:

> Images haunt. There is a whole mythology built on this fact: Cézanne painting till his eyes bled, Wordsworth wandering the Lake Country hills in an impassioned daze. Blake describes it very well, and so did the colleague of Tu Fu who said to him, "It is like being alive twice."

Let's look at some images so we can see how precisely they reproduce the person, place, or thing in question, and also how they represent something more than just the thing itself: how the person, place, or thing has accumulated *meaning* through the rendering.

> I was there when the blind went down, one of those dirty brown roller affairs, throwing a ball for a little white dog as chance would have it. I happened to look up and there it was. All over and done with, at last. I sat on for a few moments with the ball in my hand and the dog yelping and pawing at me. [*Pause.*] Moments. Her moments, my moments. [*Pause.*] The dog's moments. [*Pause.*] In the end I held it out to him and he took it in his mouth, gentle, gentle. A small, old, black hard solid rubber ball. [*Pause.*] I shall feel it, in my hand, until my dying day. [*Pause.*] I might have kept it. [*Pause.*] But I gave it to the dog. [*Pause.*] Ah, well . . .

In this play, "Krapp's Last Tape" by Samuel Beckett, we experience the moment that a man's mother died captured in a series of concrete images: the blind going down, the ball being held in the hand, and the dog yelping for it. The specifics of the blind, the ball, and the dog help us comprehend the reality of the mother's death, and what it means to the narrator.

> The space between the fireplace and the door to the kitchen is filled with shelves and a shallow cupboard. The tea cart is kept under the stairs. Then comes the door to the coat closet, the inside of which is painted a particularly beautiful shade of Chinese red, and the door to the hall. On the sliding door cabinet (we have turned the corner now and are moving toward the windows) there is a pottery lamp with a wide perforated gray paper shade

and such a long thin neck that it seems to be trying to turn into a crane. Also a record player that plays only 78s and has to be wound after every record. The oil painting over the couch is of a rock quarry in Maine, and we have discovered that it changes according to the time of day and the color of the sky. It is particularly alive after a snowfall.

In this vivid passage from "The Thistles in Sweden" by William Maxwell, we see the room in great detail, and the imagery arouses intense emotions—we feel the narrator's longing for the days when he could actually be in this room, his yearning for the past, and what it represents to him now, in the present day.

Imagery That Works on Two Levels

The notion that imagery works on two levels is a critical one. On the one hand, you want to portray the way things *are* in the world of your story or creative nonfiction piece. You want to describe the small town, or the mountains, or the scene in the restaurant in the city, and you want the reader to be able to experience it as deeply as if he or she were there themselves. On the other hand, there is really no such thing as a completely objective image: just think of how things look differently on a day you are blissfully happy, and on a day you are rather blue.

Imagery is your way *in* to material. It's your way of reaching down into your subconscious and finding out what you really think about a person, place, thing, event. By describing it honestly and completely, and not leaving out anything, no matter how seemingly incongruous, you are finally *writing*. This is what writing is all about. And it centers around the senses, and your ability to create complex, messy images that bring a situation to life—specifically the life *you* re-create through them.

Here's a passage from John Gardner's *The Art of Fiction* that succinctly lays out the role of imagery in fiction:

> Consider the following as a possible exercise in description: Describe a barn as seen by a man whose son has just been killed in a war. Do not mention the son, or war, or death. Do not mention the man who does the seeing. [. . .] If the writer works hard, and if he has the talent to be a writer, the result of his work should be a powerful and disturbing image, a faithful description of some apparently real barn but one from which the reader gets a sense of the father's emotion; though exactly what that emotion is he may not be able to pin down.

A critical part of this passage is when Gardner stresses that "no amount of intellectual study can determine for the writer what he will include." *No amount of intellectual study*. We're talking right (intuitive) brain needed here, not left (logical) brain:

> And one of the things he will discover, inevitably, is that the images of death and loss that come to him are not necessarily those we might expect. The hack mind leaps instantly to images of, for instance, darkness, heaviness, decay. But those may not be at all the kinds of images that drift into the mind that has emptied itself of all but the desire to "tell the truth"; that is, to get the feeling down in concrete details.

What Gardner rather judgmentally calls the "hack mind" we might call the inexperienced writer, who feels that death must necessarily have to do with "darkness, heaviness, decay." But we know from our discussion of sentimentality in Chapter 1 that more surprising images may come out of this exercise; the barn might be bathed in a glorious light, or be a dull mud brown under a clouded sky.

And here's a passage by Shakespeare that comments beautifully on the dual nature of images (from *Hamlet*, Act 2, Scene 2):

> HAMLET: I have of late—but wherefore I know not—lost all my mirth, forgone all custom of exercises; and indeed it goes so heavily with my disposition that this goodly frame the earth seems to me a sterile promontory; this most excellent canopy, the air, look you, this brave o'erhanging firmament, this majestical roof fretted with golden fire—why it appeareth nothing to me but a foul and pestilent congregation of vapors.

Hamlet is saying that if not for his mood, the world would look a completely different place to him—the images themselves would be completely altered, even though he would be looking at the very same world.

Let's look at two more examples:

> The flashlight beams explored her body, causing its whiteness to gleam. Her breasts were floppy; her nipples looked shriveled. Her belly appeared inflated by gallons of water. For a moment, a beam focused on her mound of pubic hair which was overlapped by the swell of her belly, and then moved almost shyly away down her legs, and the cops all glanced at us—at you, especially—above their lights; and you hugged your blanket closer as if they might confiscate it as evidence or to use as a shroud.

In this first passage, from "We Didn't" by Stuart Dybek, we get a sense of the fear of sensuality that haunts the story, a fear of what sex, and desiring sex, can do to people. We're immersed in the sensory experience of what is happening—and we feel the emotional undercurrents as well.

The new boy was Quadberry. He came in, but he was meek, and when he tuned up he put his head almost on the floor, bending over trying to be inconspicuous. The girls in the band had wanted him to be handsome, but Quadberry refused and kept himself in such hiding among the sax section that he was neither handsome, ugly, cute or anything. What he was was pretty near invisible, except for the bell of his horn, the all but closed eyes, the Arabian nose, the brown hair with its halo of white ends, the desperate oralness, the giant reed punched into his face, and hazy Quadberry, loving the wound in a private dignified ecstasy.

In this second passage, from "Testimony of Pilot" by Barry Hanna, we get a vivid picture of the sax player that puts us right there in the scene—we can really *see* him—but the image is also imbued with a sense of the player's desperation, his obsession with his instrument, and how this estranges him from his fellow students.

Writers of popular works (both fiction and nonfiction) tend to do well on the concrete side of things: they bounce their characters around from New York to London and Paris and in and out of restaurants and beds and whatnot, but somehow it doesn't add up to much emotionally. At the other end of the spectrum you have well-meaning beginning writers whose prose is filled with intense emotions and insightful moments of clarity, or epiphanies, but which lack the concrete to make it real. It is only when we marry the two that we get truly compelling fiction and creative nonfiction.

On Seeing the General in the Particular

The German philosopher Goethe wrote: "There is a great difference, whether the poet seeks the particular for the sake of the general, or sees the general in the particular."

What is he saying? He was talking about symbols, and imagery, and is a bit cryptic, but let me paraphrase: that there is a big difference between whether I say,

"Living in San Francisco is a great experience, and by way of illustrating it, I'm going to tell you something that happened to me on the way to school today."

or,

"This thing happened to me on the way to school today. I want to tell you about it. I want to tell you about it in great detail. Do you think this has something to do with living in San Francisco?"

In the first case, I am trying to bolster, or prove, a generalization (living in San Francisco is a great experience) by using a specific example. In the second case, I want to see if a general picture can arise from a specific event—but the event comes first, not the generalization.

What's the difference? It's the difference between trying to categorize things neatly and trying to observe things the way they really are.

Let's start with a statement that fits neatly within the "box":

Living in San Francisco is a really great experience.

If we think in terms of this generalization, then we will automatically begin looking for details and experiences that fit neatly within the "box" of this general statement. When approaching writing in this way, we'll try (unconsciously, for the most part) to keep things clean, to keep things simple. If things don't fit, we'll adjust them or leave them out. We do this all the time in real life, and are applauded for it: finding examples to suit a situation, we of course choose examples that prove whatever point we are trying to make. We've been trained to do that. So when I think about living in San Francisco as a "great experience" I might think of afternoons spent in Golden Gate Park, delicious lunches in Chinatown, shopping expeditions along Union Street. I'm choosing details that fit a preconceived, *general* idea that I have in mind. It might make for a pretty travelogue, but it's not particularly interesting. It certainly doesn't show the teeming life of the city itself.

But what happens if we first seek the *particular*? If I first come up with particular instances of what it's like to live in San Francisco without worrying about some general conclusion first?

- I went to the Gay Pride march, which attracted more than 1,000,000 people. Up and down Market Street, all you could see was an ocean of humanity, bright colors, waving signs.

- There are homeless people on the corner of California and Polk begging for food. Many of them are painfully thin, with sores on their arms and legs.

- Once I saw someone fall off a streetcar. It was in Chinatown, and he didn't seem upset by it, just picked himself up and walked off.

- My next-door neighbor, a lifetime San Francisco resident, shocked me by making a racist remark.

Suddenly, it's a lot harder to put all these particulars in a nice neat box. Things keep jumping out, refusing to be easily categorized. And, as we learned in Chapter 2, messy is good, complex is good. Even if you managed to see something general in these particulars (which is something we want people to do—to see the universality in our writing) it would be a *complex* conclusion they would come to. By going from the particular to the general, and not the other way around, you ensure that you will avoid oversimplistic views, and thus sentimentality.

So, by paying attention to what is small, by thinking small, a much more complex and less easily categorized picture begins to emerge—a messy picture, if you will. And rather than being alarmed by this, we should be gratified, because messiness and chaos are hallmarks of something that has the potential to be really interesting, and worth exploring further. (How many tepid articles have we read about the perky uniqueness of our home towns, after all? How interesting is *that*?)

To use another example, look at the difference between

"If you want to see what drink can do to a woman, look at my sister Sally."

and

"Look at my sister Sally. Look at her. *Look closely.*"

In the one case we've come up with a generalization, an implied hypothesis that "drink is a very bad thing," and so when we start to think of particulars, we naturally come up with details that illustrate that point.

Drink is a very bad thing.

- My sister Sally always has a headache in the morning.
- She doesn't always remember what day it is.
- She doesn't seem to enjoy her children the way she used to.

On the other hand, we can come up with a list of observations that characterize a woman, who may have a drinking problem but who is a woman first, a stereotypical problem drinker second (or, hopefully, not at all):

"Look at my sister Sally. Look at her. *Look closely.*"

- She seems happiest when she's had a few drinks, but before she's had too many.
- She loves her work and is always at her desk by 7:45 exactly.
- I once saw her run to meet her six-year-old daughter at school, heave her up in the air, and twirl her around, all with great joy on her face.
- She is beloved by all who know her. On her birthday, the presents come pouring in, from acquaintances as well as lifelong friends. A lot of the presents are bottles of liquor.

Instead of an essay on the dangers of drink (and, I agree, they are many) a portrait of a real woman begins to appear. And although we might agree, at the end, that this woman would be better off not drinking, we have a much better sense of the complexity of the human being that lies underneath the problem when we seek the particular, not for the sake of the general, but for its own sake. It's the difference between emphasizing the concept, and emphasizing what *is* and—most importantly—what can't be categorized.

All good, even great, writing must do this—nonfiction as well as fiction. If your goal is to make something *true*, that's where the things that don't make sense, don't quite add up, begin to creep in. It's only when we reinvent the experience through the particular, *this* man and *this* woman, or *this* woman and *this* woman, or *this* man and *this* man, and render the specifics and the ambiguities of that *exact* interaction, that we rise above the bane of every writer, which is to not be exact.

Not dog, but the black dog. Or better, *that* black dog with the white spot on its right ear.

Not house, but *this* house: with the broken front-door lock and the tomato bushes with fruit just beginning to ripen and the lone banana peel left on the lawn by a neighborhood child.

It's an apparent contradiction, and there is nothing more common than for a beginning writing student to say, "I want the reader to identify with the story by imagining the first car he or she ever owned, so I'm not going to describe this car in detail." No. It's one of the mysteries of writing that in order to evoke a universal reaction or emotion you must use the tools of specificity.

One way that I tell my students to try thinking small is by considering the biblical proverb: "It is as easy for a camel to get through a needle's eye as for a rich man to get into the kingdom of heaven."

If the detail is too large, too general, it won't make it through the "eye" and it won't make it to the kingdom of "narrative heaven" in which a text resonates with strong emotion for the reader. Only after it has made it through this needle's eye (through being small) can your concrete detail begin to expand in the mind and approach universality.

On Crowding the Reader Out of His Own Space

"What you're trying to do when you write is to crowd the reader out of his own space and occupy it with yours, in a good cause. You're trying to take over his sensibility and deliver an experience that moves from mere information," wrote the novelist Robert Stone. Below is a series of passages that are first written more generally, and then written tighter, smaller. See which ones crowd you most particularly out of your own space into the space prepared for you by the writer.

"He's crude," Laura told her sister as they wandered around the place trying to find some eggs. They found some fake ones and then some real ones. The fake ones had cheap jewelry in them; the real ones had either the beginnings or endings of stupid riddles pasted onto them. They also found chocolates in the form of naked women.

"He's crude," Laura told her sister as they wandered around the swimming pool, looking halfheartedly for eggs. The first they'd found was plastic and contained a cheap necklace and pendant: turned one way, Betty Boop smiled under her long lashes; turned the other way, her mouth became an "O" and her dotted dress disappeared. They found hard-boiled eggs with the beginnings of riddles on them ("How many Catholics does it take to change a light bulb?") or with the answers ("Because it was a *hung* jury.") and they found chocolates in the shape of naked women—buxom, foil-wrapped little candies nestled in the tender crocuses.

[from "Naked Ladies" by Antonya Nelson]

The servant came in, she seemed proud of what she was carrying, but it only turned out to be an underdone leg of rather tough mutton and a pile of overcooked vegetables.

Here the girl came in. She wore an air of importance derived apparently from the dish she carried, for it was covered with a great metal cover. She raised the cover with a flourish. There was a leg of mutton underneath. "Let's dine," Sara said. "I'm hungry," he added. They sat down and she took the carving-knife and made a long incision. A thin trickle of red juice ran out; it was underdone. She looked at it. Then she lifted the lids of the vegetable dishes. There was a slabbed-down mass of cabbage in one oozing green water; in the other yellow potatoes that looked hard.

[from *The Years* by Virginia Woolf]

You can see, in both these cases, that the second version works much better: the details are sharper, more particular, more apt to crowd you into a specific emotional and physical space prepared for you by the writer.

Don't Lose Any of Your Senses

An interesting exercise, after you've tried to describe something on the page, is to go through it and see what senses you have used to create the image. Chances are, you'll be depending primarily (if not completely) on the sense of sight alone. Yet imagery has to do with all five senses, not just one.

Let's walk through an exercise in which we start with a visual image, but gradually add the other four senses—see how much more satisfying and complex the image is when we are through.

> She was tall, thin, and gawky. Her hair fell straight to her waist and her feet were stuck into the oddest shoes. They looked like black boats, and her bony white ankles protruded out of them like pale masts.

Now add another sense—smell, perhaps:

> She was tall, thin, and gawky. Her hair smelled of violet and her feet were stuck into the oddest shoes you've ever seen: they looked like black boats, and her bony white ankles protruded out of them like pale masts.

And another—this time, touch:

> She was tall, thin, and gawky. Her hair smelled of violet and her feet were stuck into the oddest shoes you've ever seen: they looked like black boats, and her bony white ankles protruded out of them like pale masts. Once I'd inadvertently brushed against her arm, and an electrical shock had buzzed through me, as though she was pulsing with a hidden current.

And let's not forget sound:

> She was tall, thin, and gawky. Her hair smelled of violet, and her feet were stuck into the oddest shoes you've ever seen: they looked like black boats, and her bony white ankles protruded out of them like pale masts. When she walked you heard kallump *kaalumph*. Once I'd inadvertently brushed against her arm, and an electrical shock had buzzed through me, as though she were pulsing with a hidden current.

And finally, taste (this is a difficult one):

> She was tall, thin, and gawky. Her hair smelled of violet, and her feet were stuck into the oddest shoes you've ever seen: they looked like black boats, and her bony white ankles protruded out of them like pale masts. When she walked you heard kallump *kaalumph*. Once I'd inadvertently brushed against her arm, and an electrical shock had buzzed through me, as though she were pulsing with a hidden current. When we kissed, I tasted mint toothpaste.

See how much richer the final piece of writing is than the first one. One of the best exercises on imagery is to imagine yourself blind and describe the objects of the world around you without the sense of vision. It really makes the other senses come alive—it *forces* the other senses to come alive.

Use of Concrete Details in Creative Nonfiction

As we've noted, paying attention to concrete sensory details does not just fall into the domain of fiction. Rather, thinking small and particularly is just as critical with creative nonfiction. Just because something is factual (and we proclaim that it is factual) doesn't relieve us of the burden of making it real for our readers.

Here are some examples of fine concrete writing from noteworthy creative nonfiction pieces. Notice how firmly grounded they are in the sensory experience; how thoroughly we are drawn into the specific concrete *place* of the nonfictional world.

> It is dark now. In Rush Springs, the Homecoming game is in progress. The scoreboard lights say ten minutes left in the second quarter, the Redskins leading by two. I park on the highway. The stadium lights up the pitch-black night. Everybody's there: men with their feet up on a fence rail, smoking; women selling tickets, talking to their daughters. Let loose in the warm night air, kids run around like wild things.
>
> At half-time, I drive into the parking lot and buy a ticket. The band— mostly white children in red and black uniforms—has marched out and plays "Ebb Tide." Convertibles circle the field, as Homecoming maids perched atop the back seats smile and wave. They have a lot of hair, frizzed up, fanned out, shiny with goo. Their cars stop at the fifty-yard line, where each maid is escorted through a flower-decked arbor. The queen and king are crowned, flashbulbs pop.

In this excerpt, from "The Shadow Knows" by Beverly Lowry, you can see and smell and practically touch the visceral images from a high-school football game. The writer captures the excitement and nostalgia perfectly through her command of concrete sensory detail.

> Suppressed perhaps were the labors of my childhood as the eldest daughter of seven, tri-folding clouds of diapers, running bed linens through the mangle, stirring Catholic school uniform shirts in pots of starch. Lost were the babies' cries, the slow-thickening puddings and white sauce, mounds of socks to be matched, and toddlers watched never closely enough. Left behind me, Saturday mornings scrubbing foyer and bath tiles with Fels Naphtha, taking pails of oil soap to the rows of wooden dining chairs. I made lunch for the first "little ones" when I was six, and by seven baked my first loaf of bread. So standing evenings at the open window over foaming dishes I began subliminally to narrate a bearable selfhood. During endless hours of menial work, I spoke to God, who surrounded me, then to voices in books, and finally to fields and sky, where a presence was. Writing, I thought, formed itself elsewhere and passed through me, coming out of my hands. It was

mysterious and foreign, but the experience of its making could not be compared to anything else. In the act of writing, there was heightened being,
which could be remembered as ecstatic. There was, first, what could be said,
and later, the way of saying, which was superior to the said.

From "Emergence" by Carolyn Forché comes the tale of one writer's
beginnings, as born in the sights and sounds and smells of being the eld-
est of seven children in a Catholic household. Notice how she vividly
evokes the feelings and frustrations of the era through the use of concrete
details: the pails of oil soap and the slow-thickening puddings and the
mismatched socks all add up to give the piece weight, and to convince us
her emotions are true, and valid.

Use and Abuse of Metaphor

If you go over the images we've looked at thus far, you might notice something: very few metaphors, or comparisons. For the most part, the passages quoted in this book thus far have largely been content with
describing things as they *are* rather than what they are *like*. But metaphor,
or comparison, can be a very powerful tool to use in our creative work.

Chekhov, to his brother, on the subject of using metaphor:

> Evoke a moonlit night by writing that on the mill dam the glass fragments
> of a broken bottle flashed like a bright little star; and that the black shadow
> of a dog or a wolf rolled along like a ball.

Let's first define our terms. A metaphorical statement is a comparison
of two unlike things. A simile is a metaphorical statement (or a comparison of two unlike things) using *like* or *as*. The basic difference between a
simile and a metaphor is that one is explicit and one implied.

Some examples of similes, where the comparison is explicit:

- My love *is like* a red red rose. (Byron)
- Clouds *like* great gray brains. (Denis Johnson)
- A face *as* broad and *as* innocent *as* a cabbage. (Flannery O'Connor)
- The weather *as* cool and gray *as* wash water. (George Garrett)

In a metaphor, on the other hand, the comparison is implied:

- These are the dog days of summer. (Shakespeare)
- What do the sightless windows see, I wonder, when the sun throws
  passersby against them? (William Gass)
- . . . and Murphy can feel her shy skeleton waltzing away with him in a fit
  of ribbons, the bursting bouquets of a Christmas they are going to spend
  apart . . . (Mark Costello)

Writers use metaphorical statements (both metaphors and similes) to add extra power to a description. We're asking our readers to make a comparison in their mind that evokes a response that somehow deepens our understanding of the person, place, or thing being described.

Just look at the metaphorical statements in the poem "Tulips" by Sylvia Plath, which first compares a bunch of tulips to an "awful baby" and then to a "dozen red lead sinkers":

> The tulips are too red in the first place, they hurt me.
> Even through the gift paper I could hear them breathe
> Lightly, through their white swaddlings, like an awful baby,
> Their redness talks to my wound, it corresponds.
> They are subtle: they seem to float, though they weigh me down,
> Upsetting me with their sudden tongues and their color,
> A dozen red lead sinkers round my neck.

A good metaphor gives us a little shock: it stretches our imagination by forcing us to see something in a new light, yet it also immediately *convinces* us that it is true.

There are different kinds of metaphors:

A DEAD METAPHOR is one that has been absorbed into the language to the point where we don't even notice it anymore. Dead metaphors enrich our language, making it more colloquial and colorful.
- He ran for office.
- She flew from one task to another.
- The car ran smoothly.
- The dog worried the bone.
- I am open to suggestions.

CLICHÉD SIMILES AND METAPHORS are on their way to being dead. Once they were good and fresh and riveting. If not, they wouldn't have lasted. But they haven't yet been completely absorbed into our language; there is the imaginative effort required to make that leap from the literal to the metaphorical, without the payoff—the surprise and delight of a fresh comparison that illuminates.
- She cackled like a hen.
- He raved like a lunatic.
- She ran as fast as the wind.
- His heart felt like it would burst.

Clichéd metaphors involving eyes are especially difficult to avoid for young writers—you'd be surprised how easy it is for them to creep into your prose. Again, the instinct is good: there's truth to it, we tend to look at people's eyes for expressions, for emotion, for finding things that might not be revealed in other ways: hard eyes, gentle eyes, steely eyes, cold eyes. But eyes aren't literally "hard" or "gentle" or "steely." Those are clichéd metaphors about eyes that we must be very careful not to sneak into our pieces. If you're depending too much on eye metaphors, it's usually a sign you're taking the easy way out, trying to attribute all sorts of character traits through a character's eyes, rather than focusing on other, possibly more relevant, and certainly fresher details.

CONCEIT is when two very unlike things are brought together in a non-intuitive comparison that usually requires an explanation to be understood. Metaphor is hard enough to pull off without stretching it and stretching it and stretching it—and then explaining how the comparison works to the reader. But never say never in fiction—as evidenced by this section of *Fifth Business* by Robertson Davies, in which the title is explained:

Who are you? Where do you fit into poetry and myth? Do you know? You are Fifth Business.

You don't know that that is? Well, in opera in a permanent company of the kind we keep up in Europe you must have a prima donna—always a soprano, always the heroine, often a fool; and a tenor who always plays the lover to her; and then you must have a contralto, who is a rival to the soprano, or a sorceress or something; and a basso, who is the villain or the rival or whatever threatens the tenor.

So far so good, but you cannot make a plot work without another man, and this is usually a baritone, and he is called in the profession Fifth Business, because he is the odd man out, the person who has no opposite of the other sex. And you must have Fifth Business because he is the one who knows the secret of the hero's birth, or comes to the assistance of the heroine when she thinks all is lost, or keeps the hermitess in her cell, or may even be the cause of somebody's death if that is part of the plot. The prima donna and the tenor, the contralto and the basso, get all the best music and do all the spectacular things, but you cannot manage the plot without Fifth Business! It is not spectacular, but it is a good line of work, I can tell you, and those who play it sometimes have a career that outlasts the golden voices.

PERSONIFICATION is the attribution of human characteristics to nonhuman entities. An example of personification can be found in the story "Araby" by James Joyce, when he writes:

The houses, conscious of decent lives within them, gazed at one another with brown imperturbable faces.

A SYMBOL is something specific (an object or event) that stands for something else. That is, it is not a comparison; there is a range of meaning beyond the "thing" itself. The cross stands for the crucifixion of Jesus, as well as all the ideals and beliefs of Christianity. In *Moby-Dick* the whale stands for some complex, God-like knowledge or power that must not be pursued by man.

A symbol doesn't have a comparison. It stands by itself. It must be part of the story (or poem) yet mean more than the story (or poem). It can be a shared symbol, something common to our culture, language, religion, nationality; or it can be created within the work of fiction or poetry.

It's no accident that a figure of speech is, "X *has become* a symbol," or "Y *is becoming* a symbol." A symbol is the result of the *accumulation of experience*, not just a label that can be pasted onto any object.

When Should You Use Metaphor?

Some beginning writers feel that their imagery isn't truly compelling without metaphor. But the reverse is often true. Gratuitous use of metaphors or similes can clutter up a piece of writing—especially if the metaphors are clichéd or otherwise overly familiar.

That's because sometimes beginning writers are in such a hurry to say what something is like, they fail in letting us know what it *is*. Metaphors tend to be organic—they must grow out of the story itself. Trying to impose metaphor for its own sake is to force language into something contrived, artificial, not true. And, as we've discussed, truth is what we're ultimately after when we sit down to write.

A good metaphor (or simile) resonates within the story; your readers will immediately see its truth. It should be grasped at once; you shouldn't have to stop, go back, and reread; you shouldn't have to figure it out, like a puzzle. You shouldn't (especially) be struck by the cleverness of the writer at devising such a wonderful metaphor.

All too often, we resort to metaphor when we don't know what else to do. Well, writing fiction (or poetry) is about language, and so the figurative stuff gets piled on, and things bog down, and tension lags.

There is absolutely no way to do a metaphor writing exercise, because that defeats the purpose. If it doesn't come up organically, within the creative process of the story, then it isn't worth anything. Its only value is within context. This doesn't mean you can't come up with some terrific comparisons of unlike objects. But think of metaphor as that one extra suitcase, a very heavy one, that you should always think about before you put it in the car on the way to the airport. Do you really need this?

Sometimes you'll know that a particular sentence or phrase is dying for a comparison, something to illuminate it, and you can feel it hovering, but can't quite put your finger on it. Well, okay, work on it. But don't labor, don't force it, better off sticking with a plain image—describing what something *is* using one or more of the five senses—than putting in a metaphor that is imprecise or strained.

Avoiding the "S" Word: Banishing Conscious Symbols from Your Writing

And a word of warning about symbols: a good symbol is not imposed on the story, but evolves from within it. It is not, repeat *not*, something you put in afterward because you think it will "deepen' the meaning of your story. If you haven't managed to create a deep, moving story through characterization and plot and imagery, I'd suggest that trying to beef it up through symbolism is cheating, and your reader will see through you. It's an emotional shorthand for the real work. For example, sticking in a bunch of crosses and references to Judas and last suppers, and hoping the reader "gets it," rather than fully dramatizing the emotional suffering of a deeply religious and moral man who deliberately injures his best friend, would be cheating indeed.

Imagery, on the other hand, use as often as possible. It's the heart of riveting, dramatic prose. It fulfills many purposes: not just helping the reader see and hear and taste and touch and smell and otherwise perceive the world of the story, but pushing the reader toward deeper understanding and judgment. Not just concrete detail, or beautiful concrete detail, but the exact right concrete detail. No comparison necessary.

It may be that an image is so strong, and so organic within your story or nonfiction piece, that it gradually gathers strength as the story or piece progresses, and ultimately *becomes* a symbol. But let the PhD students discover that later. When writing, we want to think in terms of images—and, certainly, about the impact and meaning of those images on the story or piece of nonfiction—but to think consciously of symbols is to invite heavy-handedness, an over-reliance on symbolism to carry the meaning of a piece rather than having all the parts of the piece working in concert together.

Imagery as Creative Source

We don't just use imagery to render the world of the story or nonfiction piece (although that is certainly one thing that it does). We can also use imagery as the impetus to creating and discovering situation, meaning, possibilities within material. Here is a section of an essay, "Method: The Mystery and the Mechanics," by Paul Scott, author of *The Raj Quartet*, that explains this concept:

> A novel is a sequence of images. In sequence these images tell a story. Its purpose is not to *tell* you but to *show* you. The words used to convey the images and the act of juxtaposing the images in a certain way are the mechanics of the novel. *But the images are what matter* [emphasis mine]. They are the novel's raw material. Images are what we are really working with, and they are infinitely complex.
>
> Constructing a novel—telling a tale, for me at any rate—is not a business of thinking of a story, arranging it in a certain order, and then finding images to fit it. The images come first. I may have a general notion of wanting to write a book about a certain time, or place, *but unless the general notion is given the impetus of an image that seems to be connected, the notion never gets off the ground* [emphasis mine].
>
> Well, there is a problem there, because as writers, our minds teem with images. We have unending stocks of these private little mysteries, and it is all too easy to think of a story, a situation, and come up with an adequate supply of mental pictures to illustrate it. I call that automatic writing. I don't decry it. It can be very effective. But it isn't my way, and in automatic writing of this kind you seldom feel, as a reader, that there is much underneath. The images conveyed are flat, two-dimensional. In fitting an image to a situation, the image lacks density, it has little ability to stand on its own, it has no inner mystery. *The situation, somehow, must be made to rise out of the image* [emphasis mine].
>
> You need, to begin with, a strong central image that yields a strong situation, or series of situations. By strong I don't necessarily mean strongly dramatic. I mean strong in the sense of tenacious, one that won't let you off the hook. Almost every one of your waking hours is spent considering it, exploring it. You can carry on a conversation and still be thinking of it—although you do tend to lose your awareness of the lapse of real time. When in the grip of this kind of image, my wife may say to me over the breakfast table, "Darling, is it raining?" Two seconds later—but actually two minutes—after she has been to the window, looked out and seen for herself that it is, I will probably say, "No, I don't think so." This is called absence of mind. But absent is exactly what the mind is not. At least it isn't absent from the place where its duty is to be—in the embryo book, wallowing through all the sticky, unmapped, unexplored regions of this extraordinary picture that so far has not been fully transformed into a *situation*.

In the Grace Paley short short story "Mother," below, there are five images that make up the story. Let's look at each of the five images and see what they convey.

One day I was listening to the AM radio. I heard a song: "Oh, I Long To See My Mother In The Doorway." By God! I said, I understand that song. I have often longed to see my mother in the doorway. As a matter of fact, she did stand frequently in various doorways looking at me. [1] She stood one day, just so, at the front door, the darkness of the hallway behind her. It was New Year's Day. She said sadly, If you come home at 4 a.m. when you're seventeen, what time will you come home when you're twenty? She asked this question without humor or meanness. She had begun her worried preparations for death. She would not be present, she thought, when I was twenty. So she wondered.

[2] Another time she stood in the doorway of my room. I had just issued a political manifesto attacking the family's position on the Soviet Union. She said, Go to sleep for godsakes, you damn fool, you and your Communist ideas. We saw them already, Papa and me, in 1905. We guessed it all.

[3] At the door of the kitchen she said, You never finish your lunch. You run around senselessly. What will become of you?

Then she died.

Naturally for the rest of my life I longed to see her, not only in doorways, in a great number of places—in the dining room with my aunts, at the window looking up and down the block, in the country garden among zinnias and marigolds, [4] in the living room with my father.

They sat in comfortable leather chairs. They were listening to Mozart. They looked at one another amazed. It seemed to them that they'd just come over on the boat. They'd just learned the first English words. It seemed to them that he had just proudly handed in a 100 percent correct exam to the American anatomy professor. It seemed as though she'd just quit the shop for the kitchen.

[5] I wish I could see her in the doorway of the living room.

She stood there a minute. Then she sat beside him. They owned an expensive record player. They were listening to Bach. She said to him, Talk to me a little. We don't talk so much anymore.

I'm tired, he said. Can't you see? I saw maybe thirty people today. All sick, all talk talk talk talk. Listen to the music, he said. I believe you once had perfect pitch. I'm tired, he said.

Then she died.

1. In this first image, we get the sense of how vividly the narrator sees her mother, how she's standing "just so" as if the narrator is gesturing toward an actual picture that *we* can see. We see the worried mother, and the relationship between the two of them.
2. In this second image we sense the impatience but also the affection (however exasperated) the mother has for her daughter, whose only

crime is that she is young and passionate. A different slant on their relationship is revealed.

3. In this third image we're back to the worried mother. The fact that this is immediately followed by the words, "Then she died" implies that this is the mother that was frozen in the narrator's mind upon death.

4. In this fourth image we see the woman, not as a mother, but as a person: an immigrant full of wonder and excitement at having succeeded in America. We also see the father for the first time, and get a glimpse of the relationship between them, and a sense of the marriage that produced the narrator.

5. In this fifth image we get the depiction of a woman, disappointed, unappreciated, lonely. That this is followed by "Then she died" again shows the narrator's enhanced understanding of her mother as a person (not as a mother) and how she regrets having failed her while she was alive.

Part 2: EXERCISES

Exercise 1: *Harper's* Index on a Personal Level

> Goal: To show how very specific, even quantifiable, details can add up to a "big picture"—in this case, a self-portrait.

Harper's *Index, May 2006*

Percentage of the 156 provisions of 2001's USA Patriot Act that were permanent in the original law: 88

Number of the sixteen remaining provisions that were made permanent by Congress in March: 14

Years by which the other two were extended: 4

Number of U.S. cities and towns so far that have passed resolutions calling for the impeachment of President Bush: 8

Ratio of the entire U.S. federal budget in 1948, adjusted for inflation, to the amount spent so far on the Iraq war: 1:1

Percentage of U.S. soldiers in Iraq who say the war was a retaliation for Saddam Hussein's role in the 9/11 attacks: 85

Chances that an American believes that the U.S. will suffer a "major terrorist attack" by next March: 2 in 3

Number of beetles that right-wing entomologists have named after Bush Administration officials: 3

Estimated number of animal and plant species known to science: 1,800,000

Estimated number of different official names that have been applied to them: 6,000,000

Rank of "Christian" among one-word descriptions of George W. Bush offered by Americans in February 2005: 15

Rank this March: 5

Number of times that Mary, Jesus's mother, is referenced by name in the Bible and the Koran, respectively: 19, 34

Percentage of U.S. megachurches that "always" or "often" use electric guitar or bass in services: 93

Percentage change last year in the number of CDs sold at Starbucks: +307

Minimum number of shopping carts that went missing from L.A.–area stores last year: 6,220,000

Years that Hillary Clinton sat on Wal-Mart's board of directors: 5

Number of "Wal-ocaust" T-shirts sold by a Georgia man before Wal-Mart ordered him to cease and desist: 1

Ratio, in the United States, of the number of Wal-Mart employees to the number of high school teachers: 1:1

Percentage change since 1940 in the average iron content of milk: –62

Percentage alcohol content in a 300-year-old whiskey recipe being revived by a Scottish distillery: 90

Months after Hamas's electoral victory that the only Palestinian brewery will release its nonalcoholic beer: 5

Estimated number of Ugandan prisoners who escaped in February while guards celebrated the president's reelection: 400

Maximum number of Africans brought to America in any single year during the trans-Atlantic slave trade: 35,000

Average number of Africans who have legally emigrated to the United States each year since 2000: 55,000

Estimated percentage share of global GDP in 1974 that came from "developed" and "emerging" nations, respectively: 61, 39

Estimated percentage from those nations today: 49, 51

Minimum number of world nations that have at least one legislator from a communist party: 27

Percentage of South Korean youth who say their country should back North Korea in the event of war with the U.S.: 48

Percentage of China's investable assets that are controlled by the richest half-percent of households: 62

Percentage of white-collar Chinese workers who have personal blogs: 52

Chances that an unprotected PC will become infected with a virus within an hour of being on the Internet: 9 in 10

Chance that a British youth reports having been bullied via text message: 1 in 7

Number of billboards with the names and faces of convicted sex offenders that Mississippi will put up this spring: 100

Percentage change last year in the number of stolen cattle recovered in Texas and Oklahoma: +104

Minimum number of ranches in Texas where one can shoot a zebra: 56

Weeks in advance that Al Qaeda operatives must request vacation time, according to seized documents: 10

Number of Harlequin novels published last year that feature love between a Western woman and an Arab sheikh: 15

Number by 2008 that will feature NASCAR races: 22

What to do: 1. First, look at the *Harper's* Index, and see how the editors choose facts and details, some of them quite small and seemingly arcane, to add up to a particular view of our society.

2. Now write down ten things about yourself that are *quantifiable* in some way, i.e., can be expressed with numbers. Look at the example for inspiration.

Below is a "composite" example of how this exercise can be done, taken from numerous student attempts over the years:

Harper's *Index for an Individual*

Years after I started menstruating that I learned to always keep a box of tampons in the house: 25

Number of sisters I have: 5

Number of sisters who are talking to me at present: 3

Average number of minutes after two of my sisters have a fight that I hear about it: 15

Chances that when my husband goes to the video store he'll return with something with the word "planet" in the title: 100 percent

Number of times I've put on *Beauty and the Beast* by Cocteau and eaten a pint of Chunky Monkey ice cream when I'm feeling blue: 17

Chances that my son will say, "But I'm not tired!" when it's bedtime: 100 percent

Hours after my sister-in-law hears about someone being sick that she also gets sick: 2

Number of unread books by my bedside table: 7

Diet Coke, water, and milk as my No. 1, 2, and 3 favorite beverages

Exercise 2: Render a Tree, Capture the Forest

Goal: To show how by selectively choosing *this* tree, then *that* tree, you can render something big—the whole forest.

What to do: 1. Read "Nebraska" by Ron Hansen (pp. 147–51) and see how he captures the entire state of Nebraska through the use of carefully chosen details.

2. By carefully choosing a dozen details—a donut shop, an interaction on a street corner between a husband and wife—attempt to capture an entire place: a town, a state, a city, a county.

The following example was provided by Susan Wood:

Northwestern Illinois had been beautiful once, you could see that. Even now, beyond the edges of our subdivision, there were traces of the rolling prairie, grasses rippling out as far as eye could see, the sun bleaching the sheaves of stalks a honey gold. But the sprawl was approaching from Chicago, 30 miles to the south. Huge bulldozers and cranes moved in, tearing raw holes in the earth, shaving off the rich topsoil and topping it with red clay in which nothing could grow. Huge mountains of dirt appeared from these excavations, bleeding bronzed trickles of water polluted by oil runoffs, discarded soda cans, and cigarette lighters. In between the large rectangular cuts in the ground that would become the basements of houses ran the roads, already finished, pristine black ribbons bordered by fresh cement curbs and punctuated with street lights that already turned on automatically when dusk fell.

Our house was one of the few that had been finished, and the only one in which humans resided. We ran wild all day among the construction sites, stealing bits of lumber to build a playhouse on our grassless yard, throwing mud bombs into the unfinished entry halls and living rooms of the houses that would one day be occupied by our neighbors. At night we'd walk along the ghostly roads, splitting up at corners and walking in different directions only to have the maze-like roads bring us back again to each other within minutes. There was an unearthly silence on those evenings. Not a bird, not a cricket; all of nature had fled as if from a war zone.

Part 3: READING AS A WRITER

The Things They Carried

TIM O'BRIEN

First Lieutenant Jimmy Cross carried letters from a girl named Martha, a junior at Mount Sebastian College in New Jersey. They were not love letters, but Lieutenant Cross was hoping, so he kept them folded in plastic at the bottom of his rucksack. In the late afternoon, after a day's march, he would dig his foxhole, wash his hands under a canteen, unwrap the letters, hold them with the tips of his fingers, and spend the last hour of light pretending. He would imagine romantic camping trips into the White Mountains in New Hampshire. He would sometimes taste the envelope flaps, knowing her tongue had been there. More than anything, he wanted Martha to love him as he loved her, but the letters were mostly chatty, elusive on the matter of love. She was a virgin, he was almost sure. She was an English major at Mount Sebastian, and she wrote beautifully about her professors and roommates and midterm exams, about her respect for Chaucer and her great affection for Virginia Woolf. She often quoted lines of poetry; she never mentioned the war, except to say, Jimmy, take care of yourself. The letters weighed ten ounces. They were signed "Love, Martha," but Lieutenant Cross understood that "Love" was only a way of signing and did not mean what he sometimes pretended it meant. At dusk, he would carefully return the letters to his rucksack. Slowly, a bit distracted, he would get up and move among his men, checking the perimeter, then at full dark he would return to his hole and watch the night and wonder if Martha was a virgin.

The things they carried were largely determined by necessity. Among the necessities or near necessities were P-38 can openers, pocket knives, heat tabs, wristwatches, dog tags, mosquito repellent, chewing gum, candy, cigarettes, salt tablets, packets of Kool-Aid, lighters, matches, sewing kits, Military Payment Certificates, C rations, and two or three canteens of water. Together, these items weighed between fifteen and twenty pounds, depending upon a man's habits or rate of metabolism. Henry Dobbins, who was a big man, carried extra rations; he was especially fond of canned peaches in heavy syrup over pound cake. Dave Jensen, who practiced field hygiene, carried a toothbrush, dental floss, and several hotel-size bars of soap he'd stolen on R&R in Sydney, Australia. Ted Lavender, who was scared, carried tranquilizers until he was shot in the head outside the village of Than Khe in mid-April. By necessity, and because it was SOP,[1] they all carried steel helmets that weighed five pounds including the liner and camouflage cover. They carried the standard fatigue jackets and trousers. Very few carried underwear. On their feet they carried jungle boots—2.1 pounds—and Dave Jensen carried three pairs of socks and a can of Dr. Scholl's foot powder as a precaution against trench foot. Until he was shot, Ted Lavender carried six or seven ounces of premium dope, which for him was a necessity. Mitchell Sanders, the RTO,[2] carried condoms. Norman Bowker carried a diary. Rat Kiley carried comic books. Kiowa, a devout Baptist, carried an illustrated New Testament that had been presented to him by his father, who taught Sunday school in Oklahoma City, Oklahoma. As a hedge against bad times, however, Kiowa also carried his grandmother's distrust of the white man, his grandfather's old hunting hatchet. Necessity dictated. Because the land was mined and booby-trapped, it was SOP for each man to carry a steel-centered, nylon-covered flak jacket, which weighed 6.7 pounds, but which on hot days seemed much heavier. Because you could die so quickly, each man carried at least one large compress bandage, usually in the helmet band for easy access. Because the nights were cold, and because the monsoons were wet, each carried a green plastic poncho that could be used as a raincoat or groundsheet or makeshift tent. With its quilted liner, the poncho weighed almost two pounds, but it was worth every ounce. In April, for instance, when Ted Lavender was shot, they used his poncho to wrap him up, then to carry him across the paddy, then to lift him into the chopper that took him away.

They were called legs or grunts.

To carry something was to "hump" it, as when Lieutenant Jimmy Cross humped his love for Martha up the hills and through the swamps. In its intransitive form, "to hump" meant "to walk," or "to march," but it implied burdens far beyond the intransitive.

Almost everyone humped photographs. In his wallet, Lieutenant Cross carried two photographs of Martha. The first was a Kodachrome snapshot signed "Love," though he knew better. She stood against a brick wall. Her eyes were gray and neutral, her lips slightly open as she stared straight-on at the camera. At night, sometimes, Lieutenant Cross wondered who had taken the picture, because he knew she had boyfriends, because he loved

---

[1] Standard operating procedure.
[2] Radiotelephone operator.

her so much, and because he could see the shadow of the picture taker spreading out against the brick wall. The second photograph had been clipped from the 1968 Mount Sebastian yearbook. It was an action shot—women's volleyball—and Martha was bent horizontal to the floor, reaching, the palms of her hands in sharp focus, the tongue taut, the expression frank and competitive. There was no visible sweat. She wore white gym shorts. Her legs, he thought, were almost certainly the legs of a virgin, dry and without hair, the left knee cocked and carrying her entire weight, which was just over one hundred pounds. Lieutenant Cross remembered touching that left knee. A dark theater, he remembered, and the movie was *Bonnie and Clyde*, and Martha wore a tweed skirt, and during the final scene, when he touched her knee, she turned and looked at him in a sad, sober way that made him pull his hand back, but he would always remember the feel of the tweed skirt and the knee beneath it and the sound of the gunfire that killed Bonnie and Clyde, how embarrassing it was, how slow and oppressive. He remembered kissing her good night at the dorm door. Right then, he thought, he should've done something brave. He should've carried her up the stairs to her room and tied her to the bed and touched that left knee all night long. He should've risked it. Whenever he looked at the photographs, he thought of new things he should've done.

What they carried was partly a function of rank, partly of field specialty.

As a first lieutenant and platoon leader, Jimmy Cross carried a compass, maps, code books, binoculars, and a .45-caliber pistol that weighed 2.9 pounds fully loaded. He carried a strobe light and the responsibility for the lives of his men.

As an RTO, Mitchell Sanders carried the PRC-25 radio, a killer, twenty-six pounds with its battery.

As a medic, Rat Kiley carried a canvas satchel filled with morphine and plasma and malaria tablets and surgical tape and comic books and all the things a medic must carry, including M&M's for especially bad wounds, for a total weight of nearly twenty pounds.

As a big man, therefore a machine gunner, Henry Dobbins carried the M-60, which weighed twenty-three pounds unloaded, but which was almost always loaded. In addition, Dobbins carried between ten and fifteen pounds of ammunition draped in belts across his chest and shoulders.

As PFCs or Spec 4s, most of them were common grunts and carried the standard M-16 gas-operated assault rifle. The weapon weighed 7.5 pounds unloaded, 8.2 pounds with its full twenty-round magazine. Depending on numerous factors, such as topography and psychology, the riflemen carried anywhere from twelve to twenty magazines, usually in cloth bandoliers, adding on another 8.4 pounds at minimum, fourteen pounds at maximum. When it was available, they also carried M-16 maintenance gear—rods and steel brushes and swabs and tubes of LSA oil—all of which weighed about a pound. Among the grunts, some carried the M-79 grenade launcher, 5.9 pounds unloaded, a reasonably light weapon except for the ammunition, which was heavy. A single round weighed ten ounces. The typical load was twenty-five rounds. But Ted Lavender, who was scared, carried thirty-four rounds when he was shot and killed outside Than Khe, and he went down under an exceptional burden, more than twenty pounds of ammunition, plus the flak jacket and helmet and rations and waters and toilet paper and tranquilizers and all the rest, plus the unweighed fear. He was dead weight. There was no twitching or flopping. Kiowa, who saw it happen, said it was like watching a rock fall, or a big sandbag or something—just boom, then down—not like the movies where the dead guy rolls around and does fancy spins and goes ass over teakettle—not like that, Kiowa said, the poor bastard just flat-fuck fell. Boom. Down. Nothing else. It was a bright morning in mid-April. Lieutenant Cross felt the pain. He blamed himself. They stripped off Lavender's canteens and ammo, all the heavy things, and Rat Kiley said the obvious, the guy's dead, and Mitchell Sanders used his radio to report one U.S. KIA[3] and to request a chopper. Then they wrapped Lavender in his poncho. They carried him out to a dry paddy, established security, and sat smoking the dead man's dope until the chopper came. Lieutenant Cross kept to himself. He pictured Martha's smooth young face, thinking he loved her more than anything, more than his men, and now Ted Lavender was dead because he loved her so much and could not stop thinking about her. When the dust-off arrived, they carried Lavender aboard. Afterward they burned Than Khe. They marched until dusk, then dug their holes, and that night Kiowa kept explaining how you had to be there, how fast it was, how the poor guy just dropped like so much concrete. Boom-down, he said. Like cement.

In addition to the three standard weapons—the M-60, M-16, and M-79—they carried whatever presented itself, or whatever seemed appropriate as a means of killing or staying alive. They carried catch-as-catch-can. At various times, in various situations, they carried M-14s and CAR-15s and

[3] Killed in action.

Swedish Ks and grease guns and captured AK-47s and Chi-Coms and RPGs and Simonov carbines and black-market Uzis and .38-caliber Smith & Wesson handguns and 66 mm LAWs and shotguns and silencers and blackjacks and bayonets and C-4 plastic explosives. Lee Strunk carried a slingshot; a weapon of last resort, he called it. Mitchell Sanders carried brass knuckles. Kiowa carried his grandfather's feathered hatchet. Every third or fourth man carried a Claymore antipersonnel mine—3.5 pounds with its firing device. They all carried fragmentation grenades—fourteen ounces each. They all carried at least one M-18 colored smoke grenade—twenty-four ounces. Some carried CS or teargas grenades. Some carried white-phosphorus grenades. They carried all they could bear, and then some, including a silent awe for the terrible power of the things they carried.

In the first week of April, before Lavender died, Lieutenant Jimmy Cross received a good-luck charm from Martha. It was a simple pebble, an ounce at most. Smooth to the touch, it was a milky-white color with flecks of orange and violet, oval-shaped, like a miniature egg. In the accompanying letter, Martha wrote that she had found the pebble on the Jersey shoreline, precisely where the land touched water at high tide, where things came together but also separated. It was this separate-but-together quality, she wrote, that had inspired her to pick up the pebble and to carry it in her breast pocket for several days, where it seemed weightless, and then to send it through the mail, by air, as a token of her truest feelings for him. Lieutenant Cross found this romantic. But he wondered what her truest feelings were, exactly, and what she meant by separate-but-together. He wondered how the tides and waves had come into play on that afternoon along the Jersey shoreline when Martha saw the pebble and bent down to rescue it from geology. He imagined bare feet. Martha was a poet, with the poet's sensibilities, and her feet would be brown and bare, the toenails unpainted, the eyes chilly and somber like the ocean in March, and though it was painful, he wondered who had been with her that afternoon. He imagined a pair of shadows moving along the strip of sand where things came together but also separated. It was phantom jealousy, he knew, but he couldn't help himself. He loved her so much. On the march, through the hot days of early April, he carried the pebble in his mouth, turning it with his tongue, tasting sea salts and moisture. His mind wandered. He had difficulty keeping his attention on the war. On occasion he would yell at his men to spread out the column, to keep their eyes open, but then he would slip away into daydreams, just pretending, walking barefoot along the Jersey shore, with Martha, carrying nothing. He would feel himself rising. Sun and waves and gentle winds, all love and lightness.

What they carried varied by mission.

When a mission took them to the mountains, they carried mosquito netting, machetes, canvas tarps, and extra bug juice.

If a mission seemed especially hazardous, or if it involved a place they knew to be bad, they carried everything they could. In certain heavily mined AOs,[4] where the land was dense with Toe Poppers and Bouncing Betties, they took turns humping a twenty-eight-pound mine detector. With its headphones and big sensing plate, the equipment was a stress on the lower back and shoulders, awkward to handle, often useless because of the shrapnel in the earth, but they carried it anyway, partly for safety, partly for the illusion of safety.

On ambush, or other night missions, they carried peculiar little odds and ends. Kiowa always took along his New Testament and a pair of moccasins for silence. Dave Jensen carried night-sight vitamins high in carotin. Lee Strunk carried his slingshot; ammo, he claimed, would never be a problem. Rat Kiley carried brandy and M&M's. Until he was shot, Ted Lavender carried the starlight scope, which weighed 6.3 pounds with its aluminum carrying case. Henry Dobbins carried his girlfriend's pantyhose wrapped around his neck as a comforter. They all carried ghosts. When dark came, they would move out single file across the meadows and paddies to their ambush coordinates, where they would quietly set up the Claymores and lie down and spend the night waiting.

Other missions were more complicated and required special equipment. In mid-April, it was their mission to search out and destroy the elaborate tunnel complexes in the Than Khe area south of Chu Lai. To blow the tunnels, they carried one-pound blocks of pentrite high explosives, four blocks to a man, sixty-eight pounds in all. They carried wiring, detonators, and battery-powered clackers. Dave Jensen carried earplugs. Most often, before blowing the tunnels, they were ordered by higher command to search them, which was considered bad news, but by and large they just shrugged and carried out orders. Because he was a big man, Henry Dobbins was excused from tunnel duty. The others would draw numbers. Before Lavender died there were seventeen men in the platoon, and whoever drew the number seventeen would strip off his gear and crawl in

---

[4]Areas of operations.

head first with a flashlight and Lieutenant Cross's .45-caliber pistol. The rest of them would fan out as security. They would sit down or kneel, not facing the hole, listening to the ground beneath them, imagining cobwebs and ghosts, whatever was down there—the tunnel walls squeezing in— how the flashlight seemed impossibly heavy in the hand and how it was tunnel vision in the very strictest sense, compression in all ways, even time, and how you had to wiggle in—ass and elbows—a swallowed-up feeling—and how you found yourself worrying about odd things—will your flashlight go dead? Do rats carry rabies? If you screamed, how far would the sound carry? Would your buddies hear it? Would they have the courage to drag you out? In some respects, though not many, the waiting was worse than the tunnel itself. Imagination was a killer.

On April 16, when Lee Strunk drew the number seventeen, he laughed and muttered something and went down quickly. The morning was hot and very still. Not good, Kiowa said. He looked at the tunnel opening, then out across a dry paddy toward the village of Than Khe. Nothing moved. No clouds or birds or people. As they waited, the men smoked and drank Kool-Aid, not talking much, feeling sympathy for Lee Strunk but also feeling the luck of the draw. You win some, you lose some, said Mitchell Sanders, and sometimes you settle for a raincheck. It was a tired line and no one laughed.

Henry Dobbins ate a tropical chocolate bar. Ted Lavender popped a tranquilizer and went off to pee.

After five minutes, Lieutenant Jimmy Cross moved to the tunnel, leaned down, and examined the darkness. Trouble, he thought—a cave-in maybe. And then suddenly, without willing it, he was thinking about Martha. The stresses and fractures, the quick collapse, the two of them buried alive under all that weight. Dense, crushing love. Kneeling, watching the hole, he tried to concentrate on Lee Strunk and the war, all the dangers, but his love was too much for him, he felt paralyzed, he wanted to sleep inside her lungs and breathe her blood and be smothered. He wanted her to be a virgin and not a virgin, all at once. He wanted to know her. Intimate secrets—why poetry? Why so sad? Why the grayness in her eyes? Why so alone? Not lonely, just alone—riding her bike across campus or sitting off by herself in the cafeteria. Even dancing, she danced alone— and it was the aloneness that filled him with love. He remembered telling her that one evening. How she nodded and looked away. And how, later, when he kissed her, she received the kiss without returning it, her eyes wide open, not afraid, not a virgin's eyes, just flat and uninvolved.

Lieutenant Cross gazed at the tunnel. But he was not there. He was buried with Martha under the white sand at the Jersey shore. They were pressed together, and the pebble in his mouth was her tongue. He was smiling. Vaguely, he was aware of how quiet the day was, the sullen paddies, yet he could not bring himself to worry about matters of security. He was beyond that. He was just a kid at war, in love. He was twenty-two years old. He couldn't help it.

A few moments later Lee Strunk crawled out of the tunnel. He came up grinning, filthy but alive. Lieutenant Cross nodded and closed his eyes while the others clapped Strunk on the back and made jokes about rising from the dead.

Worms, Rat Kiley said. Right out of the grave. Fuckin' zombie.

The men laughed. They all felt great relief.

Spook City, said Mitchell Sanders.

Lee Strunk made a funny ghost sound, a kind of moaning, yet very happy, and right then, when Strunk made that high happy moaning sound, when he went *Ahhooooo,* right then Ted Lavender was shot in the head on his way back from peeing. He lay with his mouth open. The teeth were broken. There was a swollen black bruise under his left eye. The cheekbone was gone. Oh shit, Rat Kiley said, the guy's dead. The guy's dead, he kept saying, which seemed profound—the guy's dead. I mean really.

The things they carried were determined to some extent by superstition. Lieutenant Cross carried his good-luck pebble. Dave Jensen carried a rabbit's foot. Norman Bowker, otherwise a very gentle person, carried a thumb that had been presented to him as a gift by Mitchell Sanders. The thumb was dark brown, rubbery to the touch, and weighed four ounces at most. It had been cut from a VC corpse, a boy of fifteen or sixteen. They'd found him at the bottom of an irrigation ditch, badly burned, flies in his mouth and eyes. The boy wore black shorts and sandals. At the time of his death he had been carrying a pouch of rice, a rifle, and three magazines of ammunition.

You want my opinion, Mitchell Sanders said, there's a definite moral here.

He put his hand on the dead boy's wrist. He was quiet for a time, as if counting a pulse, then he patted the stomach, almost affectionately, and used Kiowa's hunting hatchet to remove the thumb.

Henry Dobbins asked what the moral was.

Moral?

You know. *Moral.*

Sanders wrapped the thumb in toilet paper and handed it across to Norman Bowker. There was no blood. Smiling, he kicked the boy's head, watched the flies scatter, and said, It's like with that old TV show—Paladin. Have gun, will travel.

Henry Dobbins thought about it.

Yeah, well, he finally said. I don't see no moral.

There it *is*, man.

Fuck off.

They carried USO stationery and pencils and pens. They carried Sterno, safety pins, trip flares, signal flares, spools of wire, razor blades, chewing tobacco, liberated joss sticks and statuettes of the smiling Buddha, candles, grease pencils, *The Stars and Stripes*, fingernail clippers, Psy Ops[5] leaflets, bush hats, bolos, and much more. Twice a week, when the resupply choppers came in, they carried hot chow in green Mermite cans and large canvas bags filled with iced beer and soda pop. They carried plastic water containers, each with a two-gallon capacity. Mitchell Sanders carried a set of starched tiger fatigues for special occasions. Henry Dobbins carried Black Flag insecticide. Dave Jensen carried empty sandbags that could be filled at night for added protection. Lee Strunk carried tanning lotion. Some things they carried in common. Taking turns, they carried the big PRC-77 scrambler radio, which weighed thirty pounds with its battery. They shared the weight of memory. They took up what others could no longer bear. Often, they carried each other, the wounded or weak. They carried infections. They carried chess sets, basketballs, Vietnamese-English dictionaries, insignia of rank, Bronze Stars and Purple Hearts, plastic cards imprinted with the Code of Conduct. They carried diseases, among them malaria and dysentery. They carried lice and ringworm and leeches and paddy algae and various rots and molds. They carried the land itself— Vietnam, the place, the soil—a powdery orange-red dust that covered their boots and fatigues and faces. They carried the sky. The whole atmosphere, they carried it, the humidity, the monsoons, the stink of fungus and decay, all of it, they carried gravity. They moved like mules. By daylight they took sniper fire, at night they were mortared, but it was not battle, it was just the endless march, village to village, without purpose, nothing won or lost. They marched for the sake of the march. They plodded along slowly, dumbly, leaning forward against the heat, unthinking, all blood and bone, simple grunts, soldiering with their legs, toiling up the hills and down into

[5] Psychological operations.

the paddies and across the rivers and up again and down, just humping, one step and then the next and then another, but no volition, no will, because it was automatic, it was anatomy, and the war was entirely a matter of posture and carriage, the hump was everything, a kind of inertia, a kind of emptiness, a dullness of desire and intellect and conscience and hope and human sensibility. Their principles were in their feet. Their calculations were biological. They had no sense of strategy or mission. They searched the villages without knowing what to look for, not caring, kicking over jars of rice, frisking children and old men, blowing tunnels, sometimes setting fires and sometimes not, then forming up and moving on to the next village, then other villages, where it would always be the same. They carried their own lives. The pressures were enormous. In the heat of early afternoon, they would remove their helmets and flak jackets, walking bare, which was dangerous but which helped ease the strain. They would often discard things along the route of march. Purely for comfort, they would throw away rations, blow their Claymores and grenades, no matter, because by nightfall the resupply choppers would arrive with more of the same, then a day or two later still more, fresh watermelons and crates of ammunition and sunglasses and woolen sweaters—the resources were stunning—sparklers for the Fourth of July, colored eggs for Easter. It was the great American war chest—the fruits of science, the smokestacks, the canneries, the arsenals at Hartford, the Minnesota forests, the machine shops, the vast fields of corn and wheat—they carried like freight trains; they carried it on their backs and shoulders—and for all the ambiguities of Vietnam, all the mysteries and unknowns, there was at least the single abiding certainty that they would never be at a loss for things to carry.

After the chopper took Lavender away, Lieutenant Jimmy Cross led his men into the village of Than Khe. They burned everything. They shot chickens and dogs, they trashed the village well, they called in artillery and watched the wreckage, then they marched for several hours through the hot afternoon, and then at dusk, while Kiowa explained how Lavender died, Lieutenant Cross found himself trembling.

He tried not to cry. With his entrenching tool, which weighed five pounds, he began digging a hole in the earth.

He felt shame. He hated himself. He had loved Martha more than his men, and as a consequence Lavender was now dead, and this was something he would have to carry like a stone in his stomach for the rest of the war.

All he could do was dig. He used his entrenching tool like an ax, slashing, feeling both love and hate, and then later, when it was full dark, he sat at the bottom of his foxhole and wept. It went on for a long while. In part, he was grieving for Ted Lavender, but mostly it was for Martha, and for himself, because she belonged to another world, which was not quite real, and because she was a junior at Mount Sebastian College in New Jersey, a poet and a virgin and uninvolved, and because he realized she did not love him and never would.

Like cement, Kiowa whispered in the dark. I swear to God—boom-down. Not a word.

I've heard this, said Norman Bowker.

A pisser, you know? Still zipping himself up. Zapped while zipping.

All right, fine. That's enough.

Yeah, but you had to see it, the guy just—

I *heard*, man. Cement. So why not shut the fuck *up?*

Kiowa shook his head sadly and glanced over at the hole where Lieutenant Jimmy Cross sat watching the night. The air was thick and wet. A warm, dense fog had settled over the paddies and there was the stillness that precedes rain.

After a time Kiowa sighed.

One thing for sure, he said. The Lieutenant's in some deep hurt. I mean that crying jag—the way he was carrying on—it wasn't fake or anything, it was real heavy-duty hurt. The man cares.

Sure, Norman Bowker said.

Say what you want, the man does care.

We all got problems.

Not Lavender.

No, I guess not, Bowker said. Do me a favor, though.

Shut up?

That's a smart Indian. Shut up.

Shrugging, Kiowa pulled off his boots. He wanted to say more, just to lighten up his sleep, but instead he opened his New Testament and arranged it beneath his head as a pillow. The fog made things seem hollow and unattached. He tried not to think about Ted Lavender, but then he was thinking how fast it was, no drama, down and dead, and how it was hard to feel anything except surprise. It seemed un-Christian. He wished he could find some great sadness, or even anger, but the emotion wasn't there and he couldn't make it happen. Mostly he felt pleased to be alive. He liked the smell of the New Testament under his cheek, the leather and ink and paper and glue, whatever the chemicals were. He liked hearing the sounds of night. Even his fatigue, it felt fine, the stiff muscles and the prickly awareness of his own body, a floating feeling. He enjoyed not being dead. Lying there, Kiowa admired Lieutenant Jimmy Cross's capacity for grief. He wanted to share the man's pain, he wanted to care as Jimmy Cross cared. And yet when he closed his eyes, all he could think was Boom-down, and all he could feel was the pleasure of having his boots off and the fog curling in around him and the damp soil and the Bible smells and the plush comfort of night.

After a moment Norman Bowker sat up in the dark.

What the hell, he said. You want to talk, *talk*. Tell it to me.

Forget it.

No, man, go on. One thing I hate, it's a silent Indian.

For the most part they carried themselves with poise, a kind of dignity. Now and then, however, there were times of panic, when they squealed or wanted to squeal but couldn't, when they twitched and made moaning sounds and covered their heads and said Dear Jesus and flopped around on the earth and fired their weapons blindly and cringed and sobbed and begged for the noise to stop and went wild and made stupid promises to themselves and to God and to their mothers and fathers, hoping not to die. In different ways, it happened to all of them. Afterward, when the firing ended, they would blink and peek up. They would touch their bodies, feeling shame, then quickly hiding it. They would force themselves to stand. As if in slow motion, frame by frame, the world would take on the old logic—absolute silence, then the wind, then sunlight, then voices. It was the burden of being alive. Awkwardly, the men would reassemble themselves, first in private, then in groups, becoming soldiers again. They would repair the leaks in their eyes. They would check for casualties, call in dust-offs, light cigarettes, try to smile, clear their throats and spit and begin cleaning their weapons. After a time someone would shake his head and say, No lie, I almost shit my pants, and someone else would laugh, which meant it was bad, yes, but the guy had obviously not shit his pants, it wasn't that bad, and in any case nobody would ever do such a thing and then go ahead and talk about it. They would squint into the dense, oppressive sunlight. For a few moments, perhaps, they would fall silent, lighting a joint and tracking its passage from man to man, inhaling, holding in the humiliation. Scary stuff, one of them might say. But then someone else would grin or flick his eyebrows and say, Roger-dodger, almost cut me a new asshole, *almost*.

There were numerous such poses. Some carried themselves with a sort of wistful resignation, others with pride or stiff soldierly discipline or good humor or macho zeal. They were afraid of dying but they were even more afraid to show it.

They found jokes to tell.

They used a hard vocabulary to contain the terrible softness. *Greased*, they'd say. *Offed, lit up, zapped while zipping*. It wasn't cruelty, just stage presence. They were actors and the war came at them in 3-D. When someone died, it wasn't quite dying, because in a curious way it seemed scripted, and because they had their lines mostly memorized, irony mixed with tragedy, and because they called it by other names, as if to encyst and destroy the reality of death itself. They kicked corpses. They cut off thumbs. They talked grunt lingo. They told stories about Ted Lavender's supply of tranquilizers, how the poor guy didn't feel a thing, how incredibly tranquil he was.

There's a moral here, said Mitchell Sanders.

They were waiting for Lavender's chopper, smoking the dead man's dope.

The moral's pretty obvious, Sanders said, and winked. Stay away from drugs. No joke, they'll ruin your day every time.

Cute, said Henry Dobbins.

Mind-blower, get it? Talk about wiggy—nothing left, just blood and brains.

They made themselves laugh.

There it is, they'd say, over and over, as if the repetition itself were an act of poise, a balance between crazy and almost crazy, knowing without going. There it is, which meant be cool, let it ride, because oh yeah, man, you can't change what can't be changed, there it is, there it absolutely and positively and fucking well *is*.

They were tough.

They carried all the emotional baggage of men who might die. Grief, terror, love, longing—these were intangibles, but the intangibles had their own mass and specific gravity, they had tangible weight. They carried shameful memories. They carried the common secret of cowardice barely restrained, the instinct to run or freeze or hide, and in many respects this was the heaviest burden of all, for it could never be put down, it required perfect balance and perfect posture. They carried their reputations. They carried the soldier's greatest fear, which was the fear of blushing. Men killed, and died, because they were embarrassed not to. It was what had brought them to the war in the first place, nothing positive, no dreams of glory or honor, just to avoid the blush of dishonor. They died so as not to die of embarrassment.

They crawled into tunnels and walked point and advanced under fire. Each morning, despite the unknowns, they made their legs move. They endured. They kept humping. They did not submit to the obvious alternative, which was simply to close the eyes and fall. So easy, really. Go limp and tumble to the ground and let the muscles unwind and not speak and not budge until your buddies picked you up and lifted you into the chopper that would roar and dip its nose and carry you off to the world. A mere matter of falling, yet no one ever fell. It was not courage, exactly; the object was not valor. Rather, they were too frightened to be cowards.

By and large they carried these things inside, maintaining the masks of composure. They sneered at sick call. They spoke bitterly about guys who had found release by shooting off their own toes or fingers. Pussies, they'd say. Candyasses. It was fierce, mocking talk, with only a trace of envy or awe, but even so, the image played itself out behind their eyes.

They imagined the muzzle against flesh. They imagined the quick, sweet pain, then the evacuation to Japan, then a hospital with warm beds and cute geisha nurses.

They dreamed of freedom birds.

At night, on guard, staring into the dark, they were carried away by jumbo jets. They felt the rush of takeoff. *Gone!* they yelled. And then velocity, wings and engines, a smiling stewardess—but it was more than a plane, it was a real bird, a big sleek silver bird with feathers and talons and high screeching. They were flying. The weights fell off, there was nothing to bear. They laughed and held on tight, feeling the cold slap of wind and altitude, soaring, thinking *It's over, I'm gone!*—they were naked, they were light and free—it was all lightness, bright and fast and buoyant, light as light, a helium buzz in the brain, a giddy bubbling in the lungs as they were taken up over the clouds and the war, beyond duty, beyond gravity and mortification and global entanglements—*Sin loi!*[6] they yelled, *I'm sorry, motherfuckers, but I'm out of it, I'm goofed, I'm on a space cruise, I'm gone!*—and it was a restful, disencumbered sensation, just riding the light waves, sailing that big silver freedom bird over the mountains and oceans, over America, over the farms and great sleeping cities and cemeteries and highways and the golden arches of McDonald's. It was flight, a kind of fleeing, a kind of falling, falling higher and higher, spinning off the edge of the earth and beyond the sun and through the vast, silent vacuum where there were no burdens and where everything weighed exactly nothing. *Gone!* they screamed, *I'm sorry but I'm gone!* And so at night, not

---

[6] "Sorry about that!" (Vietnamese).

quite dreaming, they gave themselves over to lightness, they were carried, they were purely borne.

On the morning after Ted Lavender died, First Lieutenant Jimmy Cross crouched at the bottom of his foxhole and burned Martha's letters. Then he burned the two photographs. There was a steady rain falling, which made it difficult, but he used heat tabs and Sterno to build a small fire, screening it with his body, holding the photographs over the tight blue flame with the tips of his fingers.

He realized it was only a gesture. Stupid, he thought. Sentimental, too, but mostly just stupid.

Lavender was dead. You couldn't burn the blame.

Besides, the letters were in his head. And even now, without photographs, Lieutenant Cross could see Martha playing volleyball in her white gym shorts and yellow T-shirt. He could see her moving in the rain.

When the fire died out, Lieutenant Cross pulled his poncho over his shoulders and ate breakfast from a can.

There was no great mystery, he decided.

In those burned letters Martha had never mentioned the war, except to say, Jimmy, take care of yourself. She wasn't involved. She signed the letters "Love," but it wasn't love, and all the fine lines and technicalities did not matter.

The morning came up wet and blurry. Everything seemed part of everything else, the fog and Martha and the deepening rain.

It was a war, after all.

Half smiling, Lieutenant Jimmy Cross took out his maps. He shook his head hard, as if to clear it, then bent forward and began planning the day's march. In ten minutes, or maybe twenty, he would rouse the men and they would pack up and head west, where the maps showed the country to be green and inviting. They would do what they had always done. The rain might add some weight, but otherwise it would be one more day layered upon all the other days.

He was realistic about it. There was that new hardness in his stomach.

No more fantasies, he told himself.

Henceforth, when he thought about Martha, it would be only to think that she belonged elsewhere. He would shut down the daydreams. This was not Mount Sebastian, it was another world, where there were no pretty poems or midterm exams, a place where men died because of carelessness and gross stupidity. Kiowa was right. Boom-down, and you were dead, never partly dead.

Briefly, in the rain, Lieutenant Cross saw Martha's gray eyes gazing back at him.

He understood.

It was very sad, he thought. The things men carried inside. The things men did or felt they had to do.

He almost nodded at her, but didn't.

Instead he went back to his maps. He was now determined to perform his duties firmly and without negligence. It wouldn't help Lavender, he knew that, but from this point on he would comport himself as a soldier. He would dispose of his good-luck pebble. Swallow it, maybe, or use Lee Strunk's slingshot, or just drop it along the trail. On the march he would impose strict field discipline. He would be careful to send out flank security, to prevent straggling or bunching up, to keep his troops moving at the proper pace and at the proper interval. He would insist on clean weapons. He would confiscate the remainder of Lavender's dope. Later in the day, perhaps, he would call the men together and speak to them plainly. He would accept the blame for what had happened to Ted Lavender. He would be a man about it. He would look them in the eyes, keeping his chin level, and he would issue the new SOPs in a calm, impersonal tone of voice, an officer's voice, leaving no room for argument or discussion. Commencing immediately, he'd tell them, they would no longer abandon equipment along the route of march. They would police up their acts. They would get their shit together, and keep it together, and maintain it neatly and in good working order.

He would not tolerate laxity. He would show strength, distancing himself.

Among the men there would be grumbling, of course, and maybe worse, because their days would seem longer and their loads heavier, but Lieutenant Cross reminded himself that his obligation was not to be loved but to lead. He would dispense with love; it was not now a factor. And if anyone quarreled or complained, he would simply tighten his lips and arrange his shoulders in the correct command posture. He might give a curt little nod. Or he might not. He might just shrug and say Carry on, then they would saddle up and form into a column and move out toward the villages of Than Khe.

1. How do the concrete details affect the story? At what point does O'Brien slip in some abstractions to good effect?
2. Why tell us that Lavender is dead so early in the story? How does that

impact the suspense? Why do you want to read on if you know that Lavender is dead, i.e., you know the whole story?

3. Notice that the full story has been told by the end of the third page. Then O'Brien goes back and tells it again, in more detail. Why structure the story this way?

4. What is the story ultimately about? What happens at the end when Jimmy Cross burns the letters and decides to be a stricter leader? Is he merely facing reality, or is he substituting one fantasy (about Martha) with another (that he can control what happens to his unit by stricter behavior)?

Nebraska

RON HANSEN

The town is Americus, Covenant, Denmark, Grange, Hooray, Jerusalem, Sweetwater—one of the lesser-known moons of the Platte, conceived in sickness and misery by European pioneers who took the path of least resistance and put down roots in an emptiness like the one they kept secret in their youth. In Swedish and Danish and German and Polish, in anxiety and fury and God's providence, they chopped at the Great Plains with spades, creating green sod houses that crumbled and collapsed in the rain and disappeared in the first persuasive snow and were so low the grown-ups stooped to go inside; and yet were places of ownership and a hard kind of happiness, the places their occupants gravely stood before on those plenary occasions when photographs were taken.

And then the Union Pacific stopped by, just a camp of white campaign tents and a boy playing his Harpoon at night, and then a supply store, a depot, a pine water tank, stockyards, and the mean prosperity of the twentieth century. The trains strolling into town to shed a boxcar in the depot sideyard, or crying past at sixty miles per hour, possibly interrupting a girl in her high-wire act, her arms looping up when she tips to one side, the railtop as slippery as a silver spoon. And then the yellow and red locomotive rises up from the heat shimmer over a mile away, the August noonday warping the sight of it, but cinders tapping away from the spikes and the iron rails already vibrating up inside the girl's shoes. She steps down to the roadbed and then into high weeds as the Union Pacific pulls Wyoming coal and Georgia-Pacific lumber and snowplow blades and aslant Japanese pickup trucks through the open countryside and on to Omaha. And when it passes by, a worker she knows is opposite her, like a pedestrian at a stoplight, the sun not letting up, the plainsong of grasshoppers going on and on between them until the worker says, "Hot."

Twice the Union Pacific tracks cross over the sidewinding Democrat, the water slow as an oxcart, green as silage, croplands to the east, yards and houses to the west, a green ceiling of leaves in some places, whirlpools showing up in it like spinning plates that lose speed and disappear. In winter and a week or more of just above zero, high-school couples walk the gray ice, kicking up snow as quiet words are passed between them, opinions are mildly compromised, sorrows are apportioned. And Emil Jedlicka unslings his blue-stocked .22 and slogs through high brown weeds and snow, hunting ring-necked pheasant, sidelong rabbits, and—always suddenly—quail, as his little brother Orin sprints across the Democrat in order to slide like an otter.

July in town is a gray highway and a Ford hay truck spraying by, the hay sailing like a yellow ribbon caught in the mouth of a prancing dog, and Billy Awalt up there on the camel's hump, eighteen years old and sweaty and dirty, peppered and dappled with hay dust, a lump of chew like an extra thumb under his lower lip, his blue eyes happening on a Dairy Queen and a pretty girl licking a pale trickle of ice cream from the cone. And Billy slaps his heart and cries, "Oh! I am pierced!"

And late October is orange on the ground and blue overhead and grain silos stacked up like white poker chips, and a high silver water tower belittled one night by the sloppy tattoo of one year's class at George W. Norris High. And below the silos and water tower are stripped treetops, their gray limbs still lifted up in alleluia, their yellow leaves crowding along yard fences and sheeping along the sidewalks and alleys under the shepherding wind.

Or January and a heavy snow partitioning the landscape, whiting out the highways and woods and cattle lots until there are only open spaces and steamed-up windowpanes, and a Nordstrom boy limping pitifully in the hard plaster of his clothes, the snow as deep as his hips when the boy tips over and cannot get up until a little Schumacher girl sitting by the stoop window, a spoon in her mouth, a bowl of Cheerios in her lap, says in plain voice, "There's a boy," and her mother looks out to the sidewalk.

Houses are big and white and two stories high, each a cousin to the next, with pigeon roosts in the attic gables, green storm windows on the upper floor, and a green screened porch, some as pillowed and couched as parlors or made into sleeping rooms for the boy whose next step will be the Navy and days spent on a ship with his hometown's own population, on gray water that rises up and is allayed like a geography of cornfields, sugar beets, soybeans, wheat, that stays there and says, in its own way, "Stay." Houses are turned away from the land and toward whatever is not always, sitting across from each other like dressed-up children at a party in daylight, their parents looking on with hopes and fond expectations. Overgrown elm and sycamore trees poach the sunlight from the lawns and keep petticoats of snow around them into April. In the deep lots out back are wire clotheslines with flapping white sheets pinned to them, property lines are hedged with sour green and purple grapes, or with rabbit wire and gardens of peonies, roses, gladiola, irises, marigolds, pansies. Fruit trees are so closely planted that they cannot sway without knitting. The apples and cherries drop and sweetly decompose until they're only slight brown bumps in the yards, but the pears stay up in the wind, drooping under the pecks of birds, withering down like peppers until their sorrow is justly noticed and they one day disappear.

Aligned against an alley of blue shale rock is a garage whose doors slash weeds and scrape up pebbles as an old man pokily swings them open, teetering with his last weak push. And then Victor Johnson rummages inside, being cautious about his gray sweater and high-topped shoes, looking over paint cans, junked electric motors, grass rakes and garden rakes and a pitchfork and sickles, gray doors and ladders piled overhead in the rafters, and an old windup Victrola and heavy platter records from the twenties, on one of them a soprano singing "I'm a Lonesome Melody." Under a green tarpaulin is a wooden movie projector he painted silver and big cans of tan celluloid, much of it orange and green with age, but one strip of it preserved: of an Army pilot in jodhpurs hopping from one biplane onto another's upper wing. Country people who'd paid to see the movie had been spellbound by the slight dip of the wings at the pilot's jump, the slap of his leather jacket, and how his hair strayed wild and was promptly sleeked back by the wind. But looking at the strip now, pulling a ribbon of it up to a windowpane and letting it unspool to the ground, Victor can make out only twenty frames of the leap, and then snapshot after snapshot of an Army pilot clinging to the biplane's wing. And yet Victor stays with it, as though that scene of one man staying alive were what he'd paid his nickel for.

Main Street is just a block away. Pickup trucks stop in it so their drivers can angle out over their brown left arms and speak about crops or praise the weather or make up sentences whose only real point is their lack of complication. And then a cattle truck comes up and they mosey along with a touch of their cap bills or a slap of the door metal. High-school girls in skintight jeans stay in one place on weekends, and jacked-up cars cruise past, rowdy farmboys overlapping inside, pulling over now and then in order to give the girls cigarettes and sips of pop and grief about their lipstick. And when the cars peel out, the girls say how a particular boy measured up or they swap gossip about Donna Moriarity and the scope she permitted Randy when he came back from boot camp.

Everyone is famous in this town. And everyone is necessary. Townspeople go to the Vaughn Grocery Store for the daily news, and to the Home Restaurant for history class, especially at evensong when the old people eat graveled pot roast and lemon meringue pie and calmly sip coffee from cups they tip to their mouths with both hands. The Kiwanis Club meets here on Tuesday nights, and hopes are made public, petty sins are tidily dispatched, the proceeds from the gumball machines are tallied up and poured into the upkeep of a playground. Yutesler's Hardware has picnic items and kitchen appliances in its one window, in the manner of those prosperous men who would prefer to be known for their hobbies. And there is one crisp, white, Protestant church with a steeple, of the sort pictured on calendars; and the Immaculate Conception Catholic Church, grayly holding the town at bay like a Gothic wolfhound. And there is an insurance agency, a county coroner and justice of the peace, a secondhand shop, a handsome chiropractor named Koch who coaches the Pony League baseball team, a post office approached on unpainted wood steps outside of a cheap mobile home, the Nighthawk tavern where there's Falstaff tap beer, a green pool table, a poster recording the Cornhuskers scores, a crazy man patiently tolerated, a gray-haired woman with an unmoored eye, a boy in spectacles thick as paperweights, a carpenter missing one index finger, a plump waitress whose day job is in a basement beauty shop, an old woman who creeps up to the side door at eight in order to purchase one shot glass of whiskey.

And yet passing by, and paying attention, an outsider is only aware of what isn't, that there's no bookshop, no picture show, no pharmacy or dry cleaners, no cocktail parties, extreme opinions, jewelry or piano stores, motels, hotels, hospital, political headquarters, philosophical theories about Being and the soul.

High importance is only attached to practicalities, and so there is the Batchelor Funeral Home, where a proud old gentleman is on display in a dark brown suit, his yellow fingernails finally clean, his smeared eyeglasses in his coat pocket, a grandchild on tiptoes by the casket, peering at the lips that will not move, the sparrow chest that will not rise. And there's Tommy Seymour's for Sinclair gasoline and mechanical repairs, a green balloon dinosaur bobbing from a string over the cash register, old tires piled beneath the cottonwood, For Sale in the sideyard a Case tractor, a John Deere reaper, a hay mower, a red manure spreader, and a rusty grain conveyor, green weeds overcoming them, standing up inside them, trying slyly and little by little to inherit machinery for the earth.

And beyond that are woods, a slope of pasture, six empty cattle pens, a driveway made of limestone pebbles, and the house where Alice Sorensen pages through a child's World Book Encyclopedia, stopping at the descriptions of California, Capetown, Ceylon, Colorado, Copenhagen, Corpus Christi, Costa Rica, Cyprus.

Widow Dworak has been watering the lawn in an open raincoat and apron, but at nine she walks the green hose around to the spigot and screws down the nozzle so that the spray is a misty crystal bowl softly baptizing the ivy. She says, "How about some camomile tea?" And she says, "Yum. Oh, boy. That hits the spot." And bends to shut the water off.

The Union Pacific night train rolls through town just after ten o'clock when a sixty-year-old man named Adolf Schooley is a boy again in bed, and when the huge weight of forty or fifty cars jostles his upstairs room like a motor he'd put a quarter in. And over the sighing industry of the train, he can hear the train saying *Nebraska, Nebraska, Nebraska, Nebraska.* And he cannot sleep.

Mrs. Antoinette Heft is at the Home Restaurant, placing frozen meat patties on waxed paper, pausing at times to clamp her fingers under her arms and press the sting from them. She stops when the Union Pacific passes, then picks a cigarette out of a pack of Kools and smokes it on the back porch, smelling air as crisp as Oxydol, looking up at stars the Pawnee Indians looked at, hearing the low harmonica of big rigs on the highway, in the town she knows like the palm of her hand, in the country she knows by heart.

1. How does Hansen manage to capture the entire region in just a few pages of text?
2. What are the some of the images that spring to mind after you've read the piece?
3. What techniques does Hansen use that you could "steal" to make your own work more vivid and emotionally satisfying?

CHAPTER FOUR

The Shapely Story

Part 1: DEFINING THE SHORT STORY

Getting Started

"But is it a story?" is one of the main questions you hear in student creative writing workshops. Very frequently, it isn't—yet. Much of what we first see in early short story drafts from beginning writers are rough character sketches, theories about life, abstract ideas, anecdotes, or morality tales that fail to deliver the emotional satisfaction we expect from a completely rendered piece of short fiction.

So what *is* a short story? It's not as easy a question to answer as you might think. Indeed, a great deal of debate has taken place on what makes a story a story, and some very learned and intelligent people disagree—or have agreed to disagree—on a number of key points.

In this chapter we will focus on the shape of fiction, specifically the short story. First we'll try to define what makes a short story, and discuss some of the key narrative conventions that have accrued over the years (some of which you may have picked up from other sources). Finally, we'll have a chance to practice some of the concepts we have talked about in exercises specifically designed to help you get started on writing short fiction.

For this chapter, it is best to do one of the readings ahead of time: Francine Prose's "What Makes a Short Story?" (pp. 167–78). It will help you better understand the concepts introduced in this chapter.

Some Basic Definitions

Perhaps nothing is as daunting as reading any of the very fine books on writing and then trying to reconcile exactly what a short story *is*. After all, what possible definition can we come up with that includes stories we love by Anton Chekhov, Donald Barthelme, Alice Munro, Jorge Luis Borges, Henry James, Grace Paley, and others?

Here are just a few of the definitions you can find:

"A short piece of prose fiction having few characters and aiming at unity of effect."—*The American Heritage Dictionary*

"A shaft driven straight into the heart of human experience."—Edith Wharton

"An account of a character struggling to reach a goal."—Steven Schoen

"What you see when you look out the window."—Mavis Gallant

"A dramatic event that involves a person because he is a person, and a particular person—that is, because he shares in the general human condition and in some specific human situation."—Flannery O'Connor

Many people base their definition of a story on Aristotle's admonition that it must have a beginning, middle, and end. This is generally assumed to mean that a story follows the three-part shape of conflict, crisis, and resolution. (More on this shortly.)

Other definitions center on Edgar Allan Poe's theory that a story must achieve "a certain unique or single effect" and be readable in one sitting, "a half hour to one or two hours in its perusal." This view of the short story is perhaps best summed up by Brander Matthews in his introduction to *The Short Story*, a 1907 anthology of short fiction:

This is definite and precise beyond all misunderstanding, the short story must do one thing only, and it must do this completely and perfectly; it must not loiter or digress; it must have unity of action, unity of temper, unity of tone, unity of color, unity of effect; and it must vigilantly exclude everything that might interfere with its singleness of intention.

Former *Esquire* fiction editor Rust Hills says that "a short story tells of something that happened to someone" but modifies it to say that as a result of that "something" the character is significantly changed, or "moved," to use Hills's term. Indeed, this notion that a change must occur in a character is commonly viewed as "required" by many teachers and students of writing alike.

Before you throw up your hands in frustration, just wait: help is on the way. There is no better commentary on this issue than Francine Prose's essay, "What Makes a Short Story?" In this piece, Prose debunks most of the common platitudes regarding the short story. "The real problem is that the most obvious answer is the most correct," she writes. "We *know* what a short story is: a work of fiction of a certain length, a length with apparently no minimum."

As Joyce Carol Oates agrees in her introduction to *The Oxford Book of American Short Stories*:

> Formal definitions of the short story are commonplace, yet there is none quite democratic enough to accommodate an art that includes so much variety and an art that so readily lends itself to experimentation and idiosyncratic voices. Perhaps length alone should be the sole criterion? Whenever critics try to impose other, more subjective strictures on the genre (as on any genre) too much work is excluded.

Unlike many theorists, neither Prose nor Oates dictates that to be a "real story" a piece must contain easily identifiable components, or fulfill any given form. For Prose, there is one basic requirement other than that of length (Prose writes that some literary critics believe Joseph Conrad's "Heart of Darkness" stretches the length of a short story as far as it can go without being considered a novella): a short story cannot be summarized; it contains some irreducible germ at its heart that defies expression. In this, she is echoing the words of Flannery O'Connor and Goethe, as we discussed earlier: that true literature "resists paraphrase" and "finds the general in the particular."

Oates adds another requirement: that "no matter its mysteries or experimental properties, it achieves closure—meaning that, when it ends, the attentive reader understands why." In other words (my words), a story that is a real story delivers a unit of satisfaction to the reader that cannot be delivered by merely summarizing the events of the story. In some cases, this sense of closure might be very subtle. Joyce Carol Oates's own "Where Are You Going, Where Have You Been?" (pp. 72–86) often frustrates readers because it seems to end before the end, yet a careful reading of the work shows that it has indeed reached closure—and very powerful closure indeed.

And then we have Henry James. Although at one point, Henry James seemed to be quite certain that there were rules governing what a story was and wasn't (among other things, he wrote that a short story "can't be a 'story' in the vulgar sense of the word. It must be a picture; it must illustrate something . . ."), in his famous essay, "The Art of Fiction," James says that the "good health" of an art demands that it be "perfectly free." He was talking about novel writing (rebutting an essay that tried to lay out all the rules a novel must supposedly obey to *be* a novel), but we can extend what he says to the short story as well. James goes on to write:

> [Art] lives upon exercise, and the very meaning of exercise is freedom. The only obligation to which in advance we may hold a novel without incurring the accusation of being arbitrary, is that it be interesting. That general responsibility rests upon it, but it is the only one I can think of.

Let's continue building our definition of what a short story is by borrowing this nugget of wisdom as well: the short story has the obligation to be interesting.

So what do we have as our final, composite definition of a short story? A short work of prose, with no minimum number of words and a maximum length of, say, 20,000 words (that should be generous enough). And the only three requirements we will put on it ahead of time are that it be interesting, resist paraphrase, and end up providing some unit of satisfaction, or sense of completeness, to the reader.

The Conflict–Crisis–Resolution Model

One of the first things we must address in a section on story is the conflict–crisis–resolution model. It is so predominant that many young writers—as well as a good number of experienced teachers—feel that a story is not a real story unless it fits into this model.

According to this definition of a short story, there is always an "arc" to a narrative that looks like the diagram below:

Called the Freitag triangle after the nineteenth-century literary critic who first formulated this theory, the idea is that every story has conflict that gradually intensifies and culminates in a crisis, after which there is a resolution.

We can be even more specific and label no less than five different stages of a short story, according to Freitag: the beginning is called the *exposition*, which provides background on the characters, the setting, the situation, etc.; the next stage is called the *rising action*, during which the character(s) face increasingly intensive conflict; then the *climax*, or culmination of the conflict; after that the *falling action*, or denouement, during which the tension is palpably eased; and, finally, the *resolution*, or ending.

You can find this diagram, or one like it, in just about every book on fiction. (If you paid attention in high school, you might even remember categorizing the three kinds of conflict that are possible: man against man, man against nature, man against himself.) But while this concept might be useful when dissecting a certain type of story, it is certainly not a way of reading *all* stories. A good number of very fine stories—including many included in this book—simply do not fit into the conflict–crisis–resolution model.

Moreover, even though the conflict–crisis–resolution model might fit the majority of stories we read, I am hard-pressed to use it as an example of how to *write* them.

So this is the question: While theories like this probably cover the narrative bases in a neat, abstracted way, in what way do they help us write? How do we take an abstract model like this and make it useful for our purpose, creating art?

Let's first backtrack and look at an example of a story that *does* fit fairly well into the crisis–conflict–resolution model: John Cheever's "The Swimmer" (pp. 330–40). You'll notice that the conflict in this story would probably better be described as a series of "complications" (another word used in conjunction with the Freitag triangle), but in all other respects it conforms nicely to our needs.

We start with the *exposition*: Neddy Merrill, who "seemed to have the especial slenderness of youth," is at the Westerhazys' pool, at a Sunday afternoon party. This is the setting of the scene, the introduction of the character and his particular situation. We learn a bit about the Westerhazys and the kind of Waspy social community Neddy belongs to. Then Neddy has a brilliant idea: he is going to swim home! His idea is to swim his way home through the "Lucinda River," as he calls the network of backyard pools in his affluent suburb (after his wife). The *rising action* begins as he sets out across the various backyards. One of the first complications is manifested in the shape of a storm; Neddy must take shelter until it passes. After that, the conflicts (complications) intensify. Difficulties begin to befall Neddy; he faces, among other obstacles, a drained pool and a busy highway. ("Had you gone for a Sunday afternoon ride that day you might have seen him, close to naked, standing on the shoulders of Route 424, waiting for a chance to cross.") Then he swims through the public pool—an unpleasant experience—and indeed the whole adventure is becoming increasingly distasteful to him (the *rising action* continues to rise). People begin treating him rudely. The tension increases until he meets his *crisis*: he is rejected by an ex-mistress, who treats him scornfully at a time when he finds his physical strength has oddly dissipated. Finally, reaching home, the *falling action*: he finds his own house boarded up and abandoned, and the *resolution*: he is left alone, aged and bereft.

I've oversimplified (and, by the way, proven that you can't tell a story by summarizing the plot), but you can see how this fits roughly into the Freitag model. A good number of stories can be analyzed thus, and although none follows the formula exactly, you can make the case that this is the form most short stories take.

But now let's look at another famous story included in this book: "The Things They Carried" (pp. 131–46).

There is no exposition: the story starts abruptly with a description of what Lieutenant Jimmy Cross, an officer in Vietnam commanding a platoon, carried (love letters). This is rapidly followed by lists of what the other soldiers in the platoon carried (pocket knives, heat tabs, lighters, matches, C rations, water). We hear about the central event of the story halfway through the second paragraph: one of the men, Lavender, is shot. This would arguably be considered the climax in a traditional story. But rather than building up to it, we are told about it upfront, quite casually. The narrative then circles around and around, revisiting the shooting incident in a number of ways, all the while being periodically interrupted by the lists of the things the men carried, which gradually change from real, physical things to more abstract things, such as fear and anguish and guilt. We're put into the mind of characters other than Jimmy Cross (which complicates the story). Finally, the story ends with Jimmy Cross burning his love letters and determining to repudiate love and human emotion in favor of what he considers the more worthy goal of taking care of his men.

To try to chart this story along the conflict–crisis–resolution model is silly—and I would even venture to say that this story couldn't have been written if O'Brien had been thinking in such simplistic terms.

Linear vs. Modular Stories

Madison Smartt Bell, in his exemplary work, *Narrative Design*, makes a distinction between linear and modular story structures. In his view, "linear" stories follow the conflict–crisis–resolution model of the Freitag triangle; "modular" stories are composed as a mosaic, a design made up of component parts:

> If linear design can be understood as somehow subtractive, a process of removing the less essential material so as to reveal the movement of narrative

vectors more clearly and cleanly, then modular design is additive. The writer adds and arranges more and more modular units which may be attractive in themselves for all sorts of different reasons, but which also must serve the purpose of clarifying the overall design of the text as a whole. . . .

What modular design can do is liberate the writer from linear logic, those chains of cause and effect, strings of dominoes always falling forward.

One of the most famous examples of modular design is the story "In the Heart of the Heart of the Country" by William Gass. Although you might be able to piece together a sort of narrative (English professor has affair with student that ends, leaving him heartbroken) that's hardly what the story is *about*. (If it were, why include all the other matter in there? There is a lot of geography in there, a lot of details about the town, about the weather, the neighbors, and so on.) The material is modular; none of it depends for causality on anything else. You could conceivably move the different modules around, although there are doubtless some very specific reasons that the author arranged them precisely as he did.

Even with so-called linear stories, there are a number of reasons why thinking conflict–crisis–resolution might not be helpful. First of all is the language used: "conflict" and "rising action" bring to mind fistfights and guns and rather melodramatic events. Yet think of stories like Grace Paley's "Mother" (p. 126) or Anton Chekhov's "The Lady with the Little Dog" (pp. 284–98); to use the word "conflict" to describe how they capture and hold our attention seems incongruous. These characters desire things, *yearn* for things; they do not fight or otherwise clash in any obvious or simplistic way.

Second of all, even stories that follow this model seldom have a steady rising action that never falters. Instead, there are ebbs and flows in the story: pockets of tension built up and tension released, all of which contribute to the story's culmination. Indeed, I prefer to use a diagram I call the "earthquake model" to indicate how tension can build, subside, then build again, before arriving at the pivotal moment, or climax.

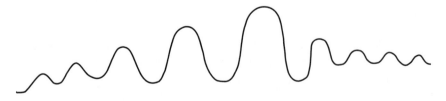

Third, and finally, abstract theory is simply not where stories come from. They come from some dark, secretive place, and from material that doesn't raise its head and jump through hoops when bidden. Knowing the so-called rules about conflict, crisis, and resolution doesn't help one *write* a good story. It may even impede you, if you feel you have to write by some formula.

Still, knowing about the conflict–crisis–resolution model can be very helpful *after* a story has been written. If the story does seem to want to fit into this general form (and most stories written today do fall within this domain), knowing the general shape of stories of this kind can be very useful in editing it.

As Madison Smartt Bell concludes:

> It's easy to get silly with these pictures [the Freitag triangle]. And indeed, most writers can get by very handily without them (or at any rate, without actually chalking them on the board) during the process of writing. The diagrams are no more than crude representations of the shape which the writer's intuition should be giving to the material as the process of composition goes forward. The Freitag triangle is a left brain superimposition over what is for the most part a right brain activity. But if intuition fails or goes astray, the triangle and its variants can be quite useful as diagnostic tools, perhaps even as problem-solving devices.

This is probably the most useful way to think of the Freitag triangle: not as a model to follow, but as a way of going back into a story and seeing how it measures up, structurally, to this conventional view of short fiction. Note my use of "conventional": this works for stories that want to be conventional conflict–crisis–resolution stories, but never, under any circumstances, should it be applied to *all* stories. If you get nothing else out of this chapter, please take this with you: you do not have to write to this conventional model.

To Epiphany or Not to Epiphany?

About that "unit of satisfaction" we talked about in the last section. How are we to achieve it?

Another common presumption about short stories, especially recently, is that a piece is not *really* a short story unless it culminates in a revelation, or "epiphany," as James Joyce described it. The idea is that a character is brought (or forced into) a state of enlightenment, experiencing a moment when he or she realizes something of great importance to his or her life. This is what Aristotle called "recognition" (and which, along with "reversal" and "suffering," made up what he considered the three parts of plot).

We can see the epiphany model at work in many stories. Two famous ones are "Araby" by James Joyce and "A & P" by John Updike. They have very similar plots: a young boy views an (unattainable) object of beauty and wishes to make a gesture, a gift, to her. The effort fails, in both stories, leaving the Joyce hero to lament, "Gazing up into the darkness I saw myself as a creature driven and derided by vanity; and my eyes burned with anguish and anger," and the Updike protagonist to conclude, "my stomach kind of fell as I felt how hard the world was going to be to me hereafter." Both are epiphanies, or moments of insight, that the characters achieve as a result of the specific events that transpire in the story. And many, many beautiful stories have been written in which an epiphany is prevalent—not the least of which is "The Things They Carried," which we just analyzed. But in his excellent essay, "Against Epiphanies," Charles Baxter points out that perhaps epiphanies are being overused:

> *Suddenly I realized . . .*
> The language of literary epiphanies naturally has something in common with the rhetoric of religious revelation. The veil of appearances is pulled aside and an inner truth is revealed. A moment of radiant vision brings forth the sensation, if not the content, of meaning.
>
> An epiphany, in a traditional religious context, was the showing forth of the divinity of the Christ child. It was, quite literally, an awful moment. Awe governed it. To adapt this solemn moment for literary purposes, as James Joyce wished to do, was a Promethean gesture: It was an attempt to steal the fires of religion and place them, still burning, in literature.

But as Baxter points out, "the loss of innocence, and the arrival of knowingness can become an addiction":

> A mode that began with moves of elegant feeling and energy, particularly in stories that have to deal with worlds within worlds of urban or small town or even familial hypocrisy, can get stale. Worse than stale: rotten. The mass production of insight, in fiction or elsewhere, is a dubious phenomenon. But because it is a private experience, it can't be debated or contested. Suddenly, it seems, everyone is having insights. Possibly we have entered the Age of Insight.
>
> Everywhere there is a glut of epiphanies. Radiance rules. But some of the insights have seemed disturbingly untrustworthy. There is a smell about them of recently molded plastic. At the level of discursive rhetoric, it is a bit like the current craze for angels. Perhaps these are not true insights at all. What then?

As Baxter observes, we can name many fine stories that possess literary epiphanies. But to view that as the *only* way to bring a story to fruition is to paint yourself into a very tight creative corner indeed.

The novelist Jim Shepard, also a teacher, noticed the same phenomenon as Baxter in his students' work:

> More and more I've been seeing stories in which the protagonists are whooshed along the little conveyor belts of their narratives to that defining moment of insight or clarification that will allow them to see with new eyes the essential emotional or spiritual furniture of their lives. The implication is nearly always that this moment of insight removes one of the last major obstacles on the road to personal fulfillment. . . .
>
> Now, as I understand it, a short story, by definition, does have a responsibility, in its closing gestures, to enlarge *our* understanding, but it seems to be increasingly difficult for writers to resist allowing their hapless *protagonist* a new understanding as well—an understanding that will set him or her on the path to a more actualized life.
>
> [from "I Know Myself Real Well. That's the Problem"]

In my own classroom, people seem to feel dissatisfied if this insight has not been provided for the character. They want revelation, they want the possibility of redemption, they want to *fix* things for the characters involved. All wonderful generous bounty to bestow on characters, but perhaps our job isn't to rescue all the characters that come under our care (our own as well as others'). Perhaps our job is simply to *render* what their predicament is, rather than solving their problems for them?

Is Change Necessary? (The Debate Continues)

The notion that *reversal* (as Aristotle called it), or change, is a requirement of a piece of fiction is also a prevalent one. That is, a character must not only realize some truth that had previously been obscure to him or her, he/she must act upon it. The character must grow or somehow be altered in some significant way for it to be considered a "real" story.

Yet in life, we are given opportunities for change all the time, and we fail to make those changes, either out of stupidity, or laziness, or even ignorance—we didn't even know the possibility for change was, well, a possibility.

The novelist John L'Heureux has a way of describing a certain type of story—he doesn't believe that all stories must follow this model—which deals with this question of to-change-or-not-to-change: "Capture a moment after which nothing can ever be the same again," he advises. This is a wonderfully flexible definition of a short story—again, for certain types of stories—because it drives home the fact that change is not necessary. Change can be offered to a character—and declined. The "crisis" of a piece can be of negative, rather than positive, action: something not done, a sin not committed, an act of grace not performed. But a moment of significance has passed, and things cannot be the same again.

In "Daughters of the Late Colonel" by Katherine Mansfield, the two adult women, mourning the death of their father, refuse to grow up; they have a chance to re-examine their lives, and perhaps determine to live them differently, but in the end are unable to break through the years of habit and repression that have smothered them for so long:

> She turned away from the Buddha with one of her vague gestures. She went over to where Josephine was standing. She wanted to say something to Josephine, something frightfully important, about—about the future and what . . .
>
> "Don't you think perhaps—" she began.
>
> But Josephine interrupted her. "I was wondering if now—" she murmured. They stopped; they waited for each other.
>
> "Go on, Con," said Josephine.
>
> "No, no, Jug, after you," said Constantia.
>
> "No, say what you were going to say. You began," said Josephine.
>
> "I'd . . . I'd rather hear what you were going to say first," said Constantia.
>
> "Don't be absurd, Con."
>
> "Really, Jug."
>
> "Connie!"
>
> "Oh, *Jug*!"
>
> A pause. Then Constantia said faintly, "I can't say what I was going to say, Jug, because I've forgotten what it was . . . that I was going to say."
>
> Josephine was silent for a moment. She stared at a big cloud where the sun had been. Then she replied shortly, "I've forgotten too."

On Not Becoming Slaves to Theory

"I feel that discussing story-writing in terms of plot, character, and theme is like trying to describe the expression on a face by saying where the eyes, nose, and mouth are," Flannery O'Connor wrote in her celebrated essay "Writing Short Stories." She continues:

> You want to know how you can actually write a good story, and further, how you can tell when you've done it; and so you want to know what the form of a short story is, as if the form were something that existed outside of each story and could be applied or imposed on the material. Of course, the more you write, the more you will realize that the form is organic; that it is something that grows out of the material, that the form of each story is unique. [. . .] The only way, I think, to learn to write short stories is to write

them, and then to try to discover what you have done. The time to think of technique is when you've actually got the story in front of you.

As we discussed in Chapter 2, one of the things that distinguishes a creative writer from, say, an accountant or a systems analyst is that the writer's process is shrouded in mystery. Writers use their own sense of not-knowing to delve into the heart of some ambiguity of personal interest. From these personal mysteries they generate prose that can then grow and, under the right circumstances, be shaped into a short story, novel, or creative nonfiction piece. But very few writers know what they are going to write beforehand. The creative mind usually doesn't work that way, as Donald Barthelme writes in his essay "Not Knowing":

> Let us suppose that someone is writing a story. From the world of conventional signs he takes an azalea bush, plants it in a pleasant park. He takes a gold pocket watch from the world of conventional signs and places it under the azalea bush. He takes from the same rich source a handsome thief and a chastity belt, places the thief in the chastity belt and lays him tenderly under the azalea, not neglecting to wind the gold pocket watch so that its ticking will, at length, awaken the now-sleeping thief. From the Sarah Lawrence campus he borrows a pair of seniors, Jacqueline and Jemima, and sets them to walking into the vicinity of the azalea bush and the handsome, chaste thief. Jacqueline and Jemima have just failed the Graduate Record Examination and are cursing God in colorful Sarah Lawrence language. What happens next?
> Of course, I don't know. *It's appropriate to say that the writer is someone who, confronted with a blank page, does not know anything* [emphasis mine].

Willa Cather, alternatively, makes the distinction between writing as an exercise "as safe and commendable as making soap or breakfast foods" and what happens when we attempt to create art, "which is always a search for something for which there is no market demand, something new and untried, *where the values are intrinsic and have nothing to do with standardized values* [emphasis mine]."

So it's always critical to keep in mind that there are no rules in fiction, only *conventions* that have been built up over the years based on the way that writers have crafted their stories. (A convention is "an established technique, practice, or device," according to *Merriam-Webster's Collegiate Dictionary*.) Conventions can be useful, because they provide successful models we can emulate and learn from, and which help guide us in the reading and writing of fiction. But too many beginning writers translate them into hard-core rules that *must* be followed. Among all the other reasons we've stated why this won't work, it's just plain impossible: as you'll see, many of the so-called rules contradict each other. Try to follow them all (just like trying to follow all the advice given in a writing workshop) and you'll either go mad or end up with a chaotic mess, rather than a story or novel.

Much of the theory that is presented in writing books can be useful *after* a story has been written. You can say, "Oh yes, so *that* explains why I was having trouble with this section." But trying to write a story by theory is a bit like trying to obtain all our bodily nourishment from air: we need oxygen, true, but that alone won't suffice for keeping us alive.

There's no doubt that writing short fiction would be easier if there were some hard-set rules. Indeed, some writers cling to the conflict–crisis–resolution model or the change model as a way of avoiding the fear, and the ambiguity of the blank page (or blank computer screen). As we'll say time and time again, any way "in" to a story is a good one, and so if it is helpful for you to think of short fiction in this way, then do it.

But it's wrong-headed to approach the writing of fiction in an overly formulaic way. I was once surprised to hear that a writer giving seminars was actually handing out this formula, ABCDE:

Action
Backstory
Crisis
Denouement
Ending

While it might be a useful *exercise* (you might even want to try it yourself) to begin a story with an action (begin in the middle), only to backtrack and fill in the blanks (we'll talk about this in the chapter on "Raising the Curtain," Chapter 11), we wouldn't want to structure every story like this. We're in the business of exploring material through writing, not filling out formulas. If you wanted formulas, you'd be reading a mathematics or chemistry textbook, not this one.

Rick DeMarinis makes a heart-warming "confession" in his book *The Art and the Craft of the Short Story*:

> I don't know how to write a short story even though I've written hundreds of them, published five collections of them, sold them to magazines, both literary and commercial. I have also taught the subject for more than twenty years in various university English departments that hired me for that purpose. But here's the thing: I don't have a set of rules, a formula, a system, that tells me how to set about writing a story of *literary quality*. I don't have a

"how." If I had such a system, one that would fit every interesting human situation, I'd write a prizewinner every day of the week. I'd make Chekhov look like a backslider. I'd make Cheever look like he was working out of laundry lists. I'd make Hemingway look punch-drunk. But the hard truth is that there is no system, no set of rules that guarantee able composition or abundant production. There is no magic formula that will make hard work, commitment, inspiration, taste, and good luck unnecessary.

If in this chapter I seemed to be arguing as much against the conventions as explaining them, it's because all too often I see a wonderfully complex beginning of a story either squashed early on by unsubtle uses of "conflict" or killed off in workshop as not fulfilling, in some obvious way, the conflict–crisis–resolution model.

Part 2: EXERCISES

Trying to assimilate what a short story is has stymied many, many very smart people. There are enough rigid definitions and so-called rules to make your head spin. The exercises in this section are to help you understand the basic concepts of what makes for a story, and to help you see past some of the so-called conventions that may stifle you as you try to write your own story.

Exercise 1: False Epiphanies I Have Had

> Goal: To examine your own thoughts and assumptions about epiphanies in fiction, and to understand that sometimes we try to force false epiphanies into our stories in order to fit a preconceived model.

What to do: 1. Think of a time when you (or a character in a story you're working on) had an epiphany—a moment when you believed, finally and absolutely, that you had the answer to something (yes, this is the woman I want to marry; no, I was never meant to be an architect; yes, it's the right thing to move to Columbus), but which turned out to be wrong. If you want, use the phrase "suddenly I realized" as a way of spurring the epiphany on.

2. Write down the precise events that led up to the epiphany (what you were doing, where you were, who you were with, etc.).

3. Now write "the morning after" by capturing a moment of doubt and uncertainty that followed the false epiphany.

As always, ground it in a specific place and time—no abstractions. (And it doesn't have to be the literal morning after—the false epiphany can be proven wrong years after it occurs, as in the example below.)

The following example was written by Christie Cochrell:

1. I realized I could love Oliver.

2. His ancient cat, all spine and tail, lays itself against me, its whole length, and I realize how much love Oliver needs, how much I can provide, because this lovely creature, his only companion, is not much longer for this world, clearly. Oliver and I have been in Italy for three weeks, and have just come home from the airport—to his home, his home of five or so years, in which the sofa is still draped with drop cloths, these boxes still to be unpacked. He is so lonely. There is the insignificant but mortal weight of this cat that has come to me immediately, gray and forlorn, there is time ahead to get to be its friend, to get lonely Oliver out of his boxes, trusting in love again.

3. The next morning, saddened at being apart for the first time in three weeks, I impulsively go to find Oliver at his favorite café (remembering his reading the *Herald Tribune* every morning in Rome). He'll be happy to see me, missing me too. I'm daring, taking this chance at love. I find him at the café, after thinking he isn't there after all, go up to the table, happily. He looks startled when I say hi quietly; then taken aback—unhappy to be interrupted in his reading, his solitary routine. After a telling moment of silence he says, politely, that I can sit down. We are as if strangers again. I know I'll never again see his lovely cat. We'll both go on being lonely apart.

Exercise 2: Opportunities Not Taken

Goal: To examine moments when change was possible, but declined.

What to do: 1. Think of a time when you (or a character) made a negative decision: chose *not* to do something, go somewhere, *not* to act in a certain way.

2. Write it down *precisely*: where were you (or your character), what were you wearing, what did you say and do?

The following was written by Steve Marvin:

My mother believes in giving me choices: she's done this since I was a baby, she read it in some book that you give kids choices, not open-ended questions. Not, "What do you want to eat?" but "Do you want to eat pizza or chicken tonight?" She's raised me this way and I guess I've gotten in the habit of thinking in terms of choices too when I've had a hard time deciding what to do about something. What exactly is the choice that I am making? And so the other night, it was late, and Joanne was over of course—her roommate is giving her trouble—and of course as usual I offered her the couch but this time she refused. Now she was upset, she was wearing that coffee-colored short short dress she wears when she wants to look hot even though she's a little too heavy for getting the right effect. She's got her ass-kicking boots on. She wants to go out, she's not ready to go to sleep and I can tell this is going to be one of the difficult nights when she won't take no for an answer. In this case I've made my choice: I want to stay home and get some sleep before class tomorrow, but she is getting madder and madder and I see my choice is between having a friend and not having a friend. In the past I've always gone along and I don't know what it was but at that moment I had an inkling that I had a real choice, because of course it was never a choice, when Joanne wants to do something, you do it, because the choice is unacceptable, which is having Joanne mad at you or having her acting nice to you, and believe me, that is not a choice. So there I am, dressed like a bum, hardly ready to go out and something in me snapped and I said, I'm not going, but she didn't even have to open her mouth, I saw that *look* and of course I went to get dressed.

Part 3: READING AS A WRITER

What Makes a Short Story?

FRANCINE PROSE

There must be more difficult questions than "What makes a short story?"

What is man, that Thou art mindful of him? What does a woman want? What is love? What walks on four legs at dawn, two legs at noon, three legs in the evening? What can you say about a twenty-five-year-old girl who died? Tell me where is fancy bred, in the heart or in the head?

Yet all of these seemingly impossible questions are, in fact, far easier to address than the deceptively straightforward matter of what constitutes the short story. For all of these classic puzzlers—except for the sphinx's riddle—suggest variant solutions and multiple possibilities, invite expansion and rumination, whereas any attempt to establish the identifying characteristics of the short story seems to require a narrowing, a winnowing, a definition by exclusion. A short story is probably this—but definitely not that.

The real problem is that the most obvious answer is the most correct. We *know* what a short story is: a work of fiction of a certain length, a length with apparently no minimum. An increasing number of anthologies feature stories of no more than a humble page, or a single flashy paragraph, and one of the most powerful stories in all of literature, Isaac Babel's "Crossing Into Poland," less than three pages long, is capacious enough to include a massive and chaotic military campaign, a soldier's night of troubled dreams, and the report of a brutal murder. Similarly, Cynthia Ozick's "The Shawl" is only four pages long.

But, nearing the opposite end of the spectrum, Robert Boswell's "The Darkness of Love" is over forty pages. After a certain point (to be on the safe side, let's say seventy or eighty pages, though one short-story theoretician has argued that Conrad's "Heart of Darkness"—not one word more or less—defines the outer limits of the form) the extended short story begins to impinge on novella territory.

Lacking anything clearer or more definitive than these vague mumblings about size, we imagine that we can begin to define the short story by distinguishing it from other forms of fiction, by explaining why it is not a sketch, a fairy tale, or a myth.

And yet some of our favorite stories seem a lot like the sort of casual anecdote we might hear a friend tell at a dinner party. Somerset Maugham, in what must have been a demented moment, claimed that many of Chekhov's great stories *were* anecdotes and not proper stories at all. ("If you try to tell one of his stories you will find that there is nothing to tell. The anecdote, stripped of its trimmings, is insignificant and often inane. It was grand for people who wanted to write a story and couldn't think of a plot to discover that you could very well manage without one.") And just to confuse things further, many fairy tales—the best of Hans Christian Andersen and the Brothers Grimm—are as carefully constructed, as densely layered, as elaborately crafted as the stories (or are they tales?) of, for example, Hawthorne and Poe.

Why do we feel so certain that a masterpiece such as Tolstoy's "The Three Hermits" is a short story, though it so clearly bears—and takes so little trouble to hide—the stamp of its origins in "an old legend current in the Volga district" and though its structure has more in common with the shaggy-dog story than with the artful, nuanced studies of Henry James, who, in fact, was quite insistent that a short story "must be an idea—it can't be a 'story' in the vulgar sense of the word. It must be a picture; it must illustrate something . . . something of the real essence of the subject."

Just to take on James, always something of a challenge, let's look at

"The Three Hermits," which could hardly be more of a "story," in the most fabulously, unashamedly "vulgar sense of the word." The protagonist, if we can call him that—we know nothing about his background or the subtler depths of his character, absolutely nothing, in short, except that he is a Bishop of the Orthodox Church—is traveling on a ship that passes near an island on which, he hears, live three monks who spend their lives in prayer. The Bishop insists on being ferried to the island, where he meets the hermits—again described with a minimum of the sort of physical and psychological description that, we have been taught, is essential for fiction in general and for the short story in particular. One of the monks is tall "with a piece of matting tied round his waist"; the second is shorter, in a "tattered peasant coat"; and the third is "very old, bent with age and wearing an old cassock." To his horror, the Bishop discovers that the hermits have their own way of praying ("Three are ye, three are we, have mercy on us") and have never heard of the Lord's Prayer.

The bulk of the story, the shaggy-dog part, concerns the Bishop's efforts to teach these comically slow learners how to pray correctly—a Herculean task that consumes the entire day and that is completed, more or less, to the visitor's satisfaction. That night, as the Bishop is sailing away from the island, he sees a light skimming toward him across the water. "Was it a seagull, or the little gleaming of some small boat?" No, in fact, the radiance is an aura surrounding the hermits, flying hand in hand over the water, desperately chasing the Bishop's boat because they have forgotten what they learned from the church official, who—educated at last—tells them, "It is not for me to teach you. Pray for us sinners."

Even in summary, this story retains some of its power to astonish and move us, and yet the full effect of reading the work in its entirety is all but lost. Which brings us to one of the few things that *can* be said about the short story: Like all great works of art, it cannot be summarized or reduced without sacrificing the very qualities that do in fact distinguish an amusing dinner-party anecdote from a great work of art—depth, resonance, harmony, plus all the less quantifiable marks of artistic creation. This is especially true of stories in which the plot line is not so clear, so succinct, so distilled to its folkloric essentials, and of writers who achieve their effects almost entirely by the use of tone, by the accretion of minute detail, and by the precise use of language.

What can we possibly—accurately—conclude about Turgenev's "Bezhin Meadow" when we hear that it concerns a few hours that the narrator spends among a group of peasant boys who scare themselves and each other by telling ghost stories? At the end of the story, we learn—in a sort of brief epilogue—that one of the boys was killed a short time after that evening on the meadow. When we hear it summarized, the plot seems sketchy and indistinct—why is this not a vignette or a "mood piece"? But when we read the story itself—a work of art that feels utterly complete and in which every sentence and phrase contributes to the whole—we are certain, beyond any doubt, that it is indeed a story. We cannot imagine anything that needs to be added or omitted.

What remains of the humor and breathtaking originality of Katherine Mansfield's "Daughters of the Late Colonel" when we describe it as a story about two childlike (but ostensibly adult) sisters attempting to get through the days following the death of their father? What survives of the many small gestures and lines of deceptively whimsical dialogue that lead us to understand that the distribution of power between the more "grown-up" sensible Josephine and the fanciful, impulsive, skittish Constantia is the same as it must have been in early childhood? What remains of Josephine's certainty that their dead father is hiding in his chest of drawers, or of his former nurse's—Nurse Andrew's—upsetting, "simply fearful" greed for butter, or of the "white, terrified" blancmange that the cook sets on the table, or of that final, elliptical moment of forgetting in which we intuit the impossible and tragic cost of remembering?

It is hard to *recognize* Chekhov's "The Lady with the Pet Dog" from the following description: A jaded womanizer falls deeply in love despite himself and for the first time, and in the course of that love affair discovers that his whole world—that he himself—has changed. How sentimental and obvious it sounds, how romantic and unconvincing. Yet when we actually read the story, we feel that it is of enormous, immeasurable consequence and resonance, and that it tells us all we need to know about Gurov and Anna's whole lives. We feel that the story's details—the slice of watermelon in the hotel room, the description of Gurov's wife's eyebrows—are as important as its "action," and that if we left out these details, the perfect but somehow fragile architecture of the story would begin to crumble.

Not much remains of the short story, retold in summary—but not *nothing*. For this also can be said, of the short story: If we find a way to describe what the story is *really* about, not its plot but its essence, what small or large part of life it has managed to translate onto the page, there is always *something* there—enough to engage us, and pique our interest.

But isn't the same true of novels? What do we lose when we try to explain what *Mrs. Dalloway* is *about*? Or when we become hopelessly enmired in the tangles—lovers, generations, narrators, stories within stories, frames within frames—of *Wuthering Heights*? Or when we say that we just read the most harrowing novel about a provincial French housewife whose life is ruined by her silly and impractical fantasies of love and romance? The answer's the same: Nearly everything, though some "germ" (to quote James again) stays ineradicably present.

A similarly illusory distinction that is often made between the short story and the novel claims that the short story—unlike its more expansive or discursive older sibling—works more often by implication, by indirection, that it more frequently achieves its results by what has *not* been said or what has been left out. But although it is undeniably true that certain stories function this way—the situation that has caused all the trouble between the lovers in Ernest Hemingway's "Hills Like White Elephants" is never directly mentioned in the course of the lovers' painful conversation—it is also true that in the greatest works of fiction, regardless of their length, every line tells us pages *more* than it appears to communicate on the surface. So even in Proust's *In Search of Lost Time*—hardly the most concise and economical of novels—each seemingly insignificant phrase and incident assumes additional meaning and resonance as the book progresses; every incident, every minor exchange takes on levels of significance that we cannot hope to apprehend until we go back and reread the whole. In fact the most important way to read—the way that teaches us most about what a great writer does, and what *we* should be doing—is to take a story apart (line by line, word by word) the way a mechanic takes apart an automobile engine, and to ask ourselves how each word, each phrase, and each sentence contributes to the entirety.

In their efforts to define the formal qualities of the short story form, critics are often driven back to invoke basic Aristotelian principles (short stories, we hear, have a beginning, a middle, and an end) and to quote the early masters of the genre, writers who must have had, one supposes, a more sharply focused view of the new frontier toward which they were heading. So introductions to anthologies, textbook chapters, and surveys of the latest developments in the academic field of "short story theory" are all fond of invoking Edgar Allan Poe's notion of the "single effect."

> A skillful literary artist has constructed a tale. If wise, he has not fashioned his thoughts to accommodate his incidents; but having conceived, with deliberate care, a certain unique or single *effect* to be wrought out, he then invents such incidents—he then combines such events as may best aid him in establishing this preconceived effect . . . in the whole composition, there should be no word written, of which the tendency, direct or indirect, is not

to the one pre-established design. And by such means, with such care and skill, a picture is at length painted which leaves in the mind of he who contemplates it with a kindred art, a sense of the fullest satisfaction. The idea of the tale has been presented unblemished, because undisturbed, and this is an end unattainable to the novel.

More recent—and also frequently quoted—is V. S. Pritchett's characteristically elegant and incisive formulation:

The novel tends to tell us everything whereas the short story tells us only one thing, and that, intensely. . . . It is, as some have said, a "glimpse through," resembling a painting or even a song which we can take in at once, yet bring the recesses and contours of larger experience to the mind.

And Chekhov—whom some readers (this one, for example) consider the greatest writer of the modern short story—had himself some very definite ideas on the necessity of keeping things simple:

In planning a story one is bound to think first about its framework; from a crowd of leading characters one selects one person only—wife or husband; one puts him on the canvas and paints him alone, making him prominent, while the others one scatters over the canvas like small coins, and the result is something like the vault of heaven: one big moon and a number of very small stars around it. . . . It is not necessary to portray many characters. . . . The center of gravity should be in two persons: him and her. [to A. P. Chekhov, 1886] . . . One must write about simple things: how Peter Semionovich married Maria Ivanovna. That is all.

Certainly this is true of his own "The Lady with the Pet Dog," in which the center of gravity seems to turn—slowly at first, and then more and more intensely—around those all-important "two persons."

No sensible reader could argue with Pritchett or Poe. But then again, few readers could explain exactly what "a single effect" is, or what precisely is the "one thing" that our favorite short story is telling us so intensely. And Chekhov should have known—and *did* know—better, since many of his most successful and beautifully realized stories encompass a good deal more than "him and her" or the nuptial arrangements of Peter Semionovich and Maria Ivanovna.

Indeed, the minute one tries to make any sweeping declarations about the proper limitations or boundaries of the short story, one thinks (as with any "rule" for the writing of fiction) of an example—a masterpiece!—that embodies the very opposite of the law that one has just proposed. So let's take just a few of the many assumptions that the casual reader—or the student hungry for some definitive parameters—might make about the short story.

Perhaps we should begin by addressing Chekhov's statement about that big moon and those very small stars, about that "him and her" whose interaction should form the core of the story. One might assume that for reasons of economy or artistic harmony, the short story should limit itself to depicting the situation of a main protagonist or at least a somewhat restricted—a *manageable*—cast of characters. And many stories do. There are only three major characters—the narrator, his wife, and the blind man—in Raymond Carver's "Cathedral." And only one character, really, in Poe's "The Pit and the Pendulum." In Flannery O'Connor's "Everything That Rises Must Converge" the "him and her" are the overbearing, heartbreaking mother and her snobbish and long-suffering son Julian. And in James Baldwin's "Sonny's Blues," the narrator and Sonny are the big moon around whom the others—Isabel, the mother and father, the other musicians—revolve.

But who, one might ask, is the "big moon" in Tim O'Brien's "The Things They Carried," or in Chekhov's own "In the Ravine," a story that focuses not on any central character, but on the life of an entire community, Ukleevo, a village that "was never free from fever, and there was boggy mud there even in summer, especially under the fences over which hung old willow-trees that gave deep shade. Here there was always a smell from the factory refuse and the acetic acid which was used in the finishing of the cotton print." In this polluted and horrifically corrupt little hamlet, the most powerful family—a clan of shopkeepers—devotes itself to lying and cheating their neighbors; their dishonesty and general depravity are repaid, eventually, by heartbreak and ruin.

The story does have a villain, the vicious Aksinya (who, as the very worst person in her family, naturally is spared the destruction that befalls the somewhat less culpable others), and a heroine, of sorts, the innocent peasant girl Lipa, who does not appear until quite a few pages into the story. Nonetheless, we feel throughout that Chekhov is less interested in depicting particular destinies than in painting a broader picture; the story is the literary equivalent of a monumental canvas, crowded with figures—Rembrandt's "Night Watch," for one. We never know exactly, we can never answer that question that writing teachers so often ask: Whose story is it?

But even the story that lacks a central character should, presumably, limit itself to a single point of view, a controlling intelligence that guides us through the narrative. Or should it? Once more the answer seems to be: not necessarily. "Sonny's Blues," "Cathedral," and John Updike's "A & P" are examples of short fictions that stay fixedly within the consciousness of their narrators. Kafka's "The Judgment" adheres more or less faithfully to the close-third-person viewpoint through which we observe the tormented last hours of Georg Bendermann.

Yet another of Kafka's stories—"The Metamorphosis"—also begins in the close third person, with the understandable astonishment of Gregor Samsa, who (when we meet him) has just woken in his bed to find that he has been transformed, overnight, into a giant insect. And there the story remains until the narrative must leave the room in which Gregor is imprisoned in order to follow the action in the other parts of the apartment and chart the effects that Gregor's peculiar transformation has had on the members of his family. Finally, after Gregor's death, the story can—for obvious reasons—no longer be told from his point of view, and a more detached omniscience describes the process by which his parents and his sister repair themselves and go on with their lives after the regrettable but unavoidable demise of the unfortunate Gregor.

Still other stories pay even less heed to the somewhat schoolmarmish admonition that they color neatly within the lines of a single perspective. In "The Lady with the Pet Dog," we feel that Chekhov is constantly shifting his—and our—distance from Gurov. Sometimes (for example, in the scene in which he watches the sunset) we feel that we are looking through his eyes, and down into his soul; at other moments (when he first sees Anna and toys with the idea of seducing her) we feel that we are watching him with a somewhat greater and more ironic remove.

Alice Munro's "Friend of My Youth" begins with a dream that the first person narrator has about her mother, and then narrates the rest of the story from the point of view of "my mother" with occasional, stabilizing swings back to that initial "I." Katherine Mansfield's "Prelude" moves seamlessly from one family member to another, exposing the innermost—tormented or fortuitously ignorant—thoughts of an extended family: a mother and father, their children, and the mother's unmarried sister. Tatiana Tolstaya's "Heavenly Flame" behaves as if it has never heard of the whole issue of point of view, and skips around from character to character, alighting from time to time on a sort of group perspective, a "we" representing the minisociety vacationing at a country house near a convalescent home. And though John Cheever's "Goodbye, My Brother" begins in the first person plural—not the royal we or the editorial we but the family we—we readers soon understand that this plural ("We are a family that is very close in spirit") is by its very nature ironic, and functions as a key to the fortress and the prison in which the narrator chooses and is forced to reside. Much of the story, in fact, is about the efforts to break away from that "we" (the Pommeroy family) so that point of view becomes, in an intriguing way, part of the plot—and the problem—of the story.

But even if the short story refuses to fall in line with any of our notions about the number and range of its characters, and the importance of a single perspective, shouldn't it observe the most (one would think) easy to follow of the Aristotelian conventions, the prescriptions concerning the length of time that the action may comfortably span? It's true that "Hills Like White Elephants" nearly restricts itself to the real time of a single conversation, and that Tillie Olsen's "I Stand Here Ironing" takes place entirely during a session at the ironing board.

On the other hand, "Sonny's Blues" moves back and forth through decades of the two main characters' histories, covering the most significant parts of the lifetimes of two men; at the same time, it fits a huge wedge of social history into the confines of a short story. And Lars Gustafsson's "Greatness Strikes Where It Pleases" takes, as its subject, the existence—and especially the inner life—of an unnamed retarded man, who grows up in the country and spends his later years in a home. In the space breaks, the black space between sections, months, days, or years elapse—blank spots that, we soon realize, matter far less than we might have supposed, since our hero has been liberated by consciousness from the narrow strictures of time:

> At the end of the '50s, his parents died. Nobody tried to explain it to him, and he didn't know in what order they died or when, but when he hadn't seen them for a few years—his mother would visit him regularly twice a year and always brought him candy and apples, an anxious lot of apples, as if the lack of apples were his problem—he started to miss them, in some vague fashion, about the way you might all of a sudden long for mustard or honey or a certain kind of floury gravy with just a taste of burned pork.

As much as we might like the short story to keep its borders modest, crisp, and neat, the form keeps defying our best efforts to wrap it up and present it in a tidy package. Pick up those helpful, instructional books—Anyone Can Write a Short Story—and you're bound to find one of those diagrams, those EKGs of the "typical plot line," its slow ascent, its peak and valley (or peaks and valleys) meant to indicate the tensing or slackening of dramatic interest.

But any attempt to draw such a chart for a story such as Bruno Schulz's "Sanitarium Under the Sign of the Hour Glass"—with its labyrinthine plot turns and disorienting switchbacks—will look less like that comprehensible medical or seismographic chart than one of those webs spun by those poor spiders whom scientists used to torment with doses of mind-altering drugs. How does one draw up a chart for "The Things They Carried," which is structured like an obsessive, repetitive list of *stuff*—the materials that a group of Vietnam soldiers are humping through the jungle—and contains, hidden inside, a story of life and death.

Some stories have huge amounts of plot—it has been said that Heinrich von Kleist's "The Marquise of O." was used, unedited, as a shooting script for Eric Rohmer's full-length film (of the same name) based on the novella. And some stories—John Updike's "A & P," Raymond Carver's "Cathedral"—have, by comparison, almost no plot at all.

The understandable longing to keep things tidy and nice and neat also leads many critics and teachers to put the "epiphany"—the burst of understanding, self-knowledge, or knowledge about the world that may occur to a character at some crucial point in the story—at the highest peak of that EKG graph, like the cherry on a sundae. Some even insist that this sort of mini-enlightenment is necessary for the short story—is, in fact, a hallmark and sine qua non of the form.

It's my understanding that the word epiphany first came into common currency—in the literary rather than the religious sense—in connection with the fiction of James Joyce, many of whose characters do seem to "get something" by the end of many of his brilliant stories. Sometimes, characters in stories do learn something. By the end of "Sonny's Blues," the narrator has had a vision (however unwelcome and unwilled) of what music means to his brother, and of what sort of musician his brother is. The recognition that her precious new hat is the very same one worn by the black woman on the bus has overwhelming—and tragic—consequences for the mother in "Everything That Rises Must Converge." Gurov learns one startling lesson after another in "The Lady with the Pet Dog," and the story ends with the realization that "the hardest part was still before" the two lovers. But just because Joyce's or Baldwin's or Chekhov's or O'Connor's characters wise up, even for a moment, doesn't mean that anyone else's characters do, or should be expected to.

One could spend pages listing short fictions in which characters come out the other end of the story every bit as benighted as they were in the first sentence. By the end of "Everything That Rises Must Converge," Julian could hardly *not* know that something has happened to change his life. But the story concludes before he—or the reader—has had a chance to intuit what that change is, or what it will mean. It's hard to say what the unnamed narrator learns in Samuel Beckett's thrilling and upsetting story "First Love." To claim that every short story should include a moment of epiphany is like insisting that every talented, marvelous dog jump through the same narrow hoop.

It is simply not true that a character always learns something in the course of a short story. Heaven forbid that someone should *have* to see life or the world in a brighter or darker light, that someone *has* to be changed—or, even worse, improved. How deadly dull it would be if that were the case for all those stories in all those anthologies—all those epistemological light bulbs going on, one right after another.

A story creates its own world, often—though not always—with clear or mysterious correspondences to our own, a world in which we are too involved to keep track of what anyone is learning. While reading the story, we enter that world. We feel that everything in it belongs there, and has not been forced on it by its reckless or capricious creator. In fact, we tend to forget the creator, who has wound the watch of the story and vanished from creation. We may feel this world is something like life and at the same time better than life, since this short-story world—unlike life—has reached some miraculous ecological balance, so that everything in that world has been put there for a reason.

Unlike most novels, great short stories make us marvel at their integrity, their economy. If we went at them with our blue pencils, we might find we had nothing to do. We would discover there was nothing that the story could afford to lose without the whole delicate structure collapsing like a soufflé or meringue. And yet we are left with a feeling of completeness, a conviction that we know exactly as much as we need to know, that all of our questions have been answered—even if we are unable to formulate what exactly those questions and answers *are.*

This sense of the artistic whole, this assurance that nothing has been left out and that nothing extraneous has been included, is part of what distinguishes the short story from other pieces of writing with which it shares certain outward characteristics—what separates it, for example, from the newspaper account, which, like the short story, most often features characters and at least some vestige of a plot. But the newspaper version of "The Lady with the Pet Dog"—MAN'S AFFAIR TURNS SERIOUS—manages to leave out every single thing that makes the story so beautiful, significant, and moving.

Everything in the story resonates at its own unique, coherent, and recognizable pitch, along with everything else in the story, creating an effect that Joyce described—quoting Aquinas, and in another context—as "wholeness, harmony, and radiance." As readers, we may feel that after finishing the story we understand something new, something solid. And we recognize the short story (what a short story *is*) in a visceral, quasi-physiological way; we feel—to paraphrase what Emily Dickinson said about poetry—as if the top of our head had come off. Maybe, that is something like what Poe meant by his unity of effect—the short work of fiction, so beautifully made that it cannot be broken down into components or spare parts. Reading a masterpiece like Chekhov's "The Lady with the Pet Dog," we cannot think of anything we would add, anything else we need to know; nor is there anything extra or superfluous.

To understand what a short story is requires reading dozens and dozens of them, far more than the examples collected in [an] anthology, more than the additional stories mentioned in this essay. By reading many and varied examples, we develop an almost instinctive sense of what a short story is, so that when we read one we recognize it, just as we recognize our own instincts and emotions. We know what a short story is, just as we know what it is to be afraid, or to fall in love.

To really communicate the entirety of what a short story has given us, of what it has done for us, of what it has helped us understand or see in a new way, would involve repeating the whole story, every one of our favorite stories [. . .] and also the stories I have mentioned above—stories that lovers of the short story should know practically by heart. It would mean quoting all those stories sentence by sentence, line by line, word by word—the only real answer to that most difficult of questions: What makes a short story?

1. Do you agree with Francine Prose's conclusions about the best way to define a short story? Why or why not?
2. Can you think of any short stories that you love (or even like) that transgress all the so-called "rules" of what makes for a short story?
3. Is there any more specific way to define the "sense of artistic whole" that Prose talks about? Why or why not?

Helping

ROBERT STONE

One gray November day, Elliot went to Boston for the afternoon. The wet streets seemed cold and lonely. He sensed a broken promise in the

"Your troubles have to do with here and now," Elliot told his client. "Fantasies aren't helpful."

His voice sounded overripe and hypocritical in his own ears. What a dreadful business, he thought. What an awful job this is. Anger was driving him crazy.

Blankenship straightened up and spoke through his tears. "This dream . . ." he said. "I'm scared."

Elliot felt ready to endure a great deal in order not to hear Blankenship's dream.

"I'm not the one you see about that," he said. In the end he knew his duty. He sighed. "O.K. All right. Tell me about it."

"Yeah?" Blankenship asked with leaden sarcasm. "Yeah? You think dreams are friggin' boring!"

"No, no," Elliot said. He offered Blankenship a tissue and Blankenship took one. "That was sort of off the top of my head. I didn't really mean it."

Blankenship fixed his eyes on dreaming distance. "There's a feeling that goes with it. With the dream." Then he shook his head in revulsion and looked at Elliot as though he had only just awakened. "So what do you think? You think it's boring?"

"Of course not," Elliot said. "A physical feeling?"

"Ya. It's like I'm floating in rubber."

He watched Elliot stealthily, aware of quickened attention. Elliot had caught dengue in Vietnam and during his weeks of delirium had felt vaguely as though he were floating in rubber.

"What are you seeing in this dream?"

Blankenship only shook his head. Elliot suffered a brief but intense attack of rage.

"Hey, Blankenship," he said equably, "here I am, man. You can see I'm listening."

"What I saw was black," Blankenship said. He spoke in an odd tremolo. His behavior was quite different from anything Elliot had come to expect from him.

"Black? What was it?"

"Smoke. The sky maybe."

"The sky?" Elliot asked.

"It was all black. I was scared."

In a waking dream of his own, Elliot felt the muscles on his neck distend. He was looking up at a sky that was black, filled with smoke-swollen clouds, lit with fires, damped with blood and rain.

"What were you scared of?" he asked Blankenship.

"I don't know," Blankenship said.

Elliot could not drive the black sky from his inward eye. It was as though Blankenship's dream had infected his own mind.

"You don't know? You don't know what you were scared of?"

Blankenship's posture was rigid. Elliot, who knew the aspect of true fear, recognized it there in front of him.

"The Nam," Blankenship said.

"You're not even old enough," Elliot told him.

Blankenship sat trembling with joined palms between his thighs. His face was flushed and not in the least ennobled by pain. He had trouble with alcohol and drugs. He had trouble with everything.

"So wherever your black sky is, it isn't Vietnam."

Things were so unfair, Elliot thought. It was unfair of Blankenship to appropriate the condition of a Vietnam veteran. The trauma inducing his post-traumatic stress had been nothing more serious than his own birth, a routine procedure. Now, in addition to the poverty, anxiety, and confusion that would always be his life's lot, he had been visited with irony. It was all arbitrary and some people simply got elected. Everyone knew that who had been where Blankenship had not.

"Because, I assure you, Mr. Blankenship, you were never there."

"Whaddaya mean?" Blankenship asked.

When Blankenship was gone Elliot leafed through his file and saw that the psychiatrists had passed him upstairs without recording a diagnosis. Disproportionately angry, he went out to the secretary's desk.

"Nobody wrote up that last patient," he said. "I'm not supposed to see people without a diagnosis. The shrinks are just passing the buck."

The secretary was a tall, solemn redhead with prominent front teeth and a slight speech disorder. "Dr. Sayyid will have kittens if he hears you call him a shrink, Chas. He's already complained. He hates being called a shrink."

"Then he came to the wrong country," Elliot said. "He can go back to his own."

The woman giggled. "He *is* the doctor, Chas."

"Hates being called a shrink!" He threw the file on the secretary's table and stormed back toward his office. "That fucking little zip couldn't give you a decent haircut. He's a prescription clerk."

The secretary looked about her guiltily and shook her head. She was used to him.

Elliot succeeded in calming himself down after a while, but the image

of the black sky remained with him. At first he thought he would be able
to simply shrug the whole thing off. After a few minutes, he picked up his
phone and dialed Blankenship's probation officer.

"The Vietnam thing is all he has," the probation officer explained. "I
guess he picked it up around."

"His descriptions are vivid," Elliot said.

"You mean they sound authentic?"

"I mean he had me going today. He was ringing my bells."

"Good for Blanky. Think he believes it himself?"

"Yes," Elliot said. "He believes it himself now."

Elliot told the probation officer about Blankenship's current arrest,
which was for showering illegally at midnight in the Wyndham Regional
High School. He asked what probation knew about Blankenship's present
relationship with his family.

"You kiddin'?" the P.O. asked. "They're all locked down. The whole
family's inside. The old man's in Bridgewater. Little Donny's in San
Quentin or somewhere. Their dog's in the pound."

Elliot had lunch alone in the hospital staff cafeteria. On the far side of
the double-glazed windows, the day was darkening as an expected snowstorm gathered. Along Route 7, ancient elms stood frozen against the gray
sky. When he had finished his sandwich and coffee, he sat staring out at
the winter afternoon. His anger had given way to an insistent anxiety.

On the way back to his office, he stopped at the hospital gift shop for a
copy of *Sports Illustrated* and a candy bar. When he was inside again, he
closed the door and put his feet up. It was Friday and he had no appoint-
ments for the remainder of the day, nothing to do but write a few letters
and read the office mail.

Elliot's cubicle in the social services department was windowless and
lined with bookshelves. When he found himself unable to concentrate on
the magazine and without any heart for his paperwork, he ran his eye
over the row of books beside his chair. There were volumes by Heinrich
Muller and Carlos Casteneda, Jones's life of Freud, and *The Golden Bough*.
The books aroused a revulsion in Elliot. Their present uselessness repelled
him.

Over and over again, detail by detail, he tried to recall his conversation
with Blankenship.

"You were never there," he heard himself explaining. He was trying to
get the whole incident straightened out after the fact. Something was
wrong. Dread crept over him like a paralysis. He ate his candy bar without tasting it. He knew that the craving for sweets was itself a bad sign.

Blankenship had misappropriated someone else's dream and made it his own. It made no difference whether you had been there, after all. The dreams had crossed the ocean. They were in the air.

He took his glasses off and put them on his desk and sat with his arms folded, looking into the well of light from his desk lamp. There seemed to be nothing but whirl inside him: Unwelcome things came and went in his mind's eye. His heart beat faster. He could not control the headlong promiscuity of his thoughts.

It was possible to imagine larval dreams traveling in suspended animation undetectable in a host brain. They could be divided and regenerate like flatworms, hide in seams and bedding, in war stories, laughter, snapshots. They could rot your socks and turn your memory into a black-and-green blister. Green for the hills, black for the sky above. At daybreak they hung themselves up in rows like bats. At dusk they went out to look for dreamers.

Elliot put his jacket on and went into the outer office, where the secretary sat frowning into the measured sound and light of her machine. She must enjoy its sleekness and order, he thought. She was divorced. Four redheaded kids between ten and seventeen lived with her in an unpainted house across from Stop & Shop. Elliot liked her and had come to find her attractive. He managed a smile for her.

"Ethel, I think I'm going to pack it in," he declared. It seemed awkward to be leaving early without a reason.

"Jack wants to talk to you before you go, Chas."

Elliot looked at her blankly.

Then his colleague, Jack Sprague, having heard his voice, called from the adjoining cubicle. "Chas, what about Sunday's games? Shall I call you with the spread?"

"I don't know," Elliot said. "I'll phone you tomorrow."

"This is a big decision for him," Jack Sprague told the secretary. "He might lose twenty-five bucks."

At present, Elliot drew a slightly higher salary than Jack Sprague, although Jack had a PhD and Elliot was simply an MSW. Different branches of the state government employed them.

"Twenty-five bucks," said the woman. "If you guys have no better use for twenty-five bucks, give it to me."

"Where are you off to, by the way?" Sprague asked.

Elliot began to answer, but for a moment no reply occurred to him. He shrugged. "I have to get back," he finally stammered. "I promised Grace."

"Was that Blankenship I saw leaving?"

Elliot nodded.

"It's February," Jack said. "How come he's not in Florida?"

"I don't know," Elliot said. He put on his coat and walked to the door. "I'll see you."

"Have a nice weekend," the secretary said. She and Sprague looked after him indulgently as he walked toward the main corridor.

"Are Chas and Grace going out on the town?" she said to Sprague. "What do you think?"

"That would be the day," Sprague said. "Tomorrow he'll come back over here and read all day. He spends every weekend holed up in this goddamn office while she does something or other at the church." He shook his head. "Every night he's at AA and she's home alone."

Ethel savored her overbite. "Jack," she said teasingly, "are you thinking what I think you're thinking? Shame on you."

"I'm thinking I'm glad I'm not him, that's what I'm thinking. That's as much as I'll say."

"Yeah, well, I don't care," Ethel said. "Two salaries and no kids, that's the way to go, boy."

Elliot went out through the automatic doors of the emergency bay and the cold closed over him. He walked across the hospital parking lot with his eyes on the pavement, his hands thrust deep in his overcoat pockets, skirting patches of shattered ice. There was no wind, but the motionless air stung; the metal frames of his glasses burned his skin. Curlicues of mud-brown ice coated the soiled snowbanks along the street. Although it was still afternoon, the street lights had come on.

The lock on his car door had frozen and he had to breathe on the keyhole to fit the key. When the engine turned over, Jussi Björling's recording of the Handel Largo filled the car interior. He snapped it off at once.

Halted at the first stoplight, he began to feel the want of a destination. The fear and impulse to flight that had got him out of the office faded, and he had no desire to go home. He was troubled by a peculiar impatience that might have been with time itself. It was as though he were waiting for something. The sensation made him feel anxious; it was unfamiliar but not altogether unpleasant. When the light changed he drove on, past the Gulf station and the firehouse and between the greens of Ilford Common. At the far end of the common he swung into the parking lot of the Packard Conway Library and stopped with the engine running. What he was experiencing, he thought, was the principle of possibility.

He turned off the engine and went out again into the cold. Behind the leaded library windows he could see the librarian pouring coffee in her tiny private office. The librarian was a Quaker of socialist principles named Candace Music, who was Elliot's cousin.

The Conway Library was all dark wood and etched mirrors, a Gothic saloon. Years before, out of work and booze-whipped, Elliot had gone to hide there. Because Candace was a classicist's widow and knew some Greek, she was one of the few people in the valley with whom Elliot had cared to speak in those days. Eventually, it had seemed to him that all their conversations tended toward Vietnam, so he had gone less and less often. Elliot was the only Vietnam veteran Candace knew well enough to chat with, and he had come to suspect that he was being probed for the edification of the East Ilford Friends Meeting. At that time he had still pretended to talk easily about his war and had prepared little discourses and picaresque anecdotes to recite on demand. Earnest seekers like Candace had caused him great secret distress.

Candace came out of her office to find him at the checkout desk. He watched her brow furrow with concern as she composed a smile. "Chas, what a surprise. You haven't been in for an age."

"Sure I have, Candace. I went to all the Wednesday films last fall. I work just across the road."

"I know, dear," Candace said. "I always seem to miss you."

A cozy fire burned in the hearth, an antique brass clock ticked along on the marble mantel above it. On a couch near the fireplace an old man sat upright, his mouth open, asleep among half a dozen soiled plastic bags. Two teenage girls whispered over their homework at a table under the largest window.

"Now that I'm here," he said, laughing, "I can't remember what I came to get."

"Stay and get warm," Candace told him. "Got a minute? Have a cup of coffee."

Elliot had nothing but time, but he quickly realized that he did not want to stay and pass it with Candace. He had no clear idea of why he had come to the library. Standing at the checkout desk, he accepted coffee. She attended him with an air of benign supervision, as though he were a Chinese peasant and she a medical missionary, like her father. Candace was tall and plain, more handsome in her middle sixties than she had ever been.

"Why don't we sit down?"

He allowed her to gentle him into a chair by the fire. They made a threesome with the sleeping old man.

"Have you given up translating, Chas? I hope not."

"Not at all," he said. Together they had once rendered a few fragments of Sophocles into verse. She was good at clever rhymes.

"You come in so rarely, Chas. Ted's books go to waste."

After her husband's death, Candace had donated his books to the Conway, where they reposed in a reading room inscribed to his memory, untouched among foreign-language volumes, local genealogies, and books in large type for the elderly.

"I have a study in the barn," he told Candace. "I work there. When I have time." The lie was absurd, but he felt the need of it.

"And you're working with Vietnam veterans," Candace declared.

"Supposedly," Elliot said. He was growing impatient with her nodding solicitude.

"Actually," he said, "I came in for the new Oxford *Classical World*. I thought you'd get it for the library and I could have a look before I spent my hard-earned cash."

Candace beamed. "You've come to the right place, Chas, I'm happy to say." He thought she looked disproportionately happy. "I have it."

"Good," Elliot said, standing. "I'll just take it, then. I can't really stay."

Candace took his cup and saucer and stood as he did. When the library telephone rang, she ignored it, reluctant to let him go. "How's Grace?" she asked.

"Fine," Elliot said. "Grace is well."

At the third ring she went to the desk. When her back was turned, he hesitated for a moment and then went outside.

The gray afternoon had softened into night, and it was snowing. The falling snow whirled like a furious mist in the headlight beams on Route 7 and settled implacably on Elliot's cheeks and eyelids. His heart, for no good reason, leaped up in childlike expectation. He had run away from a dream and encountered possibility. He felt in possession of a promise. He began to walk toward the roadside lights.

Only gradually did he begin to understand what had brought him there and what the happy anticipation was that fluttered in his breast. Drinking, he had started his evening from the Conway Library. He would arrive hung over in the early afternoon to browse and read. When the old pain rolled in with dusk, he would walk down to the Midway Tavern for a remedy. Standing in the snow outside the library, he realized that he had contrived to promise himself a drink.

Ahead, through the storm, he could see the beer signs in the Midway's window warm and welcoming. Snowflakes spun around his head like an excitement.

Outside the Midway's package store, he paused with his hand on the doorknob. There was an old man behind the counter whom Elliot remembered from his drinking days. When he was inside, he realized that the old man neither knew nor cared who he was. The package store was thick with dust; it was on the counter, the shelves, the bottles themselves. The old counterman looked dusty. Elliot bought a bottle of King William Scotch and put it in the inside pocket of his overcoat.

Passing the windows of the Midway Tavern, Elliot could see the ranks of bottles aglow behind the bar. The place was crowded with men leaving the afternoon shifts at the shoe and felt factories. No one turned to note him when he passed inside. There was a single stool vacant at the bar and he took it. His heart beat faster. Bruce Springsteen was on the jukebox.

The bartender was a club fighter from Pittsfield called Jackie G., with whom Elliot had often gossiped. Jackie G. greeted him as though he had been in the previous evening. "Say, babe?"

"How do," Elliot said.

A couple of men at the bar eyed his shirt and tie. Confronted with the bartender, he felt impelled to explain his presence. "Just thought I'd stop by," he told Jackie G. "Just thought I'd have one. Saw the light. The snow. . . ." He chuckled expansively.

"Good move," the bartender said. "Scotch?"

"Double," Elliot said.

When he shoved two dollars forward along the bar, Jackie G. pushed one of the bills back to him. "Happy hour, babe."

"Ah," Elliot said. He watched Jackie pour the double. "Not a moment too soon."

For five minutes or so, Elliot sat in his car in the barn with the engine running and his Handel tape on full volume. He had driven over from East Ilford in a baroque ecstasy, swinging and swaying and singing along. When the tape ended, he turned off the engine and poured some Scotch into an apple juice container to store providentially beneath the car seat. Then he took the tape and the Scotch into the house with him. He was lying on the sofa in the dark living room, listening to the Largo, when he heard his wife's car in the driveway. By the time Grace had made her way up the icy back-porch steps, he was able to hide the Scotch and rinse his glass clean in the kitchen sink. The drinking life, he thought, was lived moment by moment.

Soon she was in the tiny cloakroom struggling off with her overcoat. In the process she knocked over a cross-country ski, which stood propped against the cloakroom wall. It had been more than a year since Elliot had used the skis.

She came into the kitchen and sat down at the table to take off her boots. Her lean, freckled face was flushed with the cold, but her eyes looked weary. "I wish you'd put those skis down in the barn," she told him. "You never use them."

"I always like to think," Elliot said, "that I'll start the morning off skiing."

"Well, you never do," she said. "How long have you been home?"

"Practically just walked in," he said. Her pointing out that he no longer skied in the morning enraged him. "I stopped at the Conway Library to get the new Oxford *Classical World*. Candace ordered it."

Her look grew troubled. She had caught something in his voice. With dread and bitter satisfaction, Elliot watched his wife detect the smell of whiskey.

"Oh, God," she said. "I don't believe it."

Let's get it over with, he thought. Let's have the song and dance.

She sat up straight in her chair and looked at him in fear.

"Oh, Chas," she said, "how could you?"

For a moment he was tempted to try to explain it all.

"The fact is," Elliot told his wife, "I hate people who start the day cross-country skiing."

She shook her head in denial and leaned her forehead on her palm and cried.

He looked into the kitchen window and saw his own distorted image. "The fact is I think I'll start tomorrow morning by stringing head-high razor wire across Anderson's trail."

The Andersons were the Elliot's nearest neighbors. Loyall Anderson was a full professor of government at the state university, thirty miles away. Anderson and his wife were blond and both of them were over six feet tall. They had two blond children, who qualified for the gifted class in the local school but attended regular classes in token of the Andersons' opposition to elitism.

"Sure," Elliot said. "Stringing wire's good exercise. It's life-affirming in its own way."

The Andersons started each and every day with a brisk morning glide along a trail that they partly maintained. They skied well and presented a pleasing, wholesome sight. If, in the course of their adventure, they encountered a snowmobile, Darlene Anderson would affect to choke and cough, indicating her displeasure. If the snowmobile approached them from behind and the trail was narrow, the Andersons would decline to let it pass, asserting their statutory right-of-way.

"I don't want to hear your violent fantasies," Grace said.

Elliot was picturing razor wire, the Army kind. He was picturing the decapitated Andersons, their blood and jaunty ski caps bright on the white trail. He was picturing their severed heads, their earnest blue eyes and large white teeth reflecting the virginal morning snow. Although Elliot hated snowmobiles, he hated the Andersons far more.

He looked at his wife and saw that she had stopped crying. Her long, elegant face was rigid and lipless.

"Know what I mean? One string at Mommy and Daddy level for Loyall and Darlene. And a bitty wee string at kiddie level for Skippy and Samantha, those cunning little whizzes."

"Stop it," she said to him.

"Sorry," Elliot told her.

Stiff with shame, he went and took his bottle out of the cabinet into which he had thrust it and poured a drink. He was aware of her eyes on him. As he drank, a fragment from old Music's translation of *Medea* came into his mind. "Old friend, I have to weep. The gods and I went mad together and made things as they are." It was such a waste; eighteen months of struggle thrown away. But there was no way to get the stuff back in the bottle.

"I'm very sorry," he said. "You know I'm very sorry, don't you, Grace?"

The delectable Handel arias spun on in the next room.

"You must stop," she said. "You must make yourself stop before it takes over."

"It's out of my hands," Elliot said. He showed her his empty hands. "It's beyond me."

"You'll lose your job, Chas." She stood up at the table and leaned on it, staring wide-eyed at him. Drunk as he was, the panic in her voice frightened him. "You'll end up in jail again."

"One engages," Elliot said, "and then one sees."

"How can you have done it?" she demanded. "You promised me."

"First the promises," Elliot said, "and then the rest."

"Last time was supposed to be the last time," she said.

"Yes," he said, "I remember."

"I can't stand it," she said. "You reduce me to hysterics." She wrung her hands for him to see. "See? Here I am, I'm in hysterics."

"What can I say?" Elliot asked. He went to the bottle and refilled his glass. "Maybe you shouldn't watch."

"You want me to be forbearing, Chas? I'm not going to be."

"The last thing I want," Elliot said, "is an argument."

"I'll give you a fucking argument. You didn't have to drink. All you had to do was come home."

"That must have been the problem," he said.

Then he ducked, alert at the last possible second to the missile that came for him at hairline level. Covering up, he heard the shattering of glass, and a fine rain of crystals enveloped him. She had sailed the sugar bowl at him; it had smashed against the wall above his head and there was sugar and glass in his hair.

"You bastard!" she screamed. "You are undermining me!"

"You ought not to throw things at me," Elliot said. "I don't throw things at you."

He left her frozen into her follow-through and went into the living room to turn the music off. When he returned she was leaning back against the wall, rubbing her right elbow with her left hand. Her eyes were bright. She had picked up one of her boots from the middle of the kitchen floor and stood holding it.

"What the hell do you mean, that must have been the problem?"

He set his glass on the edge of the sink with an unsteady hand and turned to her. "What do I mean? I mean that most of the time I'm putting one foot in front of the other like a good soldier and I'm out of it from the neck up. But there are times when I don't think I will ever be dead enough—or dead long enough—to get the taste of this life off my teeth. That's what I mean!"

She looked at him dry-eyed. "Poor fella," she said.

"What you have to understand, Grace, is that this drink I'm having"—he raised the glass toward her in a gesture of salute—"is the only worthwhile thing I've done in the last year and a half. It's the only thing in my life that means jack shit, the closest thing to satisfaction I've had. Now how can you begrudge me that? It's the best I'm capable of."

"You'll go too far," she said to him. "You'll see."

"What's that, Grace? A threat to walk?" He was grinding his teeth. "Don't make me laugh. You, walk? You, the friend of the unfortunate?"

"Don't you hit me," she said when she looked at his face. "Don't you dare."

"You, the Christian Queen of Calvary, walk? Why, I don't believe that for a minute."

She ran a hand through her hair and bit her lip. "No, we stay," she said. Anger and distraction made her look young. Her cheeks blazed rosy against the general pallor of her skin. "In my family we stay until the fella dies. That's the tradition. We stay and pour it for them and they die."

He put his drink down and shook his head.

"I thought we'd come through," Grace said. "I was sure."

"No," Elliot said. "Not altogether."

They stood in silence for a minute. Elliot sat down at the oilcloth-covered table. Grace walked around it and poured herself a whiskey.

"You are undermining me, Chas. You are making things impossible for me and I just don't know." She drank and winced. "I'm not going to stay through another drunk. I'm telling you right now. I haven't got it in me. I'll die."

He did not want to look at her. He watched the flakes settle against the glass of the kitchen door. "Do what you feel the need of," he said.

"I just can't take it," she said. Her voice was not scolding but measured and reasonable. "It's February. And I went to court this morning and lost Vopotik."

Once again, he thought, my troubles are going to be obviated by those of the deserving poor. He said, "Which one was that?"

"Don't you remember them? The three-year-old with the broken fingers?"

He shrugged. Grace sipped her whiskey.

"I told you. I said I had a three-year-old with broken fingers, and you said, 'Maybe he owed somebody money.'"

"Yes," he said, "I remember now."

"You ought to see the Vopotiks, Chas. The woman is young and obese. She's so young that for a while I thought I could get to her as a juvenile. The guy is a biker. They believe the kid came from another planet to control their lives. They believe this literally, both of them."

"You shouldn't get involved that way," Elliot said. "You should leave it to the caseworkers."

"They scared their first caseworker all the way to California. They were following me to work."

"You didn't tell me."

"Are you kidding?" she asked. "Of course I didn't." To Elliot's surprise, his wife poured herself a second whiskey. "You know how they address the child? As 'dude.' She says to it, 'Hey, dude.'" Grace shuddered with loathing. "You can't imagine! The woman munching Twinkies. The kid smelling of shit. They're high morning, noon, and night, but you can't get anybody for that these days."

"People must really hate it," Elliot said, "when somebody tells them they're not treating their kids right."

"They definitely don't want to hear it," Grace said. "You're right." She sat stirring her drink, frowning into the glass. "The Vopotik child will die, I think."

"Surely not," Elliot said.

"This one I think will die," Grace said. She took a deep breath and puffed out her cheeks and looked at him forlornly. "The situation's extreme. Of course, sometimes you wonder whether it makes any difference. That's the big question, isn't it?"

"I would think," Elliot said, "that would be the one question you didn't ask."

"But you do," she said. "You wonder: Ought they to live at all? To continue the cycle?" She put a hand to her hair and shook her head as if in confusion. "Some of these folks, my God, the poor things cannot put Wednesday on top of Tuesday to save their lives."

"It's a trick," Elliot agreed, "a lot of them can't manage."

"And kids are small, they're handy and underfoot. They make noise. They can't hurt you back."

"I suppose child abuse is something people can do together," Elliot said.

"Some kids are obnoxious. No question about it."

"I wouldn't know," Elliot said.

"Maybe you should stop complaining. Maybe you're better off. Maybe your kids are better off unborn."

"Better off or not," Elliot said, "it looks like they'll stay that way."

"I mean our kids, of course," Grace said. "I'm not blaming you, understand? It's just that here we are with you drunk again and me losing Vopotik, so I thought why not get into the big unaskable questions." She got up and folded her arms and began to pace up and down the kitchen. "Oh," she said when her eye fell upon the bottle, "that's good stuff, Chas. You won't mind if I have another? I'll leave you enough to get loaded on."

Elliot watched her pour. So much pain, he thought; such anger and confusion. He was tired of pain, anger, and confusion; they were what had got him in trouble that very morning.

The liquor seemed to be giving him a perverse lucidity when all he now required was oblivion. His rage, especially, was intact in its salting of alcohol. Its contours were palpable and bleeding at the borders. Booze was good for rage. Booze could keep it burning through the darkest night.

"What happened in court?" he asked his wife.

She was leaning on one arm against the wall, her long, strong body flexed at the hip. Holding her glass, she stared angrily toward the invisible fields outside. "I lost the child," she said.

Elliot thought that a peculiar way of putting it. He said nothing.

"The court convened in an atmosphere of high hilarity. It may be Hate Month around here but it was buddy-buddy over at Ilford Courthouse. The room was full of bikers and bikers' lawyers. A colorful crowd. There was a lot of bonding." She drank and shivered. "They didn't think too well of me. They don't think too well of broads as lawyers. Neither does the judge. The judge has the common touch. He's one of the boys."

"Which judge?" Elliot asked.

"Buckley. A man of about sixty. Know him? Lots of veins on his nose?"

Elliot shrugged.

"I thought I had done my homework," Grace told him. "But suddenly I had nothing but paper. No witnesses. It was Margolis at Valley Hospital who spotted the radiator burns. He called us in the first place. Suddenly he's got to keep his reservation for a campsite in St. John. So Buckley threw his deposition out." She began to chew on a fingernail. "The case-workers have vanished—one's in L.A., the other's in Nepal. I went in there and got run over. I lost the child."

"It happens all the time," Elliot said. "Doesn't it?"

"This one shouldn't have been lost, Chas. These people aren't simply confused. They're weird. They stink."

"You go messing into anybody's life," Elliot said, "that's what you'll find."

"If the child stays in that house," she said, "he's going to die."

"You did your best," he told his wife. "Forget it."

She pushed the bottle away. She was holding a water glass that was almost a third full of whiskey.

"That's what the commissioner said."

Elliot was thinking of how she must have looked in court to the cherry-faced judge and the bikers and their lawyers. Like the schoolteachers who had tormented their childhoods, earnest and tight-assed, humorless and self-righteous. It was not surprising that things had gone against her.

He walked over to the window and faced his reflection again. "Your optimism always surprises me."

"My optimism? Where I grew up our principal cultural expression was the funeral. Whatever keeps me going, it isn't optimism."

"No?" he asked. "What is it?"

"I forget," she said.

"Maybe it's your religious perspective. Your sense of the divine plan."

She sighed in exasperation. "Look, I don't think I want to fight any-more. I'm sorry I threw the sugar at you. I'm not your keeper. Pick on someone your own size."

"Sometimes," Elliot said, "I try to imagine what it's like to believe that the sky is full of care and concern."

"You want to take everything from me, do you?" She stood leaning against the back of her chair. "That you can't take. It's the only part of my life you can't mess up."

He was thinking that if it had not been for her he might not have sur-vived. There could be no forgiveness for that. "Your life? You've got all this piety strung out between Monadnock and Central America. And look at yourself. Look at your life."

"Yes," she said, "look at it."

"You should have been a nun. You don't know how to live."

"I know that," she said. "That's why I stopped doing counseling. Because I'd rather talk the law than life." She turned to him. "You got everything I had, Chas. What's left I absolutely require."

"I swear I would rather be a drunk," Elliot said, "than force myself to believe such trivial horseshit."

"Well, you're going to have to do it without a straight man," she said, "because this time I'm not going to be here for you. Believe it or not."

"I don't believe it," Elliot said. "Not my Grace."

"You're really good at this," she told him. "You make me feel ashamed of my own name."

"I love your name," he said.

The telephone rang. They let it ring three times, and then Elliot went over and answered it.

"Hey, who's that?" a good-humored voice on the phone demanded.

Elliot recited their phone number.

"Hey, I want to talk to your woman, man. Put her on."

"I'll give her a message," Elliot said.

"You put your woman on, man. Run and get her."

Elliot looked at the receiver. He shook his head. "Mr. Vopotik?"

"Never you fuckin' mind, man. I don't want to talk to you. I want to talk to the skinny bitch."

Elliot hung up.

"Is it him?" she asked.

"I guess so."

They waited for the phone to ring again and it shortly did.

"I'll talk to him," Grace said. But Elliot already had the phone.

"Who are you, asshole?" the voice inquired. "What's your fuckin' name, man?"

"Elliot," Elliot said.

"Hey, don't hang up on me, Elliot. I won't put up with that. I told you go get that skinny bitch, man. You go do it."

There were sounds of festivity in the background on the other end of the line—a stereo and drunken voices.

"Hey," the voice declared. "Hey, don't keep me waiting, man."

"What do you want to say to her?" Elliot asked.

"That's none of your fucking business, fool. Do what I told you."

"My wife is resting," Elliot said. "I'm taking her calls."

He was answered by a shout of rage. He put the phone aside for a moment and finished his glass of whiskey. When he picked it up again the man on the line was screaming at him. "That bitch tried to break up my family, man! She almost got away with it. You know what kind of pain my wife went through?"

"What kind?" Elliot asked.

For a few seconds he heard only the noise of the party. "Hey, you're not drunk, are you, fella?"

"Certainly not," Elliot insisted.

"You tell that skinny bitch she's gonna pay for what she did to my family, man. You tell her she can run but she can't hide. I don't care where you go—California, anywhere—I'll get to you."

"Now that I have you on the phone," Elliot said, "I'd like to ask you a couple of questions. Promise you won't get mad?"

"Stop it!" Grace said to him. She tried to wrench the phone from his grasp, but he clutched it to his chest.

"Do you keep a journal?" Elliot asked the man on the phone. "What's your hat size?"

"Maybe you think I can't get to you," the man said. "But I can get to you, man. I don't care who you are, I'll get to you. The brothers will get to you."

"Well, there's no need to go to California. You know where we live."

"For God's sake," Grace said.

"Fuckin' right," the man on the telephone said. "Fuckin' right I know."

"Come on over," Elliot said.

"How's that?" the man on the phone asked.

"I said come on over. We'll talk about space travel. Comets and stuff. We'll talk astral projection. The moons of Jupiter."

"You're making a mistake, fucker."

"Come on over," Elliot insisted. "Bring your fat wife and your beat-up kid. Don't be embarrassed if your head's a little small."

The telephone was full of music and shouting. Elliot held it away from his ear.

"Good work," Grace said to him when he had replaced the receiver.

"I hope he comes," Elliot said. "I'll pop him."

He went carefully down the cellar stairs, switched on the overhead light, and began searching among the spiderwebbed shadows and fouled fishing line for his shotgun. It took him fifteen minutes to find it and his cleaning case. While he was still downstairs, he heard the telephone ring again and his wife answer it. He came upstairs and spread his shooting gear across the kitchen table. "Was that him?"

She nodded wearily. "He called back to play us the chainsaw."

"I've heard that melody before," Elliot said.

He assembled his cleaning rod and swabbed out the shotgun barrel. Grace watched him, a hand to her forehead. "God," she said. "What have I done? I'm so drunk."

"Most of the time," Elliot said, sighting down the barrel, "I'm helpless in the face of human misery. Tonight I'm ready to reach out."

"I'm finished," Grace said. "I'm through, Chas. I mean it."

Elliot rammed three red shells into the shotgun and pumped one forward into the breech with a satisfying report. "Me, I'm ready for some radical problem solving. I'm going to spray that no-neck Slovak all over the yard."

"He isn't a Slovak," Grace said. She stood in the middle of the kitchen with her eyes closed. Her face was chalk white.

"What do you mean?" Elliot demanded. "Certainly he's a Slovak."

"No he's not," Grace said.

"Fuck him anyway. I don't care what he is. I'll grease his ass."

He took a handful of deer shells from the box and stuffed them in his jacket pockets.

"I'm not going to stay with you. Chas. Do you understand me?"

Elliot walked to the window and peered out at his driveway. "He won't be alone. They travel in packs."

"For God's sake!" Grace cried, and in the next instant bolted for the downstairs bathroom. Elliot went out, turned off the porch light and switched on a spotlight over the barn door. Back inside, he could hear Grace in the toilet being sick. He turned off the light in the kitchen.

He was still standing by the window when she came up behind him. It seemed strange and fateful to be standing in the dark near her, holding the shotgun. He felt ready for anything.

"I can't leave you alone down here drunk with a loaded shotgun," she said. "How can I?"

"Go upstairs," he said.

"If I went upstairs it would mean I didn't care what happened. Do you understand? If I go it means I don't care anymore. Understand?"

"Stop asking me if I understand," Elliot said. "I understand fine."

"I can't think," she said in a sick voice. "Maybe I don't care. I don't know. I'm going upstairs."

"Good," Elliot said.

When she was upstairs, Elliot took his shotgun and the whiskey into the dark living room and sat down in an armchair beside one of the lace-curtained windows. The powerful barn light illuminated the length of his driveway and the whole of the back yard. From the window at which he sat, he commanded a view of several miles in the direction of East Ilford. The two-lane blacktop road that ran there was the only one along which an enemy could pass.

He drank and watched the snow, toying with the safety of his 12-gauge Remington. He felt neither anxious nor angry now but only impatient to be done with whatever the night would bring. Drunkenness and the silent rhythm of the falling snow combined to make him feel outside of time and syntax.

Sitting in the dark room, he found himself confronting Blankenship's dream. He saw the bunkers and wire of some long-lost perimeter. The rank smell of night came back to him, the dread evening and quick dusk, the mysteries of outer darkness: fear, combat, and death. Enervated by liquor, he began to cry. Elliot was sympathetic with other people's tears but ashamed of his own. He thought of his own tears as childish and excremental. He stifled whatever it was that had started them.

Now his whiskey tasted thin as water. Beyond the lightly frosted glass, illuminated snowflakes spun and settled sleepily on weighted pine boughs. He had found a life beyond the war after all, but in it he was still sitting in darkness, armed, enraged, waiting.

His eyes grew heavy as the snow came down. He felt as though he could be drawn up into the storm and he began to imagine that. He imagined his life with all its artifacts and appetites easing up the spout into white oblivion, everything obviated and foreclosed. He thought maybe he could go for that.

When he awakened, his left hand had gone numb against the trigger guard of his shotgun. The living room was full of pale, delicate light. He looked outside and saw that the storm was done with and the sky radiant and cloudless. The sun was still below the horizon.

Slowly Elliot got to his feet. The throbbing poison in his limbs served to remind him of the state of things. He finished the glass of whiskey on the windowsill beside his easy chair. Then he went to the hall closet to get a ski jacket, shouldered his shotgun, and went outside.

There were two cleared acres behind his house; beyond them a trail descended into a hollow of pine forest and frozen swamp. Across the hollow, white pastures stretched to the ridge line, lambent under the lightening sky. A line of skeletal elms weighed with snow marked the course of frozen Shawmut Brook.

He found a pair of ski goggles in a jacket pocket and put them on and set out toward the tree line, gripping the shotgun, step by careful step in the knee-deep snow. Two raucous crows wheeled high overhead, their cries exploding the morning's silence. When the sun came over the ridge, he stood where he was and took in a deep breath. The risen sun warmed his face and he closed his eyes. It was windless and very cold.

Only after he had stood there for a while did he realize how tired he had become. The weight of the gun taxed him. It seemed infinitely wearying to contemplate another single step in the snow. He opened his eyes and closed them again. With sunup the world had gone blazing blue and white, and even with his tinted goggles its whiteness dazzled him and made his head ache. Behind his eyes, the hypnagogic patterns formed a monsoon-heavy tropical sky. He yawned. More than anything, he wanted to lie down in the soft, pure snow. If he could do that, he was certain he could go to sleep at once.

He stood in the middle of the field and listened to the crows. Fear, anger, and sleep were the three primary conditions of life. He had learned that over there. Once he had thought fear the worst, but he had learned that the worst was anger. Nothing could fix it; neither alcohol nor medicine. It was a worm. It left him no peace. Sleep was the best.

He opened his eyes and pushed on until he came to the brow that overlooked the swamp. Just below, gliding along among the frozen cattails and bare scrub maple, was a man on skis. Elliot stopped to watch the man approach.

The skier's face was concealed by a red-and-blue ski mask. He wore snow goggles, a blue jumpsuit, and a red woolen Norwegian hat. As he came, he leaned into the turns of the trail, moving silently and gracefully along. At the foot of the slope on which Elliot stood, the man looked up, saw him, and slid to a halt. The man stood staring at him for a moment and then began to herringbone up the slope. In no time at all the skier stood no more than ten feet away, removing his goggles, and inside the woolen mask Elliot recognized the clear blue eyes of his neighbor, Professor Loyall Anderson. The shotgun Elliot was carrying seemed to grow heavier. He yawned and shook his head, trying unsuccessfully to clear it. The sight of Anderson's eyes gave him a little thrill of revulsion.

"What are you after?" the young professor asked him, nodding toward the shotgun Elliot was cradling.

"Whatever there is," Elliot said.

Anderson took a quick look at the distant pasture behind him and then turned back to Elliot. The mouth hole of the professor's mask filled with teeth. Elliot thought that Anderson's teeth were quite as he had imagined them earlier. "Well, Polonski's cows are locked up," the professor said. "So they at least are safe."

Elliot realized that the professor had made a joke and was smiling. "Yes," he agreed.

Professor Anderson and his wife had been the moving force behind an initiative to outlaw the discharge of firearms within the boundaries of East Ilford Township. The initiative had been defeated, because East Ilford was not that kind of town.

"I think I'll go over by the river," Elliot said. He said it only to have something to say, to fill the silence before Anderson spoke again. He was afraid of what Anderson might say to him and of what might happen.

"You know," Anderson said, "that's all bird sanctuary over there now."

"Sure," Elliot agreed.

Outfitted as he was, the professor attracted Elliot's anger in an elemental manner. The mask made him appear a kind of doll, a kachina figure or a marionette. His eyes and mouth, all on their own, were disagreeable.

Elliott began to wonder if Anderson could smell the whiskey on his breath. He pushed the little red bull's-eye safety button on his gun to Off.

"Seriously," Anderson said, "I'm always having to run hunters out of there. Some people don't understand the word 'posted.'"

"I would never do that," Elliot said, "I would be afraid."

Anderson nodded his head. He seemed to be laughing. "Would you?" he asked Elliot merrily.

In imagination, Elliot rested the tip of his shotgun barrel against Anderson's smiling teeth. If he fired a load of deer shot into them, he thought, they might make a noise like broken china. "Yes," Elliot said. "I wouldn't know who they were or where they'd been. They might resent my being alive. Telling them where they could shoot and where not."

Anderson's teeth remained in place. "That's pretty strange," he said. "I mean, to talk about resenting someone for being alive."

"It's all relative," Elliot said. "They might think, 'Why should he be alive when some brother of mine isn't?' Or they might think, 'Why should he be alive when I'm not?'"

"Oh," Anderson said.

"You see?" Elliot said. Facing Anderson, he took a long step backward. "All relative."

"Yes," Anderson said.

"That's so often true, isn't it?" Elliot asked. "Values are often relative."

"Yes," Anderson said. Elliot was relieved to see that he had stopped smiling.

"I've hardly slept, you know," Elliot told Professor Anderson. "Hardly at all. All night. I've been drinking."

"Oh," Anderson said. He licked his lips in the mouth of the mask. "You should get some rest."

"You're right," Elliot said.

"Well," Anderson said, "got to go now."

Elliot thought he sounded a little thick in the tongue. A little slow in the jaw.

"It's a nice day," Elliot said, wanting now to be agreeable.

"It's great," Anderson said, shuffling on his skis.

"Have a nice day," Elliot said.

"Yes," Anderson said, and pushed off.

Elliot rested the shotgun across his shoulders and watched Anderson withdraw through the frozen swamp. It was in fact a nice day, but Elliot took no comfort in the weather. He missed night and the falling snow.

As he walked back toward his house, he realized that now there would be whole days to get through, running before the antic energy of whiskey. The whiskey would drive him until he dropped. He shook his head in regret. "It's a revolution," he said aloud. He imagined himself talking to his wife.

Getting drunk was an insurrection, a revolution—a bad one. There would be outsize bogus emotions. There would be petty moral blackmail and cheap remorse. He had said dreadful things to his wife. He had bullied Anderson with his violence and unhappiness, and Anderson would not forgive him. There would be damn little justice and no mercy.

Nearly to the house, he was startled by the desperate feathered drumming of a pheasant's rush. He froze, and out of instinct brought the gun up in the direction of the sound. When he saw the bird break from its cover and take wing, he tracked it, took a breath, and fired once. The bird was a little flash of opulent color against the bright-blue sky. Elliot felt himself flying for a moment. The shot missed.

Lowering the gun, he remembered the deer shells he had loaded. A hit with the concentrated shot would have pulverized the bird, and he was glad he had missed. He wished no harm to any creature. Then he thought of himself wishing no harm to any creature and began to feel fond and sorry for himself. As soon as he grew aware of the emotion he was indulging, he suppressed it. Pissing and moaning, mourning and weeping, that was the nature of the drug.

The shot echoed from the distant hills. Smoke hung in the air. He turned and looked behind him and saw, far away across the pasture, the tiny blue-and-red figure of Professor Anderson motionless against the snow. Then Elliot turned again toward his house and took a few labored steps and looked up to see his wife at the bedroom window. She stood perfectly still, and the morning sun lit her nakedness. He stopped where he was. She had heard the shot and run to the window. What had she thought to see? Burnt rags and blood on the snow. How relieved was she now? How disappointed?

Elliot thought he could feel his wife trembling at the window. She was hugging herself. Her hands clasped her shoulders. Elliot took his snow goggles off and shaded his eyes with his hand. He stood in the field staring.

The length of the gun was between them, he thought. Somehow she had got out in front of it, to the wrong side of the wire. If he looked long enough he would find everything out there. He would find himself down the sight.

How beautiful she is, he thought. The effect was striking. The window was so clear because he had washed it himself, with vinegar. At the best of times he was a difficult, fussy man.

Elliot began to hope for forgiveness. He leaned the shotgun on his forearm and raised his left hand and waved to her. Show a hand, he thought. Please just show a hand.

He was cold, but it had got light. He wanted no more than the gesture. It seemed to him that he could build another day on it. Another day was all you needed. He raised his hand higher and waited.

1. How do the opening paragraphs set the tone for the story? What is that tone?
2. What purpose does Blankenship serve in the story? How would the story be different if he were not in it?
3. What are some of the "mysteries" rendered powerfully in this story? (What things do you continue to wonder about after the story has ended.)
4. What aspects about the relationship between the main character and his wife are surprising yet convincing?

CHAPTER FIVE

Why You Need to Show *and* Tell

*Or, why the most common
piece of advice given to beginning
writers is misleading*

Part 1: THE IMPORTANCE OF NARRATION

Getting Started

Show, not tell. If you've ever taken a creative writing workshop, shown a story or essay to a writer friend who has taken workshops, or read just about any beginning book on creative writing, you will have bumped into this piece of conventional wisdom.

The only problem is, it's wrong.

Well, wrong is perhaps too strong a word. Let's say that it's certainly not always right. And it could be wrong for you. Very wrong. Even if it was right for Ernest Hemingway, or is still right for Richard Ford, or for Tobias Wolff.

Part 1 of this chapter first defines the terms *showing* and *telling*. We then look at writing samples that show the broad range of ways that these two basic writing tools can be used. The exercises at the end of the chapter will give students hands-on practice in incorporating what they've learned into their own writing. Finally, in Part 3, you will have a chance to see how some masters of the short story and essay have used their own unique combinations of showing and telling.

Some Basic Definitions

Let's first take a step back and try to understand the reason this show-not-tell advice is so freely passed out. Quite frankly, it's because even experienced writers—and yes, even university professors—don't always pay attention to the real meanings of the terms they are using. Either that, or

they are trying to oversimplify a terribly complex issue in the hope of getting beginners to avoid making some basic (and common) beginning
errors. In either case, it makes sense to first define as best as we can what
we're talking about.

> SHOWING. *The American Heritage Dictionary* defines "to show" as "to cause
> or allow to be seen." In literature, "showing" is also referred to as dram-
> atizing. If something is shown, or dramatized, the reader is allowed to
> be an eyewitness (of sorts) to the events of the story, novel, or essay
> through the use of dialogue (what characters say) and action (what
> characters do or have done to them). Another way to think about show-
> ing is to think of what can be performed in a *dramatic* genre, such as the
> stage, television, or movies. Indeed, the definition of "dramatize" is "to
> be adaptable to dramatic form."

> TELLING. Also referred to as summary or narration, writers *tell* to directly
> communicate or describe to the reader what is happening in a creative
> work. That is, as a writer you can describe the setting (it was a dark and
> stormy night); you can describe the characters (she had a face as broad
> and as innocent as a cabbage); and you can even "tell" the plot by sum-
> marizing what happens at a particular point in the story, novel, or non-
> fiction piece (she told him she'd had enough, and that she was leaving
> for Peoria on the morning train).

Let's be even more precise. When a story, novel, or essay is dramatized,
or shown, the reader is presented with concrete evidence of what's happening. So what does this include? Think of anything you could witness
in the real world (a couple fighting at a restaurant), or on a stage (a
revival of *Cat on a Hot Tin Roof*), or in a movie (*Casablanca*):

- Words spoken, or dialogue between characters. ("Why did you order that?
  You know I'm a vegetarian!")
- Actions and reactions among characters. (She picks up the fork and stabs
  the tablecloth twice.)
- Basic *objective* descriptions of objects or settings that a reader would naturally see if the situation were videotaped or photographed. (It was dark
  outside the restaurant. There were twelve tables in the room, only four of
  which were occupied.)

Everything other than these things is narration, or telling. This includes
the following:

- History, or background information that supplements our knowledge of
  what's currently happening in the story, novel, or creative nonfiction piece.

- Explanations or definitions that clarify whatever things are currently happening in the story, novel, or creative nonfiction piece.
- Specific thoughts or emotions of the characters involved.
- Any analysis of or commentary on what is happening in the story, novel, or creative nonfiction piece.
- Fiddling with the "clock" of the ongoing piece, by transporting the reader backward or forward in time without showing the interim events.

Showing and telling. That pretty much covers everything creative writers do with words. You can show, or you can tell. Very basic. And understanding the difference between these two tools, and figuring out how you can best use them given your own voice and material, is a critical aspect of your development as a writer.

Why "Show, Don't Tell" Is Such Common Advice

Now let's look at an example of why "showing" is generally considered more effective than "telling." Read through the three versions of sample text below. It's a section from "Helping," a superb short story by Robert Stone (pp. 178–202), presented in three deliberately different ways. (Grateful thanks and credit for this way of explaining showing vs. telling goes to novelist John L'Heureux, of Stanford University.) The final one is Stone's actual published prose. The only thing you need to know about the situation is that the main character (named Elliot), a Vietnam vet, has recently fallen off the wagon and has spent the night in heavy drinking and fighting with his wife. At this point in the story, Elliot, still somewhat drunk and very angry and confused, has taken his shotgun outside his house.

Example 1

Elliot took his shotgun and went out into the fields behind his house. There he met his neighbor, a professor at a local college. The professor didn't seem to understand the state that Elliot was in. He taunted him about not shooting in a bird sanctuary. Elliot took the safety latch off his shotgun. He imagined filling the professor's mouth with deer shot. The professor finally seemed to grasp the idea that he was in danger. He stopped smiling. Elliot felt his anger dissipate.

You can see right away why this isn't very good. It's a clumsy, hackneyed telling of what has happened. Everything is summarized too quickly. We don't hear what words are spoken, or see any gestures or other movement by the characters. The writer has not really done his or her job—readers are forced to do all the imaginative work themselves.

All right. So this story is "told," and told poorly, and when beginning writers churn out this kind of prose, it is probably a good thing to instruct them to tell less, and show more. So a diligent student will try again, and can usually come up with something much better—much less "told"—without too much difficulty once thus directed.

Example 2

Elliot took his shotgun and went out into the field. There he met his neighbor, a professor at a local college. The shotgun Elliot was carrying seemed to grow heavier when he saw his neighbor. He yawned and shook his head, trying unsuccessfully to clear it. The sight of Anderson's eyes gave him a little thrill.

"What are you after?" the professor asked.

"Whatever there is," Elliot said.

Anderson took a quick look at the pasture behind him. Elliot could see his teeth through the mask. The mouth hole of the professor's mask filled with teeth. The professor made a joke about how a neighbor's cows were safe because they were locked up.

This infuriated Elliot. He turned the gun's safety latch to Off.

In his mind, Elliot fired a load of deer shot into the teeth.

Finally, the professor realized what danger he was in. Elliot was relieved to see that he stopped smiling.

Elliot told the professor that he'd hardly slept.

The professor finally understood he was perhaps in danger. Elliot felt his anger dissipate.

You can see how much better this is. We're beginning to actually witness what's happening in that field. It's coming to life. It's shown, or dramatized. Yes, it's still a bit sketchy, still incomplete; the reader is still forced to create most of the images in his or her own mind in order to fully visualize what's happening. But it's vastly improved. So the student is told that this is good, and perhaps to try again, to *show* even more. And maybe eventually he or she would be able to produce something like the following, which is Stone's own taut dramatic prose.

Example 3: Stone's actual text

He stood in the middle of the field and listened to the crows. Fear, anger, and sleep were the three primary conditions of life. He had learned that over there. Once he had thought fear the worst, but he had learned that the worst was anger. Nothing could fix it; neither alcohol nor medicine. It was a worm. It left him no peace. Sleep was the best.

He opened his eyes and pushed on until he came to the brow that overlooked the swamp. Just below, gliding along among the frozen cattails and bare scrub maple, was a man on skis. Elliot stopped to watch the man approach.

The skier's face was concealed by a red-and-blue ski mask. He wore snow goggles, a blue jumpsuit, and a red woolen Norwegian hat. As he came, he leaned into the turns of the trail, moving silently and gracefully along. At the foot of the slope on which Elliot stood, the man looked up, saw him, and slid to a halt. The man stood staring at him for a moment and then began to herringbone up the slope. In no time at all the skier stood no more than ten feet away, removing his goggles, and inside the woolen mask Elliot recognized the clear blue eyes of his neighbor, Professor Loyall Anderson. The shotgun Elliot was carrying seemed to grow heavier. He yawned and shook his head, trying unsuccessfully to clear it. The sight of Anderson's eyes gave him a little thrill of revulsion.

"What are you after?" the young professor asked him, nodding toward the shotgun Elliot was cradling.

"Whatever there is," Elliot said.

Anderson took a quick look at the distant pasture behind him and then turned back to Elliot. The mouth hole of the professor's mask filled with teeth. Elliot thought that Anderson's teeth were quite as he had imagined them earlier. "Well, Polonski's cows are locked up," the professor said. "So they at least are safe."

Elliot realized that the professor had made a joke and was smiling. "Yes," he agreed.

Professor Anderson and his wife had been the moving force behind an initiative to outlaw the discharge of firearms within the boundaries of East Ilford Township. The initiative had been defeated, because East Ilford was not that kind of town.

"I think I'll go over by the river," Elliot said. He said it only to have something to say, to fill the silence before Anderson spoke again. He was afraid of what Anderson might say to him and of what might happen.

"You know," Anderson said, "that's all bird sanctuary over there now."

"Sure," Elliot agreed.

Outfitted as he was, the professor attracted Elliot's anger in an elemental manner. The mask made him appear a kind of doll, a kachina figure or a marionette. His eyes and mouth, all on their own, were disagreeable.

Elliot began to wonder if Anderson could smell the whiskey on his breath. He pushed the little red bull's-eye safety button on his gun to Off.

"Seriously," Anderson said. "I'm always having to run hunters out of there. Some people don't understand the word 'posted.'"

"I would never do that," Elliot said, "I would be afraid."

Anderson nodded his head. He seemed to be laughing. "Would you?" he asked Elliot merrily.

In imagination, Elliot rested the tip of his shotgun barrel against Anderson's smiling teeth. If he fired a load of deer shot into them, he thought, they might make a noise like broken china. "Yes," Elliot said. "I wouldn't know who they were or where they'd been. They might resent my being alive. Telling them where they could shoot and where not."

Anderson's teeth remained in place. "That's pretty strange," he said. "I mean, to talk about resenting someone for being alive."

"It's all relative," Elliot said. "They might think, 'Why should he be alive when some brother of mine isn't?' Or they might think, 'Why should he be alive when I'm not?'"

"Oh," Anderson said.

"You see?" Elliot said. Facing Anderson, he took a long step backward. "All relative."

"Yes," Anderson said.

"That's so often true, isn't it?" Elliot asked. "Values are often relative."

"Yes," Anderson said. Elliot was relieved to see that he had stopped smiling.

"I've hardly slept, you know," Elliot told Professor Anderson. "Hardly at all. All night. I've been drinking."

"Oh," Anderson said. He licked his lips in the mouth of the mask. "You should get some rest."

"You're right," Elliot said.

"Well," Anderson said, "got to go now."

Elliot thought he sounded a little thick in the tongue. A little slow in the jaw.

"It's a nice day," Elliot said, wanting now to be agreeable.

"It's great," Anderson said, shuffling on his skis.

"Have a nice day," Elliot said.

"Yes," Anderson said, and pushed off.

We should all have the ability to write like this. Really fine writing. This has been shown to us, not told (well, mostly shown—read on). And it seems clear that showing is better than telling.

Or is it? Consider the following passage:

Lolita, light of my life, fire of my loins. My sin, my soul. Lo-lee-ta: the tip of the tongue taking a trip of three steps down the palate to tap, at three, on the teeth. Lo. Lee. Ta.

She was Lo, plain Lo, in the morning, standing four feet ten in one sock. She was Lola in slacks. She was Dolly at school. She was Dolores on the dotted line. But in my arms she was always Lolita.

Did she have a precursor? She did, indeed she did. In point of fact, there might have been no Lolita at all had I not loved, one summer, a certain initial girl-child. In a princedom by the sea. Oh when? About as many years before Lolita was born as my age was that summer. You can always count on a murderer for a fancy prose style.

Ladies and gentlemen of the jury, exhibit number one is what the seraphs, the misinformed, simple, noble-winged seraphs, envied. Look at this tangle of thorns.

This is the opening passage of *Lolita* by Vladimir Nabokov. Would you tell him that he's "telling" too much? Because he is—telling, that is. The first five pages or so of this acknowledged masterpiece of twentieth-century literature are completely told. There's no dramatization, no "showing," in sight. And we wouldn't have it any other way. The narration is so strong and evocative, the voice so compelling, that we wouldn't mind being told many more things in this manner.

The Show-and-Tell Balancing Act

There are many other examples of terrific telling—read the openings of classic literary works and see for yourself—so as writing advice goes, "show not tell" is perhaps not always good advice. After all, *The American Heritage Dictionary* definition of "tell" is "To give a detailed account of; narrate: *tell what happened; told us a story*" [emphasis mine], which is the essence of what we are trying to do with creative writing, right? Tell a story?

Let's look even more closely at the Stone text and deconstruct it enough to see that it's not completely shown, after all. That there's quite a lot of telling involved. (In the section below, the "telling" is in boldface.)

Example 4: Stone's Show-and-Tell Balancing Act

He stood in the middle of the field **and listened to the crows. Fear, anger, and sleep were the three primary conditions of life. He had learned that over there. Once he had thought fear the worst, but he had learned that the worst was anger. Nothing could fix it; neither alcohol nor medicine. It was a worm. It left him no peace. Sleep was the best.**

He opened his eyes **and pushed on until he came to the brow that overlooked the swamp. Just below, gliding along among the frozen cattails and bare scrub maple, was a man on skis.** Elliot stopped **to watch the man approach.**

The skier's face **was concealed by** a red-and-blue ski mask. He wore snow goggles, a blue jumpsuit, and a red **woolen Norwegian hat. As he came, he leaned into the turns of the trail, moving silently and gracefully along.** At the foot of the slope on which Elliot stood, the man looked up, saw him, and slid to a halt. The man stood staring at him for a moment and then began to herringbone up the slope. In no time at all the skier stood no more than ten feet away, removing his goggles, **and inside the woolen mask Elliot recognized the clear blue eyes of his neighbor, Professor Loyall Anderson. The** shotgun Elliot was carrying seemed to grow heavier. He yawned and shook his head, trying unsuccessfully to clear it. The sight of Anderson's eyes gave him a little thrill of revulsion.

"What are you after?" the young professor asked him, nodding toward the shotgun Elliot was cradling.

"Whatever there is," Elliot said.

Anderson took a quick look at the distant pasture behind him and then turned back to Elliot. The mouth hole of the professor's mask filled with teeth. Elliot thought that Anderson's teeth were quite as he had imagined them earlier. "Well, Polonski's cows are locked up," the professor said. "So they at least are safe."

Elliot realized that the professor had made a joke and was smiling. "Yes," he agreed.

Professor Anderson and his wife had been the moving force behind an initiative to outlaw the discharge of firearms within the boundaries of East Ilford Township. The initiative had been defeated, because East Ilford was not that kind of town.

"I think I'll go over by the river." Elliot said. He said it only to have something to say, to fill the silence before Anderson spoke again. He was afraid of what Anderson might say to him and of what might happen.

"You know," Anderson said, "that's all bird sanctuary over there now."

"Sure," Elliot agreed.

Outfitted as he was, the professor attracted Elliot's anger in an elemental manner. The mask made him appear a kind of doll, a kachina figure or a marionette. His eyes and mouth, all on their own, were disagreeable.

Elliot began to wonder if Anderson could smell the whiskey on his breath. He pushed the little red bull's-eye safety button on his gun to Off.

"Seriously," Anderson said. "I'm always having to run hunters out of there. Some people don't understand the word 'posted.'"

"I would never do that," Elliot said, "I would be afraid."

Anderson nodded his head. He seemed to be laughing. "Would you?" he asked Elliot merrily.

In imagination, Elliot rested the tip of his shotgun barrel against Anderson's smiling teeth. If he fired a load of deer shot into them, he thought, they might make a noise like broken china. "Yes," Elliot said. "I wouldn't know who they were or where they'd been. They might resent my being alive. Telling them where they could shoot and where not."

Anderson's teeth remained in place. "That's pretty strange," he said. "I mean, to talk about resenting someone for being alive."

"It's all relative," Elliot said. "They might think, 'Why should he be alive when some brother of mine isn't?' Or they might think, 'Why should he be alive when I'm not?'"

"Oh," Anderson said.

"You see?" Elliot said. Facing Anderson, he took a long step backward. "All relative."

"Yes," Anderson said.

"That's so often true, isn't it?" Elliot asked. "Values are often relative."

"Yes," Anderson said. **Elliot was relieved to see that he had stopped smiling.**

"I've hardly slept, you know," Elliot told Professor Anderson. "Hardly at all. All night. I've been drinking."

"Oh," Anderson said. He licked his lips in the mouth of the mask. "You should get some rest."

"You're right," Elliot said.

"Well," Anderson said, "got to go now."

Elliot thought he sounded a little thick in the tongue. A little slow in the jaw.

"It's a nice day," Elliot said, **wanting now to be agreeable.**

"It's great," Anderson said, shuffling on his skis.

"Have a nice day," Elliot said.

"Yes," Anderson said, and pushed off.

How do you determine what is showing and what is telling? There are two basic questions you can ask when determining if any one section of a story, novel, or nonfiction piece is narration or scene.

1. HOW OBJECTIVE IS THE "INFORMATION" BEING PRESENTED? Is it something you could witness for yourself without any help from the author? Then it's showing. Is the information being filtered or interpreted in order to push you toward a conclusion or emotional reaction that otherwise you might not have? That's telling. This is why, in the Stone text, "watched the man approach" and "concealed" are boldfaced as telling. This is information we wouldn't necessarily pick up for ourselves if the events were being played out on a movie screen. We might use different phrases, like "the man skied toward him" and "hidden," depending on our personal feelings toward the movie or situation. The fact that these specific words were chosen makes the information subjective, not objective. Likewise, we would only see a hat, not know that it was woolen or Norwegian unless told. "Elliot recognized the clear blue eyes of his neighbor, Professor Loyall Anderson" is also telling for two reasons. "Recognized" is a state we can't observe objectively, although there are a number of gestures that imply recognition, such as a start, or double take. And using "clear" to describe Anderson's eyes reveals Elliot's state of mind—his envy of his neighbor's placid state—rather than an objective showing of the facts.

2. HAS THE "CLOCK" OF THE STORY, NOVEL, OR CREATIVE NONFICTION PIECE BEEN STOPPED FOR ANY REASON? Another aspect of narration, or telling,

is that it usually involves stopping or starting the "clock" of the piece. It's the equivalent of the aside used in theatre, or a time out in a sports event: the action needs to cease temporarily in order for other information to be presented. In the case of "Helping," Robert Stone used telling to manipulate the narration clock in the following instances:

Stop the clock—you need to know that this character is imagining filling his neighbor's teeth with deershot.

Stop the clock—you should probably know that Elliot is relieved to see that his neighbor has stopped smiling.

Now that your eyes are open, you will become aware of how much "telling" is done by past and contemporary masters of fiction and creative nonfiction. Indeed, the precise mix of scene and narration that a writer chooses to use is one of the most defining elements of his or her particular "voice," or style.

Traditional Uses of Narration (Telling)

So, how do you choose when to show, and when to tell?

Traditionally, it's been assumed that you want to show the important stuff. Important behaviors, important interactions, important speeches, conversations. The convention has been that anything that changes the situation of the story, novel, or essay in a significant way should happen in "eyewitness" mode.

There are a number of reasons why this makes sense. For starters, it's human nature for readers to want to witness something for themselves in a work of creative writing. It's more immersive, more dramatic, more involving—more everything that good writing should be. Readers have a natural desire to be present when the drama heats up—they tend not to be satisfied by having key scenes summarized for them.

Narration has been used, *traditionally*, to fill in the gaps. To supplement what is being shown, or dramatized. It has traditionally been understood that showing is the cornerstone for constructing creative work, and that narration, although important, plays second fiddle. As an example, we will look at the opening of Hemingway's "Hills Like White Elephants" (pp. 356–60) which limits the use of narration to the most basic level.

The hills across the valley of the Ebro were long and white. On this side there was no shade and no trees and the station was between two lines of rails in the sun. Close against the side of the station there was a warm shadow of the building and a curtain, made of strings of bamboo beads, hung across the open door into the bar, to keep out flies. The American and the girl with him sat at a table in the shade, outside the building. It was very hot and the express from Barcelona would come in forty minutes. It stopped at this junction for two minutes and went on to Madrid.

1. Narration is used to "set the scene" or prepare the reader for what will shortly be shown. ("The hills across the valley of the Ebro were long and white.")
2. Narration is used to provide important information that would be difficult or awkward to dramatize in the existing context. (The train from Barcelona was due in forty minutes.) This can include background, history, facts, or thoughts or emotions that a character would not be able to express using the spoken word.
3. Narration is used to manipulate the interior "clock" of the story, novel, or creative nonfiction piece in order to either insert or omit certain information.

Why Narration Is Such an Important Creative Tool

Let's now look at a piece that proves how much we'd lose without the use of this very important tool. The following sample texts are excerpts from, respectively, *Peter Pan* the novella, written by J. M. Barrie, and *Peter Pan* the stage play, also written by Barrie.

Playwrights can't use narration. It's not in their box of artistic tools. Of course, they have other, extremely valuable tools that prose writers don't have access to—such as actors who can bring characters to life; real physical objects, not just descriptions; and physical gestures and actions. But playwrights don't have narration. They can't *tell* us anything, not without resorting to rather artificial devices, such as asides to the audience, or commentary by an observing chorus or narrator.

So let's look at the two versions of *Peter Pan*, and see how Barrie compensated for the fact that he was not able to utilize the tool of narration in the stage play. (Barrie wrote the play first, and the novella second.)

And first you must forget all other versions of *Peter Pan*—especially the Disney version. This is the original, and it is enchanting.

From *Peter Pan:* The Novella

[Wendy's mother] was a lovely lady, with a romantic mind and such a sweet mocking mouth. Her romantic mind was like the tiny boxes, one within the other, that come from the puzzling East, however many you discover there is always one more; and her sweet mocking mouth had one

kiss on it that Wendy could never get, though there it was, perfectly conspicuous in the right-hand corner.

The way Mr. Darling won her was this: the many gentlemen who had
been boys when she was a girl discovered simultaneously that they loved
her, and they all ran to her house to propose to her except Mr. Darling,
who took a cab and nipped in first, and so he got her. He got all of her,
except the innermost box and the kiss. He never knew about the box, and
in time he gave up trying for the kiss. Wendy thought Napoleon could
have got it, but I can picture him trying, and then going off in a passion,
slamming the door.

Mr. Darling used to boast to Wendy that her mother not only loved him
but respected him. He was one of those deep ones who know about stocks
and shares. Of course, no one really knows, but he quite seemed to know,
and he often said stocks were up and shares were down in a way that
would have made any woman respect him.

From *Peter Pan:* The Play

MICHAEL *(obstreperous):* I won't go to bed, I won't, I won't. Nana it isn't six
o'clock yet. Two minutes more, please one minute more?

*(Here the bathroom door closes on them, and Mrs. Darling, who has perhaps
heard his cry, enters the nursery. She is the loveliest lady in Bloomsbury, with
a sweet mocking mouth, and as she is going out to dinner tonight she is
already wearing her evening gown because she knows her children like to see
her in it. It is a delicious confection made by herself out of nothing and other
people's mistakes. She does not often go out to dinner, preferring when the
children are in bed to sit beside them tidying up their minds, just as if they
were drawers. If Wendy and the boys could keep awake they might see her
repacking into their proper places the many articles of the mind that have
strayed during the day, lingering humorously over some of their contents,
wondering where on earth they picked this thing up, making discoveries sweet
and not so sweet, pressing this to her cheek and hurriedly stowing that out of
sight. When they wake in the morning the naughtinesses with which they
went to bed are not, alas, blown away, but they are placed at the bottom of the
drawer; and on the top, beautifully aired, are their prettier thoughts ready for
the new day. As she enters the room she is startled to see a strange little face
outside the window and a hand groping as if it wanted to come in.)*

MRS. DARLING: Who are you? *(The unknown disappears; she hurries to the
window)* No one there. And yet I feel sure I saw a face. My children!

(She throws open the bathroom door and Michael's head appears gaily over the

bath. He splashes; she throws kisses to him and closes the door) Wendy,
John! *(she cries, and gets reassuring answers from the day nursery. She sits
down, relieved, on Wendy's bed; and Wendy and John come in, looking their
smallest size, as children tend to do to a mother suddenly in fear for them)*

JOHN *(histrionically)*: We are doing an act; we are playing at being you and
father. *(He imitates the only father who has come under his special notice)* A little less noise there.

WENDY: Now let us pretend we have a baby.

JOHN *(good-naturedly)*: I am happy to inform you, Mrs. Darling, that you
are now a mother. *(Wendy gives way to ecstasy)* You have missed the chief
thing; you haven't asked, boy or girl?

WENDY: I am so glad to have one at all, I don't care which it is.

Writing students always laugh when they compare these two versions.
Yes, it's clear that Barrie the novelist is having trouble showing and not
telling when he puts on his dramatist hat. So he crams all the lovely narration into the stage directions. The actors get this information, but the
audience obviously doesn't—not directly, at least, although Barrie can
hope that these subtle, funny observations are absorbed by the actors and
influence their performances.

How Showing and Telling Complement Each Other

Ideally, these two elements of writing are organically intertwined. That is,
what we tell doesn't just echo or repeat what we show. We use the two
together to achieve whatever effect we want. When a section of "telling"
can be eliminated without taking away from a creative work's meaning,
then by all means cut it, and allow the showing to carry the piece. But the
opposite is also true: often we can tell something more efficiently, elegantly, beautifully, or subtly than we could hope to do if dramatizing it. In
such cases, we should eliminate the dramatization, or scene, in favor of
the narration. We'll explore this in greater depth in Chapter 9.

Good Intentions, Bad Advice

So why do so many well-meaning—and competent!—creative writing
instructors use "show not tell" as their mantra?

Because good telling is difficult to do.

It goes back to what we discussed in Chapter 2: the need to be concrete,
the need for specificity. It's a relatively straightforward thing to be con-

crete when showing, or dramatizing something; after all, the characters are either there, or they aren't. They are sitting on chairs, or they are standing on the deck of a boat. They are speaking words, or they are silent; they are polishing their eyeglasses, or they are throwing coffee cups at walls. It's difficult to be abstract when showing.

Telling, however, is where the temptation to generalize or go abstract is strongest. It's my guess that when creative writing professors urge their classes to show and not to tell, they are really trying to urge students to be more concrete and specific. They see student writing that is too general or abstract, and they make the mistake of blaming the technique—narration—for the poor writing that results.

What about this version of the opening of *Lolita* (my apologies to Nabokov):

> Lolita. Oh, she was something. Really sexy. Really hot. I loved saying her name, over and over. Lolita, Lolita, Lolita. I liked the way she looked in her school uniform. She was pretty damn cute. Oh yes.

We know, having read the original, that the problem isn't that this is narration, but that it's not very good narration—certainly not comparable to the real thing that Nabokov wrote. We wouldn't necessarily want Nabokov to open his novel with a dramatized scene of Humbert Humbert acting out his passion for Lolita. But we do want to hear his narration here. A better way to think about it, perhaps, is that we want Nabokov to use his artistic judgment about where to show and where to tell, and that telling, in his expert hands, is sublime.

This is critical, because most creative writing classes today use the workshop technique in one form or another. In order for students to provide helpful advice to each other, they need to be able to correctly diagnose the problems found in the stories they review. There's a big difference between a creative piece that is truly crying out for more scenes, and a piece in which the narration is technically weak. In the first case, we want to urge the writer to show more. In the latter case, we want the writer to practice his or her narration techniques in order to employ narration more successfully in future creative work.

In short, let's not shoot the messenger. Just because a particular narration passage does not succeed is not a reason to ban all telling. Instead, our job is to try to make it better. Some cases in point:

> *Version A:* My father is old, and his heart is failing. He still is quite lucid, intellectually, however, and so we have many good conversations even

though he mostly stays in bed these days. He used to be a doctor, and he thinks about his condition in a very scientific way. Today he is in a great deal of pain, and I've propped him up with lots of pillows. He is dying, and we both know it, so when he asks me for one last favor, I agree.

Version B: My father is eighty-six years old and in bed. His heart, that bloody motor, is equally old and will not do certain jobs any more. It still floods his head with brainy light. But it won't let his legs carry the weight of his body around the house. Despite my metaphors, this muscle failure is not due to his old heart, he says, but to a potassium shortage. Sitting on one pillow, leaning on three, he offers last-minute advice and makes a request.

[from "A Conversation With My Father" by Grace Paley]

Version A: It's her job to wash him whenever he needs it, so every few days she wets a washcloth and does so. She has to be very gentle because he is burned so badly. In some places his skin looks purple, at other places the bone shows through. Even though he must be in a great deal of pain, sometimes he smiles at her.

She's been doing this for months, and so she is very familiar with his body. It's so thin it reminds her of Christ as he was crucified. She thinks of him as someone very good, even holy. He is very patient, and lies still, looking up at the ceiling quietly whenever she washes him.

Version B: Every four days she washes his black body, beginning at the destroyed feet. She wets a washcloth and holding it above his ankles squeezes the water onto him, looking up as he murmurs, seeing his smile. Above the shins the burns are worst. Beyond purple. Bone.

She has nursed him for months and she knows the body well, the penis sleeping like a seahorse, the thin tight hips. Hipbones of Christ, she thinks. He is her despairing saint. He lies flat on his back, no pillow, looking up at the foliage painted onto the ceiling, its canopy of branches, and above that, blue sky.

[from The English Patient by Michael Ondaatje]

The Showing-Telling Continuum

It can be very helpful to think about showing and telling as representing the two extreme ends of the same continuum. In this next section, we'll look at how various stories fall along this line.

Let's start at the "pure showing" end. It's rare (off-stage) to find creative work that is purely shown, or dramatized. The following is from *A Thousand Acres*, the Pulitzer Prize–winning novel by Jane Smiley. The boldfaced parts are the narration—that's what is being told. Everything else is shown—the reader is an eyewitness to what occurs. The telling is kept to a minimum.

designed for working girls over fifty, who weighed from 165 to 200 pounds. His mother was one of the slimmer ones, but she said ladies did not tell their age or weight. She would not ride the buses by herself at night since they had been integrated, and because the reducing class was one of her few pleasures, necessary for her health, and *free*, she said Julian could at least put himself out to take her, considering all she did for him. Julian did not like to consider all she did for him, but every Wednesday night he braced himself and took her.

She was **almost ready to go**, standing before the hall mirror, putting on her hat, while he, his hands behind him, **appeared pinned to the door frame, waiting like Saint Sebastian for the arrows to begin piercing him. The hat was new and had cost her seven dollars and a half.** She kept saying, "Maybe I should have paid that for it. No, I shouldn't have. I'll take it off and return it tomorrow. I shouldn't have bought it."

Julian raised his eyes **to heaven.** "Yes, you should have bought it," he said. "Put it on and let's go." **It was a hat.** A purple velvet flap came down on one side of it and stood up on the other; the rest of it was green **and looked like a cushion with the stuffing out. He decided it was less comical than jaunty and pathetic. Everything that gave her pleasure was small and depressed him.**

And, in fact, although the entire story takes place on a single evening and could have been dramatized, like Hemingway's "Hills Like White Elephants" (pp. 356–60), using dialogue and gesture, O'Connor makes the deliberate choice to tell us many things: that Julian considered himself a martyr for what he was doing for his mother; that it was a hideous hat; and finally, and most importantly, O'Connor reaches into Julian's mind and comes out with that lovely line of narration "Everything that gave her pleasure was small and depressed him." Just think what the passage would have been like without those things—it would seem much flatter and less rich.

Finally, the following is a complete short story (this kind of piece is sometimes called a "short short") called "Scratch Music," by C. D. Wright. It is pure narration—what we often call a "voice" story, because it really sounds like a character talking without interruption by other characters or events. There's no dramatization whatsoever, but since the voice is so compelling, the piece succeeds.

How many threads have I broken with my teeth. How many times have I looked at the stars and felt ill. Time here is divided into before and since your shuttering in 1978. I remember hanging onto the hood of the big-fendered Olds with a mess of money in my purse. Call that romance. Some memory precedes you: when I wanted lederhosen because I'd read *Heidi*. And how I wanted my folks to build a fallout shelter so I could arrange the cans. And coveting mother's muskrat. I remember college. And being in Vista; I asked the librarian in Banks, the state's tomato capital, if she had any black literature and she said they used to have *Lil Black Sambo* but the white children tore out pages and wrote ugly words inside. Someone said if I didn't like Banks I should go to Moscow. I said, Come on, let's go outside and shoot the hoop. I've got a jones to beat your butt. I haven't changed. Now if I think of the earth's origins, I get vertigo. When I think of its death, I fall, I've picked up a few things, I know if you want songbirds, plant berry trees. If you don't want birds, buy a rubber snake. I remember that town with the Alcoa plant I toured. The manager kept referring to the workers as Alcoans, I thought of hundreds of flexible metal beings bent over assemblages. They sparked. What would I do in Moscow. I have these dreams—relatives loom over my bed. We should put her to sleep Lonnie says, Go home old girl, go home, my aunt says. Why should I go home before her I want to say. But I am bereft. So how is Life in The Other World. Do you get the news. Are you allowed a pet. But I wanted to show you how I've grown, what I know: I keep my bees far from the stable, they can't stand how horses smell. And I know sooner or later an old house will need a new roof. And more than six years have whistled by since you blew your heart out like the porch light. Reason and meaning don't step into another lit spot like a well-meaning stranger with a hat. And mother's mother who has lived in the same house ten times six years, told me. We didn't know we had termites until they swarmed. Then we had to pull up the whole floor. "Too late, no more . . ." you know the poem. But you, you bastard. You picked up a gun in winter as if it were a hat and you were leaving a restaurant; full, weary, and thankful to be spending the evening with no one.

Here's the continuum with the stories mapped out according to their use of scene and narration:

Pure Showing				Pure Telling
"Hills Like White Elephants	*A Thousand Acres*	*The Shipping News*	"Everything That Rises Must Converge"	"Scratch Music"

Let's be very clear: it's not that it's important to clinically dissect all showing and telling. In fact, sometimes it's very difficult to do so. The point is to recognize that *both* are important, both make up what we call creative writing, and to universally declare that more of one is good, and less of the other is better, is to impose rigid thinking on our own creative process as well as that of others.

Showing and Telling in Creative Nonfiction

The same precepts about showing and telling hold true in creative nonfiction as they do in fiction: the balance of the showing and the telling is a critical part of a writer's style, or voice, and there is no one "right" way to achieve that balance. Each writer needs to find it out for himself or herself.

Here's a passage from *This Boy's Life* by Tobias Wolff, in which we see about an equal mix of showing and telling. As before, the telling (narration) is boldfaced:

Mr. Howard stopped talking. He leaned back, blinking a little as if he had dozed off. He did not speak, nor did I. I didn't want Huff to know I was there. Huff had certain rituals of greeting that I was anxious to avoid, and if he sensed he was embarrassing me he would never let me get away. He would sink my ship but good. So I kept my head down and my mouth shut while Huff and the other boy talked about the fight, and about the girl the two boys had been fighting over. They talked about another girl. Then they talked about eating pussy. Huff took the floor on this subject, and showed no sign of giving it up. He went on at length. I heard boys hold forth like this all the time, and I did it myself, but now I thought I'd better show some horror. I frowned and shook my head **and stared down at the tabletop.**

"Shall we go?" Mr. Howard asked.

I did not want to break cover but I had no choice. I got up and walked past Huff's booth. Mr. Howard behind me. **Though I kept my face averted I was sure that Huff would see me, and as I moved toward the door I was waiting to hear him shout, "Hey! Dicklick!" The shout never came.**

Mr. Howard drove around Concrete for a while before taking me back to school. He was curious about the cement plant, and disappointed that I could tell him nothing about what went on inside it. He was quiet for a time. Then he said, "You should know that a boys' school can be a pretty rough-and-tumble place."

I said that I could take care of myself.

"I don't mean physically rough," Mr. Howard said. "Boys talk about all kinds of things. Even at a school like Hill you don't hear a whole lot of boys sitting around at night talking about Shakespeare. They're going to talk about other things. Sex, whatever. And they're going to take the gloves off."

I said nothing.

"You can't expect everyone to be, you know, an Eagle Scout."

"I don't," I said.

"I'm just saying that life in a boys' school can come as a bit of a shock to someone who's led a sheltered life." **I began to make an answer, but Mr.**

Howard said, "Let me just say one more thing. You're obviously doing a great job here. With your grades and so on you should be able to get into an excellent college later on. I'm not sure that a prep school is exactly the right move for you. You might end up doing yourself more harm than good. It's something to consider."

Part 2: EXERCISES

Since determining the particular mix of showing and telling that is right for you is a major part of finding your voice as a writer, the following exercises provide you with ways to experiment and see what feels comfortable.

You may well find that you do one thing well, and the other not as well. This could be a hint that your talent is in showing, for example. But it shouldn't mean that you neglect telling, or narration. In fact, not having such a strong command of narration might be the best reason to practice it—keep in mind that you are still developing as a writer (and will continue to develop for the rest of your life) and that you should be practicing all aspects of craft all the time as a way to continue to grow as an artist.

Exercise 1: Tell Me a Story

Goal: To practice the techniques of showing and telling, and to understand the artistic as well as technical differences between scene and narration.

What to do: 1. If possible, find an audience and begin with oral storytelling: talk (briefly) about something you witnessed in the past week or month. (You could have been an uninvolved bystander, or involved in the event.)

2. Next, take fifteen minutes to write a pure narration (telling) version of the event in question.

3. Next, do a pure scene version.

4. Finally, write a version that is a combination of both scene and narration.

5. If possible, do this in a group, and read each version out loud (the sharing of these exercises is critical for enabling you to learn from your colleagues).

Here's an example of scene versus narration done by Paul Wood:

Pure Narration:

My mother and I were having an argument. Like all our arguments, it was purportedly about something very specific—in this case, who was the winner of the 1986 World Series—yet it seemed to indicate something of the larger issues facing us. We tended to mystify each other, my mother and me, and we got closest to one another in our arguments, when we could crystallize or at least point to something concrete between us that we didn't agree on. Most of the time we existed in a floating state of nebulous bewilderment. She said the Yankees had won. I said the Orioles. That was basically all there was to our argument: each stating the position over and over again, each stating for evidence such things like our personal emotions about the outcome. She said she knew it was the Yankees because she had visited New York that year (she hated New York) and had come back with a Yankees T-shirt for me and my father. I said I knew it was the Orioles because the fact that they were *birds* had impressed itself upon my teenaged mind. I remembered thinking, I told her, how strange it was that birds were the national baseball champions.

Pure Scene:

"Yankees," my mother said. "The Yankees won that year."

"No," I told her. "In 1986, it was the Orioles. I'm sure it was."

"The Yankees," she repeated.

"The Orioles," I said.

"Are we just going to keep this up all night?" she asked.

"We may," I said. "We just may. Unless you have some hard-core evidence to the contrary . . . ?"

"I remember it was the Yankees, because I'd just come back from a visit to that godforsaken place," she said.

"You mean New York?" I asked.

"Shush. Yes. New York. I had just come back, and I brought home two Yankee T-shirts: one for you and one for your father. Later, I remembered thinking how remarkably far-sighted that had been of me."

"Well, I have a memory of my own regarding the World Series from that year," I told her. "I remember thinking how wimpy it was that the champions were *birds*. Birds, for Christsakes."

"Don't swear," she said.

"I'm just saying, it struck me as ironic that the birds had beaten any number of fiercer animals," I said. "It was irony that would not have escaped anyone's notice who was in a noticing mood."

Scene and Narration:

"Yankees," my mother said. "The Yankees won that year."

"No," I told her. "In 1986 it was the Orioles. I'm sure it was." To which my mother had nothing to say except to repeat her earlier assertion. No, she was sure it was the Yankees. I was equally sure it was the Orioles. We both repeated our positions a number of times without gaining an inch in the other's viewpoint. We tended to mystify each other, my mother and me, and we got closest to one another in our arguments, when we could crystallize or at least point to something concrete between us that we didn't agree on. Most of the time we existed in a floating state of nebulous bewilderment. She asked me if we were going to keep it up all night.

"We may," I said. "We just may. Unless you have some hard-core evidence to the contrary . . . ?"

"I remember it was the Yankees, because I'd just come back from a visit to that godforsaken place," she said.

"You mean New York?" I asked.

"Shush. Yes. New York. I had just come back, and I brought home two Yankee T-shirts: one for you and one for your father. Later, I remembered thinking how remarkably far-sighted that had been of me." I said I knew it was the Orioles because the fact that they were *birds* had impressed itself upon my teenaged mind. I remembered thinking, I told her, how strange it was that birds were the national baseball champions.

"That proves nothing," she said.

Exercise 2: What Everyone Knows / What I Know

Goal: To practice using narration to move from public knowledge to private knowledge.

What to do: 1. Think of a place, person, or event (something that happened) that you are intimately familiar with (if possible, that you have intimate knowledge of that no one else does).

2. Next, do a freewrite using the first sentence "What everyone knows about X is . . ." where X is the person, place, or event.

3. After this step has been concluded, write a second piece beginning with the sentence, "But what *I* know about X is . . ." where you reveal your special private knowledge or unique perspective.

The following exercise was written by Jenna Philpott:

What everyone knows about her is that she buys expensive shoes and wears them. Tod's. Gucci. Choo. Her boss and her underlings all know her quip, "The pain of a beautiful three-hour shoe can keep you awake for a twelve-hour day!" She calls her nanny at 10 a.m. and 4 p.m. and rubs her sore feet during those calls. She gives a generous bonus to her household help each Christmas and summer vacation. "I'm not cheap." Cocktail hour has returned after the birth of her child, "Weekends at four if you can make it!" Everyone knows they haven't really been invited and won't ever go.

What *I* know is that her daughter is deaf and blind. No pictures of the girl beside the woman and her husband. A grin for Aspen! Two grins for Tahiti! A kiss for Iceland! Her daughter lies on her back on the floor surrounded by toys she can neither see nor hear. The infant starts to squirm when the cleaning lady vacuums an arc around her. The vibrations stir something in her brain, "Others are near!" I also know that the woman's vacation days are her daughter's surgery days. This Friday her daughter's right eye will be removed, its pressure too great for a brain to develop. If the child recovers well, heart surgery is on the docket the day before Thanksgiving.

Part 3: READING AS A WRITER

Brownies

ZZ PACKER

By the end of our first day at Camp Crescendo, the girls in my Brownie troop had decided to kick the asses of each and every girl in Brownie Troop 909. Troop 909 was doomed from the first day of camp; they were white girls, their complexions like a blend of ice cream: strawberry, vanilla. They turtled out from their bus in pairs, their rolled-up sleeping bags chromatized with Disney characters—Sleeping Beauty, Snow White, Mickey Mouse—or the generic ones cheap parents bought—washed-out rainbows, unicorns, curly-eyelashed frogs. Some clutched Igloo coolers and still others held onto stuffed toys like pacifiers, looking all around them like tourists determined to be dazzled.

Our troop wended its way past their bus, past the ranger station, past the colorful trail guide drawn like a treasure map, locked behind glass.

"Man, did you smell them?" Arnetta said, giving the girls a slow once-over. "They smell like Chihuahuas. *Wet* Chihuahuas." Although we had passed their troop by yards, Arnetta raised her nose in the air and grimaced.

Arnetta said this from the very rear of the line, far away from Mrs. Margolin, who strung our troop behind her like a brood of obedient ducklings. Mrs. Margolin even looked like a mother duck—she had hair cropped close to a small ball of a head, almost no neck, and huge, miraculous breasts. She wore enormous belts that looked like the kind weight lifters wear, except hers were cheap metallic gold or rabbit fur or covered with gigantic fake sunflowers. Often these belts would become nature lessons in and of themselves. "See," Mrs. Margolin once said to us, pointing to her belt. "This one's made entirely from the feathers of baby pigeons."

The belt layered with feathers was uncanny enough, but I was more disturbed by the realization that I had never actually *seen* a baby pigeon. I searched for weeks for one, in vain—scampering after pigeons whenever I was downtown with my father.

But nature lessons were not Mrs. Margolin's top priority. She saw the position of troop leader as an evangelical post. Back at the AME church where our Brownie meetings were held, she was especially fond of imparting religious aphorisms by means of acrostics—Satan was the "Serpent Always Tempting And Noisome"; she'd refer to the Bible as "Basic Instructions Before Leaving Earth." Whenever she occasionally quizzed us on these at the beginning of the Brownie meeting, expecting to hear the acrostics parroted back to her, only Arnetta's correct replies soared over our vague mumblings. "Jesus?" Mrs. Margolin might ask expectantly, and Arnetta alone would dutifully answer, "Jehovah's Example, Saving Us Sinners."

Arnetta made a point of listening to Mrs. Margolin's religious talk and giving her what she wanted to hear. Because of this, Arnetta could have blared through a megaphone that the white girls of Troop 909 were "wet Chihuahuas" without arousing so much as a blink from Mrs. Margolin. Once Arnetta killed the troop goldfish by feeding it a French fry covered in ketchup, and when Mrs. Margolin demanded an explanation, Arnetta claimed that the goldfish had been eyeing her meal for *hours*, until—giving in to temptation—it had leapt up and snatched the whole golden fry from her fingertips.

"*Serious* Chihuahua," Octavia added—though neither Arnetta nor Octavia could *spell* "Chihuahua" or had ever *seen* a Chihuahua. Trisyllabic words had gained a sort of exoticism within our fourth-grade set at Woodrow Wilson Elementary. Arnetta and Octavia, compelled to outdo each other, would flip through the dictionary, determined to work the vulgar-sounding ones like "Djibouti" and "asinine" into conversation.

"*Caucasian* Chihuahuas," Arnetta said.

That did it. Drema and Elise doubled up on each other like inextricably entwined kites; Octavia slapped the skin of her belly; Janice jumped straight up in the air, then did it again, just as hard, as if to slam-dunk her own head. No one had laughed so hard since a boy named Martez had stuck his pencil in the electric socket and spent the whole day with a strange grin on his face.

"Girls, girls," said our parent helper, Mrs. Hedy. Mrs. Hedy was Octavia's mother. She wagged her index finger perfunctorily, like a windshield wiper. "Stop it now. Be good." She said this loudly enough to be heard, but lazily, nasally, bereft of any feeling or indication that she meant to be obeyed, as though she would say these words again at the exact same pitch if a button somewhere on her were pressed.

But the girls didn't stop laughing; they only laughed louder. It was the word "Caucasian" that had got them all going. One day at school, about a month before the Brownie camping trip, Arnetta had turned to a boy wearing impossibly high-ankled floodwater jeans, and said "What are *you? Caucasian?*" The word took off from there, and soon everything was Caucasian. If you ate too fast, you ate like a Caucasian; if you ate too slow, you ate like a Caucasian. The biggest feat anyone at Woodrow Wilson could do was to jump off the swing in midair, at the highest point in its arc, and if you fell (like I had, more than once) instead of landing on your feet, knees bent Olympic-gymnast-style, Arnetta and Octavia were prepared to comment. They'd look at each other with the silence of passengers who'd narrowly escaped an accident, then nod their heads, and whisper with solemn horror and haughtiness, "*Caucasian.*"

Even the only white kid in our school, Dennis, got in on the Caucasian act. That time when Martez stuck the pencil in the socket, Dennis had pointed, and yelled, "That was *so* Caucasian!"

Living in the south suburbs of Atlanta, it was easy to forget about whites. Whites were like those baby pigeons: real and existing, but rarely thought about. Everyone had been to Rich's to go clothes shopping, everyone had seen white girls and their mothers coo-cooing over dresses; everyone had gone to the downtown library and seen white businessmen swish by importantly, wrists flexed in front of them to check the time on their watches as though they would change from Clark Kent into Superman any second. But those images were as fleeting as cards shuffled in a deck, whereas the ten white girls behind us—*invaders*, Arnetta would later call them—were instantly real and memorable, with their long shampoo-commercial hair, as straight as spaghetti from the box. This alone was reason for envy and hatred. The only black girl most of us had ever seen with hair that long was Octavia, whose hair hung past her butt like a Hawaiian hula dancer's. The sight of Octavia's mane prompted other girls to listen to her reverentially, as though whatever she had to say would somehow activate their own follicles. For example, when, on the first day of camp, Octavia made as if to speak, a silence began. "Nobody," Octavia said, "calls us niggers."

At the end of that first day, when half of our troop made its way back to the cabin after tag-team restroom visits, Arnetta said she'd heard one of the girls in Troop 909 call Daphne a nigger. The other half of the girls and I were helping Mrs. Margolin clean up the pots and pans from the ravioli dinner. When we made our way to the restrooms to wash up and brush our teeth, we met up with Arnetta midway.

"Man, I completely heard the girl," Arnetta reported. "Right, Daphne?"

Daphne hardly ever spoke, but when she did her voice was petite and tinkly, the voice one might expect from a shiny new earring. She'd written a poem once, for Langston Hughes Day, a poem brimming with all the teacher-winning ingredients—trees and oceans, sunsets and moons—but what cinched the poem for the grown-ups, snatching the win from Octavia's musical ode to Grandmaster Flash and the Furious Five, were Daphne's last lines:

> You are my father, the veteran
> When you cry in the dark
> It rains and rains and rains in my heart

She'd worn clean, though faded, jumpers and dresses when Chic jeans were the fashion, but when she went up to the dais to receive her prize journal, pages trimmed in gold, she wore a new dress with a velveteen bodice and a taffeta skirt as wide as an umbrella. All the kids clapped, though none of them understood the poem. I'd read encyclopedias the way others read comics, and I didn't get it. But those last lines pricked me, they were so eerie, and as my father and I ate cereal, I'd whisper over my Froot Loops, like a mantra, *"You are my father, the veteran. You are my father, the veteran, the veteran, the veteran,"* until my father, who acted in plays as Caliban and Othello and was not a veteran, marched me up to my teacher one morning, and said, "Can you tell me what the hell's wrong with this kid?"

I had thought Daphne and I might become friends, but she seemed to grow spooked by me whispering those lines to her, begging her to tell me what they meant, and I had soon understood that two quiet people like us were better off quiet alone.

"Daphne? Didn't you hear them call you a nigger?" Arnetta asked, giving Daphne a nudge.

The sun was setting through the trees, and their leafy tops formed a canopy of black lace for the flame of the sun to pass through. Daphne shrugged her shoulders at first, then slowly nodded her head when Arnetta gave her a hard look.

Twenty minutes later, when my restroom group returned to the cabin, Arnetta was still talking about Troop 909. My restroom group had passed by some of the 909 girls. For the most part, they had deferred to us, waving us into the restrooms, letting us go even though they'd gotten there first.

We'd seen them, but from afar, never within their orbit enough to see whether their faces were the way all white girls appeared on TV—pony-tailed and full of energy, bubbling over with love and money. All I could see was that some rapidly fanned their faces with their hands, though the heat of the day had long passed. A few seemed to be lolling their heads in slow circles, half-purposefully, as if exercising the muscles of their necks, half-ecstatically, rolling their heads about like Stevie Wonder.

"We can't let them get away with that," Arnetta said, dropping her voice to a laryngitic whisper. "We can't let them get away with calling us niggers. I say we teach them a lesson." She sat down cross-legged on a sleeping bag, an embittered Buddha, eyes glimmering acrylic black. "We can't go telling Mrs. Margolin, either. Mrs. Margolin'll say something about doing unto others and the path of righteousness and all. Forget that shit." She let her eyes flutter irreverently till they half closed, as though ignoring an insult not worth returning. We could all hear Mrs. Margolin outside, gathering the last of the metal campware.

Nobody said anything for a while. Arnetta's tone had an upholstered confidence that was somehow both regal and vulgar at once. It demanded a few moments of silence in its wake, like the ringing of a church bell or the playing of taps. Sometimes Octavia would ditto or dissent whatever Arnetta had said, and this was the signal that others could speak. But this time Octavia just swirled a long cord of hair into pretzel shapes.

"Well?" Arnetta said. She looked as if she had discerned the hidden severity of the situation and was waiting for the rest of us to catch up. Everyone looked from Arnetta to Daphne. It was, after all, Daphne who had supposedly been called the name, but Daphne sat on the bare cabin floor, flipping through the pages of the Girl Scout handbook, eyebrows arched in mock wonder, as if the handbook were a catalogue full of bright and startling foreign costumes. Janice broke the silence. She clapped her hands to broach her idea of a plan.

"They gone be sleeping," she whispered conspiratorially, "then we gone sneak into they cabin, then we gone put daddy longlegs in they sleeping bags. Then they'll wake up. Then we gone beat 'em up till they flat as frying pans!" She jammed her fist into the palm of her hand, then made a sizzling sound.

Janice's country accent was laughable, her looks homely, her jumpy acrobatics embarrassing to behold. Arnetta and Octavia volleyed amused, arrogant smiles whenever Janice opened her mouth, but Janice never caught the hint, spoke whenever she wanted, fluttered around Arnetta and Octavia futilely offering her opinions to their departing backs. Whenever Arnetta and Octavia shooed her away, Janice loitered until the two would finally sigh, "What *is* it, Miss Caucasoid? What do you want?"

"Oh shut up, Janice," Octavia said, letting a fingered loop of hair fall to her waist as though just the sound of Janice's voice had ruined the fun of her hair twisting.

"All right," Arnetta said, standing up. "We're going to have a secret meeting and talk about what we're going to do."

The word "secret" had a built-in importance. Everyone gravely nodded her head. The modifier form of the word had more clout than the noun. A secret meant nothing; it was like gossip: just a bit of unpleasant knowledge about someone who happened to be someone other than yourself. A secret *meeting*, or a secret *club*, was entirely different.

That was when Arnetta turned to me, as though she knew doing so was both a compliment and a charity.

"Snot, you're not going to be a bitch and tell Mrs. Margolin, are you?"

I had been called "Snot" ever since first grade, when I'd sneezed in class and two long ropes of mucus had splattered a nearby girl.

"Hey," I said. "Maybe you didn't hear them right—I mean—"

"Are you gonna tell on us or not?" was all Arnetta wanted to know, and by the time the question was asked, the rest of our Brownie troop looked at me as though they'd already decided their course of action, me being the only impediment. As though it were all a simple matter of patriotism.

Camp Crescendo used to double as a high school band and field hockey camp until an arching field hockey ball landed on the clasp of a girl's metal barrette, knifing a skull nerve, paralyzing the right side of her body. The camp closed down for a few years, and the girl's teammates built a memorial, filling the spot on which the girl fell with hockey balls, upon which they had painted—all in nail polish—get-well tidings, flowers, and hearts. The balls were still stacked there, like a shrine of ostrich eggs embedded in the ground.

On the second day of camp, Troop 909 was dancing around the mound of nail polish–decorated hockey balls, their limbs jangling awkwardly, their cries like the constant summer squeal of an amusement park. There was a stream that bordered the field hockey lawn, and the girls from my troop settled next to it, scarfing down the last of lunch: sandwiches made from salami and slices of tomato that had gotten waterlogged from the melting ice in the cooler. From the stream bank, Arnetta eyed the Troop 909 girls, scrutinizing their movements to glean inspiration for battle.

"Man," Arnetta said, "we could bum-rush them right now if that damn lady would *leave*."

The 909 troop leader was a white woman with the severe pageboy hairdo of an ancient Egyptian. She lay sprawled on a picnic blanket, sphinxlike, eating a banana, sometimes holding it out in front of her like a microphone. Beside her sat a girl slowly flapping one hand like a bird with a broken wing. Occasionally, the leader would call out the names of girls who'd attempted leapfrogs and flips, or of girls who yelled too loudly or strayed far from the circle.

"I'm just glad Big Fat Mama's not following us here," Octavia said. "At least we don't have to worry about her." Mrs. Margolin, Octavia assured us, was having her Afternoon Devotional, shrouded in mosquito netting, in a clearing she'd found. Mrs. Hedy was cleaning mud from her espadrilles in the cabin.

"I handled them." Arnetta sucked on her teeth and proudly grinned. "I told her we was going to gather leaves."

"Gather leaves," Octavia said, nodding respectfully. "That's a good one. They're so mad-crazy about this camping thing." She looked from ground to sky, sky to ground. Her hair hung down her back in two braids like a squaw's. "I mean, I really don't know why it's even called *camping*—all we ever do with Nature is find some twigs and say something like, 'Wow, this fell from a tree.'" She then studied her sandwich. With two disdainful fingers, she picked out a slice of dripping tomato, the sections congealed with red slime. She pitched it into the stream embrowned with dead leaves and the murky effigies of other dead things, but in the opaque water a group of small silver-brown fish appeared. They surrounded the tomato and nibbled.

"Look!" Janice cried. "Fishes! Fishes!" As she scrambled to the edge of the stream to watch, a covey of insects threw up tantrums from the wheatgrass and nettle, a throng of tiny electric machines, all going at once. Octavia snuck up behind Janice as if to push her in. Daphne and I exchanged terrified looks. It seemed as though only we knew that Octavia was close enough—and bold enough—to actually push Janice into the stream. Janice turned around quickly, but Octavia was already staring serenely into the still water as though she were gathering some sort of courage from it. "What's so funny?" Janice said, eyeing them all suspiciously.

Elise began humming the tune to "Karma Chameleon," all the girls joining in, their hums light and facile. Janice began to hum, against everyone else, the high-octane opening chords of "Beat It."

"I love me some Michael Jackson," Janice said when she'd finished humming, smacking her lips as though Michael Jackson were a favorite meal. "I will marry Michael Jackson."

Before anyone had a chance to impress upon Janice the impossibility of this, Arnetta suddenly rose, made a sun visor of her hand, and watched Troop 909 leave the field hockey lawn.

"Dammit!" she said. "We've got to get them *alone*."

"They won't ever be alone," I said. All the rest of the girls looked at me. If I spoke even a word, I could count on someone calling me Snot, but everyone seemed to think that we could beat up these girls; no one entertained the thought that they might fight *back*. "The only time they'll be unsupervised is in the bathroom."

"Oh shut up, Snot," Octavia said.

But Arnetta slowly nodded her head. "The bathroom," she said. "The bathroom," she said, again and again. "The bathroom! The bathroom!" She cheered so blissfully that I thought for a moment she was joking.

According to Octavia's watch, it took us five minutes to hike to the restrooms, which were midway between our cabin and Troop 909's. Inside, the mirrors above the sinks returned only the vaguest of reflections, as though someone had taken a scouring pad to their surfaces to obscure the shine. Pine needles, leaves, and dirty flattened wads of chewing gum covered the floor like a mosaic. Webs of hair matted the drain in the middle of the floor. Above the sinks and below the mirrors, stacks of folded white paper towels lay on a long metal counter. Shaggy white balls of paper towels sat on the sink tops in a line like corsages on display. A thread of floss snaked from a wad of tissues dotted with the faint red-pink of blood. One of those white girls, I thought, had just lost a tooth.

The restroom looked almost the same as it had the night before, but it somehow seemed stranger now. We had never noticed the wooden rafters before, coming together in great V's. We were, it seemed, inside a whale, viewing the ribs of the roof of its mouth.

"Wow. It's a mess," Elise said.

"You can say that again."

Arnetta leaned against the doorjamb of a restroom stall. "This is where they'll be again," she said. Just seeing the place, just having a plan, seemed to satisfy her. "We'll go in and talk to them. You know, 'How you doing?

How long will you be here?' that sort of thing. Then Octavia and I are gonna tell them what happens when they call any one of us a nigger."

"I'm going to say something, too," Janice said.

Arnetta considered this. "Sure," she said. "Of course. Whatever you want."

Janice pointed her finger like a gun at Octavia and rehearsed the line she'd thought up, "'We're gonna teach you a *lesson.*' That's what I'm going to say." She narrowed her eyes like a TV mobster. "'We're gonna teach you little girls a lesson!'"

With the back of her hand, Octavia brushed Janice's finger away. "You couldn't teach me to shit in a toilet."

"But," I said, "what if they say, 'We didn't say that. We didn't call anyone a N-I-G-G-E-R'?"

"Snot," Arnetta sighed. "Don't think. Just fight. If you even know how."

Everyone laughed while Daphne stood there. Arnetta gently laid her hand on Daphne's shoulder. "Daphne. You don't have to fight. We're doing this for you."

Daphne walked to the counter, took a clean paper towel, and carefully unfolded it like a map. With this, she began to pick up the trash all around. Everyone watched.

"C'mon," Arnetta said to everyone. "Let's beat it." We all ambled toward the restroom doorway, where the sunshine made one large white rectangle of light. We were immediately blinded and shielded our eyes with our hands, our forearms.

"Daphne?" Arnetta asked. "Are you coming?"

We all looked back at the girl, who was bending, the thin of her back hunched like a maid caught in stage limelight. Stray strands of her hair were lit nearly transparent, thin fiber-optic threads. She did not nod yes to the question, nor did she shake her head no. She abided, bent. Then she began again, picking up leaves, wads of paper, the cotton fluff innards from a torn stuffed toy. She did it so methodically, so exquisitely, so humbly, she must have been trained. I thought of those dresses she wore, faded and old, yet so pressed and clean; I then saw the poverty in them, I then could imagine her mother, cleaning the houses of others, returning home, weary.

"I guess she's not coming."

We left her, heading back to our cabin, over pine needles and leaves, taking the path full of shade.

"What about our secret meeting?" Elise asked.

Arnetta enunciated in a way that defied contradiction: "We just had it."

Just as we caught sight of our cabin, Arnetta violently swerved away from Octavia. "You farted," she said.

Octavia began to sashay, as if on a catwalk, then proclaimed, in a Hollywood-starlet voice, "My farts smell like perfume."

It was nearing our bedtime, but in the lengthening days of spring, the sun had not yet set.

"Hey, your mama's coming," Arnetta said to Octavia when she saw Mrs. Hedy walk toward the cabin, sniffling. When Octavia's mother wasn't giving bored, parochial orders, she sniffled continuously, mourning an imminent divorce from her husband. She might begin a sentence, "I don't know what Robert will do when Octavia and I are gone. Who'll buy him cigarettes?" and Octavia would hotly whisper "*Mama*" in a way that meant: Please don't talk about our problems in front of everyone. Please shut up.

But when Mrs. Hedy began talking about her husband, thinking about her husband, seeing clouds shaped like the head of her husband, she couldn't be quiet, and no one could ever dislodge her from the comfort of her own woe. Only one thing could perk her up—Brownie songs. If the rest of the girls were quiet, and Mrs. Hedy was in her dopey sorrowful mood, she would say, "Y'all know I like those songs, girls. Why don't you sing one?" Everyone would groan except me and Daphne. I, for one, liked some of the songs.

"C'mon, everybody," Octavia said drearily. "She likes 'The Brownie Song' best."

We sang, loud enough to reach Mrs. Hedy:

> I've something in my pocket;
> It belongs across my face.
> And I keep it very close at hand in a most convenient place.
> I'm sure you couldn't guess it
> If you guessed a long, long while.
> So I'll take it out and put it on—
> It's a great big Brownie Smile!

"The Brownie Song" was supposed to be sung as though we were elves in a workshop, singing as we merrily cobbled shoes, but everyone except me hated the song and sang it like a maudlin record, played at the most sluggish of rpms.

"That was good," Mrs. Hedy said, closing the cabin door behind her. "Wasn't that nice, Linda?"

"Praise God," Mrs. Margolin answered without raising her head from the chore of counting out Popsicle sticks for the next day's session of crafts.

"Sing another one," Mrs. Hedy said, with a sort of joyful aggression, like a drunk I'd once seen who'd refused to leave a Korean grocery.

"God, Mama, get over it," Octavia whispered in a voice meant only for Arnetta, but Mrs. Hedy heard it and started to leave the cabin.

"Don't go," Arnetta said. She ran after Mrs. Hedy and held her by the arm. "We haven't finished singing." She nudged us with a single look. "Let's sing 'The Friends Song.' For Mrs. Hedy."

Although I liked some of the songs, I hated this one:

> Make new friends
> But keep the o-old,
> One is silver
> And the other gold.

If most of the girls in my troop could be any type of metal, they'd be bunched-up wads of tinfoil maybe, or rusty iron nails you had to get tetanus shots for.

"No, no, no," Mrs. Margolin said before anyone could start in on "The Friends Song." "An uplifting song. Something to lift her up and take her mind off all these earthly burdens."

Arnetta and Octavia rolled their eyes. Everyone knew what song Mrs. Margolin was talking about, and no one, no one, wanted to sing it.

"Please, no," a voice called out. "Not 'The Doughnut Song.'"

"Please not 'The Doughnut Song,'" Octavia pleaded.

"I'll brush my teeth twice if I don't have to sing 'The Doughnut—'"

"Sing!" Mrs. Margolin demanded.

We sang:

> Life without Jesus is like a do-ough-nut!
> Like a do-ooough-nut!
> Like a do-ooough-nut!
> Life without Jesus is like a do-ough-nut!
> There's a hole in the middle of my soul!

There were other verses, involving other pastries, but we stopped after the first one and cast glances toward Mrs. Margolin to see if we could gain a reprieve. Mrs. Margolin's eyes fluttered blissfully, half-asleep.

"Awww," Mrs. Hedy said, as though giant Mrs. Margolin were a cute baby. "Mrs. Margolin's had a long day."

"Yes indeed," Mrs. Margolin answered. "If you don't mind, I might just go to the lodge where the beds are. I haven't been the same since the operation."

I had not heard of this operation, or when it had occurred, since Mrs. Margolin had never missed the once-a-week Brownie meetings, but I could see from Daphne's face that she was concerned, and I could see that the other girls had decided that Mrs. Margolin's operation must have happened long ago in some remote time unconnected to our own. Nevertheless, they put on sad faces. We had all been taught that adulthood was full of sorrow and pain, taxes and bills, dreaded work and dealings with whites, sickness, and death.

"Go right ahead, Linda," Mrs. Hedy said. "I'll watch the girls." Mrs. Hedy seemed to forget about divorce for a moment; she looked at us with dewy eyes, as if we were mysterious, furry creatures. Meanwhile, Mrs. Margolin walked through the maze of sleeping bags until she found her own. She gathered a neat stack of clothes and pajamas slowly, as though doing so were almost painful. She took her toothbrush, her toothpaste, her pillow. "All right!" Mrs. Margolin said, addressing us all from the threshold of the cabin. "Be in bed by nine." She said it with a twinkle in her voice, as though she were letting us know she was allowing us to be naughty and stay up till nine-fifteen.

"C'mon, everybody," Arnetta said after Mrs. Margolin left. "Time for us to wash up."

Everyone watched Mrs. Hedy closely, wondering whether she would insist on coming with us since it was night, making a fight with Troop 909 nearly impossible. Troop 909 would soon be in the bathroom, washing their faces, brushing their teeth—completely unsuspecting of our ambush.

"We won't be long," Arnetta said. "We're old enough to go to the restroom by ourselves."

Mrs. Hedy pursed her lips at this dilemma. "Well, I guess you Brownies are almost Girl Scouts, right?"

"Right!"

"Just one more badge," Drema said.

"And about," Octavia droned, "a million more cookies to sell." Octavia looked at all of us. *Now's our chance*, her face seemed to say, but our chance to do *what* I didn't exactly know.

Finally, Mrs. Hedy walked to the doorway where Octavia stood, dutifully waiting to say good-bye and looking bored doing it. Mrs. Hedy held Octavia's chin. "You'll be good?"

"Yes, Mama."

"And remember to pray for me and your father? If I'm asleep when you get back?"

"Yes, Mama."

When the other girls had finished getting their toothbrushes and washcloths and flashlights for the group restroom trip, I was drawing pictures of tiny birds with too many feathers. Daphne was sitting on her sleeping bag, reading.

"You're not going to come?" Octavia asked.

Daphne shook her head.

"I'm also gonna stay, too," I said. "I'll go to the restroom when Daphne and Mrs. Hedy go."

Arnetta leaned down toward me and whispered so that Mrs. Hedy, who had taken over Mrs. Margolin's task of counting Popsicle sticks, couldn't hear. "No, Snot. If we get in trouble, you're going to get in trouble with the rest of us."

We made our way through the darkness by flashlight. The tree branches that had shaded us just hours earlier, along the same path, now looked like arms sprouting menacing hands. The stars sprinkled the sky like spilled salt. They seemed fastened to the darkness, high up and holy, their places fixed and definite as we stirred beneath them.

Some, like me, were quiet because we were afraid of the dark; others were talking like crazy for the same reason.

"Wow," Drema said, looking up. "Why are all the stars out here? I never see stars back on Oneida Street."

"It's a camping trip, that's why," Octavia said. 'You're supposed to see stars on camping trips."

Janice said, "This place smells like the air freshener my mother uses."

"These woods are *pine*," Elise said. "Your mother probably uses pine air freshener."

Janice mouthed an exaggerated "Oh," nodding her head as though she just then understood one of the world's great secrets.

No one talked about fighting. Everyone was afraid enough just walking through the infinite deep of the woods. Even without seeing anyone's face, I could tell this wasn't about Daphne being called a nigger. The word that had started it all seemed melted now into some deeper, unnameable feeling. Even though I didn't want to fight, was afraid of fighting, I felt as though I were part of the rest of the troop, as though I were defending something. We trudged against the slight incline of the path, Arnetta leading the way. I wondered, looking at her back, what she could be thinking.

"You know," I said, "their leader will be there. Or they won't even be there. It's dark already. Last night the sun was still in the sky. I'm sure they're already finished."

"Whose flashlight is this?" Arnetta said, shaking the weakening beam of the light she was holding. "It's out of batteries.' "

Octavia handed Arnetta her flashlight. And that's when I saw it. The bathroom was just ahead.

But the girls were there. We could hear them before we could see them.

"Octavia and I will go in first so they'll think there's just two of us. Then wait till I say, 'We're gonna teach you a lesson,' " Arnetta said. "Then bust in. That'll surprise them."

"That's what I was supposed to say," Janice said.

Arnetta went inside, Octavia next to her. Janice followed, and the rest of us waited outside.

They were in there for what seemed like whole minutes, but something was wrong. Arnetta hadn't given the signal yet. I was with the girls outside when I heard one of the Troop 909 girls say, "NO. That did NOT happen!"

That was to be expected, that they'd deny the whole thing. What I hadn't expected was *the voice* in which the denial was said. The girl sounded as though her tongue were caught in her mouth. "That's a BAD word!" the girl continued. "We don't say BAD words!"

"Let's go in," Elise said.

"No," Drema said. "I don't want to. What if we get beat up?"

"Snot?" Elise turned to me, her flashlight blinding. It was the first time anyone had asked my opinion, though I knew they were just asking because they were afraid.

"I say we go inside, just to see what's going on."

"But Arnetta didn't give us the signal," Drema said. "She's supposed to say, 'We're going to teach you a lesson,' and I didn't hear her say it."

"C'mon," I said. "Let's just go in."

We went inside. There we found the white girls, but about five girls were huddled up next to one big girl. I instantly knew she was the owner of the voice we'd heard. Arnetta and Octavia inched toward us as soon as we entered.

"Where's Janice?" Elise asked, then we heard a flush. "Oh."

"I think," Octavia said, whispering to Elise, "they're retarded."

"We ARE NOT retarded!" the big girl said, though it was obvious that she was. That they all were. The girls around her began to whimper.

"They're just pretending," Arnetta said, trying to convince herself. "I know they are."

Octavia turned to Arnetta. "Arnetta. Let's just leave."

Janice came out of a stall, happy and relieved, then she suddenly remembered her line, pointed to the big girl, and said, "We're gonna teach you a lesson."

"Shut up, Janice," Octavia said, but her heart was not in it. Arnetta's face was set in a lost, deep scowl. Octavia turned to the big girl, and said loudly, slowly, as if they were all deaf, "We're going to leave. It was nice meeting you, okay? You don't have to tell anyone that we were here. Okay?"

"Why not?" said the big girl, like a taunt. When she spoke, her lips did not meet, her mouth did not close. Her tongue grazed the roof of her mouth, like a little pink fish. "You'll get in trouble. I know. I know."

Arnetta got back her old cunning. "If you said anything, then you'd be a tattletale."

The girl looked sad for a moment, then perked up quickly. A flash of genius crossed her face: "I *like* tattletale."

"It's all right, girls. It's gonna be all right!" the 909 troop leader said. It was as though someone had instructed all of Troop 909 to cry at once. The troop leader had girls under her arm, and all the rest of the girls crowded about her. It reminded me of a hog I'd seen on a field trip, where all the little hogs would gather about the mother at feeding time, latching on to her teats. The 909 troop leader had come into the bathroom shortly after the big girl threatened to tell. Then the ranger came, then, once the ranger had radioed the station, Mrs. Margolin arrived with Daphne in tow.

The ranger had left the restroom area, but everyone else was huddled just outside, swatting mosquitoes.

"Oh. They *will* apologize," Mrs. Margolin said to the 909 troop leader, but Mrs. Margolin said this so angrily, I knew she was speaking more to us than to the other troop leader. "When their parents find out, every one a them will be on punishment."

"It's all right. It's all right," the 909 troop leader reassured Mrs. Margolin. Her voice lilted in the same way it had when addressing the girls. She smiled the whole time she talked. She was like one of those TV cooking show women who talk and dice onions and smile all at the same time.

"See. It could have happened. I'm not calling your girls fibbers or anything." She shook her head ferociously from side to side, her Egyptian-style pageboy flapping against her cheeks like heavy drapes. "It *could* have happened, see. Our girls are *not* retarded. They are *delayed* learners." She said this in a syrupy instructional voice, as though our troop might be delayed learners as well. "We're from the Decatur Children's Academy. Many of them just have special needs."

"Now we won't be able to walk to the bathroom by ourselves!" the big girl said.

"Yes you will," the troop leader said, "but maybe we'll wait till we get back to Decatur—"

"I don't want to wait!" the girl said. "I want my Independence patch!"

The girls in my troop were entirely speechless. Arnetta looked as though she were soon to be tortured but was determined not to appear weak. Mrs. Margolin pursed her lips solemnly and said, "Bless them, Lord. Bless them."

In contrast, the Troop 909 leader was full of words and energy. "Some of our girls are echolalic—" She smiled and happily presented one of the girls hanging on to her, but the girl widened her eyes in horror and violently withdrew herself from the center of attention, as though she sensed she were being sacrificed for the village sins. "Echolalic," the troop leader continued. "That means they will say whatever they hear, like an echo—that's where the word comes from. It comes from 'echo.'" She ducked her head apologetically. "I mean, not all of them have the most *progressive* of parents, so if they heard a bad word they might have repeated it. But I guarantee it would not have been *intentional*."

Arnetta spoke. "I saw her say the word. I heard her." She pointed to a small girl, smaller than any of us, wearing an oversized T-shirt that read: EAT BERTHA'S MUSSELS.

The troop leader shook her head and smiled. "That's impossible. She doesn't speak. She can, but she doesn't."

Arnetta furrowed her brow. "No. It wasn't her. That's right. It was *her*."

The girl Arnetta pointed to grinned as though she'd been paid a compliment. She was the only one from either troop actually wearing a full uniform: the mocha-colored A-line shift, the orange ascot, the sash covered with patches, though all the same one—the Try-It patch. She took a few steps toward Arnetta and made a grand sweeping gesture toward the sash. "See," she said, full of self-importance, "I'm a Brownie." I had a hard time imagining this girl calling anyone a "nigger"; the girl looked perpetually delighted, as though she would have cuddled up with a grizzly if someone had let her.

•   •   •

On the fourth morning, we boarded the bus to go home.

The previous day had been spent building miniature churches from Popsicle sticks. We hardly left the cabin. Mrs. Margolin and Mrs. Hedy guarded us so closely, almost no one talked for the entire day.

Even on the day of departure from Camp Crescendo, all was serious and silent. The bus ride began quietly enough. Arnetta had to sit beside Mrs. Margolin, Octavia had to sit beside her mother. I sat beside Daphne, who gave me her prize journal without a word of explanation.

"You don't want it?"

She shook her head no. It was empty.

Then Mrs. Hedy began to weep. "Octavia," Mrs. Hedy said to her daughter without looking at her, "I'm going to sit with Mrs. Margolin. All right?"

Arnetta exchanged seats with Mrs. Hedy. With the two women up front, Elise felt it safe to speak. "Hey," she said, then she set her face into a placid vacant stare, trying to imitate that of a Troop 909 girl. Emboldened, Arnetta made a gesture of mock pride toward an imaginary sash, the way the girl in full uniform had done. Then they all made a game of it, trying to do the most exaggerated imitations of the Troop 909 girls, all without speaking, all without laughing loud enough to catch the women's attention.

Daphne looked at her shoes, white with sneaker polish. I opened the journal she'd given me. I looked out the window, trying to decide what to write, searching for lines, but nothing could compare with the lines Daphne had written, *"My father, the veteran,"* my favorite line of all time. The line replayed itself in my head, and I gave up trying to write.

By then, it seemed as though the rest of the troop had given up making fun of the 909 girls. They were now quietly gossiping about who had passed notes to whom in school. For a moment the gossiping fell off, and all I heard was the hum of the bus as we sped down the road and the muffled sounds of Mrs. Hedy and Mrs. Margolin talking about serious things.

"You know," Octavia whispered, "why did *we* have to be stuck at a camp with retarded girls? You know?"

"*You* know why," Arnetta answered. She narrowed her eyes like a cat. "My mama and I were in the mall in Buckhead, and this white lady just kept looking at us. I mean, like we were foreign or something. Like we were from China."

"What did the woman say?" Elise asked.

"Nothing," Arnetta said. "She didn't say nothing."

A few girls quietly nodded their heads.

"There was this time," I said, "when my father and I were in the mall and—"

"Oh, shut up, Snot," Octavia said.

I stared at Octavia, then rolled my eyes from her to the window. As I watched the trees blur, I wanted nothing more than to be through with it all: the bus ride, the troop, school—all of it. But we were going home. I'd see the same girls in school the next day. We were on a bus, and there was nowhere else to go.

"Go on, Laurel," Daphne said to me. It was the first time she'd spoken the whole trip, and she'd said my name. I turned to her and smiled weakly so as not to cry, hoping she'd remember when I'd tried to be her friend, thinking maybe that her gift of the journal was an invitation of friendship. But she didn't smile back. All she said was, "What happened?"

I studied the girls, waiting for Octavia to tell me to "shut up" again before I even had a chance to utter another word, but everyone was amazed that Daphne had spoken. I gathered my voice. "Well," I said. "My father and I were in this mall, but *I* was the one doing the staring." I stopped and glanced from face to face. I continued. "There were these white people dressed like Puritans or something, but they weren't Puritans. They were Mennonites. They're these people who, if you ask them to do a favor, like paint your porch or something, they have to do it. It's in their rules."

"That sucks," someone said.

"C'mon," Arnetta said. "You're lying."

"I am not."

"How do you know that's not just some story someone made up?" Elise asked, her head cocked, full of daring. "I mean, who's gonna do whatever you ask?"

"It's not made up. I know because when I was looking at them, my father said, 'See those people. If you ask them to do something, they'll do it. Anything you want.'"

No one would call anyone's father a liar. Then they'd have to fight the person, but Drema parsed her words carefully. "How does your *father* know that's not just some story? Huh?"

"Because," I said, "he went up to the man and asked him would he paint our porch, and the man said, 'Yes.' It's their religion."

"Man, I'm glad I'm a Baptist," Elise said, shaking her head in sympathy for the Mennonites.

"So did the guy do it?" Drema asked, scooting closer to hear if the story got juicy.

"Yeah," I said. "His whole family was with him. My dad drove them to our house. They all painted our porch. The woman and girl were in bonnets and long, long skirts with buttons up to their necks. The guy wore this weird hat and these huge suspenders."

"Why," Arnetta asked archly, as though she didn't believe a word, "would someone pick a *porch*? If they'll do anything, why not make them paint the whole *house*? Why not ask for a hundred bucks?"

I thought about it, and I remembered the words my father had said about them painting our porch, though I had never seemed to think about his words after he'd said them.

"He said," I began, only then understanding the words as they uncoiled from my mouth, "it was the only time he'd have a white man on his knees doing something for a black man for free."

I remembered the Mennonites bending like Daphne had bent, cleaning the restroom. I remembered the dark blue of their bonnets, the black of their shoes. They painted the porch as though scrubbing a floor. I was already trembling before Daphne asked quietly, "Did he thank them?"

I looked out the window. I could not tell which were the thoughts and which were the trees. "No," I said, and suddenly knew there was something mean in the world that I could not stop.

Arnetta laughed. "If I asked them to take off their long skirts and bonnets and put on some jeans, they would do it?"

And Daphne's voice—quiet, steady: "Maybe they would. Just to be nice."

1. How is dialogue used in this story? How important are the scenes (as opposed to the narration)?
2. How does the dialogue characterize the narrator—both in what she says herself and how she responds to what other people say?
3. What do you think of the colloquialism of the dialogue? Does it work for you? Does it seem realistic?

Winner Take Nothing

BERNARD COOPER

When I received word informing me I'd won the PEN/Ernest Hemingway Award for my first book, I held the letter in trembling hands while the following thoughts, in precisely this order, shot through my head:

I won the Ernest Hemingway Award!

I don't deserve it.

My father has heard of Ernest Hemingway!

There I stood, elated by a last-ditch chance to impress my dad.

Not that my father disapproved of my being a writer; he understood it to the extent that he could understand my gambling with my life in order to pursue a profession he found frivolous and fiscally unsound. Whenever I mentioned to him that I'd had something published in a magazine or literary journal, the first question he'd ask was "How much they pay you?" A retired attorney, he probably thought of "they" as a faceless jury, twelve arbiters of taste. He'd pose this question with considerable enthusiasm, arching his white eyebrows, his face a picture of impending pride. Imagine telling a man who keeps a wad of twenties in a gold money clip shaped like a dollar sign that, after working on a piece of writing for months, you've been compensated with a complimentary copy of the publication. "You're kidding," he'd say, shaking his head as if I'd told him I'd been duped in a shell game.

Over the years, I'd cultivated a certain temperance when sharing literary news with my father: I'd come to consider it unfortunate but not devastating that he was unable to recognize the arc—or was it the bump?—of my career. Still, I ached to have him slap me on the back, wanted to hear his unstinting praise and in it the honeyed pronouncement: son.

To this end, I once gave him an essay of mine to read. It was a brief reminiscence about my mother, who, up until her death, dreamed of writing a book into which she'd cram every anecdote she could think of, starting with her emigration from Russia to the United States at the age of two. She never wrote so much as a word, but the persistence of her wish struck me as oddly noble, and the tone of the piece was, I believed, unmistakably fond. And so, one night at the Brass Pan, the restaurant where my father and I occasionally met for dinner, I handed him the pages, neatly stapled. Before I let go of the manuscript (feeling him tug it from across the table was the closest I'd come to his tangible enthusiasm), I told him I hoped he'd enjoy reading it.

Days went by. Weeks. Months. For nearly half a year, in all the times we saw each other or spoke on the phone, he never mentioned the essay, and pride prevented me from coming right out and asking whether he'd read it. If it hadn't been for a chokingly potent vodka tonic I drank during one of our dinners, I might not have asked him to this day.

"Dad, you've never mentioned the essay I wrote about Mom."

"Well," sighed my father, shrugging his shoulders. "What can I tell you? You wrote down your opinion."

In the dim light of the restaurant, he looked anything but adversarial, his brown eyes peering at me over the rim of his bifocals. I took another swig of vodka. My father, I had to admit, had managed perfectly well without literature, and I had no illusions that writing, especially mine, could enrich his life. At eighty-six he chiefly read *TV Guide*, a map by which he navigated nights in front of the Sony console, its huge screen the only source of light. He also subscribed to *Consumer Reports*, but largely, I think, to sustain through retirement the image he had of himself as a citizen with buying power. The issues were stacked on a shelf next to his law books—and a yellowing paperback copy of *The Snows of Kilimanjaro*.

My father wasn't the first person I called with news of the award, but when I dialed his number and invoked the name of Hemingway, his "Oh!" was as round and buoyant as a bubble. For a moment, I thought the elusive approval I'd wanted might be close at hand, compensation for his years of disinterest in my work. In much of that work, I'd tried to capture the moodiness with which he'd presided over my childhood: a C on my report card, say, could meet with his indifference or detonate his rage. One never knew what familial infraction or offhand remark might cause him to suddenly leave the room and brood for hours. He was also capable of lavish generosity and bursts of goofy humor, and whenever these traits prevailed, I finally felt at peace with a man whose livelihood was, as he liked to put it, suing the pants off people.

"Listen," he said, "we'll fly to New York for the award ceremony, share a room and take in some Broadway shows." I was stunned by his offer, and more than a little touched. Since he had no compunction about expressing bemusement at my small successes, it never occurred to me that he might need to take an active part in my large ones.

I told my father that nothing could make me happier than knowing he was proud of me, and terrific as a trip with him sounded, I wouldn't have time to go to Broadway shows or give him the attention he deserved. Besides, I'd already made plans to go with Brian, the man I'd lived with for many years, our hotel and flight already booked. I offered to take my father to the Brass Pan so we could celebrate properly, and suggested the three of us take a vacation together another time, when I could relax and we could really enjoy ourselves. "I hope you understand," I said.

After I stopped talking, I gave my little speech high marks; it had been, I thought, a good mixture of respect and autonomy. But the longer he remained silent, the more aware I became of the telephone's static, a sound growing vast, oceanic. "Dad?"

"Fine," he said. "If that's what you want."

•   •   •

The plane flight, as always, made me claustrophobic. But when panic finally gave way to the Valium I'd taken twenty minutes before takeoff, my hands and feet grew rubbery, the view of earth abstract.

Once inside the terminal at JFK, the firm ground acted as a conduit, diffusing fear. At the baggage claim, watching luggage spill onto the carousel, it finally dawned on me that I had survived the flight to receive an award. Sunlight burned through a bank of windows. People swarmed toward a fleet of cabs and were whisked away to meetings and reunions. Possibility charged the air, dense, electric. In my happiness, I turned to Brian and faced my father.

At first I thought I might be drugged or dreaming, though by then, only the mildest trace of Valium remained in my system. I looked at him and couldn't speak, the entire busy terminal contracting to a point the size of his face. Was he omnipresent like Santa Claus or God? Dad looked back and blithely smiled.

"Surprise," he said.

"How . . .?" I sputtered.

"Your plane. I went first class."

Suddenly, I understood that all the questions he'd asked about the details of my trip—time of departure, name of the airline—questions I'd interpreted as paternal concern, were part of a perfectly executed plan.

Brian, who at first had been as incredulous as I, rushed in to fill the conspicuous silence. He shook my father's hand. "Are you staying at our hotel?" he asked.

I recalled with a start that we'd booked a room at a gay hotel. "I'm at the Warwick," said my father. "Quite a fancy place, according to the Automobile Club." Two familiar carryalls were making aimless circles in the periphery of my vision, and before I knew what I was doing, I yanked them off the carousel. Vacillating between guilt and fury, I felt like a small unstable electron. "We're leaving," I announced. I fled toward the taxi stand, leaving Brian no choice but to dash after me.

"Share a ride?" my father shouted. I didn't look back.

Once we settled into our hotel room, I began to worry that I'd acted rashly. Had I been a different person, I might have poked my father in the ribs and teased him for being a stubborn coot. But to be a different person I would have to have been raised by a different dad. Mine was an old Jewish genie who materialized wherever he willed and granted any wish—as long as it was his.

When I called the Warwick, my father answered on the second ring. "We'd better have a talk," I said.

"It's your dime."

"I thought you understood I wanted to do this on my own."

"Fine. I'll pack my goddamn bags and go home."

"No. I want you to stay now that you're here. I'm just trying to explain why I reacted the way I did at the airport."

"Now you explained it. Is that what you wanted to talk about?"

There had to be more. During the cab ride, I'd rehearsed ways to tell him that his surprise was an intrusion disguised as kindness, a success usurped. But now I couldn't recall what I'd wanted to say or understand why we each found it so important to win the other's capitulation.

"We'll have lunch tomorrow," he said.

The dining room at the Warwick, with its ambient chimes of silverware and ice, offered a quiet retreat from the city. My father looked small and harmless as he sat waiting for us at a table. He peered around the spacious room, bifocals flashing, hands folded before him in a boyish pose, almost contrite. As Brian and I walked toward the table, it struck me that my father was not at all the giant of the nursery I was prone to imagine; when I didn't have the actual man before me, he ballooned into myth.

A somewhat leery conviviality arose as we sat down.

"So, Mr. Cooper," asked Brian, "what have you been doing?"

My father toyed with the silverware. "Nothing much. I watched a little TV."

"What did you watch, Dad?"

"How about that. I can't remember."

Brian and I looked at each other.

"Is there anybody you know in New York you could go to dinner with tonight?" Please, I prayed.

"I got relatives in Jersey. Or used to twenty years ago. I should look them up next time I'm here." His hearing aid squealed with feedback, and he fiddled with its tiny dial.

"The thing is, Dad, we can't go to dinner with you tonight."

"I know," he said curtly. "You're very busy."

The maître d' brought us huge glossy menus, the covers printed to look like marble. I opened mine, expecting an engraving of the Ten Commandments: Thou shalt honor thy father, who gazeth at the entrées. Without lifting his eyes from the menu, he waved his hand in a gesture of largesse. "Get whatever you want. Sky's the limit."

•   •   •

The next day, I added an additional paragraph to my acceptance speech. In it I thanked my father for reading me stories as a child. His rapt voice had transported me, I wrote, and his enthusiasm for telling tales had introduced me to the power of language. I wasn't certain whether my father had, in fact, read me stories as a child, but neither he nor I would object to the sentimental prospect. Collusion, after all, would be a kind of bond.

At the ceremony that evening, half a dozen awards were handed out. Almost every author who received one had written a speech identical to mine, a sort of apologia in which they expressed surprise at having won and either implied or insisted they were undeserving. The motif of modesty had been exhausted by the time I walked up to the podium, but I'd already revised my speech that morning and was too nervous to change it again. When I came to the part about my father, I looked up from the wrinkled sheet of paper, eager to find him and make eye contact, but I had to look back quickly for fear of losing my place. The paragraph I'd added struck me as a little schmaltzy, and I worried that my apparent sentimentality would discourage people in the audience from buying my book. In the end, it didn't really matter; my homage was meant for Dad's ears alone, and reading it aloud righted the night.

Or so I thought. Immediately after the ceremony, I found my father milling in the crowd and raced up to ask him how he'd liked my speech. "Couldn't hear a damn thing," he said, chuckling at his rotten luck. His hearing aid, unable to distinguish between foreground and background noises, had amplified both. From the rear of the auditorium, my dad could see me reading in the distance, but he heard ubiquitous coughs and whispers, crackling leather coats, the rubbery acoustics of someone chewing gum.

In the year that followed, I began to publish essays and memoirs in a few well-paying magazines. My income was still meager by any standard except my own, but at last I could speak my father's language, a lexicon of hard cold cash.

By that time, however, it had become difficult for him to react to news of my solvency with anything but the foggiest acknowledgment. At the mention of money, he'd look at me wistfully, nod his head, then look away. My father was going broke from the lawsuits he'd recently filed against neighbors and in-laws and strangers. Vines and retaining walls trespassed on his property. A relative missed a payment on a loan. An uninsured idiot dented his fender. Someone blundered, someone would pay, someone would rue the day he was born. He represented himself in court and lost each case. The judges were corrupt, he'd claim, his witnesses inarticulate. Defeat never seemed to give him pause or lessen his zeal for prosecution.

Dad remained fairly amiable during our dinners, and I found it flattering to be one of the few people in his life exempt from litigation. Some nights, when the waitress at the Brass Pan asked for his order, my father stiffened and eyed her with suspicion, tense as a man being cross-examined. She'd hover above him, pencil poised, while he blinked and slowly returned to his senses, finally lifting his tremulous hand and pointing to an entrée on the menu. His decline was apparent in visit after visit. Time took a belated toll, as though weariness had waited until now to irrevocably claim his face; his eyes were puzzled, hair unkempt, chin bristling with patches of stubble.

Eventually, he grew too distracted by his legal battles to return my phone calls. On the rare occasions when we spoke, he said he was too busy to meet me for dinner. More often than not, the answering machine picked up after several rings and played its unassailable refrain: I am not at home at this present time.

After months of an elusiveness he couldn't be coaxed out of, I drove over to my father's house one afternoon to ask why he hadn't returned my calls. Dad answered the door of his Spanish-style house, blinking, beleaguered, but glad to see me. At my insistence, we sat in the dining room to talk. Briefs and appeals and depositions were scattered across the mahogany table, his makeshift desk. Pencils and paper napkins saved his place in the law books he hadn't opened for years, piled now in precarious stacks.

"Are you sure you're not angry at me about something?" I asked. "Because if you are . . ."

My father laughed, fiddled with his hearing aid. "What makes you think I'm angry?"

"You're so . . . unavailable these days."

"How many times do I have to tell you? I'm busy. Swamped. Do you need me to spell it out for you?" He rose to his feet, and I thought he might start to sound out the letters. "You have no idea. No goddamn concept."

I stood too, trying to rise above the childlike vantage point that came with being seated. "All I'm saying is that you have to eat dinner anyway, and we might as well . . ."

"Who says?"

"What?"

"Who says I have to eat dinner? Where is it written? Is it written here?" He hefted a law book and let it slam back onto the table. Stray papers jumped and fluttered. I made a move to calm him down, but he began to prowl around the table, stirring up the sunlit dust. "Don't you ever tell me what to do!"

"Having dinner is not something to do! I mean, it is something to do, but I'm not telling you to do it." At a loss for logic, I was barking back.

"Don't you raise your voice at me!" He rushed up and grabbed the back of my shirt, a hank of fabric twisted in his grip. "I'm eighty-six years old," he shouted. "I'm an old man, and I can do whatever the hell I want whenever the hell I want." He pushed me toward the door, breathing hard, his face red and alien with effort.

"Dad?"

"That's right," he said. When he opened the door, the daylight was blinding. "Don't ever forget that I'm your father. Now get the hell out and don't come back."

Since high school, I've been both taller and stronger than my father, but just as we reached the threshold of the door it occurred to me that I might flatter him into relenting if I let my body be heaved outside as though from an admirable, manly force. Instead of resisting or fighting back, I yielded to his elderly arms.

Acquiescence didn't help. Before the door slammed shut behind me, I turned and glimpsed his indignant figure retreating within my childhood house. The door hit the jamb with a deafening bang, the birds falling silent for half a second before going back to their usual racket.

Daily I relived the particulars: the shirt taut across my chest, the heat of his breath on the back of my neck, the flood of light as the door swung wide. The sheer abruptness and implausibility of what had happened made me worry that perhaps I'd said something inadvertently thoughtless or cruel—a spark to his incendiary temper.

In lieu of an explanation, I started making hypothetical changes in the story. Suppose I hadn't mentioned dinner. Suppose I hadn't raised my voice. Suppose we'd stood instead of sat. Say the day had been cooler, the hour later, the dust motes churning in another direction. Would the outcome of my visit have been any different?

Several nights a week, I had to drive past my boyhood house on the way home from teaching, and the closer I came, the greater its magnetic pull. More than once, I turned the steering wheel at the last minute, aiming my car through a tunnel of trees and parking across the street from his house. The urge to spy on my father was unexplainable, as deep and murky as the darkness it required.

Throughout the first year of our estrangement, my entreaties and apologies and furious demands for contact were recited into his answering machine. On a few occasions, he picked up the phone and then slammed it down at the sound of my voice.

By the second year, resignation took hold. I'd lost the desire to drive by his house or reach him by phone. I recalled that afternoon less often, and when I did, I refused to probe the memory for meaning.

By the third year, his absence settled inside me like a stone, impervious to hope or hurt.

"I realize this phone call must come as an unpleasant surprise," the social worker told me. "But I believe your father's deterioration is significant enough to make legal guardianship a necessary step."

Mr. Gomez assured me that I didn't have to make up my mind right away; it would be several months before the case came before a judge. An anonymous caller had phoned Adult Protective Services to say my father needed help. If I assumed responsibility, my father's Social Security checks would be placed in a trust, and he'd need my permission for every expenditure: medicine, groceries, clothes.

"Careful monetary management is especially crucial in your father's case," said Mr. Gomez. "As you may know, the bank has begun foreclosure on his house."

"I had no idea."

Mr. Gomez cleared his throat. "On a positive note, I should also tell you that your father spoke with great pride about your many accomplishments. What's the name of the book you wrote? He couldn't remember."

I mumbled the title to Mr. Gomez, promised to give our discussion some thought, and said goodbye. I'd become so guarded against any emotion having to do with my father that the prospect of seeing him again roused only a dull ambivalence. After three years, I'd finally decided it was I who didn't want contact with him, a decision that redefined circumstance and made my exile bearable. And now, out of the blue, the county urged a reunion, reminding me (as if I needed to be reminded) that the man was my inescapable relation.

I'd been writing when the phone rang.

"Bernard?"

"Dad?" Saying the word made my mouth go dry.

"I sold the house, and the people who bought it want to move in pretty soon, so I've been cleaning out closets, and I came across all sorts of drawings and photos of yours. You wanna come get them? Is four-thirty good?"

"Four-thirty's good." My assent was automatic, though I wasn't sure I was ready to see him.

"OK. See you later."

"Wait," I blurted. "How have you been?"

"Fine. And you?"

Three years. "I'm fine too."

"Good," he said. "As long as you're fine." His harried voice softened. "Well," he said, "I'm really swamped."

After I'd hung up the phone, I realized he hadn't said hello.

I approached the house with apprehension; who knew what condition I'd find him in? His Cadillac sat in the driveway, dented and missing strips of chrome. Since I'd last spied on the house two years ago, the first-floor windows had been covered with bars. The front door stood behind a wrought-iron grate, and no matter how decorative its design, it made the house look forbidding, aloof.

No sooner had I rung the doorbell than my father appeared behind the bars, jangling keys like a castle keep. All the while, he burbled greetings in the high-pitched voice of his jovial persona. Arms folded across my chest, I couldn't act as if things had been normal, not without damaging a sense of reality that, especially in my father's presence, could founder and bend like a little boy's. "Come on in," he said, unlocking the grate. I found his hospitality suspicious, and much as I wanted to make amends, I also wanted to run the other way. I'd come to think of my boyhood house as a place I'd never visit again, and now that I stood on the verge of return, I practically had to astral-project and give myself a push from behind.

The house was even more crammed with memorabilia than I remembered. He must have strewn souvenirs about the rooms as he cleaned out the closets, a last-minute effort to make his mark on the home he had to forfeit. A velvet painting of JFK hung above the fireplace. A birdcage he'd won on a cruise contained a windup canary whose jerky movements and monotonous song he insisted on demonstrating as soon as I walked in the door. In a sign of either delight or dementia, he watched it warble with childlike glee.

Piled on the coffee table, old boxes contained the egg-tempera paintings I'd done in elementary school, the colors still vibrant though the paint had turned as powdery as talcum. Crude landscapes and blotchy figures called back the distant triumph of being able to shape the world and contain it on a piece of paper. Pictures from photo booths showed a mugging ten-year-old who bore as much resemblance to me now as I to my father; I wanted to warn that oblivious boy of what was to come. I couldn't look at the stuff for long, and I gathered up the boxes, ready to go.

"Sit," said my father. I did.

"What's new?"

"Lots."

"Written any more books of yours?"

"Yes."

"Have they won those Hemingway awards?"

"That's only for a first book."

"I see," he said. "Tell me what else has been going on." He leaned forward in the chair, cocked his good ear in my direction.

"Look, I appreciate your willingness to get together with me, but I think I deserve to know why you haven't spoken to me in three years."

His brows furrowed in puzzlement. "You live, things happen, you go on. That's the way it works."

"That's not the way it works for me."

"Well, the truth of the matter is that you were getting irritated with me about my hearing aid. You were always screaming, 'What? What? I can't hear you! Turn up your damn ear!'"

"First of all, Dad, *you're* the one who shouts 'What? I can't hear you.' Second, I'd never scold you because you're hard of hearing."

"I'm telling you, that's what happened."

"It didn't."

"Did."

"OK. Suppose it did. Is that any reason not to speak to me for three years?"

My father sat back, stared into space, gave the question due consideration. "Yes," he said, lurching forward. "Yes, it is." He looked at his feet, then back at me. "I've lived in this house for fifty years. Do you remember when we moved in?"

"I wasn't born yet."

"Do you remember what day it was?"

It seemed pointless to repeat myself. "Tuesday?" I guessed.

"No," he said. "It was your mother's birthday. Boy, that was a long time ago. I sold the place to two very nice guys. By the way, how's that friend of yours, what's his name?"

"Brian's fine, he . . ."

"What do I need all these rooms for, anyway? It was either sell the house or get kicked out on the street."

I shook my head in commiseration, pretending to know nothing about the foreclosure.

"Some crazy social worker said I shouldn't handle the sale myself. But I showed him. Closed escrow on my own, then told Hernandez to take a hike."

I stopped myself from blurting "Gomez."

"The kicker," he continued, "is that I paid someone to report me to the guy in the first place."

"What!"

"See," said my father. "You do shout 'What.'" He bristled a moment, shifted in his seat. "It was the only way to save myself. If they said I was soft in the head, the bank couldn't foreclosure."

"Did you know that Gomez called me?"

"I figured he might." My father sighed. "I got a pretty penny for the place, but I owe a lot, too. There are liens and things. A second mortgage. I'm looking at a mobile home in Oxnard. Not the best, but it's what I can afford. And it almost looks like a regular house. You'll come up and visit." He stared at me a moment. "You sure have grown since the last time I saw you."

"Dad, I've been this tall since high school."

"Taller than me?"

"For years," I said.

He shrugged his shoulders. "Then I guess I'm shrinking."

After loading the boxes into my car, I came back inside the kitchen to say goodbye. "I have something for you," my father said. He beamed at me and stepped aside. Atop the counter, a pink bakery box yawned open to reveal an enormous cake, its circumference studded with ripe strawberries. Slivered almonds, toasted gold, had been evenly pressed into a mortar of thick white frosting, every spare surface dotted with florets. In the center was written, in goopy blue script, *Papa Loves Bernard*. For a second, I thought there'd been some mistake. I'd never called my father Papa. Dad, yes. Pop, perhaps. The nickname didn't mesh with the life I knew. If the years of silence between us had an inverse, that cloying, layered cake was it.

My father had begun yanking open drawers and kitchen cabinets, offering me anything that might not fit into his new trailer, which was just about most of what he owned: a punch-bowl set, napkin rings—artifacts from his life with my mother, a life of friends and fancy repasts. His barrage of offers was frenzied, desperate. All the while, I politely declined. "This is more than enough," I said, gazing at the cake. I knew a bite would be dense with sugar, a spongy glut. Yet it looked delectable sitting in his kitchen, Betty Crocker's Sunday bonnet. While my father jettisoned old possessions, I swiped a finger across the frosting and debated whether to taste it.

1. What is the mix of scene versus narration in this piece? How well does this balance work?
2. The piece spans a great deal of time. How does the author start and stop the clock of the essay?
3. Can you point to some sections of narration that are convincing because of their specificity?

CHAPTER SIX

Who's Telling This Story, Anyway?

Part 1: INTRODUCTION TO POINT OF VIEW

Getting Started

In Chapter 5, we talked about the difference between scene and narration, how narration is also called "telling," and why "show not tell," despite being a popular piece of advice, isn't always the best way to go. Sometimes you'll want to tell your readers things directly—narrate things. And even if you like to keep narrative to a bare minimum, it's almost a given that you'll have *some* telling to do. You might want to set the scene ("the prairie was hot and dry and the ground shimmered in the heat"), or start or stop the clock of the story ("later that same day," or "ten years passed without incident"). All this requires telling.

To do this telling, or narration, you must have a *narrator*. Pretty basic. Someone must be telling those parts of the story that can't be witnessed first-hand in scenes. This is called *point of view*, and the point of view is one of the key things you must decide when you sit down and try to get your story or nonfiction material onto paper.

This is what we're going to talk about in this chapter. First, we're going to define "narrator," then we're going to talk about the different narrative choices you have when settling on a point of view. You'll then be given some exercises—complete with student examples—to practice the different kinds of point of view. Finally, we have some readings that illustrate the different points of view you can choose when writing your story, novel, or creative nonfiction piece.

Some Basic Definitions

First, let's define "narrator." It's important to understand that this is where there is a key difference between writing fiction and nonfiction: in fiction, a narrator is different from the author. The author is writing the words. The narrator is the *intelligence* that is *telling the story*. In fiction, the author controls the narrator, but is not synonymous with the narrator.

> NOTE: This is different in nonfiction. In nonfiction, the author and the narrator are the same. There's no convention that differentiates the nonfiction author from the narrator of the story. More on this later.

A brief warning: when you read about fiction writing and point of view in many textbooks, the word "narrator" is used in various ways. It's more than a little confusing. Some texts might even tell you that the only stories that have narrators are those with first-person narrators (an "I" who is telling the story). I disagree. For the purposes of this textbook, therefore, *every* made-up story or novel has a narrator. Even if the story is being told by an invisible and bodiless intelligence which never personally enters the story as a character, and which appears to be godlike in its scope of knowledge, I want to refer to that as the narrator. Some people assume and/or insist that it is the author, that we're getting the author's perception of the world. That might be true sometimes. But it's untrue enough of the time in fiction for us never to assume that. So we will always talk about the *narrator* of the story or novel, not the author, when we talk about fiction.

Think of it this way: it's like the relationship between a puppeteer and a puppet. They might sometimes raise their right hands at the same time, or move to the left simultaneously, but they are not the same. The author controls the narrator, but is not synonymous with him or her.

So what are our choices of narrators? Simple. Well, deceptively simple. Just three:

First person
Second person
Third person

Let's move on and define these terms and look at some examples.

First Person

First person point of view is possibly the most popular point of view for beginning writers. With it, the narrative is being told by an actual character within the piece, an "I." In nonfiction, this "character" is the author, relating something that has happened to him or her. In fiction this character is made up, not real.

So the first person narrator is a character—made up, in fiction—who is telling the story. Again, in fiction, we never assume that it's the author, even if the narrator tells you, "I am writing this down for you. I am the author." If the narrator were the author, it would be nonfiction. It would be someone telling of a real experience.

There are actually two kinds of first person narrators we can look at. First, there's a narrator who is *directly* involved in the story or nonfiction piece. Someone who is intimately and obviously affected by what is happening. Second, there's a first person "observer." A character that is standing back, saying, "I have a story to tell you, about something I witnessed, but I was not directly involved."

A fine distinction, but let's look at examples of both.

> "Tell me things I won't mind forgetting," she said. "Make it useless stuff or skip it."
>
> I began. I told her insects fly through rain, missing every drop, never getting wet. I told her no one in America owned a tape recorder before Bing Crosby did. I told her the shape of the moon is like a banana—you see it looking full, you're seeing it end-on.
>
> The camera made me self-conscious and I stopped. It was trained on us from a ceiling mount—the kind of camera banks use to photograph robbers. It played our image to the nurses down the hall in Intensive Care. "Go on, girl," she said. "you get used to it."
>
> I had my audience. I went on.

This is obviously first person of the involved kind. The narrator (a character, made up) is telling a story that directly involves her. (This is from the excellent story "In the Cemetery Where Al Jolson Is Buried" by Amy Hempel.) We know, in a story of this kind, to be looking at the narrator as key to what the story's about; it's "her" story, because all the events and emotions are filtered through her point of view. We're interested, ultimately, in the impact of the events of the story on the narrator, because that's where our attention is being focused. It's pretty unambiguous in that regard.

Now, a famous example of a detached first person narrator:

> In my younger and more vulnerable years my father gave me some advice that I've been turning over in my mind ever since.
>
> "Whenever you feel like criticizing any one," he told me, "just remember

that all the people in this world haven't had the advantages that you've had."

He didn't say any more, but we've always been unusually communicative in a reserved way, and I understood that he meant a great deal more than that. In consequence, I'm inclined to reserve all judgments, a habit that has opened up many curious natures to me, and also made me the victim of not a few veteran bores. The abnormal mind is quick to detect and attach itself to this quality when it appears in a normal person, and so it came about that in college I was unjustly accused of being a politician, because I was privy to the secret griefs of wild, unknown men. Most of the confidences were unsought—frequently, I have feigned sleep, preoccupation, or a hostile levity when I realized by some unmistakable sign that an intimate revelation was quivering on the horizon; for the intimate revelations of young men, or at least the terms in which they express them, are usually plagiaristic and marred by obvious suppressions. Reserving judgments is a matter of infinite hope. I am still a little afraid of missing something if I forget that, as my father snobbishly suggested, and I snobbishly repeat, a sense of the fundamental decencies is parceled out unequally at birth.

And, after boasting this way of my tolerance, I come to the admission that it has a limit. Conduct may be founded on the hard rock or the wet marshes, but after a certain point I don't care what it's founded on. When I came back from the East last autumn I felt that I wanted the world to be in uniform and at a sort of moral attention forever; I wanted no more riotous excursions with privileged glimpses into the human heart.

Probably every American, at one point or another, has read *The Great Gatsby*—most of us for the first time in high school. We tend to remember it as the story of the doomed love affair between the mysterious, flamboyant Gatsby and the beautiful (and married) Daisy, and we sometimes forget it's told by a first person narrator, Nick, a distant cousin of Daisy who is a transplant from the Midwest and who witnesses the entire riotous affair. It's a terrific example of a *detached* first person narrator.

Whose Story Is It?

Now, here's the important part. Whose story is it when we have a first person narrator? This is an important question, and one that invariably comes up when we sit down to analyze a story, novel, or nonfiction piece.

What do we mean when we ask that question? We're asking, who are we primarily focused upon, who does the piece end up being *about*? The answer with an involved first person narrator is easy: the narrator. It's about him or her. But what about first person observer, you might ask? And the answer one comes back to, almost inevitably, even with the most detached first person narrators, is that the piece is ultimately about that narrator. Nick in *The Great Gatsby* is detached. In this opening section, as we saw, he goes to great lengths to talk about his propensity to be told the stories of "wild, unknown men" and boasts about his tolerance for being an observer of all sorts of humanity. You might say he pats himself on the back a little bit about his abilities as a detached, nonjudgmental listener (even as he makes judgments all over the place—even to the point of saying that some of his confidants have "abnormal minds"). A little later in the book, he says, "Everyone suspects himself of at least one of the cardinal virtues, and this is mine: I am one of the few honest people that I have ever known."

As it turns out, the book really revolves around Nick. Despite all his disclaimers that he's just an innocent bystander, it's about Nick's involvement in the events of the summer, and his propensity to fool himself by calling himself honest. By the end of the book, it's the impact of the events on *Nick* that matters—on his moral fiber, on his ability to think honestly about himself.

This is one of the conventions of modern creative writing, and, to be honest, I cannot think of many exceptions. When you have a first person narrator, when you have a character telling a story—no matter how detached or impartial he or she seems to be—it's *that* person's story. Somehow, it's the effect on that narrator that is the important thing—even when the events being observed are as dramatic as in *The Great Gatsby*—that, ultimately, is the point of the story or nonfiction piece, even if it's a subtle point. Otherwise, why not tell the story straight? Why filter it, unless there's a point to having it filtered? Why not just tell it from a straight third person point of view?

Here's another first person narrator from Richard Shelton's short short "The Stones," in which the narrator starts out very present but ends up dropping out of the story altogether:

> I love to go out on summer nights and watch the stones grow. I think they grow better here in the desert, where it is warm and dry, than almost anywhere else. Or perhaps it is only that the young ones are more active here.
>
> Young stones tend to move about more than their elders consider good for them. Most young stones have a secret desire which their parents had before them but have forgotten ages ago. And because this desire involves water, it is never mentioned. The older stones disapprove of water and say, "Water is a gadfly who never stays in one place long enough to learn anything." But the young stones try to work themselves into a position, slowly and without their elders noticing it, in which a sizable stream of water during a summer

storm might catch them broadside and unknowing, so to speak, and push them along over a slope or down an arroyo. In spite of the danger this involves, they want to travel and see something of the world and settle in a new place, far from home, where they can raise their own dynasties away from the domination of their parents.

And although family ties are very strong among stones, many of the more daring ones have succeeded, and they carry scars to prove to their children that they once went on a journey, helter-skelter and high water, and traveled perhaps fifteen feet, an incredible distance. As they grow older, they cease to brag about such clandestine adventures.

It is true that old stones get to be very conservative. They consider all movement either dangerous or downright sinful. They remain comfortable where they are and often get fat. Fatness, as a matter of fact, is a mark of distinction.

And on summer nights, after the young stones are asleep, the elders turn to a serious and frightening subject—the moon, which is always spoken of in whispers. "See how it glows and whips across the sky, always changing its shape," one says. And another says, "Feel how it pulls at us, urging us to follow." And a third whispers, "It is a stone gone mad."

Why make it first person? Why not tell this straight third person ("Stones grow better in the desert, where it is warm and dry, than almost anywhere else")? Because this story is, ultimately, about the narrator's experience of the stones, about his/her (we never know the sex of the narrator) own thoughts and fantasies about what stones believe and feel and act like. The story has meaning because of what is *projected* onto the stones by the first person narrator.

And then there's this famous story of Alice Munro's, "Meneseteung," which has such a disguised first person narrator that we almost forget she is there:

In 1879 Almeda Roth was still living in the house at the corner of Pearl and Dufferin streets, the house her father had built for his family. The house is there today; the manager of the liquor store lives in it. It's covered with aluminum siding; a closed-in porch has replaced the veranda. The woodshed, the fence, the gates, the privy, the barn—all these are gone. A photograph taken in the 1880s shows them all in place. The house and fence look a little shabby, in need of paint, but perhaps that is just because of the bleached-out look of the brownish photograph. The lace-curtained windows look like white eyes. No big shade tree is in sight, and, in fact, the tall elms that overshadowed the town until the 1950s, as well as the maples that shade it now, are skinny young trees with rough fences around them to protect them from the cows. Without the shelter of those trees, there is a great exposure—backyards, clotheslines, woodpiles, patchy sheds and barns and privies—all bare, exposed, provisional-looking. . . . The town has taken root, it's not going to vanish, yet it still has some of the look of an encampment. And, like an encampment, it's busy all the time—full of people, who, within the town, usually walk wherever they're going; full of animals, which leave horse buns, cow pats, dog turds that ladies have to hitch up their skirts for; full of the noise of building and of drivers shouting at their horses and of the trains that come in several times a day.

I read about that life in the *Vidette*.

This is a story about (again) an unnamed first person narrator, going through old newspaper archives and other historical artifacts, ferreting out the details of a dead poet's life. We see the narrator taking the bare-bones facts and filling in the blanks out of her imagination. She's fantasizing, in effect, what it must have been like to be Almeda Roth, to have lived in that town and in that place with those kinds of personages. Indeed, ultimately, it is about *her* (the narrator's) fantasies—and also about the stories we tell ourselves—as much as or more than it is about the dead poet Almeda Roth.

Here's another interesting variation on first person narration: *plural first person*, i.e., there's a group of people telling the story. "*We* did this, *we* saw that." This is relatively rare, but here are two examples:

> Whenever we saw Mrs. Lisbon we looked in vain for some sign of the beauty that must have once been hers. But the plump arms, the brutally cut steel-wool hair, and the librarian's glasses foiled us every time. We saw her only rarely, in the morning, fully dressed though the sun hadn't come up, stepping out to snatch up the dewy milk cartons, or on Sundays when the family drove in their paneled station wagon.

Notice the use of "we" in this excerpt from the novel *The Virgin Suicides* by Jeffrey Eugenides. And here's another plural first person narrator, from William Faulkner's "A Rose For Emily":

> When Miss Emily Grierson died, our whole town went to her funeral: the men through a sort of respectful affection for a fallen monument, the women mostly out of curiosity to see the inside of her house, which no one save an old manservant—a combined gardener and cook—had seen in at least ten years.

As always, our eye is on the first person narrator when figuring out what the story is about. Just because in these examples it's a *group* of people (in the first case, a group of young men who have worshipped a family of girls from afar; in the second, an entire town that has been interested in this eccentric old woman for decades) doesn't alter that basic rule: it's the narrators' story, ultimately. Think about it: otherwise, why filter the story through that consciousness? Why not just tell it straight, without interjecting a character (or, in this case, characters) between the reader and the story? Because, ultimately, the story is about the narrators. This is one of the strongest conventions (not rules; there are no rules) of fiction writing: when in doubt, in a first person story, look at the narrator for clues as to what the story is really about.

Second Person

Second person is one of the more complex points of view, and it is rarely used. In second person, the narrator speaks via a "you," who can be one of four types of characters:

1. The "you" is actually an *inverted* form of first person. That is, it is a first person narrator referring to himself or herself as "you"—usually because they are dissociating themselves from distasteful thoughts, actions, or memories. For example, "You really don't like yourself very much when you act like this."
2. The "you" refers to a specific character, so that the piece, in effect, becomes a monologue addressed to a person or persons. For example. "David, you didn't realize how much damage you could cause, you obviously weren't thinking when you stole that letter from my desk."
3. The "you" is a direct address to the reader: "And you people, you who are reading this book . . ."
4. The "you" can also, occasionally, be an attempt to turn the reader into an active character in the story. "You walk into the room. You are aware that something is wrong. You can't figure out what it is."

Let's look at each of these kinds of second person narrator in turn.

The first use of second person, as inverted first person, is, in fact, the most common.

You're not the kind of guy who would be at a place like this at this time of the morning. But here you are, and you cannot say that the terrain is entirely unfamiliar, although the details are fuzzy. You are at a nightclub talking to a girl with a shaved head. The club is either Heartbreak or the Lizard Lounge. All might come clear if you could just slip into the bathroom and do a little more Bolivian Marching Powder. Then again, it might not. A small voice inside you insists that this epidemic lack of clarity is a result of too much of that already. The night has already turned on that imperceptible pivot where 2 a.m. changes to 6 a.m. You know this moment has come and gone, but you are not yet willing to concede that you have crossed the line beyond which all is gratuitous damage and the palsy of unraveled nerve endings.

This famous example of second person, from the novel *Bright Lights, Big City* by Jay McInerney, has a narrator who is so distanced from himself, so psychologically removed from his actions (and wanting so much not to take responsibility for them) that he refers to himself as "you."

And here's another example of this kind of second person narrator, from Lorrie Moore's "How to Be a Writer":

> First, try to be something, anything, else. A movie star/astronaut. A movie star/missionary. A movie star/kindergarten teacher. President of the World. Fail miserably. It is best if you fail at an early age—say fourteen. Early, critical disillusionment is necessary so that at fifteen you can write long haiku sequences about thwarted desire. It is a pond, a cherry blossom, a wind brushing against sparrow wing leaving for mountain. Count the syllables. Show it to your mom. She is tough and practical. She has a son in Vietnam and a husband who may be having an affair. She believes in wearing brown because it hides spots. She'll look briefly at your writing, then back up at you with a face blank as a donut. She'll say: "How about emptying the dishwasher?" Look away. Shove the forks in the fork drawer. Accidentally break one of the freebie gas station glasses. This is the required pain and suffering. This is only for starters.

You see that these are both really characters referring to themselves as "you." It's really a variation of first person, in that a character is telling us a story, it's just that he or she prefers to distance himself or herself. Most commonly, it's a way of showing a character that is alienated from himself or herself, and has trouble identifying with the thoughts and actions he or she is engaged in. This is certainly the case with these two examples. In *Bright Lights, Big City*, the first example, the main character is so far removed from himself that he can't admit to himself the destructive behavior he's engaged in. In "How to Be a Writer," a young woman distances herself from reality (in a humorous way) in order not to face up to certain truths about her life.

The second use of second person, that of direct address to a specific character or character, is used in stories that are written as either oral monologues or letters. Below is an example:

> You must be aware, first, that because Susan is my girlfriend pretty much everything she discusses with you she also discusses with me. She tells me what she said and what you said. We have been seeing each other for about six months now and I am pretty familiar with her story, or stories. Similarly, with your responses, at least the general pattern. I know, for example, that my habit of referring to you as "the sandman" annoys you but let me assure you that I mean nothing unpleasant by it. It is simply a nickname. The refer-

ence is to the old rhyme: "Sea-sand does the sandman bring / Sleep to end the day / He dusts the children's eyes with sand / And steals their dreams away."

You notice that here, too, there's a first person narrator involved in this form of second person. Even if the first person narrator is hidden behind the "you"—even if the words "I" or "me" never appear—he or she is there, close by. In this case, in this very funny story, "The Sandman" by Donald Barthelme, the first person narrator is a man who is writing a letter to his girlfriend's shrink.

The third example of second person is also usually a first person narrator who has slipped temporarily into second person; nineteenth-century novelists, for example, were fond of occasionally slipping into second person to address the reader directly. But this is usually not sustained beyond a sentence or two. For example, Dear reader, you might be wondering what happened; yes, I married him!

The fourth type of second person is very rare in fiction, although it is seen quite frequently in nonfiction, particularly in feature journalism as published in daily papers and monthly magazines. There are cases when it is used in fiction (as we'll see below), but it's a very unusual use of this point of view.

> You are always in danger in the forest, where no people are. Step between the portals of the great pines where the shaggy branches tangle about you, trapping the unwary traveler in nets as if the vegetation itself were in plot with the wolves who live there, as though the wicked trees go fishing on behalf of their friends—step between the gateposts of the forest with the great trepidation and infinite precautions, for if you stray from the path for one instant, the wolves will eat you. They are grey as famine, they are as unkind as plague.
>
> [from "The Company of Wolves" by Angela Carter]

Do you see how the writer is making you, the reader, into a character in the story? You are being instructed to step through the forest, and warned, directly, of the dangers to you if you should do so.

Second person point of view is not widely used. It can work, but it's a little gimmicky, and runs the danger of getting tiresome except in shorter pieces. Still, you can experiment with it, and see what you think for yourself.

Third Person

Third person point of view is the most complex point of view. In it, the narrator is a disembodied intelligence who does *not* appear directly in the piece as a character. Rather, he or she exists above the story or nonfiction piece, observing it from outside.

Third person point of view is actually a continuum of possible narrators, based on how much the third person narrator *knows*. Let's look at this continuum of *knowledge* as it pertains to point of view:

Limited Third Person

Omniscient	Direct Observer
Godlike	Fly on Wall

At one end is unlimited knowledge, an omniscient narrator. He or she sees all, knows all: knows what characters are thinking, what they are feeling, what happened in the past, what will happen in the future. This is a godlike being with unlimited powers of observation and knowledge of the world of the story or novel.

Anything to the right of this is a *limited third person* narrator. That is, the knowledge of the narrator has been limited in some way. A limited third person narrator is not omniscient—she or he does not have unlimited powers. He or she might only be able to see what one character is thinking or feeling; or may only know what characters are thinking, not what they are feeling; or may only have knowledge of the past, but no knowledge of the future. There are all sorts of ways that a narrator's knowledge can be "limited."

At the far right side of the spectrum is the most *limited* knowledge. Called a "direct observer," this kind of third-person narrator is like a fly on the wall—he or she can see and hear what is going on, but that's it: no powers to read into characters' hearts or minds, no power to interpret thoughts or explain emotions, no power to explain history or predict the future.

Exactly where on this spectrum your third person narrator resides—if you choose this point of view—is completely up to you. And as you'll see, this makes for a lot of potential choices.

Let's look at some examples of these different kinds of third person narrators.

> Elizabeth listened in silence, but was not convinced; their behavior at the assembly had not been calculated to please in general; and with more quickness of observation and less pliancy of temper than her sister, and with a judgment too unassailed by any attention to herself, she was very little disposed to approve them.

They were in fact very fine ladies, not deficient in good humour when they were pleased, not in the power of being agreeable when they chose it, but proud and conceited. They were rather handsome, had been educated in one of the first private seminaries in town, had a fortune of twenty thousand pounds, were in the habit of spending more than they ought, and of associating with people of rank, and were therefore in every respect entitled to think well of themselves, and meanly of others. They were of a respectable family in the north of England; a circumstance more deeply impressed on their memories than that their brother's fortune and their own had been acquired by trade.

Mr. Bingley inherited property to the amount of nearly a hundred thousand pounds from his father, who had intended to purchase an estate, but did not live to do it. Mr. Bingley intended it likewise, and sometimes made choice of his county; but as he was now provided with a good house and the liberty of a manor, it was doubtful to many of those who best knew the easiness of his temper, whether he might not spend the remainder of his days at Netherfield, and leave the next generation to purchase.

His sisters were very anxious for his having an estate of his own; but, though he was now established only as a tenant, Miss Bingley was by no means unwilling to preside at his table—nor was Mrs. Hurst, who had married a man of more fashion than fortune, less disposed to consider his house as her home when it suited her.

[from *Pride and Prejudice* by Jane Austen]

Pride and Prejudice is a wonderful example of omniscient third person point of view: we are put into the minds of various characters, and we are given judgments of them. Beautiful judgments. That is, notice that your omniscient narrator doesn't need to be unbiased and neutral. He or she can be a judgmental or cynical narrator, can have opinions and express them freely, even to the point of liking or disdaining individual characters, or the actions they engage in.

At the other end of the spectrum we have what is conventionally called the "direct observer." He or she has very, very limited access: this kind of narrator usually is able to see and hear, but is given no other access to the characters. No thoughts, let alone an interpretation of those thoughts, let alone judgment of those thoughts. Just what the proverbial fly on the wall could see and hear. Let's look again at "Hills Like White Elephants" by Ernest Hemingway:

The hills across the valley of the Ebro were long and white. On this side there was no shade and no trees and the station was between two lines of rails in the sun. Close against the side of the station there was the warm shadow of the building and a curtain, made of strings of bamboo beads, hung across the open door into the bar, to keep out flies. The American and the girl with him sat at a table in the shade, outside the building. It was very hot and the express from Barcelona would come in forty minutes. It stopped at this junction for two minutes and went on to Madrid.

It is not common to have narrators this limited. Most narrators, especially in short fiction, are closer to the middle of the continuum.

But here is another case where many of the books about writing don't serve you very well: as we explained above, there are all sorts of variations of limited third person narrators. Yet in most writing books, limited third person is said to be the case when the knowledge of the narrator is limited to the heart and mind of a single character. But there are many ways that a narrator's knowledge can be less than that possessed by some God-knows-all-sees-all omniscient narrator. Here are just a few:

1. It can be limited to just the thoughts of a character, but not the emotions.
2. It can see beyond those thoughts and actually perceive the emotions.
3. It can peek into the subconscious—things that the character(s) are not aware of—but not have any powers to relate past events.

Or any variation thereof. All limited third person means is that you have chosen to limit the knowledge of your narrator in some way.

Let's look at some examples of limited third person narrators.

> Now is the time for drastic action. He contemplates taking Wayne's hand, then checks himself. He has never done anything in her presence to indicate that the sexuality he confessed to five years ago was a reality and not an invention. Even now, he and Wayne might as well be friends, college roommates. Then Wayne, his savior, with a single, sweeping gesture, reaches for his hand, and clasps it, in the midst of a joke he is telling about Saudi Arabians. By the time he is laughing, their hands are joined. Neil's throat contracts; his heart begins to beat violently. He notices his mother's eyes flicker, glance downward; she never breaks the stride of her sentence. The dinner goes on and every taboo nurtured since childhood falls quietly away.
>
> [from "Territory" by David Leavitt]

Here we're limited to the heart and mind of a single character—the other characters are opaque to us, we cannot see through the surface of their external behavior. This is the most common type of limited third person narrator.

Here's another example of a third person limited narrator—but this one is interesting because the character that the narrator is limited to observing changes as the story progresses; the narrative insight into thoughts and emotions is passed from one character to another, like a ball. See how it starts out third person omniscient, then turns into third person limited for one character after another:

> None of them knew the color of the sky. Their eyes glanced level, and were fastened upon the waves that swept toward them. These waves were of the hue of slate, save for the tops, which were of foaming white, and all of the men knew the colors of the sea. The horizon narrowed and widened and dipped and rose, and at all times its edge was jagged with waves that seemed thrust up in points like rocks.
>
> Many a man ought to have a bath-tub larger than the boat which here rode upon the sea. These waves were most wrongfully and barbarously abrupt and tall, and each froth-top was a problem in small boat navigation.
>
> The cook squatted in the bottom and looked with both eyes at the six inches of gunwale which separated him from the ocean. His sleeves were rolled over his fat forearms, and the two flaps of his unbuttoned vest dangled as he bent to bail out the boat. Often he said: "Gawd! That was a narrow clip." As he remarked it he invariably gazed eastward over the broken sea.
>
> The oiler, steering with one of the two oars in the board, sometimes raised himself suddenly to keep clear of water that swirled in over the stern. It was a thin little boat and it seemed often ready to snap.
>
> The correspondent, pulling at the other oar, watched the waves and wondered why he was there.
>
> The injured captain, lying in the bow, was at this time buried in that profound dejection and indifference which comes, temporarily, at least, to even the bravest and most enduring when, willy nilly, the firm fails, the army loses, the ship goes down.
>
> [from "The Open Boat" by Stephen Crane]

You can see how the narrator "travels" from one character to another, giving us information about each one in equal parts. There's another interesting limitation that the author has chosen: the third person narrator cannot give us any information about the world of the story other than what is happening on the boat. This is not a narrator who can tell us, "Not far away, on shore, a group of men was preparing a rescue mission." No, this narrator is physically rooted in a particular place and time, and so our knowledge of the world of the story is limited in that way.

Here's another way to think about this whole idea of knowledge as it pertains to third person narrators: think of it as standing in a house that borders a big open field. With an omniscient narrator, you are standing in front of a large clear window that allows you to view a scene that stretches for miles in every direction. With limited third person narrator, you have a smaller window that gives you access to a smaller view of the world of the story. The more limited your narrator, the smaller your window, and the less you can see (and hear, feel, etc.). It's as simple as that.

As we said above, the most common way of limiting a third person narrator is by limiting his or her powers to seeing the inner life (thoughts, feelings) of just one character. But this is not the only way. A third person narrator could be limited in that he or she could read the thoughts of all the characters, but not their underlying emotions—or could state their emotions, but not analyze *why* they were feeling the way they did. Any combination of knowledge is possible: there are as many possible third person narrators out there as there are possible first person narrators.

A Word about Attitude

It's also important to understand that a third person narrator doesn't have to be a bland, middle-of-the-road, so-called "objective" reporter of what goes on. He or she can have *attitude*. Judgment. Comment editorially on what is happening, approve or disapprove of what characters are like. "She was a rubbishy little creature and she knew it," is a wonderful line of third person narrative from E. M. Forster's *Howards End*. Likewise, "he, his hands behind him, appeared pinned to the door frame, waiting like Saint Sebastian for the arrows to begin piercing him," is a very funny observation of a character by one of Flannery O'Connor's third person narrators. Give your third person narrators *personality*. A Texas accent. Opinions about the world, about politics. Whatever you choose is fair game.

Distance and Point of View

Now, it's important to understand that it's not just knowledge that affects your point of view. *Distance* is also a factor. In other words, a narrator, in addition to knowing more or less about the world of the story or novel or nonfiction piece, can be at greater or lesser distance from it.

A very popular point of view these days, especially in short stories, is *close* third person point of view. (It's also referred to as *third person intimate*.) This is when the narrator is so close to the action, to what's happening, that the narration can be indistinguishable from first person in many ways.

Let's first look at some examples of close third person narrators. Note that the relative closeness of a narrator is independent of the *knowledge* that narrator possesses. You can have a very limited third person narrator who is far from the story or novel, or you can have an omniscient narrator who is very close to the action of the story. Let's examine what we have below in terms of both knowledge and distance:

> Although Bertha Young was thirty she still had moments like this when she wanted to run instead of walk, to take dancing steps on and off the pavement, to bowl a hoop, to throw something up in the air and catch it again, or to stand still and laugh at—nothing—at nothing, simply.
>
> What can you do if you are thirty and, turning the corner of your own street you are overcome, suddenly, by a feeling of bliss—absolute bliss!—as though you'd suddenly swallowed a bright piece of that late afternoon sun and it burned in your bosom, sending out a little shower of sparks into every particle, into every finger and toe . . . ?
>
> Oh, is there no way you can express it without being "drunk and disorderly"? How idiotic civilization is! Why be given a body if you have to keep it shut up in a case like a rare, rare fiddle?
>
> [from "Bliss" by Katherine Mansfield]

This story has a close limited third person narrator—a narrator who happens to be limited (in knowledge) to the thoughts and feelings of just one character, but who is very, very close to that character—so close as to be practically identical to first person at certain times in the text. The last paragraph, for example, has no "she thought" attached to the text, yet these are clearly the thoughts of the character; that shows how deeply embedded we are in this character's mind.

Here's another example:

> The dream was set in Shady Hill—she dreamed that she woke in her own bed. Donald was always gone. She was at once aware of the fact that the bomb had exploded. Mattress stuffing and a trickle of brown water were coming through a big hole in the ceiling. The sky was gray—lightless— although there were in the west a few threads of red light, like those charming vapor trails we see in the air after the sun has set. She didn't know if these were vapor trails or some part of that force that would destroy the marrow in her bones. The gray air seemed final. The sky would never shine with light again. From her window she could see a river, and now, as she watched, boats began to come upstream. At first, there were only two or three. Then there were tens, and then there were hundreds. There were outboards, excursion boats, yachts, schooners with auxiliary motors; there were even rowboats. The number of boats grew until the water was covered with them, and the noise of motors rose to a loud din. The jockeying for position in this retreat up the river became aggressive, then savage.
>
> [from "The Wrysons" by John Cheever]

This happens to be an omniscient narrator (you can't tell from this section, but the narrator can see into the hearts and minds of all the characters in the story) who is also very, very close: so close that we melt into the reality of Irene Wryson's dream just as if it was reality.

Now, what about this example?

> Christina Goering's father was an American industrialist of German parentage and her mother was a New York lady of a very distinguished family. Christina spent the first half of her life in a very beautiful house (not more than an hour from the city) which she had inherited from her mother. It was in this house that she had been brought up as a child with her sister Sophie.
>
> As a child Christina had been very much disliked by other children. She had never suffered particularly because of this, having led, even at a very early age, an active inner life that curtailed her observation of whatever went on around her, to such a degree that she never picked up the mannerisms then in vogue, and at the age of ten was called old-fashioned by other little girls. Even then she wore the look of certain fanatics who think of themselves as leaders without once having gained the respect of a single human being.
>
> Christina was troubled horribly by ideas which never would have occurred to her companions, and at the same time took for granted a position in society which any other child would have found unbearable. Every now and then a schoolmate would take pity on her and try to spend some time with her, but far from being grateful for this, Christina would instead try her best to convert her new friend to the cult of whatever she believed in at the time. [. . .] She was in the habit of going through many mental struggles—generally of a religious nature—and she preferred to be with other people and organize games. These games, as a rule, were very moral, and often involved god. However, no one else enjoyed them and she was obliged to spend a great part of the day alone.
>
> [from *Two Serious Ladies* by Jane Bowles]

This is a very distant third person omniscient: the narrator sees all, knows all, and is able to make value judgments about the characters. But the tone is very distant, despite this omniscience.

To see an example of a very distant, very limited third person narrator, go to p. 356 and look at "Hills Like White Elephants." In that, not only are we working with the most limited third person narrator possible, the narrator is also very far removed from the characters.

Finally, how about this one?

> Robbie wanted to say, You're talking about something you've read, now. They'll be too ashamed to have Bernadette or the baby around; this is Que-

bec. But he was too tired to offer a new field of discussion. He was as tired as if they had been talking for hours. He said, "I suppose this Vermont place, this school or whatever it is, has got to be paid for."

"It certainly does." Nora looked tight and cold at this hint of stinginess. It was unnatural for her to be in the wrong, still less to remain on the defensive. She had taken the position now that even if Robbie were not responsible, he had somehow upset Bernadette. In some manner, he could be found guilty and made to admit it. She would find out about it later. Meanwhile, she felt morally bound to make him pay.

"Will it be expensive, do you think?"

She gave him a look, but he said nothing more.

[from "Bernadette" by Mavis Gallant]

You see how we get the thoughts and feelings of Robbie, and then we move to Nora and get her perspective. Our omniscient third person narrator has the ability to move about at will and give us information about what's going on in the hearts and minds of both characters. But we don't actually get very close to the characters. We're being kept at a distance, we're not as intimately involved as in some of the other examples.

Shifts in Narrative Distance

The previous section might imply that you have to pick a distance and stick to it throughout a story. Nothing could be further from the truth. In good fiction, shifts in distance are common. They must also be carefully controlled. Often, at the beginning of a story, we find the narrative distance fairly large. Often, distance will decrease—sometimes collapsing to the point of nonexistence—in order to allow the author to more thoroughly investigate the heart or mind of a character. A skillful writer will know how to pan in and pan out, just like a skilled camera operator on a movie set.

It was too hot. She went inside the house and turned on the radio to drown out the quiet. She sat on the edge of her bed, barefoot, and listened for an hour and a half to a program called XYZ Sunday Jamboree, record after record of hard, fast, shrieking songs she sang along with, interspersed by exclamations from "Bobby King": "An' look here you girls at Napoleon's—Son and Charley want you to pay real close attention to this song coming up!"

And Connie paid close attention herself, bathed in a glow of slow-pulsed joy that seemed to rise mysteriously out of the music itself and lay languidly about the airless little room, breathed in and breathed out with each gentle rise and fall of her chest.

In this scene, from "Where Are You Going, Where Have You Been?" by Joyce Carol Oates (pp. 72–86) you can see how the distance starts out very close ("It was too hot" puts us directly in Connie's mind) but then the distance lengthens, and we pull back a bit to get information about her going inside the house and listening to the radio. Then the distance closes in again, putting us right in the heart of Connie, what she's thinking and feeling. This is one of the advantages of third person intimate: you can have all the advantages of first person (being intimate) and still pull back and get more of a perspective on the larger world.

But it's important to note that sudden shifts in distance can be disconcerting for your readers. If you've been referring to the character as "Doris" and she suddenly becomes "Mrs. Mannerling," that is an obvious sudden shift that will jolt the reader. John Gardner in his book *The Art of Fiction* calls this sudden change a problem in "psychic distance":

> Careless shifts in psychic distance can also be distracting. By psychic distance we mean the distance the reader feels between himself and the events in the story. Compare the following examples, the first meant to establish great psychic distance, the next meant to establish slightly less, and so on until in the last example, psychic distance, theoretically at least, is nil.
>
> 1. It was winter of the year 1853. A large man stepped out of a doorway.
> 2. Henry J. Warburton had never much cared for snowstorms.
> 3. Henry hated snowstorms.
> 4. God how he hated these damn snowstorms.
> 5. Snow. Under your collar, down inside your shoes, freezing and plugging up your miserable soul . . .

The point isn't that narrative distance needs to stay constant, but that shifts in distance need to be carefully managed so as not to jolt the reader out of what Gardner calls "the dream of the story."

Choosing a Point of View for Your Creative Work

Now: what form of point of view do you choose? You might hope there is some objective, quantifiable way of choosing a point of view, but unfortunately it doesn't work that way. Often, the choice of a point of view is a completely intuitive one; the writer may not know why he or she chose first person, or third person limited, only feels that the choice is the right one for a particular story.

Still, there are some conventionally accepted pros and cons of each kind of point of view. Let's look at some of them, and see how they hold up under analysis.

A FIRST PERSON POINT OF VIEW: The conventionally stated advantage of this is that it provides immediacy, involves the reader, pulls him or her in, is helpful in getting sympathy for the main character (who happens to be the narrator).

The disadvantage: very limited scope. You only have the eyes, ears, and brains of that character. Everything is filtered through him or her.

Another disadvantage: Is it possible to be *too* close to a story? We're going to be talking about unreliable narrators later, in Chapter 7, but I want to point out that, especially when you are writing about a very emotionally charged situation, putting it in first person can work against you. You can risk losing your reader. Victim stories fall into this category. Sometimes, if you are trying to garner sympathy or understanding for a character, the last thing you want to do is put it in first person. The narrator can be seen as self-serving, pitying, or whining. You risk it becoming maudlin. Nothing will eliminate sympathy faster than having to listen to a character whine—even if he or she really has been victimized in some horrifying way.

With an OMNISCIENT NARRATOR, the advantages of course are that you have the "big window" onto the terrain of the story or nonfiction piece: your readers can see all, do all, go back to the beginning of time, take time out to give a lecture on nautical knots (*The Shipping News*) or the correct way to skin a whale (*Moby-Dick*) or whatever else you choose.

The conventionally accepted disadvantage of an omniscient narrator: it can be too much, can contain too much information, can distract the reader from what really matters in the story or nonfiction piece.

LIMITED THIRD: A very popular choice, especially in the last few decades. The conventional wisdom is that it focuses the reader's attention on what matters, narrows down the scope of the story to make it manageable. And, of course, using shifts in narrative distance, you can easily get into the heart and mind of a character, just like first person, yet you have the advantage of pulling back, panning the camera, if you will, to show us more of the world of the story or nonfiction piece.

Again, keep in mind that the amount of knowledge you give the narrator (either unlimited, as in omniscient, or very limited, as in direct observer or first person) is separate from the *distance* that narrator can invoke in the tone. Just because very close third person narrators are generally linked to those that are limited in knowledge doesn't mean that you have to follow that route. You can choose a limited third person narrator who is distant from the events of the story, or an omniscient narrator who is extremely close to the events. It's up to you.

Interestingly enough, an oft-heard piece of advice in creative writing workshops is "change the point of view," as if changing the point of view is a panacea for all sorts of problems.

Sometimes when this advice is given (to change the point of view from first person to third person, say, or vice versa), it has to do with the narrative *distance*: readers feel uncomfortable with the distance that the narrator has from the events in the story (either too close or too distant), and think that changing the point of view will fix that. But as we've seen, distance is independent of knowledge. Even first person point of view can be distant if the character is alienated from himself or herself. Here's an example to prove this point:

> I sat down in the waiting area across the hall. In forty-five minutes the nurse came out and said to me, "Michelle is comfortable now."
> "Is she dead?"
> "Of course not."
> "I kind of wish she was."
> She looked frightened. "I don't know what you mean."
> I went in through the curtain to see Michelle. She smelled bad.
> "How are you feeling?"
> "I feel fine."
> "What did they stick up you?"
> "What?" she said. "*What?*"
> The nurse said, "Hey. Out of here. Out of here."
> She went through the curtain and came back with a big black guy wearing a starched white shirt and one of those phony gold badges. "I don't think this man needs to be in the building," she said to him, and then she said to me, "Would you like to wait outside, sir?"
> "Yeah yeah yeah," I said, and all the way down the big stairs and out the front I said "Yeah yeah yeah yeah yeah yeah yeah."
> It was raining outdoors and most of the Catholics were squashed up under an awning next door with their signs held overhead against the weather. They splashed holy water on my cheek and on the back of my neck, and I didn't feel a thing. Not for many years.

In this passage, from "Dirty Wedding" by Denis Johnson, we have a first person narrator who is so distanced from his own thoughts and emotions that he's put up a shield against allowing any feelings to seep into his consciousness. We're kept at a distance because he keeps himself at a distance. Likewise, as we saw above, you can have omniscient third person narrators with a collapsed distance: we're embedded in the hearts and minds of the characters, as closely as if the point of view were first person.

Point of View and Creative Nonfiction

All these various points of view and conventions go for creative nonfiction writing as well as fictional prose. You can have first, second, or third person narrators; and your third person narrators can vary along the two spectrums of knowledge and distance.

Here's an example of a first person nonfiction piece:

> I am a man who tilts. When I am sitting, my head slants to the right; when walking, the upper part of my body reaches forward to catch a sneak preview of the street. One way or another, I seem to be off-center—or "uncentered," to use the jargon of holism. My lousy posture, a tendency to slump or put myself into lazy, contorted misalignments, undoubtedly contributes to lower back pain. For a while, I correct my bad habits, do morning exercises, sit straight, breathe deeply, but always an inner demon that insists on approaching the world askew resists perpendicularity.

"Portrait of My Body" by Phillip Lopate is clearly about the narrator. Indeed, it could hardly be more personal. The narrator (who is synonymous with the author in this case) broods at length about the various aspects of his physical body, both positive and negative attributes. It's a wonderful example of first person *involved*.

Here's an example of a nonfiction piece with a first person *observer*:

> There is only one known portrait of Robert Carter III. He posed for it sometime around 1749 in Thomas Hudson's London studio, and when one looks at the result two and a half centuries later, it is easy enough to imagine what the painter was thinking. Probably Carter was just another country gentleman—this one a little young, with that flat American accent making him seem more like a Scot or an Ulsterman—and Hudson knew that type, knew its vanities. And so Carter appears to us in a billowing gold suit and green cape, brown hair neatly tied back, smirking, a mask dangling from the tapered fingers of his left hand. He looks as if he is on his way to a ball, a lifetime of balls, except for a pair of huge dark eyes that suggest something else, something open and unfinished, something that resisted being posed as the young patriarch on the rise . . .

In this essay, "The Anti-Jefferson" by Andrew Levy, we have a nonfiction piece that is purportedly about a man who freed his slaves in apparent contradiction to his own fiduciary interests, but it is actually told by a first person narrator who imposes himself and his opinions and interests throughout the piece. (At another point, the author/narrator writes: "By the time I saw that portrait, on a postcard reproduction that the Virginia Historical Society no longer sells, it was the summer of 1998 and I was six months deep into the what and the why, the eyes, and the mask.")

Here's a nonfiction example of second person point of view:

> I know you are tired. I am tired too. Will you walk along the edge of the desert with me? I would like to show you what lies before us.

All my life I have wanted to trick blood from a rock. I have dreamed about raising the devil and cutting him in half. I have thought too about never being afraid of anything at all. This is where you come to do those things.

I know what they tell you about the desert but you mustn't believe them. This is no deathbed. Dig down, the earth is moist. Boulders have turned to dust here, the dust feels like graphite. You can hear a man breathe at a distance of twenty yards. You can see out there to the edge where the desert stops and the mountains begin. You think it is perhaps ten miles. It is more than a hundred. Just before the sun sets all the colors will change. Green will turn to blue, red to gold.

[from *Desert Notes* by Barry Lopez]

Finally, here's an example of a third person narrator in a creative non-fiction piece: "It was a time of hope, that was the thing," an excerpt from *The White Blackbird*, a life of the painter Margarett Sargent by her granddaughter, Honor Moore:

"There were five, six, or seven remotely happy years," Margie said of her parents' marriage. "It was a terribly abnormal, strained, difficult, tenuous relationship," said young Shaw. And Harry, his twin: "I never knew any happiness between them, ever."

At the end of her life, Marjorie did not believe Margarett had ever loved her, and when she described Isabel Pell, the woman whose visits to Prides supplanted hers, she used the word "wicked." Margarett would never have admitted she treated Marjorie callously, would have described herself as "devoted"—"incredulous" at her friend's indignation. In 1926, leaving out the tension in their friendship, she did a watercolor called *The Quilt*—Marjorie asleep, beautiful and dreamily rendered in pale washes, both hands resting carefully on her chest, the quilt covering her a splash of vividly painted squares, an opening path.

Common Point of View Problems

One of the most common ways to break with point of view conventions is to be telling the story from one point of view, and then suddenly shift to another. For instance, if we're following the action of a story from the point of view of one of the characters and suddenly we get what one of the other characters is thinking or feeling, that can be very disconcerting. In general, once you establish your point of view, you're going to want to stick with it. The point isn't to follow some esoteric rule, but to avoid jolting your readers out of the story. When such a jolt occurs, some would argue that there is a point of view error that needs to be fixed. But while this might be the case some, or even most, of the time, you can read stories—good stories—in which the point of view shifts, say from one kind of limited third person to another kind of limited third person. In such cases, we assume that the author felt it important enough to risk jolting the reader to get some additional information into the text. Does it work? Does the author get away with it? Only the reader can say.

Here's an example of a shift in point of view that might be considered an error:

> Claire sat on the bus, wringing her hands and trying not to cry. This was going to be her first time away from home, and she was already homesick. Already the lure of camp from reading those brochures was fading. She moved slightly in her seat to allow room for a young man about her own age who was carrying what looked to be a heavy satchel. He looked at Claire and felt pity, so he took out of his pocket a piece of chocolate and offered it to her.

Do you see how we suddenly shift from a third person point of view limited to Claire to one that includes insight into what the young man is feeling? Whether this is an error or something that adds to the story is only something that readers of the complete story can decide. The point of view police will always decry this sort of shift, but the fact remains that many fine stories embody shifts of this kind. It's entirely about what you can get away with.

Of course, if we are suddenly getting information, or access to a conversation, or reading a letter or overhearing a phone call that your narrator has no way of knowing about, that's a pretty obvious error. You must either cut it, or figure out some way of getting that information filtered through your narrator. For example, she can overhear a telephone conversation; or he can be told about an argument; or she can read someone else's letter.

More subtle errors: all of a sudden, the narrator will make a value judgment, or a leap of logic, that is markedly different from what he or she was capable of before, *for no plausible reason.* CAUTION: I'm not saying a character has to be consistent, that's something else altogether. Your character can act in different ways at different times for myriad reasons. Your character can grow. Change. Regress. But if there's an implausible leap of knowledge or insight or wisdom by a previously limited point of view character, that could be a point of view problem.

Keep in mind that this is just an introduction to point of view, which is a marvelously complex topic. We'll continue on in Chapter 7 when we talk about point of view and *reliability.*

Part 2: EXERCISES

Choosing the point of view is one of the most important things you will do when writing your story, novel, or nonfiction piece. You have many, many choices—although sometimes it won't feel like a choice. Sometimes you'll just make a leap of faith when it comes to the point of view. Other times, you'll need to question it, explore and experiment.

Exercise 1: Change Point of View and Dance: Experiments in Narration

Goal: To show you how changing the point of view dramatically affects how the material reads. (It's not just a case of doing a universal search and replace of "I" for "he" or "she." Different things enter or come out of the material depending on the point of view that you use.)

What to do: 1. Pick an incident that happened to you in the past month or so—something that has stuck in your mind, although for what reason you're not quite sure.

2. Tell about the event in three different ways: first person point of view, second person point of view, and third person *omniscient* point of view.

The following passage was written by Steven Marvin:

I was sitting at the bus station waiting for a bus downtown. My wife was with me, we were going to a department store to buy stuff for our child, who was to be born in about six weeks. I still hadn't gotten used to the sight of my wife's swollen belly, and the fact that *I* had done that to her—sometimes I felt like I was going to get into trouble, that I had done something really, really wrong—when I felt a sharp pain in my stomach. Really sharp, like a knife pushing in from the outside. I doubled over in pain. My wife, of course, was very concerned, and actually knelt down in front of me, her great belly brushing against the dirty floor of the station.

You are sitting in a bus station. You are with your wife. She is heavy with your child. You've done enough reading to know that bad things lie ahead for her. And you're getting off scot free. Today is what you've come in your mind to call "D-Day. You've agreed to buy the diapers, and the underwear, and the clothes, and all the other things you'll need to bring the baby home from the hospital. You've already been given a ton of stuff by friends and family. Then suddenly there is a pain in your stomach. Is this what giving birth is like, you wonder briefly, but not for long; the pain is too intense.

Your immensely pregnant wife is kneeling on the dirty linoleum floor in front of you. You can hardly breathe. What is happening?

The young couple was sitting quietly together in the bus terminal. You would have thought they'd been married for decades, the way they leaned against each other calmly, no passion or excitement, just calm support. The woman was very pregnant. She looked happy, but a little worried; her hands clasped her backpack hard and occasionally she swallowed hard. It was hard to guess at what the young man was thinking. He wore a zipped-up black sweatshirt with the hood up over his head, making him look a little like a pointy-headed elf. He was carrying a shopping bag that seemed to be filled with papers. Occasionally, he reached out with his right hand and brushed his knuckles against the cheekbone of his wife. Then, suddenly, he bent over, grabbing his stomach. The woman panicked, first standing up, letting her backpack slide to the floor, then bending down over her husband, and finally kneeling before him in a supplicating manner.

Exercise 2: Using Point of View as a Way "In" to Difficult Material

Goal: To play with point of view as a way to gain access to material that has previously been difficult to write about.

What to do: 1. Pick an incident or event that you've tried to write about, or which you've hesitated to write about because it is so personal or difficult.

2. First, write it in the first person point of view. Just write it straight out, no matter how difficult (or how poor a job you might think you're doing).

3. Now write it in third person omniscient point of view, meaning that there is a narrator who knows all and sees all and who is commenting on what is happening according to the "truth" of the incident. Don't be shy about making judgments or otherwise commenting on the thoughts or actions of your characters: a third person omniscient narrator, after all, sees all and knows all.

Here's a passage from an exercise by John Garcia.

I've been trying to write about the stroke my father had about a month ago. It wasn't a severe one; he's getting all his faculties back, his slowed speech is just temporary, the doctors say, but it was still scary and it was a wake-up call. He's seventy-four, but I'd been used to thinking of him as immortal. The bastard. The same bastard who'd made my life miserable growing up. Things have calmed down a lot lately, of course. We no longer fight—what's there to fight about? My tattoos are there, they're not going anywhere; I no longer use all the piercings in my body, just my right ear, and of course I have a good job. The fact that I still lead what he considered a rootless existence is a sticking point, but when I drop by to visit he actually seems glad to see me. I think he's bored in his retirement. Terribly bored. He was always so full of energy, but now he just naps on the couch and flips through the channels of his satellite TV.

John's first view of his father after the stroke was a terrifying one: his father, the strong, the mighty, the invincible, lying quiet and still in the hospital room. Asleep. He was drooling out of the right side of his mouth. His left arm was thrown up against his chest, as though he was warding off some attack. John's heart throbbed with pity and anger. The old bastard. He sat down. His mother was holding his father's hand. She had stopped crying, but she was far from calm. What would she do if he died? She didn't even know where the checkbook was. She didn't know their credit card companies—he took care of all that. John felt a sudden sharp stab of fear and loss as he began to comprehend what this could mean for his mother—and for him.

Part 3: READING AS A WRITER

The Lady with the Little Dog

ANTON CHEKHOV

Translated by Richard Pevear and Larissa Volokhonsky

I

The talk was that a new face had appeared on the embankment: a lady with a little dog. Dmitri Dmitrich Gurov, who had already spent two weeks in Yalta and was used to it, also began to take an interest in new faces. Sitting in a pavilion at Vernet's, he saw a young woman, not very tall, blond, in a beret, walking along the embankment; behind her ran a white spitz.

And after that he met her several times a day in the town garden or in the square. She went strolling alone, in the same beret, with the white spitz; nobody knew who she was, and they called her simply "the lady with the little dog."

"If she's here with no husband or friends," Gurov reflected, "it wouldn't be a bad idea to make her acquaintance."

He was not yet forty, but he had a twelve-year-old daughter and two sons in school. He had married young, while still a second-year student, and now his wife seemed half again his age. She was a tall woman with dark eyebrows, erect, imposing, dignified, and a thinking person, as she called herself. She read a great deal, used the new orthography, called her husband not Dmitri but Dimitri, but he secretly considered her none too bright, narrow-minded, graceless, was afraid of her, and disliked being at home. He had begun to be unfaithful to her long ago, was unfaithful often, and, probably for that reason, almost always spoke ill of women, and when they were discussed in his presence, he would say of them:

"An inferior race!"

It seemed to him that he had been taught enough by bitter experience to call them anything he liked, and yet he could not have lived without the "inferior race" even for two days. In the company of men he was bored, ill at ease, with them he was taciturn and cold, but when he was among women, he felt himself free and knew what to talk about with them and how to behave; and he was at ease even being silent with them. In his appearance, in his character, in his whole nature there was something attractive and elusive that disposed women towards him and enticed them; he knew that, and he himself was attracted to them by some force.

Repeated experience, and bitter experience indeed, had long since taught him that every intimacy, which in the beginning lends life such pleasant diversity and presents itself as a nice and light adventure, inevitably, with decent people—especially irresolute Muscovites, who are slow starters—grows into a major task, extremely complicated, and the situation finally becomes burdensome. But at every new meeting with an interesting woman, this experience somehow slipped from his memory, and he wanted to live, and everything seemed quite simple and amusing.

And so one time, towards evening, he was having dinner in the garden, and the lady in the beret came over unhurriedly to take the table next to his. Her expression, her walk, her dress, her hair told him that she belonged to decent society, was married, in Yalta for the first time, and alone, and that she was bored here . . . In the stories about the impurity of local morals there was much untruth, he despised them and knew that these stories were mostly invented by people who would eagerly have sinned themselves had they known how; but when the lady sat down at the next table, three steps away from him, he remembered those stories of easy conquests, of trips to the mountains, and the tempting thought of a quick, fleeting liaison, a romance with an unknown woman, of whose very name you are ignorant, suddenly took possession of him.

He gently called the spitz, and when the dog came over, he shook his finger at it. The spitz growled. Gurov shook his finger again.

The lady glanced at him and immediately lowered her eyes.

"He doesn't bite," she said and blushed.

"May I give him a bone?" and, when she nodded in the affirmative, he asked affably: "Have you been in Yalta long?"

"About five days."

"And I'm already dragging through my second week here."

They were silent for a while.

"The time passes quickly, and yet it's so boring here!" she said without looking at him.

"It's merely the accepted thing to say it's boring here. The ordinary man lives somewhere in his Belevo or Zhizdra and isn't bored, then he comes here: 'Ah, how boring! Ah, how dusty!' You'd think he came from Granada."

She laughed. Then they went on eating in silence, like strangers; but after dinner they walked off together—and a light, bantering conversation began, of free, contented people, who do not care where they go or what they talk about. They strolled and talked of how strange the light was on the sea; the water was of a lilac color, so soft and warm, and over it the moon cast a golden strip. They talked of how sultry it was after the hot day. Gurov told her he was a Muscovite, a philologist by education, but worked in a bank; had once been preparing to sing in an opera company, but had dropped it, owned two houses in Moscow . . . And from her he learned that she grew up in Petersburg, but was married in S., where she had now been living for two years, that she would be staying in Yalta for about a month, and that her husband might come to fetch her, because he also wanted to get some rest. She was quite unable to explain where her husband served—in the provincial administration or the zemstvo[1] council—and she herself found that funny. And Gurov also learned that her name was Anna Sergeevna.

Afterwards, in his hotel room, he thought about her, that tomorrow she would probably meet him again. It had to be so. Going to bed, he recalled that still quite recently she had been a schoolgirl, had studied just as his daughter was studying now, recalled how much timorousness and angularity there was in her laughter, her conversation with a stranger—it must have been the first time in her life that she was alone in such a situation, when she was followed, looked at, and spoken to with only one secret

_____
[1] County council.

purpose, which she could not fail to guess. He recalled her slender, weak neck, her beautiful gray eyes.

"There's something pathetic in her all the same," he thought and began to fall asleep.

II

A week had passed since they became acquainted. It was Sunday. Inside it was stuffy, but outside the dust flew in whirls, hats blew off. They felt thirsty all day, and Gurov often stopped at the pavilion, offering Anna Sergeevna now a soft drink, now ice cream. There was no escape.

In the evening when it relented a little, they went to the jetty to watch the steamer come in. There were many strollers on the pier; they had come to meet people, they were holding bouquets. And here two particularities of the smartly dressed Yalta crowd distinctly struck one's eye: the elderly ladies were dressed like young ones, and there were many generals.

Owing to the roughness of the sea, the steamer arrived late, when the sun had already gone down, and it was a long time turning before it tied up. Anna Sergeevna looked at the ship and the passengers through her lorgnette, as if searching for acquaintances, and when she turned to Gurov, her eyes shone. She talked a lot, and her questions were abrupt, and she herself immediately forgot what she had asked; then she lost her lorgnette in the crowd.

The smartly dressed crowd was dispersing, the faces could no longer be seen, the wind had died down completely, and Gurov and Anna Sergeevna stood as if they were expecting someone else to get off the steamer. Anna Sergeevna was silent now and smelled the flowers, not looking at Gurov.

"The weather's improved towards evening," he said. "Where shall we go now? Shall we take a drive somewhere?"

She made no answer.

Then he looked at her intently and suddenly embraced her and kissed her on the lips, and he was showered with the fragrance and moisture of the flowers, and at once looked around timorously—had anyone seen them?

"Let's go to your place . . ." he said softly.

And they both walked quickly.

Her hotel room was stuffy and smelled of the perfumes she had bought in a Japanese shop. Gurov, looking at her now, thought: "What meetings there are in life!" From the past he had kept the memory of carefree, good-natured women, cheerful with love, grateful to him for their happiness, however brief; and of women—his wife, for example—who loved without sincerity, with superfluous talk, affectedly, with hysteria, with an expression as if it were not love, not passion, but something more significant; and of those two or three very beautiful, cold ones, in whose faces a predatory expression would suddenly flash, a stubborn wish to take, to snatch from life more than it could give, and these were women not in their first youth, capricious, unreasonable, domineering, unintelligent, and when Gurov cooled towards them, their beauty aroused hatred in him, and the lace of their underwear seemed to him like scales.

But here was all the timorousness and angularly of inexperienced youth, a feeling of awkwardness, and an impression of bewilderment, as if someone had suddenly knocked at the door. Anna Sergeevna, the "lady with the little dog," somehow took a special, very serious attitude towards what had happened, as if it were her fall—so it seemed, and that was strange and inopportune. Her features drooped and faded, and her long hair hung down sadly on both sides of her face, she sat pondering in a dejected pose, like the sinful woman in an old painting.

"It's not good," she said. "You'll be the first not to respect me now."

There was a watermelon on the table in the hotel room. Gurov cut himself a slice and unhurriedly began to eat it. At least half an hour passed in silence.

Anna Sergeevna was touching, she had about her a breath of the purity of a proper, naive, little-experienced woman; the solitary candle burning on the table barely lit up her face, but it was clear that her heart was uneasy.

"Why should I stop respecting you?" asked Gurov. "You don't know what you're saying yourself."

"God forgive me!" she said, and her eyes filled with tears. "This is terrible."

"It's like you're justifying yourself."

"How can I justify myself? I'm a bad, low woman, I despise myself and am not even thinking of any justification. It's not my husband I've deceived, but my own self! And not only now, I've been deceiving myself for a long time. My husband may be an honest and good man, but he's a lackey! I don't know what he does there, how he serves, I only know that he's a lackey. I married him when I was twenty, I was tormented by curiosity, I wanted something better. I told myself there must be a different life. I wanted to live! To live and live . . . I was burning with curiosity . . . you won't understand it, but I swear to God that I couldn't control myself any longer, something was happening to me, I couldn't restrain myself, I told my husband I was ill and came here . . . And here I go about as if in a daze, as if I'm out of my mind . . . and now I've become a trite, trashy woman, whom anyone can despise."

Gurov was bored listening, he was annoyed by the naive tone, by this repentance, so unexpected and out of place; had it not been for the tears in her eyes, one might have thought she was joking or playing a role.

"I don't understand," he said softly, "what is it you want?"

She hid her face on his chest and pressed herself to him.

"Believe me, believe me, I beg you . . ." she said. "I love an honest, pure life, sin is vile to me, I myself don't know what I'm doing. Simple people say, 'The unclean one beguiled me.' And now I can say of myself that the unclean one has beguiled me."

"Enough, enough . . ." he muttered.

He looked into her fixed, frightened eyes, kissed her, spoke softly and tenderly, and she gradually calmed down, and her gaiety returned. They both began to laugh.

Later, when they went out, there was not a soul on the embankment, the town with its cypresses looked completely dead, but the sea still beat noisily against the shore; one barge was rocking on the waves, and the lantern on it glimmered sleepily.

They found a cab and drove to Oreanda.

"I just learned your last name downstairs in the lobby: it was written on the board—von Dideritz," said Gurov. "Is your husband German?"

"No, his grandfather was German, I think, but he himself is Orthodox."

In Oreanda they sat on a bench not far from the church, looked down on the sea, and were silent. Yalta was barely visible through the morning mist, white clouds stood motionless on the mountaintops. The leaves of the trees did not stir, cicadas called, and the monotonous, dull noise of the sea, coming from below, spoke of the peace, of the eternal sleep that awaits us. So it had sounded below when neither Yalta nor Oreanda were there, so it sounded now and would go on sounding with the same dull indifference when we are no longer here. And in this constancy, in this utter indifference to the life and death of each of us, there perhaps lies hidden the pledge of our eternal salvation, the unceasing movement of life on earth, of unceasing perfection. Sitting beside the young woman, who looked so beautiful in the dawn, appeased and enchanted by the view of this magical décor—sea, mountains, clouds, the open sky—Gurov reflected that, essentially, if you thought of it, everything was beautiful in this world, everything except for what we ourselves think and do when we forget the higher goals of being and our human dignity.

Some man came up—it must have been a watchman—looked at them, and went away. And this detail seemed such a mysterious thing, and also beautiful. The steamer from Feodosia could be seen approaching in the glow of the early dawn, its lights out.

"There's dew on the grass," said Anna Sergeevna after a silence.

"Yes. It's time to go home."

They went back to town.

After that they met on the embankment every noon, had lunch together, dined, strolled, admired the sea. She complained that she slept poorly and that her heart beat anxiously, kept asking the same questions, troubled now by jealousy, now by fear that he did not respect her enough. And often on the square or in the garden, when there was no one near them, he would suddenly draw her to him and kiss her passionately. Their complete idleness, those kisses in broad daylight, with a furtive look around and the fear that someone might see them, the heat, the smell of the sea, and the constant flashing before their eyes of idle, smartly dressed, well-fed people, seemed to transform him; he repeatedly told Anna Sergeevna how beautiful she was, and how seductive, was impatiently passionate, never left her side, while she often brooded and kept asking him to admit that he did not respect her, did not love her at all, and saw in her only a trite woman. Late almost every evening they went somewhere out of town, to Oreanda or the cascade; these outings were successful, their impressions each time were beautiful, majestic.

They were expecting her husband to arrive. But a letter came from him in which he said that his eyes hurt and begged his wife to come home quickly. Anna Sergeevna began to hurry.

"It's good that I'm leaving," she said to Gurov. "It's fate itself."

She went by carriage, and he accompanied her. They drove for a whole day. When she had taken her seat in the express train and the second bell had rung, she said:

"Let me have one more look at you . . . One more look. There."

She did not cry, but was sad, as if ill, and her face trembled.

"I'll think of you . . . remember you," she said. "God be with you. Don't think ill of me. We're saying good-bye forever, it must be so, because we should never have met. Well, God be with you."

The train left quickly, its lights soon disappeared, and a moment later the noise could no longer be heard, as if everything were conspiring on purpose to put a speedy end to this sweet oblivion, this madness. And, left alone on the platform and gazing into the dark distance, Gurov listened to the chirring of the grasshoppers and the hum of the telegraph wires with a feeling as if he had just woken up. And he thought that now there was one more affair or adventure in his life, and it, too, was now over, and all that was left was the memory . . . He was touched, saddened, and felt some slight remorse; this young woman whom he was never to see again had not been happy with him; he had been affectionate with her, and sincere, but all the same, in his treatment of her, in his tone and caresses, there had been a slight shade of mockery, the somewhat coarse arrogance of a happy man, who was, moreover, almost twice her age. She had all the while called him kind, extraordinary, lofty; obviously, he had appeared to her not as he was in reality, and therefore he had involuntarily deceived her . . .

Here at the station there was already a breath of autumn, the wind was cool.

"It's time I headed north, too," thought Gurov, leaving the platform. "High time!"

III

At home in Moscow everything was already wintry, the stoves were heated, and in the morning, when the children were getting ready for school and drinking their tea, it was dark, and the nanny would light a lamp for a short time. The frosts had already set in. When the first snow falls, on the first day of riding in sleighs, it is pleasant to see the white ground, the white roofs; one's breath feels soft and pleasant, and in those moments one remembers one's youth. The old lindens and birches, white with hoarfrost, have a good-natured look, they are nearer one's heart than cypresses and palms, and near them one no longer wants to think of mountains and the sea.

Gurov was a Muscovite. He returned to Moscow on a fine, frosty day, and when he put on his fur coat and warm gloves and strolled down Petrovka, and when on Saturday evening he heard the bells ringing, his recent trip and the places he had visited lost all their charm for him. He gradually became immersed in Moscow life, now greedily read three newspapers a day and said that he never read the Moscow newspapers on principle. He was drawn to restaurants, clubs, to dinner parties, celebrations, and felt flattered that he had famous lawyers and actors among his clients, and that at the Doctors' Club he played cards with a professor. He could eat a whole portion of selyanka[2] from the pan . . .

A month would pass and Anna Sergeevna, as it seemed to him, would

---

[2] Meat stewed with pickled cabbage and served in a pan.

be covered by mist in his memory and would only appear to him in dreams with a touching smile, as other women did. But more than a month passed, deep winter came, and yet everything was as clear in his memory as if he had parted with Anna Sergeevna only the day before. And the memories burned brighter and brighter. Whether from the voices of his children doing their homework, which reached him in his study in the evening quiet, or from hearing a romance, or an organ in a restaurant, or the blizzard howling in the chimney, everything would suddenly rise up in his memory: what had happened on the jetty, and the early morning with mist on the mountains, and the steamer from Feodosia, and the kisses. He would pace the room for a long time, and remember, and smile, and then his memories would turn to reveries, and in his imagination the past would mingle with what was still to be. Anna Sergeevna was not a dream, she followed him everywhere like a shadow and watched him. Closing his eyes, he saw her as if alive, and she seemed younger, more beautiful, more tender than she was; and he also seemed better to himself than he had been then, in Yalta. In the evenings she gazed at him from the bookcase, the fireplace, the corner, he could hear her breathing, the gentle rustle of her skirts. In the street he followed women with his eyes, looking for one who resembled her . . .

And he was tormented now by a strong desire to tell someone his memories. But at home it was impossible to talk of his love, and away from home there was no one to talk with. Certainly not among his tenants nor at the bank. And what was there to say? Had he been in love then? Was there anything beautiful, poetic, or instructive, or merely interesting, in his relations with Anna Sergeevna? And he found himself speaking vaguely of love, of women, and no one could guess what it was about, and only his wife raised her dark eyebrows and said:

"You know, Dimitri, the role of fop doesn't suit you at all."

One night, as he was leaving the Doctors' Club together with his partner, an official, he could not help himself and said:

"If you only knew what a charming woman I met in Yalta!"

The official got into a sleigh and drove off, but suddenly turned around and called out:

"Dimitri Dmitrich!"

"What?"

"You were right earlier: the sturgeon was a bit off!"

Those words, so very ordinary, for some reason suddenly made Gurov indignant, struck him as humiliating, impure. Such savage manners, such faces! These senseless nights, and such uninteresting, unremarkable days!

Frenzied card-playing, gluttony, drunkenness, constant talk about the same thing. Useless matters and conversations about the same thing took for their share the best part of one's time, the best of one's powers, and what was left in the end was some sort of curtailed, wingless life, some sort of nonsense, and it was impossible to get away or flee, as if you were sitting in a madhouse or a prison camp!

Gurov did not sleep all night and felt indignant, and as a result had a headache all the next day. And the following nights he slept poorly, sitting up in bed all the time and thinking, or pacing up and down. He was sick of the children, sick of the bank, did not want to go anywhere or talk about anything.

In December, during the holidays, he got ready to travel and told his wife he was leaving for Petersburg to solicit for a certain young man—and went to S. Why? He did not know very well himself. He wanted to see Anna Sergeevna and talk with her, to arrange a meeting, if he could.

He arrived at S. in the morning and took the best room in the hotel, where the whole floor was covered with gray army flannel and there was an inkstand on the table, gray with dust, with a horseback rider, who held his hat in his raised hand, but whose head was broken off. The hall porter gave him the necessary information: von Dideritz lives in his own house on Staro-Goncharnaya Street, not far from the hotel; he has a good life, is wealthy, keeps his own horses, everybody in town knows him. The porter pronounced it "Dridiritz."

Gurov walked unhurriedly to Staro-Goncharnaya Street, found the house. Just opposite the house stretched a fence, long, gray, with spikes.

"You could flee from such a fence," thought Gurov, looking now at the windows, now at the fence.

He reflected: today was not a workday, and the husband was probably at home. And anyhow it would be tactless to go in and cause embarrassment. If he sent a message, it might fall into the husband's hands, and that would ruin everything. It would be best to trust to chance. And he kept pacing up and down the street and near the fence and waited for his chance. He saw a beggar go in the gates and saw the dogs attack him, then, an hour later, he heard someone playing a piano, and the sounds reached him faintly, indistinctly. It must have been Anna Sergeevna playing. The front door suddenly opened and some old woman came out, the familiar white spitz running after her. Gurov wanted to call the dog, but his heart suddenly throbbed, and in his excitement he was unable to remember the spitz's name.

He paced up and down, and hated the gray fence more and more, and now he thought with vexation that Anna Sergeevna had forgotten him, and was perhaps amusing herself with another man, and that that was so natural in the situation of a young woman who had to look at this cursed fence from morning till evening. He went back to his hotel room and sat on the sofa for a long time, not knowing what to do, then had dinner, then took a long nap.

"How stupid and upsetting this all is," he thought, when he woke up and looked at the dark windows: it was already evening. "So I've had my sleep. Now what am I to do for the night?"

He sat on the bed, which was covered with a cheap, gray, hospital-like blanket, and taunted himself in vexation:

"Here's the lady with the little dog for you . . . Here's an adventure for you . . . Yes, here you sit."

That morning, at the train station, a poster with very big lettering had caught his eye: it was the opening night of *The Geisha*. He remembered it and went to the theater.

"It's very likely that she goes to opening nights," he thought.

The theater was full. And here, too, as in all provincial theaters generally, a haze hung over the chandeliers, the gallery stirred noisily; the local dandies stood in the front row before the performance started, their hands behind their backs; and here, too, in the governor's box, the governor's daughter sat in front, wearing a boa, while the governor himself modestly hid behind the portière, and only his hands could be seen; the curtain swayed, the orchestra spent a long time tuning up. All the while the public came in and took their seats, Gurov kept searching greedily with his eyes.

Anna Sergeevna came in. She sat in the third row, and when Gurov looked at her, his heart was wrung, and he realized clearly that there was now no person closer, dearer, or more important for him in the whole world; this small woman, lost in the provincial crowd, not remarkable for anything, with a vulgar lorgnette in her hand, now filled his whole life, was his grief, his joy, the only happiness he now wished for himself; and to the sounds of the bad orchestra, with its trashy local violins, he thought how beautiful she was. He thought and dreamed.

A man came in with Anna Sergeevna and sat down next to her, a young man with little side-whiskers, very tall, stooping; he nodded his head at every step, and it seemed he was perpetually bowing. This was probably her husband, whom she, in an outburst of bitter feeling that time in Yalta, had called a lackey. And indeed, in his long figure, his side-whiskers, his little bald spot, there was something of lackeyish modesty; he had a sweet smile, and the badge of some learned society gleamed in his buttonhole, like the badge of a lackey.

During the first intermission the husband went to smoke; she remained in her seat. Gurov, who was also sitting in the stalls, went up to her and said in a trembling voice and with a forced smile:

"How do you do?"

She looked at him and paled, then looked again in horror, not believing her eyes, and tightly clutched her fan and lorgnette in her hand, obviously struggling with herself to keep from fainting. Both were silent. She sat, he stood, alarmed at her confusion, not venturing to sit down next to her. The tuning-up violins and flutes sang out, it suddenly became frightening, it seemed that people were gazing at them from all the boxes. But then she got up and quickly walked to the exit, he followed her, and they both went confusedly through corridors and stairways, going up, then down, and the uniforms of the courts, the schools, and the imperial estates flashed before them, all with badges; ladies flashed by, fur coats on hangers, a drafty wind blew, drenching them with the smell of cigar stubs. And Gurov, whose heart was pounding, thought: "Oh, Lord! Why these people, this orchestra . . ."

And just then he suddenly recalled how, at the station in the evening after he had seen Anna Sergeevna off, he had said to himself that everything was over and they would never see each other again. But how far it still was from being over!

On a narrow, dark stairway with the sign "To the Amphitheater," she stopped.

"How you frightened me!" she said, breathing heavily, still pale, stunned. "Oh, how you frightened me! I'm barely alive. Why did you come? Why?"

"But understand, Anna, understand . . ." he said in a low voice, hurrying. "I beg you to understand . . ."

She looked at him with fear, with entreaty, with love, looked at him intently, the better to keep his features in her memory.

"I've been suffering so!" she went on, not listening to him. "I think only of you all the time, I've lived by my thoughts of you. And I've tried to forget, to forget, but why, why did you come?"

Further up, on the landing, two high-school boys were smoking and looking down, but Gurov did not care, he drew Anna Sergeevna to him and began kissing her face, her cheeks, her hands.

"What are you doing, what are you doing!" she repeated in horror, pushing him away from her. "We've both lost our minds. Leave today, leave at once . . . I adjure you by all that's holy, I implore you . . . Somebody's coming!"

Someone was climbing the stairs.

"You must leave . . ." Anna Sergeevna went on in a whisper. "Do you hear, Dmitri Dmitrich? I'll come to you in Moscow. I've never been happy, I'm unhappy now, and I'll never, never be happy, never! Don't make me suffer still more! I swear I'll come to Moscow. But we must part now! My dear one, my good one, my darling, we must part!"

She pressed his hand and quickly began going downstairs, turning back to look at him, and it was clear from her eyes that she was indeed not happy . . . Gurov stood for a little while, listened, then, when everything was quiet, found his coat and left the theater.

IV

And Anna Sergeevna began coming to see him in Moscow. Once every two or three months she left S., and told her husband she was going to consult a professor about her female disorder—and her husband did and did not believe her. Arriving in Moscow, she stayed at the Slavyansky Bazaar and at once sent a man in a red hat to Gurov. Gurov came to see her, and nobody in Moscow knew of it.

Once he was going to see her in that way on a winter morning (the messenger had come the previous evening but had not found him in). With him was his daughter, whom he wanted to see off to school, which was on the way. Big, wet snow was falling.

"It's now three degrees above freezing, and yet it's snowing," Gurov said to his daughter. "But it's warm only near the surface of the earth, while in the upper layers of the atmosphere the temperature is quite different."

"And why is there no thunder in winter, papa?"

He explained that, too. He spoke and thought that here he was going to a rendezvous, and not a single soul knew of it or probably would ever know. He had two lives: an apparent one, seen and known by all who needed it, filled with conventional truth and conventional deceit, which perfectly resembled the lives of his acquaintances and friends, and another that went on in secret. And by some strange coincidence, perhaps an accidental one, everything that he found important, interesting, necessary, in which he was sincere and did not deceive himself, which constituted the core of his life, occurred in secret from others, while everything that made up his lie, his shell, in which he hid in order to conceal the truth—for instance, his work at the bank, his arguments at the club, his "inferior race," his attending official celebrations with his wife—all this was in full view. And he judged others by himself, did not believe what he saw, and always supposed that every man led his own real and very interesting life under the cover of secrecy, as under the cover of night. Every personal existence was upheld by a secret, and it was perhaps partly for that reason that every cultivated man took such anxious care that his personal secret should be respected.

After taking his daughter to school, Gurov went to the Slavyansky Bazaar. He took his fur coat off downstairs, went up, and knocked softly at the door. Anna Sergeevna, wearing his favorite gray dress, tired from the trip and the expectation, had been waiting for him since the previous evening; she was pale, looked at him and did not smile, and he had barely come in when she was already leaning on his chest. Their kiss was long, lingering, as if they had not seen each other for two years.

"Well, how is your life there?" he asked. "What's new?"

"Wait, I'll tell you . . . I can't."

She could not speak because she was crying. She turned away from him and pressed a handkerchief to her eyes.

"Well, let her cry a little, and meanwhile I'll sit down," he thought, and sat down in an armchair.

Then he rang and ordered tea; and then, while he drank tea, she went on standing with her face turned to the window . . . She was crying from anxiety, from a sorrowful awareness that their life had turned out so sadly; they only saw each other in secret, they hid from people like thieves! Was their life not broken?

"Well, stop now," he said.

For him it was obvious that this love of theirs would not end soon, that there was no knowing when. Anna Sergeevna's attachment to him grew ever stronger, she adored him, and it would have been unthinkable to tell her that it all really had to end at some point; and she would not have believed it.

He went up to her and took her by the shoulders to caress her, to make a joke, and at that moment he saw himself in the mirror.

His head was beginning to turn gray. And it seemed strange to him that he had aged so much in those last years, had lost so much of his good looks. The shoulders on which his hands lay were warm and trembled. He felt compassion for this life, still so warm and beautiful, but probably already near the point where it would begin to fade and wither, like his own life. Why did she love him so? Women had always taken him to be other than he was, and they had loved in him, not himself, but a man their imagination had created, whom they had greedily sought all their lives; and then, when they had noticed their mistake, they had still loved him. And not one of them had been happy with him. Time passed, he met women, became intimate, parted, but not once did he love; there was anything else, but not love.

And only now, when his head was gray, had he really fallen in love as one ought to—for the first time in his life.

He and Anna Sergeevna loved each other like very close, dear people, like husband and wife, like tender friends; it seemed to them that fate itself had destined them for each other, and they could not understand why he had a wife and she a husband; and it was as if they were two birds of passage, a male and a female, who had been caught and forced to live in separate cages. They had forgiven each other the things they were ashamed of in the past, they forgave everything in the present, and they felt that this love of theirs had changed them both.

Formerly, in sad moments, he had calmed himself with all sorts of arguments, whatever had come into his head, but now he did not care about any arguments, he felt deep compassion, he wanted to be sincere, tender . . .

"Stop, my good one," he said, "you've had your cry—and enough . . . Let's talk now, we'll think up something."

Then they had a long discussion, talked about how to rid themselves of the need for hiding, for deception, for living in different towns and not seeing each other for long periods. How could they free themselves from these unbearable bonds?

"How? How?" he asked, clutching his head. "How?"

And it seemed that, just a little more—and the solution would be found, and then a new, beautiful life would begin; and it was clear to both of them that the end was still far, far off, and that the most complicated and difficult part was just beginning.

1. What kind of narrator does this story have? How much does he/she know? What is his/her distance from the events of the story?
2. What are the pivotal moments of the story? Is there an epiphany? Or multiple epiphanies? Point out those places where the character Gurov is enlightened, or realizes some truth about his situation.
3. What is the "resolution" of the story? What do you make of resolutions like this (where nothing is really resolved)?

Moonrise

PENNY WOLFSON

At the Center for Creative Photography in Tucson, Arizona, my husband, Joe, and I are looking at prints of *Moonrise, Hernandez, New Mexico*, by Ansel Adams. A slender young man in a suit has brought us, as requested, three versions of this famous photograph. He dons a pair of white gloves before removing the $14\,^1/_{20} \times 18\,^1/_{20}$ enlargements from their Plexiglas sheaths, opens the hinged glass viewing case in front of us, and places the photographs carefully, lovingly, on a slanted white board inside. He stands there while we examine the pictures; when we are finished, he will repeat the process in reverse.

I don't know exactly where Hernandez, New Mexico, is, but it reminds me a bit of Sacaton, ninety miles northwest of here, the Pima Indian village where Joe is a government doctor and where we have lived since July of 1983. Now it's December. We have made the trip to Tucson expressly to view the Ansel Adams photos, though we did not imagine that there would be so many prints from the same negative.

In *Moonrise* two thirds of the space is usurped by a rich black sky; a gibbous moon floats like a hot-air balloon in an otherworldly—and yet absolutely southwestern—landscape. A gauzy strip of low clouds or filtered light drifts along the horizon; distant mountains are lit by waning sun or rising moon. Only in the bottom third of the photo, among scrubby earth and sparsely scattered trees, does human settlement appear: a small collection of modest adobe houses and one larger adobe church. Around the edge of the village white crosses rise from the ground at many angles; at first glance they resemble clotheslines strung with sheets or socks, but on more careful examination it is obvious that they mark graves.

The prints differ greatly in quality from the reproductions one usually sees, and also differ slightly from one another: here we see a more defined darkness, burnt in by the photographer, there a variation in exposure, a grainier texture. But that does not change the essential meaning of the photograph, a meaning one never forgets in the Southwest: Nature dominates. Human life is small, fragile, and finite. And yet, still, beautiful.

I. Falling, 1998

I am at the Grand Union in Dobbs Ferry, New York, with my son Ansel, who is thirteen years old. It's raining. He begged to come, so I brought him, not really wanting to, because I had to bring his wheelchair, too: it weighs more than two hundred pounds and isn't easy to maneuver into the minivan, even with the ramp. I have to wrestle the motorized chair until it faces forward and then, bending and squeezing into the narrow confines of the van, I have to fasten it to the floor with several clasps. By the time I have done this even once, I'm irritable. A trip to the supermarket means doing it twice and undoing it twice.

Anyway, we've finished our shopping, and we leave the supermarket. Ansel is in his chair, without his hooded yellow raincoat from L. L. Bean, because he has decided that at his age a raincoat is babyish, not cool. He's afraid people at school will laugh at him. Maybe this is true, I say, but I think it's stupid. Why get wet when you can stay dry? Needless to say, I lose this argument.

Before loading the groceries I open the van door so that Ansel can get in the front seat, where he always sits if Joe isn't with us. He parks his chair at a distance from the minivan, so that I'll have room for the ramp, and starts to rise, laboriously. No, "rise" sounds too easy, like smoke going up a flue, airy, like yeast bread rising in the oven. Ansel does not rise. He shifts sideways in the seat and pulls himself up heavily, propping his eighty pounds against the armrest for balance. He leans with his left arm, twists his right shoulder around to straighten up, and brings his hip and buttocks to a partly standing position. Actually he's sort of bent in half, with his hands still on the chair's joystick. There is a moment of imbalance. His feet are planted far apart, farther out than his hips, and he needs to bounce back and forth a few times to bring his feet together. Finally he's up. He begins walking toward the door in his waddling, tiptoe way. His spine is curved quite a bit from scoliosis, his stomach is forward, his hands are out at his sides chest-high, his fingers outstretched.

His balance is so tenuous that his five-year-old brother, Toby, can knock him down. Sometimes Ansel will bellow, "I'm tired of everyone always leaving things all over the floor! Don't they know I'll fall?" It's true that we're a little careless about this. But Ansel will trip over anything—an unevenness in the sidewalk, the dog's water dish, some bits of food on the floor, things expected and unexpected—and sometimes over nothing. Sooner or later he falls. It's part of the routine. And the older he gets, the more he falls.

Now, in the Grand Union parking lot, he falls. Who knows why—it could be the wet ground. He's in the skinny aisle of asphalt between our car and the one parked next to us. He falls, and it's pouring, and I'm still loading grocery bags into the back.

"Mom!" he calls at me, half barking, half crying. "I fell!" There's such anguish, such anger, in his voice when he falls, and such resignation. He never thinks I hear him.

And why am I suddenly so angry? Such terrible impatience rises in me now. Am I really such a witch, such a bad mother, that when I'm loading groceries and my son falls, I don't have the time or patience to cope? Why am I so angry?

"Wait a minute," I say. "I'll be there in a minute."

So he sits on the wet pavement between the cars. I know his sweatpants are at this moment soaking through. I can see that the wheelchair, waiting to be rolled up the ramp, needing to be pushed and yanked into position, is also getting wet. Its foamy nylon seat will need drying out later.

A middle-aged blond woman has wheeled her shopping cart into the lot and approaches us. "Can I help?"

No, you definitely cannot help, runs through my head. This is both true and self-righteous. Physically, the job is not meant for two; it's easier for me to do on my own. How would we two, and Ansel, even fit between the cars?

I grit my teeth and smile and say, "No, no thanks, really. I can do it." People always seem puzzled and upset when they see him fall. It's so sudden, an instant crumpling, without warning. They can't see the weakness, the steady deterioration of his pelvis. Maybe someone would fall this way if he'd been hit hard in the solar plexus; I don't know. But Ansel's feet give way for no apparent reason, and he's down.

The blond woman has heard me, but she keeps standing there, her hands clamped around the handle of her cart, her eyes moving from Ansel to the grocery bags to me. I know she means to be helpful, and in a way I do want something from her—pity? an acknowledgment that I am more noble than she? But mostly I want her to go away. *Don't look at me. Don't watch this.*

"Mom! Where *are* you?"

I turn from the blond woman; she fades away. "OK, I'm coming," I say. I try to wedge myself between the cars so that I can retrieve Ansel. There's a special way to pick him up: you have to come from behind and grab him under the arms, raise him so that his toes dangle just above the ground, and then set his feet down precisely the right distance apart.

I'm in pretty good shape, but Ansel is dead weight. Another child could help you, could put his hands around your neck. His feet would come off the ground at even the suggestion of lifting. But Ansel is pulling me down, his limp shoulders, his heavy leg braces, his sodden pants, his clumsy sneakers. I can't hold him. My own sneakers slip on the wet pavement.

2. Chaos, 1999

The New York Academy of Medicine, on 103rd Street and Fifth Avenue, is not exactly in the slums, but it's not really the Upper East Side either. On a dreary, drizzly morning I park at the Metropolitan Museum garage, on Eightieth Street, and walk up Madison, past Banana Republic and Ann Taylor and patisseries and fancy meat purveyors and little French children's-clothing shops that display sashed dresses with hand-embroidered yokes in their windows. But above 96th Street, near the Mount Sinai Hospital complex, the scenery and the people change abruptly; everything's older and more rundown. Street peddlers hawk books, batteries, Yankees caps, cheap scarves, acrylic ski caps, five-dollar handbags. I see an obese black man leaning on a cane, harried-looking workers with Mount Sinai badges, a woman exiting a hospital building through a revolving door carrying crutches.

Eleven years ago, when Ansel was three, doctors diagnosed in him a form of muscular dystrophy called Duchenne, which rapidly destroys muscle tissue, confining its victims to wheelchairs by adolescence and invariably resulting in early death. Like hemophilia, it is almost always transmitted to sons from asymptomatic "carrier" mothers. In my extended family, which produced an overwhelming number of daughters and almost no sons for two generations, the existence of the Duchenne gene—or, more correctly, the existence of an altered gene that doesn't properly code for a particular muscle protein—was unknown, a subterranean truth. My mother and sister and I, all carriers without outward signs, never guessed at this defect in our genetic heritage.

Joe and I gave our son, conceived and born in Arizona, the name of the great photographer we admired, Ansel Adams, who had died earlier that year. The name seemed apt; Ansel was, as people often told us, prettier than a picture, amber-haired and round-eyed, with a perpetually quizzical but serene countenance and the build of a slender but sturdy miniature football player. For two years he developed normally, reaching all the benchmarks on or close to schedule. He was an engaging and beautiful boy, gifted, one suspected, in some intangible way. When his teacher in nursery school began to point out Ansel's deficits in language and in gross motor skills (he couldn't master rudimentary grammar, couldn't alternate legs on the stairs), we refused to see any problem. It was impossible for us to believe that this perfectly wonderful child, our child, was not perfect at all, that he was in fact handicapped and would become progressively more handicapped.

It took a year for us to accept his differentness, to have him profession-
ally evaluated, to reach a diagnosis. And although we have been to dozens
of doctors and have dealt with every aspect of his disease, it has taken me
eleven years to get up the nerve to come here, to the Academy of Medicine, and look squarely at what will happen to Ansel in a future I have not
yet completely faced.

The library reading room is large and quiet, with a high ceiling and a
faded tapestry on the wall behind me. At a long oak table beneath a grand
chandelier, surrounded by busts of famous scientists, all men, who peer
down from atop the bookshelves, I sit nervously waiting for the books I've
requested. It makes sense, I suppose, that Louis Pasteur sits head and
shoulders above the lesser-knowns.

But not even Pasteur, I remind myself, could have cured muscular dystrophy. Nor could any of the nineteenth-century doctors who described
the disease, including the English physicians Charles Bell, Edward
Meryon, and William Gowers and the French neurologist G. B. A.
Duchenne, after whom the most common form of muscular dystrophy is
named. And despite hundreds, perhaps thousands, of studies completed
and articles written and compiled in prestigious journals such as *Muscle
and Nerve* and *The Lancet* and the *Journal of the American Medical Association*,
sitting right here in the bound volumes surrounding me in this rarefied
room, no one, even in this century, has found a way to save my son.

A young woman arrives with my books: a general text on Duchenne
muscular dystrophy from 1993 by a British geneticist named Alan E. H.
Emery, and two books by Duchenne himself, one from the 1870s and
crumbling with age, called *A Treatise on Localized Electrization* (*De l'électri-
sation localisée*, first published in 1855), and one translated in the 1950s,
Physiology of Motion. But I find the writings of the great doctor inscrutable
and bizarre, filled with stuff about electrical impulses and pictures of
strange apparatus; Duchenne devised such instruments as the "dynamo-
meter," or strength gauge, and the harpoon biopsy needle, which he used
to study muscles in his patients at different stages in their short lives
(before that, muscle tissue was mostly observed at autopsy). Duchenne's
books have nearly no narrative; they consist mostly of pages and pages of
minute drawings and observations of every muscle in the human body,
with one- and two-page sections such as "Motions of the Thumb" and
"Flexion of the Forearm." One forgets that before this century medicine
was largely descriptive, and that one of the main questions about muscular dystrophy was whether it was primarily neurological—affecting the
spine and nerves—or truly muscular. Duchenne confirmed that the dis-

ease had no neurogenic basis. Nevertheless, there was something obsessive if not downright nutty about him—or maybe my impatient twentieth-century mother's mind fails to grasp the connections between his
results and his writings.

But when I open Emery's book, *Duchenne Muscular Dystrophy*, everything else vanishes. I read between lines; I am transfixed, by turns elated
and restless. For the first time in eleven years I look at pictures of boys in
the advanced stages of the disease. There are obese boys and skeletal boys
looking like Auschwitz victims, their spines twisted and their emaciated
arms and legs dangling. There is a boy with grotesquely enlarged muscles
throughout his body; he resembles a deformed child bodybuilder, a waxy
muscle-bound doll, a strange, surprised balloon boy. In many cases no
attempt has been made to conceal the identities of these boys; their faces
are in clear view, and their misshapen bodies are naked, so one can see the
deterioration clearly. There is something vulgar and vulnerable about the
nakedness of these boys, their genitalia seeming in some instances particularly underdeveloped compared with the rest of their bodies and often
too frankly exposed. At home I don't see my son naked, as I used to when
he was little; I glimpse only the outward signs of deterioration—the thick-
veined calves, the legs bruised by falls, the callused, deformed feet, the
increasingly swayed back, the heels that can no longer reach the floor. I
focus on his face: despite its fleshy roundness, caused by steroids, it is still
beautiful to me, with its alert, quizzical eyes and arched eyebrows, its stubborn mouth (how easily it registers disgust or frustration or delight!), its
straight, broad nose with a suggestion of freckles, its crown of chestnut hair.

I study an engraving from 1879 of a boy in three positions rising from
the floor, in what doctors call a Gowers' maneuver, named after the physician. In the first scene the boy is on his hands and knees; in the second his
rump is raised into the air and his two hands press on the ground for support; in the third he rests a hand on his thigh to balance himself. Here I
experience the oddest feeling—a thrill of identification. Yes! There it is,
exactly. My child. So true, so utterly Ansel. But obviously true of other
boys, too, over hundreds or thousands of years. I feel less lonely, in a way,
but I can't deny what's in the photographs. And there's no denying the
statistics either: 90 percent of boys with Duchenne die by the age of
twenty. At sixteen about half are dead. A nine-year-old we know who has
Duchenne can no longer walk. Should I feel happy or sad knowing that
Ansel is at the far end of the curve?

Some pages I barely glance at—I know the early symptoms, and I have
already witnessed some of the decay in Ansel. I know that there is a "pro-

gressive weakness of movement, first affecting the lower limbs and then later the upper limbs" and "a gradual increase in the size of many affected muscles." I have seen that the "lumbar lordosis becomes more exaggerated and the waddling gait increases"; I see the shortening of the heel cords.

But as the disease progresses, Emery's book reminds me, the breakdown intensifies: "Muscle weakness becomes more profound, contractures develop, particularly . . . of the elbows, knees, and hips . . . movements of the shoulders and wrists also become limited. The talus bone [protrudes] prominently under the skin." Finally all hell breaks loose: "Thoracic deformity . . . restricts adequate pulmonary airflow . . . a severe kyphoscoliosis [curvature of the spine] develops . . . a gradual deterioration begins in pulmonary function with reduced maximal inspiratory and expiratory pressures. By the later stages there is a significant reduction in total lung capacity." In other words, the spine contorts, compressing the chest cavity; the respiratory and heart muscles weaken; and eventually the child can't breathe. Less commonly, the heart gives out.

In a chapter called "Management," I review the paltry fixes: knee orthoses; braces that extend from ankle to groin; stretching exercises; steroids (the author, writing in 1993, downplayed their importance); wheelchairs; standing frames; rigid body jackets; the "Luque operation," which involves inserting two rods in the spine; tenotomy, or cutting the Achilles and other tendons; finally, assisted ventilation and drainage of the lungs. Some sound radical, some gruesome; at any rate, they are only Band-Aids, short-term measures that extend life perhaps one year, perhaps two. Sooner or later, usually by their mid-twenties, all boys with Duchenne succumb. Of 144 patients Emery studied, only sixteen made it to their twenty-fifth birthdays.

Every night, hands in his pockets for balance, on tiptoe, his jaw set in a grimace, his feet hesitantly reaching and shuffling, leaning longer on the right than on the left, Ansel stumbles along the hallway between his bedroom and the living room, willing himself to walk. It is unheard of—a fifteen-year-old with Duchenne walking. "Amazing," I tell him, "amazing," as he collapses in his wheelchair. We know it can't last forever, but we keep our fingers crossed.

Sunday morning I wake up, descend the stairs, begin boiling water for coffee. From the stove I get a glimpse of the cabinets that Joe fixed the day before: two low storage cupboards whose doors had been yanked off by the harsh sweep of Ansel's wheelchair. For weeks the jumble of our kitchen had been exposed, its internal disorder revealed. On Saturday, Joe finally mended them, filling in the holes and jimmying the hardware. The doors hung a bit askew, leaving an empty space like a knocked-out front tooth. Still, for the moment they stayed in place.

But now I see that one door has come loose at its hinges again; it hangs perilously from a single screw. Inside the darkness, chaos.

3. Moonrise, 2000

Ansel and I are on 165th Street in Washington Heights, on our way to the doctor at the Neurological Institute. I picked him up at school, and he told me he loves me, as he does at least once a day, and then we drove here and parked in the Kinney lot, where, because of our "handicapped" placard, the attendants let us squeeze into a ground-level spot.

This is the neighborhood where Joe and I first lived together, in medical-school housing in one of the huge modern buildings making up The Towers, which overlook the George Washington Bridge. We did not particularly get along with our multiple roommates, and we did not always like each other, but it was our first home, and it holds memories: the "Man in the Pan" early-morning lectures at which the doctors-in-training studied dissected organs; the late Sunday nights when I searched for Joe and his friend Peter, who were studying for a Monday exam in the recesses of the vast Health Sciences Library; the white-coated world of the medical complex, with people waiting in line for treatment, and the marble floor of Columbia-Presbyterian Hospital, through which I walked when coming home from the subway. I had just read Malcolm X's great book about his life, and I was always aware of our closeness to the Audubon Ballroom, where Malcolm was shot, and also of the darkness and danger of the 168th Street subway station, where several rapes and murders had taken place. My sister's boyfriend, who worked in a microbiology lab at Presbyterian, had been stabbed in the heart on the train on his way to work. He recovered, because he was taken to the emergency room quickly, but he had a scary, knotty scar on his chest where the mugger's knife had gone in.

There are sweet memories, too, mostly associated with food: the French toast at the Haven coffee shop, around the corner, and the farmer's cheese from the old Daitch Dairy (a remnant of the aging Jewish community), and the old-fashioned luncheonette on Fort Washington, where a soda jerk whipped up chocolate malteds made with Breyer's ice cream. The apartment in The Towers was where I held a successful surprise party for Joe; I managed to concoct Julia Child's fanciest chocolate cake, le Marquis, without his ever noticing. It was also where I had to deliver the news to Joe that his adored stepfather had died suddenly, at forty-eight, of a heart attack.

We are supposed to see Dr. DeVivo at least once a year, but it has been a year and some months since our last visit. When Ansel and I arrive, we are told to sit in a secluded, empty waiting room, where he does his math homework and I glance at a magazine called *Healthy Kids*. Joe arrives—in a suit, because he is now the head of family practice at the Catholic Medical Centers, in Brooklyn and Queens—and a receptionist says that we are in the wrong waiting room. We go and sit for another twenty minutes in a much more crowded room. A small boy in a stroller cries, seemingly over-tired and cranky; his mother, in a foreign language, tries to soothe him. He has tiny white braces on his legs, but I can't make out what his problem is. I never ask, "Why are you here?" although I always want to know. It sounds too much like "What are you in for?"

When DeVivo, a white-haired, stocky man, enters the room, I am not sure I recognize him, it's been so long. But he is wearing a white coat, and he seems to be in charge, so we follow him into his large office at the end of the hallway. I am very conscious that on our last visit Ansel walked from the waiting room to the office, and I remember the look of surprise on the doctor's face: how amazing that a fourteen-year-old with Duchenne could still walk! Now Ansel wheels his way down the long corridor, and I am the one surprised that he could have walked so far so recently.

Joe, Ansel, and I sit in three upholstered chairs facing DeVivo, who sits behind a massive desk. I remember suddenly how poorly Joe did in his neurology rotation in medical school; how he didn't like the neurologists—they were too cerebral and academic, he felt. DeVivo's manner is restrained, and when he speaks, he addresses Ansel first. He asks Ansel about school, about his clarinet lessons (the doctor plays trombone), and gets only a typical teenager's grunts. The pleasantries aside, he gets to what's important: "Tell me, Ansel, how do you feel, physically, compared with the last time I saw you?"

"Well, I use the wheelchair more," Ansel says. "I get out of the wheelchair three or four times a day and stretch, and then I walk a few steps. That's all. I can't really walk more than that."

He doesn't say it sadly, just as fact; but Joe and I and the doctor know it is sad, and it sits heavy in the air, a presence among us. I think of Ansel at five, walking into town with me because he suddenly wanted to bake cookies and we had to buy cookie cutters. He walked slowly, but he walked all the way, a quarter of a mile in each direction.

For a moment no one else can speak. There isn't anything to say, is there? He gets worse. He will die. Even if it's slow, it will happen. It's a whole life, not a half-life, divided infinitely. Sooner or later it will not be there.

But in one way it's not sad. Ansel has spoken, after all, and we have all listened. He is no longer a small child but the voice of authority. Who can know the answers but Ansel? He has a deep voice and a little trace of a mustache on his upper lip. He and the neurologist discuss the best course of therapy, his medications (would Ansel agree to take three enzyme capsules a day, rather than the one he has been taking?), and his adherence to a low-salt, low-fat diet.

Joe, DeVivo, and Ansel retreat to the examining room that adjoins the office, where the table, made for small children, is too high for Ansel to mount. I stay behind, aware that he will not want his mother present when the doctor prods private parts or asks personal questions. I also don't want to see the fat that spills over the elastic of his underpants or the angry calluses on his feet when he removes his splints and shoes and socks. I'd rather look at the stack of magazines on luxury-home renovation, at the wall of books at the back of the room, at the color photos of racing sailboats—this must be one of the doctor's hobbies. I look out the dirty window of the Neurological Institute, half a block away from our old apartment at The Towers. It is strange to be here, looking out at a past that contained not even a flicker of Ansel. Why is it unthinkable to look at a future without him?

Joe and I are on the street on a Sunday afternoon, late. The forsythia is in bloom; there is yellow everywhere, and a dark sky with just a strip of light over the Palisades. Joe wants to know what I am writing: it is about Ansel's growing up and deteriorating all at once, the "unnaturalness" of a child's beginning to die just when he is beginning to flower.

Joe rejects this, furious. "What are you saying—because it's not average, not the norm, it's unnatural? That's like saying homosexuality is unnatural." I see his eyes flash behind his glasses. "What's unnatural about it?" he says. "It is in fact the natural order of things, that mutations occur. That's who we are, who we have to be, as humans."

"So you have no feelings about Ansel's getting worse?" I demand tearfully.

He purses his lips angrily, forcing air through them. "Of course I have feelings about it. But why is it necessarily sadder for someone to die young than old? Is it sadder for Ansel to die than a ninety-year-old man who's never done anything, who has nothing to show for his life? Anyway, Ansel's not dead. I can't mourn for him. And I refuse to see my life as a tragedy!"

"Well, that's what I'm writing about," I say. "And I'm sorry if you don't think it's sad!" Then I can't speak for ten minutes. I stride along next to Joe, up the hill beside the Food Emporium, and I don't look at him. I am too stubborn and angry. How can he say that a dying child is not heart-rending? How about that boy Zachy, the only child of one of Joe's colleagues, who died at eight or nine of a brain tumor? Wasn't that worse, more tragic, than, say, my father's death at seventy-three? Wasn't my father's life, in concrete and substantial ways, long *enough*, whereas Zachy's was not?

At the top of the hill, thinking back on Zachy's death and its aftermath—his stunned parents sitting shiva in the apartment; the boy's baseball card collection still visible in his bedroom—I can no longer hold on to my anger at Joe. I see him simply as a fellow sufferer: trying to construct meaning from ill fate, to find solace in the destruction of his firstborn. He is just groping for a spiritual handhold. This is Joe, used to such loss (two fathers and a mother, all young, all loved), soothing himself, explaining to himself, as a child might, why death comes. And this is just the other half of me.

In six months Ansel will be old enough to drive. In September he will be sixteen, able in New York State to take that step toward adulthood—obtaining a learner's permit. Even though we don't have the details yet, even though his father is not convinced that he can physically operate a motor vehicle, Ansel and I talk about driving as a reality—how he will take over the wheelchair van and I will buy a tiny red Miata, the car of my dreams. He is not as crazy about cars as some teenage boys are, but one day when he and I see a cab-yellow sixties Camaro idling at the corner of Cedar Street and Broadway in the town where we live, his left eyebrow lifts, he peers at me sideways, and he says, "Wow." He's ready.

In the books on muscular dystrophy one learns that there are three markers: the onset of disease, confinement to a wheelchair, death. Ansel is approaching the date of confinement. He will be there, I am sure, by his sixteenth birthday.

I have panic attacks nearly every night. Awakened by some minor provocation—for instance, my daughter, Diana, enters the room to check the time—I turn over, sit up, and quite suddenly experience dread; there is no other word. I blink my eyes, because I am sure I'm going blind, and scratch my middle fingertip with my thumbnail, to assure myself that I'm not paralyzed. I try to take the pulse in my wrist, but I'm too scared and can't count right. I am outside my body, physically detached, at the end of a long passageway, drowning—all those melodramatic scenarios of what it's like to die.

Seven years ago, when I was in labor with Toby, a nurse injected me with Stadol, a painkiller, and I became distant and paranoid like this. I held on to Joe's hand, literally for dear life. "Tell me I am not dying," I said over and over, to hear my own voice and to hear him respond. *What an irony*, I thought then, *to die giving birth!*

Now my heart seems to be racing in my head, but my blood is glacial, cold and slow. I have finally gone over the edge! The fear feeds on itself. I get dressed so that I can be ready to drive to the emergency room, if need be.

Sitting on the edge of the bed, sure of my own doom, I wonder suddenly, *Am I trying to experience my own death in place of Ansel's? Am I the sacrifice?*

It is the middle of March, and every moment pulls me two ways. In a community church in White Plains, New York, that looks like a cross between a pagoda and an airline terminal, I sit with Joe, Diana, and Toby in a fan-shaped room filled with folding chairs. It is a kind of backward room, because one enters by way of the stage and descends to seats. Ansel, who will be performing with an ensemble from his music school, can wheel onto the stage but not into the audience, so after he plays, Joe will have to carry him down the steps.

When the woodwinds come onstage and are seated, Ansel seems taller than the others, though he's actually quite short, because for the first time he is playing from his wheelchair. Usually he transfers, with difficulty, to a regular chair, but it was thought that the amount of time before the next group came on was too brief to allow for that. I can see Ansel now and then between the arms of the conductor. He is puffing out his big cheeks, like Dizzy Gillespie on the horn. He loves the clarinet, the instrument he chose when he began music lessons at school, in the fifth grade. Joe was against it. "What's the point," he asked, "when all boys with muscular dystrophy develop breathing difficulties? He won't be able to play for more than a couple of years; it will just be frustrating." As he does with nearly everything, Ansel stood firm, and got his way, and it is good that he did. Clarinet-playing is his breathing therapy as well as his joy, and it may be the reason his lungs show no deterioration yet.

He progressed slowly when he took lessons at the public school, but as soon as he began at the music school, he flourished. Under the guidance of a gifted teacher Ansel has become a disciplined music student who, after many days and nights of mistakes, false starts, and practice, practice, practice, can be depended on to produce a fine sound. When he leaves his bedroom door open, I enjoy the lovely strains of the Weber clarinet concertino or of a Hindemith sonata. He is not a virtuoso; he is more of a plodder, but he plods well. He has learned to respect the difficulty of the task and the beauty of the result.

Sitting at the concert, I feel the pleasure of his playing, but seeing him in the wheelchair, I cannot shake the feeling of loss, a loss that feels sharpest when I love him most. I know that when boys become confined to their wheelchairs, their chests and lungs become constricted. Wind is the first thing to go. *Who knows which way the wind blows? Who knows where my love goes, how my love grows, where the time goes?* Despite my best efforts, despite my pride in Ansel (that serious, stubborn, laboring face!), a tear wells up in the corner of my eye. I shift my glasses so that Diana will not see. She does anyway.

"Mom, why are you crying?" she asks. I shake my head. "Ansel?" she whispers urgently. I nod, and wordlessly I put my arm around her shoulder—her bare, cool, pubescent shoulder, upon which I perhaps place too great a burden—and hold her close to me. Later Ansel sits with me, and Diana sits alone all the way in back. Joe has pulled Toby out, because he is complaining so much about being at a concert. The Festival Orchestra, sounding very professional despite being jerkily led by a very thin, very young conductor, plays Bach. In the midst of the quite proper, cultivated audience, Ansel and I dip and bounce our heads and shoulders to the rhythms. Near the end Ansel whispers, "Have you noticed everybody else here is completely still, no one else but you and me is moving to the music?" I have.

I keep with me much of the time a letter from a friend of a friend whose boy died of Duchenne at twenty-four. Even though I have never met her, I identify with this mother, because her boy did well; he must have been an outlier, like Ansel, to live to such a ripe old age. My son "was the absolute center of my life," she wrote. "Now I feel like the woman in the Hopper painting *Cape Cod Morning*, looking out the bay window, wondering what will come next."

Ansel has been away from the house for almost the entire weekend, attending a model U.N. at a nearby high school Friday night, all day Saturday, and Sunday morning. We are not used to his being away, and Diana and I both feel his absence. The question seems to be not "Is this what it will be like when he's away at college?" but "Is this what it will be like when he is dead?"

"Ansel is what makes the house happy," Diana says later that week, and I think back to the moment of his birth, when I heard a sound that reminded me of the popping of a champagne cork. I think of his name: a variation of Anschel, a diminutive of Asher, which in Hebrew means "happy."

Diana and I try to think about what makes Ansel fun. "He's just a very up person," she says, which is odd, because he is also a big complainer, a class-A kvetch. "Puns," I say. "Remember when he wrote that story about the teenage monster who wasn't frightening enough because he didn't have enough 'scaritonin'?"

"Non sequiturs," Diana offers, and it's true. I used to call Ansel the king of non sequiturs. We might all be having a conversation about, say, the fact that the Lobster Roll is the only restaurant worth going to in the Hamptons. The rest of us might consider the topic exhausted and move rapidly on to two or three unrelated topics. We might be talking about the book I am reading for my psychology class in graduate school or about how boring Toby finds the second grade. And then, maybe half an hour later, sometimes a day later, Ansel will pipe up with "There is that Mexican place in East Hampton," as though there has been not even a tiny break in the conversation. His neuroses are funny too, I say: for instance, he worries about global warming every time the temperature in winter is above average. Everyone else is enjoying the sun, but Ansel is worried! And he always worries about being worried: "Should I be worried?" He is so much like me, and like my father, that I can't help laughing at the reflection.

I am aware that having a limited future makes Ansel freer. Next year, for example, he plans to enroll in the vocational-training program offered by the school system, even though he is on an academic track. The vocational program includes culinary arts, and Ansel knows that is what he wants. Isn't food what he thinks about all the time? The taste of a blood orange or a fresh fig may be the most important, most commented-on part of his day. In English he has chosen "luxury foods" for his special project; he writes of the high cost of hunting for truffles, of the packaging of caviar, of the pleasure of watching the guys behind the counter at Zabar's slice lox. He faithfully reads the "Dining Out" section of the *New York Times* and leafs through the Penzys Spices catalog.

He doesn't care that taking culinary arts each morning at a location in northern Westchester County will seriously limit his academic program. He does not want to sit through another year of science, even though it would "look better" on his college applications. He has no time to waste.

Ansel calls a meeting with me and his guidance counselor and the director of the program, the last of whom he informs, "I can't do something without being serious about it. Otherwise I just don't think it's worth doing." When the director describes the culinary-arts program, which is almost completely hands-on cooking, the corners of Ansel's mouth curve into a little smile, and the guidance counselor, who knows him well, says, "I don't often see that look in Ansel's eyes."

It is apparent that cooking is what he must do. Being a public program, the vocational-training class must accommodate him, so he will probably have an aide for lifting heavy pots off the stove and similar tasks. It seems exciting, although I am a bit concerned that Ansel may miss out on two years of science, French, and math, which are given in the morning, when he will be off school grounds. After the meeting I stay behind to speak with his counselor.

"How would it be if he just does culinary arts for one year, not two?" I ask. Ansel would like to start the program this September, his junior year, but I think it will be better for college-admission purposes if he waits until his senior year.

"Yes, I assumed one year," the counselor says, adding, "Preferably his junior year."

I am surprised. "Because . . . ?"

"Because I know culinary arts will be in the morning next year; I'm not sure about the following year. And that would be better as far as academics go. Because he has to take history and English. Also . . ."

I know the other reason. She lets me say it. "Because we don't know where he will be physically in two years. This may be the only year he can do it."

I meet an old friend in the city for lunch. We walk to the restaurant, and she rattles on about the short story she is writing. I cannot open my mouth; I am sure I will start to cry. For two weeks I have been up every night with shoulder pain: a pinched nerve, probably brought on by a slipped disc. Yesterday my kitchen was gutted in advance of a major renovation for Ansel's benefit, and there are still bent nails sticking up from the floor every few inches.

My friend tells me about her latest challenge: her therapist has asked her, "What do you want?" As in life.

"Want," I say, almost sneering, and as I open my mouth, everything spills out, and in a little Vietnamese restaurant on Third Avenue, I start weeping. "Who cares what you want?" I say accusingly, and I am frightened by my feeling, which comes out so raw and powerful and pitiless. "I want my son to live a long life. So what?" Every word is a choking effort, my tongue swollen and sore, my throat like gravel. Why bother wanting?

I have two dreams. In the first one, two cars are driving fast in the left lane of the highway, in the wrong direction. Everyone in our car can see as we approach them that this is a very dangerous thing. But it's too late to stop. The cars crash head-on into other cars just in front of us, and I can see the drivers thrown aside, into the air, the cars tin-can crushed. But we are saved. We only witness the horror and move on. We don't even stop. What can we do?

In the second dream Ansel and I come upon a red-rock canyon in the middle of a southwestern desert. We are not really surprised; we have been expecting to find the canyon. It has a lip of rock across its entrance, so we cannot see beyond, its contents are secret. But once we get inside, we are aware of water and sand, and a very beautiful light glinting off beach umbrellas. We are at the ocean. Ansel can walk. We stake out our place on the sand. We have brought our lunch and a blanket, and we sit together and eat: crusty French bread, a wedge of Parmigiano-Reggiano from Todaro Brothers, slices of ripe mango. We are happy.

When Ansel rises from the table today, his legs tremble as he transfers to the wheelchair. Our house is in complete disorder: dining table and refrigerator and microwave are all sitting in the living room, because the kitchen renovation is not complete. The shelves in the living room hold two-by-fours; a sugar bowl; strips of insulation; our good silverware in a blue felt Bloomingdale's bag; a tin candy box filled with paper clips, packing tape, nail clippers, misplaced trinkets and bits of toys, Pokémon cards, and Monopoly hotels.

After dinner Ansel is sitting at the table drinking tea and trying to read *Treasure Island*, which he finds difficult because of the antiquated language and because he has been interrupted over and over again by Diana and Toby, who are bored. I am in the next room, also reading, when I hear a commotion: Ansel is screaming and weeping, "Stop! Stop! I can't stand it, stop!" in a weird, high, animal-like shriek. When I run in, I see that he has taken his empty teacup and begun to bang it over and over again on the table; while I watch, horrified, he puts the cup down and begins to bang his forehead rhythmically.

"What happened?" I demand angrily of Diana. "What *happened?!*" I am stamping my foot, the rage spilling out of me. "What did you do?"

"I didn't do anything!" she retorts. "He was burping again—which he always does!—and I told him he was disgusting and he went crazy! God! You blame me for everything!"

Now Ansel begins to shriek again. "I'm an idiot! I'm an idiot! I did it because I'm an idiot!" His cheeks are big and red, and he can't catch his breath, and he begins to whimper. Embarrassment, comprehension, a normal sibling fight turned abnormal—a fifteen-year-old acting like a three-year-old.

"Pick him up," I say quietly to Joe, who has come in from the next room. "Pick him up and carry him into his room."

Later I ask Ansel, "What is it like—that anger? Are you on another planet, like I used to be when I had temper tantrums when I was a kid?" I know that anger is a locked box, but it is also freedom—a soaring, powerful white light.

"I don't know," he says. "I don't know. I just think if I scream and scream and scream maybe I'll stop being angry. Maybe I'll get it all out of me."

"Is there so much anger?" I ask. "What's it about?"

"Please, Mom." He turns his head away. "Please. Let's not talk about it anymore."

Another day he comes home from school depressed. "I'm worried about dying," he says. I honestly don't know what to say. Since when am I so wise anyway? I'm tired, and I worry about dying too. Driving home fast on the Saw Mill River Parkway, I sometimes think, *What will happen to my kids if I die?* It is always Ansel's face I see; how could he forgive me?

So I don't respond, not really, and later, when he is putting together the pieces of his clarinet, he wails melodramatically, "I'm so depressed, and no one cares!" Now I feel compelled to react, so I go into his room. He continues: "I was depressed in the first place, and then when I got to health class my teacher had written 'The Stages of Grief' up on the blackboard—we're studying death—and it just made me more depressed . . . And then we saw part of *Schindler's List*, clips of the movie . . ."

"Did you see the part with the little girl in the red coat who is wandering around the ghetto and then gets shot?" I ask, thinking this had upset him.

He looks at me. "She doesn't get shot, Mom. She hides in the building . . ."

"But she does, Ans. Eventually she does get shot."

"Nope," he says. "You're wrong, Mom. You forgot."

I don't want to contradict him again, though I know I'm right. I think of his great capacity for denial. I remember something the physician John

Bach wrote in an article about boys with muscular dystrophy: "Successful adaptation does not depend upon an accurate perception of reality."

This morning I catch sight of Toby's torso while he is dressing. He is seven and a half, slender and small, built like a dancer. He has that nice square chest that a boy is supposed to have, with a line running down the center from breastbone to belly. Ansel would have been beautiful too, perhaps more so. I remember a photo from the summer before Ansel began taking prednisone to slow down the deterioration of his muscles, when he could still walk, ploddingly, up the unrailed front steps. A blue-purple T-shirt, a sun-tinted face: a quite handsome eleven-year-old. Before the chipmunk cheeks, puffy from steroids. That must have been the summer before the wheelchair. My beautiful son.

Ansel's independent reading this month: Mark Twain's *Roughing It*; most of Phillip Lopate's *The Art of the Personal Essay*; "The Snows of Kilimanjaro" and other stories by Ernest Hemingway; M. F. K. Fisher's *A Cordiall Water*; *The Red Badge of Courage*, by Stephen Crane; *National Geographic*; S. J. Perelman's *Chicken Inspector no. 23*. His selection of a project for social studies, any "ism": Dadaism. Favorite music: Louis Armstrong, Thelonious Monk, show tunes, the Buena Vista Social Club.

Ansel and I are sitting in the living room, late. Everyone else has gone to sleep. He is doing his daily exercises: leaning with his palms against the back of the couch, pushing his heels down toward the floor, one at a time, to lengthen the Achilles tendons, trying to stay mobile for as long as possible. He has had a tough day, and he is very tired. Earlier he asked Joe to carry him to the bathroom (he usually walks), and when he got there he fell trying to reach the toilet.

"I don't know why I'm having so much trouble," he says to me later. "Do you think I'm just tired? Why should I be so tired?"

"I don't know, Ans. It may just be the disease. It's getting worse, I guess. That's really crummy, isn't it?"

He doesn't say anything. He is cutting his toenails, concentrating on the task of keeping all the parings in one pile on the coffee table. "Isn't it?" I repeat.

He looks up. "No. I think everything that happens has a reason."

"I guess that's because you believe in God," I say.

"I used to get depressed thinking about this stuff," he continues, seeming to ignore my remark. "But then I realized it doesn't help. So I don't think about it anymore."

I ask him at another time, "Do you think about the fact that you may not have as many years as other people?"

"No, Mom. I just want to be happy."

Ansel says everything that happens has a reason. He uses the toilet in the middle of the night and flushes it, and the flood of water in the pipes wakes up our collie in the basement, and she begins barking, and I wake up, and it is a quarter to four.

In a way I'm not tired, so I get up and go down to the basement, where the dog is kenneled. She is wide awake and on her feet, waiting expectantly, as though we planned a rendezvous. She nips my heels and tries to push through my legs as we mount the stairs. Then she shoots outside, and I follow.

It's warm out, and completely calm; the three-quarters moon is immense and neon yellow, hanging over the Palisades, nearly merging with the horizon. It seems otherworldly, like—and I know this is a ridiculous thought—an object from outer space. In other words, it appears as it is—completely apart from, oblivious of, anything human.

I don't know if it's rising or setting. Joe will be able to tell me in the morning, but right now I don't want to know, not yet. I stand there with the mystery of the moon for some time, with the thrill of knowing its beauty—having it to myself for a few rare moments—while the dog sniffs under damp leaves, looking for a place to pee.

When she is finished, I take her back to the basement and give her a full bowl of water, which she drinks thirstily. I go to sleep easily, somehow fulfilled. Ansel says everything has a reason. He is fifteen. In two hours it will be daylight.

1. What kind of narrator does this essay have?
2. In what way does the essay reflect the narrator's "story"?
3. How would this be different if the author had chosen to tell this using a third person narrator?

CHAPTER SEVEN

How Reliable Is This Narrator?

Part 1: HOW POINT OF VIEW AFFECTS OUR UNDERSTANDING OF A STORY

Getting Started

Now that you understand the different point of view choices that you have, and how they can vary according to our two axes—knowledge and distance—you inevitably come to the issue of *reliability*. Okay, so this narrator is telling me this story. How trustworthy is he or she? How much of this story do I believe?

In this chapter, we'll look at issues of reliability, particularly as related to first and third person narrators. Then, you will have some exercises so you can practice what you've read about. Finally, we have a story with a narrator who may or may not be unreliable.

How We Judge the Integrity of the Stories We Hear and Read

Whether you realize it or not, every time someone tells you something, you are evaluating the integrity of the information. In life, we size up the people around us, and have pretty strong judgments about their biases, the limits of their knowledge, or their ability to understand complex or abstract thought. We factor all that into our willingness to "buy" what someone tells us.

It's the same with what we read. We question the reliability of the narrator, the teller of the story, novel, or nonfiction piece. We allow our assessment of reliability to affect our digestion of the work.

There are different issues of reliability based on the point of view types of options you have. We'll examine them individually.

First Person Point of View and Reliability

If you choose a first person narrator, you're going to run into the issue of reliability. Even the most reliable, the most honest, the most straightforward, intelligent, and moral first person narrator is going to have limitations.

What are some of these limitations? Unless you are writing science fiction, or some other kind of nonrealistic prose, the following limitations generally apply:

1. Geographic: The narrator, who is a character in the story, or the author of the nonfiction piece, can only be in one place at a time.
2. Temporal: They can only exist at one time period.
3. Physical: They are limited by their (human or otherwise) bodies, and the abilities of those bodies.
4. Intellectual: Their intellect almost certainly has limitations, even if they are highly intelligent.
5. Experiential: They can only have so much knowledge of the world, only so much personal experience at their disposal.
6. Moral/spiritual: A narrator can be quite intelligent and experienced but morally deficient.
7. Emotional: What we frequently refer to today as "emotional intelligence" can figure into a character's abilities and limitations.

Okay, so limitations are going to exist for any first person narrator. In fiction, you need to know what those limitations are, and how they affect your story.

In nonfiction, this issue is a little trickier. In nonfiction, since the author is synonymous with the narrator, the limitations of the narrator are those of the author. And since very few authors would want their credibility questioned, unreliability in a nonfiction piece is generally not considered a good thing—unlike in fiction, when unreliability in a narrator can be an integral part of the story.

IMPORTANT: In fiction, the more you decide to limit your narrator's honesty, intelligence, moral judgment, etc., the more it will distort your story. Not only will you have a distorted story or novel, but also you will have to have some way of showing the reader that you, *the author*, are aware of the limitations of the narrator and how they distort the piece. You must give readers clues as to how to compare what the narrator tells them with what the reality of your story truly is.

Let's look at some examples:

Through the fence, between the curling flower spaces, I could see them hitting. They were coming toward where the flag was and I went along the fence. Luster was hunting in the grass by the flower tree. They took the flag out, and they were hitting. Then they put the flag back and they went to the table, and he hit and the other hit. Then they went on, and I went along the fence. Luster came away from the flower tree and we went along the fence and they stopped and we stopped and I looked through the fence while Luster was hunting in the grass.

"Here, caddie." He hit. They went away across the pasture. I held to the fence and watched them going away.

"Listen at you, now," Luster said. "Aint you something, thirty-three years old, going on that way. After I done went all the way to town to buy you that cake. Hush up that moaning. Aint you going to help me find that quarter so I can go to the show tonight."

They were hitting little, across the pasture. I went along the fence to where the flag was. It flapped on the bright grass and the trees.

"Come on," Luster said. "We done looked there. They aint no more coming right now. Lets go down to the branch and find that quarter before them niggers finds it."

It was red, flapping on the pasture. Then there was a bird slanting and tilting on it. Luster threw. The flag flapped on the bright grass and the trees. I held onto the fence.

"Shut up that moaning," Luster said. "I cant make them come if they aint coming, can I. If you dont hush up, mammy aint going to have no birthday for you. If you dont hush, you know what I going to do. I going to eat that cake all up. Eat them candles, too. Eat all them thirty-three candles. Come on, lets go down to the branch. I got to find my quarter. Maybe you can find one of they balls. Here. Here they is. Way over yonder. See." He came to the fence and pointed his arm. "See them. They aint coming back here no more. Come on."

We went along the fence and came to the garden fence where our shadows were. My shadow was higher than Luster's on the fence.

[from *The Sound and the Fury* by William Faulkner]

The title of this book comes from Shakespeare: "Life is a tale told by an idiot, full of sound and fury, signifying nothing." It's told by a whole series of unreliable narrators, of whom Benjy, the retarded man, is just one. None are quite as dramatically unreliable (in one sense, anyway) as Benjy. But if you read through the excerpt again, carefully, you'll see that although we are getting physical things described without a context that easily allows us to make sense of it, the physical descriptions seem to be accurate (if you haven't figured it out yet, Benjy is watching a game of golf being played). We're also getting dialogue that seems to be reliable—it gives us clues about what is going on. Gradually, a picture of what is happening arises, based on the descriptions of what is happening and the dialogue. (Benjy is watching a game of golf, he's crying and making a fuss, and his keeper, Luster, is trying to quiet him down. It happens to be Benjy's birthday; he is thirty-three years old today.)

Always, with an unreliable narrator, we are asking ourselves (whether we know it or not): What information are we getting that we can trust? What can't we trust? In this case, Benjy is telling us the truth, to the best of his ability. He's very honest, observant, intuitive. He just doesn't have the ability to assimilate and analyze and explain things. But he reports things honestly and accurately, and his judgment in many ways is more to be trusted than any of the other more "normal" characters to be found in the book.

And now, a convention alert: Generally, even when we have an unreliable narrator, the aspects of scene—the showing—tend to be reliable, trustworthy. That is, when we have a scene consisting of dialogue and action, the convention is that we are seeing things the way they actually happened. We're hearing what is actually being said. The convention (never a rule: there are no rules in fiction) is that *showing*, or scene, is reliable. It's the *telling*, or narrative, that is potentially unreliable.

Makes sense, right? After all, scenes are the things that you get in "eyewitness" mode. So you see, in *The Sound and the Fury*, how this works. When we are *shown* something, we can assume it really happened. When we are *told* something is when we are on potentially shaky ground.

What is the reason for this?

Because if we don't get some hard-core evidence of reality somewhere in a story or novel, some way of knowing what is actually going on, we are going to be dreadfully confused. Thus scenes have traditionally acted as a "reality check" with unreliable narrators.

This is, again, not a fast rule. If you want, transgress this rule. Transgress any so-called rule! But if you are going to put a scene on the page, and it contains lies or distortions or untruths, you have to find a way of letting the reader know that and figure out what reality is. That's tricky. Making the scene reliable is a sure-fire method of doing this.

Now, interpreting what is said, or how people looked, or how they said something has always been fair game for distortion. But generally speaking, if a physical action is described, or words in quotation marks are provided in a scene—even by a very unreliable first person narrator—we are supposed to believe them.

By the way, Faulkner didn't have enough faith either in his readers or in his writing to leave it alone. He provided what was basically a summary of all the events, as an appendix, so that readers would know what *really* happened.

As far as why Faulkner chose a whole series of unreliable narrators to tell his story, here are his own words:

> I tried first to tell it with one brother [Benjy] and that wasn't enough. That was Section One. I tried it with another brother, and that wasn't enough. That was Section Two. I tried the third brother, because Caddy was still to me too beautiful and too moving to reduce her to telling what was going on, that it would be more passionate to see her through somebody else's eyes, I thought. And that failed and I tried myself—the fourth section—[using omniscient third person point of view] to try and tell what happened and I still failed.

Here's another example of an unreliable narrator. Can you tell what can be believed from this section?

> They're out there.
>
> Black boys in white suits up before me to commit sex acts in the hall and get it mopped up before I can catch them.
>
> They're mopping when I come out the dorm, all three of them sulky and hating everything, the time of day, the place they're at here, the people they got to work around. When they hate like this, better if they don't see me. I creep along the wall quiet as dust in my canvas shoes, but they got special sensitive equipment detects my fear and they all look up, all three at once, eyes glittering out of the black faces like the hard glitter of radio tubes out of the back of an old radio.
>
> "Here's the Chief. The *soo*-pah Chief, fellas. Ol' Chief Broom. Here you go, Chief Broom . . ."
>
> Stick a mop in my hand and motion to the spot they aim for me to clean today, and I go. One swats the backs of my legs with a broom handle to hurry me past.
>
> "Haw, you look at 'im shag it? Big enough to eat apples off my head an' he mind me like a baby."
>
> They laugh and I hear them mumbling behind me, heads close together. Hum of black machinery, humming hate and death and other hospital secrets. They don't bother not talking out loud about their hate secrets when I'm nearby because they think I'm deaf and dumb. Everybody thinks

so. I'm cagey enough to fool them that much. If my being half Indian ever helped me in any way in this dirty life, it helped me being cagey, helped me all these years.

I'm mopping near the ward door when a key hits it from the other side and I know it's the Big Nurse by the way the lockworks cleave to the key, soft and swift and familiar she been around locks so long. She slides through the door with a gust of cold and locks the door behind her and I see her fingers trail across the polished steel—tip of each finger the same color as her lips. Funny orange. Like the tip of a soldering iron. Color so hot or so cold if she touches you with it, you can't tell which.

She's carrying her woven wicker bag like the ones the Umpqua tribe sells out along the hot August highway, a bag shape of a tool box with a hemp handle. She's had it all the years I been here. It's a loose weave and I can see inside it; there's no compact or lipstick or woman stuff, she's got that bag full of a thousand parts she aims to use in her duties today—wheels and gears, cogs polished to a hard glitter, tiny pills that gleam like porcelain, needles, forceps, watchmakers' pliers, rolls of copper wire.

The opening of *One Flew Over the Cuckoo's Nest* by Ken Kesey shows us we are in the hands of a very unreliable first person narrator indeed. Special sensitive equipment? A thousand parts—including wheels and gears, cogs, needles, forceps—in a nurse's personal handbag? Unlikely. Yet *some* of it seems plausible. The men mopping the hallway. The woman sweeping into the hospital, full of confidence and bringing with her a cold fear . . . These seem to ring true. And in fact we can glean from this very unreliable narrator a sense of what is happening, a lot of it from the dialogue, which we know, by convention, to trust, but also from a sense of the emotional truth inherent in the observations.

Which leads us to one of the key reasons that you might choose to employ an unreliable narrator: sometimes-unreliable narrators can be used to get at deeper truths. Much of what they tell us is obviously not true and obviously distorted. But in a case like this, where clearly we're not supposed to take what he says literally, in some way an unreliable narrator can get at more important information. In this case, Chief Broom has a clearer view of what is going on in the mental hospital than anyone else. He sees the danger posed by the often malicious staff to the inmates—especially those inmates who rock the boat. It's exaggerated, and paranoid, but it's very real. In this case, the facts are less important than the truth that emerges from the narrative.

Interestingly enough, we learn that the physical objects described in this novel are not necessarily trustworthy, as they are in *The Sound and the*

Fury. Chief Broom doesn't always describe real things (for starters, he talks about a "fog machine" that the staff brings in when they want to befuddle the inmates). Over time, we learn to judge what we can believe of Chief Broom's assessments and what we can't believe. When the fog machine is working, for example, it's a sign that he's picking up on some tension in the institution, something happening at the intuitive level (he's a very intuitive character). So we learn in what way to interpret even his most seemingly untrustworthy statements.

Third Person Point of View and Reliability

Now here's an important piece of information: when a third person narrator tells us something about a story, or novel, it is, *by convention*, always true. Take a moment to think about this. Remember, it's not a character, with flaws (human or otherwise), like with a first person narrator. No, this is an outsider, not involved in the story, not a human character but a disembodied intelligence telling us about the events of the story or novel. And when the third person narrator speaks, according to convention, it is always the truth. Always reliable.

So if that is the case, what do you make of this opening to a very famous story?

> When Gregor Samsa woke up one morning from unsettling dreams, he found himself changed in his bed into a monstrous vermin. He was lying on his back as hard as armor plate, and when he lifted his head a little, he saw his vaulted brown belly, sectioned by arch-shaped ribs, to whose dome the cover, about to slide off completely, could barely cling. His many legs, pitifully thin compared with the size of the rest of him, were waving helplessly before his eyes.
> "What's happened to me?" he thought. It was no dream.

What's going on here? People don't turn into cockroaches overnight. We know this. Yet it's a third person narrator. How are we to make sense of a story that begins like this?

Well, we have four options to consider when we're told something that doesn't make sense to us (given that we know that a third person narrator is, by definition, always reliable):

1. We're in a world in which this implausible, improbable, unbelievable thing is real. We're being asked, according to Coleridge's famous phrase, to make a "willing suspension of disbelief." This is of course perfectly valid. As creators of our fictional worlds, we can make the sky

pink and pigs fly. Anything we want. So when our readers read in John Cheever's "The Swimmer" (pp. 330–40) that the winter constellations could be seen at the end of a summer's day, it is because *in that world* it was possible. In this particular case, we have to consider the possibility that this is a world in which people *can* turn into cockroaches.

2. A second possibility is that we're in a character's mind, through the use of very close third person point of view. In other words, we're seeing the world from an unreliable character's perspective even though we're in third person. It's a distance thing, as we discussed in Chapter 6. In effect, our third person narrator has been "possessed" by a character in the story, and can only tell us what that character sees and believes. Stories of unpleasant or implausible events that end with a character waking up and realizing "it was all a dream" fall into this category. So do stories in which we find out, at some point, that the character is insane.

3. A third possibility is that we've entered the realm of metafiction: mocking the conventions, turning the conventions on their heads. This kind of writing attempts to draw attention to the writing itself, or to the ridiculous nature of conventions, or of tradition, in order to say something about art, the creative process, the artificiality of fictional form, etc. The characters aren't what is important—or not what's primarily important. The author is deliberately playing with the conventions for reasons of his or her own.

4. Finally, there's the possibility (it must be considered) that the author simply made a mistake. (Oops, people can't turn into cockroaches.) This is a bad thing. The last thing we want is for the *author* to lose credibility with his or her readers.

In the case of Franz Kafka's "The Metamorphosis" our choice is between the first and second options above: either this is a world in which young men can inexplicably turn into cockroaches, or we're in the mind of an unreliable (mad or dreaming) character. As it turns out, reading into the story further, we can eliminate the second possibility; Gregor has indeed been turned into a giant insect, and his life is terribly plagued as a result.

Let's examine the second possibility a little closer: What happens when distance has indeed collapsed and we're in the mind of a character through third person intimate point of view?

> The kettle is about to boil, and the telephone rings. He dries his hands slowly and goes to answer it, expecting Mandy Navarrete's fourth child. Christmas Day, a long silent day, will end now with a long unpleasant night.

There was a time when deliveries excited him; during the gene-pool study he looked forward to those infant eyes, and setting up his camera and lights. But there is nothing to study now. Mandy Navarrete is all muscles and resistance, a woman who delivers in her own time. Her grandmother Concepcion Navarrete was his first grade teacher. She was similarly muscular, and disapproved of his family.

He lifts the receiver slowly on the fourth or fifth ring. The voice speaks in hurried Spanish but he answers in English because he knows they can understand. He hasn't spoken Spanish since the day he married Alice. "There is plenty of time," he says. "I know this process. We don't need to be in a panic."

He hears silence, static, several different voices and questions and then the same voice again, emphatically repeating its word. *Secuestrada.* Kidnapped.

"Who is this?"

He listens. The voice is very distant and often breaks. It is a woman, a friend of his daughter. He tries to understand which daughter they mean. *Secuestrada.* Codi has been away for a few days, but this voice is saying, "Hollie." Someone is keeping her. She was in the field alone, with her horse, when they came to blow up the building. He understands none of this.

Hollie, the woman insists, as if trying to wake him from sleep. Are you the father? We are very much afraid.

[from *Animal Dreams* by Barbara Kingsolver]

You can see, in this excerpt, how the third person narration leads us to believe one thing (that the doctor is waiting to deliver a child), when actually we are in the mind of an unreliable narrator through use of close third person point of view. The character in question is elderly, senile, and terribly unreliable. He believes he is still a practicing doctor although he has not delivered a baby in decades. Eventually the third person narrator pulls back and lets us see how we have been fooled by the close narrative distance.

Sometimes you can spend quite a bit of time wondering whether you are in a strange world, with its own rules—i.e., the omniscient narrator is simply explaining the laws of a different universe, where people can turn into cockroaches—or whether you have entered into the mind of one character or another. Let's look at another example:

Riding up the winding road of Saint Agnes Cemetery in the back of the rattling old truck, Francis Phelan became aware that the dead, even more than the living, settled down in neighborhoods. The truck was suddenly surrounded by fields of monuments and cenotaphs of kindred design and striking size, all guarding the privileged dead. But the truck moved on and the limits of mere privilege became visible, for here now came the acres of truly prestigious death: illustrious men and women, captains of life without their diamonds, furs, carriages, and limousines, but buried in pomp and glory, vaulted in great tombs built like heavenly safe deposit boxes, or parts of the Acropolis. And ah yes, here too, inevitably, came the flowing masses, row upon row of them under simple headstones and simpler crosses. Here was the neighborhood of the Phelans.

Francis's mother twitched nervously in her grave as the truck carried him nearer to her; and Francis's father lit his pipe, smiled at his wife's discomfort, and looked out from his own bit of sod to catch a glimpse of how much his son had changed since the train accident.

Francis's father smoked roots of grass that died in the periodic droughts afflicting the cemetery. He stored the root essence in his pockets until it was brittle to the touch, then pulverized it between his fingers and packed his pipe. Francis's mother wove crosses from the dead dandelions and other deep-rooted weeds; careful to preserve their fullest length, she wove them while they were still in the green stage of death, then ate them with an insatiable revulsion.

"Look at that tomb," Francis said to his companion. "Ain't that somethin'? That's Arthur T. Grogan. I saw him around Albany when I was a kid. He owned all the electricity in town."

"He ain't got much of it now," Rudy said.

"Don't bet on it," Francis said. "Them kind of guys hang onto a good thing."

This is from *Ironweed* by William Kennedy, which won the Pulitzer Prize. We're in the mind of Francis Phelan, seeing the world from his point of view through the use of close, limited third person point of view. These ghosts are Francis's ghosts: only he can see them, and interact with them, and they appear to him throughout the book. Are they for real? Or are we seeing the world through an unreliable character's point of view? You should read the book yourself to find out what you think, but I think we're supposed to believe in the ghosts. They're too authoritative, know too much about the history of Albany, about Francis's family—they know things that Francis doesn't know, which makes them infinitely credible. So this is a world in which a character gets visits from ghosts from his past, who inform him of things, or accuse him, or otherwise interact with him. He is not dreaming, and he is not insane. The ghosts are real (even though no one else can see or hear them).

Again, the rules of narration are yours to set. I'm telling you the various conventions. But you are the one making a contract with your reader, and the only stipulation is that you make the terms of the contract clear, and that you don't break the contract. Consistency. Let there be logic. That logic can be complex—it can be, like in James Joyce's work, so convoluted that it keeps scholars guessing for decades as to who is narrating any particular section, and what he or she knows. But it has to be there.

Part 2: EXERCISES

Determining the reliability of your narrator is one of the critical aspects of working with both first and third person points of view. It's important for first person point of view because any character, no matter how intelligent or morally upright or experienced, is going to have limitations; third person because if you decide to play with reliability through manipulating the narrative distance, you need to have a way of showing what the truth is.

Exercise 1: He Said, She Said

Goal: To show how different characters' perceptions of an event can differ based on their individual biases.

What to do: 1. Choose two characters who are in a situation in which one confronts the other as having done something wrong, or broken the rules in some way.

2. Tell about the incident from both perspectives, using first person point of view each time. Show how each character distorts things in his/her favor.

Here's an example of how this exercise might be completed, by Perry Stuart:

POV 1:

I was walking down the street when suddenly, out of nowhere, came a car, going way over the speed limit (which is 35 on residential streets, but 25 on our street because we have a school here). A cat happened to be crossing the road at the same time, and whoosh! Suddenly there was a screech and the car had stopped, but no cat in sight. I was sure that the cat was dead, I was sure I had heard the thump, it wouldn't have surprised me if the cat had dragged itself off bleeding to die on its own, only no blood, no sign of the cat. The driver was unrepentant. "Stupid animal," he said, thinking I was sympathetic to him. "You'd think they'd learn to stay out of the way of traffic." Well, I certainly told him off! I was enraged! I told him that I would take his license plate and report him to the police. He was unmoved by my anger, just put his foot on the gas and zoomed on.

POV 2:

It was one of those streets that you're not supposed to go down unless you actually live there. "Closed to local traffic" is what the sign said. There used to be speed bumps, but they took them out, too many complaints. But it was the fastest way to the freeway and I was late (of course) and this job really mattered to me, but I wasn't going that fast, perhaps 40 miles an hour, which I think is below the speed limit on these streets, when a black and white cat suddenly streaked out into the road in front of me. Holy cow! Of course, I slammed on the brakes, and waited for that sickening thud (I hate that part of it). There was a guy standing there, who'd witnessed the whole thing. I could tell he was just as shocked as I was. "Stupid animal," I told him, and he agreed. He added, quite mildly, that perhaps I was going a little over the speed limit, and I told him that the speed limit was too slow on these streets, which were wide enough to go at least 10 miles an hour faster. He didn't say anything, but I could tell he agreed. I said goodbye and powered myself out of there. Still no sign of the cat, but who cares? The little bastards have nine lives, after all.

Exercise 2: See What I See, Hear What I Hear

> Goal: To focus on the concrete details that are solid evidence of the reality of a particular creative world.

What to do: 1. Place your character in a situation that should be familiar but isn't (imagine that your character has temporary amnesia and is doubting his or her grasp of reality, and is looking for clues as to what reality is).
2. Write about the situation using concrete sensory details to show your reader what reality is.

Here's a couple of passages by Carl Czyzewski that dramatize how this exercise might be done:

> I was aware of a few things right away. That I was inside a room, a room in a house by the looks of it. There was a sofa, a yellow tapestry-like covering to it, I could feel the rough texture of the material with my fingers. When I sat down, it held my weight firmly, with bounce. At my feet, a luxurious oriental carpet on top of a hardwood floor, polished to a high gleam. A man sitting across from me, he seemed to be talking, but the meaning of the words escaped me. Just meaningless syllables.

> There was a bench. That was a reality. He could feel its cold, hard surface. Droplets of something damp on top. Dew? Someone's tears? He shuddered

at the thought. A slight movement out of the corner of his eye. No. Concentrate on facts. There was the bench. And over here. A tree. There was the coolness of standing under its branches, out of the hot sun. The sun. The brightness. The ground he was walking on, the newspaper he held in his hand. "I am going for a walk," he said out loud, as if to verify that he existed.

Part 3: READING AS A WRITER

The Swimmer

JOHN CHEEVER

It was one of those midsummer Sundays when everyone sits around saying, "I *drank* too much last night." You might have heard it whispered by the parishioners leaving church, heard it from the lips of the priest himself, struggling with his cassock in the *vestiarium*, heard it from the golf links and the tennis courts, heard it from the wildlife preserve where the leader of the Audubon group was suffering from a terrible hangover. "I *drank* too much," said Donald Westerhazy. "We all *drank* too much," said Lucinda Merrill. "It must have been the wine," said Helen Westerhazy. "I *drank* too much of that claret."

This was the edge of the Westerhazys' pool. The pool, fed by an artesian well with a high iron content, was a pale shade of green. It was a fine day. In the west there was a massive stand of cumulus cloud so like a city seen from a distance—from the bow of an approaching ship—that it might have had a name. Lisbon. Hackensack. The sun was hot. Neddy Merrill sat by the green water, one hand in it, one around a glass of gin. He was a slender man—he seemed to have the especial slenderness of youth—and while he was far from young he had slid down his banister that morning and given the bronze backside of Aphrodite on the hall table a smack, as he jogged toward the smell of coffee in his dining room. He might have been compared to a summer's day, particularly the last hours of one, and while he lacked a tennis racket or a sail bag the impression was definitely one of youth, sport, and clement weather. He had been swimming and now he was breathing deeply, stertorously as if he could gulp into his lungs the components of that moment, the heat of the sun, the intenseness of his pleasure. It all seemed to flow into his chest. His own house stood in Bullet Park, eight miles to the south, where his four beautiful daughters would have had their lunch and might be playing tennis. Then it occurred to him that by taking a dogleg to the southwest he could reach his home by water.

His life was not confining and the delight he took in this observation could not be explained by its suggestion of escape. He seemed to see, with a cartographer's eye, that string of swimming pools, that quasi-subterranean stream that curved across the county. He had made a discovery, a contribution to modern geography; he would name the stream Lucinda after his wife. He was not a practical joker nor was he a fool but he was determinedly original and had a vague and modest idea of himself as a legendary figure. The day was beautiful and it seemed to him that a long swim might enlarge and celebrate its beauty.

He took off a sweater that was hung over his shoulders and dove in. He had an inexplicable contempt for men who did not hurl themselves into pools. He swam a choppy crawl, breathing either with every stroke or every fourth stroke and counting somewhere well in the back of his mind the one-two one-two of a flutter kick. It was not a serviceable stroke for long distances but the domestication of swimming had saddled the sport with some customs and in his part of the world a crawl was customary. To be embraced and sustained by the light green water was less a pleasure, it seemed, than the resumption of a natural condition, and he would have liked to swim without trunks, but this was not possible, considering his project. He hoisted himself up on the far curb—he never used the ladder— and started across the lawn. When Lucinda asked where he was going he said he was going to swim home.

The only maps and charts he had to go by were remembered or imaginary but these were clear enough. First there were the Grahams, the Hammers, the Lears, the Howlands, and the Crosscups. He would cross Ditmar Street to the Bunkers and come, after a short portage, to the Levys, the Welchers, and the public pool in Lancaster. Then there were the Hallorans, the Sachses, the Biswangers, Shirley Adams, the Gilmartins, and the Clydes. The day was lovely, and that he lived in a world so generously supplied with water seemed like a clemency, a beneficence. His heart was high and he ran across the grass. Making his way home by an uncommon route gave him the feeling that he was a pilgrim, an explorer, a man with a destiny, and he knew that he would find friends all along the way; friends would line the banks of the Lucinda River.

He went through a hedge that separated the Westerhazys' land from the Grahams', walked under some flowering apple trees, passed the shed that housed their pump and filter, and came out at the Grahams' pool. "Why, Neddy," Mrs. Graham said, "what a marvelous surprise. I've been trying to get you on the phone all morning. Here, let me get you a drink." He saw then, like any explorer, that the hospitable customs and traditions of the natives would have to be handled with diplomacy if he was ever going to reach his destination. He did not want to mystify or seem rude to the Grahams nor did he have the time to linger there. He swam the length of their pool and joined them in the sun and was rescued, a few minutes later, by the arrival of two carloads of friends from Connecticut. During the uproarious reunions he was able to slip away. He went down by the front of the Grahams' house, stepped over a thorny hedge, and crossed a vacant lot to the Hammers'. Mrs. Hammer, looking up from her roses, saw him swim by although she wasn't quite sure who it was. The Lears heard him splashing past the open windows of their living room. The Howlands and the Crosscups were away. After leaving the Howlands' he crossed Ditmar Street and started for the Bunkers', where he could hear, even at that distance, the noise of a party.

The water refracted the sound of voices and laughter and seemed to suspend it in midair. The Bunkers' pool was on a rise and he climbed some stairs to a terrace where twenty-five or thirty men and women were drinking. The only person in the water was Rusty Towers, who floated there on a rubber raft. Oh, how bonny and lush were the banks of the Lucinda River! Prosperous men and women gathered by the sapphire-colored waters while caterer's men in white coats passed them cold gin. Overhead a red de Haviland trainer was circling around and around and around in the sky with something like the glee of a child in a swing. Ned felt a passing affection for the scene, a tenderness for the gathering, as if it was something he might touch. In the distance he heard thunder. As soon as Enid Bunker saw him she began to scream: "Oh, look who's here! What a marvelous surprise! When Lucinda said you couldn't come I thought I'd *die*." She made her way to him through the crowd, and when they had finished kissing she led him to the bar, a progress that was slowed by the fact that he stopped to kiss eight or ten other women and shake the hands of as many men. A smiling bartender he had seen at a hundred parties gave him a gin and tonic and he stood by the bar for a moment, anxious not to get stuck in any conversation that would delay his voyage. When he seemed about to be surrounded he dove in and swam close to the side to avoid colliding with Rusty's raft. At the far end of the pool he bypassed the Tomlinsons with a broad smile and jogged up the garden path. The gravel cut his feet but this was only unpleasantness. The party was confined to the pool, and as he went toward the house he heard the brilliant, watery sound of voices fade, heard the noise of a radio from the Bunkers' kitchen, where someone was listening to a ball game. Sunday afternoon. He made his way through the parked cars and down the grassy border of their driveway to Alewives Lane. He did not want to be seen on the road in his bathing trunks but there was no traffic and he made the short distance to the Levys' driveway, marked with a PRIVATE PROPERTY sign and a green tube for the *New York Times*. All the doors and windows of the big house were open but there were no signs of life; not even a dog barked. He went around the side of the house to the pool and saw that the Levys had only recently left. Glasses and bottles and dishes of nuts were on a table at the deep end, where there was a bathhouse or gazebo, hung with Japanese lanterns. After swimming the pool he got himself a glass and poured a drink. It was his fourth or fifth drink and he had swum nearly half the length of the Lucinda River. He felt tired, clean, and pleased at that moment to be alone; pleased with everything.

It would storm. The stand of cumulus cloud—that city—had risen and darkened, and while he sat there he heard the percussiveness of thunder again. The de Haviland trainer was still circling overhead and it seemed to Ned that he could almost hear the pilot laugh with pleasure in the afternoon; but when there was another peal of thunder he took off for home. A train whistle blew and he wondered what time it had gotten to be. Four? Five? He thought of the provincial station at that hour, where a waiter, his tuxedo concealed by a raincoat, a dwarf with some flowers wrapped in newspaper, and a woman who had been crying would be waiting for the local. It was suddenly growing dark; it was that moment when the pinheaded birds seemed to organize their song into some acute and knowledgeable recognition of the storm's approach. Then there was a fine noise of rushing water from the crown of an oak at his back, as if a spigot there had been turned. Then the noise of fountains came from the crowns of all the tall trees. Why did he love storms, what was the meaning of his excitement when the door sprang open and the rain wind fled rudely up the stairs, why had the simple task of shutting the windows of an old house seemed fitting and urgent, why did the first watery notes of a storm wind have for him the unmistakable sound of good news, cheer, glad tidings? Then there was an explosion, a smell of cordite, and rain lashed the Japanese lanterns that Mrs. Levy had bought in Kyoto the year before last, or was it the year before that?

He stayed in the Levys' gazebo until the storm had passed. The rain had cooled the air and he shivered. The force of the wind had stripped a maple of its red and yellow leaves and scattered them over the grass and the water. Since it was midsummer the tree must be blighted, and yet he felt a peculiar sadness at this sign of autumn. He braced his shoulders, emptied his glass, and started for the Welchers' pool. This meant crossing the Lindleys' riding ring and he was surprised to find it overgrown with grass and all the jumps dismantled. He wondered if the Lindleys had sold their horses or gone away for the summer and put them out to board. He seemed to remember having heard something about the Lindleys and their horses but the memory was unclear. On he went, barefoot through the wet grass, to the Welchers', where he found their pool was dry.

This breach in his chain of water disappointed him absurdly, and he felt like some explorer who seeks a torrential headwater and finds a dead stream. He was disappointed and mystified. It was common enough to go away for the summer but no one ever drained his pool. The Welchers had definitely gone away. The pool furniture was folded, stacked, and covered with a tarpaulin. The bathhouse was locked. All the windows of the house were shut, and when he went around to the driveway in front he saw a FOR SALE sign nailed to a tree. When had he last heard from the Welchers—when, that is, had he and Lucinda last regretted an invitation to dine with them? It seemed only a week or so ago. Was his memory failing or had he so disciplined it in the repression of unpleasant facts that he had damaged his sense of the truth? Then in the distance he heard the sound of a tennis game. This cheered him, cleared away all his apprehensions and let him regard the overcast sky and the cold air with indifference. This was the day that Neddy Merrill swam across the county. That was the day! He started off then for his most difficult portage.

Had you gone for a Sunday afternoon ride that day you might have seen him, close to naked, standing on the shoulders of Route 424, waiting for a chance to cross. You might have wondered if he was the victim of foul play, had his car broken down, or was he merely a fool. Standing barefoot in the deposits of the highway—beer cans, rags, and blowout patches— exposed to all kinds of ridicule, he seemed pitiful. He had known when he started that this was a part of his journey—it had been on his maps—but confronted with the lines of traffic, worming through the summery light, he found himself unprepared. He was laughed at, jeered at, a beer can was thrown at him, and he had no dignity or humor to bring to the situation. He could have gone back, back to the Westerhazys', where Lucinda would still be sitting in the sun. he had signed nothing, vowed nothing, pledged nothing, not even to himself. Why, believing as he did, that all human obduracy was susceptible to common sense, was he unable to turn back? Why was he determined to complete his journey even if it meant putting his life in danger? At what point had this prank, this joke, this piece of horseplay become serious? He could not go back, he could not even recall with any clearness the green water at the Westerhazys', the sense of inhaling the day's components, the friendly and relaxed voices saying that they had *drunk* too much. In the space of an hour, more or less, he had covered a distance that made his return impossible.

An old man, tooling down the highway at fifteen miles an hour, let him get to the middle of the road, where there was a grass divider. Here he was exposed to the ridicule of the northbound traffic, but after ten or fifteen minutes he was able to cross. From here he had only a short walk to the Recreation Center at the edge of the village of Lancaster, where there were some handball courts and a public pool.

The effect of the water on voices, the illusion of brilliance and suspense, was the same here as it had been at the Bunkers' but the sounds here were louder, harsher, and more shrill, and as soon as he entered the crowded enclosure he was confronted with regimentation. "ALL SWIMMERS MUST TAKE A SHOWER BEFORE USING THE POOL. ALL SWIMMERS MUST USE THE FOOTBATH. ALL SWIMMERS MUST WEAR THEIR IDENTIFICATION DISKS." He took a shower, washed his feet in a cloudy and bitter solution, and made his way to the edge of the water. It stank of chlorine and looked to him like a sink. A pair of lifeguards in a pair of towers blew police whistles at what seemed to be regular intervals and abused the swimmers through a public address system. Neddy remembered the sapphire water at the Bunkers' with longing and thought that he might contaminate himself—damage his own prosperousness and charm—by swimming in this murk, but he reminded himself that he was an explorer, a pilgrim, and that this was merely a stagnant bend in the Lucinda River. He dove, scowling with distaste, into the chlorine and had to swim with his head above water to avoid collisions, but even so he was bumped into, splashed, and jostled. When he got to the shallow end both lifeguards were shouting at him: "Hey, you, you without the identification disk, get outa the water." He did, but they had no way of pursuing him and he went through the reek of suntan oil and chlorine out through the hurricane fence and passed the handball courts. By crossing the road he entered the wooded part of the Halloran estate. The woods were not cleared and the footing was treacherous and difficult until he reached the lawn and the clipped beech hedge that encircled their pool.

The Hallorans were friends, an elderly couple of enormous wealth who seemed to bask in the suspicion that they might be Communists. They were zealous reformers but they were not Communists, and yet when they were accused, as they sometimes were, of subversion, it seemed to gratify and excite them. Their beech hedge was yellow and he guessed this had been blighted like the Levys' maple. He called hullo, hullo, to warn the Hallorans of his approach, to palliate his invasion of their privacy. The Hallorans, for reasons that had never been explained to him, did not wear bathing suits. No explanations were in order, really. Their nakedness was a detail in their uncompromising zeal for reform and he stepped politely out of his trunks before he went through the opening in the hedge.

Mrs. Halloran, a stout woman with white hair and a serene face, was reading the *Times*. Mr. Halloran was taking beech leaves out of the water with a scoop. They seemed not surprised or displeased to see him. Their pool was perhaps the oldest in the country, a fieldstone rectangle, fed by a brook. It had no filter or pump and its waters were the opaque gold of the stream.

"I'm swimming across the county," Ned said.

"Why, I didn't know one could," exclaimed Mrs. Halloran.

"Well, I've made it from the Westerhazys'," Ned said. "That must be about four miles."

He left his trunks at the deep end, walked to the shallow end, and swam this stretch. As he was pulling himself out of the water he heard Mrs. Halloran say, "We've been *terribly* sorry to hear about all your misfortunes, Neddy."

"My misfortunes?" Ned asked. "I don't know what you mean."

"Why we heard that you'd sold the house and that your poor children . . ."

"I don't recall having sold the house," Ned said, "and the girls are at home."

"Yes," Mrs. Halloran sighed. "Yes . . ." Her voice filled the air with an unseasonable melancholy and Ned spoke briskly. "Thank you for the swim."

"Well, have a nice trip," said Mrs. Halloran.

Beyond the hedge he pulled on his trunks and fastened them. They were loose and he wondered if, during the space of an afternoon, he could have lost some weight. He was cold and he was tired and the naked Hallorans and their dark water had depressed him. The swim was too much for his strength but how could he have guessed this, sliding down the banister that morning and sitting in the Westerhazys' sun? His arms were lame. His legs felt rubbery and ached at the joints. The worst of it was the cold in his bones and the feeling that he might never be warm again. Leaves were falling down around him and he smelled wood smoke on the wind. Who would be burning wood at this time of the year?

He needed a drink. Whiskey would warm him, pick him up, carry him through the last of his journey, refresh his feeling that it was original and valorous to swim across the county. Channel swimmers took brandy. He needed a stimulant. He crossed the lawn in front of the Hallorans' house and went down a little path to where they had built a house for their only daughter, Helen, and her husband, Eric Sachs. The Sachses' pool was small and he found Helen and her husband there.

"Oh, *Neddy*," Helen said. "Did you lunch at Mother's?"

"Not *really*," Ned said. "I *did* stop to see your parents." This seemed to be explanation enough. "I'm terribly sorry to break in on you like this but I've taken a chill and I wonder if you'd give me a drink."

"Why, I'd *love* to," Helen said, "but there hasn't been anything in this house to drink since Eric's operation. That was three years ago."

Was he losing his memory, had his gift for concealing painful facts let him forget that he had sold his house, that his children were in trouble, and that his friend had been ill? His eyes slipped from Eric's face to his abdomen, where he saw three pale, sutured scars, two of them at least a foot long. Gone was his navel, and what, Neddy thought, would the roving hand, bed-checking one's gifts at 3 a.m., make of a belly with no navel, no link to birth, this breach in the succession?

"I'm sure you can get a drink at the Biswangers'," Helen said. "They're having an enormous do. You can hear it from here. Listen!"

She raised her head and from across the road, the lawns, the gardens, the woods, the fields, he heard again the brilliant noise of voices over water. "Well, I'll get wet," he said, still feeling that he had no freedom of choice about his means of travel. He dove into the Sachses' cold water, and gasping, close to drowning, made his way from one end of the pool to the other. "Lucinda and I want *terribly* to see you," he said over his shoulder, his face set toward the Biswangers'. "We're sorry it's been so long and we'll call you *very* soon."

He crossed some fields to the Biswangers' and the sounds of revelry there. They would be honored to give him a drink, they would be happy to give him a drink. The Biswangers invited him and Lucinda for dinner four times a year, six weeks in advance. They were always rebuffed and yet they continued to send out their invitations, unwilling to comprehend the rigid and undemocratic realities of their society. They were the sort of people who discussed the price of things at cocktails, exchanged market tips during dinner, and after dinner told dirty stories to mixed company. They did not belong to Neddy's set—they were not even on Lucinda's Christmas card list. He went toward their pool with feelings of indifference, charity, and some unease, since it seemed to be getting dark and these were the longest days of the year. The party when he joined it was noisy and large. Grace Biswanger was the kind of hostess who asked the optometrist, the veterinarian, the real-estate dealer, and the dentist. No one was swimming and the twilight, reflected on the water of the pool, had a wintry gleam. There was a bar and he started for this. When Grace Biswanger saw him she came toward him, not affectionately as he had every right to expect, but bellicosely.

"Why, this party has everything," she said loudly, "including a gate crasher."

She could not deal him a social blow—there was no question about this and he did not flinch. "As a gate crasher," he asked politely, "do I rate a drink?"

"Suit yourself," she said. "You don't seem to pay much attention to invitations."

She turned her back on him and joined some guests, and he went to the bar and ordered a whiskey. The bartender served him but he served him rudely. His was a world in which the caterer's men kept the social score, and to be rebuffed by a part-time barkeep meant that he had suffered some loss of social esteem. Or perhaps the man was new and uninformed. Then he heard Grace at his back say: "They went for broke overnight— nothing but income—and he showed up drunk one Sunday and asked us to loan him five thousand dollars . . ." She was always talking about money. It was worse than eating your peas off a knife. He dove into the pool, swam its length, and went away.

The next pool on his list, the last but two, belonged to his old mistress, Shirley Adams. If he had suffered any injuries at the Biswangers' they would be cured here. Love—sexual roughhouse in fact—was the supreme elixir, the painkiller, the brightly colored pill that would put the spring back into his step, the joy of life in his heart. They had had an affair last week, last month, last year. He couldn't remember. It was he who had broken it off, his was the upper hand, and he stepped through the gate of the wall that surrounded her pool with nothing so considered as self-confidence. It seemed in a way to be his pool, as the lover, particularly the illicit lover, enjoys the possessions of his mistress with an authority unknown to holy matrimony. She was there, her hair the color of brass, but her figure, at the edge of the lighted, cerulean water, excited in him no profound memories. It had been, he thought, a lighthearted affair, although she had wept when he broke it off. She seemed confused to see him and he wondered if she was still wounded. Would she, God forbid, weep again?

"What do you want?" she asked.

"I'm swimming across the county."

"Good Christ. Will you ever grow up?"

"What's the matter?"

"If you've come here for money," she said, "I won't give you another cent."

"You could give me a drink."

"I could but I won't. I'm not alone."

"Well, I'm on my way."

He dove in and swam the pool, but when he tried to haul himself up onto the curb he found that the strength in his arms and shoulders had gone, and he paddled to the ladder and climbed out. Looking over his shoulder he saw, in the lighted bathhouse, a young man. Going out onto the dark lawn he smelled chrysanthemums or marigolds—some stubborn autumnal fragrance—on the night air, strong as gas. Looking overhead he saw that the stars had come out, but why should he seem to see Andromeda, Cepheus, and Cassiopeia? What had become of the constellations of midsummer? He began to cry.

It was probably the first time in his adult life that he had ever cried, certainly the first time in his life that he had ever felt so miserable, cold, tired, and bewildered. He could not understand the rudeness of the caterer's barkeep or the rudeness of a mistress who had come to him on her knees and showered his trousers with tears. He had swum too long, he had been immersed too long, and his nose and his throat were sore from the water. What he needed then was a drink, some company, and some clean, dry clothes, and while he could have cut directly across the road to his home he went on to the Gilmartins' pool. Here, for the first time in his life, he did not dive but went down the steps into the icy water and swam a hobbled sidestroke that he might have learned as a youth. He staggered with fatigue on his way to the Clydes' and paddled the length of their pool, stopping again and again with his hand on the curb to rest. He climbed up the ladder and wondered if he had the strength to get home. He had done what he wanted, he had swum the county, but he was so stupefied with exhaustion that his triumph seemed vague. Stooped, holding on to the gateposts for support, he turned up the driveway of his own house.

The place was dark. Was it so late that they had all gone to bed? Had Lucinda stayed at the Westerhazys' for supper? Had the girls joined her there or gone someplace else? Hadn't they agreed, as they usually did on Sunday, to regret all their invitations and stay at home? He tried the garage doors to see what cars were in but the doors were locked and rust came off the handles onto his hands. Going toward the house, he saw the force of the thunderstorm had knocked one of the rain gutters loose. It hung down over the front door like an umbrella rib, but it could be fixed in the morning. The house was locked, and he thought that the stupid cook or the stupid maid must have locked the place up until he remembered that it had been some time since they had employed a maid or a cook. He shouted, pounded on the door, tried to force it with his shoulder, and then, looking in at the windows, saw that the place was empty.

1. When do you first realize that this story might not be told completely in a realistic mode?
2. How does Cheever gradually draw us into the fantastical nature of the events of the story?
3. There are two possible explanations for the aspects of the story that don't make sense (from a view of "reality" as we know it). What are they? What do you believe?

CHAPTER EIGHT

You Talking to Me?

Part 1: CRAFTING EFFECTIVE DIALOGUE

Getting Started

From the moment we are born, language envelops us, instructs us. Right away we begin the complex process of absorbing vocabulary, grammar, and meaning as communicated by the spoken word. Speech is integral to how we live—and, not surprisingly, is a critical part of how we communicate using the written word as well.

Open just about any book—fiction or nonfiction—and chances are you'll find dialogue in it. Some of this dialogue will be short and terse; some, expansive and lyrical. You'll find different characters using different idioms, syntax, grammar, vocabulary. You'll find dialogue that sounds like what you'd hear at the local coffee shop, and dialogue that no one on earth has ever spoken, yet which somehow works within the context of the story, novel, or nonfiction piece.

Learning to craft good dialogue is one of the most critical aspects of learning to write good fiction and creative nonfiction. Without understanding how to render on the page a realistic approximation of how real people talk to (and at) each other, you will fail to develop one of the key tools you have for generating truly compelling creative work.

In this chapter, we will first examine what good dialogue should accomplish. We will look at a number of examples—from prose pieces, both fiction and creative nonfiction, as well as from dramatic works written for theater (we can learn a lot from theater, since in drama, words *are* action). Then you will have a chance to practice what we've discussed in exercises. Finally, you will be exposed to some examples of good dialogue in the reading for this chapter.

What Dialogue Is Good For

Dialogue isn't just the words your characters speak to each other. Good dialogue works on a number of different levels. Here are the main things you want to accomplish with it:

1. Adds to the reader's knowledge of the situation. (Knowledge is different from facts.)
2. Keeps the piece moving forward.
3. Reveals something about the speaker's personality, both directly and indirectly. (What is *not* being said is called the subtext—read on.)
4. Dramatizes relationships between characters.

> IMPORTANT: Good dialogue is not necessarily realistic dialogue. You do not want to copy what you heard on the street. You want to make it *sound* natural, but that doesn't mean it *is* natural. It takes careful editing to create natural-sounding dialogue. Generally, that means paying attention to the rhythm of sentences. Varying the length of sentences. Making a conscious effort to be non-grammatical (people seldom speak in full sentences). More on this later in the chapter.

Dialogue needs to be extremely specific. We're leery of (and bored by) characters who talk in generalities or abstractions. "I think I'm in love with you, darling," is always suspect. "Oh my God, so *that's* the way you brush your teeth!" is a wonderful piece of dialogue that I've borrowed from a friend of mine who is writing a story about the beginning of a love affair.

Every character should speak differently. Each should have a distinct way of phrasing, of opinion, of subject matter. Extremely clever dialogue that bounces back and forth effortlessly between characters is no good if one or more of the characters is saying things they wouldn't or couldn't say.

> "C'mon, Jane, make an effort."
> "What do you mean, make an effort? I'm working as hard as I can. I still just don't get it."
> "It's simple: you just multiply the length by the width and you get the total area in square inches."
> "I'm sorry, I'm sorry, I still don't understand. What are square inches?"
> "Arggh! Let's start over from the beginning."

From this passage we can tell that the first speaker is impatient, and a little patronizing, the second speaker unsure and apologetic. All through the spoken word—we didn't need even a word of narrative to help us understand what the characters were thinking or feeling.

Also, dialogue for a particular character can change depending on:

1. Who he or she is talking to (if the character is talking to more than one person, the matter gets even more complicated).
2. Whether the characters are in a private or a public place.
3. The mood of the speaker (angry: might say things harsher than usual; frightened: might try to placate the listener).

For example, we talk differently to our friends than we do to our mothers. Likewise, our words will vary depending on whether we are annoyed, or impatient, or saddened by something. All the things that affect character will affect dialogue.

In short: dialogue reflects character, so anything that affects a character will affect the dialogue (more on this in Chapter 10, on characterization).

What Dialogue Is Not

Let's explain what dialogue *isn't*.

1. Not an important source of facts about a piece.
   So not:

   "You've missed your 8:34 train to San Francisco, and if you think I'm going to drive you 34 miles to your job at the law firm of Harris and Sullivan, for the fifth time since we were mistakenly married at your parents' summer house in the Hamptons three years ago, you're mistaken."

   Instead:

   "You missed it again."
   "Oh, no. Can't be!"
   "Just look at the time."
   "It's the damn clock. I told you not to buy one with a snooze button."
   "Yes, my fault. As always."

2. Not good for describing people, places, or objects.
   So not:

   "My, you look stunning in your gold lame gown with beads around the collar that shimmers when you walk sexily around the room."

   Instead:

   "Wow."
   "What?"
   "That dress, what's it made of? It kind of glows. Wow."

3. Absolutely no substitute for direct narrative. If you have basic facts to supply to the reader, if in doubt, put it in narrative.

Above all, make sure you don't have "empty" scenes, like the following, that could be replaced with a few sentences of narrative:

"Hello, may I speak to Amy?"

"This is Amy."

"Hi, Amy, how are you? I know you're my sister, but I haven't seen you in three weeks."

"I know, Gail. I feel bad about that. I was afraid you were still mad about the fact that I ripped your favorite sweater. How about meeting for coffee this afternoon?"

"Fine. Café Verona, at noon?"

"Sounds great. See you there."

"Bye."

Instead:

Ann hadn't seen her sister Gail in three weeks, not since Gail had borrowed Ann's vintage red beaded sweater only to let her cat unravel one of the sleeves. They decided to meet on neutral ground: Café Verona at noon.

4. It *especially* should not be used for extended brooding by a character.

"I can't help wondering, why were we put on this planet? We are specks of humanity, drowning in our despair, with no joy, no hope, nothing to bring us salvation in our pathetic, small lives."

No. If in doubt, always put it in narrative. *Tell* us ("Arnold went on a rant of philosophical brooding that all the others mostly tuned out") rather than waste our time in an empty scene.

A Word about Attribution

We need to know who is talking when words are spoken in a piece. Most of the time, you should use the word "said." If you can, drop it. But don't worry about it being repetitive, as it is so much a part of fiction that it is virtually invisible. Do not—repeat, do not—feel you need to use substitutes such as "hissed," "threatened," "exploded," "smirked," "sneered," "chuckled," "growled," etc. Take them out. Use "said" or occasionally (as appropriate) "shouted" or "yelled" or "whispered."

Also, most of the time, using adverbs to describe how something was said is unnecessary. It can even weaken the effect of the dialogue ("she said angrily," "he said hopefully," "I said happily"). Word choices and carefully chosen gestures can be much more effective than mere adverbs can be.

So not:

"What are you talking about," he asked angrily.

Instead:

"What the hell are you talking about?" he asked, slamming the Bible down onto the table so that the glasses tinkled.

You can see how much more effective it is to use gesture and choose your spoken words carefully than to simply add an adverb at the end of a dialogue tag.

Five Important Tips on Dialogue

So you want to write better dialogue? Here are five important tips that will immediately make your dialogue better:

1. Gesture is a part of dialogue.
2. Dialogue is what characters *do* to one another.
3. Silence is a part of dialogue.
4. Dialogue is not necessarily grammatically correct.
5. Make the world part of your dialogue.

Let's now go over each of these points in detail:

1. Gesture is a part of dialogue. Using gesture to show *how* something is said can be one of the most effective means of writing dialogue you will come across. Consider the following excerpt from "Hills Like White Elephants" (the entire story can be found at the end of this chapter, on pp. 356–60). The gestures are boldfaced.

The woman brought two glasses of beer and two felt pads. She put the felt pads and the beer glasses on the table and looked at the man and the girl. The girl was looking off at the line of hills. They were white in the sun and the country was brown and dry.

"They look like white elephants," she said.

"I've never seen one," **the man drank his beer**.

"No, you wouldn't have."

"I might have," the man said. "Just because you say I wouldn't have doesn't prove anything."

The girl looked at the bead curtain. "They've painted something on it," she said. "What does it say?"

Notice how the gestures inform the way the dialogue is spoken. When the man drinks his beer after saying, "I've never seen one," he is dismissing what the girl says. When the girl looks at the bead curtain, she is trying to change the subject to defuse the tension between them. In both cases, the gestures inform the words spoken to such an extent that they can be considered extensions of the dialogue.

In general, having your characters *do* something while they're speaking adds verisimilitude to the exchange; we rarely just sit there, frozen, as we speak to one another. We're either fidgeting—with our wedding rings, our watches—or we're in the middle of another activity, like kneading bread or fixing a car. In such cases, it is natural for gestures and actions that are part of the scene to enter into the dialogue itself.

2. Dialogue is what characters do to one another. Think in terms of verbal sparring. In our stories and novels and creative nonfiction pieces, characters rarely, if ever, come to actual blows. But they do come to words. If you think of dialogue as a *physical* exchange between characters, you'll fare much better at crafting effective prose speech. In the example below, from "Silver Water," by Amy Bloom, we see how the jargon spouted by the therapist is met with contempt and hostility by the family seeking therapy. They are definitely "doing things" to the therapist in exchange for what they perceive as his insincerity.

> Mr. Walker said, "I wonder why it is that everyone is so entertained by Rose behaving inappropriately."
>
> Rose burped and then we all laughed. This was the seventh family therapist we had seen, and none of them had lasted very long. Mr. Walker, unfortunately, was determined to do right by us.
>
> "What do you think of Rose's behavior, Violet?" They did this sometimes. In their manual it must say, If you think the parents are too weird, try talking to the sister.
>
> "I don't know. Maybe she's trying to get you to stop talking about her in the third person."
>
> "Nicely put," my mother said.
>
> "Indeed," my father said.
>
> "Fuckin' A," Rose said.
>
> "Well, this is something that the whole family agrees upon," Mr. Walker said, trying to act as if he understood or even liked us.
>
> "This was not a successful intervention, Ferret Face," Rose said.

3. Silence is a part of dialogue. When a character refuses to answer a remark or question, or looks off into the distance, or even pauses just slightly, that is part of a verbal communication. Indeed, silence can be one of the most powerful tools you have when constructing effective dialogue. In the passage that follows, from "The Museum of Science and Industry Story" by David Mamet, we see how silence works to indicate how the character is listening and responding to the person on the other end of the phone.

ALBERT: Hello? *(brief pause as he listens)* Where *are* you? *(brief pause after each phrase as he listens)*

Albert.

Albert *Litko.*

(As ALBERT talks we see the Museum lights being extinguished, one by one until he is sitting in the dark.)

At the Museum.

Waiting for *you.*

Well, we *did.*

We certainly *did.*

Well, *I* thought we did.

I'm sorry, too.

At the Museum, I told you.

(SILENCE)

It's okay. *(pause)* Well, what are you doing *tonight?*

Oh. *(long pause)*

What are you doing *tomorrow* night?

Oh.

No. I'm not. I'm not.

No. Don't be silly.

No. Okay.

So, how do we write silence into our dialogue? Sometimes you might want to simply put in a line of narrative—"There was quiet for a moment"—but sometimes you might want to be more subtle than that. Here are some other ways of infusing silence or pauses into your dialogue:

· Insert some sensory clues to what is happening during the silence. "The clock ticked away" is a cliché, as is "A dog barked in the distance." But these are examples of the kind of sensory clues you can provide (in narrative) that creates a pause, or brief silence.

"Are you sure about this, Anne?" he asked. "Really sure?"

"They could hear the wind rustling through the trees outside. An ant crawled along the counter between them.

"Yes," she said, finally. "I'm sure."

- Provide a descriptive passage of the setting (place) that the scene is taking place in.

"I'm sure I could make you h-h-h-happy," he said, stuttering a bit. "I'm a very hard w-w-w-worker."

The sky over his head was a deep, deep blue; there were cows in the fields and the few houses that could be seen seemed to blend into the grayish-brown landscape.

"I know, I just can't quite *see* it," she said. "It eludes me."

- Provide the character with an (unspoken) thought that is a reaction to the dialogue at hand.

"I've got a sixth sense for these things," she said. "I know how to make money. It's in my blood."

Right, he thought as he looked at her sullen face. I'm really going to give you my life's savings.

"And what would you do first?" he asked.

- Provide a character with an association, like a memory (flashback) related to the dialogue at hand.

"You must have been a pretty cute kid," he said.

After he spoke, she had a sudden image of herself at age seven, standing on the threshold of the house, holding on to her dog's leash and pulling back, not gently, in order to keep the dog inside.

"Not particularly," she said.

4. Dialogue is not necessarily grammatically correct. People generally don't speak in complete sentences with perfect grammar. Plus, there's often a rhythm or cadence to the language that defies conventional syntax. Instead of worrying about getting the grammar right, focus instead on varying sentence length (interposing shortened sentences among longer ones is generally considered very effective) and on the *music* of the words. In the passage that follows, from Anthony Burgess's *A Clockwork Orange*, even though the language is foreign to us

(Burgess made up his own language for this piece, a combination of cockney and Russian) we can hear the music and rhythm of the sentences, and how they flow.

"We got worried," said Georgie. "There we were, awaiting and peeting away at the old knify moloko, and you had not turned up. So then Pete here thought how you might have been like offended by some veshch or other, so round we come to your abode. That's right, Pete, right?"

"Oh, yes, right," said Pete.

"Apy polly loggies," I said, careful. "I had something of a pain in the gulliver so had to sleep. I was not wakened when I gave orders for wakening. Still, here we all are, ready for what the old nochy offers, yes?" I seemed to have picked up that yes? from P. R. Deltoid, my Post-Corrective Adviser. Very strange.

"Sorry about the pain," said Georgie, like very concerned. "Using the gulliver too much like, maybe. Giving orders and discipline and such, perhaps. Sure the pain is going? Sure you'll not be happier going back to the bed?" And they all had a bit of a malenky grin.

5. Make the world part of your dialogue. As we learned in talking about silence, above, you can indicate pauses or silence by involving the sensory world of the story, novel, or nonfiction piece in your dialogue. In a general way, however, it's a good idea to interject sensory cues from the "real" world into the words spoken. After all, as we've also discussed, dialogue never takes place in a vacuum. There are always things going on around the speakers: sounds and sights and smells and other sensory details that can be incorporated into the dialogue in order to provide for a more immersive experience.

"I'm ready. I've been ready for ten minutes. What's taking you so long?" she asked. She was standing in the hallway of their small apartment, wrapping a scarf around her neck as she watched him pull on his shirt.

"Give me a break, I only woke up thirty minutes ago," he said. He threw first one tie, then another, onto the disheveled bed, before finding the one he wanted from the overstuffed closet.

"Whose fault is that?" she asked. She was finished with her scarf and was now waiting, her hand on the front brass doorknob, polished to a sheen by frequent use.

"Yes, of course, of course, it is my fault, always my fault," he said as he put on his jacket in front of the bathroom mirror. It had a crack running up the left side that distorted his face a little. He grimaced and then strode out to meet his wife.

You can see how including narrative that involves the sensory world of the story, novel, or nonfiction piece deepens the experience of reading the dialogue.

On Subtext

Dialogue also reveals much by what *isn't* being said. Characters conceal things. They partially conceal things. They outright lie. They exaggerate. They rephrase.

When it's at its best, dialogue must exist on two levels: what is actually being said, which must pertain to the plot or general events of the piece; and what is being implied or revealed, which is the subtext, or emotional undercurrent. In the best creative works, the two go hand in hand.

Here's an example of what is meant by subtext from the novel *Remember Me* by Fay Weldon:

> Listen now, carefully, to the conversation of this mother and daughter. Madeleine and Hilary talk in riddles, as families do, even families as small and circumscribed as this one, using the everyday objects of their lives as symbols of their discontent:
>
> 1. HILARY: Mum, I can't find my shoes again.
> 2. MADELEINE (*looking*): They'll be where you took them off. (*finding*) Here they are.
> 3. HILARY: Not those old brown things. My new red ones.
> 4. MADELEINE: You can't possibly wear these to school. They're ridiculous. They'll cripple your feet.
> 5. HILARY: No they won't. Everyone wears platforms!
> 6. MADELEINE: In that case, everyone will be going around in plaster casts, and serve them right.
> 7. HILARY: You only don't like them because Lily [her father's new wife] bought them for me.
> 8. MADELEINE: I don't like them because they are ugly and ridiculous.
> 9. HILARY: I can't find the other ones. And anyway, I'm late. Please, Mum? They're my feet.
>
> Which, being translated, is:
>
> 1. HILARY: Why is this place always such a mess?
> 2. MADELEINE: Why are you such a baby?
> 3. HILARY: You know nothing about me.
> 4. MADELEINE: I know everything about you.
> 5. HILARY: I want to be like other people.
> 6. MADELEINE: Other people aren't worth being like.
> 7. HILARY: I know all about you, don't think I don't.

8. MADELEINE: You force me to tell the truth. Our whole situation is ugly and ridiculous and I despair of it.
9. HILARY: Then let me find my own way out of it, please.

So HILARY defeats her mother, as the children of guilty mothers do, and goes off to school wearing the red shoes with platform heels.

In "Hills Like White Elephants" (pp. 356–60) the subtext becomes clear after hearing the man repeat "I don't want you to do anything that you don't want to" several times; what he is really saying is, "I am *absolutely determined* that you are going to do this" (have an abortion). He's saying one thing, but meaning another: the very definition of subtext in dialogue.

A Word about Dialect

Sometimes you'll want to do something to the dialogue to indicate that a character is speaking less than perfect English. He or she might have an accent, for example. Or have an imperfect command of grammar. It's a bit out of fashion right now to spell out phonetically such deviations in speech. Typically, today, writers prefer to *suggest* that a character has an unusual speech pattern (foreign accent, lisp, etc.) through word choice, syntax (word placement within the sentence), content (reflecting a foreign way of viewing the world) or narrative. The reason: writing in dialect (or misspelling words in order to indicate pronunciation) can be more distracting than illuminating.

For example, rather than writing:

"He'th a velly thilly perthon, Jameth ith," she lisped.

Instead write:

Doris had trouble articulating the letters "r" and "s," something that James found oddly attractive. When he overheard Doris say to her mother, "He's a very silly person, James is," and heard his own name pronounced "Jameth," he shuddered with pleasure. That night, he lay awake in bed repeating, "Jameth, Jameth, Jameth." It seemed to him that Doris had caused him to be both reborn as well as renamed, and that Jameth was a better, kinder man than James ever could hope to be.

Here's an example of some very realistic sounding dialogue (from *Invisible Man* by Ralph Ellison) that uses syntax and word choice and a few deliberately phonetically spelled words to indicate that the characters are speaking other than what one might consider to be proper English:

And the big dark woman saying, *Boy, is you all right, what's wrong?* In a husky voiced contralto. And me saying, *I'm all right, just weak,* and trying to stand, and her saying, *Why don't y'all stand back and let the man breathe? Stand back there y'all,* and now echoed by an official tone, *Keep moving, break it up.* And she on one side and a man on the other, helping me to stand and the policeman saying, *Are you all right?* And me answering, *Yes, I just felt weak, must have fainted but all right now,* and him ordering the crowd to move on and the others moving on except the man and woman and him saying, *You sure you okay, daddy,* and me nodding yes, and her saying, *Where you live son, somewhere around here?* And me telling her Men's House and her looking at me shaking her head saying, *Men's House, Men's House, shucks that ain't no place for nobody in your condition what's weak and needs a woman to keep an eye on you awhile* and me saying, *But I'll be all right now,* and her, *Maybe you will and maybe you won't. I live just up the street and round the corner, you better come on round and rest till you feel stronger. I'll phone Men's House and tell em where you at.* And me too tired to resist and already she had one arm and was instructing the fellow to take the other and we went, me between them, inwardly rejecting and yet accepting her bossing, hearing, *You take it easy, I'll take care of you like I done a heap of others, my name's Mary Rambo, everybody knows me round this part of Harlem, you heard of me, ain't you?*

However, never say never in fiction, which is why some very fine writers choose to write in dialect. Here's a section of *Far Tortuga*, a novel by Peter Matthiessen written entirely in dialect (and with no attribution—you have to figure out not only what the characters are saying, but who is saying it):

> Domn good thing it was de land of opportunity, cause Desmond took every last centavo dat dey had fore he let'm off of de boat.
>
> I remember one time—Copm Bennie, I b'lieve it was—he wanted to lease dat old shark scow dat Desmond had, and Desmond demanded three hundred pounds for ten days. I told Bennie, I say, Mon, if dat vessel worth thirty pounds a day after all de crewin paid, why in de hell ain't Desmond out dere fishin sharks three hundred and sixty-five days in de year?
>
> Well, dere is one thing Desmond know and dat is sharks.
>
> I told you why—cause he a shark his*self*.
>
> (quietly) Hear dat? Come to Desmond Eden, Raib can hear you in a god-dom hurricane.
>
> (louder) You been in dat sharkskin game dere, ain't you Copm? On de Sponnish shore? I heard you was running guns dere, bringing back shark-skin.

Using Placeholders

Sometimes it can be difficult to come up with compelling, believable dialogue with pulsing subtext on the spot, that does all the things dialogue should do. A technique that works well for my students is, when in doubt, write out what needs to be *communicated*. Use what I call a *placeholder* or "serviceable" dialogue, with the understanding that you will go back later and change it.

Here's an example of how that might work. Say you want to write some dialogue that features an argument between a mother and daughter over the daughter staying out too late the previous night. You might start with serviceable dialogue that communicates the basic information, only later swapping it for better, more concise and spontaneous-sounding words.

Placeholder text:

> "You can't just defy my orders and do whatever you please," Susan told her daughter.
>
> "Why not?" her daughter said.
>
> "You are always defying me," Susan said. "I won't have it. You shouldn't have stayed out so late last night. I was worried about you. And what will the neighbors think?"
>
> "You are so self-centered that you think this is all about you. All you care about is what other people think."
>
> "What am I to do with you? You really frustrate me. You make me feel like a failure as a mother."
>
> "Maybe just leave me alone. I'm old enough to do what I want."

Notice how this scopes out the general things that need to be said between the mother and daughter, but how it's not particularly spontaneous-sounding. It's also a little too direct; it would make more sense to have the characters talk by way of something else, more indirectly.

Real dialogue (substituted later):

> "You can't do this to me," Susan told her daughter.
>
> "To you? This is about you?" her daughter asked.
>
> "Of course not. No. What I meant was, I was very clear: you were not to stay out past midnight."
>
> "You were clear all right. But clarity isn't everything."
>
> "What do you mean?"
>
> "I mean, credibility counts. And you have none. None whatsoever."
>
> "I'm the mother here."
>
> "Maybe you shouldn't be," her daughter said.

Now, notice how this sounds like more of what a mother and daughter, sparring, would sound like. It conveys all the necessary information and emotion, but does so in a much more spontaneous and believable way.

Dialogue in Creative Nonfiction Writing

Good dialogue is good dialogue, whether found in fiction or creative nonfiction. Below is an excerpt from *The Same River Twice*, a memoir by Chris Offutt, where you see that gesture and silence are built into this scene, with its vivid and spontaneous-sounding dialogue.

As a full-fledged kinker, I had access to the forbidden zone of performer alley. Here the clowns played chess, the aerialists disdained anyone confined to earth, and the dwarfs spent most of their time baiting the Parrot Lady. They constantly threatened to pluck her, and commented quite openly on her presumed skill at fellatio.

One Sunday, in a community so religious the circus wasn't allowed to admit the public until well past noon, the heat rose to ninety-eight. Only the aerialist and the Parrot Lady had trailers with air-conditioning. The rest of us sat semiclothed in available shade. A dwarf began crooning a love song on the Parrot Lady's aluminum steps. She opened her door with enough force to smack it against the trailer. The dwarfs retreated like tumbleweed.

"A bird in hand," one said.

"Is worth a hand in the bush," said the other.

"I got a sword she can't swallow."

"Get lost, you little pissants," the Parrot Lady said. She leaned against the doorjamb in the shimmering heat. "Hey, Walrus Man," she called. "Come here."

All the kinkers blinked from a doze, staring at me, then at her. I stumbled to her trailer as if moving through fog. My clothes clung to me.

"Save me a sandwich," said one of the dwarfs.

The air-conditioned trailer made the sweat cold on my body. She motioned me to a couch. Gingham curtains hung from each window, and an autographed picture of Elvis Presley sat on a tiny TV. The room was very small, very neat.

"Thirsty?" she said. "Like a drink?"

I nodded and she poured clear liquid from a pitcher into a glass, added ice and an olive.

"Nothing better in summer than a martini," she said.

Not wanting her to know that I'd never sampled such an exotic drink, I drank it in one chug and asked for another. She lifted her eyebrows and poured me one. I drank half for the sake of civility.

"The one thing I hate more than dwarfs," she said, "is the circus."

Part 2: EXERCISES

Exercise 1: Nonverbal Communication

Goal: To practice incorporating gesture and silence (non-responses) into dialogue, as responses.

What to do: 1. Think of a situation involving two characters, one who is trying to convince the other of something that he/she doesn't agree with.

2. Write the scene, using gesture and silence to indicate reluctance to comply or outright disagreement. HINT: Silence can be implied in many ways, as you can see from the sample writing below, as well as stated directly, using narrative.

The following passage was written by Cybele Unger:

"I'm telling you, Carol, this is a cinch. Easy as pie. A sure-fire investment," he said.

Carol hesitated for a moment before answering. "Sure-fire," she said.

"Yes! Absolutely certain!"

Carol picked up her fork and twirled it absently in her right hand. "But the stock market isn't doing so well these days," she said, eventually. "Everyone knows that. How can you be so sure this will work?"

"I'm telling you, it's unbeatable. Larry says so."

There was silence for a moment before Carol replied, flatly. "Larry says so."

"Will you stop repeating what I say? It's driving me nuts. Yes, Larry says so. And he knows."

The kitchen clock ticked away ten, twenty seconds.

"Carol? Did you hear what I said?"

"I heard you."

"Well, how about it?"

Carol sighed, and continued playing with her fork. "I guess so," she said finally.

Exercise 2: Them's Fighting Words

Goal: To understand dialogue as part of the action of a scene.

What to do: 1. Think of a situation in which one character is angry with another character for breaking the rules in some way.

2. Write out the scene in the form of dialogue in which the characters "fight" each other with words.

Daniel Tsui wrote the following passage in response to the exercise prompt:

"That's *it*. You're gonna get it."

"No, I'm not. It's no big deal. Mom never used that dish anyway. She'll never notice."

"She'll notice if I tell her."

"You wouldn't."

"Just watch me."

"I'll watch you, and then you can watch me tell her about the five dollars that disappeared from her purse last week."

"You have no proof."

"Who needs proof? It'll be enough to plant the seed of suspicion. She'll wonder. That'll be enough."

"She won't be able to punish me. Let her wonder."

"And then, next time you want something from her, watch her hesitate. Like that ski trip coming up in two weeks. I'm gonna enjoy watching you beg."

"You bastard."

"You started it."

Part 3: READING AS A WRITER

Hills Like White Elephants

ERNEST HEMINGWAY

The hills across the valley of the Ebro were long and white. On this side there was no shade and no trees and the station was between two lines of rails in the sun. Close against the side of the station there was the warm shadow of the building and a curtain, made of strings of bamboo beads, hung across the open door into the bar, to keep out flies. The American and the girl with him sat at a table in the shade, outside the building. It was very hot and the express from Barcelona would come in forty minutes. It stopped at this junction for two minutes and went on to Madrid.

"What should we drink?" the girl asked. She had taken off her hat and put it on the table.

"It's pretty hot," the man said.

"Let's drink beer."

"*Dos cervezas*," the man said into the curtain.

"Big ones?" a woman asked from the doorway.

"Yes. Two big ones."

The woman brought two glasses of beer and two felt pads. She put the felt pads and the beer glasses on the table and looked at the man and the girl. The girl was looking off at the line of hills. They were white in the sun and the country was brown and dry.

"They look like white elephants," she said.

"I've never seen one," the man drank his beer.

"No, you wouldn't have."

"I might have," the man said. "Just because you say I wouldn't have doesn't prove anything."

The girl looked at the bead curtain. "They've painted something on it," she said. "What does it say?"

"Anis del Toro. It's a drink."

"Could we try it?"

The man called "Listen" through the curtain. The woman came out from the bar.

"Four reales."

"We want two Anis del Toro."

"With water?"

"Do you want it with water?"

"I don't know," the girl said. "Is it good with water?"

"It's all right."

"You want them with water?" asked the woman.

"Yes, with water."

"It tastes like licorice," the girl said and put the glass down.

"That's the way with everything."

"Yes," said the girl. "Everything tastes of licorice. Especially all the things you've waited so long for, like absinthe."

"Oh, cut it out."

"You started it," the girl said. "I was being amused. I was having a fine time."

"Well, let's try and have a fine time."

"All right. I was trying. I said the mountains looked like white elephants. Wasn't that bright?"

"That was bright."

"I wanted to try this new drink: That's all we do, isn't it—look at things and try new drinks?"

"I guess so."

The girl looked across at the hills.

"They're lovely hills," she said. "They don't really look like white elephants. I just meant the coloring of their skin through the trees."

"Should we have another drink?"

"All right."

The warm wind blew the bead curtain against the table.

"The beer's nice and cool," the man said.

"It's lovely," the girl said.

"It's really an awfully simple operation, Jig," the man said. "It's not really an operation at all."

The girl looked at the ground the table legs rested on.

"I know you wouldn't mind it, Jig. It's really not anything. It's just to let the air in."

The girl did not say anything.

"I'll go with you and I'll stay with you all the time. They just let the air in and then it's all perfectly natural."

"Then what will we do afterward?"

"We'll be fine afterward. Just like we were before."

"What makes you think so?"

"That's the only thing that bothers us. It's the only thing that's made us unhappy."

The girl looked at the bead curtain, put her hand out, and took hold of two of the strings of beads.

"And you think then we'll be all right and be happy."

"I know we will. You don't have to be afraid. I've known lots of people that have done it."

"So have I," said the girl. "And afterward they were all so happy."

"Well," the man said, "if you don't want to you don't have to. I wouldn't have you do it if you didn't want to. But I know it's perfectly simple."

"And you really want to?"

"I think it's the best thing to do. But I don't want you to do it if you don't really want to."

"And if I do it you'll be happy and things will be like they were and you'll love me?"

"I love you now. You know I love you."

"I know. But if I do it, then it will be nice again if I say things are like white elephants, and you'll like it?"

"I'll love it. I love it now but I just can't think about it. You know how I get when I worry."

"If I do it you won't ever worry?"

"I won't worry about that because it's perfectly simple."

"Then I'll do it. Because I don't care about me."

"What do you mean?"

"I don't care about me."

"Well, I care about you."

"Oh, yes. But I don't care about me. And I'll do it and then everything will be fine."

"I don't want you to do it if you feel that way."

The girl stood up and walked to the end of the station. Across, on the other side, were fields of grain and trees along the banks of the Ebro. Far away, beyond the river, were mountains. The shadow of a cloud moved across the field of grain and she saw the river through the trees.

"And we could have all this," she said. "And we could have everything and every day we make it more impossible."

"What did you say?"

"I said we could have everything."

"We can have everything."

"No, we can't."

"We can have the whole world."

"No, we can't."

"We can go everywhere."

"No, we can't. It isn't ours any more."

"It's ours."

"No, it isn't. And once they take it away, you never get it back."

"But they haven't taken it away."

"We'll wait and see."

"Come on back in the shade," he said. "You mustn't feel that way."

"I don't feel any way," the girl said. "I just know things."

"I don't want you to do anything that you don't want to do—"

"Nor that isn't good for me," she said. "I know. Could we have another beer?"

"All right. But you've got to realize—"

"I realize," the girl said. "Can't we maybe stop talking?"

They sat down at the table and the girl looked across at the hills on the dry side of the valley and the man looked at her and at the table.

"You've got to realize," he said, "that I don't want you to do it if you don't want to. I'm perfectly willing to go through with it if it means anything to you."

"Doesn't it mean anything to you? We could get along."

"Of course it does. But I don't want anybody but you. I don't want any one else. And I know it's perfectly simple."

"Yes, you know it's perfectly simple."

"It's all right for you to say that, but I do know it."

"Would you do something for me now?"

"I'd do anything for you."

"Would you please please please please please please please stop talking?"

He did not say anything but looked at the bags against the wall of the station. There were labels on them from all the hotels where they had spent nights.

"But I don't want you to," he said, "I don't care anything about it."

"I'll scream," the girl said.

The woman came out through the curtains with two glasses of beer and put them down on the damp felt pads. "The train comes in five minutes," she said.

"What did she say?" asked the girl.

"That the train is coming in five minutes."

The girl smiled brightly at the woman, to thank her.

"I'd better take the bags over to the other side of the station," the man said. She smiled at him.

"All right. Then come back and we'll finish the beer."

He picked up the two heavy bags and carried them around the station to the other tracks. He looked up the tracks but could not see the train. Coming back, he walked through the barroom, where people waiting for the train were drinking. He drank an Anis at the bar and looked at the people. They were all waiting reasonably for the train. He went out through the bead curtain. She was sitting at the table and smiled at him.

"Do you feel better?" he asked.

"I feel fine," she said. "There's nothing wrong with me. I feel fine."

1. Point out places where word choice, syntax, and gesture help us understand *how* something is said.
2. Point out places where the adage "dialogue is what characters do to one another" rings true.
3. Point out places where the dialogue is deliberately nongrammatical in order to make it sound spontaneous and reveal emotion.

Inside the Bunker

JOHN SACK

The people who say the Holocaust didn't happen asked me to speak at their recent international conference. The invitation surprised me, for I am a Jew who's written about the Holocaust and (for chrissakes, I feel like adding) certainly hasn't denied it. To my eyes, however, the invitation, which came from the Institute for Historical Review in Orange County, California, the central asylum for the delusion that the Germans didn't kill any Jews and that the Holocaust is, quote unquote, the Hoax of the Twentieth Century, was not just a wonderment; it was also a golden opportunity, a golden-engraved temptation. We journalists usually sit at the outer edge of occasions: behind the bar in courtrooms, far off the floor of Congress, well out of passing or pitching range at football or baseball games. We are the beggars at banquet halls, waiting for the brass bell and the two-second bite, and the institute offered me what every journalist hungers for: the feast of unhampered access. Its letter was a safe-conduct pass to a country so fogbound that you and I can't discern it. Who are the Holocaust deniers? What are they like behind closed doors? And why are they motionless stones as avalanches of evidence crash onto them, roaring, *You're wrong, you're wrong*? I'd been invited to mingle with them like a mole in Hitler's Eagle's Nest and then ascend to a lectern to tell them off, and I wrote the institute saying that, yes, I'd come.

I flew on a Friday to John Wayne Airport in Orange County and called up the institute, asking, "Where will the conference be?" Until then I hadn't known, for the institute feared that I might divulge it to the Jewish Defense League, a group the FBI has called active terrorists, and that the league might initiative violence. It had done so at other conferences to other speakers. One had been punched, punched by a fist also holding a cherry pie, one had been beaten up, and one had been beaten up in Paris, Vichy, Lyon, and Stockholm. A man who's older than me—I'm seventy— this last man had been maced, thrown to the ground, and kicked in the head because of his imprudent belief that the Holocaust didn't take place. For six weeks his jaw had been wired and he'd eaten through a soda straw. All three men, the leading lights of denial, would speak at this weekend's conference, and the institute didn't want to see their freedom of speech or their bodies imperiled by Jews who conducted chants of "Nazis!" "Neo-Nazis!" or "Anti-Semites!" or by Jews who threw punches. On the phone, an institute employee told me where the conference was but said, "Don't tell anyone."

Knowing where to go, I took a courtesy van to a palm-filled hotel with a Japanese footbridge over a rambling pool, the sun glinting off its rippling water. A few deniers (who'd also called up the institute and been told, "Don't tell") were down in the open-air lobby, making hollow jokes about the threat, possibly imminent, possibly not, of the Jewish Defense

League. "I'm checking everything out," a man from Adelaide, Australia, laughed to me.

"Should I have concerns about my security here?" a tall and broad-shouldered man from New York, an Italian, asked me.

"Are you concerned about it?"

"Now that I'm out of the closet, yes. The people around me say I should be. Do you think my life's in jeopardy here?"

"We'll soon find out," I said. "The Jewish Defense League is right here in California and, I'm sure, know we're around."

"Heh," said the man from New York.

By six o'clock the lobby was full. The deniers (by Saturday there'd be 140) were about three-quarters men and one-quarter women. Most were white, but one was African-American. One was bald, but none were razor-shaved skinheads. Many wore beards, one a white bushy one like Santa Claus's. Most wore slacks and short-sleeved shirts, but a few wore jackets, blazers, or business suits, one a safari suit, and one a white suit like Mark Twain's. Two wore T-shirts that said, NO HOLES? NO HOLOCAUST!, a text whose exegesis I'd get on Saturday. The conversations I heard were about nutrition ("I was raised on raw milk") and about paddle wheelers ("You know, like in *Show Boat*. You haven't seen it? I suggest you rent it"). All in all, the deniers that day and that weekend seemed the most middling of Middle Americans. Or better: despite their take on the Holocaust, they were affable, open-minded, intelligent, intellectual. Their eyes weren't fires of unapproachable certitude, and their lips weren't lemon twists of astringent hate. Nazis and neo-Nazis they didn't seem to be.

Nor did they seem anti-Semites. I'm sure many anti-Semites say the Holocaust didn't happen (even as they take delight that it really did), but I don't believe I met any that weekend. The only debatably anti-Semitic comment that I heard was on Friday night, when I dined in the downstairs restaurant with a prominent denier in a NO HOLES? NO HOLOCAUST! shirt, an Alabama man whose name is Dr. Robert Countess. A gangling scholar of classical Greek and classical Hebrew, he had taught history at the University of Alabama and had retired to a farm outside Huntsville, where he plays major league Ping-Pong and collects old Peugeots; he has twenty-two, some dating back to the Crash. While scarcely cranky, he had a cranky-sounding voice, and in the open-air restaurant he was practically grinding gears as he discoursed on the Septuagint and as I, not Countess, brought up the Jewish sacred scrolls, the Talmud. "What's called the Talmud," Countess lectured—"*talmud* being the participle form of *lamad*, in Hebrew *learn*—developed in Babylonia as rabbis reflected on certain pas-

sages in the Torah. Some of these rabbis engaged in a syncretism, a bringing together, of Babylonian paganism with the religion of Abraham, Isaac,
and Jacob. So if you read much of the Talmud, and Elda will tell you her
favorite story—"

"No," said Elda, Countess's wife, who was dining with us.

"It's unbelievable, but it's in the Talmud," said Countess.

"No, no. I don't want to tell it," said Elda, embarrassed.

"Go ahead and tell it," Countess entreated.

"Well," said Elda, blushing, "it's in the Talmud that if a Jewish man's
repairing the roof, and if his sister-in-law is down below, and if he falls
onto her and she becomes pregnant—"

"He falls off the roof in such a way—" Countess said, laughing.

"Can you picture it? Then the child won't be a bastard," said Elda. The
tale would be anti-Semitic rubbish if it weren't indeed in the Talmud (in
Yevamot, and again in Bava Kamma) and if the Countesses were just
amused and not also appalled. "You and I laugh about this," said Countess, "but I sit in stark amazement saying, Jews aren't stupid people! How
can they go along with this?"

"The answer is, We don't," I explained. By bedtime on Friday, my
impression of the Countesses was like my impression of UFO devotees.
Everyone in America believes in one or another ridiculous thing. Me, I
belong to the International Society for Cryptozoology, and I firmly believe
that in Lake Tele, in the heart of the Congo, there is a living, breathing
dinosaur. Admittedly, this is trivial compared with Holocaust denial, but
fifteen years ago I even went to the Congo to photograph it. I didn't—I
didn't even see it—but I still believe in it. Other people believe more
momentous things, and the Countesses and the other deniers believe that
the Holocaust didn't happen. Like me in the Congo, they're wrong, wrong,
wrong, but to say that emphatically isn't to say (as some people do) that
they're odious, contemptible, despicable. To say that they're rats (as does
Deborah Lipstadt, the author of *Denying the Holocaust*) is no more correct
than to say it of people who, in their ignorance, believe the less pernicious
fallacy that Oswald didn't kill Kennedy. Oh, did I hit a soft spot there?

The conference started on Saturday. In the center of the lobby stood a Kentia palm and in concentric circles around it were peace lilies, crotons, bird-
of-paradise flowers, and happy conference-goers. Young and old, they
talked like any Americans at any professional conference: they talked of
the weather, their homes, their children ("One is a lawyer, another a businessman. For their sake I'm still in the closet"). On the hour, more and

more were wearing the NO HOLES? NO HOLOCAUST! shirts in red, green, and gray as they seated themselves on bridge chairs to listen to speakers in the shuttered darkness of the garden ballroom. "It's one heck of a nice conference," I heard someone say.

Now about "No holes? No Holocaust!" The first thing to know is that no one at that palm-filled hotel would deny that Hitler hated the Jews, that Hitler sent them to concentration camps, and that Hitler said, "I want to annihilate the Jews" as hundreds of thousands died in (as one denier called them) godforsaken hellholes like Auschwitz. It may surprise you, but no one at that hotel would deny that hundreds of thousands of Jews died of typhus, dysentery, starvation, and exhaustion at Auschwitz or that their corpses went to the constant flames of five crematoriums night and day. These deniers even call this the Holocaust, and what they deny is that some of the Jews died of something other than natural causes, that some went to rooms that the Germans poured cyanide (or at four other camps, carbon monoxide) into. The Jews, say the Holocaust deniers, weren't *murdered*, and the Germans didn't deliberately murder them.

Tens of thousands of witnesses disagree. Jews who once stood at the railroad depot at Auschwitz say that the Germans told them, "Go right," and told their mothers, fathers, and children, "Go left," and say that they never saw those mothers, fathers, and children again. I and the rest of the world believe that the Jews who went left went to cyanide chambers, but the deniers believe they went to other parts of Auschwitz or, by train, to other concentration camps. "Part of the Jews remained in Auschwitz," a speaker (another scholar, a man who speaks seventeen languages, including Chinese) said at the ballroom lectern one day. "The rest were transported farther. Many opted to stay in the Soviet Union." Tens of thousands of witnesses saw the cyanide chambers, too, saw the lilac-colored cyanide pellets cascade onto the Jews, but almost all of these witnesses died in five minutes, without being able to testify to it. A few indeed testified, among them two Auschwitz commandants. One said that children under twelve and people over fifty-five were cyanided daily, and one said, "At least 2,500,000 victims were executed by gassing," then backed off to 1,200,000. Some doctors at Auschwitz testified. One doctor said, "When the doors were opened, bodies fell out," and one doctor said, "The *Inferno*, by Dante, is in comparison almost comedy." Some Jews who toted bodies to the crematoriums testified. One said, "We found heaps of naked bodies, doubled up. They were pinkish and in places red. Some were covered with greenish marks, and saliva ran from their mouths. Others were bleeding from the nose. There was excrement on many of them," and one said,

one had troubled himself to see if seven to eight hundred people could fit on twenty-five square meters until Provan, in Monongahela, read these words in the *Confessions*: "More than half are children." *Well, if I've got one thing*, thought Provan, *it's children*, and he put down the book and took his five children and one big baby doll into an upstairs bedroom. "What are you doing?" asked Mrs. Provan.

"An experiment: how many kids can fit in a gas chamber."

"You shouldn't use the kids like that. It's sorta gruesome."

"Aw, it won't hurt them," said Provan in his down-home voice, and he had the kids strip to their underwear. He packed them into a corner, then with two dressers corralled them into a square of sixteen by sixteen inches. Then, setting them free, he used an electronic calculator to calculate to his astonishment that he could fit 891 children into the gas chamber at Belzec. Tears came to Provan's eyes, for he saw the *Confessions* differently now. Its author, he saw, wouldn't say something so impossible, incredible, nonsensical, something no one would believe for a half century, if he himself hadn't witnessed it. Gerstein, the SS man, had seen Jews die at Belzec ("One hears them weeping, sobbing"), and the Holocaust had indeed happened.

Provan did two more experiments even as Mrs. Provan, a sort of Cesare Cremonini—the colleague of Galileo's who wouldn't look into Galileo's telescope—told him, "You shouldn't." In one, he used five kids, three mannequins, and one doll, and in the other, five kids, three adults—a printer, a minister, and an Italian woman who said, "You're nuts, but I'll do it"— all with their clothes on, and the doll, and he calculated that seven hundred fathers, mothers, children, and babies would fit in the chamber at Belzec. And last March, he used the same scientific method on the "No holes? No Holocaust!" hypothesis, going with some of his children (he had nine by now) to one collapsed chamber at Auschwitz. The witnesses there had said the holes were alongside the central columns, and Provan used a forty-dollar metric measuring tape to find where the columns had been and found—well, whaddya know?—those celebrated holes. No longer were they twenty-five by twenty-five centimeters, as the witnesses had said. Now, with the roof blown up, they were larger, and Provan photographed them, came home to Monongahela, wrote up a monograph, printed it at his print shop, and printed a cover that, in gold letters, with the exclamation point demoted to a question mark, said, NO HOLES? NO HOLOCAUST? He then flew to Orange County and appeared at the palm-filled hotel on Saturday afternoon.

Not even washing up, he sat with childlike delight on a flowery lobby love seat by the Kentia palm, handing his two dozen spiral-bound copies to the illuminati of Holocaust denial. If he expected encomiums, he misunderstood human nature, which clings to established beliefs as though to a life preserver without which we'd sink to the jet-black depths of the Mindanao Trough. "You have a bent toward evil," the chief denier from Australia, a man of German ancestry, told Provan. "You slander the German people. You believe in the Holocaust." "But Charles, if I may call you Charles, bring me the *pudding*," said the chief denier alive, a Frenchman who coined the "No holes? No Holocaust!" motto. "Bring me the holes of twenty-five by twenty-five centimeters."

"Oh, I can't," said Provan.

"Where do you see a square of twenty-five by twenty-five?"

"Oh, not anymore. But this hole is big enough to have held it."

"But you don't have a square of twenty-five centimeters."

"I admit that."

"This cannot convince me," the Frenchman said.

The angriest denier was David Irving, the British historian who'd said in London that a photograph of a hole would drive such a metaphorical hole in his case that he couldn't defend it. Irving, who isn't allowed at Auschwitz and may have been jealous of an amateur's access, sat at the open-air downstairs restaurant in front of a caesar salad. On spotting Provan, he turned black, and his words came like chisel chips. "I'm hopping mad," Irving said. "If I were an SS man and somebody said, 'Knock some holes in that ceiling, will you? We're going to start putting cyanide in,' I'd make those holes in the middle of some empty area. I wouldn't put them—bang, bang, bang, bang—next to the load-bearing pillars. What were the load-bearing pillars for? Just cosmetic purposes?" Provan, twenty years younger, stood like a boy called down to the principal's office, looking abashed, and Irving continued, "The Germans spend God knows how many hundreds of thousands of pounds building this? And then they allow some jerk with a sledgehammer to punch holes next to the load-bearing pillars? I'm having lunch," said Irving abruptly, and he attacked his salad without a whit of his ardent convictions voided by Provan's photographs. Of course, the deniers would say it's Provan and I whose convictions weren't voided by Irving, and it may be a hundred years before we know whose views prevail. "We have won," an SS man told Primo Levi at Auschwitz. "There may be suspicions, but there will be no certainties, because we'll destroy the evidence together with you."

Provan, the only speaker (other than me) who believed that the Holocaust happened, spoke in the ballroom later on. He spoke about a Jewish coroner at Auschwitz and not about his "No holes? No Holocaust?" mono-graph or his one other epoch-making discovery. In the cyanide chambers at Auschwitz, there are no cyanide stains, and the deniers, though they've never worn a T-shirt saying NO CYANIDE? NOBODY DIED! call this another proof that what we call cyanide chambers were, in fact, innocuous morgues. But according to Provan, the chambers have no stains because the Germans painted their walls.

Sixteen other speakers spoke on Saturday, Sunday, and Monday, for this was a holiday weekend, and I counted six who'd run afoul of the law because of their disbelief in the Holocaust and the death apparatus at Auschwitz. To profess this in anyone's earshot is illegal not just in Ger-many but in Holland, Belgium, France, Spain, Switzerland, Austria, Poland, and Israel, where denying the Holocaust can get you five years while denying God can get you just one. One speaker, David Irving, had been fined $18,000 for saying aloud in Germany that one of the cyanide chambers at Auschwitz is a replica built by the Poles after the war. A replica it truly is, but truth in these matters is no defense in Germany. Another speaker, a Frenchman, had been fined in France, and another speaker, a German, had been sentenced to fourteen months in Germany but, his land-lord evicting him, his wife deserting him, had fled to England. Another speaker, an Australian, had come from seven months in a German jail for writing in Australia (alas, on the Internet, which Germans in Germany can read) that there were no cyanide chambers at Auschwitz. In his defense, he'd called an expert witness, but the man couldn't testify or he'd be jailed, too, the victim of the self-same law. The fifth speaker was a Swiss, a man I'd once roomed with (I'd met many deniers previously) and fed the kan-garoos with in South Australia. He'll go to jail for three months in Switzer-land for questioning the Auschwitz cyanide chambers.

In the United States, thank God, we have the First Amendment. But even in that shuttered ballroom in California, the sixth speaker couldn't say all he wanted to—couldn't, for example, say the Germans didn't kill the Jews deliberately. A few hours earlier, he and I had debated this at a waffle breakfast, debated it in audible voices with no qualms of being arrested, indicted, or imprisoned by federal marshals. "But what about Eichmann?" I'd asked him. "He wrote that Hitler ordered the physical destruction of the Jews. He wrote about *Vergasungslager*, gassing camps."

"John. The man was in Israeli captivity."

"Well, what about *during* the war? Hans Frank, the governor general of Poland, said to exterminate all the Jews, without exception."

"He was only *quoted* as saying that, John."

"And what about Goebbels? He said a barbaric method was being employed against the Jews. And Himmler? He said the SS knew what a hundred, five hundred, one thousand corpses were like."

"John, I don't know. They might have said it," the sixth speaker told me. "But it isn't true that genocide was a German national policy." A few hours later, the speaker didn't dare repeat this up in the ballroom, for he's a Canadian citizen and his speech was carried live on the Internet in Canada, and if he said what he'd said over waffles, he'd have been prosecuted in Canada. Already he'd been tried twice as well as hit, beaten, bombed, engulfed by a $400,000 fire, and told, "We'll cut your testicles off."

The man's name is Ernst Zündel. He's round-faced and red-faced like in a Hals, he's eternally jolly, and he was born in Calmbach, Germany. If you saw the recent movie about the Holocaust deniers, *Mr. Death*, he's the man in the hard hat who says, "We Germans will not go down in history as genocidal maniacs. *We. Will. Not.*" He has become a hero to anti-Semites and, like every denier, has been called anti-Semitic himself, but it's just as honest to say that the Jews who (along with God) oversee the Jewish community are in fact anti-Zündelic, anti-Countessic, anti-Irvingic, and, in one word, anti-denieric. The normal constraints of time, temperance, and truth do not obstruct some Jewish leaders from their nonstop vituperation of Holocaust deniers. "They're morally ugly. They're morally sick," said Elie Wiesel on PBS. They bombard us with disinformation, said Abraham Foxman, the national director of the Anti-Defamation League, on the op-ed page of the *New York Times*. "Holocaust deniers," said Foxman, spreading disinformation himself, "would have [us] believe there were no concentration camps." Myself, I disagree with these Jewish leaders. Most deniers, most attendees in their slacks and shorts at the palm-filled hotel, were like Zündel: people who, as Germans, had chosen to comfort themselves with the wishful thinking that none of their countrymen in the 1940s were genocidal maniacs.

I can sympathize with the Germans, for I've seen a bit of this wishful thinking among some Jews. Seven years ago, I ruefully reported in my book *An Eye for an Eye* that thousands of Jews who'd survived the Holocaust had rounded up Germans and beaten, whipped, tortured, and murdered them—German men, women, children, and babies—in concentration camps run by Jews. This little holocaust was corroborated by *60 Minutes* and the *New York Times* but not by Jewish leaders. They, pardon the expression, denied it, writing reviews whose titles were "The Big Lie" and "False Witness" and "Do Me a Favor—Don't Read This Book." If Jews feel pressed to deny what happened to sixty thousand Germans, then Jews might forgive the Germans, like Zündel, who choose to deny what happened to six million Jews.

Instead, Jewish leaders hound them. Astronomers don't spill rivers of ink denouncing the UFO fanatics, whose theories are much less malignant but whose legions are much more numerous than the dozen dozen deniers at that international conference, their first in six slow-moving years. But for various reasons (for reparations, for the survival of Israel, or for real apprehensions that it could happen again), Jewish leaders want the Holocaust to be front and center in America's consciousness. In this they've succeeded spectacularly. Americans who aren't senior citizens think it was partly to save the Jews that we declared war on Germany, though that was no factor at all. Americans who don't know if one hundred thousand, two hundred thousand, or one million of our own soldiers died (and surely don't know that fifty million people died in China) know exactly how many Jews died in World War II. Once, said Michael Berenbaum, the former research director of the U.S. Holocaust Memorial Museum, "the Holocaust was a side story of World War II. Now one thinks of World War II as a background story [to] the Holocaust." Among many ways Jewish leaders accomplished this was to tap out an SOS, an all-points alarm, whenever in any dark corner they spotted a knavish denier.

They may have adopted this from Jakob Böhme, a German mystic of Shakespeare's time. Böhme once said, "Nothing becomes manifest without opposition, for if it has nothing to oppose it, it slowly moves away from itself and does not return." Lest the Holocaust become unmanifest, lest the Holocaust move away from itself, Jewish leaders constantly point to the opposition, the bogeyman, the bugaboo, the otherwise ineffectual squad of Holocaust deniers. But there's a double edge to Böhme's sword: by opposing, opposing, opposing them in print, on the radio, and on TV, Jewish leaders make the deniers manifest, too. The deniers survive because they are being persecuted. They survive to spread their doctrine to the true Jew-haters of the world.

My own speech was on Monday afternoon. It was about *An Eye for an Eye*, which the Germans among the deniers wanted to hear about so they could share their parents' guilt with the Jews, their parents' victims. No longer did I want to tell the deniers off, but I did want to edify them (and I did) that I and the Jews in *An Eye for an Eye* devoutly believe that the Holocaust happened. But also I wanted to say something therapeutic, to say something about hate. At the hotel, I'd seen none of it, certainly less than I'd seen when Jews were speaking of Germans. No one had ever said anything remotely like Elie Wiesel, "Every Jew, somewhere in his being, should set aside a zone of hate—healthy, virile hate—for what persists in the Germans," and no one had said anything like Edgar Bronfman, the president of the World Jewish Congress. A shocked professor told Bronfman once, "You're teaching a whole generation to hate thousands of Germans," and Bronfman replied, "No, I'm teaching a whole generation to hate *millions* of Germans." Jew hatred like that German hatred, or like the German hatred on every page of *Hitler's Willing Executioners*, I saw absolutely none of, but I saw that some people, all Germans, had had to struggle to suppress it.

"The tone of the Jewish establishment," said Zündel at another breakfast in the airy downstairs restaurant, "is so strident, offensive, grating, so denigrating of Germans, there's going to be—" He stopped short.

"We are so sick of the Holocaust!" a German woman with us took up. "Gentiles have it thrown in their faces morning, noon, and night without relief. Do the Jewish people know that?"

"They convict us, imprison us, make us into outcasts," said Zündel, who is now being prosecuted in Canada for, among other things, truthfully saying that Germans didn't make soap out of Jews. "Teachers lose their jobs. Professors lose their tenure, and I say this isn't good for the Jewish community."

"I see dissatisfaction," said the German woman, "that I shudder about. I think the Jewish community has to try to lessen it. This censorship! This terrorism!" In no way did her or Zündel's jaw get twisted like a twisted rubber band into the outward contours of hate, but the woman's quivered at the edges somewhat.

So at the lectern in the grand ballroom on Monday, I spoke about hate. "There are," I said, "eighty-five thousand books about the Holocaust. And none has an honest answer to How could the *Germans* do it? The people who gave us Beethoven, the Ninth Symphony, the Ode to Joy, *Alle Menschen werden Brüder*, all men become brothers. How could the Germans perpetrate the Holocaust? This mystery, we've got to solve it, or we'll keep having genocides in Cambodia, Bosnia, Zaire. Well," I said, "what I report in *An Eye for an Eye* is Lola"—the heroine, the commandant of a terrible prison in Gleiwitz, Germany—"Lola has solved it. The Jews have solved it. Because in their agony, their despair, their insanity, if you will, they felt they became like the Germans—the Nazis—themselves. And if I'd been there," I said, "I'd have become one, too, and now I understand why. A lot of Jews, understandably, were full of hate in 1945, they were volcanoes full of red-hot hate. They thought if they spit out the hate at the Germans, then they'd be rid of it.

"No," I continued. "It doesn't work that way. Let's say I'm in love with someone. I don't tell myself, Uh-oh, I've got inside of me two pounds of love, and if I love her and *love* her, then I'll use all of my love up—I'll be all out of love. No, I understand and we all understand that love is a paradoxical thing, that the more we send out, the more we've got. So why don't we understand that about hate? If we hate, and we act on that hate, then we hate even more later on. If we spit out a drop of hate, we stimulate the saliva glands and we produce a drop and a quarter of it. If we spit that out, we produce a drop and a half, then two drops, three, a teaspoon, tablespoon, a Mount Saint Helens. The more we send out, the more we've got, until we are perpetual-motion machines, sending out hate and hate until we've created a holocaust." I then said emphatically, "You don't have to be a German to become like that. You can be a Serb, a Hutu, a Jew—you can be an American. *We* were the ones in the Philippines. *We* were the ones in Vietnam. *We* were the ones in Washington, D.C., for ten thousand years the home of the Anacostia Indians. They had one of their campgrounds at what now is the United States Holocaust Memorial Museum.

"We all have it in us to become like Nazis," I said. "Hate, as Lola discovered, is a muscle, and if we want to be monsters, all we have to do is exercise it. To hate the Germans, to hate the Arabs, to hate the Jews. The longer we exercise it, the bigger it gets, as if every day we curl forty pounds and, far from being worn out, in time we are curling fifty, sixty, we are the Mr. Universe of Hate, the Heinrich Himmler. We all can be hate-full people, hateful people. We can destroy the people we hate, *maybe*, but we surely destroy ourselves."

The people who say the Holocaust didn't happen applauded. Loud and long they applauded, and a number of German deniers stood up. Some asked questions about Auschwitz, like why did I think that Germans *meant* for Jews to die? But one from Berlin, named Wolfgang, later confessed to me, "I believe that Auschwitz became unsanitary. The Jews were worked very hard, I grant you that. They died. And they had to be gotten rid of. And after they died, the SS put them into crematoriums. I won't deny that. And maybe to scare some, the SS told them, 'You're next, you're going to go up in smoke.' And maybe . . ."

The conference ended on Monday. No one was ever attacked by the Jewish Defense League. The deniers (revisionists, they call themselves) meet next in Cincinnati, and they have invited me to be the keynote speaker there. I've said yes.

1. How does dialogue add to the essay? Would the essay have the same impact if there were no dialogue in it? Why or why not?
2. How does the author make the dialogue sound spontaneous? What techniques does he use?
3. How is the dialogue used to characterize the various speakers, as well as move the essay forward?

CHAPTER NINE

The Plot Thickens

Part 1: FIGURING OUT WHAT HAPPENS NEXT

Getting Started

Now, after a detour, we're back where we were at the end of Chapter 4: thinking about the shape of fiction. In Chapter 4 we reviewed some of the various definitions of the short story, went over some of the more common ones, and finally came up with our own. But we weren't quite done with the topic. Some of the conventions we were talking about—such as conflict–crisis–resolution and epiphanies—are key elements of plot.

"What is plot?" the short story writer Grace Paley once asked rhetorically, before promptly answering herself: "first one thing happens, then another thing, then another . . ." And of course, although she is right, there is more we can say that will be helpful as you work on your short story or novel.

We'll start, as before, with some basic definitions. Then we'll look at a number of different plotting techniques. Then we'll go over some exercises you can do to help you plot your short story or novel. Finally, a reading that is strong in plot will illustrate some of the points of this text.

Story vs. Plot: Some Basic Definitions

Let's start by going back to the basics. What are we trying to do when we write our story or novel? The most-quoted source on this topic is E. M. Forster, in *Aspects of the Novel:*

> Let us listen to three voices. If you ask one type of man, "What does a novel do?" he will reply placidly: "Well—I don't know—it seems a funny sort of question to ask—a novel's a novel—well, I don't know—I suppose it

kind of tells a story, so to speak." He is quite good-tempered and vague, and probably driving a motor-bus at the same time and paying no more attention to literature than it merits. Another man, whom I visualize as on a golf-course, will be aggressive and brisk. He will reply: "What does a novel do? Why, tell a story of course, and I've no use for it if it didn't. I like a story. Very bad taste on my part, no doubt, but I like a story. You can take your art, you can take your literature, you can take your music, but give me a good story. And I like a story to be a story, mind, and my wife's the same." And a third man he says in a sort of drooping regretful voice, "Yes—oh dear, yes—the novel tells a story." I respect and admire the first speaker. I detest and fear the second. And the third is myself. Yes—oh dear, yes—the novel tells a story. That is the fundamental aspect without which it could not exist. That is the highest factor common to all novels, and I wish that it was not so, that it could be something different—melody, or perception of the truth, not this low atavistic form.

Later, he elaborates on the difference between story and plot:

Let us define a plot. We have defined a story as a narrative of events arranged in their time-sequence. A plot is also a narrative of events, the emphasis falling on causality. "The king died and then the queen died" is a story. "The king died, and then the queen died of grief" is a plot. The time-sequence is preserved, but the sense of causality overshadows it. [. . .] If it is in a story we say, "and then?" If it is in a plot we ask "why?" That is the fundamental difference.

So, what is he saying? First of all, let's be clear: he's using the word "story" in a different way than we have been. He says that the story is a set of events in chronological order—the events that keep our readers asking, "and then?"—while plot is something more sophisticated, something that delves into the interior mystery of the piece. To put it another way (a way that mirrors the way we've been talking about creative writing in this book), the story part of a piece can be easily summarized (first this happened, then that happened, then *that* happened) while the plot is part of that aspect of the short story or novel that *resists paraphrase* (sound familiar?).

Other critics who have tried to define plot focus more closely on the idea of *causality* that Forster raises. Everything must happen for a reason, and everything that happens must have consequences, and those consequences lead to other consequences until (frequently) the whole thing snowballs and culminates in a crisis. For short fiction, this is where Poe's definition of a short story as having unity of purpose usually kicks in. A novel can have many threads, so this theory goes; a short story has only one. (See Chapter 4 for more information about Poe's ideas.)

But although these things might be true in many, or even most, cases, it's not true in all, as Francine Prose reminds us in her essay, "What Makes a Short Story?" (pp. 167–78). But I think we can agree that the events that take place in a novel or short story have to add up to some *effect*, or, to put it the way we put it in Chapter 4, *unit of satisfaction* (in the case of a novel, it might be a very large unit, or even, indeed, a multifaceted unit). In other words, for that "attentive reader" that we all desire there is a sense of completeness, or closure, as a result of this particular sequence of events, and well-written stories or novels waste nothing: every event (or what we will call "plot point") contributes in some way to this end effect.

So plot, as we will define it, is that series of events, arranged in a particular order, which brings about the desired final effect of a short story or novel. True, this is a very bare-bones definition. But that is critical. Just as our definition of a short story was delicately wrought lest we exclude any of the fine stories that have been written over the years, let us do the same with plot. And we're going to go out on a limb here and say that even in so-called plotless stories this definition of plot is fulfilled. Because even in so-called plotless stories *things happen*—they must, or they wouldn't be stories, they'd be abstract ruminations. Things have to happen, and they usually happen to people, although in some cases to members of the animal kingdom, or sometimes even to objects or even places. (In such cases, we often say that the object or the place *is* a character.)

A Word about Causality

Why did I leave out the word *causality* when formulating our definition of plot? It seems as though that would be a prime determinant of the plot points chosen. And it is, it is—but I'd rather imply it (after all, we do say that the series of events *brings about* the desired effect) than build it more directly into the definition. Again, we want to keep the definition a bit loose and fluid because we are trying to think of the definition as leaving nothing out, but also as being of use to us when we sit down to write.

To put too much stress on the fact that every plot point *must* have its own particular consequence is to undermine the subtlety of many stories and novels. The problem with thinking too simplistically in terms of causality is that it can cause us to think in direct, linear terms—John had a poor childhood and therefore he thrived on accumulating riches of all kinds, which led to his downfall as a materialistic narcissist—whereas we know that life (along with most short stories and novels) is subtler than that. All too often, in a workshop, someone begins criticism with the dreadful phrase "I want to know why . . ."—demanding that sort of simplistic linear movement. Yet we know that human nature—and most short stories and novels, at least the ones we're concentrating on in this book, are about human nature—is more complicated. Mere straws *can* break elephants' backs.

Let's look at a scene from Robert Stone's "Helping" (pp. 178–202) to see the subtlety of causality in fiction.

This is a scene in which the main character, Elliot, just before he falls off the proverbial wagon, goes to visit a cousin of his who works in the library. To the uninitiated eye, this scene might seem superfluous; how does it contribute to bringing us to the final scene of Elliot waiting for a redemptive gesture from his wife? But let's take a closer look.

Elliot stops by the Conway Library to visit his cousin, Candace. He "watched her brow furrow with concern as she composed a smile." A cozy fire is burning; an antique clock is ticking: a very comfortable scene. Elliot can't remember why he came, but he quickly "realized that he did not want to stay and pass it [the time] with Candace." Still, he sits down with Candace and chats awkwardly. Then he thinks of something to ask for, a reason for being there that might dissipate the awkwardness: the new Oxford *Classical World*. Candace and Elliot have tea together. Then, before she can get the book for him, he takes the opportunity to sneak out when she answers the phone.

What's the point of this scene? What does it "cause" to happen? Nothing obvious. Yet Elliot's irritation and distress is amplified, not relaxed, as a result of his visit with what seems to be a caring and solicitous friend. If Elliot had gone directly from work to the liquor store (if, in fact, this scene in the library had been omitted) it would have cheapened the effort he'd been making all those months. It would be too easy. It was as if he had to make one last attempt to stay sober before allowing his "heart to leap up for no good reason" once he has left the library. The tension has been tightened, and we get a sense of the struggle, and of the inefficacy of his usual coping devices, to help him in his extreme condition.

We see, in other words, that this scene contributes, and contributes enormously, to the plot, yet the ways in which it does so are subtle and complex. There *is* cause and effect, but it doesn't hit you over the head.

Moreover, most writers work more by intuition rather than carefully plotting out cause and effect (although as a plotting exercise, that can be very useful). And although it is true that in many beginning stories, certain events might not make a contribution to the plot, in which case they may have to be tweaked or rethought, sometimes a writer will have no more than an urgent sense that *this* has to happen *here*, and the causality works itself out subconsciously.

But there are many reasons why beginning writers might want to avoid elucidating too explicitly that *this* happened directly *because* of that.

Why did the boy beat his dog? the workshop asks. So the writer puts in an unhappy childhood. There. Causality. Or, why did the girl break off the engagement? the workshop wants to know. She seemed happy enough with her fiancé, after all. So why? *Why?* These are valid questions to ask— but never, ever demand that the writer invent some linear, simplistic "reason" for what can be very complexly motivated behaviors.

Render *How*–Don't Try to Answer *Why*

Remember that our job isn't, as we discussed in Chapter 2, to solve the mysteries around us, but to *render* them precisely. So instead of dramatizing the *why* down to the last possible causal factor (the girl's father had blue eyes, her fiancé had brown ones, the match was therefore incompatible in her mind) to the point of oversimplifying via pop psychology the complex bundles of thoughts and emotions that are human beings, we depict *how* they acted. Don't try to explain *why* the engagement disintegrated, demonstrate *how* it fell apart. If your story is convincing, we'll have a sense of why, without the oversimplification that often accompanies so much beginning fiction.

In the excerpt below, we see a young girl falling in love with a cad. We see *how* it happens, in the story "A Simple Heart" by Gustave Flaubert; we're not told *why* she's susceptible, it's played out in front of us. Yet the causality is there: there's something about the original, horrifying encounter that makes her susceptible to this dubious young man the second time she meets him.

> One August evening—she was eighteen at the time—they took her off to the fete at Colleville. From the start she was dazed and bewildered by the noise of the fiddles, the lamps in the trees, the medley of gaily colored dresses, the gold crosses and lace, and the throng of people jigging up and down. She was standing shyly on one side when a smart young fellow, who had been leaning on the shaft of a cart, smoking his pipe, came up and asked her to dance. He treated her to cider, coffee, griddle-cake, and a silk neckerchief, and imagining that she knew what he was after, offered to see her home. At the edge of a field of oats, he pushed her roughly to the ground. Thoroughly frightened, she started screaming for help. He took to his heels.
>
> Another night, on the road to Beaumont, she tried to get past a big, slow-moving wagon loaded with hay, and as she was squeezing by she recognized Theodore.
>
> He greeted her quite calmly, saying that she must forgive him for the way he had behaved to her, as "it was the drink that did it."

She did not know what to say in reply and felt like running off.

Straight away he began talking about the crops and the notabilities of the commune, saying that his father had left Colleville for the farm at Les Ecots, so that they were now neighbors.

"Ah!" she said.

He added that his family wanted to see him settle but that he was in no hurry and was waiting to find a wife to suit his fancy. She lowered her head. Then he asked her if she was thinking of getting married. She answered with a smile that it was mean of him to make fun of her.

"But I'm not making fun of you!" he said. "I swear I'm not!"

He put his left arm round her waist and she walked on supported by his embrace. Soon they slowed down. There was a gentle breeze blowing, the stars were shining, the huge load of hay was swaying about in front of them, and the four horses were raising clouds of dust as they shambled along. Then without being told, they turned off to the right. He kissed her once more and she disappeared into the darkness.

On Metafiction

It's difficult to talk about plot in any meaningful context without talking about character as well. But before we can talk about character and plot, one must first make a pro forma nod toward a type of fiction that can frequently avoid character altogether: metafiction.

By definition, metafiction is fiction about fiction: rather than trying to illuminate the human condition, as the vast majority of stories and novels attempt to do, metafiction is about examining the creative act, or about questioning the conventions of fiction. Writers of metafiction include John Barth, Donald Barthelme, Italo Calvino, and Jorge Luis Borges.

For the purposes of this chapter, however, we will be skipping metafiction in favor of discussing *character-based fiction*, that is, fiction that attempts to say something about characters, or the human condition.

Character-Based Plotting

If we're focused on character-based fiction, as we generally are in this book, then plot is the specific series of events that befalls a character or a set of characters. And so, if plot is what happens to characters, and if we want those things that happen to have significance, it stands to reason that somehow plot reflects character, and vice versa. If characters take action (or refuse to take an action), if they put themselves in positions of danger, or refuse to put themselves in positions of danger, that is your plot. We'll save those dreadful words "in character" for Chapter 10, when we talk about characterization. Let's just assume for now that if your character does something, then she or he is capable of doing that; likewise, if they fail to do something, then it is *possible* (not necessarily determined, but possible) for them to fail to do that particular thing.

Along these lines, the writer John Gardner provides one of the most elegant definitions of plot and character ever formulated:

> In the place of the classical writer's clear distinction between the outside world and the inside world—"situation" on one hand and "character" on the other—modern writers see outer reality and inner reality as interpenetrating: The world is whatever we feel it to be, so that the situation character must deal with is partly character.

Let's look at an example of a story in which "the situation character must deal with is partly character."

In Denis Johnson's "Emergency" (pp. 47–56), the character has placed himself in an emergency room in a hospital; he works there, he has *chosen* to be there. He has also taken drugs, and has chosen to make a friend of a rather dubious character named George. These choices he made (as a result of the character he is) naturally lead to his joyride to the county fair and to the adventure with the bunnies. And the bunnies would not have been squashed if he were not the type of person who would forget that they were there, and let them roll around to the back of his shirt and be squashed. Throughout this story, we see plot unfolding as a result of choices (actions or reactions, conscious and unconscious) that this character makes.

How do we use this idea that character and plot are intertwined when we write? By asking ourselves the simple question: What can I *do* to my character to unsettle or move or stress or stretch him or her in some way? Sometimes that involves being mean to our characters; sometimes extraordinarily nice (in the story, "The Handsomest Drowned Man in the World" by Gabriel García Márquez, an incredibly wonderful thing happens to a town, thus setting events in motion).

In either case, plot is what we, as authors, *do* to our characters in order to elicit particular responses. More on this when we work on our exercises for this chapter.

On Conflict

You cannot read about plot without running into that central word "conflict." A story or a novel must have *conflict*, we're told, or it doesn't (can't) hold the reader's interest. And this is true: a story or novel without conflict is a story or novel without much of anything interesting happening in it.

The problem, as we talked about in Chapter 4, comes in the nature of the word "conflict." It can be too violent, too direct; and although doubtless there are writers who sit down and wonder, "What conflict can I put in my story?" there are many others who work in a subtler vein. The *American Heritage Dictionary*'s definition of conflict is, firstly, a "striking or dashing together; violent collision; as, a *conflict* of elements or waves"; and secondly, "a strife for the mastery; hostile contest; battle; struggle; fighting."

Many, if not most, writers work on a more subtle level than that. Philip Roth writes about placing a character in a "situation," for example. Others talk about plot being the intersection between "character and circumstance." One definition that I use to help writers who are working along the conventional conflict–crisis–resolution model is to say that plot is "that series of events that causes your character to crack open in some way." (Change is not necessary; change can be declined, but to bring that character to that potential opening-up point can be a very interesting thing to do—again, if you are working in a more traditional short story form.)

Desire is also very powerful. Making your character want something that is somehow out of reach can create a very compelling plot.

Let's look at some of the opening "conflicts" of stories and see how ill-suited they are to being described using that conventional term:

"Girl" by Jamaica Kincaid: A mother tells her daughter to wash the white clothes on Monday and the colored clothes on Tuesday.

"Follow the Eagle" by William Kotzwinkle: Two men, half-drunk and exuberant, ride their motorcycles toward the Colorado River one bright sunshine-filled morning.

"Souvenir" by Jayne Anne Phillips: A woman forgets to send a Valentine's Day card to her mother.

"Pet Milk" by Stuart Dybek: A man sits drinking his coffee and thinking about his grandmother, long dead.

As E. M. Forster points out, plot isn't as easy as just coming up with a "conflict":

the plot, instead of finding human beings more or less cut to its requirements, as they are in the drama, finds them enormous, shadowy and intractable, and three-quarters hidden like an iceberg. In vain it points out to these unwieldy creatures the advantages of the triple process of complication, crisis, and solution so persuasively expounded by Aristotle. A few of them rise and comply, and a novel which ought to have been a play is the result. But there is no general response. They want to sit apart and brood or something, and the plot (whom I here visualize as a sort of higher government official) is concerned at their lack of public spirit.

And as Charles Baxter wrote in his essay "On Defamiliarization":

Anyone who writes stories or novels or poems with some kind of narrative structure often imagines a central character, then gives that character a desire or a fear or perhaps some kind of goal and sets another character in a collision course with that person. The protagonist collides with an antagonist. All right: we know where we are. We often talk about this sort of dramatic conflict as if it were all unitary, all of one kind: One person wants something, another person wants something else, and conflict results. But this is not, I think, the way most stories actually work. Not everything is a contest. We are not always fighting our brothers for our share of the worldly goods. Many good stories have no antagonist at all. My friends on the lawn don't tell their stories that way. Actual conflict can be a fairly minor element in most stories, written or told. A more appropriate question might be, "What's emerging here?" or "What's showing up?"

Other writers are even more dismissive of formal plots. John Cheever said in an interview published in the *Paris Review*:

I don't work with plots. I work with intuition, apprehension, dreams, concepts. Characters and events come simultaneously to me. Plot implies narrative and a lot of crap. It is a calculated attempt to hold the reader's interest at the sacrifice of moral conviction. Of course, one doesn't want to be boring . . . one needs an element of suspense. But a good narrative is a rudimentary structure, rather like a kidney.

So, think in terms of conflict (man against man, man against nature, man against himself) if that is helpful to you. If not, try one of these other "ways in" to your story:

- Your character wants something (desires something) that she or he is not getting.
- You want to capture a moment after which nothing can ever be the same.
- You want to find the right events, in the right order, to cause your character(s) to crack open in some way.
- Your character finds himself/herself intersecting with circumstances that are too much for him/her.
- You want to place your character in a "situation."

Analyzing Plot Points

In workshop, we frequently talk about *plot points* which are, in the most basic terms, the things that happen (again, for the most part to characters, human or otherwise). If you look at some of the finest work of fiction (both short fiction and novels) you'll notice that if the writers were thinking only in simplistic terms of conflict–crisis–resolution, these are hardly the plot points they'd come up with.

Let's look at the plot points of the story at the end of this chapter, "Sonny's Blues" by James Baldwin We'll see that there's a basic "story" (to use the term the way E. M. Forster uses it) that differs from the basic plot in that in the plot the story is told out of sequence, to wring the greatest impact from the events depicted.

First, here are the plot points as Baldwin renders them:

1. Protagonist reads about the arrest of his brother Sonny in the newspaper.
2. Class lets out, and the laughter of children who "aren't really children" reaches his ears.
3. Someone from the block, Sonny's friend, comes by to talk about Sonny.
4. Protagonist receives letter from Sonny.
5. Protagonist meets Sonny when he comes back to New York after being released from jail.
6. They take a cab ride home, going through the park.
7. Flashback to father, a drunk who nevertheless loved his family.
8. Flashback to the last time the protagonist saw his mother alive, when he hears story (from his mother) about his father losing a brother when young.
9. Flashback: After mother's funeral, (still in past) protagonist talks to Sonny about his desire to be a musician.
10. Flashback: Later, away at the army, protagonist hears news of Sonny from his fiancée, Isabel.
11. Flashback: Sonny joins the Navy.
12. Flashback: Protagonist has an "awful fight" with Sonny and they don't speak for months.
13. Memory of the time that little Gracie died.
14. Back to present (right after what happens in #6 above); now Sonny is living with protagonist and his family. Protagonist talks to Sonny about music, drugs.
15. Protagonist goes to nightclub with Sonny, sees his brother for what he really is.

Now, here are the events in chronological order (the "story," if you will. See how they are placed out of order according to the *plot*:

7. Father was a self-destructive drunk who nevertheless loved his family, especially Sonny.
8. Last time protagonist saw his mother alive, they had a conversation about the family, Sonny, the father—specifically, that the father had once lost a brother.
10. Later, in the army, protagonist hears news about Sonny from his fiancée, Isabel.
9. After mother's funeral, protagonist talks to Sonny about his desire to be a musician.
11. Sonny joins the Navy.
12. Protagonist has a "awful fight" with Sonny and they don't speak for months.
1. Protagonist reads about Sonny's arrest in the newspaper.
2. Class lets out, and the laughter of children who "aren't really children" reaches his ears.
3. Someone from the block, Sonny's friend, comes by to talk about Sonny.
13. Little Gracie dies.
4. Protagonist receives letter from Sonny, who is in prison.
5. Protagonist meets Sonny when he comes back to New York after being released from jail.
6. They take a cab ride home, going through the park.
14. The brothers have a discussion about drugs, music.
15. Protagonist goes to nightclub with Sonny.

Notice that the opening plot point, where the protagonist reads about Sonny in the paper, actually happens very late in the "story" when viewed as a simple chronology. And yes, there is causality: there is a reason for arranging the sequence as Baldwin does. As readers, we end up asking *why* and *how*, which is what we do with a plot, rather than *and then?*, which we tend to do with a simple story (as Forster defines it). We want to know what happens next, and we are sophisticated enough to know that "what happens next" might be something that happened ten years ago. Memory, in the form of flashbacks, is an important aspect of plot.

Joyce Carol Oates's story "Where Are You Going, Where Have You Been?" (pp. 72–86) almost always puzzles young readers when they read it for the first time. "Where's the ending?" they cry, because they haven't realized that the story is effectively over: we're not sure what is going to happen to Connie (we're pretty sure it won't be a good thing), but the author has wrapped up what, for her, was the interesting part, which is that Connie acquiesced and was easily led to her doom. She makes a generous gesture: to spare her family, she goes quietly, like a lamb to what we assume is the slaughter.

The plot points of "Where Are You Going, Where Have You Been?" are relatively simple:

1. Connie spars with her mother, her sister, rebels in usual teenage ways.
2. Connie goes to the shopping plaza with her best girlfriend.
3. One night in midsummer they lie about going to the movies, instead going to the drive-in restaurant where the older kids hang out.
4. A boy named Eddie comes in to talk to them.
5. A boy with shaggy black hair and a convertible jalopy painted gold grins at her and says, "Gonna get you, baby."
6. Connie spends three hours with Eric, eating and then parking and making out in an alley.
7. The summer continues the same way, Connie spending evenings with various boys.
8. Connie has a conversation with her mother regarding the Pettinger girl and some more conflict with her.
9. One Sunday Connie gets up late and refuses to go to a family barbecue. She lies around the house, listening to the music on the radio.
10. A car comes up the drive, it's the guy with the dark hair; they talk for a while before he turns threatening.
11. Connie prepares to leave the house to go with him.

This is done in strict chronological order, but notice that although there are certainly plot points that could be labeled "conflict" (#3, #5, and #8, for example) most of the plot points are more subtle than that. But all are putting pressure on the character, all leading up to the final moment when Connie goes with Arnold Friend to her doom.

Avoiding *Scènes à Faire*: Recognizing Clichéd Plot Twists

We've talked about clichés in several places already: overly familiar language we simply called "clichés," and overly familiar characters we call stereotypes. Now we also have overly familiar plots, which we will call, because it's convenient, *scènes à faire*.

"*Scènes à faire*" is French for "scenes to make" and it is a filmmakers' term as well as (increasingly) a legal one. In recent years, every hit movie has, as a matter of course, lawsuits filed against its makers for "stealing" the plot from someone else's book or screenplay. The courts have decided that copyright protection cannot be extended for *scènes à faire*. Legally, as the court defined them in *Alexander v. Haley*, a 1978 copyright case against the miniseries of Alex Haley's *Roots*, *scènes à faire* are "incidents, characters or settings which are as a practical matter indispensable, or at least standard, in the treatment of a given topic." As Tad Friend explained it in "Copy Cats," a *New Yorker* piece:

> Thus the court suggested that when one is writing about slavery one would almost perforce include, among other things, "attempted escapes, flights through the woods pursued by baying dogs, the sorrowful or happy singing of slaves." Another court held that a realistic portrait of cops in the South Bronx would necessarily contain "drunks, prostitutes, vermin, and derelict cars." . . .
>
> The notion of *scènes à faire* is capacious enough to include the manner in which a reasonable person might develop an idea even if another reasonable person had earlier developed the same idea in the same way. For instance, if dinosaurs were reanimated, they obviously have to be kept far away from the nearest nursery school. So a writer who claimed that he had banished his velociraptors to a remote island before Michael Crichton did the same in *Jurassic Park* got nowhere in court: the judge ruled that "placing dinosaurs on a prehistoric island far from the mainland amounts to no more than a *scène à faire* in a dinosaur adventure story."
>
> The well-known Hollywood lawyer Bert Fields, who is defending Fox Searchlight Pictures in a copyright suit against *The Full Monty*, breezily explains the film's similarities to a play called *Ladies Night* by offering a similar argument. "Once you've got the idea of male strippers," he says, "it's all *scènes à faire*; you've got the inevitable scene when they first put on a G-string, the inevitable scene when someone's naked body is shown as rather unattractive. You've got to have a problem for each of the six guys, so one guy having impotence just goes with the territory."

Obviously, the last thing you ever want to write is a *scène à faire*, or piece of boilerplate! In fact, if you find yourself thinking that you "must" have a particular scene because the type of story demands it, question that instinct. Must you have the breakup scene in a relationship? You might want to, but anything that feels obligatory might just be considered a *scène à faire*, and maybe you should try to substitute something else. Whatever you do, it must not be what would be used in any other story or novel. In plot, as in every other aspect of creative writing, we aim to *surprise*, to confound expectations.

Part 2: EXERCISES

Exercise 1: What's Behind the Door of Room 101?

Goal: To figure out a character's particular vulnerabilities and play on them in a scene-building exercise.

What to do: 1. First, read the following excerpt from *1984* by George Orwell:

> "You asked me once," said O'Brien, "what was in Room 101. I told you that you know the answer already. Everyone knows it. The thing that is in Room 101 is the worst thing in the world.
>
> "The worst thing in the world varies from individual to individual. It may be burial alive, or death by fire, or by drowning, or by impalement, or fifty other deaths. *There are cases where it is some quite trivial thing, not fatal.*" [emphasis mine]

2. Imagine what is behind the door of Room 101 for your character. It cannot be an abstraction: it must be something real, something physical that can happen to your character (though not necessarily realistic; it can be fantastical or improbable). So not fear, or even fear of heights, but an example of how that might manifest itself in a real *thing* (standing on the edge of a 100-story building, for example).

   HINT: Try to be subtle, and come up with a fear that *defines*. That is, not a "standard" fear that anyone might have (fear of walking down dark alleys, fear of strangers carrying guns), but one that is irrational and somewhat unique to your character in that not everyone would understand or sympathize.

3. Write a scene (or have a narrator describe a situation) in which your character faces something that *reminds* him or her of the worst thing in the world. Not the thing itself, but a tangential "trigger" that brings on an exceedingly anxious reaction. Do not mention the "worst thing" itself. Just describe the physical thing or event that sets off your character, and how he/she reacts.

Here's an example of what you might write for this exercise:

What's behind the door of Room 101: Being crushed by a heavy object.

Her kids were watching one of those colorfully violent Saturday cartoon shows, one where oddly shaped animals chased each other using a variety of improbable vehicles. Periodically, one of the characters would fall off a cliff, or get run over by a steamroller, or get put through a mechanical wringer. Her kids, especially her small daughter, howled with laughter as pancake-thin dogs and cats attempted to regain their proper shapes. But Marilyn felt her chest constrict. Her fingers began to tingle. One of the flat cats put a finger in its mouth and blew, puffing itself up into its proper shape again. A dog stretched out one paw, then another, and watched them spring back into shape. Marilyn found it hard to breathe. She walked over to the television set, and, over the outraged howls of her children, snapped it off.

Exercise 2: "By the Time You Read This..."

Goal: To focus on the *small* things that can happen, plot-wise, and to open up your mind to possibilities.

What to do: 1. Fix your mind on your main character (or one of your main characters) in a story you are writing.
2. Have the character sit down to write a letter to someone he/she is intimate with, who happens to be not close by at the moment. (It can be an email, if that helps you work, but make it be an email that won't be read for at least twenty-four hours, as an immediate reading of the email would destroy the point of the exercise.)
3. Begin the letter, "By the time you read this" and make a detailed list of all the things that will have happened by the time the intended recipient of the letter actually reads it.

Here's a composite example (written by a number of students over the years) on how this exercise might be completed:

By the time you read this...

• The chicken will be roasted, the garlic and rosemary scent spread throughout the house, the new potatoes baked until their skins are crisp.

• The baby will have been bathed, and smell sourly of her grandfather's Old Spice shaving cologne that she insists must be rubbed on her back before she allows herself to be dressed.

• At least three more moths will have found a way into the house, and will be circling around the face of Dan Rather on the TV, reporting the latest agonies suffered in the final moments in the lives of the ValueJet crash victims.

• The cat will have insisted on having her belly scratched, and will have shown her appreciation by gently biting the hand that strokes her.

- The bottle of Merlot will be half empty.
- The phone will have rung twice, and not answered either time. No message will have been left.
- 2,000 miles away, a seventy-four-year-old woman will have been given an injection of morphine, will have nibbled on a Graham Wheat Thin, will have spit it up, will have crushed angrily the stem of a tulip from the bouquet of flowers delivered to her room that day, will have cursed her doctor, and turned her back upon the senile roommate who will croak like a frog throughout the night ahead.

Part 3: READING AS A WRITER

Sonny's Blues

JAMES BALDWIN

I read about it in the paper, in the subway, on my way to work. I read it, and I couldn't believe it, and I read it again. Then perhaps I just stared at it, at the newsprint spelling out his name, spelling out the story. I stared at it in the swinging lights of the subway car, and in the faces and bodies of the people, and in my own face, trapped in the darkness which roared outside.

It was not to be believed and I kept telling myself that, as I walked from the subway station to the high school. And at the same time I couldn't doubt it. I was scared, scared for Sonny. He became real to me again. A great block of ice got settled in my belly and kept melting there slowly all day long, while I taught my classes algebra. It was a special kind of ice. It kept melting, sending trickles of ice water all up and down my veins, but it never got less. Sometimes it hardened and seemed to expand until I felt my guts were going to come spilling out or that I was going to choke or scream. This would always be at a moment when I was remembering some specific thing Sonny had once said or done.

When he was about as old as the boys in my classes his face had been bright and open, there was a lot of copper in it; and he'd had wonderfully direct brown eyes, and great gentleness and privacy. I wondered what he looked like now. He had been picked up, the evening before, in a raid on an apartment downtown, for peddling and using heroin.

I couldn't believe it: but what I mean by that is that I couldn't find any room for it anywhere inside me. I had kept it outside me for a long time. I hadn't wanted to know. I had had suspicions, but I didn't name them, I kept putting them away. I told myself that Sonny was wild, but he wasn't crazy. And he'd always been a good boy, he hadn't ever turned hard or evil or disrespectful, the way kids can, so quick, so quick, especially in Harlem. I didn't want to believe that I'd ever see my brother going down, coming to nothing, all that light in his face gone out, in the condition I'd already seen so many others. Yet it had happened and here I was, talking about algebra to a lot of boys who might, every one of them for all I knew, be popping off needles every time they went to the head. Maybe it did more for them than algebra could.

I was sure that the first time Sonny had ever had horse, he couldn't have been much older than these boys were now. These boys, now, were living as we'd been living then, they were growing up with a rush and their heads bumped abruptly against the low ceiling of their actual possibilities. They were filled with rage. All they really knew were two darknesses, the darkness of their lives, which was now closing in on them, and the darkness of the movies, which had blinded them to that other darkness, and in which they now, vindictively, dreamed, at once more together than they were at any other time, and more alone.

When the last bell rang, the last class ended, I let out my breath. It seemed I'd been holding it for all that time. My clothes were wet—I may have looked as though I'd been sitting in a steam bath, all dressed up, all afternoon. I sat alone in the classroom a long time. I listened to the boys outside, downstairs, shouting and cursing and laughing. Their laughter struck me for perhaps the first time. It was not the joyous laughter which—God knows why—one associates with children. It was mocking and insular, its intent to denigrate. It was disenchanted, and in this, also, lay the authority of their curses. Perhaps I was listening to them because I was thinking about my brother and in them I heard my brother. And myself.

One boy was whistling a tune, at once very complicated and very simple, it seemed to be pouring out of him as though he were a bird, and it sounded very cool and moving through all that harsh, bright air, only just holding its own through all those other sounds.

I stood up and walked over to the window and looked down into the courtyard. It was the beginning of the spring and the sap was rising in the boys. A teacher passed through them every now and again, quickly, as though he or she couldn't wait to get out of that courtyard, to get those boys out of their sight and off their minds. I started collecting my stuff. I thought I'd better get home and talk to Isabel.

The courtyard was almost deserted by the time I got downstairs. I saw this boy standing in the shadow of a doorway, looking just like Sonny. I almost called his name. Then I saw that it wasn't Sonny, but somebody we used to know, a boy from around our block. He'd been Sonny's friend. He'd never been mine, having been too young for me, and, anyway, I'd never liked him. And now, even though he was a grown-up man, he still hung around that block, still spent hours on the street corners, was always high and raggy. I used to run into him from time to time and he'd often work around to asking me for a quarter or fifty cents. He always had some real good excuse, too, and I always gave it to him, I don't know why.

But now, abruptly, I hated him. I couldn't stand the way he looked at me, partly like a dog, partly like a cunning child. I wanted to ask him what the hell he was doing in the school courtyard.

He sort of shuffled over to me, and he said, "I see you got the papers. So you already know about it."

"You mean about Sonny? Yes, I already know about it. How come they didn't get you?"

He grinned. It made him repulsive and it also brought to mind what he'd looked like as a kid. "I wasn't there. I stay away from them people."

"Good for you." I offered him a cigarette and I watched him through the smoke. "You come all the way down here just to tell me about Sonny?"

"That's right." He was sort of shaking his head and his eyes looked strange, as though they were about to cross. The bright sun deadened his damp dark brown skin and it made his eyes look yellow and showed up the dirt in his kinked hair. He smelled funky. I moved a little away from him and I said, "Well, thanks. But I already know about it and I got to get home."

"I'll walk you a little ways," he said. We started walking. There were a couple of kids still loitering in the courtyard and one of them said goodnight to me and looked strangely at the boy beside me.

"What're you going to do?" he asked me. "I mean, about Sonny?"

"Look. I haven't seen Sonny for over a year. I'm not sure I'm going to do anything. Anyway, what the hell *can* I do?"

"That's right," he said quickly, "ain't nothing you can do. Can't much help old Sonny no more, I guess."

It was what I was thinking and so it seemed to me he had no right to say it.

"I'm surprised at Sonny, though," he went on—he had a funny way of talking, he looked straight ahead as though he were talking to himself—"I thought Sonny was a smart boy, I thought he was too smart to get hung."

"I guess he thought so too," I said sharply, "and that's how he got hung. And how about you? You're pretty goddamn smart, I bet."

Then he looked directly at me, just for a minute. "I ain't smart," he said. "If I was smart, I'd have reached for a pistol a long time ago."

"Look. Don't tell *me* your sad story, if it was up to me, I'd give you one." Then I felt guilty—guilty, probably, for never having supposed that the poor bastard *had* a story of his own, much less a sad one, and I asked, quickly, "What's going to happen to him now?"

He didn't answer this. He was off by himself some place. "Funny thing," he said, and from his tone we might have been discussing the quickest way to get to Brooklyn, "when I saw the papers this morning, the first thing I asked myself was if I had anything to do with it. I felt sort of responsible."

I began to listen more carefully. The subway station was on the corner, just before us, and I stopped. He stopped, too. We were in front of a bar and he ducked slightly, peering in, but whoever he was looking for didn't seem to be there. The juke box was blasting away with something black and bouncy and I half watched the barmaid as she danced her way from the juke box to her place behind the bar. And I watched her face as she laughingly responded to something someone said to her, still keeping time to the music. When she smiled one saw the little girl, one sensed the doomed, still-struggling woman beneath the battered face of the semi-whore.

"I never *give* Sonny nothing," the boy said finally, "but a long time ago I come to school high and Sonny asked me how it felt." He paused, I couldn't bear to watch him, I watched the barmaid, and I listened to the music which seemed to be causing the pavement to shake. "I told him it felt great." The music stopped, the barmaid paused and watched the juke box until the music began again. "It did."

All this was carrying me some place I didn't want to go. I certainly didn't want to know how it felt. It filled everything, the people, the houses, the music, the dark, quicksilver barmaid, with menace; and this menace was their reality.

"What's going to happen to him now?" I asked again.

"They'll send him away some place and they'll try to cure him." He shook his head. "Maybe he'll even think he's kicked the habit. Then they'll let him loose"—he gestured, throwing his cigarette into the gutter. "That's all."

"What do you mean, that's *all*?"

But I knew what he meant.

"I *mean*, that's *all*." He turned his head and looked at me, pulling down the corners of his mouth. "Don't you know what I mean?" he asked, softly.

"How the hell *would* I know what you mean?" I almost whispered it, I don't know why.

"That's right," he said to the air, "how would *he* know what I mean?" He turned toward me again, patient and calm, and yet I somehow felt him shaking, shaking as though he were going to fall apart. I felt that ice in my guts again, the dread I'd felt all afternoon; and again I watched the barmaid, moving about the bar, washing glasses, and singing. "Listen. They'll let him out and then it'll just start all over again. That's what I mean."

"You mean—they'll let him out. And then he'll just start working his way back in again. You mean he'll never kick the habit. Is that what you mean?"

"That's right," he said, cheerfully. "*You* see what I mean."

"Tell me," I said at last, "why does he want to die? He must want to die, he's killing himself, why does he want to die?"

He looked at me in surprise. He licked his lips. "He don't want to die. He wants to live. Don't nobody want to die, ever."

Then I wanted to ask him—too many things. He could not have answered, or if he had, I could not have borne the answers. I started walking. "Well, I guess it's none of my business."

"It's going to be rough on old Sonny," he said. We reached the subway station. "This is your station?" he asked. I nodded. I took one step down. "Damn!" he said, suddenly. I looked up at him. He grinned again. "Damn it if I didn't leave all my money home. You ain't got a dollar on you, have you? Just for a couple of days, is all."

All at once something inside gave and threatened to come pouring out of me. I didn't hate him any more. I felt that in another moment I'd start crying like a child.

"Sure," I said. "Don't sweat." I looked in my wallet and didn't have a dollar, I only had a five. "Here," I said. "That hold you?"

He didn't look at it—he didn't want to look at it. A terrible closed look came over his face, as though he were keeping the number on the bill a secret from him and me. "Thanks," he said, and now he was dying to see me go. "Don't worry about Sonny. Maybe I'll write him or something."

"Sure," I said. "You do that. So long."

"Be seeing you," he said. I went on down the steps.

And I didn't write Sonny or send him anything for a long time. When I finally did, it was just after my little girl died, he wrote me back a letter which made me feel like a bastard.

Here's what he said:

Dear brother,

You don't know how much I needed to hear from you. I wanted to write you many a time but I dug how much I must have hurt you and so I didn't write. But now I feel like a man who's been trying to climb up out of some deep, real deep and funky hole and just saw the sun up there, outside. I got to get outside.

I can't tell you much about how I got here. I mean I don't know how to tell you. I guess I was afraid of something or I was trying to escape from something and you know I have never been very strong in the head (smile). I'm glad Mama and Daddy are dead and can't see what's happened to their son and I swear if I'd known what I was doing I would never have hurt you so, you and a lot of other fine people who were nice to me and who believed in me.

I don't want you to think it had anything to do with me being a musician. It's more than that. Or maybe less than that. I can't get anything straight in my head down here and I try not to think about what's going to happen to me when I get outside again. Sometime I think I'm going to flip and *never* get outside and sometime I think I'll come straight back. I tell you one thing, though, I'd rather blow my brains out than go through this again. But that's what they all say, so they tell me. If I tell you when I'm coming to New York and if you could meet me, I sure would appreciate it. Give my love to Isabel and the kids and I was sure sorry to hear about little Gracie. I wish I could be like Mama and say the Lord's will be done, but I don't know it seems to me that trouble is the one thing that never does get stopped and I don't know what good it does to blame it on the Lord. But maybe it does some good if you believe it.

Your brother,
Sonny

Then I kept in constant touch with him and I sent him whatever I could and I went to meet him when he came back to New York. When I saw him many things I thought I had forgotten came flooding back to me. This was because I had begun, finally, to wonder about Sonny, about the life that Sonny lived inside. This life, whatever it was, had made him older and thinner and it had deepened the distant stillness in which he had always moved. He looked very unlike my baby brother. Yet, when he smiled, when we shook hands, the baby brother I'd never known looked out from the depths of his private life, like an animal waiting to be coaxed into the light.

"How you been keeping?" he asked me.

"All right. And you?"

"Just fine." He was smiling all over his face. "It's good to see you again."

"It's good to see you."

The seven years' difference in our ages lay between us like a chasm: I wondered if these years would ever operate between us as a bridge. I was remembering, and it made it hard to catch my breath, that I had been there when he was born; and I had heard the first words he had ever spoken. When he started to walk, he walked from our mother straight to me. I caught him just before he fell when he took the first steps he ever took in this world.

"How's Isabel?"

"Just fine. She's dying to see you."

"And the boys?"

"They're fine, too. They're anxious to see their uncle."

"Oh, come on. You know they don't remember me."

"Are you kidding? Of course they remember you."

He grinned again. We got into a taxi. We had a lot to say to each other, far too much to know how to begin.

As the taxi began to move, I asked, "You still want to go to India?"

He laughed. "You still remember that. Hell, no. This place is Indian enough for me."

"It used to belong to them," I said.

And he laughed again. "They damn sure knew what they were doing when they got rid of it."

Years ago, when he was around fourteen, he'd been all hipped on the idea of going to India. He read books about people sitting on rocks, naked, in all kinds of weather, but mostly bad, naturally, and walking barefoot through hot coals and arriving at wisdom. I used to say that it sounded to me as though they were getting away from wisdom as fast as they could. I think he sort of looked down on me for that.

"Do you mind," he asked, "if we have the driver drive alongside the park? On the west side—I haven't seen the city in so long."

"Of course not," I said. I was afraid that I might sound as though I were humoring him, but I hoped he wouldn't take it that way.

So we drove along, between the green of the park and the stony, lifeless elegance of hotels and apartment buildings, toward the vivid, killing streets of our childhood. These streets hadn't changed, though housing projects jutted up out of them now like rocks in the middle of a boiling sea. Most of the houses in which we had grown up had vanished, as had the stores from which we had stolen, the basements in which we had first tried sex, the rooftops from which we had hurled tin cans and bricks. But houses exactly like the houses of our past yet dominated the landscape, boys exactly like the boys we once had been found themselves smothering in these houses, came down into the streets for light and air and found themselves encircled by disaster. Some escaped the trap, most didn't. Those who got out always left something of themselves behind, as some animals amputate a leg and leave it in the trap. It might be said, perhaps, that I had escaped, after all, I was a school teacher; or that Sonny had, he hadn't lived in Harlem for years. Yet, as the cab moved uptown through streets which seemed, with a rush, to darken with dark people, and as I covertly studied Sonny's face, it came to me that what we both were seeking through our separate cab windows was that part of ourselves which had been left behind. It's always at the hour of trouble and confrontation that the missing member aches.

We hit 110th Street and started rolling up Lenox Avenue. And I'd known this avenue all my life, but it seemed to me again, as it had seemed on the day I'd first heard about Sonny's trouble, filled with a hidden menace which was its very breath of life.

"We almost there," said Sonny.

"Almost." We were both too nervous to say anything more.

We live in a housing project. It hasn't been up long. A few days after it was up it seemed uninhabitably new, now, of course, it's already rundown. It looks like a parody of the good, clean, faceless life—God knows the people who live in it do their best to make it a parody. The beat-looking grass lying around isn't enough to make their lives green, the hedges will never hold out the streets, and they know it. The big windows fool no one, they aren't big enough to make space out of no space. They don't bother with the windows, they watch the TV screen instead. The playground is most popular with the children who don't play at jacks, or skip rope, or roller skate, or swing, and they can be found in it after dark. We moved in partly because it's not too far from where I teach, and partly for the kids; but it's really just like the houses in which Sonny and I grew up. The same things happen, they'll have the same things to remember. The moment Sonny and I started into the house I had the feeling that I was simply bringing him back into the danger he had almost died trying to escape.

Sonny has never been talkative. So I don't know why I was sure he'd be dying to talk to me when supper was over the first night. Everything went fine, the oldest boy remembered him, and the youngest boy liked him, and Sonny had remembered to bring something for each of them; and Isabel, who is really much nicer than I am, more open and giving, had gone to a lot of trouble about dinner and was genuinely glad to see him. And she's always been able to tease Sonny in a way that I haven't. It was nice to see her face so vivid again and to hear her laugh and watch her make Sonny laugh. She wasn't, or, anyway, she didn't seem to be, at all uneasy or embarrassed. She chatted as though there were no subject which had to be avoided and she got Sonny past his first, faint stiffness. And thank God she was there, for I was filled with that icy dread again. Everything I did seemed awkward to me, and everything I said sounded freighted with hidden meaning. I was trying to remember everything I'd heard about dope addiction and I couldn't help watching Sonny for signs. I wasn't doing it out of malice. I was trying to find out something about my brother. I was dying to hear him tell me he was safe.

"Safe!" my father grunted, whenever Mama suggested trying to move to a neighborhood which might be safer for children. "Safe, hell! Ain't no place safe for kids, nor nobody."

He always went on like this, but he wasn't, ever, really as bad as he sounded, not even on weekends, when he got drunk. As a matter of fact, he was always on the lookout for "something a little better," but he died before he found it. He died suddenly, during a drunken weekend in the middle of the war, when Sonny was fifteen. He and Sonny hadn't ever got on too well. And this was partly because Sonny was the apple of his father's eye. It was because he loved Sonny so much and was frightened for him, that he was always fighting with him. It doesn't do any good to fight with Sonny. Sonny just moves back, inside himself, where he can't be reached. But the principal reason that they never hit it off is that they were so much alike. Daddy was big and rough and loud-talking, just the opposite of Sonny, but they both had—that same privacy.

Mama tried to tell me something about this, just after Daddy died. I was home on leave from the army.

This was the last time I ever saw my mother alive. Just the same, this picture gets all mixed up in my mind with pictures I had of her when she was younger. The way I always see her is the way she used to be on a Sunday afternoon, say, when the old folks were talking after the big Sunday dinner. I always see her wearing pale blue. She'd be sitting on the sofa. And my father would be sitting in the easy chair, not far from her. And the living room would be full of church folks and relatives. There they sit, in chairs all around the living room, and the night is creeping up outside, but nobody knows it yet. You can see the darkness growing against the windowpanes and you hear the street noises every now and again, or maybe the jangling beat of a tambourine from one of the churches close by, but it's real quiet in the room. For a moment nobody's talking, but every face looks darkening, like the sky outside. And my mother rocks a little from the waist, and my father's eyes are closed. Everyone is looking at something a child can't see. For a minute they've forgotten the children. Maybe a kid is lying on the rug, half asleep. Maybe somebody's got a kid in his lap and is absent-mindedly stroking the kid's head. Maybe there's a kid, quiet and big-eyed, curled up in a big chair in the corner. The silence, the darkness coming, and the darkness in the faces frightens the child obscurely. He hopes that the hand which strokes his forehead will never stop—will never die. He hopes that there will never come a time when the old folks won't be sitting around the living room, talking about where they've come from, and what they've seen, and what's happened to them and their kinfolk.

But something deep and watchful in the child knows that this is bound to end, is already ending. In a moment someone will get up and turn on the light. Then the old folks will remember the children and they won't talk any more that day. And when light fills the room, the child is filled with darkness. He knows that every time this happens he's moved just a little closer to that darkness outside. The darkness outside is what the old folks have been talking about. It's what they've come from. It's what they endure. The child knows that they won't talk any more because if he knows too much about what's happened to *them*, he'll know too much too soon, about what's going to happen to *him*.

The last time I talked to my mother, I remember I was restless. I wanted to get out and see Isabel. We weren't married then and we had a lot to straighten out between us.

There Mama sat, in black, by the window. She was humming an old church song, *Lord, you brought me from a long ways off.* Sonny was out some-where. Mama kept watching the streets.

"I don't know," she said, "if I'll ever see you again, after you go off from here. But I hope you'll remember the things I tried to teach you."

"Don't talk like that," I said, and smiled. "You'll be here a long time yet."

She smiled, too, but she said nothing. She was quiet for a long time. And I said, "Mama, don't you worry about nothing. I'll be writing all the time, and you be getting the checks. . . ."

"I want to talk to you about your brother," she said, suddenly. "If any-thing happens to me he ain't going to have nobody to look out for him."

"Mama," I said, "ain't nothing going to happen to you *or* Sonny. Sonny's all right. He's a good boy and he's got good sense."

"It ain't a question of his being a good boy," Mama said, "nor of his having good sense. It ain't only the bad ones, nor yet the dumb ones that gets sucked under." She stopped, looking at me. "Your Daddy once had a brother," she said, and she smiled in a way that made me feel she was in pain. "You didn't never know that, did you?"

"No," I said, "I never knew that," and I watched her face.

"Oh, yes," she said, "your Daddy had a brother." She looked out of the window again. "I know you never saw your Daddy cry. But *I* did—many a time, through all these years."

I asked her, "What happened to his brother? How come nobody's ever talked about him?"

This was the first time I ever saw my mother look old.

"His brother got killed," she said, "when he was just a little younger than you are now. I knew him. He was a fine boy. He was maybe a little full of the devil, but he didn't mean nobody no harm."

Then she stopped and the room was silent, exactly as it had sometimes been on those Sunday afternoons. Mama kept looking out into the streets.

"He used to have a job in the mill," she said, "and, like all young folks, he just liked to perform on Saturday nights. Saturday nights, him and your father would drift around to different places, go to dances and things like that, or just sit around with people they knew, and your father's brother would sing, he had a fine voice, and play along with himself on his guitar. Well, this particular Saturday night, him and your father was coming home from some place, and they were both a little drunk and there was a moon that night, it was bright like day. Your father's brother was feeling kind of good, and he was whistling to himself, and he had his guitar slung over his shoulder. They was coming down a hill and beneath them was a road that turned off from the highway. Well, your father's brother, being always kind of frisky, decided to run down this hill, and he did, with that guitar banging and clanging behind him, and he ran across the road, and he was making water behind a tree. And your father was sort of amused at him and he was still coming down the hill, kind of slow. Then he heard a car motor and that same minute his brother stepped from behind the tree, into the road, in the moonlight. And he started to cross the road. And your father started to run down the hill, he says he don't know why. This car was full of white men. They was all drunk, and when they seen your father's brother they let out a great whoop and holler and they aimed the car straight at him. They was having fun, they just wanted to scare him, the way they do sometimes, you know. But they was drunk. And I guess the boy, being drunk, too, and scared, kind of lost his head. By the time he jumped it was too late. Your father says he heard his brother scream when the car rolled over him, and he heard the wood of that guitar when it give, and he heard them strings go flying, and he heard them white men shouting, and the car kept on a-going and it ain't stopped till this day. And, time your father got down the hill, his brother weren't nothing but blood and pulp."

Tears were gleaming on my mother's face. There wasn't anything I could say.

"He never mentioned it," she said, "because I never let him mention it before you children. Your Daddy was like a crazy man that night and for many a night thereafter. He says he never in his life seen anything as dark as that road after the lights of that car had gone away. Weren't nothing, weren't nobody on that road, just your Daddy and his brother and that busted guitar. Oh, yes. Your Daddy never did really get right again. Till the day he died he weren't sure but that every white man he saw was the man that killed his brother."

She stopped and took out her handkerchief and dried her eyes and looked at me.

"I ain't telling you all this," she said, "to make you scared or bitter or to make you hate nobody. I'm telling you this because you got a brother. And the world ain't changed."

I guess I didn't want to believe this. I guess she saw this in my face. She turned away from me, toward the window again, searching those streets.

"But I praise my Redeemer," she said at last, "that He called your Daddy home before me. I ain't saying it to throw no flowers at myself, but, I declare, it keeps me from feeling too cast down to know I helped your father get safely through this world. Your father always acted like he was the roughest, strongest man on earth. And everybody took him to be like that. But if he hadn't had *me* there—to see his tears!"

She was crying again. Still, I couldn't move. I said, "Lord, Lord, Mama, I didn't know it was like that."

"Oh, honey," she said, "there's a lot that you don't know. But you are going to find it out." She stood up from the window and came over to me. "You got to hold on to your brother," she said, "and don't let him fall, no matter what it looks like is happening to him and no matter how evil you gets with him. You going to be evil with him many a time. But don't you forget what I told you, you hear?"

"I won't forget," I said. "Don't you worry, I won't forget. I won't let nothing happen to Sonny."

My mother smiled as though she were amused at something she saw in my face. Then, "You may not be able to stop nothing from happening. But you got to let him know you's *there*."

•   •   •

Two days later I was married, and then I was gone. And I had a lot of things on my mind and I pretty well forgot my promise to Mama until I got shipped home on a special furlough for her funeral.

And, after the funeral, with just Sonny and me alone in the empty kitchen, I tried to find out something about him.

"What do you want to do?" I asked him.

"I'm going to be a musician," he said.

For he had graduated, in the time I had been away, from dancing to the juke box to finding out who was playing what, and what they were doing with it, and he had bought himself a set of drums.

"You mean, you want to be a drummer?" I somehow had the feeling that being a drummer might be all right for other people but not for my brother Sonny.

"I don't think," he said, looking at me very gravely, "that I'll ever be a good drummer. But I think I can play a piano."

I frowned. I'd never played the role of the older brother quite so seriously before, had scarcely ever, in fact, *asked* Sonny a damn thing. I sensed myself in the presence of something I didn't really know how to handle, didn't understand. So I made my frown a little deeper as I asked: "What kind of musician do you want to be?"

He grinned. "How many kinds do you think there are?"

"Be *serious*," I said.

He laughed, throwing his head back, and then looked at me. "I *am* serious."

"Well, then, for Christ's sake, stop kidding around and answer a serious question. I mean, do you want to be a concert pianist, you want to play classical music and all that, or—or what?" Long before I finished he was laughing again. "For Christ's *sake*, Sonny!"

He sobered, but with difficulty. "I'm sorry. But you sound so—*scared*!" and he was off again.

"Well, you may think it's funny now, baby, but it's not going to be so funny when you have to make your living at it, let me tell you *that*." I was furious because I knew he was laughing at me and I didn't know why.

"No," he said, very sober now, and afraid, perhaps, that he'd hurt me, "I don't want to be a classical pianist. That isn't what interests me. I mean"—he paused, looking hard at me, as though his eyes would help me to understand, and then gestured helplessly, as though perhaps his hand would help—"I mean, I'll have a lot of studying to do, and I'll have to study *everything*, but, I mean, I want to play *with*—jazz musicians." He stopped. "I want to play jazz," he said.

Well, the word had never before sounded as heavy, as real, as it sounded that afternoon in Sonny's mouth. I just looked at him and I was probably frowning a real frown by this time. I simply couldn't see why on earth he'd want to spend his time hanging around nightclubs, clowning around on bandstands, while people pushed each other around a dance floor. It seemed—beneath him, somehow. I had never thought about it before, had never been forced to, but I suppose I had always put jazz musicians in a class with what Daddy called "good-time people."

"Are you *serious*?"

"Hell, *yes*, I'm serious."

He looked more helpless than ever, and annoyed, and deeply hurt.

I suggested, helpfully: "You mean—like Louis Armstrong?"

His face closed as though I'd struck him. "No. I'm not talking about none of that old-time, down home crap."

"Well, look, Sonny, I'm sorry, don't get mad. I just don't altogether get it, that's all. Name somebody—you know, a jazz musician you admire."

"Bird."

"Who?"

"Bird! Charlie Parker! Don't they teach you nothing in the goddamn army?"

I lit a cigarette. I was surprised and then a little amused to discover that I was trembling. "I've been out of touch," I said. "You'll have to be patient with me. Now. Who's this Parker character?"

"He's just one of the greatest jazz musicians alive," said Sonny, sullenly, his hands in his pockets, his back to me. "Maybe *the* greatest," he added, bitterly, "that's probably why *you* never heard of him."

"All right," I said, "I'm ignorant. I'm sorry. I'll go out and buy all the cat's records right away, all right?"

"It don't," said Sonny, with dignity, "make any difference to me. I don't care what you listen to. Don't do me no favors."

I was beginning to realize that I'd never seen him so upset before. With another part of my mind I was thinking that this would probably turn out to be one of those things kids go through and that I shouldn't make it seem important by pushing it too hard. Still, I didn't think it would do any harm to ask: "Doesn't all this take a lot of time? Can you make a living at it?"

He turned back to me and half leaned, half sat, on the kitchen table. "Everything takes time," he said, "and—well, yes, sure, I can make a living at it. But what I don't seem to be able to make you understand is that it's the only thing I want to do."

"Well, Sonny," I said, gently, "you know people can't always do exactly what they *want* to do—"

"*No*, I don't know that," said Sonny, surprising me. "I think people *ought* to do what they want to do, what else are they alive for?"

"You getting to be a big boy," I said desperately, "it's time you started thinking about your future."

"I'm thinking about my future," said Sonny, grimly. "I think about it all the time."

I gave up. I decided, if he didn't change his mind, that we could always talk about it later. "In the meantime," I said, "you got to finish school." We had already decided that he'd have to move in with Isabel and her folks. I knew this wasn't the ideal arrangement because Isabel's folks are inclined to be dicty and they hadn't especially wanted Isabel to marry me. But I didn't know what else to do. "And we have to get you fixed up at Isabel's."

There was a long silence. He moved from the kitchen table to the window. "That's a terrible idea. You know it yourself."

"Do you have a *better* idea?"

He just walked up and down the kitchen for a minute. He was as tall as I was. He had started to shave. I suddenly had the feeling that I didn't know him at all.

He stopped at the kitchen table and picked up my cigarettes. Looking at me with a kind of mocking, amused defiance, he put one between his lips. "You mind?"

"You smoking already?"

He lit the cigarette and nodded, watching me through the smoke. "I just wanted to see if I'd have the courage to smoke in front of you." He grinned and blew a great cloud of smoke to the ceiling. "It was easy." He looked at my face. "Come on, now. I bet you was smoking at my age, tell the truth."

I didn't say anything but the truth was on my face, and he laughed. But now there was something very strained in his laugh. "Sure. And I bet that ain't all you was doing."

He was frightening me a little. "Cut the crap," I said. "We already decided that you was going to go and live at Isabel's. Now what's got into you all of a sudden?"

"*You* decided it," he pointed out. "*I* didn't decide nothing." He stopped in front of me, leaning against the stove, arms loosely folded. "Look, brother. I don't want to stay in Harlem no more, I really don't." He was very earnest. He looked at me, then over toward the kitchen window. There was something in his eyes I'd never seen before, some thoughtfulness, some worry all his own. He rubbed the muscle of one arm. "It's time I was getting out of here."

"Where do you want to *go*, Sonny?"

"I want to join the army. Or the navy, I don't care. If I say I'm old enough, they'll believe me."

Then I got mad. It was because I was so scared. "You must be crazy. You goddamn fool, what the hell do you want to go and join the *army* for?"

"I just told you. To get out of Harlem."

"Sonny, you haven't even finished *school*. And if you really want to be a musician, how do you expect to study if you're in the *army*?"

He looked at me, trapped, and in anguish. "There's ways. I might be able to work out some kind of deal. Anyway, I'll have the G.I. Bill when I come out."

"*If* you come out." We stared at each other. "Sonny, please. Be reasonable. I know the setup is far from perfect. But we got to do the best we can."

"I ain't learning nothing in school," he said. "Even when I go." He turned away from me and opened the window and threw his cigarette out into the narrow alley. I watched his back. "At least, I ain't learning nothing you'd want me to learn." He slammed the window so hard I thought the glass would fly out, and turned back to me. "And I'm sick of the stink of these garbage cans!"

"Sonny," I said, "I know how you feel. But if you don't finish school now, you're going to be sorry later that you didn't." I grabbed him by the shoulders. "And you only got another year. It ain't so bad. And I'll come back and I swear I'll help you do *whatever* you want to do. Just try to put up with it till I come back. Will you please do that? For me?"

He didn't answer and he wouldn't look at me.

"Sonny. You hear me?"

He pulled away. "I hear you. But you never hear anything *I* say."

I didn't know what to say to that. He looked out of the window and then back at me. "OK," he said, and sighed. "I'll try."

Then I said, trying to cheer him up a little, "They got a piano at Isabel's. You can practice on it."

And as a matter of fact, it did cheer him up for a minute. "That's right," he said to himself. "I forgot that." His face relaxed a little. But the worry, the thoughtfulness, played on it still, the way shadows play on a face which is staring into the fire.

But I thought I'd never hear the end of that piano. At first, Isabel would write me, saying how nice it was that Sonny was so serious about his music and how, as soon as he came in from school, or wherever he had been when he was supposed to be at school, he went straight to that piano and stayed there until suppertime. And, after supper, he went back to that piano and stayed there until everybody went to bed. He was at the piano all day Saturday and all day Sunday. Then he bought a record player and started playing records. He'd play one record over and over again, all day long sometimes, and he'd improvise along with it on the piano. Or he'd play one section of the record, one chord, one change, one progression, then he'd do it on the piano. Then back to the record. Then back to the piano.

Well, I really don't know how they stood it. Isabel finally confessed that it wasn't like living with a person at all, it was like living with sound. And the sound didn't make any sense to her, didn't make any sense to any of them—naturally. They began, in a way, to be afflicted by this presence that was living in their home. It was as though Sonny were some sort of god, or monster. He moved in an atmosphere which wasn't like theirs at all. They fed him and he ate, he washed himself, he walked in and out of their door; he certainly wasn't nasty or unpleasant or rude, Sonny isn't any of those things; but it was as though he were all wrapped up in some cloud, some fire, some vision all his own; and there wasn't any way to reach him.

At the same time, he wasn't really a man yet, he was still a child, and they had to watch out for him in all kinds of ways. They certainly couldn't throw him out. Neither did they dare to make a great scene about that piano because even they dimly sensed, as I sensed, from so many thousands of miles away, that Sonny was at that piano playing for his life.

But he hadn't been going to school. One day a letter came from the school board and Isabel's mother got it—there had, apparently, been other letters but Sonny had torn them up. This day, when Sonny came in, Isabel's mother showed him the letter and asked where he'd been spending his time. And she finally got it out of him that he'd been down in Greenwich Village, with musicians and other characters, in a white girl's apartment. And this scared her and she started to scream at him and what came up, once she began—though she denies it to this day—was what sacrifices they were making to give Sonny a decent home and how little he appreciated it.

Sonny didn't play the piano that day. By evening, Isabel's mother had calmed down but then there was the old man to deal with, and Isabel herself. Isabel says she did her best to be calm but she broke down and started crying. She says she just watched Sonny's face. She could tell, by watching him, what was happening with him. And what was happening was that they penetrated his cloud, they had reached him. Even if their fingers had been a thousand times more gentle than human fingers ever are, he could hardly help feeling that they had stripped him naked and were spitting on that nakedness. For he also had to see that his presence, that music, which was life or death to him, had been torture for them and that they had endured it, not at all for his sake, but only for mine. And Sonny couldn't take that. He can take it a little better today than he could then but he's still not very good at it and, frankly, I don't know anybody who is.

The silence of the next few days must have been louder than the sound of all the music ever played since time began. One morning, before she went to work, Isabel was in his room for something and she suddenly realized that all of his records were gone. And she knew for certain that he was gone. And he was. He went as far as the navy would carry him. He finally sent me a postcard from some place in Greece and that was the first I knew that Sonny was still alive. I didn't see him any more until we were both back in New York and the war had long been over.

He was a man by then, of course, but I wasn't willing to see it. He came by the house from time to time, but we fought almost every time we met. I didn't like the way he carried himself, loose and dreamlike all the time, and I didn't like his friends, and his music seemed to be merely an excuse for the life he led. It sounded just that weird and disordered.

Then we had a fight, a pretty awful fight, and I didn't see him for months. By and by I looked him up, where he was living, in a furnished room in the Village, and I tried to make it up. But there were lots of people in the room and Sonny just lay on his bed, and he wouldn't come downstairs with me, and he treated these other people as though they were his family and I weren't. So I got mad and then he got mad, and then I told him that he might just as well be dead as live the way he was living. Then he stood up and he told me not to worry about him any more in life, that he *was* dead as far as I was concerned. Then he pushed me to the door and the other people looked on as though nothing were happening, and he slammed the door behind me. I stood in the hallway, staring at the door. I heard somebody laugh in the room and then the tears came to my eyes. I started down the steps, whistling to keep from crying, I kept whistling to myself, *You going to need me, baby, one of these cold, rainy days.*

I read about Sonny's trouble in the spring. Little Grace died in the fall. She was a beautiful little girl. But she only lived a little over two years. She died of polio and she suffered. She had a slight fever for a couple of days, but it didn't seem like anything and we just kept her in bed. And we would certainly have called the doctor, but the fever dropped, she seemed to be all right. So we thought it had just been a cold. Then, one day, she was up, playing, Isabel was in the kitchen fixing lunch for the two boys when they'd come in from school, and she heard Grace fall down in the living room. When you have a lot of children you don't always start running when one of them falls, unless they start screaming or something. And, this time, Grace was quiet. Yet, Isabel says that when she heard that *thump* and then that silence, something happened in her to make her afraid. And she ran to the living room and there was little Grace on the floor, all twisted up, and the reason she hadn't screamed was that she couldn't get her breath. And when she did scream, it was the worst sound, Isabel says, that she'd ever heard in all her life, and she still hears it sometimes in her dreams. Isabel will sometimes wake me up with a low, moaning, strangled sound and I have to be quick to awaken her and hold her to me and where Isabel is weeping against me seems a mortal wound.

I think I may have written Sonny the very day that little Grace was buried. I was sitting in the living room in the dark, by myself, and I suddenly thought of Sonny. My trouble made his real.

One Saturday afternoon, when Sonny had been living with us, or, anyway, been in our house, for nearly two weeks, I found myself wandering aimlessly about the living room, drinking from a can of beer, and trying to work up the courage to search Sonny's room. He was out, he was usually out whenever I was home, and Isabel had taken the children to see their grandparents. Suddenly I was standing still in front of the living room window, watching Seventh Avenue. The idea of searching Sonny's room made me still. I scarcely dared to admit to myself what I'd be searching for. I didn't know what I'd do if I found it. Or if I didn't.

On the sidewalk across from me, near the entrance to a barbecue joint, some people were holding an old-fashioned revival meeting. The barbecue cook, wearing a dirty white apron, his conked hair reddish and metallic in the pale sun, and a cigarette between his lips, stood in the doorway, watching them. Kids and older people paused in their errands and stood there, along with some older men and a couple of very tough-looking women who watched everything that happened on the avenue, as though they owned it, or were maybe owned by it. Well, they were watching this, too. The revival was being carried on by three sisters in black, and a brother. All they had were their voices and their Bibles and a tambourine. The brother was testifying and while he testified two of the sisters stood together, seeming to say, amen, and the third sister walked around with the tambourine outstretched and a couple of people dropped coins into it. Then the brother's testimony ended and the sister who had been taking up the collection dumped the coins into her palm and transferred them to the pocket of her long black robe. Then she raised both hands, striking the tambourine against the air, and then against one hand, and she started to sing. And the two other sisters and the brother joined in.

It was strange, suddenly, to watch, though I had been seeing these street meetings all my life. So, of course, had everybody else down there. Yet, they paused and watched and listened and I stood still at the window. *"Tis the old ship of Zion,"* they sang, and the sister with the tambourine kept a steady, jangling beat, *"it has rescued many a thousand!"* Not a soul under the sound of their voices was hearing this song for the first time, not one of them had been rescued. Nor had they seen much in the way of rescue work being done around them. Neither did they especially believe in the holiness of the three sisters and the brother, they knew too much about them, knew where they lived, and how. The woman with the tambourine, whose voice dominated the air, whose face was bright with joy, was divided by very little from the woman who stood watching her, a cigarette between her heavy, chapped lips, her hair a cuckoo's nest, her face scarred and swollen from many beatings, and her black eyes glittering like coal. Perhaps they both knew this, which was why, when, as rarely, they addressed each other, they addressed each other as Sister. As the singing filled the air the watching, listening faces underwent a change, the eyes focusing on something within; the music seemed to soothe a poison out of them; and time seemed, nearly, to fall away from the sullen, belligerent, battered faces, as though they were fleeing back to their first condition, while dreaming of their last. The barbecue cook half shook his head and smiled, and dropped his cigarette and disappeared into his joint. A man fumbled in his pockets for change and stood holding it in his hand impatiently, as though he had just remembered a pressing appointment further up the avenue. He looked furious. Then I saw Sonny, standing on the edge of the crowd. He was carrying a wide, flat notebook with a green cover, and it made him look, from where I was standing, almost like a schoolboy. The coppery sun brought out the copper in his skin, he was very faintly smiling, standing very still. Then the singing stopped, the tambourine turned into a collection plate again. The furious man dropped in his coins and vanished, so did a couple of the women, and Sonny dropped some change in the plate, looking directly at the woman with a little smile. He started across the avenue, toward the house. He has a slow, loping walk, something like the way Harlem hipsters walk, only he's imposed on this his own half-beat. I had never really noticed it before.

I stayed at the window, both relieved and apprehensive. As Sonny disappeared from my sight, they began singing again. And they were still singing when his key turned in the lock.

"Hey," he said.

"Hey, yourself. You want some beer?"

"No. Well, maybe." But he came up to the window and stood beside me, looking out. "What a warm voice," he said.

They were singing *If I could only hear my mother pray again!*

"Yes," I said, "and she can sure beat that tambourine."

"But what a terrible song," he said, and laughed. He dropped his note-book on the sofa and disappeared into the kitchen. "Where's Isabel and the kids?"

"I think they went to see their grandparents. You hungry?"

"No." He came back into the living room with his can of beer. "You want to come some place with me tonight?"

I sensed, I don't know how, that I couldn't possibly say no. "Sure. Where?"

He sat down on the sofa and picked up his notebook and started leafing through it. "I'm going to sit in with some fellows in a joint in the Village."

"You mean, you're going to play, tonight?"

"That's right." He took a swallow of his beer and moved back to the window. He gave me a sidelong look. "If you can stand it."

"I'll try," I said.

He smiled to himself and we both watched as the meeting across the way broke up. The three sisters and the brother, heads bowed, were singing *God be with you till we meet again*. The faces around them were very quiet. Then the song ended. The small crowd dispersed. We watched the three women and the lone man walk slowly up the avenue.

"When she was singing before," said Sonny, abruptly, "her voice reminded me for a minute of what heroin feels like sometimes—when it's in your veins. It makes you feel sort of warm and cool at the same time. And distant. And—and sure." He sipped his beer, very deliberately not looking at me. I watched his face. "It makes you feel—in control. Some-times you've got to have that feeling."

"Do you?" I sat down slowly in the easy chair.

"Sometimes." He went to the sofa and picked up his notebook again. "Some people do."

"In order," I asked, "to play?" And my voice was very ugly, full of con-tempt and anger.

"Well"—he looked at me with great, troubled eyes, as though, in fact, he hoped his eyes would tell me things he could never otherwise say—"they *think* so. And *if* they think so—!"

"And what do *you* think?" I asked.

He sat on the sofa and put his can of beer on the floor. "I don't know," he said, and I couldn't be sure if he were answering my question or pursuing his thoughts. His face didn't tell me. "It's not so much to *play*. It's to *stand* it, to be able to make it at all. On any level." He frowned and smiled: "In order to keep from shaking to pieces."

"But these friends of yours," I said, "they seem to shake themselves to pieces pretty goddamn fast."

"Maybe." He played with the notebook. And something told me that I should curb my tongue, that Sonny was doing his best to talk, that I should listen. "But of course you only know the ones that've gone to pieces. Some don't—or at least they haven't *yet* and that's just about all *any* of us can say." He paused. "And then there are some who just live, really, in hell, and they know it and they see what's happening and they go right on. I don't know." He sighed, dropped the notebook, folded his arms. "Some guys, you can tell from the way they play, they on something *all* the time. And you can see that, well, it makes something real for them. But of course," he picked up his beer from the floor and sipped it and put the can down again, "they *want* to, too, you've got to see that. Even some of them that say they don't—*some*, not all."

"And what about you?" I asked—I couldn't help it. "What about you? Do *you* want to?"

He stood up and walked to the window and remained silent for a long time. Then he sighed. "Me," he said. Then: "While I was downstairs before, on my way here, listening to that woman sing, it struck me all of a sudden how much suffering she must have had to go through—to sing like that. It's *repulsive* to think you have to suffer that much."

I said: "But there's no way not to suffer—is there, Sonny?"

"I believe not," he said and smiled, "but that's never stopped anyone from trying." He looked at me. "Has it?" I realized, with this mocking look, that there stood between us, forever, beyond the power of time or forgiveness, the fact that I had held silence—so long!—when he had needed human speech to help him. He turned back to the window. "No, there's no way not to suffer. But you try all kinds of ways to keep from drowning in it, to keep on top of it, and to make it seem—well, like *you*. Like you did something, all right, and now you're suffering for it. You know?" I said nothing. "Well you know," he said, impatiently, "why *do* people suffer? Maybe it's better to do something to give it a reason, *any* reason."

"But we just agreed," I said, "that there's no way not to suffer. Isn't it better, then, just to—take it?"

"But nobody just takes it," Sonny cried, "that's what I'm telling you! *Everybody* tries not to. You're just hung up on the *way* some people try— it's not *your* way!"

The hair on my face began to itch, my face felt wet. "That's not true," I said, "that's not true. I don't give a damn what other people do, I don't even care how they suffer. I just care how *you* suffer." And he looked at me. "Please believe me," I said, "I don't want to see you—die—trying not to suffer."

"I won't," he said, flatly, "die trying not to suffer. At least, not any faster than anybody else."

"But there's no need," I said, trying to laugh, "is there? in killing yourself."

I wanted to say more, but I couldn't. I wanted to talk about will power and how life could be—well, beautiful. I wanted to say that it was all within; but was it? or, rather, wasn't that exactly the trouble? And I wanted to promise that I would never fail him again. But it would all have sounded—empty words and lies.

So I made the promise to myself and prayed that I would keep it.

"It's terrible sometimes, inside," he said, "that's what's the trouble. You walk these streets, black and funky and cold, and there's not really a living ass to talk to, and there's nothing shaking, and there's no way of getting it out—that storm inside. You can't talk it and you can't make love with it, and when you finally try to get with it and play it, you realize *nobody's* listening. So *you've* got to listen. You got to find a way to listen."

And then he walked away from the window and sat on the sofa again, as though all the wind had suddenly been knocked out of him. "Sometimes you'll do *anything* to play, even cut your mother's throat." He laughed and looked at me. "Or your brother's." Then he sobered. "Or your own." Then: "Don't worry. I'm all right now and I think I'll *be* all right. But I can't forget—where I've been. I don't mean just the physical place I've been, I mean where I've *been*. And *what* I've been."

"What have you been, Sonny?" I asked.

He smiled—but sat sideways on the sofa, his elbow resting on the back, his fingers playing with his mouth and chin, not looking at me. "I've been something I didn't recognize, didn't know I could be. Didn't know anybody could be." He stopped, looking inward, looking helplessly young, looking old. "I'm not talking about it now because I feel *guilty* or anything like that—maybe it would be better if I did, I don't know. Anyway, I can't really talk about it. Not to you, not to anybody," and now he turned and faced me. "Sometimes, you know, and it was actually when I was most *out* of the world, I felt that I was in it, that I was *with* it, really, and I could play or I didn't really have to *play*, it just came out of me, it was there. And I don't know how I played, thinking about it now, but I know I did awful things, those times, sometimes, to people. Or it wasn't that I *did* anything to them—it was that they weren't real." He picked up the beer can; it was empty; he rolled it between his palms: "And other times—well, I needed a fix, I needed to find a place to lean, I needed to clear a space to *listen*—and I couldn't find it, and I—went crazy, I did terrible things to *me*, I was terrible *for* me." He began pressing the beer can between his hands, I watched the metal begin to give. It glittered, as he played with it, like a knife, and I was afraid he would cut himself, but I said nothing. "Oh well. I can never tell you. I was all by myself at the bottom of something, stinking and sweating and crying and shaking, and I smelled it, you know? *my* stink, and I thought I'd die if I couldn't get away from it and yet, all the same, I knew that everything I was doing was just locking me in with it. And I didn't know," he paused, still flattening the beer can, "I didn't know, I still *don't* know, something kept telling me that maybe it was good to smell your own stink, but I didn't think that *that* was what I'd been trying to do—and—who can stand it?" and he abruptly dropped the ruined beer can, looking at me with a small, still smile, and then rose, walking to the window as though it were the lodestone rock. I watched his face, he watched the avenue. "I couldn't tell you when Mama died—but the reason I wanted to leave Harlem so bad was to get away from drugs. And then, when I ran away, that's what I was running from—really. When I came back, nothing had changed, I hadn't changed, I was just—older." And he stopped, drumming with his fingers on the windowpane. The sun had vanished, soon darkness would fall. I watched his face. "It can come again," he said, almost as though speaking to himself. Then he turned to me. "It can come again," he repeated. "I just want you to know that."

"All right," I said, at last. "So it can come again. All right."

He smiled, but the smile was sorrowful. "I had to try to tell you," he said.

"Yes," I said. "I understand that."

"You're my brother," he said, looking straight at me, and not smiling at all.

"Yes," I repeated, "yes. I understand that."

He turned back to the window, looking out. "All that hatred down there," he said, "all that hatred and misery and love. It's a wonder it doesn't blow the avenue apart."

We went to the only nightclub on a short, dark street, downtown. We squeezed through the narrow, chattering, jam-packed bar to the entrance of the big room, where the bandstand was. And we stood there for a moment, for the lights were very dim in this room and we couldn't see. Then, "Hello, boy," said a voice and an enormous black man, much older than Sonny or myself, erupted out of all that atmospheric lighting and put an arm around Sonny's shoulder. "I been sitting right here," he said, "waiting for you."

He had a big voice, too, and heads in the darkness turned toward us.

Sonny grinned and pulled a little away, and said, "Creole, this is my brother. I told you about him."

Creole shook my hand. "I'm glad to meet you, son," he said, and it was clear that he was glad to meet me *there*, for Sonny's sake. And he smiled, "You got a real musician in *your* family," and he took his arm from Sonny's shoulder and slapped him, lightly, affectionately, with the back of his hand.

"Well. Now I've heard it all," said a voice behind us. This was another musician, and a friend of Sonny's, a coal-black, cheerful-looking man, built close to the ground. He immediately began confiding to me, at the top of his lungs, the most terrible things about Sonny, his teeth gleaming like a lighthouse and his laugh coming up out of him like the beginning of an earthquake. And it turned out that everyone at the bar knew Sonny, or almost everyone; some were musicians, working there, or nearby, or not working, some were simply hangers-on, and some were there to hear Sonny play. I was introduced to all of them and they were all very polite to me. Yet, it was clear that, for them, I was only Sonny's brother. Here, I was in Sonny's world. Or, rather: his kingdom. Here, it was not even a question that his veins bore royal blood.

They were going to play soon and Creole installed me, by myself, at a table in a dark corner. Then I watched them, Creole, and the little black man, and Sonny, and the others, while they horsed around, standing just below the bandstand. The light from the bandstand spilled just a little short of them and, watching them laughing and gesturing and moving about, I had the feeling that they, nevertheless, were being most careful not to step into that circle of light too suddenly: that if they moved into the light too suddenly, without thinking, they would perish in flame. Then, while I watched, one of them, the small, black man, moved into the light and crossed the bandstand and started fooling around with his drums. Then—being funny and being, also, extremely ceremonious—Creole took Sonny by the arm and led him to the piano. A woman's voice called Sonny's name and a few hands started clapping. And Sonny, also being funny and being ceremonious, and so touched, I think, that he could have cried, but neither hiding it nor showing it, riding it like a man, grinned, and put both hands to his heart and bowed from the waist.

Creole then went to the bass fiddle and a lean, very bright-skinned brown man jumped up on the bandstand and picked up his horn. So there they were, and the atmosphere on the bandstand and in the room began to change and tighten. Someone stepped up to the microphone and announced them. Then there were all kinds of murmurs. Some people at the bar shushed others. The waitress ran around, frantically getting in the last orders, guys and chicks got closer to each other, and the lights on the bandstand, on the quartet, turned to a kind of indigo. Then they all looked different there. Creole looked about him for the last time, as though he were making certain that all his chickens were in the coop, and then he—jumped and struck the fiddle. And there they were.

All I know about music is that not many people ever really hear it. And even then, on the rare occasions when something opens within, and the music enters, what we mainly hear, or hear corroborated, are personal, private, vanishing evocations. But the man who creates the music is hearing something else, is dealing with the roar rising from the void and imposing order on it as it hits the air. What is evoked in him, then, is of another order, more terrible because it has no words, and triumphant, too, for that same reason. And his triumph, when he triumphs, is ours. I just watched Sonny's face. His face was troubled, he was working hard, but he wasn't with it. And I had the feeling that, in a way, everyone on the bandstand was waiting for him, both waiting for him and pushing him along. But as I began to watch Creole, I realized that it was Creole who held them all back. He had them on a short rein. Up there, keeping the beat with his whole body, wailing on the fiddle, with his eyes half closed, he was listening to everything, but he was listening to Sonny. He was having a dialogue with Sonny. He wanted Sonny to leave the shoreline and strike out for the deep water. He was Sonny's witness that deep water and drowning were not the same thing—he had been there, and he knew. And he wanted Sonny to know. He was waiting for Sonny to do the things on the keys which would let Creole know that Sonny was in the water.

And, while Creole listened, Sonny moved, deep within, exactly like someone in torment. I had never before thought of how awful the relationship must be between the musician and his instrument. He has to fill it, this instrument, with the breath of life, his own. He has to make it do what he wants it to do. And a piano is just a piano. It's made out of so much wood and wires and little hammers and big ones, and ivory. While there's only so much you can do with it, the only way to find this out is to try; to try and make it do everything.

And Sonny hadn't been near a piano for over a year. And he wasn't on much better terms with his life, not the life that stretched before him now. He and the piano stammered, started one way, got scared, stopped; started another way, panicked, marked time, started again; then seemed to have found a direction, panicked again, got stuck. And the face I saw on Sonny I'd never seen before. Everything had been burned out of it, and, at the same time, things usually hidden were being burned in, by the fire and fury of the battle which was occurring in him up there.

Yet, watching Creole's face as they neared the end of the first set, I had the feeling that something had happened, something I hadn't heard. Then they finished, there was scattered applause, and then, without an instant's warning, Creole started into something else, it was almost sardonic, it was "Am I Blue." And, as though he commanded, Sonny began to play. Something began to happen. And Creole let out the reins. The dry, low, black man said something awful on the drums, Creole answered, and the drums talked back. Then the horn insisted, sweet and high, slightly detached perhaps, and Creole listened, commenting now and then, dry, and driving, beautiful and calm and old. Then they all came together again, and Sonny was part of the family again. I could tell this from his face. He seemed to have found, right there beneath his fingers, a damn brand-new piano. It seemed that he couldn't get over it. Then, for awhile, just being happy with Sonny, they seemed to be agreeing with him that brand-new pianos certainly were a gas.

Then Creole stepped forward to remind them that what they were playing the blues. He hit something in all of them, he hit something in me, myself, and the music tightened and deepened, apprehension began to beat the air. Creole began to tell us what the blues were all about. They were not about anything very new. He and his boys up there were keeping it new, at the risk of ruin, destruction, madness, and death, in order to find new ways to make us listen. For, while the tale of how we suffer, and how we are delighted, and how we may triumph is never new, it always must be heard. There isn't any other tale to tell, it's the only light we've got in all this darkness.

And this tale, according to that face, that body, those strong hands on those strings, has another aspect in every country, and a new depth in every generation. Listen, Creole seemed to be saying, listen. Now these are Sonny's blues. He made the little black man on the drums know it, and the bright, brown man on the horn. Creole wasn't trying any longer to get Sonny in the water. He was wishing him Godspeed. Then he stepped back, very slowly, filling the air with the immense suggestion that Sonny speak for himself.

Then they all gathered around Sonny and Sonny played. Every now and again one of them seemed to say, amen. Sonny's fingers filled the air with life, his life. But that life contained so many others. And Sonny went all the way back, he really began with the spare, flat statement of the opening phrase of the song. Then he began to make it his. It was very beautiful because it wasn't hurried and it was no longer a lament. I seemed to hear with what burning he had made it his, with what burning we had yet to make it ours, how we could cease lamenting. Freedom lurked around us and I understood, at last, that he could help us to be free if we would listen, that he would never be free until we did. Yet, there was no battle in his face now. I heard what he had gone through, and would continue to go through until he came to rest in earth. He had made it his: that long line, of which we knew only Mama and Daddy. And he was giving it back, as everything must be given back, so that, passing through death, it can live forever. I saw my mother's face again, and felt, for the first time, how the stones of the road she had walked on must have bruised her feet. I saw the moonlit road where my father's brother died. And it brought something else back to me, and carried me past it. I saw my little girl again and felt Isabel's tears again, and I felt my own tears begin to rise. And I was yet aware that this was only a moment, that the world waited outside, as hungry as a tiger, and that trouble stretched above us, longer than the sky.

Then it was over. Creole and Sonny let out their breath, both soaking wet, and grinning. There was a lot of applause and some of it was real. In the dark, the girl came by and I asked her to take drinks to the bandstand. There was a long pause, while they talked up there in the indigo light and after awhile I saw the girl put a Scotch and milk on top of the piano for Sonny. He didn't seem to notice it, but just before they started playing again, he sipped from it and looked toward me, and nodded. Then he put it back on top of the piano. For me, then, as they began to play again, it glowed and shook above my brother's head like the very cup of trembling.

1. What effect is created by telling certain aspects of the story "out of sequence"? How would this be a different story if the events were simply told in chronological order?
2. Is there an epiphany in this story? Do any of the characters change in any way? If yes, explain how.

CHAPTER TEN

Recognizable People

Part 1: CREATING SURPRISING-YET-CONVINCING CHARACTERS

Getting Started

As we've said before, this book is mainly concerned with creative work that says something about the human condition—what we call character-based fiction and creative nonfiction. Characters are thus central to what we do every time we sit down and put pen to paper or begin typing on the keyboard. We want to create real people: characters that live and breathe and act in believable ways—and, most important, characters whom our readers will find worth caring about.

So, given that characters are so critical, how do we render compelling and believable characters on the page? This chapter is about just that: tips and techniques for creating characters that fulfill the dual requirement of being both surprising *and* convincing.

Character is so important to the kind of writing we're aspiring to accomplish that, really, *everything* is ultimately about character: showing and telling, dialogue, plot, concrete details . . . everything we've been discussing thus far in this book revolves around strong and compelling characters. This chapter therefore cannot hope to capture everything there is to say about characterization, but instead provides an overview of characterization that is backed up by each and every other chapter in this book.

We will start out by defining what a character is, then we will look at ways in which character is revealed, both directly and indirectly. You'll have a chance to do some exercises that help you define and reveal character. Finally, you'll get to read some pieces in which the characterization is particularly vivid and compelling.

Flat vs. Round Characters

When we pick up a book of fiction or creative nonfiction to read, one of the things we're most focused on (whether we realize it or not) is character. Yes, plot is important, and so are scene and narration, and point of view, and all the other things we've been discussing in this book, but whether the characters are compelling or not is really the bottom line. Consciously or subconsciously, we have our radar switched on in order to detect signs of life. After all, characters are supposed to be human beings (mostly—we'll leave writing about animals and science fiction out for now). They are people with physical features (red hair, size nine shoes), mental talents (good at math, terrible at French), and complex emotional attributes. They have histories, pasts, memories, hopes, and dreams. Even if all of this isn't made explicit in the piece itself, readers can *feel* the presence of a real, live, breathing character on the page. Nowhere else is Hemingway's famous iceberg theory more appropriate: with characters, only 10 percent of what the author knows about the character actually appears in the story or nonfiction piece—but if he or she doesn't know the other 90 percent, then that will be apparent to the reader: the character will appear lifeless, not believable, *flat* in someway.

The first thing we therefore need to define is the difference between flat and round characters. Flat characters are also called stereotypes, and the hallmark of flat characters is that they are incapable of surprising us; they act in a prescribed way, and are utterly consistent, without complexity. Thus the loving mother, the evil stepfather, the cruel boss, the happy prostitute—these are all examples of flat characters that lack the complexity and emotional depth of the real people we know.

A round character is the opposite of this: he or she is capable of *surprising* us—with unexpected fits of anger or an uplifting sense of humor or a snide remark about a presumed friend. But a round character also *convinces* us. As E. M. Forster says, if a character never surprises us, then he or she is flat; if they surprise but do not convince us, they are only flat pretending to be round.

An example of a fully rounded character is Gurov in Chekhov's "The Lady with the Little Dog" (pp. 284–98). Gurov surprises us because he is capable of falling in love with Anna; he tries, but finds he cannot just treat her as another run-of-the-mill affair. Let's read the passage where Gurov realizes he has actually fallen in love with the woman with whom he thought he was just going to have a brief vacation dalliance:

> Anna Sergeevna came in. She sat in the third row, and when Gurov looked at her, his heart was wrung, and he realized clearly that there was now no person closer, dearer, or more important for him in the whole world; this small woman, lost in the provincial crowd, not remarkable for anything, with a vulgar lorgnette in her hand, now filled his whole life, was his grief, his joy, the only happiness he now wished for himself; and to the sounds of the bad orchestra, with its trashy local violins, he thought how beautiful she was. He thought and dreamed.

Likewise, Connie, from "Where Are You Going, Where Have You Been?" (pp. 72–86), is a round character because she is capable—as selfish and ambivalent about her family as she is—of making a sacrifice on their behalf and going with Arnold Friend so he won't carry out his threat of hurting them. Here's the passage where she makes this sacrifice:

> She put out her hand against the screen. She watched herself push the door slowly open as if she were back safe somewhere in the other doorway, watching this body and this head of long hair moving out into the sunlight where Arnold Friend waited.

It sounds like having a flat character in your piece would be a bad thing, and indeed a piece of creative work would be dull and ultimately fail to succeed if all the characters were flat. To be accused of having flat characters is to be accused of having dull and predictable work—something no one wants to hear. Yet not all the characters—especially in a longer piece—need to be fully rounded. Sometimes the waiter needs to just bring the food to the table, not surprise us with his private joys and sorrows. Usually, however, we want our stories and nonfiction pieces to be populated by round characters.

Eschewing the General in Favor of the Particular

With characters as well as other aspects of creative writing, we always reject general statements in favor of ones that are particular and precise. Real people don't act in "general" ways. Although "in general" people attending funerals act sad or bereaved, and people attending weddings or christenings are generally happy, these things are not necessarily true of the *particular*. As Gustave Flaubert, writing to Guy de Maupassant, said:

When you pass a grocer seated at his shop door, a tailor smoking his pipe, a stand of hackney coaches, show me that grocer and that tailor, their attitude, their whole physical appearance, including also by a skillful description their whole moral nature, so that I cannot confound them with any other grocer or any other janitor; make me see, in one word, that a certain cab horse does not resemble the fifty others that follow or preceded it . . . there are not in the whole world two grains of sand, two specks, two hands, or two noses exactly alike.

Let's look at some examples of times that characters act in ways that are unique, and much more particular than what we'd expect if we thought of a "general" reaction to the prompting situations.

Milo heaved himself up from the sofa, ready for the drive back to New York. It is the same way he used to get off the sofa that last year he lived here. He would get up, dress for work, and not even go into the kitchen for breakfast—just sit, sometimes in his coat as he was sitting just now, and at the last minute he would push himself up and go out to the driveway, usually without a good-bye, and get in the car and drive off either very fast or very slowly. I liked it better when he made the tires spin in the gravel when he took off.

In this story, "The Cinderella Waltz" by Ann Beattie, we see the particular way that a man acts when his marriage is ending—and the very particular reaction of the narrator, the soon-to-be ex-wife (who would prefer that he show anger rather than this resigned, passive sadness). Contrast that with Andre Dubus's "A Father's Story," in which a man tries to keep the memories of his ex-wife and children alive in the house as long as possible:

There were no clothes or cosmetics, but potted plants endured my neglectful care as long as they could, and slowly died; I did not kill them on purpose, to exorcise the house of her, but I could not remember to water them. For weeks, because I did not use it much, the house was as neat as she had kept it, though dust layered the order she had made. The kitchen went first: I got the dishes in and out of the dishwasher and wiped the top of the stove, but did not return cooking spoons and pot holders to their hooks on the wall, and soon the burners and oven were caked with spillings, the refrigerator had more space and was spotted with juices. The living room and my bedroom went next; I did not go into the children's rooms except on bad nights when I went from room to room and looked and touched and smelled, so they did not lose their order until a year later when the kids came for six weeks.

And in another Ann Beattie story, "Find and Replace," we have the highly particular way that a woman acts (and decides to present herself to the world) upon the death of her husband. In her case, we also see her characterized by her possessions, especially what she wears:

> My mother's face was still quite pink. Shortly before my father's death, after she had a little skin cancer removed from above her lip, she went to the dermatologist for microdermabrasion. She was wearing the requisite hat with a wide brim and Ari Onassis sunglasses. She had on her uniform: shorts covered with a flap, so that it looked as if she were wearing a skirt, and a T-shirt embellished with sequins. Today's featured a lion with glittering black ears and, for all I knew, a correctly colored nose. Its eyes, which you might think would be sequins, were painted on. Blue.

In each of these cases, we don't see general or "expected" behavior in the situation in question; we see highly specific actions and thoughts that characterize these particular characters.

Consistency as the Hobgoblin of Characters

Once we understand about flat and round characters, it follows that one of the first things we have to say about characters is that *consistency* is not necessarily a virtue. True, we won't believe in a character whose behavior is all over the map, yet any character who fails to surprise us *at all* will also fail the test of being a believable, round character. Both are equally flawed in terms of characterization.

Think about it: Do you know of any living person who is completely consistent in his or her thoughts, words, and deeds? Who never strays from doing the expected, day after day after day? A person who is completely consistent is dead. A completely consistent character is flat.

What we are striving for, after all, is *complexity*. Human beings are indefinitely multifaceted, and behave in ways that are seemingly contradictory. A man may love his family very much, yet act in ways that put them in danger—or even harm them himself. A woman may value her job, yet continually put it in jeopardy by seemingly senseless self-destructive behaviors.

Often in a workshop there comes the phrase "not acting in character." The speaker of this phrase usually means it critically, as a bad thing, yet I've found that it can mean one of two things: either that the character is surprising the reader by something he or she is doing (which is good), or that the character is surprising us but not convincing us by that surprise (which is indeed a problem). If, for example, a seemingly hard-boiled, cynical man is suddenly capable of true love, we will invariably be surprised; whether we are convinced that this change is possible is up to the skill of the writer. A less sophisticated reader (and critic) will be troubled by the surprising behavior; a more sophisticated reader will take a moment to judge whether that surprising behavior has been convincingly rendered.

Ways of Defining Character

As with all other aspects of writing compelling fiction and nonfiction, you can create characterizations by either showing or telling, or (what is more likely) some combination of the two. As we've talked about in Chapter 6, neither is "correct"; effective characterization can be created either way. Here are the various ways that characters can be defined and revealed: as you'll see, some of these involve straight "telling" by narrators; others can be shown, or dramatized, in scenes; and others use a combination of both showing and telling.

1. **What the character looks like.** This is one of the most basic ways of introducing and defining character: through description of his or her physical characteristics via straight narrative. It is rare, although not unheard of, to create compelling characterization without *some* degree of narrative description of this type. This type of characterization method can also include descriptions of a character's *environment* as well as *possessions*.

> The doctor was a handsome, big-shouldered man with a tanned face. He wore a three-piece blue suit, a striped tie, and ivory cufflinks. His gray hair was combed along the sides of his head, and he looked as if he had just come from a concert.

Here, in "A Small, Good Thing" by Raymond Carver, we have a direct "telling" description of a doctor: not only what he looks like and what he is wearing, but also the aura about him; "he looked as if he had just come from a concert" is as revealing a phrase as the concrete details used to render his person on the page. Pretty straightforward.

> Aged and frail, Granny is three-quarters succumbed to the mortality the ache in her bones promises her and almost ready to give in entirely. A boy came out from the village to build up her hearth for the night an hour ago and the kitchen crackles with busy firelight. She has her Bible for company, she is a pious old woman. She is propped up on several pillows in the bed set into the wall peasant-fashion, wrapped up in the patchwork quilt she made before she was married, more years ago than she cares to remember. Two china spaniels with liver-colored blotches on their coats and black noses

sit on either side of the fireplace. There is a bright rug of woven rags on the pantiles. The grandfather clock ticks away her eroding time.

Here, in "The Company of Wolves" by Angela Carter, we get a portrait of a character (the granny in the traditional "Little Red Riding Hood" story) that is based more on her possessions than on a physical description of the woman herself, yet it is highly effective; we can see her in her bed, we know things about her from the objects she has surrounded herself with, and she becomes a living, breathing person by the end of this brief paragraph.

> A rarity for another reason—a librarian who did not look like one, who wore a Borsalino fedora, his a classic of thirty years, a Bogart raincoat, English boots John Major would covet, a black silk shirt, a vintage tie.
>
> Never as dashing as he wished to appear, however. Slight, short, and for several years now the bronze-color curls gone gray and the romantically drooping eyelids of his youth now faded flags at half mast.

In this story, "Who Is It Can Tell Me Who I Am?" by Gina Berriault, we get another physical description, but with added complexity because the narrator tells us that the character is aging—and aging unhappily—and the imagery mirrors this mournful reality.

2. What the character says. The words that come out of a character's mouth, in dialogue, are a very powerful means of characterization. Not only *what* a character says (the content), but also the *manner* in which he or she says it, is critical. This includes the vocabulary, syntax, use or misuse of words, and general diction as well as any gesture or emotionally charged way in which a character delivers a line of dialogue. The use of subtext—what *isn't* being said, or what is being avoided—is also a rich mining ground for characterization. We discussed all of these things in depth in Chapter 8, but here are some further examples:

> "I always wondered what a gold mine would look like when I saw it," Edna said, still laughing, wiping a tear from her eye.
>
> "Me too," I said. "I was always curious about it."
>
> "We're a couple of fools, aren't we, Earl? she said, unable to quit laughing completely. "We're two of a kind."
>
> "It might be a good sign, though," I said.
>
> "How could it be? It's not our gold mine. There aren't any drive-up windows." She was still laughing.
>
> "We've seen it," I said, pointing. "That's it right there. It may mean we're getting closer. Some people never see it at all."

"In a pig's eye, Earl," she said. "You and me see it in a pig's eye."
And she turned and got in the cab to go.

In this story, "Rock Springs" by Richard Ford, we learn about the characters not only through what they say, but how they say it. The use of gesture and particular speech syntax poignantly dramatizes the easy camaraderie that this doomed relationship possesses right before the end, and shows how the different ways they view their misfortune defines them as individual characters.

3. What the character does (how she or he acts). "Actions speak louder than words," goes the old adage, and this can be true in characterization as well as real life. How a character behaves, both alone and in response to actions from other characters, is a critical aspect of characterization. Let's look at some examples:

Wing Biddlebaum talked much with his hands. The slender expressive fingers, forever active, forever striving to conceal themselves in his pockets, behind his back, came forth and became the piston rods of his machinery of expression.

The story of Wing Biddlebaum is a story of hands. Their restless activity, like unto the beating of the wings of an imprisoned bird, had given him his name. Some obscure poet of the town had thought of it. The hands alarmed their owner. He wanted to keep them hidden away and looked with amazement at the quiet inexpressive hands of other men who worked beside him in the fields, or passed, driving sleepy teams on country roads.

In "Hands," by Sherwood Anderson, we get a sense of this man not only from the way he moves his hands, but from his reaction to the response his hands get from neighbors and townspeople. Then, in the following passage, from "Taking Care" by Joy Williams, we see how the tenderness and responsibility a man feels as he takes care of a baby paints a moving picture of a rich, compelling character:

Jones has the baby on his lap and he is feeding her. The evening meal is lengthy and complex. First he must give her vitamins, then, because she has a cold, a dropper of liquid aspirin. This is followed by a bottle of milk, eight ounces, and a portion of strained vegetables. He gives her a rest now so that the food can settle. On his hip, she rides through the rooms of the huge house as Jones turns lights off and on. He comes back to the table and gives her a little more milk, a half jar of strained chicken and a few spoonfuls of dessert, usually cobbler, buckle, or pudding. The baby enjoys all equally. She is good. She eats rapidly and neatly. Sometimes she grasps the spoon, turns it around and thrusts the wrong end into her mouth. Of course there is nothing that cannot be done incorrectly. Jones adores the baby.

Finally, in this next passage, from "In the Heart of the Heart of the Country" by William Gass, we get a description of a man through the eyes of his neighbor, characterized by the way he behaves as well as by his possessions:

From spring through fall, Billy collects coal and wood and puts the lumps and pieces in piles near his door, for keeping warm is his one work. I see him most often on mild days sitting on his doorsill in the sun. I notice he's squinting a little, which is perhaps the reason he doesn't cackle as I pass. His house is the size of a single garage and very old. It shed its paint with its youth and its boards are a warped and weathered gray. So is Billy. He wears a short lumpy faded black coat when it's cold, otherwise he always goes about in the same loose, grease-spotted shirt and trousers. I suspect his galoshes were yellow once, when they were new.

4. What the character thinks or feels. Depending on the point of view, you may be able to convey what your character thinks or feels directly on the page (as opposed to indirectly, through implication, by what he or she says or does). This can also be a very powerful tool for characterization, especially if a character speaks or acts in a way that is different from what he or she is really thinking or feeling.

How was she going to get everything fed?—that was her problem. The dogs had to be fed. There wasn't enough hay in the barn for the horses and the cow. If she didn't feed the chickens how could they lay eggs? Without eggs to sell how could she get things in town, things she had to have to keep the life of the farm going? Thank heaven, she did not have to feed her husband—in a certain way. That hadn't lasted long after their marriage and after the babies came. Where he went on his long trips she did not know. Sometimes he was gone from home for weeks, and after the boy grew up they went off together.

In this piece, "Death in the Woods" by Sherwood Anderson, the character's worries define her, and her thoughts betray her real feelings about her husband and family life.

She sat a long time with her coffee, waiting for minutes to pass, considering how many meals she and her mother ate alone. Similar times of day, hundreds of miles apart. Women by themselves. The last person Kate had eaten breakfast with had been someone she'd met in a bar. He was passing through town. He liked his fried eggs gelatinized in the center, only slightly runny, and Kate had studiously looked away as he ate. The night before he'd looked down from above her as he finished and she still moved under him. "You're still wanting," he'd said. "That's nice." Mornings now, Kate saw her own face in the mirror and was glad she'd forgotten his name. When she looked at her reflection from the side, she saw a faint etching of lines beside her mouth. She hadn't slept with anyone for five weeks, and the skin beneath her eyes had taken on a creamy darkness.

Here a woman's thoughts move swiftly from eating alone, to comparisons with her mother, to a memory of a one-night stand, to regrets and longing for intimacy. In this case, it's the association of ideas that provides a strong characterization in the story "Souvenir" by Jayne Anne Phillips.

On Sunday she is ready by four-thirty. She doesn't know what the afternoon holds; there are surely no places for "high tea"—a colonial tradition—in Cedar Falls, Iowa. If he takes her back to his place, it will mean he has invited other guests. From his voice she can tell Dr. Chatterji likes to do things correctly. She has dressed herself in a peach-colored nylon georgette sari, jade drop-earrings, and a necklace. The color is good on dark skin. She is not pretty, but she does her best. Working at it is a part of self-respect. In the mid-seventies, when American women felt rather strongly about such things, Maya had been in trouble with her women's group at Duke. She was too feminine. She had tried to explain the world she came out of. Her grandmother had been married off at the age of five in a village now in Bangladesh. Her great-aunt had been burned to death over a dowry problem. She herself had been trained to speak softly, arrange flowers, sing, be pliant. If she were to seduce Ted Suminski, she thinks as she waits in the front yard for Dr. Chatterji, it would be minor heroism. She has broken with the past. But.

In this story, "The Tenant" by Bharati Mukherjee, we get a woman's thoughts about a blind date she is about to go on, and (again) the association of her ideas as they follow one upon the other, is what matters. We get a sense of who she is from observing the way she looks, to recalling that she is not pretty but "does her best," to memories of being an undergraduate in a strange world that didn't understand her culture.

Character and Plot

As we discussed in Chapter 9, plot is simply those things that happen in order to bring about a certain effect, or final outcome. Character is a big part of plot, because things that happen are usually happening to characters. There are a number of ways that characters and plot intersect.

1. Character can take action (create a plot point by acting). This is the most obvious way that character and plot relate to each other: a character does something, and the story (or creative nonfiction piece) is one step closer to completion.

> I won't bore you with the details. The begging, the crawling over glass, the crying. Let's just say that after two weeks of this, of my driving out to her house, sending her letters, and calling her at all hours of the night, we put it back together. Didn't mean I ever ate with her family again or that her girl-friends were celebrating. Those *cabronas*, they were like, *No, jamas*, never. Even Magda wasn't too hot on the rapprochement at first, but I had the momentum of the past on my side. When she asked me, "Why don't you leave me alone?" I told her the truth: "It's because I love you, *mami*." I know this sounds like a load of doo-doo, but it's true: Magda's my heart. I didn't want her to leave me; I wasn't about to start looking for a girlfriend because I'd fucked up one lousy time.

In this story, "The Sun, the Moon, the Stars" by Junot Díaz, we see how the narrator's obsession with his girlfriend—and his obsessive personality generally—drive the plot forward. Likewise, in the following story, "The Rich Brother" by Tobias Wolff, the character Pete decides to take on a hitchhiker, which in turn triggers other events; in effect, his arrogance and sense of invincibility develop the story:

> Pete still had it in mind to brush him off, but he didn't do that. Instead he unlocked the door for him. He wanted to see what would happen. It was an adventure, but not a dangerous adventure. The man might steal Pete's ash-tray but he wouldn't kill him. If Pete got killed on the road it would be by some spiritual person in a sweatsuit, someone with his eyes on the far hori-zon and a wet Try God T-shirt in his duffel bag.
>
> As soon as they left the parking lot the man lit a cigar. He blew a cloud of smoke over Pete's shoulder and sighed with pleasure. "Put it out," Pete told him.
>
> "Of course," the man said. Pete looked into the rearview mirror and saw the man take another long puff before dropping the cigar out the window. "Forgive me," he said. "I should have asked. Name's Webster, by the way."

2. Character can be acted upon (by others, by God, by nature, etc.) and create further plot points by *reacting*. If characters can act, they can also be acted upon: things can happen to them independently of their own actions—and their reactions to those things can cause the plot to unfold even more.

I first met Malcolm at a party, a small dull awkward party after a recital at which he and one or two others had been performing. I was twenty at the time. The recital had not much interested me, as I do not care for music, and had gone through a sense of duty to my hostess who was teaching me Elizabethan literature and who had asked me during a tutorial if I would like tickets. Unable to say no, I had naturally said yes. The program consisted of music played on various ancient instruments such as viols and lutes and harpsichords, and I kept hoping that it was instructive, as it was certainly not enjoyable, or so I thought until Malcolm sang. The first song he sang did not impress me particularly—it was one of those Fa la la, Hey Nonny Nonny lyrics, and he sang it with rather a feeble plaintive charm as though he knew it balanced on the edge of foolishness. He had an interesting face, though not a noticeable one. I wouldn't have picked him out from a group of people to stare at, but singled out as he was by a solo performance and the surrounding dullness of the proceedings, he repaid attention. He had a thin, sensitive girl's face; fair, rather wavy hair, with a part and a forelock; he was small and slight and had a kind of pleasing intensity about him, a nervous energy, a performer's energy. Although he looked very young, it was indefinably clear that he was not as young as he looked and that he would continue to look the same for the next fifteen years.

In this excerpt from a novel, *The Waterfall* by Margaret Drabble, we get the narrator reacting to meeting her future husband at a recital, and her rather passive attraction to him drives the plot forward. In the following extract from, "The Rudy Elmenhurst Story" by Julia Alvarez, the character's reaction to a romantic overture by a fellow student causes the plot to unfold further:

That night there was a knock on my door. I was in my nightgown already, doing our assignment, a love poem in the form of a sonnet. I'd been reading it out loud pretty dramatically, trying to get the accents right, so I felt embarrassed to be caught. I asked who it was. I didn't recognize the name. Rudy? "The guy who borrowed your pencil," the voice said through the closed door. Strange, I thought, ten-thirty at night. I hadn't yet caught on to some of the strategies. "Did I wake you up?" he wanted to know when I opened the door. "No, no," I said, laughing apologetically. This guy I had sworn never to talk to after he had embarrassed me in class, but my politeness training ran on automatic. I excused myself for not asking him in. "I'm doing my homework." That wasn't an excuse in the circles he ran in. We stood at the door for a long moment, he looking over my shoulder into my room for an invitation. "I just came to return your pencil." He held it out, a small red stub in his palm. "Just to return that?" I said, calling his bluff. He grinned, dimples making parentheses at the corners of his lips as if his smile were a secret between us. "Yeah," he said, and again he had that intent look in his eye, and again he looked over my shoulder. I picked the pencil out of his palm and was glad it had been sharpened to a stub so he couldn't see my name in gold letters inscribed on the side. "Thank you," I said, shifting my weight on my feet and touching the doorknob, little moves, polite preliminaries to closing the door.

3. Character can remember things (flashbacks). One very rich source of characterization-driven plotting can be found in flashbacks, giving the reader information about what is traditionally called "backstory," or the past of the story. Flashbacks are very important to plot—which, you remember, is those events *arranged in the proper order the writer thinks best*, not necessarily chronological order. In the following passage, from Stephen Dixon's novel *Interstate*, this character has a flashback while driving that leads to him taking significant action later in the plot:

Driving home, thinking of his mother and him when he was little more than a baby, a photo. First only his mother for a moment. Doesn't know where the thought came from or why the picture popped in. But suddenly—forgets what he was thinking of just before her, probably nothing much of anything—there was her face and neck and open-collar top of the summer dress she was wearing in the photo and then the whole photo, backdrop and concrete ground and crossed knees included, her shoes and his bare feet, even the white border or frame or outline with the notched or jagged edges or whatever one calls them when they're by design kind of frayed, the style for years then, which he knows has a name because he recently read it in an article on photography but forgets or never recorded it in his head. Something he saw on the road set off the thought?

4. Character can imagine things. An often unremarked-upon aspect of plot is that plot points can be created by a character's imagining of things: either a fantasy, a daydream, a dream, or a projection.

He began to imagine various unlikely ways by which he could teach her a lesson. He might make friends with some distinguished Negro professor or lawyer and bring him home to spend the evening. He would be entirely justified but her blood pressure would rise to 300 . . . He imagined his mother lying desperately ill and his being able to secure only a Negro doctor for her. He toyed with that idea for a few minutes and then dropped it for a momentary vision of himself participating as a sympathizer in a sit-in demonstration. This was possible but he did not linger with it. Instead he approached the ultimate horror. He brought home a beautiful suspiciously Negroid woman. Prepare yourself, he said. There is nothing you can do about it. This is the woman I've chosen. She's intelligent, dignified, even good, and she's suffered and she hasn't thought it *fun*. No persecute us, go ahead and persecute us. Drive her out of here, but remember you're driving me too. His eyes were narrowed and through the indignation he had generated, he saw his mother across the aisle, purple-faced, shrunken to the dwarf-like proportions of her moral nature, sitting like a mummy beneath the ridiculous banner of her hat.

In this story, "Everything That Rises Must Converge" by Flannery O'Connor, the son's fantasies boil his thoughts into a cauldron of ill will that causes him to treat his mother even worse than he had been doing previously—and also prepare him (and the reader) for what is coming at the end of the story.

Wants and Needs

Everyone needs things: food, water, shelter. And everyone wants things: love, money, friendship, material possessions. Many writers believe that a key determinant of a good characterization is the depiction of what the character wants and needs (two different things). Indeed, you could say that this is the basis of all characterization: what a character desires is what drives him or her to act (or react, or not act), and therefore what determines the heart of a story or nonfiction piece.

Here are some examples of characters who urgently *desire* something. In the first passage, from *The Joy Luck Club* by Amy Tan, it's as simple as a young girl desperately wanting a good present from a grab bag:

> Having watched the older children opening their gifts, I already knew that the big gifts were not necessarily the nicest ones. One girl my age got a large coloring book of biblical characters, while a less greedy girl who selected a smaller box received a glass vial of lavender toilet water. The sound of the box was also important. A ten-year-old boy had chosen a box that jangled when he shook it. It was a tin globe of the world with a slit for inserting money. He must have thought it was full of dimes and nickels, because when he saw that it had just ten pennies, his face fell with such undisguised disappointment that his mother slapped the side of his head and led him out of the hall, apologizing to the crowd for her son who had such bad manners he couldn't appreciate such a fine gift.
>
> As I peered into the sack, I quickly fingered the remaining presents, testing their weight, imagining what they contained. I chose a heavy compact one that was wrapped in shiny silver foil and a red satin ribbon. It was a

twelve-pack of Life Savers and I spent the rest of the party arranging and rearranging the candy tubes in the order of my favorites.

In the following story, "Friendly Skies" by T. Coraghessan Boyle, the main character is so frightened by what is happening aboard the aircraft that all she wants is to reach safe ground again. This need for safety drives her actions for the rest of the story.

> She was so frightened that she could only nod, her head filled with the sucking dull hiss of the air jets and the static of the speakers. The man leaned across her and squinted through the gray aperture of the window to the wing beyond. "Fuck, that's all we need. There's no way I'm going to make my connection now."
>
> She didn't understand. Connection? Didn't he realize they were going to die?
>
> She braced herself and murmured a prayer. Voices rose in alarm. Her eyes felt as if they were going to implode in their sockets. But then the flames flickered and dimmed, and she felt the plane lifted up as if in the palm of some celestial hand, and for all the panic, the dimly remembered prayers, the cries and shouts, and the sudden potent reek of urine, the crisis was over almost as soon as it had begun. "I hate to do this to you, folks," the captain drawled, "but it looks like we're going to have to turn around and take her back to LAX."

Finally, in the famous story "The Metamorphosis," by Franz Kafka, we have Gregor, who has mysteriously turned into a giant cockroach, wanting, above all things, not to be a burden to his family. His obsequiousness prevails throughout the story.

> It was late at night when the light finally went out in the living room, and now it was easy for Gregor to tell that his parents and his sister had stayed up so long, since, as he could distinctly hear, all three were now retiring on tiptoes. Certainly no one would come in to Gregor until the morning; and so he had ample time to consider undisturbed how best to rearrange his life. But the empty high-ceilinged room in which he was forced to lie flat on the floor made him nervous, without his being able to tell why—since it was, after all, the room in which he had lived for the past five years—and turning half unconsciously and not without a slight feeling of shame, he scuttled under the couch where, although his back was a little crushed and he could not raise his head any more, he immediately felt very comfortable and was only sorry that his body was too wide to go completely under the couch.
>
> There he stayed the whole night, which he spent partly in a sleepy trance, from which hunger pangs kept waking him with a start, partly in worries and vague hopes, all of which, however, led to the conclusion that for the

time being he would have to lie low and, by being patient and showing his family every possible consideration, help them bear the inconvenience which he simply had to cause them in his present condition.

Characters in Relationships

How characters behave and think and feel when in a relationship with other characters is a key point of characterization. Often, a character will think and act (and speak) differently depending on who else is around. Think of the way you behave when you're around your friends vs. your parents, or your teacher (if you're in school). You talk differently, you act differently, you may even think and feel differently (a reprimand from a social peer feels different from one from a boss, for example).

Here are some examples of character revealed through interaction with others.

> His heart, that bloody motor, is equally old and will not do certain jobs anymore. It still floods his head with brainy light. But it won't let his legs carry the weight of his body around the house. Despite my metaphors, this muscle failure is not due to his old heart, he says, but to a potassium short-age. Sitting on one pillow, leaning on three, he offers last-minute advice and makes a request.
>
> [from "A Conversation With My Father" by Grace Paley]

We feel the affection between the father and daughter (the daughter is describing the father in this first-person story), also his need to be med-ically precise about things that the narrator (a writer) uses language to describe.

> "Please feel the doorknob," I said. She did so without the slightest hesita-tion and this was a lovely gesture on her part, a thing that made me wish to rise up and embrace her, though I was very tired and did not move.
>
> [from "A Good Scent from a Distant Mountain" by Robert Olen Butler]

Again, we get a sense of the affection between the two characters (also a father and a daughter, only this time it is the father who is the narrator), as well as a sense of how tired the aged narrator feels.

> Anna was not in lilac, as Kitty had so urgently wished, but in a black, low-cut velvet gown, showing her full throat and shoulders, that looked as though they were carved in old ivory, and her rounded arms, with tiny, slen-der wrists. The whole gown was trimmed with Venetian guipure. On her head, among her black hair—her own, with no false additions—was a little wreath of pansies, and a bouquet of the same in the black ribbon of her sash

among white lace. Her coiffure was not striking. All that was noticeable was the little willful tendrils of her curly hair that would always break free about her neck and temples.

Kitty had been seeing Anna every day; she adored her, and had pictured her invariably in lilac. But now seeing her in black, she felt she had not fully seen Anna's charm. She saw her now as someone quite new and surprising, now she understood that Anna could not have been in lilac.

Anna turned with a soft smile of protection toward Kitty. With a flying glance, and a movement of her head, hardly perceptible, but understood by Kitty, she signified approval of Kitty's dress and looks. "You came into the room dancing," Anna said.

In this except from *Anna Karenina* by Leo Tolstoy, we see the protective nature of the relationship that the older woman feels for the younger, and the admiration bordering on adoration that the younger woman feels for the older.

When he had to get up to go to the bathroom he moved like a ninety-year-old. He couldn't stand straight, but was all bent out of shape, and shuffled. I helped him put on clean clothes. When he lay down on the bed again, a sound of pain came out of him, like tearing thick paper. I went around the room putting things away. He asked me to come sit by him and said I was going to drown him if I went on crying. "You'll submerge the entire North American continent," he said. I can't remember what he said, but he made me laugh finally. It is hard to remember things Simon says, and hard not to laugh when he says them. This is not merely the partiality of affection: He makes everybody laugh. I doubt that he intends to. It is just that a mathematician's mind works differently from other people's. Then when they laugh, that pleases him.

[from "The New Atlantis" by Ursula K. Le Guin]

Here we get a sense of the affection that the well man has for the sick man, how deeply he is pained by the illness, and his sense of impending loss.

Character in Creative Nonfiction

The same techniques apply to developing and revealing character in nonfiction as in fiction. Here are some examples:

Henry Wideman was a short, thick, dark man whose mahogany color passed onto Daddy, blended with the light, bright skin of John and Freeda French's daughter Bette to produce the brown we were. Do you remember anything about him, or were you too young? Have you ever wondered how the city appeared through his eyes, the eyes of a rural black boy far from

- Fine-tipped pen
- Cell phone
- Discount coupon for Jiffy Lube
- Torn half of a movie ticket for a porno movie
- Program for an art gallery opening

Exercise 2: Sins of Commission, Sins of Omission

Goal: To learn more about your character by a) finding out what "sins" he or she has committed while simultaneously b) discovering what he or she thinks is a sin.

What to do: 1. Choose a character, and fix him/her in your mind.
2. Write down two lists: one of the sins of omission (the things he/she didn't do) and one of the sins of commission (what he/she *did* do) that are on his/her conscience.

The following passage was written in response to the exercise prompt by James Hanafee:

Sins of Omission

- Didn't acknowledge distress in sister's voice when I called her last Sunday. Pretended the dog was peeing on the carpet and that I needed to hang up when it seemed as though she was about to say something serious.
- Didn't smile at my son when he showed me the family portrait he'd drawn because my bald spot was so prominently displayed.
- Didn't thank wife for making dinner even though it was my turn to cook because no one else has a "meal schedule" posted on their refrigerator.
- Didn't cancel the brunch reservations for twelve people at Emilio's, even though we had decided not to go a week previously.
- Didn't clean the dead insects out of the kids' pool before daughter swam.

Sins of Commission

- Left the Sunday *New York Times* in disarray even though my husband hadn't read it yet.
- Speeded up and refused to let elderly man merge into my lane on 101, even though he was signaling correctly.
- Put together the broken TV remote control in such a way that the next person who picked it up would think they broke it.
- Threw away neighbor's mail that was put in our mailbox by accident.

- Ate a handful of red flame seedless grapes while shopping at Whole Foods without paying for them.
- Made sarcastic comments throughout the broadcast of the season finale of *Star Trek Voyager*, even though it was the highlight of retired father's week.

Exercise 3: Seven or Eight Things I Know about Him/Her

Goal: To "slant" at a character by coming up with small, odd details from his/her life.

What to do: 1. Read "7 or 8 Things I Know About Her" by Michael Ondaatje (below).
2. Fix a character in your mind.
3. Write seven or eight brief "facts" about that character, his/her family, his/her surroundings—but try to avoid the sorts of things that you would include in a traditional biography. You can parallel the headings found in the original prose poem, if you like.

7 or 8 Things I Know about Her—A Stolen Biography

MICHAEL ONDAATJE

The Father's Guns

After her father died they found nine guns in the house. Two in his clothing drawers, one under the bed, one in the glove compartment of the car, etc. Her brother took their mother out onto the prairie with a revolver and taught her to shoot.

The Bird

For a while in Topeka parrots were very popular. Her father was given one in lieu of a payment and kept it with him at all times because it was the fashion. It swung above him in the law office and drove back with him in the car at night. At parties friends would bring their parrots and make them perform what they had been taught: the first line from *Twelfth Night*, a bit of Italian opera, cowboy songs, or a surprisingly good rendition of Russ Colombo singing "Prisoner of Love." Her father's parrot could only imitate the office typewriter, along with the *ching* at the end of each line. Later it broke its neck crashing into a bookcase.

The Bread

Four miles out of Topeka on the highway—the largest electric billboard in the state of Kansas. The envy of all Missouri. It advertised bread and the electrical image of a knife cut slice after slice. These curled off endlessly. "Meet you at the bread," "See you at the loaf," were common phrases. Aroused couples would park there under the stars on the open night prairie. Virtue was lost, "kissed all over by every boy in Wichita." Poets, the inevitable visiting writers, were taken to see it, and it hummed over the seductions in cars, over the nightmares of girls in bed. Slice after slice fell towards the earth. A feeding of the multitude in this parched land on the way to Dorrance, Kansas.

First Criticism

She is two weeks old, her mother takes her for a drive. At the gas station the mechanic is cleaning the windshield and watches them through the glass. Wiping his hands he puts his head in the side window and says, "Excuse me for saying this but I know what I'm talking about—that child has a heart condition."

Listening In

Overhear her in the bathroom, talking to a bug: "I don't want you on me, honey." 8 a.m.

Self-Criticism

"For a while there was something about me that had a dubious quality. Dogs would not take meat out of my hand. The town bully kept handcuffing me to trees."

Fantasies

Always one fantasy. To be traveling down the street and a man in a clean white suit (the detail of "clean" impresses me) leaps into her path holding flowers and sings to her while an invisible orchestra accompanies his solo. All her life she has waited for this, and it never happens.

Reprise

In 1956 the electric billboard in Kansas caught fire and smoke plumed into a wild sunset. Bread on fire, broken glass. Birds flew towards it above the cars that circled round to watch. And last night, past midnight, her excited phone call. Her hometown is having a marathon to benefit the symphony. She pays $4 to participate. A tuxedoed gentleman begins the race with a clash of cymbals and she takes off. Along the route at frequent intervals are quartets who play for her. When they stop for water a violinist performs a solo. So here she comes. And there I go, stepping forward in my white suit, with a song in my heart.

The following was written by Jenna Philpott:

Her mother's cans

After she died, they found, in the basement of her mother's house, thousands of cans, carefully stripped of their paper labels and washed and dried, stacked neatly in shining towers up to six feet high.

The cat

Since all the other members of her family were extremely allergic to animal fur, the only pet she could have as a child was a turtle. The turtles kept dying but since they all looked alike her parents secretly replaced them in the middle of the night so she had a single, long-aged turtle from the age of seven to seventeen, when she left for school.

The bridge

There was a bridge that led over a small inlet of the Bay, and a coming-of-age ritual for all graduating seniors in high school was to jump off the bridge en masse the day before graduation day. It was a town event; the bridge was unofficially closed off (strangers who came by were politely asked to wait or go around the peninsula) and everyone stood on the banks of the inlet to cheer them on. She was horribly frightened, and if someone hadn't pushed her off she would not have had to nerve to do it.

First criticism

Her father, watching her playing with a small stuffed rabbit, holding it up to her face and rubbing it against it and laughing, said, "That child is going to be terribly lonely."

Listening in

"Are you nuts, you?" overheard in the car as she looked at herself in the rearview mirror.

Self-criticism

"When I was young I didn't know how to dance. All the other children loved to jump up and down to the music, but I didn't know how, so I always hid behind my parents until the music stopped. I learned to hate music early and associate it with humiliation."

Fantasies

Just one fantasy: To walk into a classroom on the day of an examination and to sit down calmly, and in control and know that she will excel.

Part 3: READING AS A WRITER

Surrounded by Sleep

AKHIL SHARMA

One August afternoon, when Ajay was ten years old, his elder brother, Aman, dove into a pool and struck his head on the cement bottom. For three minutes, he lay there unconscious. Two boys continued to swim, kicking and splashing, until finally Aman was spotted below them. Water had entered through his nose and mouth. It had filled his stomach. His lungs collapsed. By the time he was pulled out, he could no longer think, talk, chew, or roll over in his sleep.

Ajay's family had moved from India to Queens, New York, two years earlier. The accident occurred during the boys' summer vacation, on a visit with their aunt and uncle in Arlington, Virginia. After the accident, Ajay's mother came to Arlington, where she waited to see if Aman would recover. At the hospital, she told the doctors and nurses that her son had been accepted into the Bronx High School of Science, in the hope that by highlighting his intelligence she would move them to make a greater effort on his behalf. Within a few weeks of the accident, the insurance company said that Aman should be transferred to a less expensive care facility, a long-term one. But only a few of these were any good, and those were full, and Ajay's mother refused to move Aman until a space opened in one of them. So she remained in Arlington, and Ajay stayed too, and his father visited from Queens on the weekends when he wasn't working. Ajay was enrolled at the local public school and in September he started fifth grade.

Before the accident, Ajay had never prayed much. In India, he and his brother used to go with their mother to the temple every Tuesday night, but that was mostly because there was a good *dosa* restaurant nearby. In America, his family went to a temple only on important holy days and birthdays. But shortly after Ajay's mother came to Arlington, she moved into the room that he and his brother had shared during the summer and made an altar in a corner. She threw an old flowered sheet over a cardboard box that had once held a television. On top she put a clay lamp, an incense-stick holder, and postcards depicting various gods. There was also a postcard of Mahatma Gandhi. She explained to Ajay that God could take any form; the picture of Mahatma Gandhi was there because he had appeared to her in a dream after the accident and told her that Aman would recover and become a surgeon. Now she and Ajay prayed for at least half an hour before the altar every morning and night.

At first she prayed with absolute humility. "Whatever you do will be good because you are doing it," she murmured to the postcards of Ram and Shivaji, daubing their lips with water and rice. Mahatma Gandhi got only water, because he did not like to eat. As weeks passed and Aman did not recover in time to return to the Bronx High School of Science for the first day of classes, his mother began doing things that called attention to her piety. She sometimes held the prayer lamp until it blistered her palms. Instead of kneeling before the altar, she lay face down. She fasted twice a week. Her attempts to sway God were not so different from Ajay's performing somersaults to amuse his aunt, and they made God seem human to Ajay.

One morning as Ajay knelt before the altar, he traced an Om, a crucifix, and a Star of David into the pile of the carpet. Beneath these he traced an S, for Superman, inside an upside-down triangle. His mother came up beside him.

"What are you praying for?" she asked. She had her hat on, a thick gray knitted one that a man might wear. The tracings went against the weave of the carpet and were darker than the surrounding nap. Pretending to examine them, Ajay leaned forward and put his hand over the S. His mother did not mind the Christian and Jewish symbols—they were for commonly recognized gods, after all—but she could not tolerate his praying to Superman. She'd caught him doing so once several weeks earlier and had become very angry, as if Ajay's faith in Superman made her faith in Ram ridiculous. "Right in front of God," she had said several times.

Ajay, in his nervousness, spoke the truth. "I'm asking God to give me a hundred percent on the math test."

His mother was silent for a moment. "What if God says you can have the math grade but then Aman will have to be sick a little while longer?" she asked.

Ajay kept quiet. He could hear cars on the road outside. He knew that his mother wanted to bewail her misfortune before God so that God would feel guilty. He looked at the postcard of Mahatma Gandhi. It was a black-and-white photo of him walking down a city street with an enormous crowd trailing behind him. Ajay thought of how, before the accident, Aman had been so modest that he would not leave the bathroom until he was fully dressed. Now he had rashes on his penis from the catheter that drew his urine into a translucent bag hanging from the guardrail of his bed.

His mother asked again, "Would you say, 'Let him be sick a little while longer'?"

"Are you going to tell me the story about Uncle Naveen again?" he asked.

"Why shouldn't I? When I was sick, as a girl, your uncle walked seven times around the temple and asked God to let him fail his exams just as long as I got better."

"If I failed the math test and told you that story, you'd slap me and ask what one has to do with the other."

His mother turned to the altar. "What sort of sons did you give me, God?" she asked. "One you drown, the other is this selfish fool."

"I will fast today so that God puts some sense in me," Ajay said, glancing away from the altar and up at his mother. He liked the drama of fasting.

"No, you are a growing boy." His mother knelt down beside him and said to the altar, "He is stupid, but he has a good heart."

Prayer, Ajay thought, should appeal with humility and an open heart to some greater force. But the praying that he and his mother did felt sly and confused. By treating God as someone to bargain with, it seemed to him, they prayed as if they were casting a spell.

This meant that it was possible to do away with the presence of God entirely. For example, Ajay's mother had recently asked a relative in India to drive a nail into a holy tree and tie a saffron thread to the nail on Aman's behalf. Ajay invented his own ritual. On his way to school each morning, he passed a thick tree rooted half on the sidewalk and half on the road. One day Ajay got the idea that if he circled the tree seven times, touching the north side every other time, he would have a lucky day. From then on he did it every morning, although he felt embarrassed and always looked around beforehand to make sure no one was watching.

One night Ajay asked God whether he minded being prayed to only in need.

"You think of your toe only when you stub it," God replied. God looked like Clark Kent. He wore a gray cardigan, slacks, and thick glasses, and had a forelock that curled just as Ajay's did.

God and Ajay had begun talking occasionally after Aman drowned. Now they talked most nights while Ajay lay in bed and waited for sleep. God sat at the foot of Ajay's mattress. His mother's mattress lay parallel to his, a few feet away. Originally God had appeared to Ajay as Krishna, but Ajay had felt foolish discussing brain damage with a blue god who held a flute and wore a dhoti.

"You're not angry with me for touching the tree and all that?"

"No. I'm flexible."

"I respect you. The tree is just a way of praying to you," Ajay assured God.

God laughed. "I am not too caught up in formalities."

Ajay was quiet. He was convinced that he had been marked as special by Aman's accident. The beginnings of all heroes are distinguished by misfortune. Superman and Batman were both orphans. Krishna was separated from his parents at birth. The god Ram had to spend fourteen years in a forest. Ajay waited to speak until it would not appear improper to begin talking about himself.

"How famous will I be?" he asked finally.

"I can't tell you the future," God answered.

Ajay asked, "Why not?"

"Even if I told you something, later I might change my mind."

"But it might be harder to change your mind after you have said something will happen."

God laughed again. "You'll be so famous that fame will be a problem."

Ajay sighed. His mother snorted and rolled over.

"I want Aman's drowning to lead to something," he said to God.

"He won't be forgotten."

"I can't just be famous, though. I need to be rich too, to take care of Mummy and Daddy and pay Aman's hospital bills."

"You are always practical." God had a soulful and pitying voice, and God's sympathy made Ajay imagine himself as a truly tragic figure, like Amitabh Bachchan in the movie *Trishul*.

"I have responsibilities," Ajay said. He was so excited at the thought of his possible greatness that he knew he would have difficulty sleeping. Perhaps he would have to go read in the bathroom.

"You can hardly imagine the life ahead," God said.

Even though God's tone promised greatness, the idea of the future frightened Ajay. He opened his eyes. There was light coming from the street. The room was cold and had a smell of must and incense. His aunt and uncle's house was a narrow two-story home next to a four-lane road. The apartment building with the pool where Aman had drowned was a few blocks up the road, one in a cluster of tall brick buildings with stucco fronts. Ajay pulled the blanket tighter around him. In India, he could not have imagined the reality of his life in America: the thick smell of meat in the school cafeteria, the many television channels. And, of course, he could not have imagined Aman's accident, or the hospital where he spent so much time.

The hospital was boring. Vinod, Ajay's cousin, picked him up after school and dropped him off there almost every day. Vinod was twenty-two. In addition to attending county college and studying computer programming, he worked at a 7-Eleven near Ajay's school. He often brought Ajay hot chocolate and a comic from the store, which had to be returned, so Ajay was not allowed to open it until he had wiped his hands.

Vinod usually asked him a riddle on the way to the hospital "Why are manhole covers round?" It took Ajay half the ride to admit that he did not know. He was having difficulty talking. He didn't know why. The only time he could talk easily was when he was with God. The explanation he gave himself for this was that just as he couldn't chew when there was too much in his mouth he couldn't talk when there were too many thoughts in his head.

When Ajay got to Aman's room, he greeted him as if he were all right. "Hello, lazy. How much longer are you going to sleep?" His mother was always there. She got up and hugged Ajay. She asked how school had been, and he didn't know what to say. In music class, the teacher sang a song about a sailor who had bared his breast before jumping into the sea. This had caused the other students to giggle. But Ajay could not say the word *breast* to his mother without blushing. He had also cried. He'd been thinking of how Aman's accident had made his own life mysterious and confused. What would happen next? Would Aman die or would he go on as he was? Where would they live? Usually when Ajay cried in school, he was told to go outside. But it had been raining, and the teacher had sent him into the hallway. He sat on the floor and wept. Any mention of this would upset his mother. And so he said nothing had happened that day.

Sometimes when Ajay arrived his mother was on the phone, telling his father that she missed him and was expecting to see him on Friday. His father took a Greyhound bus most Fridays from Queens to Arlington, returning on Sunday night in time to work the next day. He was a bookkeeper for a department store. Before the accident, Ajay had thought of his parents as the same person: MummyDaddy. Now, when he saw his father praying stiffly or when his father failed to say hello to Aman in his hospital bed, Ajay sensed that his mother and father were quite different people. After his mother got off the phone, she always went to the cafeteria to get coffee for herself and Jell-O or cookies for him. He knew that if she took her coat with her, it meant that she was especially sad. Instead of going directly to the cafeteria, she was going to go outside and walk around the hospital parking lot.

That day, while she was gone, Ajay stood beside the hospital bed and balanced a comic book on Aman's chest. He read to him very slowly. Before turning each page, he said, "Okay, Aman?"

Aman was fourteen. He was thin and had curly hair. Immediately after the accident, there had been so many machines around his bed that only one person could stand beside him at a time. Now there was just a single waxy yellow tube. One end of this went into his abdomen; the other, blocked by a green bullet-shaped plug, was what his Isocal milk was poured through. When not being used, the tube was rolled up and bound by a rubber band and tucked beneath Aman's hospital gown. But even with the tube hidden, it was obvious that there was something wrong with Aman. It was in his stillness and his open eyes. Once, in their house in Queens, Ajay had left a plastic bowl on a radiator overnight and the sides had drooped and sagged so that the bowl looked a little like an eye. Aman reminded Ajay of that bowl.

Ajay had not gone with his brother to the swimming pool on the day of the accident, because he had been reading a book and wanted to finish it. But he heard the ambulance siren from his aunt and uncle's house. The pool was only a few minutes away, and when he got there a crowd had gathered around the ambulance. Ajay saw his uncle first, in shorts and an undershirt, talking to a man inside the ambulance. His aunt was standing beside him. Then Ajay saw Aman on a stretcher, in blue shorts with a plastic mask over his nose and mouth. His aunt hurried over to take Ajay home. He cried as they walked, although he had been certain that Aman would be fine in a few days: in a Spider-Man comic he had just read, Aunt May had fallen into a coma and she had woken up perfectly fine. Ajay had cried simply because he felt crying was called for by the seriousness of the occasion. Perhaps this moment would mark the beginning of his future greatness. From that day on, Ajay found it hard to cry in front of his family. Whenever tears started coming, he felt like a liar. If he loved his brother, he knew, he would not have thought about himself as the ambulance had pulled away, nor would he talk with God at night about becoming famous.

When Ajay's mother returned to Aman's room with coffee and cookies, she sometimes talked to Ajay about Aman. She told him that when Aman was six he had seen a children's television show that had a character named Chunu, which was Aman's nickname, and he had thought the show was based on his own life. But most days Ajay went into the lounge to read. There was a TV in the corner and a lamp near a window that looked out over a parking lot. It was the perfect place to read. Ajay liked fantasy novels where the hero, who was preferably under the age of twenty-five, had an undiscovered talent that made him famous when it was revealed. He could read for hours without interruption, and sometimes when Vinod came to drive Ajay and his mother home from the hospital it was hard for him to remember the details of the real day that had passed.

One evening when he was in the lounge, he saw a rock star being interviewed on *Entertainment Tonight*. The musician, dressed in a sleeveless undershirt that revealed a swarm of tattoos on his arms and shoulders, had begun to shout at the audience, over his interviewer, "Don't watch me! Live your life! I'm not you!" Filled with a sudden desire to do something, Ajay hurried out of the television lounge and stood on the sidewalk in front of the hospital entrance. But he did not know what to do. It was cold and dark and there was an enormous moon. Cars leaving the parking lot stopped one by one at the edge of the road. Ajay watched as they waited for an opening in the traffic, their brake lights glowing.

"Are things getting worse?" Ajay asked God. The weekend before had been Thanksgiving. Christmas soon would come, and a new year would start, a year during which Aman would not have talked or walked. Suddenly Ajay understood hopelessness. Hopelessness felt very much like fear. It involved a clutching in the stomach and a numbness in the arms and legs.

"What do you think?" God answered.

"They seem to be."

"At least Aman's hospital hasn't forced him out."

"At least Aman isn't dead. At least Daddy's Greyhound bus has never skidded off a bridge." Lately Ajay had begun talking much more quickly to God than he used to. Before, when he had talked to God, Ajay would think of what God would say in response before he said anything. Now Ajay spoke without knowing how God might respond.

"You shouldn't be angry at me." God sighed. God was wearing his usual cardigan. "You can't understand why I do what I do."

"You should explain better, then."

"Christ was my son. I loved Job. How long did Ram have to live in a forest?"

"What does that have to do with me?" This was usually the cue for discussing Ajay's prospects. But hopelessness made the future feel even more frightening than the present.

"I can't tell you what the connection is, but you'll be proud of yourself."
They were silent for a while.

"Do you love me truly?" Ajay asked.

"Yes."

"Will you make Aman normal?" As soon as Ajay asked the question, God ceased to be real. Ajay knew then that he was alone, lying under his blankets, his face exposed to the cold dark.

"I can't tell you the future," God said softly. These were words that Ajay already knew.

"Just get rid of the minutes when Aman lay on the bottom of the pool. What are three minutes to you?"

"Presidents die in less time than that. Planes crash in less time than that."

Ajay opened his eyes. His mother was on her side and she had a blanket pulled up to her neck. She looked like an ordinary woman. It surprised him that you couldn't tell, looking at her, that she had a son who was brain-dead.

In fact, things were getting worse. Putting away his mother's mattress and his own in a closet in the morning, getting up very early so he could use the bathroom before his aunt or uncle did, spending so many hours in the hospital—all this had given Ajay the reassuring sense that real life was in abeyance, and that what was happening was unreal. He and his mother and brother were just waiting to make a long-delayed bus trip. The bus would come eventually to carry them to Queens, where he would return to school at P.S. 20 and to Sunday afternoons spent at the Hindi movie theater under the trestle for the 7 train. But now Ajay was starting to understand that the world was always real, whether you were reading a book or sleeping, and that it eroded you every day.

He saw the evidence of this erosion in his mother, who had grown severe and unforgiving. Usually when Vinod brought her and Ajay home from the hospital, she had dinner with the rest of the family. After his mother helped his aunt wash the dishes, the two women watched theological action movies. One night, in spite of a headache that had made her sit with her eyes closed all afternoon, she ate dinner, washed dishes, sat down in front of the TV. As soon as the movie was over, she went upstairs, vomited, and lay on her mattress with a wet towel over her forehead. She asked Ajay to massage her neck and shoulders. As he did so, Ajay noticed that she was crying. The tears frightened Ajay and made him angry, "You shouldn't have watched TV," he said accusingly.

"I have to," she said. "People will cry with you once, and they will cry with you a second time. But if you cry a third time, people will say you are boring and always crying."

Ajay did not want to believe what she had said, but her cynicism made him think that she must have had conversations with his aunt and uncle that he did not know about. "That's not true," he told her, massaging her scalp. "Uncle is kind. Auntie Aruna is always kind."

"What do you know?" She shook her head, freeing herself from Ajay's fingers. She stared at him. Upside down, her face looked unfamiliar and terrifying. "If God lets Aman live long enough, you will become a stranger too. You will say, 'I have been unhappy for so long because of Aman, now I don't want to talk about him or look at him.' Don't think I don't know you," she said.

Suddenly Ajay hated himself. To hate himself was to see himself as the opposite of everything he wanted to be: short instead of tall, fat instead of thin. When he brushed his teeth that night, he looked at his face: his chin was round and fat as a heel. His nose was so broad that he had once been able to fit a small rock in one nostril.

His father was also being eroded. Before the accident, Ajay's father loved jokes—he could do perfect imitations—and Ajay had felt lucky to have him as a father. (Once, Ajay's father had convinced his own mother that he was possessed by the ghost of a British man.) And even after the accident, his father had impressed Ajay with the patient loyalty of his weekly bus journeys. But now his father was different.

One Saturday afternoon, as Ajay and his father were returning from the hospital, his father slowed the car without warning and turned into the dirt parking lot of a bar that looked as though it had originally been a small house. It had a pitched roof with a black tarp. At the edge of the lot stood a tall neon sign of an orange hand lifting a mug of sudsy golden beer. Ajay had never seen anybody drink except in the movies. He wondered whether his father was going to ask for directions to somewhere, and if so, to where.

His father said, "One minute," and they climbed out of the car.

They went up wooden steps into the bar. Inside, it was dark and smelled of cigarette smoke and something stale and sweet. The floor was linoleum like the kitchen at his aunt and uncle's. There was a bar with stools around it, and a basketball game played on a television bolted against the ceiling, like the one in Aman's hospital room.

His father stood by the bar waiting for the bartender to notice him. His father had a round face and was wearing a white shirt and dark dress pants, as he often did on the weekend, since it was more economical to have the same clothes for the office and home.

The bartender came over. "How much for a Budweiser?" his father asked.

It was a dollar fifty. "Can I buy a single cigarette?" He did not have to buy; the bartender would just give him one. His father helped Ajay up onto a stool and sat down himself. Ajay looked around and wondered what would happen if somebody started a knife fight. When his father had drunk half his beer, he carefully lit the cigarette. The bartender was standing at the end of the bar. There were only two other men in the place. Ajay was disappointed that there were no women wearing dresses slit all the way up their thighs. Perhaps they came in the evenings.

His father asked him if he had ever watched a basketball game all the way through.

"I've seen the Harlem Globetrotters."

His father smiled and took a sip. "I've heard they don't play other teams, because they can defeat everyone else so easily."

"They only play against each other, unless there is an emergency—like in the cartoon, when they play against the aliens to save the Earth," Ajay said.

"Aliens?"

Ajay blushed as he realized his father was teasing him.

When they left, the light outside felt too bright. As his father opened the car door for Ajay, he said, "I'm sorry." That's when Ajay first felt that his father might have done something wrong. The thought made him worry. Once they were on the road, his father said gently, "Don't tell your mother."

Fear made Ajay feel cruel. He asked his father, "What do you think about when you think of Aman?"

Instead of becoming sad, Ajay's father smiled. "I am surprised by how strong he is. It's not easy for him to keep living. But even before, he was strong. When he was interviewing for high school scholarships, one interviewer asked him, 'Are you a thinker or a doer?' He laughed and said, 'That's like asking, "Are you an idiot or a moron?"' "

From then on they often stopped at the bar on the way back from the hospital. Ajay's father always asked the bartender for a cigarette before he sat down, and during the ride home he always reminded Ajay not to tell his mother.

Ajay found that he himself was changing. His superstitions were becoming extreme. Now when he walked around the good-luck tree he punched it, every other time, hard, so that his knuckles hurt. Afterward, he would hold his breath for a moment longer than he thought he could bear, and ask God to give the unused breaths to Aman.

In December, a place opened in one of the good long-term care facilities. It was in New Jersey. This meant that Ajay and his mother could move back to New York and live with his father again. This was the news Ajay's father brought when he arrived for a two-week holiday at Christmas.

Ajay felt the clarity of panic. Life would be the same as before the accident but also unimaginably different. He would return to P.S. 20, while Aman continued to be fed through a tube in his abdomen. Life would be Aman's getting older and growing taller than their parents but having less consciousness than even a dog, which can become excited or afraid.

Ajay decided to use his devotion to shame God into fixing Aman. The fact that two religions regarded the coming December days as holy ones suggested to Ajay that prayers during this time would be especially potent. So he prayed whenever he thought of it—at his locker, even in the middle of a quiz. His mother wouldn't let him fast, but he started throwing away the lunch he took to school. And when his mother prayed in the morning, Ajay watched to make sure that she bowed at least once toward each of the postcards of deities. If she did not, he bowed three times to the possibly offended god on the postcard. He had noticed that his father finished his prayers in less time than it took to brush his teeth. And so now, when his father began praying in the morning, Ajay immediately crouched down beside him, because he knew his father would be embarrassed to get up first. But Ajay found it harder and harder to drift into the rhythm of sung prayers or into his nightly conversations with God. How could chanting and burning incense undo three minutes of a sunny August afternoon? It was like trying to move a sheet of blank paper from one end of a table to the other by blinking so fast that you started a breeze.

On Christmas Eve his mother asked the hospital chaplain to come to Aman's room and pray with them. The family knelt together beside Aman's bed. Afterward the chaplain asked her whether she would be attending Christmas services. "Of course, Father," she said.

"I'm also coming," Ajay said.

The chaplain turned toward Ajay's father, who was sitting in a wheelchair because there was nowhere else to sit.

"I'll wait for God at home," he said.

That night, Ajay watched *It's a Wonderful Life* on television. To him, the movie meant that happiness arrived late, if ever. Later, when he got in bed and closed his eyes, God appeared. There was little to say.

"Will Aman be better in the morning?"

"No."

"Why not?"

"When you prayed for the math exam, you could have asked for Aman to get better, and instead of your getting an A, Aman would have woken."

This was so ridiculous that Ajay opened his eyes. His father was sleeping nearby on folded-up blankets. Ajay felt disappointed at not feeling guilt. Guilt might have contained some hope that God existed.

When Ajay arrived at the hospital with his father and mother the next morning, Aman was asleep, breathing through his mouth while a nurse poured a can of Isocal into his stomach through the yellow tube. Ajay had not expected that Aman would have recovered; nevertheless, seeing him that way put a weight in Ajay's chest.

The Christmas prayers were held in a large, mostly empty room: people in chairs sat next to people in wheelchairs. His father walked out in the middle of the service.

Later, Ajay sat in a corner of Aman's room and watched his parents. His mother was reading a Hindi women's magazine to Aman while she shelled peanuts into her lap. His father was reading a thick red book in preparation for a civil service exam. The day wore on. The sky outside grew dark. At some point Ajay began to cry. He tried to be quiet. He did not want his parents to notice his tears and think that he was crying for Aman, because in reality he was crying for how difficult his own life was.

His father noticed first. "What's the matter, hero?"

His mother shouted, "What happened?" and she sounded so alarmed it was as if Ajay were bleeding.

"I didn't get any Christmas presents. I need a Christmas present," Ajay shouted. "You didn't buy me a Christmas present." And then, because he had revealed his own selfishness, Ajay let himself sob. "You have to give me something. I should get something for all this." Ajay clenched his hands and wiped his face with his fists. "Each time I come here I should get something."

His mother pulled him up and pressed him into her stomach. His father came and stood beside them. "What do you want?" his father asked.

Ajay had no prepared answer for this.

"What do you want?" his mother repeated.

The only thing he could think was "I want to eat pizza and I want candy."

His mother stroked his hair and called him her little baby. She kept wiping his face with a fold of her sari. When at last he stopped crying, they decided that Ajay's father should take him back to his aunt and uncle's. On the way, they stopped at a mini-mall. It was a little after five, and the streetlights were on. Ajay and his father did not take off their winter coats as they ate, in a pizzeria staffed by Chinese people. While he chewed, Ajay closed his eyes and tried to imagine God looking like Clark Kent, wearing a cardigan and eyeglasses, but he could not. Afterward, Ajay and his father went next door to a magazine shop and Ajay got a bag of Three Musketeers bars and a bag of Reese's peanut butter cups, and then he was tired and ready for home.

He held the candy in his lap while his father drove in silence. Even through the plastic, he could smell the sugar and chocolate. Some of the houses outside were dark, and others were outlined in Christmas lights.

After a while Ajay rolled down the window slightly. The car filled with wind. They passed the building where Aman's accident had occurred. Ajay had not walked past it since the accident. When they drove by, he usually looked away. Now he tried to spot the fenced swimming pool at the building's side. He wondered whether the pool that had pressed itself into Aman's mouth and lungs and stomach had been drained, so that nobody would be touched by its unlucky waters. Probably it had not been emptied until fall. All summer long, people must have swum in the pool and sat on its sides, splashing their feet in the water, and not known that his brother had lain for three minutes on its concrete bottom one August afternoon.

1. How does the author characterize Ajay, the main character?
2. What techniques does he use to define the relationships between the characters? How does he make those relationships both surprising and convincing?
3. What picture emerges of the culture of these characters?

No Name Woman

MAXINE HONG KINGSTON

"You must not tell anyone," my mother said, "what I am about to tell you. In China your father had a sister who killed herself. She jumped into the family well. We say that your father has all brothers because it is as if she had never been born.

"In 1924 just a few days after our village celebrated seventeen hurry-up weddings—to make sure that every young man who went 'out on the road' would responsibly come home—your father and his brothers and your grandfather and his brothers and your aunt's new husband sailed for America, the Gold Mountain. It was your grandfather's last trip. Those lucky enough to get contracts waved goodbye from the decks. They fed and guarded the stowaways and helped them off in Cuba, New York, Bali, Hawaii. 'We'll meet in California next year,' they said. All of them sent money home.

"I remember looking at your aunt one day when she and I were dressing; I had not noticed before that she had such a protruding melon of a stomach. But I did not think, 'She's pregnant,' until she began to look like other pregnant women, her shirt pulling and the white tops of her black pants showing. She could not have been pregnant, you see, because her husband had been gone for years. No one said anything. We did not discuss it. In early summer she was ready to have the child, long after the time when it could have been possible.

"The village had also been counting. On the night the baby was to be born the villagers raided our house. Some were crying. Like a great saw, teeth strung with lights, files of people walked zigzag across our land, tearing the rice. Their lanterns doubled in the disturbed black water, which drained away through the broken bunds. As the villagers closed in, we could see that some of them, probably men and women we knew well, wore white masks. The people with long hair hung it over their faces. Women with short hair made it stand up on end. Some had tied white bands around their foreheads, arms, and legs.

"At first they threw mud and rocks at the house. Then they threw eggs and began slaughtering our stock. We could hear the animals scream their deaths—the roosters, the pigs, a last great roar from the ox. Familiar wild heads flared in our night windows; the villagers encircled us. Some of the faces stopped to peer at us, their eyes rushing like searchlights. The hands flattened against the panes, framed heads, and left red prints.

"The villagers broke in the front and the back doors at the same time, even though we had not locked the doors against them. Their knives dripped with the blood of our animals. They smeared blood on the doors and walls. One woman swung a chicken, whose throat she had slit, splattering blood in red arcs about her. We stood together in the middle of our house, in the family hall with the pictures and tables of the ancestors around us, and looked straight ahead.

"At that time the house had only two wings. When the men came back, we would build two more to enclose our courtyard and a third one to begin a second courtyard. The villagers pushed through both wings, even your grandparents' rooms, to find your aunt's, which was also mine until the men returned. From this room a new wing for one of the younger families would grow. They ripped up her clothes and shoes and broke her combs, grinding them underfoot. They tore her work from the loom. They scattered the cooking fire and rolled the new weaving in it. We could hear them in the kitchen breaking our bowls and banging the pots. They overturned the great waist-high earthenware jugs; duck eggs, pickled fruits, vegetables burst out and mixed in acrid torrents. The old woman from the next field swept a broom through the air and loosed the spirits-of-the-broom over our heads. 'Pig.' 'Ghost.' 'Pig,' they sobbed and scolded while they ruined our house.

"When they left, they took sugar and oranges to bless themselves. They cut pieces from the dead animals. Some of them took bowls that were not broken and clothes that were not torn. Afterward we swept up the rice and sewed it back up into sacks. But the smells from the spilled preserves lasted. Your aunt gave birth in the pigsty that night. The next morning when I went for the water, I found her and the baby plugging up the family well.

"Don't let your father know that I told you. He denies her. Now that you have started to menstruate, what happened to her could happen to you. Don't humiliate us. You wouldn't like to be forgotten as if you had never been born. The villagers are watchful."

Whenever she had to warn us about life, my mother told stories that ran like this one, a story to grow up on. She tested our strength to establish realities. Those in the emigrant generations who could not reassert brute survival died young and far from home. Those of us in the first American generations have had to figure out how the invisible world the emigrants built around our childhoods fits in solid America.

The emigrants confused the gods by diverting their curses, misleading them with crooked streets and false names. They must try to confuse their offspring as well, who, I suppose, threaten them in similar ways—always trying to get things straight, always trying to name the unspeakable. The Chinese I know hide their names; sojourners take new names when their lives change and guard their real names with silence.

Chinese-Americans, when you try to understand what things in you are Chinese, how do you separate what is peculiar to childhood, to poverty, insanities, one family, your mother who marked your growing with stories, from what is Chinese? What is Chinese tradition and what is the movies?

If I want to learn what clothes my aunt wore, whether flashy or ordinary, I would have to begin, "Remember Father's drowned-in-the-well sister?" I cannot ask that. My mother has told me once and for all the useful parts. She will add nothing unless powered by Necessity, a riverbank that guides her life. She plants vegetable gardens rather than lawns; she carries the odd-shaped tomatoes home from the fields and eats food left for the gods.

Whenever we did frivolous things, we used up energy; we flew high kites. We children came up off the ground over the melting cones our parents brought home from work and the American movie on New Year's Day—*Oh, You Beautiful Doll* with Betty Grable one year, and *She Wore a Yellow Ribbon* with John Wayne another year. After the one carnival ride each, we paid in guilt; our tired father counted his change on the dark walk home.

Adultery is extravagance. Could people who hatch their own chicks and eat the embryos and the heads for delicacies and boil the feet in vinegar for party food, leaving only the gravel, eating even the gizzard lining—could such people engender a prodigal aunt? To be a woman, to have a daughter in starvation time was a waste enough. My aunt could not have been the lone romantic who gave up everything for sex. Women in the old China did not choose. Some man had commanded her to lie with him and be his secret evil. I wonder whether he masked himself when he joined the raid on her family.

Perhaps she had encountered him in the fields or on the mountain where the daughters-in-law collected fuel. Or perhaps he first noticed her in the marketplace. He was not a stranger because the village housed no strangers. She had to have dealings with him other than sex. Perhaps he worked an adjoining field, or he sold her the cloth for the dress she sewed and wore. His demand must have surprised, then terrified her. She obeyed him; she always did as she was told.

When the family found a young man in the next village to be her husband, she had stood tractably beside the best rooster, his proxy, and promised before they met that she would be his forever. She was lucky that he was her age and she would be the first wife, an advantage secure now. The night she first saw him, he had sex with her. Then he left for America. She had almost forgotten what he looked like. When she tried to envision him, she only saw the black and white face in the group photograph the men had had taken before leaving.

The other man was not, after all, much different from her husband. They both gave orders: she followed. "If you tell your family, I'll beat you. I'll kill you. Be here again next week." No one talked sex, ever. And she might have separated the rapes from the rest of living if only she did not have to buy her oil from him or gather wood in the same forest. I want her fear to have lasted just as long as rape lasted so that the fear could have been contained. No drawn-out fear. But women at sex hazarded birth and hence lifetimes. The fear did not stop but permeated everywhere. She told the man, "I think I'm pregnant." He organized the raid against her.

On nights when my mother and father talked about their life back home, sometimes they mentioned an "outcast table" whose business they still seemed to be settling, their voices tight. In a commensal tradition, where food is precious, the powerful older people made wrongdoers eat alone. Instead of letting them start separate new lives like the Japanese, who could become samurais and geishas, the Chinese family, faces averted but eyes glowering sideways, hung on to the offenders and fed them leftovers. My aunt must have lived in the same house as my parents and eaten at an outcast table. My mother spoke about the raid as if she had seen it, when she and my aunt, a daughter-in-law to a different household, should not have been living together at all. Daughters-in-law lived with their husbands' parents, not their own; a synonym for marriage in Chinese is "taking a daughter-in-law." Her husband's parents could have sold her, mortgaged her, stoned her. But they had sent her back to her own mother and father, a mysterious act hinting at disgraces not told me. Perhaps they had thrown her out to deflect the avengers.

She was the only daughter; her four brothers went with her father, husband, and uncles "out on the road" and for some years became western men. When the goods were divided among the family, three of the brothers took land, and the youngest, my father, chose an education. After my grandparents gave their daughter away to her husband's family, they had dispensed all the adventure and all the property. They expected her alone to keep the traditional ways, which her brothers, now among the barbarians, could fumble without detection. The heavy, deep-rooted women were to maintain the past against the flood, safe for returning. But the rare urge west had fixed upon our family, and so my aunt crossed boundaries not delineated in space.

The work of preservation demands that the feelings playing about in one's guts not be turned into action. Just watch their passing like cherry blossoms. But perhaps my aunt, my forerunner, caught in a slow life, let dreams grow and fade and after some months or years went toward what persisted. Fear at the enormities of the forbidden kept her desires delicate, wire and bone. She looked at a man because she liked the way the hair was tucked behind his ears, or she liked the question-mark line of a long torso curving at the shoulder and straight at the hip. For warm eyes or a soft voice or a slow walk—that's all—a few hairs, a line, a brightness, a sound, a pace, she gave up family. She offered us up for a charm that vanished with tiredness, a pigtail that didn't toss when the wind died. Why, the wrong lighting could erase the dearest thing about him.

It could very well have been, however, that my aunt did not take subtle enjoyment of her friend, but, a wild woman, kept rollicking company. Imagining her free with sex doesn't fit, though. I don't know any women like that, or men either. Unless I see her life branching into mine, she gives me no ancestral help.

To sustain her being in love, she often worked at herself in the mirror, guessing at the colors and shapes that would interest him, changing them frequently in order to hit on the right combination. She wanted him to look back.

On a farm near the sea, a woman who tended her appearance reaped a reputation for eccentricity. All the married women blunt-cut their hair in flaps about their ears or pulled it back in tight buns. No nonsense. Neither style blew easily into heart-catching tangles. And at their weddings they displayed themselves in their long hair for the last time. "It brushed the backs of my knees," my mother tells me. "It was braided, and even so, it brushed the backs of my knees."

At the mirror my aunt combed individuality into her bob. A bun could have been contrived to escape into black streamers blowing in the wind or in quiet wisps about her face, but only the older women in our picture album wear buns. She brushed her hair back from her forehead, tucking the flaps behind her ears. She looped a piece of thread, knotted into a circle between her index fingers and thumbs, and ran the double strand across her forehead. When she closed her fingers as if she were making a pair of shadow geese bite, the string twisted together catching the little hairs. Then she pulled the thread away from her skin, ripping the hairs out neatly, her eyes watering from the needles of pain. Opening her fingers, she cleaned the thread, then rolled it along her hairline and the tops of her eyebrows. My mother did the same to me and my sisters and herself. I used to believe that the expression "caught by the short hairs" meant a captive held with a depilatory string. It especially hurt at the temples, but my mother said we were lucky we didn't have to have our feet bound when we were seven. Sisters used to sit on their beds and cry together, she said, as their mothers or their slaves removed the bandages for a few minutes each night and let the blood gush back into their veins. I hope that the man my aunt loved appreciated a smooth brow, that he wasn't just a tits-and-ass man.

Once my aunt found a freckle on her chin, at a spot that the almanac said predestined her for unhappiness. She dug it out with a hot needle and washed the wound with peroxide.

More attention to her looks than these pullings of hairs and pickings at spots would have caused gossip among the villagers. They owned work clothes and good clothes, and they wore good clothes for feasting the new seasons. But since a woman combing her hair hexes beginnings, my aunt rarely found an occasion to look her best. Women looked like great sea snails—the corded wood, babies, and laundry they carried were the whorls on their backs. The Chinese did not admire a bent back; goddesses and warriors stood straight. Still there must have been a marvelous freeing of beauty when a worker laid down her burden and stretched and arched.

Such commonplace loveliness, however, was not enough for my aunt. She dreamed of a lover for the fifteen days of New Year's, the time for families to exchange visits, money, and food. She plied her secret comb. And sure enough she cursed the year, the family, the village, and herself.

Even as her hair lured her imminent lover, many other men looked at her. Uncles, cousins, nephews, brothers would have looked, too, had they been home between journeys. Perhaps they had already been restraining their curiosity, and they left, fearful that their glances, like a field of nesting birds, might be startled and caught. Poverty hurt, and that was their first reason for leaving. But another, final reason for leaving the crowded house was the never-said.

She may have been unusually beloved, the precious only daughter, spoiled and mirror gazing because of the affection the family lavished on her. When her husband left, they welcomed the chance to take her back from the in-laws; she could live like the little daughter for just a while longer. There are stories that my grandfather was different from other people, "crazy ever since the little Jap bayoneted him in the head." He used to put his naked penis on the dinner table, laughing. And one day he brought home a baby girl, wrapped up inside his brown western-style greatcoat. He had traded one of his sons, probably my father, the youngest, for her. My grandmother made him trade back. When he finally got a daughter of his own, he doted on her. They must have all loved her, except perhaps my father, the only brother who never went back to China, having once been traded for a girl.

Brothers and sisters, newly men and women, had to efface their sexual color and present plain miens. Disturbing hair and eyes, a smile like no other, threatened the ideal of five generations living under one roof. To focus blurs, people shouted face to face and yelled from room to room. The immigrants I know have loud voices, unmodulated to American tones even after years away from the village where they called their friendships out across the fields. I have not been able to stop my mother's screams in public libraries or over telephones. Walking erect (knees straight, toes pointed forward, not pigeon-toed, which is Chinese-feminine) and speaking in an inaudible voice, I have tried to turn myself American-feminine. Chinese communication was loud, public. Only sick people had to whisper. But at the dinner table, where the family members came nearest one another, no one could talk, not the outcasts nor any eaters. Every word that falls from the mouth is a coin lost. Silently they gave and accepted food with both hands. A preoccupied child who took his bowl with one hand got a sideways glare. A complete moment of total attention is due everyone alike. Children and lovers have no singularity here, but my aunt used a secret voice, a separate attentiveness.

She kept the man's name to herself throughout her labor and dying; she did not accuse him that he be punished with her. To save her inseminator's name she gave silent birth.

He may have been somebody in her own household, but intercourse with a man outside the family would have been no less abhorrent. All the village were kinsmen, and the titles shouted in loud country voices never let kinship be forgotten. Any man within visiting distance would have been neutralized as a lover—"brother," "younger brother," "older brother"—one hundred and fifteen relationship titles. Parents researched birth charts probably not so much to assure good fortune as to circumvent incest in a population that has but one hundred surnames. Everybody has eight million relatives. How useless then sexual mannerisms, how dangerous.

As if it came from an atavism deeper than fear, I used to add "brother" silently to boys' names. It hexed the boys, who would or would not ask me to dance, and made them less scary and as familiar and deserving of benevolence as girls.

But, of course, I hexed myself also—no dates. I should have stood up, both arms waving, and shouted out across libraries, "Hey, you! Love me back." I had no idea, though, how to make attraction selective, how to control its direction and magnitude. If I made myself American-pretty so that the five or six Chinese boys in the class fell in love with me, everyone else—the Caucasian, Negro, and Japanese boys—would too. Sisterliness, dignified and honorable, made much more sense.

Attraction eludes control so stubbornly that whole societies designed to organize relationships among people cannot keep order, not even when they bind people to one another from childhood and raise them together.

Among the very poor and the wealthy, brothers married their adopted sisters, like doves. Our family allowed some romance, paying adult brides' prices and providing dowries so that their sons and daughters could marry strangers. Marriage promises to turn strangers into friendly relatives—a nation of siblings.

In the village structure, spirits shimmered among the live creatures, balanced and held in equilibrium by time and land. But one human being flaring up into violence could open up a black hole, a maelstrom that pulled in the sky. The frightened villagers, who depended on one another to maintain the real, went to my aunt to show her a personal, physical representation of the break she had made in the "roundness." Misallying couples snapped off the future, which was to be embodied in true offspring. The villagers punished her for acting as if she could have a private life, secret and apart from them.

If my aunt had betrayed the family at a time of large grain yields and peace, when many boys were born, and wings were being built on many houses, perhaps she might have escaped such severe punishment. But the men—hungry, greedy, tired of planting in dry soil—had been forced to leave the village in order to send food-money home. There were ghost plagues, bandit plagues, wars with the Japanese, floods. My Chinese brother and sister had died of an unknown sickness. Adultery, perhaps only a mistake during good times, became a crime when the village needed food.

The round moon cakes and round doorways, the round tables of graduated sizes that fit one roundness inside another, round windows and rice bowls—these talismans had lost their power to warn this family of the law: a family must be whole, faithfully keeping the descent line by having sons to feed the old and the dead, who in turn look after the family. The villagers came to show my aunt and her lover-in-hiding a broken house. The villagers were speeding up the circling of events because she was too shortsighted to see that her infidelity had already harmed the village, that waves of consequences would return unpredictably, sometimes in disguise, as now, to hurt her. This roundness had to be made coin-sized so that she would see its circumference: punish her at the birth of her baby. Awaken her to the inexorable. People who refused fatalism because they could invent small resources insisted on culpability. Deny accidents and wrest fault from the stars.

After the villagers left, their lanterns now scattering in various directions toward home, the family broke their silence and cursed her. "Aiaa, we're going to die. Death is coming. Death is coming. Look what you've done. You've killed us. Ghost! Dead ghost! Ghost! You've never been born." She ran out into the fields, far enough from the house so that she could no longer hear their voices, and pressed herself against the earth, her own land no more. When she felt the birth coming, she thought that she had been hurt. Her body seized together. "They've hurt me too much," she thought. "This is gall, and it will kill me." With forehead and knees against the earth, her body convulsed and then relaxed. She turned on her back, lay on the ground. The black well of sky and stars went out and out and out forever; her body and her complexity seemed to disappear. She was one of the stars, a bright dot in blackness, without home, without a companion, in eternal cold and silence. An agoraphobia rose in her, speeding higher and higher, bigger and bigger; she would not be able to contain it; there would be no end to fear.

Flayed, unprotected against space, she felt pain return, focusing her body. This pain chilled her—a cold, steady kind of surface pain. Inside, spasmodically, the other pain, the pain of the child, heated her. For hours she lay on the ground, alternately body and space. Sometimes a vision of normal comfort obliterated reality: she saw the family in the evening gambling at the dinner table, the young people massaging their elders' backs. She saw them congratulating one another, high joy on the mornings the rice shoots came up. When these pictures burst, the stars drew yet further apart. Black space opened.

She got to her feet to fight better and remembered that old-fashioned women gave birth in their pigsties to fool the jealous, pain-dealing gods, who do not snatch piglets. Before the next spasms could stop her, she ran to the pigsty, each step a rushing out into emptiness. She climbed over the fence and knelt in the dirt. It was good to have a fence enclosing her, a tribal person alone.

Laboring, this woman who had carried her child as a foreign growth that sickened her every day, expelled it at last. She reached down to touch the hot, wet, moving mass, surely smaller than anything human, and could feel that it was human after all—fingers, toes, nails, nose. She pulled it up on to her belly, and it lay curled there, butt in the air, feet precisely tucked one under the other. She opened her loose shirt and buttoned the child inside. After resting, it squirmed and thrashed and she pushed it up to her breast. It turned its head this way and that until it found her nipple. There, it made little snuffling noises. She clenched her teeth at its preciousness, lovely as a young calf, a piglet, a little dog.

She may have gone to the pigsty as a last act of responsibility: she would protect this child as she had protected its father. It would look after her soul, leaving supplies on her grave. But how would this tiny child without family find her grave when there would be no marker for her anywhere, neither in the earth nor the family hall? No one would give her a family hall name. She had taken the child with her into the wastes. At its birth the two of them had felt the same raw pain of separation, a wound that only the family pressing tight could close. A child with no descent line would not soften her life but only trail after her, ghostlike, begging her to give it purpose. At dawn the villagers on their way to the fields would stand around the fence and look.

Full of milk, the little ghost slept. When it awoke, she hardened her breasts against the milk that crying loosens. Toward morning she picked up the baby and walked to the well.

Carrying the baby to the well shows loving. Otherwise abandon it. Turn its face into the mud. Mothers who love their children take them along. It was probably a girl; there is some hope of forgiveness for boys.

"Don't tell anyone you had an aunt. Your father does not want to hear her name. She has never been born." I have believed that sex was unspeakable and words so strong and fathers so frail that "aunt" would do my father mysterious harm. I have thought that my family, having settled among immigrants who had also been their neighbors in the ancestral land, needed to clean their name, and a wrong word would incite the kinspeople even here. But there is more to this silence: they want me to participate in her punishment. And I have.

In the twenty years since I heard this story I have not asked for details nor said my aunt's name; I do not know it. People who can comfort the dead can also chase after them to hurt them further—a reverse ancestor worship. The real punishment was not the raid swiftly inflicted by the villagers, but the family's deliberately forgetting her. Her betrayal so maddened them, they saw to it that she would suffer forever, even after death. Always hungry, always needing, she would have to beg food from other ghosts, snatch and steal it from those whose living descendants give them gifts. She would have to fight the ghosts massed at crossroads for the buns a few thoughtful citizens leave to decoy her away from village and home so that the ancestral spirits could feast unharassed. At peace, they could act like gods, not ghosts, their descent lines providing them with paper suits and dresses, spirit money, paper houses, paper automobiles, chicken, meat, and rice into eternity—essences delivered up in smoke and flames, steam and incense rising from each rice bowl. In an attempt to make the Chinese care for people outside the family, Chairman Mao encourages us now to give our paper replicas to the spirits of outstanding soldiers and workers, no matter whose ancestors they may be. My aunt remains forever hungry. Goods are not distributed evenly among the dead.

My aunt haunts me—her ghost drawn to me because now, after fifty years of neglect, I alone devote pages of paper to her, though not origamied into houses and clothes. I do not think she always means me well. I am telling on her, and she was a spite suicide, drowning herself in the drinking water. The Chinese are always very frightened of the drowned one, whose weeping ghost, wet hair hanging and skin bloated, waits silently by the water to pull down a substitute.

1. What techniques does the author use to define the character of the aunt for us?
2. How do we simultaneously get a picture of the narrator as she describes the aunt?
3. What picture emerges of an entire culture from this character study?

CHAPTER ELEVEN

Raising the Curtain

Part 1: BEGINNING YOUR STORY, NOVEL, OR NONFICTION PIECE

Getting Started

"A bad beginning makes for a bad ending," wrote Euripides, and indeed few things are as critical as knowing when to raise the curtain on your story, novel, or nonfiction piece. If you start too early, you might bore your readers with a lot of unnecessary history or "backstory"; if you start too late, you might rob your readers of valuable context.

In this chapter we will first talk about what a good opening must accomplish; we'll talk about your "contract" with your reader, and how to make sure that any promises you make (implicit or explicit) are delivered upon. We'll look at a number of openings of pieces and talk about what makes them praiseworthy. And we'll show you some time-honored techniques for opening a piece that you can learn from. You'll get a chance to practice the ideas we talk about, and, finally, read a piece that has an especially riveting opening.

Your Contract with the Reader

One of the most critical things you have to understand about openings is that they are promises: they make pledges about everything from the subject matter (what the story or novel or nonfiction piece is going to be about), to the tone (serious or humorous or ironic), to the fabric, or "world" in which the piece is placed. They also, not incidentally, provide some sense of what's at stake. Perhaps most importantly of all, a good opening has to convince a reader to keep on reading. That is the lowest common denominator, and the highest determinant of success: Will the reader turn the page? If yes, that's a good starting point; if no, nothing else matters.

Now, a promise, or contract, doesn't mean there are no surprises. As we discussed in Chapter 1, fiction should be full of surprises and delights: that's why we read on—to see what happens next. If we know what happens next, we stop reading. It's as simple as that.

But unless you are entering the realm of metafiction (the point of which is to examine the writing of fiction, or the artificiality of the form) you are promising the reader some things within the context of a *particular creative world*. That is, you are making a promise about what will be delivered and in what form it will be delivered and in what context. To break this promise (again, except for stories that fit into the category of metafiction) is to disappoint or frustrate your reader.

This is a tricky subject, because it can lead people to think that if, say, they start out in a realistic mode and gradually work in magic (the way John Cheever does, for example), the contract has been broken. Yet the contract can be a subtle one: it can leave open the *opportunity* for certain things or the implication that some things might be possible.

But above all, no tricks in an opening. "A shot rang out" is only a good opening under very specific circumstances. Likewise, any mystery that turns out to be extraneous to the story. "A writer has to discriminate wisely between the attention-getting device that soon becomes fairly irrelevant to the story and the beginning that genuinely gathers the reader into the arms of the story," said Robie Macauley and George Lanning, coauthors of *Technique in Fiction*. And Raymond Carver talks about the need to avoid unnecessary mystery and tricks in his book *Fires*:

> I overheard the writer Geoffrey Wolff say "No cheap tricks" to a group of writing students. That should go on a three-by-five card. I'd amend it a little. "No tricks." Period. I hate tricks. At the first sign of a trick or a gimmick in a piece of fiction, a cheap trick or even an elaborate trick, I tend to look for cover. Tricks are ultimately boring, and I get bored easily. Extremely clever chi-chi writing or just plain tomfoolery writing puts me to sleep. Writers don't need tricks or gimmicks or even necessarily need to be the smartest fellows on the block. At the risk of appearing foolish, a writer sometimes needs to be able to just stand and gape at this or that thing—a sunset or an old shoe—in absolute and simple amazement . . .

Characteristics of a Good Opening

What are the characteristics of a good opening? They're very basic.

1. Keeps the reader wondering, "What happens next?" As we mentioned above, this is the most basic requirement of any piece of creative work—fiction or nonfiction—and it is particularly relevant in the opening. As E. M. Forster wrote in *Aspects of the Novel*:

> Neanderthal man listened to stories, if one may judge by the shape of his skull. The primitive audience was an audience of shock-heads, gaping round the campfire, fatigued with contending against the mammoth or the woolly rhinoceros, and only kept awake by suspense. What would happen next? The novelist droned on, and as soon as his audience guessed what happened next, they either fell asleep or killed him. We can estimate the dangers incurred when we think of the career of Scheherazade in somewhat later times. Scheherazade avoided her fate because she knew how to wield the weapon of suspense—the only literary tool that has any effect upon tyrants and savages. Great writer though she was—exquisite in her descriptions, tolerant in her judgments, ingenious in her incidents, advanced in her morality, vivid in her delineations of character, expert in her knowledge of three Oriental capitals—it was yet on none of these gifts that she relied when trying to save her life from her intolerable husband. They were but incidental. She only survived because she managed to keep the king wondering what would happen next

So: Does your reader want to know what happens next? That's the most basic question you need to ask yourself as you establish the opening of your piece.

2. Establishes the tone of the piece. Is it fantastical? Realistic? Ironic? Humorous? Whatever the tone of the piece, every word must be saturated with it from the very beginning. A common problem one sees in beginning work is that a story will begin in one vein—say, serious and realistic—and then turn to slapstick comedy, or science fiction, or some other kind of tone. Whatever the *feeling* you want your readers to get from the piece should be apparent from the very first sentence.

3. Immerses the reader in the physical world of the piece. "First sentences are doors to worlds," wrote Ursula Le Guin, reminding us that every piece has a place in the concrete world of sensory perception. Where does the piece take place? At what point in time? What's the physical terrain: A house? A boat on the open sea? Mountains? Suburbia? Whatever the physical setting of the piece, it should be apparent from the very first word.

4. Introduces characters and situations. Finally, an opening introduces characters. Who will we be finding out about (or journeying with) on this narrative path? What is their situation; what exactly is *happening* that should cause us to be interested?

Unbalancing Acts

One good way to think about openings is to think in terms of *balance*. Either things are out of kilter, or they will soon be; there's an imbalance, or a missing link, some mystery about what is happening that draws us into the story. It can be subtle, as shown below, but it has to be there. Let's look at some examples of what keeps us enough off balance to want to read more and regain our equilibrium.

> I saw her but four times, though I remember them vividly; she made her impression on me. I thought her very pretty and very interesting—a touching specimen of a type with which I had had other and perhaps less charming associations. I'm sorry to hear of her death, and yet when I think of it why *should* I be? The last time I saw her she was certainly not . . . ! But it will be of interest to take our meetings in order.

In this story, "Four Meetings" by Henry James, what keeps us off balance—and therefore interested—is the narrator's apparently ambiguous feelings toward the character he is going to relate a tale about. And for another intriguing fact, she's dead—death is always interesting: we want to know how, and when, and in what way it matters to the narrator—and then there's that unfinished line, "The last time I saw her she was certainly not . . . !" There's a sense of mystery that propels us into the story.

Now, another example of an opening rich with possibilities:

> The woman in front of him was eating roasted peanuts that smelled so good that he could barely contain his hunger. He could not even sleep and wished they'd hurry and begin the bingo game. There, on his right, two fellows were drinking wine out of a bottle wrapped in a paper bag, and he could hear soft gurgling in the dark. His stomach gave a low, gnawing growl. "If this was down South," he thought, "all I'd have to do is lean over and say, 'Lady, gimme a few of those peanuts, please ma'am,' and she'd pass me the bag and never think nothing of it." Or he could ask the fellows for a drink in

the same way. Folks down South stuck together that way; they didn't even have to know you. But up here it was different.

In this story, "King of the Bingo Game" by Ralph Ellison, we get a sense of someone out of his realm, unhappy and a misfit. He's hungry for more than food, he wants companionship and a kind word, but he's not getting any of what he wants (and if you remember from our chapter on plot, Chapter 9, having a character want something is a very compelling way to push your story forward).

And what about this?

> You had to know Travis Houpart not to like him, that was the thing. When people first encountered him, women especially, they thought they'd met a man worth meeting. The mustache was so trim, that reassuring dark brown, then the Christlike eyes, clear as scorched butter. The whole of him was so regular-featured and even-toned that the voice was no surprise, warm and crisp as a newscaster's, telling mild jokes and deflecting any question you might ask.
>
> He bought me a drink on a night I needed one, a night I was down.

In this piece, "Mauser" by Louise Erdrich, we're kept off balance in all sorts of ways. We're first warned about this character, Travis Houpart; there's the tension that arises because of the difference between the way he looks (interesting and decent) and his apparent unsavoriness. Then there is also the suggestion that he preyed on the narrator at a point when she was vulnerable, all of which whets the appetite and keeps us reading on.

Starting in the Middle

"Begin in the middle of things," advised Horace. *In medias res*. Chekhov advised young writers to tear up the first three pages of what they'd written, which amounts to the same thing. Beginning in the middle means that the piece already has a sense of momentum, of things in motion. Let's look at some examples.

> "Hey, look at that? You know what that is?" the Wizard says. "That's a goddamn red-winged blackbird. Miss Watts saw four of 'em last week at her feeder. You know what that means?"
>
> Rensselaer blinks and checks his jockstrap, where he has stuffed two small brown packages. He is an unbelievably skinny twelve-year-old with a dreamy smile and a fine, caramel-colored face. It makes the older boy's face look almost blue.

" 'Spring,' asshole."

"Where is the old witch?" Rensselaer asks mildly. They are in Miss Watts's backyard, but she isn't around and he can't feel her little beady eyes creeping out at them from a window.

"She's at Boston City Hospital right this goddamn minute. She's got a dropped bladder and they're tying the whole thing up," the Wizard says.

In this story, "The Wizard" by C. S. Godshalk, we join the two main characters in the middle of an adventure. We're told just enough to be interested . . . and we have lots of questions. What are the two small brown packages? Who is Miss Watts and why are the boys in her backyard? We haven't gotten a lengthy exposition that lays out clearly what is happening, but we're engaged; we're *there* and that's what counts.

And what about this opening?

Gasping for air, his legs weak from the climb up the stairs, Ernest stopped outside the room surprised to find the door wide open, almost sorry he had made it before the police. An upsurge of nausea, a wave of suffocation forced him to suck violently for breath as he stepped into Gordon's room—his *own* two decades before.

Tinted psychedelic emerald, the room looked like a hippie pad posing for a photograph in *Life*, but the monotonous electronic frenzy he heard was the seventeen-year locusts, chewing spring leaves outside. He wondered whether the sedative had so dazed him that he had stumbled into the wrong room. No, now, as every time in his own college years when he had entered this room, what struck him first was the light falling through the leaded, green-stained windowglass. As the light steeped him in the ambience of the early forties, it simultaneously illuminated the artifacts of the present. Though groggy from the sedative, he experienced intermittent moments of startling clarity when he saw each object separately.

Empty beer can pyramids.

James Dean, stark poster photograph.

Records leaning on orange crate.

Life-sized redheaded girl, banjo blocking her vagina, lurid color.

Rolltop desk, swivel chair, typewriter.

Poster photograph of a teenage hero he didn't recognize.

Large CORN FLAKES carton.

In "No Trace" by David Madden, we've jumped into the middle of a story where something important has already happened—after all, this character wanted to get to the room before the police did—although we don't know what, and the narrator is already in the middle of some sort of emotional crisis (we know this because of the sedative he's taken). And as with the other stories that begin in the middle, we're caught, hooked, and already being swept along in the stream of events.

Beginning with Action

In Chapter 4, I spoke about being surprised by a formula for writing stories prescribed by a workshop leader who said stories should follow the ABCDE pattern: Action, Backstory, Conflict, Denouement, Ending. But although it shouldn't be done all the time, and certainly not in a formulaic manner, sometimes you *will* want to try to open with an action. "Plays and short stories are similar in that both start when all but the action is finished," the playwright August Wilson said, so let's look at some examples of what he meant by this.

> Murphy's drunk on the bright verge of still another Christmas and a car door slams. Then he's out in the headlights and in bed waking up the next afternoon with Annie kissing his crucified right fist. It's blue and swollen, and when he tries to move it, it tingles, it pains and Annie says, How did you hurt your hand? Did you hit somebody?
>
> Murphy waits while that question fades on her mouth, then the room glitters and he sniffs the old fractured acid of remorse asking: Was I sick?
>
> Yes.
>
> Where?
>
> On the floor. And you fell out of bed twice. It was so terrible I don't think I could stand it if it happened again promise me you won't get drunk anymore, Glover had to teach both of your classes this morning you frighten me when you're this way and you've lost so much weight you should have seen yourself last night lying naked on the floor like something from a concentration camp in your own vomit you were so white you were blue
>
> Is the color of Annie's eyes as Murphy sinks into the stars and splinters of the sheets with her, making love to her and begging her forgiveness which she gives and gives until Murphy can feel her shy skeleton waltzing away with his in a fit of ribbons, the bursting bouquets of a Christmas they are going to spend apart.

In this story, "Murphy's Xmas" by Mark Costello, we begin with action—the title character is drunk, even to the point of blacking out—and the pace of the story never flags as it moves forward (indeed, unlike the ABCDE formula mentioned above, it never goes back for any "backstory" but just moves relentlessly ahead).

When Martha Hale opened the storm door and got a cut of the north wind, she ran back for her big woolen scarf. As she hurriedly wound that round her head, her eye made a scandalized sweep of her kitchen. It was no ordinary thing that called her away—it was probably farther from ordinary than anything that had ever happened in Dickson County. But what her eye took in was that her kitchen was in no shape for leaving: her bread all ready for mixing, half the flour sifted and half unsifted.

In this story, "A Jury of Her Peers" by Susan Glaspell, we start with a deceptively simple action, the opening of a storm door, and the feel of wind, which gives the story a nice launching pad for what follows; the language is fresh and alive, and we move ahead from the action, wondering what this non-ordinary thing is that could have happened. Like the previous example, in this story there's no going back for "backstory": the story merely unfolds from this point on.

But action isn't always the best way to start. Let's take a look at some examples that begin with lengthy expositions or narrative. They're just as compelling, due to the fresh and specific nature of the details.

This blind man, an old friend of my wife's, he was on his way to spend the night. His wife had died. So he was visiting the dead wife's relatives in Connecticut. He called my wife from his in-laws'. Arrangements were made. He would come by train, a five-hour trip, and my wife would meet him at the station. She hadn't seen him since she worked for him one summer in Seattle ten years ago. But she and the blind man had kept in touch. They made tapes and mailed them back and forth. I wasn't enthusiastic about his visit. He was no one I knew. And his being blind bothered me. My idea of blindness came from the movies, in the movies, the blind moved slowly and never laughed. Sometimes they were led by seeing-eye dogs. A blind man in my house was not something I looked forward to.

In this story, "Cathedral" by Raymond Carver, instead of getting action we get an explanation of the situation, with the narrator's feelings just bluntly "told" to us. There's no dramatization. Just a setting of the physical and emotional scene. But it works as an opening because of the sense of curiosity we have about this curmudgeonly man (the narrator), and about how the unwelcome visit will turn out for him and his wife.

And how about this one:

Flo said to watch for White Slavers. She said this was how they operated: an old woman, a motherly or grandmotherly sort, made friends while riding beside you on a bus or train. She offered you candy, which was drugged. Pretty soon you began to droop and mumble, were in no condition to speak for yourself. Oh, help, the woman said, my daughter (granddaughter) is sick, please somebody help me get her off so that she can recover in the fresh air. Up stepped a polite gentleman, pretending to be a stranger, offering assistance. Together, at the next stop, they hustled you off the train or bus, and that was the last the ordinary world ever saw of you. They kept you a prisoner in the White Slave place (to which you had been transported drugged and bound so you wouldn't even know where you were), until such time as you were thoroughly degraded and in despair, your insides torn up by drunken men and invested with vile disease, your mind destroyed by drugs, your hair and teeth fallen out. It took about three years for you to get to this state. You wouldn't want to go home, then, maybe couldn't remember home, or find your way if you did. So they let you out on the streets.

Flo took ten dollars and put it in a little cloth bag, which she sewed to the strap of Rose's slip. Another thing likely to happen was that Rose would get her purse stolen.

In this story, "Wild Swans" by Alice Munro, we also begin with non-action: with a lengthy lecture by the character Flo as to the dangers of traveling alone, and what would happen to a young girl taken by the so-called White Slavers. The action doesn't begin until the very end of the passage, but the narrative is odd enough, and compelling enough, to keep us reading.

On the Nature of Suspense

What is suspense? *Merriam-Webster's Collegiate Dictionary* defines it as "mental uncertainty" or "pleasant excitement as to a decision or outcome." And isn't this what we've been talking about in this chapter? The need, in an opening, to keep readers in a state of "pleasant excitement" so that they'll read on?

It's important to understand precisely what creates literary suspense: a reader's partial (or imperfect) awareness that something of dramatic significance is about to occur. John Gardner wrote, in *The Art of Fiction*, that

[suspense must be achieved] in a piece of fiction just *before* the discovery of a body. You might perhaps describe the character's approach to the body he will find, or the location, or both. The purpose of the exercise is to develop the technique of at once *attracting the reader toward the paragraph to follow— making him want to skip ahead, and holding him on this paragraph by virtue of its interest* [emphasis mine]. Without the ability to write such foreplay paragraphs, one can never achieve real suspense.

Let's look at some examples of openings that have this attribute of "partial knowledge" built into them.

> Every night that winter he said aloud into the dark of the pillow: Half past
> four! Half-past four! Till he felt his brain had gripped the words and held
> them fast. Then he fell asleep at once, as if a shutter had fallen; and lay with
> his face turned to the clock so that he could see it first thing when he woke.

In this story, "A Sunrise on the Veld" by Doris Lessing, we wonder, what
is this "half past four"? We're intrigued by our partial knowledge of the
situation, and want to read on.

> A woman I don't know is boiling tea the Indian way in my kitchen. There are
> a lot of women I don't know in my kitchen, whispering and moving tact-
> fully. They open doors, rummage through the pantry, and try not to ask me
> where things are kept. They remind me of when my sons were small, on
> Mother's Day or when Vikram and I were tired, and they would make big,
> sloppy omelets. I would lie in bed pretending I didn't hear them.

Something has clearly happened, something that makes people want to
help the narrator, and treat her as if she were particularly delicate or vulnerable, in this story, "The Management of Grief" by Bharati Mukherjee.
The fact that we don't know what has happened—yet—whets our
appetite to hear more.

Beginning Your Creative Nonfiction Piece

> My father drank. He drank as a gut-punched boxer gasps for breath, as a
> starving dog gobbles food—compulsively, secretly, in pain and trembling. I
> use the past tense not because he ever quit drinking but because he quit liv-
> ing. That is how the story ends for my father, age sixty-four, heart bursting,
> body cooling and forsaken on the linoleum of my brother's trailer. The story
> continues for my brother, my sister, my mother, and me, and will continue
> so long as memory holds.

In this nonfiction piece, "Under the Influence" by Scott Russell Sanders,
we begin with the death: we know, as the text tells us, how one particular
aspect of the story ends. But this is in reality just the beginning of the story
for the survivors—the people who have to make sense of the life that has
just been extinguished.

> During the fall of 1984 I worked for three weekends as a caterer's assistant
> in Southern California. Like lots of others seeking their fortunes in L.A., I
> was working by day as a temporary typist in a Hollywood film studio. I was
> moonlighting with the caterer because, like lots of others, I was going broke
> on my typist's wages.

This piece engages our interest because of the tension of simple survival:

Will the narrator make it financially? There's also the implication that something happened of significance during the three weekends in 1984. We're intrigued, and so we read on in this excellent nonfiction piece, "Do He Have Your Number, Mr. Jeffrey" by Gayle Pemberton.

> One holds the knife as one holds the bow of a cello or a tulip—by the stem. Not palmed nor gripped nor grasped, but lightly, with the tips of the fingers. The knife is not for pressing. It is for drawing across the field of skin. Like a slender fish, it waits, at the ready, then, go! It darts, followed by a fine wake of red. The flesh parts, falling away to yellow globules of fat. Even now, after so many times, I still marvel at its power.

In this nonfiction piece ("The Knife" by Richard Selzer) we start with action: a surgeon's knife being held in the palm, then being used to make an incision. Right away, we're dropped into the piece: urgently and swiftly, with no looking back.

> For about fifteen minutes I have been sitting chin in hand in front of the typewriter, staring out at the snow. Trying to be honest with myself, trying to figure out why writing this seems to me so dangerous an act, filled with fear and shame, and why it seems so necessary.

In this nonfiction essay, "Split at the Root" by Adrienne Rich, we begin smack in the middle of a writer attempting to write the piece in question. We're intrigued: like her, we want to know why the act of writing feels so "dangerous"—we've embarked on a journey that we'll be taking with the writer (always an interesting technique to use) and so we eagerly go along for the ride.

Part 2: EXERCISES

A good beginning is critical to your story, novel, or nonfiction piece. Without a compelling opening, your readers might lose interest—and you will lose them. Getting the reader to turn the page is just one thing that a good opening will do. The other things outlined in this chapter—introducing the characters, establishing a tone and sense of place and sense of what the story or nonfiction piece is about—are equally important.

Exercise 1: Give It Your Best Shot

Goal: To see what happens when you begin a story (or novel or piece of creative nonfiction) with your best material rather than "saving" it up.

What to do: 1. Take a piece you've been working on.

2. Take the best, most exciting material from the piece.

3. Begin the piece with this material.

Here's an example of how to complete this exercise, written by Tom Bowker:

Original opening:

We were on our way to our grandparents' house. It was a dull day in all respects: the weather was dull, heavy clouds hid the sun but refused to release any rain, there was not a hint of wind and the humidity was so intense that it curled my hair into tiny tendrils on my forehead and behind my ears. My parents weren't speaking with each other, again. This time the fight had been over olives, whether they should be put in a salad or not. Last night my mother had put them in a salad for a dinner party and my father had glowered throughout the entire meal.

Revision:

My grandfather reached his right hand upward as if to reach for the bread, or salt, and he died. Just like that. He slowly collapsed: first his head, interestingly enough, then his shoulders, and his hand last of all, as if he were raising it at school like a polite child waiting to be heard.

Here's another example, written by Susan Jamison:

Original opening:

My brothers, as far as I remember, never spoke to each other. They marched silently through the house, spaced regularly. They could have been clones of one another. They took the same courses, went out for the same sports, read the same books, watched the same television shows. My father took great pride in this; he thought it showed the strength of the breeding. "No environmental factors, here," he said. "Genetics all the way." My brothers, as far as I could see, ignored him. But it is true that they had the same tastes. When older, they bought gray or beige Honda compact cars, married blond women or women who dyed their hair blond, worked in number-intensive jobs like accounting or finance.

Revision:

When my oldest brother was arrested, it came as a complete shock. Matthew! He of the gentle face and the hobby of breeding cockatiels—not to sell, but for the pleasure of hand-feeding the babies and giving them as gifts. It turned out he'd been selling drugs to schoolchildren out of his garage. We were all in shock. If Matthew could go bad, anything was possible.

Exercise 2: Start in the Middle

Goal: To see what happens if you follow Horace's advice and start something in the middle.

What to do: 1. Take a piece you've been working on, and choose an event that occurs in the middle of the piece.
2. Write a new opening based on this "middle."

Here's an example of this exercise, contributed by Mary O'Connor:

Original opening:

When we first moved to the house on Walnut Avenue, there was no grass, no trees, nothing: just our house, surrounded by a sea of dirt. The other houses weren't built yet; there were just the bare cement foundations that would eventually grow up to be the houses of our neighbors and playmates. The roads had been laid, however, and the streetlights installed, so one got the sense of this immense expanse of roadways and streaming lights, cutting through the mud and dirt as far as the eye could see in any direction.

Revision:

It was the third day that my little sister Ruby got bit by the black widow spider. She couldn't talk yet, so we weren't sure what happened, but she was crying, and there was a huge red welt on her arm growing larger by the second. My mother first did the "now don't make a fuss" thing before we managed to convince her something was really wrong. Ruby had stopped crying but she was having trouble breathing and she was holding her arm out as though it was a slab of rancid meat she'd picked up off the floor.

Here's another one, written by Susan Jamison:

Original opening:

Jane's boss told her that she had been chosen to attend the seminar in Tampa. Jane moaned and groaned and tried to get out of it, but she was stuck: everyone else had called in their favors, and Jane had nothing in her favor, not seniority, not talent, not what her boss called get-up-and-go. So there she was: on her way to Florida in the middle of August.

Revision:

Stewardesses always dismayed Jane. She wanted them to be ashamed of themselves, and they rarely were. Lately, they had been becoming more and more human: less makeup, long red talons for nails disappearing. Some even looked grandmotherly. On her flight to Tampa, one had had a discreet button pinned to her uniform: It Happens, but if you looked closer, you saw a faint "sh" before the "it." Jane found this extraordinary. This same stewardess told a businessman not to be a baby when he complained about not having a pillow. The one today was from the old mold, and was extraordinarily nice to Jane, who could never understand airline tickets: what was the part that was valuable, and what part needed to be thrown away. She was constantly losing the important part of the ticket, and having to go to the airline ticket counter and explain her problem.

Exercise 3: Make Them Squirm

> Goal: To practice wielding the weapon of suspense to keep your readers reading.

What to do: 1. Choose a piece you are working on.
2. Write a first few paragraphs that leave the reader in doubt of something important that is going on.

This passage was written by Thomas Kilhearn:

What could I say? It wasn't the first time I had done it, just the first time I had been caught. And the shame was pushing down on me so I could hardly swallow, but that was nothing new; I had felt this deep crushing shame when I had gotten off scot-free, without any witnesses to my transgressions, in the past. And this wasn't really that bad, was it? I sometimes have trouble keeping perspective on things, my mother tells me.

This example of the exercise was written by Jane Towson:

The night he left, I had fallen asleep as he began putting all our books in alphabetical order. Several times he woke me up to ask me questions. "In biography, do you want the books to be listed under the person being written about, or the person writing?" he asked. After the books he started on the records, then on the food in the pantry. At some point I fell asleep. When I awoke, every piece of electronic equipment we owned was gone. So was my husband. There was no note. When I opened the refrigerator, I found the food there alphabetized, too. An avocado stared me in the face.

Part 3: READING AS A WRITER

People Like That Are the Only People Here:
Canonical Babbling in Peed Onk

LORRIE MOORE

A beginning, an end: there seems to be neither. The whole thing is like a cloud that just lands and everywhere inside it is full of rain. A start: the Mother finds a blood clot in the Baby's diaper. What is the story? Who put this here? It is big and bright, with a broken khaki-colored vein in it. Over the weekend, the Baby had looked listless and spacey, clayey and grim. But today he looks fine—so what is this thing, startling against the white diaper, like a tiny mouse heart packed in snow? Perhaps it belongs to someone else. Perhaps it is something menstrual, something belonging to the Mother or to the Babysitter, something the Baby has found in a wastebasket and for his own demented baby reasons stowed away here. (Babies: they're crazy! What can you do?) In her mind, the Mother takes this away from his body and attaches it to someone else's. There. Doesn't that make more sense?

Still, she phones the clinic at the children's hospital. "Blood in the diaper," she says, and, sounding alarmed and perplexed, the woman on the other end says, "Come in now."

Such pleasingly instant service! Just say "blood." Just say "diaper." Look what you get!

In the examination room, pediatrician, nurse, head resident—all seem less alarmed and perplexed than simply perplexed. At first, stupidly, the Mother is calmed by this. But soon, besides peering and saying "Hmmmm," the pediatrician, nurse, and head resident are all drawing their mouths in, bluish and tight—morning glories sensing noon. They fold their arms across their white-coated chests, unfold them again and jot things down. They order an ultrasound. Bladder and kidneys. "Here's the card. Go downstairs; turn left."

In Radiology, the Baby stands anxiously on the table, naked against the Mother as she holds him still against her legs and waist, the Radiologist's cold scanning disc moving about the Baby's back. The Baby whimpers, looks up at the Mother. *Let's get out of here*, his eyes beg. *Pick me up!* The Radiologist stops, freezes one of the many swirls of oceanic gray, and clicks repeatedly, a single moment within the long, cavernous weather map that is the Baby's insides.

"Are you finding something?" asks the Mother. Last year, her uncle Larry had had a kidney removed for something that turned out to be benign. These imaging machines! They are like dogs, or metal detectors: they find everything, but don't know what they've found. That's where the surgeons come in. They're like the owners of the dogs. "Give me that," they say to the dog. "What the heck is that?"

"The surgeon will speak to you," says the Radiologist.

"Are you finding something?"

"The surgeon will speak to you," the Radiologist says again. "There seems to be something there, but the surgeon will talk to you about it."

"My uncle once had something on his kidney," says the Mother. "So they removed the kidney and it turned out the something was benign."

The Radiologist smiles a broad, ominous smile. "That's always the way it is," he says. "You don't know exactly what it is until it's in the bucket."

"'In the bucket,'" the Mother repeats.

The Radiologist's grin grows scarily wider—is that even possible? "That's doctor talk," he says.

"It's very appealing," says the Mother. "It's a very appealing way to talk." Swirls of bile and blood, mustard and maroon in a pail, the colors of an African flag or some exuberant salad bar: *in the bucket*—she imagines it all.

"The Surgeon will see you soon," he says again. He tousles the Baby's ringletty hair. "Cute kid," he says.

"Let's see now," says the Surgeon in one of his examining rooms. He has stepped in, then stepped out, then come back in again. He has crisp, frowning features, sharp bones, and a tennis-in-Bermuda tan. He crosses his blue-cottoned legs. He is wearing clogs.

The Mother knows her own face is a big white dumpling of worry. She is still wearing her long, dark parka, holding the Baby, who has pulled the hood up over her head because he always thinks it's funny to do that. Though on certain windy mornings she would like to think she could look vaguely romantic like this, like some French Lieutenant's Woman of the Prairie, in all of her saner moments she knows she doesn't. Ever. She knows she looks ridiculous—like one of those animals made out of twisted party balloons. She lowers the hood and slips one arm out of the sleeve. The Baby wants to get up and play with the light switch. He fidgets, fusses, and points.

"He's big on lights these days," explains the Mother.

"That's okay," says the Surgeon, nodding toward the light switch. "Let him play with it." The Mother goes and stands by it, and the Baby begins turning the lights off and on, off and on.

"What we have here is a Wilms' tumor," says the Surgeon, suddenly plunged into darkness. He says "tumor" as if it were the most normal thing in the world.

"Wilms'?" repeats the Mother. The room is quickly on fire again with light, then wiped dark again. Among the three of them here, there is a long silence, as if it were suddenly the middle of the night. "Is that apostrophe *s* or *s* apostrophe?" the Mother says finally. She is a writer and a teacher. Spelling can be important—perhaps even at a time like this, though she has never before been at a time like this, so there are barbarisms she could easily commit and not know.

The lights come on: the world is doused and exposed.

"*S* apostrophe," says the Surgeon. "I think." The lights go back out, but the Surgeon continues speaking in the dark. "A malignant tumor on the left kidney."

Wait a minute. Hold on here. The Baby is only a baby, fed on organic applesauce and soy milk—a little prince!—and he was standing so close to her during the ultrasound. How could he have this terrible thing? It must have been *her* kidney. A fifties kidney. A DDT kidney. The Mother clears her throat. "Is it possible it was my kidney on the scan? I mean, I've never heard of a baby with a tumor, and, frankly, I was standing very close." She would make the blood hers, the tumor hers; it would all be some treacherous, farcical mistake.

"No, that's not possible," says the Surgeon. The light goes back on.

"It's not?" says the Mother. Wait until it's *in the bucket,* she thinks. Don't be so sure. *Do we have to wait until it's in the bucket to find out a mistake has been made?*

"We will start with a radical nephrectomy," says the Surgeon, instantly thrown into darkness again. His voice comes from nowhere and everywhere at once. "And then we'll begin with chemotherapy after that. These tumors usually respond very well to chemo."

"I've never heard of a baby having chemo," the Mother says. *Baby* and *Chemo,* she thinks: they should never even appear in the same sentence together, let alone the same life. In her other life, her life before this day, she had been a believer in alternative medicine. Chemotherapy? Unthinkable. Now, suddenly, alternative medicine seems the wacko maiden aunt to the Nice Big Daddy of Conventional Treatment. How quickly the old girl faints and gives way, leaves one just standing there. Chemo? Of course: chemo! Why by all means: chemo. Absolutely! Chemo!

The Baby flicks the switch back on, and the walls reappear, big wedges of light checkered with small framed watercolors of the local lake. The Mother has begun to cry: all of life has led her here, to this moment. After this, there is no more life. There is something else, something stumbling and unlivable, something mechanical, something for robots, but not life. Life has been taken and broken, quickly, like a stick. The room goes dark again, so that the Mother can cry more freely. How can a baby's body be stolen so fast? How much can one heaven-sent and unsuspecting child endure? Why has he not been spared this inconceivable fate?

Perhaps, she thinks, she is being punished: too many babysitters too early on. ("Come to Mommy! Come to Mommy-Babysitter!" she used to say. But it was a joke!) Her life, perhaps, bore too openly the marks and wigs of deepest drag. Her unmotherly thoughts had all been noted: the panicky hope that his nap would last longer than it did; her occasional desire to kiss him passionately on the mouth (to make out with her baby!); her ongoing complaints about the very vocabulary of motherhood, how it degraded the speaker ("Is this a poopie onesie! Yes, it's a very poopie one-sie!"). She had, moreover, on three occasions used the formula bottles as flower vases. She twice let the Baby's ears get fudgy with wax. A few after-noons last month, at snacktime, she placed a bowl of Cheerios on the floor for him to eat, like a dog. She let him play with the Dust-Buster. Just once, before he was born, she said, "Healthy? I just want the kid to be rich." A joke, for God's sake! After he was born she announced that her life had become a daily sequence of mind-wrecking chores, the same ones over and over again, like a novel by Mrs. Camus. Another joke! These jokes will kill you! She had told too often, and with too much enjoyment, the story of how the Baby had said "Hi" to his high chair, waved at the lake waves, shouted "Goody-goody-goody" in what seemed to be a Russian accent, pointed at his eyes and said "Ice." And all that nonsensical baby talk: wasn't it a stitch? "Canonical babbling," the language experts called it. He recounted whole stories in it—totally made up, she could tell. He embroi-dered; he fished; he exaggerated. What a card! To friends, she spoke of his eating habits (carrots yes, tuna no). She mentioned, too much, his sidesplitting giggle. Did she have to be so boring? Did she have no con-sideration for others, for the intellectual demands and courtesies of human society? Would she not even attempt to be more interesting? It was a crime against the human mind not even to try.

Now her baby, for all these reasons—lack of motherly gratitude, motherly judgment, motherly proportion—will be taken away.

The room is fluorescently ablaze again. The Mother digs around in her parka pocket and comes up with a Kleenex. It is old and thin, like a mashed flower saved from a dance; she dabs it at her eyes and nose.

"The Baby won't suffer as much as you," says the Surgeon.

And who can contradict? Not the Baby, who in his Slavic Betty Boop voice can say only *mama, dada, cheese, ice, bye-bye, outside, boogie-boogie, goody-goody, eddy-eddy,* and *car.* (Who is Eddy? They have no idea.) This will not suffice to express his mortal suffering. Who can say what babies do with their agony and shock? Not they themselves. (Baby talk: isn't it a stitch?) They put it all no place anyone can really see. They are like a different race, a different species: they seem not to experience pain the way *we* do. Yeah, that's it: their nervous systems are not as fully formed, and *they just don't experience pain the way we do.* A tune to keep one humming through the war. "You'll get through it," the Surgeon says.

"How?" asks the Mother. "How does one get through it?"

"You just put your head down and go," says the Surgeon. He picks up his file folder. He is a skilled manual laborer. The tricky emotional stuff is not to his liking. The babies. The babies! What can be said to console the parents about the babies? "I'll go phone the oncologist on duty to let him know," he says, and leaves the room.

"Come here, sweetie," the Mother says to the Baby, who has toddled off toward a gum wrapper on the floor. "We've got to put your jacket on." She picks him up and he reaches for the light switch again. Light, dark. Peek-aboo: where's baby? Where did baby go?

At home, she leaves a message—"Urgent! Call me!"—for the Husband on his voice mail. Then she takes the Baby upstairs for his nap, rocks him in the rocker. The Baby waves good-bye to his little bears, then looks toward the window and says, "Bye-bye, outside." He has, lately, the habit of waving good-bye to everything, and now it seems as if he senses an imminent departure, and it breaks her heart to hear him. *Bye-bye!* She sings low and monotonously, like a small appliance, which is how he likes it. He is drowsy, dozy, drifting off. He has grown so much in the last year, he hardly fits in her lap anymore; his limbs dangle off like a pietà. His head rolls slightly inside the crook of her arm. She can feel him falling backward into sleep, his mouth round and open like the sweetest of poppies. All the lullabies in the world, all the melodies threaded through with maternal melancholy now become for her—abandoned as a mother can be by working men and napping babies—the songs of hard, hard grief. Sitting there, bowed and bobbing, the Mother feels the entirety of her love as worry and heartbreak. A quick and irrevocable alchemy: there is no longer one unworried scrap left for happiness. "If you go," she keens low into his soapy neck, into the ranunculus coil of his ear, "we are going with you. We are nothing without you. Without you, we are a heap of rocks. We are gravel and mold. Without you, we are two stumps, with nothing any longer in our hearts. Wherever this takes you, we are following. We will be there. Don't be scared. We are going, too. That is that."

"Take Notes," says the Husband, after coming straight home from work, midafternoon, hearing the news, and saying all the words out loud—*surgery, metastasis, dialysis, transplant*—then collapsing in a chair in tears. "Take notes. We are going to need the money."

"Good God," cries the Mother. Everything inside her suddenly begins to cower and shrink, a thinning of bones. Perhaps this is a soldier's readiness, but it has the whiff of death and defeat. It feels like a heart attack, a failure of will and courage, a power failure: a failure of everything. Her face, when she glimpses it in a mirror, is cold and bloated with shock, her eyes scarlet and shrunk. She has already started to wear sunglasses indoors, like a celebrity widow. From where will her own strength come? From some philosophy? From some frigid little philosophy? She is neither stalwart nor realistic and has trouble with basic concepts, such as the one that says events move in one direction only and do not jump up, turn around, and take themselves back.

The Husband begins too many of his sentences with "What if." He is trying to piece everything together like a train wreck. He is trying to get the train to town.

"We'll just take all the steps, move through all the stages. We'll go where we have to go. We'll hunt; we'll find; we'll pay what we have to pay. What if we can't pay?"

"Sounds like shopping."

"I cannot believe this is happening to our little boy," he says, and starts to sob again. "Why didn't it happen to one of us? It's so unfair. Just last week, my doctor declared me in perfect health: the prostate of a twenty-year-old, the heart of a ten-year-old, the brain of an insect—or whatever it was he said. What a nightmare this is."

What words can be uttered? You turn just slightly and there it is: the death of your child. It is part symbol, part devil, and in your blind spot all along, until, if you are unlucky, it is completely upon you. Then it is a fierce little country abducting you; it holds you squarely inside itself like a cellar room—the best boundaries of you are the boundaries of it. Are there windows? Sometimes aren't there windows?

The Mother is not a shopper. She hates to shop, is generally bad at it, though she does like a good sale. She cannot stroll meaningfully through anger, denial, grief, and acceptance. She goes straight to bargaining and stays there. How much? She calls out to the ceiling, to some makeshift construction of holiness she has desperately, though not uncreatively, assembled in her mind and prayed to; a doubter, never before given to prayer, she must now reap what she has not sown; she must assemble from scratch an entire altar of worship and begging. She tries for noble abstractions, nothing too anthropomorphic, just some Higher Morality, though if this particular Highness looks something like the manager at Marshall Field's, sucking a Frango mint, so be it. Amen. Just tell me what you want, requests the Mother. And how do you want it? More charitable acts? A billion starting now. Charitable thoughts? Harder, but of course! Of course! I'll do the cooking, honey; I'll pay the rent. Just tell me. *Excuse me?* Well, if not to you, to whom do I speak? Hello? To whom do I have to speak around here? A higher-up? A superior? Wait? I can wait. I've got all day. I've got the whole damn day.

The Husband now lies next to her in bed, sighing. "Poor little guy could survive all this, only to be killed in a car crash at the age of sixteen," he says.

The wife, bargaining, considers this. "We'll take the car crash," she says.

"What?"

"Let's Make a Deal! Sixteen Is a Full Life! We'll take the car crash. We'll take the car crash, in front of which Carol Merrill is now standing."

Now the Manager of Marshall Field's reappears. "To take the surprises out is to take the life out of life," he says.

The phone rings. The Husband gets up and leaves the room.

"But I don't want these surprises," says the Mother. "Here! You take these surprises!"

"To know the narrative in advance is to turn yourself into a machine," the Manager continues. "What makes humans human is precisely that they do not know the future. That is why they do the fateful and amusing things they do: who can say how anything will turn out? Therein lies the only hope for redemption, discovery, and—let's be frank—fun, fun, fun!

There might be things people will get away with. And not just motel tow-els. There might be great illicit loves, enduring joy, faith-shaking accidents with farm machinery. But you have to not know in order to see what sto-ries your life's efforts bring you. The mystery is all."

The Mother, though shy, has grown confrontational. "Is this the kind of bogus, random crap they teach at merchandising school? We would like fewer surprises, fewer efforts and mysteries, thank you. K through eight; can we just get K through eight?" It now seems like the luckiest, most beautiful, most musical phrase she's ever heard: K through eight. The very lilt. The very thought.

The Manager continues, trying things out. "I mean, the whole concep-tion of 'the story,' of cause and effect, the whole idea that people have a clue as to how the world works is just a piece of laughable metaphysical colonialism perpetrated upon the wild country of time."

Did they own a gun? The Mother begins looking through drawers.

The Husband comes back into the room and observes her. "Ha! The Great Havoc that is the Puzzle of all Life!" he says of the Marshall Field's management policy. He has just gotten off a conference call with the insur-ance company and the hospital. The surgery will be Friday. "It's all just some dirty capitalist's idea of a philosophy."

"Maybe it's just a fact of narrative and you really can't politicize it," says the Mother. It is now only the two of them.

"Whose side are you on?"

"I'm on the Baby's side."

"Are you taking notes for this?"

"No."

"You're not?"

"No. I can't. Not this! I write fiction. This isn't fiction."

"Then write nonfiction. Do a piece of journalism. Get two dollars a word."

"Then it has to be true and full of information. I'm not trained. I'm not that skilled. Plus, I have a convenient personal principle about artists not abandoning art. One should never turn one's back on a vivid imagination. Even the whole memoir thing annoys me."

"Well, make things up, but pretend they're real."

"I'm not that insured."

"You're making me nervous."

"Sweetie, darling, I'm not that good. I can't *do this*. I can do—what can I do? I can do quasi-amusing phone dialogue. I can do succinct descrip-tions of weather. I can do screwball outings with the family pet. Sometimes

I can do those. Honey, I only do what I can. I do *the careful ironies of day-dream.* I do *the marshy ideas upon which intimate life is built.* But this? Our baby with cancer? I'm sorry. My stop was two stations back. This is irony at its most gaudy and careless. This is a Hieronymus Bosch of facts and figures and blood and graphs. This is a nightmare of narrative slop. This cannot be designed. This cannot even be noted in preparation for a design—"

"We're going to need the money."

"To say nothing of the moral boundaries of pecuniary recompense in a situation such as this—"

"What if the other kidney goes? What if he needs a transplant? Where are the moral boundaries there? What are we going to do, have bake sales?"

"We can sell the house. I hate this house. It makes me crazy."

"And we'll live—where again?"

"The Ronald McDonald place. I hear it's nice. It's the least McDonald's can do."

"You have a keen sense of justice."

"I try. What can I say?" She pauses. "Is all this really happening? I keep thinking that soon it will be over—the life expectancy of a cloud is supposed to be only twelve hours—and then I realize something has occurred that can never ever be over."

The Husband buries his face in his hands: "Our poor baby. How did this happen to him?" He looks over and stares at the bookcase that serves as the nightstand. "And do you think even one of these baby books is any help?" He picks up the Leach, the Spock, the *What to Expect.* "Where in the pages or index of any of these does it say 'chemotherapy' or 'Hickman catheter' or 'renal sarcoma'? Where does it say 'carcinogenesis'? You know what these books are obsessed with? *Holding a fucking spoon.*" He begins hurling the books off the night table and against the far wall.

"Hey," says the Mother, trying to soothe. "Hey, hey, hey." But compared to his stormy roar, her words are those of a backup singer—a Shondell, a Pip—a doo-wop ditty. Books, and now more books, continue to fly.

Take Notes.

Is *fainthearted* one word or two? Student prose has wrecked her spelling.

It's one word. Two words—*Faint Hearted*—what would that be? The name of a drag queen.

Take Notes. In the end, you suffer alone. But at the beginning you suffer with a whole lot of others. When your child has cancer, you are instantly whisked away to another planet: one of bald-headed little boys. Pediatric Oncology. Peed Onk. You wash your hands for thirty seconds in antibacterial soap before you are allowed to enter through the swinging doors. You put paper slippers on your shoes. You keep your voice down. A whole place has been designed and decorated for your nightmare. Here is where your nightmare will occur. We've got a room all ready for you. We have cots. We have refrigerators. "The children are almost entirely boys," says one of the nurses. "No one knows why. It's been documented, but a lot of people out there still don't realize it." The little boys are all from sweet-sounding places—Janesville and Appleton—little heartland towns with giant landfills, agricultural runoff, paper factories, Joe McCarthy's grave (Alone, a site of great toxicity, thinks the Mother. The soil should be tested).

All the bald little boys look like brothers. They wheel their IVs up and down the single corridor of Peed Onk. Some of the lively ones, feeling good for a day, ride the lower bars of the IV while their large, cheerful mothers whiz them along the halls. *Wheee!*

The Mother does not feel large and cheerful. In her mind, she is scathing, acid-tongued, wraith-thin, and chain-smoking out on a fire escape somewhere. Beneath her lie the gentle undulations of the Midwest, with all its aspirations to be—to be what? To be Long Island. How it has succeeded! Strip mall upon strip mall. Lurid water, poisoned potatoes. The Mother drags deeply, blowing clouds of smoke out over the disfigured cornfields. When a baby gets cancer, it seems stupid ever to have given up smoking. When a baby gets cancer, you think, Whom are we kidding? Let's all light up. When a baby gets cancer, you think, Who came up with *this* idea? What celestial abandon gave rise to *this*? Pour me a drink, so I can refuse to toast.

The Mother does not know how to be one of these other mothers, with their blond hair and sweatpants and sneakers and determined pleasantness. She does not think that she can be anything similar. She does not feel remotely like them. She knows, for instance, too many people in Greenwich Village. She mail-orders oysters and tiramisu from a shop in SoHo. She is close friends with four actual homosexuals. Her husband is asking her to Take Notes.

Where do these women get their sweatpants? She will find out.

She will start, perhaps, with the costume and work from there.

She will live according to the bromides. Take one day at a time. Take a positive attitude. *Take a hike!* She wishes that there were more interesting things that were useful and true, but it seems now that it's only the boring things that are useful and true. *One day at a time.* And *at least we have our health.* How ordinary. How obvious. One day at a time. You need a brain for that?

While the Surgeon is fine-boned, regal, and laconic—they have correctly guessed his game to be doubles—there is a bit of the mad, overcaffeinated scientist to the Oncologist. He speaks quickly. He knows a lot of studies and numbers. He can do the math. Good! Someone should be able to do the math! "It's a fast but wimpy tumor," he explains. "It typically metastasizes to the lung." He rattles off some numbers, time frames, risk statistics. Fast but wimpy: the Mother tries to imagine this combination of traits, tries to think and think, and can only come up with Claudia Osk from the fourth grade, who blushed and almost wept when called on in class, but in gym could outrun everyone in the quarter-mile fire-door-to-fence dash. The Mother thinks now of this tumor as Claudia Osk. They are going to get Claudia Osk, make her sorry. All right! Claudia Osk must die. Though it has never been mentioned before, it now seems clear that Claudia Osk should have died long ago. Who was she anyway? So conceited: not letting anyone beat her in a race. Well, hey, hey, hey: don't look now, Claudia!

The Husband nudges her. "Are you listening?"

"The chances of this happening even just to one kidney are one in fifteen thousand. Now given all these other factors, the chances on the second kidney are about one in eight."

"One in eight," says the Husband. "Not bad. As long as it's not one in fifteen thousand."

The Mother studies the trees and fish along the ceiling's edge in the Save the Planet wallpaper border. Save the Planet. Yes! But the windows in this very building don't open and diesel fumes are leaking into the ventilating system, near which, outside, a delivery truck is parked. The air is nauseous and stale.

"Really," the Oncologist is saying, "of all the cancers he could get, this is probably the best."

"We win," says the Mother.

"*Best*, I know, hardly seems the right word. Look, you two probably need to get some rest. We'll see how the surgery and histology go. Then we'll start with chemo the week following. A little light chemo: vincristine and—"

"Vincristine?" interrupts the Mother. "Wine of Christ?"

"The names are strange, I know. The other one we use is actinomycin-D. Sometimes called 'dactinomycin.' People move the *D* around to the front."

"They move the *D* around to the front," repeats the Mother.

"Yup!" the Oncologist says. "I don't know why—they just do!"

"Christ didn't survive his wine," says the Husband.

"But of course he did," says the Oncologist, and nods toward the Baby, who has now found a cupboard full of hospital linens and bandages and is yanking them all out onto the floor. "I'll see you guys tomorrow, after the surgery." And with that, the Oncologist leaves.

"Or, rather, Christ *was* his wine," mumbles the Husband. Everything he knows about the New Testament, he has gleaned from the soundtrack of *Godspell*. "His blood was the wine. What a great beverage idea."

"A little light chemo. Don't you like that one?" says the Mother. "*Eine kleine* dactinomycin. I'd like to see Mozart write that one up for a big wad o' cash."

"Come here, honey," the Husband says to the Baby, who has now pulled off both his shoes.

"It's bad enough when they refer to medical science as 'an inexact science,'" says the Mother. "But when they start referring to it as 'an art,' I get extremely nervous."

"Yeah. If we wanted art, Doc, we'd go to an art museum." The Husband picks up the Baby. "You're an artist," he says to the Mother, with the taint of accusation in his voice. "They probably think you find creativity reassuring."

The Mother sighs. "I just find it inevitable. Let's go get something to eat." And so they take the elevator to the cafeteria, where there is a high chair, and where, not noticing, they all eat a lot of apples with the price tags still on them.

Because his surgery is not until tomorrow, the Baby likes the hospital. He likes the long corridors, down which he can run. He likes everything on wheels. The flower carts in the lobby! ("Please keep your boy away from the flowers," says the vendor. "We'll buy the whole display," snaps the Mother, adding, "Actual children in a children's hospital—unbelievable, isn't it?") The Baby likes the other little boys. Places to go! People to see! Rooms to wander into! There is Intensive Care. There is the Trauma Unit. The Baby smiles and waves. What a little Cancer Personality! Bandaged citizens smile and wave back. In Peed Onk, there are the bald little boys to play with. Joey, Eric, Tim, Mort, and Tod (Mort! Tod!). There is the four-year-old, Ned, holding his little deflated rubber ball, the one with the intriguing curling hose. The Baby wants to play with it. "It's mine. Leave it alone," says Ned. "Tell the Baby to leave it alone."

"Baby, you've got to share," says the Mother from a chair some feet away.

Suddenly, from down near the Tiny Tim Lounge, comes Ned's mother, large and blond and sweatpanted. "Stop that! Stop it!" she cries out, dashing toward the Baby and Ned and pushing the Baby away. "Don't touch that!" she barks at the Baby, who is only a Baby and bursts into tears because he has never been yelled at like this before.

Ned's mom glares at everyone. "This is drawing fluid from Neddy's liver!" She pats at the rubber thing and starts to cry a little.

"Oh my God," says the Mother. She comforts the Baby, who is also crying. She and Ned, the only dry-eyed people, look at each other. "I'm so sorry," she says to Ned and then to his mother. "I'm so stupid. I thought they were squabbling over a toy."

"It does look like a toy," agrees Ned. He smiles. He is an angel. All the little boys are angels. Total, sweet, bald little angels, and now God is trying to get them back for himself. Who are they, mere mortal women, in the face of this, this powerful and overwhelming and inscrutable thing, God's will? They are the mothers, that's who. You can't have him! they shout every day. You dirty old man! *Get out of here! Hands off!*

"I'm so sorry," says the Mother again. "I didn't know."

Ned's mother smiles vaguely. "Of course you didn't know," she says, and walks back to the Tiny Tim Lounge.

The Tiny Tim Lounge is a little sitting area at the end of the Peed Onk corridor. There are two small sofas, a table, a rocking chair, a television and a VCR. There are various videos: *Speed, Dune,* and *Star Wars.* On one of the lounge walls there is a gold plaque with the singer Tiny Tim's name on it: his son was treated once at this hospital and so, five years ago, he donated money for this lounge. It is a cramped little lounge, which, one suspects, would be larger if Tiny Tim's son had actually lived. Instead, he died here, at this hospital and now there is this tiny room which is part gratitude, part generosity, part *fuck-you.*

Sifting through the videocassettes, the Mother wonders what science fiction could begin to compete with the science fiction of cancer itself—a tumor with its differentiated muscle and bone cells, a clump of wild nothing and its mad, ambitious desire to be something: something inside you, instead of you, another organism, but with a monster's architecture, a demon's sabotage and chaos. Think of leukemia, a tumor diabolically taking liquid form, better to swim about incognito in the blood. George Lucas, direct that!

Sitting with the other parents in the Tiny Tim Lounge, the night before the surgery, having put the Baby to bed in his high steel crib two rooms down, the Mother begins to hear the stories: leukemia in kindergarten, sarcomas in Little League, neuroblastomas discovered at summer camp. "Eric slid into third base, but then the scrape didn't heal." The parents pat one another's forearms and speak of other children's hospitals as if they were resorts. "You were at St. Jude's last winter? So were we. What did you think of it? We loved the staff." Jobs have been quit, marriages hacked up, bank accounts ravaged; the parents have seemingly endured the unendurable. They speak not of the *possibility* of comas brought on by the chemo, but of the *number* of them. "He was in his first coma last July," says Ned's mother. "It was a scary time, but we pulled through."

Pulling through is what people do around here. There is a kind of bravery in their lives that isn't bravery at all. It is automatic, unflinching, a mix of man and machine, consuming and unquestionable obligation meeting illness move for move in a giant even-steven game of chess—an unending round of something that looks like shadowboxing, though between love and death, which is the shadow? "Everyone admires us for our courage," says one man. "They have no idea what they're talking about."

I could get out of here, thinks the Mother. I could just get on a bus and go, never come back. Change my name. A kind of witness relocation thing.

"Courage requires options," the man adds.

The Baby might be better off.

"There are options," says a woman with a thick suede headband. "You could give up. You could fall apart."

"No, you can't. Nobody does. I've never seen it," says the man. "Well, not *really* fall apart." Then the lounge falls quiet. Over the VCR someone has taped the fortune from a fortune cookie. "Optimism," it says, "is what allows a teakettle to sing though up to its neck in hot water." Underneath, someone else has taped a clipping from a summer horoscope. "Cancer rules!" it says. Who would tape this up? Somebody's twelve-year-old brother. One of the fathers—Joey's father—gets up and tears them both off, makes a small wad in his fist.

There is some rustling of magazine pages.

The Mother clears her throat. "Tiny Tim forgot the wet bar," she says.

Ned, who is still up, comes out of his room and down the corridor, whose lights dim at nine. Standing next to her chair, he says to the Mother, "Where are you from? What is wrong with your baby?"

In the tiny room that is theirs, she sleeps fitfully in her sweatpants, occasionally leaping up to check on the Baby. This is what the sweatpants are for: leaping. In case of fire. In case of anything. In case the difference between day and night starts to dissolve, and there is no difference at all, so why pretend? In the cot beside her, the Husband, who has taken a sleeping pill, is snoring loudly, his arms folded about his head in a kind of origami. How could either of them have stayed back at the house, with its empty high chair and empty crib? Occasionally the Baby wakes and cries out, and she bolts up, goes to him, rubs his back, rearranges the linens. The clock on the metal dresser shows that it is five after three. Then twenty to five. And then it is really morning, the beginning of this day, nephrectomy day. Will she be glad when it's over, or barely alive, or both? Each day this week has arrived huge, empty, and unknown, like a spaceship, and this one especially is lit a bright gray.

"He'll need to put this on," says John, one of the nurses, bright and early, handing the Mother a thin greenish garment with roses and teddy bears printed on it. A wave of nausea hits her; this smock, she thinks, will soon be splattered with—with what?

The Baby is awake but drowsy. She lifts off his pajamas. "Don't forget, *bubeleh*," she whispers, undressing and dressing him. "We will be with you every moment, every step. When you think you are asleep and float-ing off far away from everybody, Mommy will still be there." If she hasn't fled on a bus. "Mommy will take care of you. And Daddy, too." She hopes the Baby does not detect her own fear and uncertainty, which she must hide from him, like a limp. He is hungry, not having been allowed to eat, and he is no longer amused by this new place, but worried about its hard-ships. Oh, my baby, she thinks. And the room starts to swim a little. The Husband comes in to take over. "Take a break," he says to her. "I'll walk him around for five minutes."

She leaves but doesn't know where to go. In the hallway, she is approached by a kind of social worker, a customer-relations person, who had given them a video to watch about the anesthesia: how the parent accompanies the child into the operating room, and how gently, nicely the drugs are administered.

"Did you watch the video?"

"Yes," says the Mother.

"Wasn't it helpful?"

"I don't know," says the Mother.

"Do you have any questions?" asks the video woman. "Do you have any questions?" asked of someone who has recently landed in this fearful, alien place seems to the Mother an absurd and amazing little courtesy. The very specificity of a question would give a lie to the overwhelming strangeness of everything around her.

"Not right now," says the Mother. "Right now, I think I'm just going to go to the bathroom."

When she returns to the Baby's room, everyone is there: the surgeon, the anesthesiologist, all the nurses, the social worker. In their blue caps and scrubs, they look like a clutch of forget-me-nots, and forget them, who could? The Baby, in his little teddy-bear smock, seems cold and scared. He reaches out and the Mother lifts him from the Husband's arms, rubs his back to warm him.

"Well, it's time!" says the Surgeon, forcing a smile.

"Shall we go?" says the Anesthesiologist.

What follows is a blur of obedience and bright lights. They take an elevator down to a big concrete room, the anteroom, the greenroom, the backstage of the operating room. Lining the walls are long shelves full of blue surgical outfits. "Children often become afraid of the color blue," says one of the nurses. But of course. Of course! "Now, which one of you would like to come into the operating room for the anesthesia?"

"I will," says the Mother.

"Are you sure?" asks the Husband.

"Yup." She kisses the Baby's hair. "Mr. Curlyhead," people keep calling him here, and it seems both rude and nice. Women look admiringly at his long lashes and exclaim, "Always the boys! Always the boys!"

Two surgical nurses put a blue smock and a blue cotton cap on the Mother. The Baby finds this funny and keeps pulling at the cap. "This way," says another nurse, and the Mother follows. "Just put the Baby down on the table."

In the video, the mother holds the baby and fumes are gently waved under the baby's nose until he falls asleep. Now, out of view of camera or social worker, the Anesthesiologist is anxious to get this under way and not let too much gas leak out into the room generally. The occupational hazard of this, his chosen profession, is gas exposure and nerve damage, and it has started to worry him. No doubt he frets about it to his wife every night. Now he turns the gas on and quickly clamps the plastic mouthpiece over the baby's cheeks and lips.

The Baby is startled. The Mother is startled. The Baby starts to scream and redden behind the plastic, but he cannot be heard. He thrashes. "Tell him it's okay," says the nurse to the Mother.

Okay? "It's okay," repeats the Mother, holding his hand, but she knows he can tell it's not okay, because he can see not only that she is still wearing that stupid paper cap but that her words are mechanical and swallowed, and she is biting her lips to keep them from trembling. Panicked, he attempts to sit. He cannot breathe; his arms reach up. *Bye-bye, outside.* And then, quite quickly, his eyes shut; he untenses and has fallen not *into* sleep but aside to sleep, an odd, kidnapping kind of sleep, his terror now hidden someplace deep inside him.

"How did it go?" asks the social worker, waiting in the concrete outer room. The Mother is hysterical. A nurse has ushered her out.

"It wasn't at all like the filmstrip!" she cries. "It wasn't like the filmstrip at all!"

"The filmstrip? You mean the video?" asks the social worker.

"It wasn't like that at all! It was brutal and unforgivable."

"Why that's terrible," she says, her role now no longer misinformational but janitorial, and she touches the Mother's arm, though the Mother shakes it off and goes to find the Husband.

She finds him in the large mulberry Surgery Lounge, where he has been taken and where there is free hot chocolate in small Styrofoam cups. Red cellophane garlands festoon the doorways. She has totally forgotten it is as close to Christmas as this. A pianist in the corner is playing "Carol of the Bells," and it sounds not only unfestive but scary, like the theme from *The Exorcist.*

There is a giant clock on the far wall. It is a kind of porthole into the operating room, a way of assessing the Baby's ordeal: forty-five minutes for the Hickman implant; two and a half hours for the nephrectomy. And then, after that, three months of chemotherapy. The magazine on her lap stays open at a ruby-hued perfume ad.

"Still not taking notes," says the Husband.

"Nope."

"You know, in a way, this is the kind of thing you've *always* written about."

"You are really something, you know that? This is life. This isn't a 'kind of thing.'"

"But this is the kind of thing that fiction is: it's the unlivable life, the strange room tacked onto the house, the extra moon that is circling the earth unbeknownst to science."

"I told you that."

"I'm quoting you."

She looks at her watch, thinking of the Baby. "How long has it been?"

"Not long. Too long. In the end, maybe those're the same things."

"What do you suppose is happening to him right this second?"

Infection? Slipping knives? "I don't know. But you know what? I've gotta go. I've gotta just walk a bit." The Husband gets up, walks around the lounge, then comes back and sits down.

The synapses between the minutes are unswimmable. An hour is thick as fudge. The Mother feels depleted; she is a string of empty tin cans attached by wire, something a goat would sniff and chew, something now and then enlivened by a jolt of electricity.

She hears their names being called over the intercom. "Yes? Yes?" She stands up quickly. Her words have flown out before her, an exhalation of birds. The piano music has stopped. The pianist is gone. She and the Husband approach the main desk, where a man looks up at them and smiles. Before him is a Xeroxed list of patients' names. "That's our little boy right there," says the Mother, seeing the Baby's name on the list and pointing at it. "Is there some word? Is everything okay?"

"Yes," says the man. "Your boy is doing fine. They've just finished with the catheter, and they are moving on to the kidney."

"But it's been two hours already! Oh my God, did something go wrong? What happened? What went wrong?"

"Did something go wrong?" The Husband tugs at his collar.

"Not really. It just took longer than they expected. I'm told everything is fine. They wanted you to know."

"Thank you," says the Husband. They turn and walk back toward where they were sitting.

"I'm not going to make it." The Mother sighs, sinking into a fake leather chair shaped somewhat like a baseball mitt. "But before I go, I'm taking half this hospital out with me."

"Do you want some coffee?" asks the Husband.

"I don't know," says the Mother. "No, I guess not. No. Do you?"

"Nah, I don't, either, I guess," he says.

"Would you like part of an orange?"

"Oh, maybe, I guess, if you're having one." She takes an orange from her purse and just sits there peeling its difficult skin, the flesh rupturing beneath her fingers, the juice trickling down her hands, stinging the hangnails. She and the Husband chew and swallow, discreetly spit the seeds into Kleenex, and read from photocopies of the latest medical research, which they begged from the intern. They read, and underline, and sigh and close their eyes, and after some time, the surgery is over. A nurse from Peed Onk comes down to tell them.

"Your little boy's in recovery right now. He's doing well. You can see him in about fifteen minutes."

•   •   •

How can it be described? How can any of it be described? The trip and the story of the trip are always two different things. The narrator is the one who has stayed home, but then, afterward, presses her mouth upon the traveler's mouth, in order to make the mouth work, to make the mouth say, say, say. One cannot go to a place and speak of it; one cannot both see and say, not really. One can go, and upon returning make a lot of hand motions and indications with the arms. The mouth itself, working at the speed of light, at the eye's instructions, is necessarily struck still; so fast, so much to report, it hangs open and dumb as a gutted bell. All that unsayable life! That's where the narrator comes in. The narrator comes with her kisses and mimicry and tidying up. The narrator comes and makes a slow, fake song of the mouth's eager devastation.

It is a horror and a miracle to see him. He is lying in his crib in his room, tubed up, splayed like a boy on a cross, his arms stiffened into cardboard "no-no's" so that he cannot yank out the tubes. There is the bladder catheter, the nasal-gastric tube, and the Hickman, which, beneath the skin, is plugged into his jugular, then popped out his chest wall and capped with a long plastic cap. There is a large bandage taped over his abdomen. Groggy, on a morphine drip, still he is able to look at her when, maneuvering through all the vinyl wiring, she leans to hold him, and when she does, he begins to cry, but cry silently, without motion or noise. She has never seen a baby cry without motion or noise. It is the crying of an old person: silent, beyond opinion, shattered. In someone so tiny, it is frightening and unnatural. She wants to pick up the Baby and run—out of there, out of there. She wants to whip out a gun: *No-no's, eh? This whole thing is what I call a no-no.* Don't you touch him! she wants to shout at the surgeons and the needle nurses. Not anymore! No more! No more! She would crawl up and lie beside him in the crib if she could. But instead, because of all his intricate wiring, she must lean and cuddle, sing to him, songs of peril and flight: "We gotta get out of this place, if it's the last thing we ever do. We gotta get out of this place . . . there's a better life for me and you."

Very 1967. She was eleven then and impressionable.

The Baby looks at her, pleadingly, his arms splayed out in surrender. To where? Where is there to go? Take me! Take me!

That night, postop night, the Mother and Husband lie afloat in the cot together. A fluorescent lamp near the crib is kept on in the dark. The Baby breathes evenly but thinly in his drugged sleep. The morphine in its first flooding doses apparently makes him feel as if he were falling backward—or so the Mother has been told—and it causes the Baby to jerk, to catch himself over and over, as if he were being dropped from a tree. "Is this right? Isn't there something that should be done?" The nurses come in hourly, different ones—the night shifts seem strangely short and frequent. If the Baby stirs or frets, the nurses give him more morphine through the Hickman catheter, then leave to tend to other patients. The Mother rises to check on him in the low light. There is gurgling from the clear plastic suction tube coming out of his mouth. Brownish clumps have collected in the tube. What is going on? The Mother rings for the nurse. Is it Renée or Sarah or Darcy? She's forgotten.

"What, what is it?" murmurs the Husband, waking up.

"Something is wrong," says the Mother. "It looks like blood in his N-G tube."

"What?" The Husband gets out of bed. He, too, is wearing sweatpants.

The nurse—Valerie—pushes open the heavy door to the room and enters quietly. "Everything okay?"

"There's something wrong here. The tube is sucking blood out of his stomach. It looks like it may have perforated his stomach and that now he's bleeding internally. Look!"

Valerie is a saint, but her voice is the standard hospital saint voice: an infuriating, pharmaceutical calm. It says, Everything is normal here. Death is normal. Pain is normal. Nothing is abnormal. So there is nothing to get excited about. "Well now, let's see." She holds up the plastic tube and tries to see inside it. "Hmmm," she says. "I'll call the attending physician."

Because this is a research and teaching hospital, all the regular doctors are at home sleeping in their Mission-style beds. Tonight, as is apparently the case every weekend night, the attending physician is a medical student. He looks fifteen. The authority he attempts to convey, he cannot remotely inhabit. He is not even in the same building with it. He shakes everyone's hands, then strokes his chin, a gesture no doubt gleaned from some piece of dinner theater his parents took him to once. As if there were an actual beard on that chin! As if beard growth on that chin were even possible! *Our Town! Kiss Me Kate! Barefoot in the Park!* He is attempting to convince, if not to impress.

"We're in trouble," the Mother whispers to the Husband. She is tired, tired of young people grubbing for grades. "We've got Dr. 'Kiss Me Kate,' here."

The Husband looks at her blankly, a mix of disorientation and divorce.

The medical student holds the tubing in his hands. "I don't really see anything," he says.

He flunks! "You don't?" The Mother shoves her way in, holds the clear tubing in both hands. "That," she says. "Right here and here." Just this past semester, she said to one of her own students, "If you don't see how this essay is better than that one, then I want you just to go out into the hallway and stand there until you do." Is it important to keep one's voice down? The Baby stays asleep. He is drugged and dreaming, far away.

"Hmmm," says the medical student. "Perhaps there's a little irritation in the stomach."

"A little irritation?" The Mother grows furious. "This is blood. These are clumps and clots. This stupid thing is sucking the life right out of him!" Life! She is starting to cry.

They turn off the suction and bring in antacids, which they feed into the Baby through the tube. Then they turn the suction on again. This time on low.

"What was it on before?" asks the Husband.

"High" says Valerie. "Doctor's orders, though I don't know why. I don't know why these doctors do a lot of the things they do."

"Maybe they're . . . not all that bright?" suggests the Mother. She is feeling relief and rage simultaneously: there is a feeling of prayer and litigation in the air. Yet essentially, she is grateful. Isn't she? She thinks she is. And still, and still: look at all the things you have to do to protect a child, a hospital merely an intensification of life's cruel obstacle course.

The Surgeon comes to visit on Saturday morning. He steps in and nods at the Baby, who is awake but glazed from the morphine, his eyes two dark unseeing grapes. "The boy looks fine," the Surgeon announces. He peeks under the Baby's bandage. "The stitches look good," he says. The Baby's abdomen is stitched all the way across like a baseball. "And the other kidney, when we looked at it yesterday face-to-face, looked fine. We'll try to wean him off the morphine a little, and see how he's doing on Monday." He clears his throat. "And now," he says, looking about the room at the nurses and medical students, "I would like to speak with the Mother, alone."

The Mother's heart gives a jolt. "Me?"

"Yes," he says, motioning, then turning.

She gets up and steps out into the empty hallway with him, closing the door behind her. What can this be about? She hears the Baby fretting a little in his crib. Her brain fills with pain and alarm. Her voice comes out as a hoarse whisper. "Is there something—"

"There is a particular thing I need from you," says the Surgeon, turning and standing there very seriously.

"Yes?" Her heart is pounding. She does not feel resilient enough for any more bad news.

"I need to ask a favor."

"Certainly," she says, attempting very hard to summon the strength and courage for this occasion, whatever it is; her throat has tightened to a fist.

From inside his white coat, the surgeon removes a thin paperback book and thrusts it toward her. "Will you sign my copy of your novel?"

The Mother looks down and sees that it is indeed a copy of a novel she has written, one about teenaged girls.

She looks up. A big, spirited grin is cutting across his face. "I read this last summer," he says, "and I still remember parts of it! Those girls got into such trouble!"

Of all the surreal moments of the last few days, this, she thinks, might be the most so.

"Okay," she says, and the Surgeon merrily hands her a pen.

"You can just write 'To Dr.—' Oh, I don't need to tell you what to write."

The Mother sits down on a bench and shakes ink into the pen. A sigh of relief washes over and out of her. Oh, the pleasure of a sigh of relief, like the finest moments of love; has anyone properly sung the praises of sighs of relief? She opens the book to the title page. She breathes deeply. What is he doing reading novels about teenaged girls, anyway? And why didn't he buy the hardcover? She inscribes something grateful and true, then hands the book back to him.

"Is he going to be okay?"

"The boy? The boy is going to be fine," he says, then taps her stiffly on the shoulder. "Now you take care. It's Saturday. Drink a little wine."

Over the weekend, while the Baby sleeps, the Mother and Husband sit together in the Tiny Tim Lounge. The Husband is restless and makes cafeteria and sundry runs, running errands for everyone. In his absence, the other parents regale her further with their sagas. Pediatric cancer and chemo stories: the children's amputations, blood poisoning, teeth flaking like shale, the learning delays and disabilities caused by chemo frying the young, budding brain. But strangely optimistic codas are tacked on—endings as stiff and loopy as carpenter's lace, crisp and empty as lettuce, reticulate as a net—ah, words. "After all that business with the tutor, he's better now, and fitted with new incisors by my wife's cousin's husband, who did dental school in two and a half years, if you can believe that. We hope for the best. We take things as they come. Life is hard."

"Life's a big problem," agrees the Mother. Part of her welcomes and invites all their tales. In the few long days since this nightmare began, part of her has become addicted to disaster and war stories. She wants only to hear about the sadness and emergencies of others. They are the only situations that can join hands with her own; everything else bounces off her shiny shield of resentment and unsympathy. Nothing else can even stay in her brain. From this, no doubt, the philistine world is made, or should one say recruited? Together, the parents huddle all day in the Tiny Tim Lounge—no need to watch *Oprah*. They leave Oprah in the dust. Oprah has nothing on them. They chat matter-of-factly, then fall silent and watch *Dune* or *Star Wars*, in which there are bright and shiny robots, whom the Mother now sees not as robots at all but as human beings who have had terrible things happen to them.

Some of their friends visit with stuffed animals and soft greetings of "Looking good" for the dozing baby, though the room is way past the stuffed-animal limit. The Mother arranges, once more, a plateful of Mint Milano cookies and cups of take-out coffee for guests. All her nutso pals stop by— the two on Prozac, the one obsessed with the word *penis* in the word *happiness*, the one who recently had her hair foiled green. "Your friends put the *de* in *fin de siècle*," says the husband. Overheard, or recorded, all marital conversation sounds as if someone must be joking, though usually no one is.

She loves her friends, especially loves them for coming, since there are times they all fight and don't speak for weeks. Is this friendship? For now and here, it must do and is, and is, she swears it is. For one, they never offer impromptu spiritual lectures about death, how it is part of life, its natural ebb and flow, how we all must accept that, or other such utterances that make her want to scratch out some eyes. Like true friends, they take no hardy or elegant stance loosely choreographed from some broad perspective. They get right in there and mutter "Jesus Christ!" and shake their heads. Plus, they are the only people who not only will laugh at her stupid jokes but offer up stupid ones of their own. *What do you get when you cross Tiny Tim with a pit bull?* A child's illness is a strain on the mind. They know how to laugh in a fluty, desperate way— unlike the people who are more her husband's friends and who seem just to deepen their sorrowful gazes, nodding their heads with Sympathy. How exiling and estranging are everybody's Sympathetic Expressions! When anyone laughs, she thinks, Okay! Hooray: a buddy. In disaster as in show business.

Nurses come and go; their chirpy voices both startle and soothe. Some of the other Peed Onk parents stick their heads in to see how the Baby is and offer encouragement.

Green Hair scratches her head. "Everyone's so friendly here. Is there someone in this place who isn't doing all this airy, scripted optimism—or are people like that the only people here?"

"It's Modern Middle Medicine meets the Modern Middle Family," says the Husband. "In the Modern Middle West."

Someone has brought in take-out lo mein, and they all eat it out in the hall by the elevators.

Parents are allowed use of the Courtesy Line.

"You've got to have a second child," says a different friend on the phone, a friend from out of town. "An heir and a spare. That's what we did. We had another child to ensure we wouldn't off ourselves if we lost our first."

"Really?"

"I'm serious."

"A formal suicide? Wouldn't you just drink yourself into a lifelong stupor and let it go at that?'

"Nope. I knew how I would do it even. For a while, until our second came along, I had it all planned."

"What did you plan?"

"I can't go into too much detail, because—Hi, honey!—the kids are here now in the room. But I'll spell out the general idea: R-O-P-E."

Sunday evening, she goes and sinks down on the sofa in the Tiny Tim Lounge next to Frank, Joey's father. He is a short, stocky man with the currentless, flatlined look behind the eyes that all the parents eventually get here. He has shaved his head bald in solidarity with his son. His little boy has been battling cancer for five years. It is now in the liver, and the rumor around the corridor is that Joey has three weeks to live. She knows that Joey's mother, Heather, left Frank years ago, two years into the cancer, and has remarried and had another child, a girl named Brittany. The Mother sees Heather here sometimes with her new life—the cute little girl and the new, young, full-haired husband who will never be so maniacally and debilitatingly obsessed with Joey's illness the way Frank, her first husband, was. Heather comes to visit Joey, to say hello and now good-bye, but she is not Joey's main man. Frank is.

Frank is full of stories—about the doctors, about the food, about the nurses, about Joey. Joey, affectless from his meds, sometimes leaves his room and comes out to watch TV in his bathrobe. He is jaundiced and bald, and though he is nine, he looks no older than six. Frank has devoted the last four and a half years to saving Joey's life. When the cancer was first diagnosed, the doctors gave Joey a 20 percent chance of living six more months. Now here it is, almost five years later, and Joey's still here. It is all due to Frank, who, early on, quit his job as vice president of a consulting firm in order to commit himself totally to his son. He is proud of everything he's given up and done, but he is tired. Part of him now really believes things are coming to a close, that this is the end. He says this without tears. There are no more tears.

"You have probably been through more than anyone else on this corridor," says the Mother.

"I could tell you stories," he says. There is a sour odor between them, and she realizes that neither of them has bathed for days.

"Tell me one. Tell me the worst one." She knows he hates his ex-wife and hates her new husband even more.

"The worst? They're all the worst. Here's one: one morning, I went out for breakfast with my buddy—it was the only time I'd left Joey alone ever; left him for two hours is all—and when I came back, his N-G tube was full of blood. They had the suction on too high, and it was sucking the guts right out of him."

"Oh my God. That just happened to us," said the Mother.

"It did?"

"Friday night."

"You're kidding. They let that happen again? I gave them such a chewing-out about that!"

"I guess our luck is not so good. We get your very worst story on the second night we're here."

"It's not a bad place, though."

"It's not?"

"Naw. I've seen worse. I've taken Joey everywhere."

"He seems very strong." Truth is, at this point, Joey seems like a zombie and frightens her.

"Joey's a fucking genius. A biological genius. They'd given him six months, remember."

The Mother nods.

"Six months is not very long," says Frank. "Six months is nothing. He was four and a half years old."

All the words are like blows. She feels flooded with affection and mourning for this man. She looks away, out the window, out past the hospital parking lot, up toward the black marbled sky and the electric eyelash of the moon. "And now he's nine," she says. "You're his hero."

"And he's mine," says Frank, though the fatigue in his voice seems to overwhelm him. "He'll be that forever. Excuse me," he says, "I've got to go check. His breathing hasn't been good. Excuse me."

"Good news and bad," says the Oncologist on Monday. He has knocked, entered the room, and now stands there. Their cots are unmade. One wastebasket is overflowing with coffee cups. "We've got the pathologist's report. The bad news is that the kidney they removed had certain lesions, called 'rests,' which are associated with a higher risk for disease in the other kidney. The good news is that the tumor is stage one, regular cell structure, and under five hundred grams, which qualifies you for a national experiment in which chemotherapy isn't done but your boy is monitored with ultrasound instead. It's not all that risky, given that the patient's watched closely, but here is the literature on it. There are forms to sign, if you decide to do that. Read all this and we can discuss it further. You have to decide within four days."

Lesions? Rests? They dry up and scatter like M&M's on the floor. All she hears is the part about no chemo. Another sigh of relief rises up in her and spills out. In a life where there is only the bearable and the unbearable, a sigh of relief is an ecstasy.

"No chemo?" says the Husband. "Do you recommend that?"

The Oncologist shrugs. What casual gestures these doctors are permitted! "I know chemo. I like chemo," says the Oncologist. "But this is for you to decide. It depends how you feel."

The Husband leans forward. "But don't you think that now that we have the upper hand with this thing, we should keep going? Shouldn't we stomp on it, beat it, smash it to death with the chemo?"

The Mother swats him angrily and hard. "Honey, you're delirious!" She whispers, but it comes out as a hiss. "This is our lucky break!" Then she adds gently, "We don't want the Baby to have chemo."

The Husband turns back to the Oncologist. "What do *you* think?"

"It could be," he says, shrugging. "It could be that this is your lucky break. But you won't know for sure for five years."

The Husband turns back to the Mother. "Okay," he says. "Okay."

The Baby grows happier and strong. He begins to move and sit and eat. Wednesday morning, they are allowed to leave, and leave without chemo. The Oncologist looks a little nervous. "Are you nervous about this?" asks the Mother.

"Of course I'm nervous." But he shrugs and doesn't look that nervous. "See you in six weeks for the ultrasound," he says, waves and then leaves, looking at his big black shoes as he does.

The Baby smiles, even toddles around a little, the sun bursting through the clouds, an angel chorus crescendoing. Nurses arrive. The Hickman is taken out of the Baby's neck and chest; antibiotic lotion is dispensed. The Mother packs up their bags. The Baby sucks on a bottle of juice and does not cry.

"No chemo?" says one of the nurses. "Not even a *little* chemo?"

"We're doing watch and wait," says the Mother.

The other parents look envious but concerned. They have never seen any child get out of there with his hair and white blood cells intact.

"Will you be okay?" asks Ned's mother.

"The worry's going to kill us," says the Husband.

"But if all we have to do is worry," chides the Mother, "every day for a hundred years, it'll be easy. It'll be nothing. I'll take all the worry in the world, if it wards off the thing itself."

"That's right," says Ned's mother. "Compared to everything else, compared to all the actual events, the worry is nothing."

The Husband shakes his head. "I'm such an amateur," he moans.

"You're both doing admirably," says the other mother. "Your baby's lucky, and I wish you all the best."

The Husband shakes her hand warmly. "Thank you," he says. "You've been wonderful."

Another mother, the mother of Eric, comes up to them. "It's all very hard," she says, her head cocked to one side. "But there's a lot of collateral beauty along the way."

Collateral beauty? Who is entitled to such a thing? A child is ill. No one is entitled to any collateral beauty!

"Thank you," says the Husband.

Joey's father, Frank, comes up and embraces them both. "It's a journey," he says. He chucks the Baby on the chin. "Good luck, little man."

"Yes, thank you so much," says the Mother. "We hope things go well with Joey." She knows that Joey had a hard, terrible night.

Frank shrugs and steps back. "Gotta go," he says. "Good-bye!"

"Bye," she says, and then he is gone. She bites the inside of her lip, a bit tearily, then bends down to pick up the diaper bag, which is now stuffed with little animals; helium balloons are tied to its zipper. Shouldering the thing, the Mother feels she has just won a prize. All the parents have now vanished down the hall in the opposite direction. The Husband moves close. With one arm, he takes the Baby from her; with the other, he rubs her back. He can see she is starting to get weepy.

"Aren't these people nice? Don't you feel better hearing about their lives?" he asks.

Why does he do this, form clubs all the time; why does even this society of suffering soothe him? When it comes to death and dying, perhaps someone in this family ought to be more of a snob.

"All these nice people with their brave stories," he continues as they make their way toward the elevator bank, waving good-bye to the nursing staff as they go, even the Baby waving shyly. *Bye-bye! Bye-bye!* "Don't you feel consoled, knowing we're all in the same boat, that we're all in this together?"

But who on earth would want to be in this boat? the Mother thinks. This boat is a nightmare boat. Look where it goes: to a silver-and-white room, where, just before your eyesight and hearing and your ability to touch or be touched disappear entirely, you must watch your child die.

Rope! Bring on the rope.

"Let's make our own way," says the Mother, "and not in this boat."

Woman Overboard! She takes the Baby back from the Husband, cups the Baby's cheek in her hand, kisses his brow and then, quickly, his flowery mouth. The Baby's heart—she can hear it—drums with life. "For as long as I live," says the Mother, pressing the elevator button—up or down, everyone in the end has to leave this way—"I never want to see any of these people again."

There are the notes.

Now where is the money?

1. How does the story open? What keeps you reading?
2. How is the story structured? Is there a conflict–crisis–resolution? If so, what is the crisis?
3. What keeps the tension in the story high? What techniques does the author use to keep you interested?

CHAPTER TWELVE

What's This Creative Work Really About?

Part 1: THE ART OF TRANSFERRING TRUE EMOTIONS ONTO SENSORY EVENTS

Getting Started

Sooner or later, we need to take a step back from our writing and ask the big question: What's the meaning of this story or nonfiction piece? Yes, it's about a boy going to visit his dying uncle, or it's a journal about the first few months of a child's life; but on a deeper, emotional level, what's it really *about*?

In many textbooks this is called *theme*, but I thought we'd avoid using that word because (again) it has us thinking in terms of abstractions: love or beauty or death rather than the particulars of the highly specific situations we have chosen to creatively investigate. And of course, no story or nonfiction piece that is worth its weight in words can be easily paraphrased—we would never want to be able to easily sum up what a piece is about just like that. That would indicate a major problem with the piece: a lack of complexity, depth, and resonance—all the things that make a creative piece worth reading.

In this chapter, we'll first review the precept that all writing must exist on two levels: in the sensory world, and in a world that embraces a complex emotional and intellectual subtext. Then we will talk about what we can do to join these two equally important aspects together. We'll try some exercises that will help us understand how to do this successfully. Finally, I've included some readings that illustrate this particular aspect of writing creatively.

Many Different Answers to the Same Question

Trying to figure out the meaning of a piece can be a difficult challenge. For example, take a story we've read in this book: "Emergency" by Denis Johnson (pp. 47–56), you could correctly answer the question "What is this story about?" with any number of responses. It's a story about man who takes drugs and goes for a joyride in the country. It's a story about redemption. It's a story about longing for a time that has been lost forever. It's a story about friendship. It's a story about a guy who continually messes up. And so forth.

Nothing except the text itself can give someone a full understanding of what stories like this are "about." As Flannery O'Connor says:

> Some people have the notion that you read the story and then climb out of it into the meaning, but for the fiction writer himself the whole story is the meaning, because it is an experience, not an abstraction.

Because it is an experience, it must exist in *this* world, the world of the five senses. But it must also have resonance at a deeper emotional level. This dual nature of creative writing is what this chapter focuses on.

Writing about What Matters

In a way, we're back to what we were talking about at the beginning of this book, in Chapter 2: the need to write about what matters. If a subject doesn't resonate for us, personally, if we don't find it irresistibly interesting, then the result will be utter dullness for the reader, no matter how skillfully we are able to render things on the page.

Things to write about come from many many places: images, overheard conversations, memories, stories told to you by others, etc. Something moves you, intrigues you. There is mystery there for you. Something worth exploring.

As we've talked about ad infinitum, that "something" should be very, very specific. Not abstract, not theoretical, not general. And that something must do three things:

1. It must resonate with true emotion *for you*.
2. It must remain active and mysterious and complex *even after* you've successfully gotten it on the page.
3. It must be rendered with the five senses.

As we learned in Chapter 3, when discussing literary images, and in Chapter 8, when discussing dialogue, writing always exists on two levels:

- What happens in the world of the senses (plot, storyline, words spoken)
- What is really going on (emotional and intellectual subtext)

Sometimes the top aspect is "given" to us. With very little or no tweaking, we can make a story or nonfiction piece work simply by writing down something that actually happened to us. The meaning of the events is perfectly intelligible to whoever reads it; the emotional subtext is magically tied to the events of the piece. This *does* happen.

But more frequently, that simply doesn't work. We wonder, "Why doesn't this thing that happened to me carry the emotional weight I want it to when I relate it to others? I'm telling the story just as it happened to me, yet people don't seem to 'get' this important thing I'm trying to get across."

This can happen because of a problem in marrying the surface world of the piece with the subtext: you haven't successfully *transferred* the emotional and intellectual complexity of the intended subtext onto the sensory-based objects and events themselves.

It's the opposite of abstraction, what we're talking about here. To *abstract* something is to dissociate something from a particular object. In other words, you move away from the very particular scene of a mother interacting with her truculent daughter and extrapolate "mother love." That's the reverse of what we do in writing; we are talking about the act of *association*, about the skill and, yes, talent required to associate complex meaning with those most mundane of all things: sensory objects, people, and events.

Transference: Borrowing from Freud

A key part of Sigmund Freud's theory of psychoanalysis had to do with the idea of *transference*. The idea is that we commonly take emotions that we are feeling and transfer them onto other people. For example, we feel angry but can't bear to acknowledge that anger. So we transfer that emotion onto other people, and get the inexplicable feeling that other people are mad *at us*. In the psychoanalytic relationship, emotions transferred in such an undeserving way onto the analyst would give clues as to what the patient was really feeling inside (theoretically, at least, since the analyst won't have "earned" the visceral reactions of the patient to him or her, it provides a way to isolate and examine the emotions being transferred).

This is exactly what we do in writing. We take emotional meaning and *transfer* it onto people, places, or things. Thus, with Little Red Riding

Hood, a walk through the woods becomes much more than just a simple walk through the woods—it becomes one filled with emotional as well as physical danger and the potential loss of innocence.

Our very important goal as writers is to transfer *by whatever means possible* important and complex emotions onto the sensory objects and events we've chosen to render in our story or nonfiction piece.

We use the narrative skills we've learned about in this book (description, scene, narrative, dialogue, etc.) to effect a *transformation* so that the importance and truth of the event is transferred to the page. Our goal: to render the emotional truth (not necessarily the facts; it depends on whether we are writing fiction or nonfiction) of the original experience.

So there are actually three steps to the writing process:

1. We **notice something** that deserves to be written about.
2. We **discover** the emotional heart of our material through writing (remember moving from "triggering" to "real" subject, from Chapter 2).
3. We **render** our material in such a way that the emotion/truth is apparent (we are transferring/attaching concrete sensory details to correspond with emotions).

In this way, you get at both what has happened (what has been observed, witnessed, reacted to), and what it "means" (the emotional subtext).

In fiction, of course, we make up things when we do this. In nonfiction, we stick to facts. But in both cases, we must accomplish the same thing: attach meaning and emotions to sensory objects.

We Are Made of Dust

If this sounds familiar, that's because in a way we're back to where we were at the beginning of Chapter 3: focusing intently on concrete details. Without the details—without remembering, as Flannery O'Connor admonished us, that "we are made of dust"—our work is theoretical, abstract, empty, and devoid of interest.

That's because you can't attach an emotion to an abstraction or intellectual idea. There's no "stickiness" there. It won't work. Emotions need to be attached to things of this world: things as mundane as tables and chairs and trees and flowers. Innocuous things . . . until we've imbued them with the power of our imagination.

What these images should (must) be: the outward manifestation of interior movement, or emotions. Not just physical objects, but truth. Below, in the story "Paul's Case" by Willa Cather, we see how physical details like new linen and flowers carry emotional weight; these objects have come to mean much more than just their surface physical attributes.

> When he was shown to his sitting room on the eighth floor, he saw at a glance that everything was as it should be; there was but one detail in his mental picture that the place did not realize, so he rang for the bell boy and sent him down for flowers. He moved about nervously until the boy returned, putting away his new linen and fingering it delightedly as he did so. When the flowers came, he put them hastily into water, and then tumbled into a hot bath. Presently, he came out of his white bathroom, resplendent in his new silk underwear, and playing with the tassels of his red robe. The snow was whirling so fiercely outside his windows that he could scarcely see across the street; but within, the air was deliciously soft and fragrant. He put the violets and jonquils on the table beside the couch, and threw himself down with a long sigh, covering himself with a Roman blanket. He was thoroughly tired; he had been in such haste, he had stood up to such a strain, covered so much ground in the last twenty-four hours, that he wanted to think about how it had all come about. Lulled by the sound of the wind, the warm air, and the cool fragrance of the flowers, he sank into deep, drowsy retrospection.

Photography provides an obvious example of this. As an art form, photography isn't just about capturing an exact replica of the thing itself, but is after something deeper, some truth. When Edward Weston photographed peppers, he was photographing much more than a vegetable: something sensuous and beguiling and almost sexual in nature.

We want emotions to be forever and unalterably linked to those objects and events we choose. A key thing to remember is that popular fiction, in many cases, is all about the surface events: who marries whom, who makes money, who kills, who dies, etc. On the other hand, I've seen much "serious" but poorly written fiction that's all emotional subtext: the writer feels so intensely and wants to cram so much *feeling* into a piece, but forgets that we are made of dust, and require things of the sensory world to carry our meaning. What we want is a marriage of the two.

The Road to Universality

It's one of the contradictions of writing, this need for specificity. Especially when we want to make a difference, we want to matter, we want everyone to feel the universality of what we are saying, we don't want it just to apply to this particular situation, we don't want it to be *just* a story about a girl fly-fishing with her grandfather, but something more, something that brings meaning to others.

Here's an example (from Margaret Atwood's "Significant Moments in the Life of My Mother") in which the author renders the house where the narrator's mother grew up. Although it is unmistakably the house of the narrator's mother, and no other house, still there is universality about it; it gives us a sense that we, too, have been there and understand the emotional undertones of the place:

> In this house there were many rooms. Although I have been there, although I have seen the house with my own eyes, I still don't know how many. Parts of it were closed off, or so it seemed; there were back staircases. Passages led elsewhere. Five children lived in it, two parents, a hired man, and a hired girl, whose name and faces kept changing. The structure of the house was hierarchical, with my grandfather at the top, but its secret life— the life of pie crusts, clean sheets, the box of rags in the linen closet, the loaves in the oven—was female. The house, and all through it, the air was heavy with things that were known but not spoken. Like a hollow log, a drum, a church, it amplified, so that conversations whispered in it sixty years ago can be half-heard even today.

But It's the Truth! And Other Common Pleas for Clemency

It's very common, in a creative writing workshop, to hear the criticism that a piece is just not believable. People express skepticism about coincidences, character behavior, plot twists, or other aspects of a story or nonfiction piece that has been put up for discussion. And a common response to this sort of criticism is, "But it really happened this way!"

How can it be that things that really happened can be less believable than other, made-up events?

The answer is simple: the piece has not been rendered in a way that makes it believable to readers. For example, in "Emergency" by Denis Johnson, a whole slew of events must converge for the main character to find himself in the emotional space he's in by the end of the story. There are the drugs he's consumed, of course. His sleepless state. The successful "operation" his drug-addled friend performs in the emergency room. Getting lost in the snowstorm. Rescuing (and then killing) the baby rabbits. His current longing—for the story is told from some point in the distant future—for this simpler, happier time in his life.

You could argue that without any of these events, or emotional preparations, the moment of reckoning for him would not be credible. Certainly it would not have the emotional weight it does.

Creative Nonfiction: On Being True as Well as Factual

Nonfiction is different from fiction, because by definition you are dealing with facts, not made-up events. So how do you deal with a complaint that a particular event or series of events is not convincing or compelling?

The same principle applies to nonfiction as to fiction: somehow, you have failed to transfer the emotional meaning onto the events of the piece. Sometimes this means we have left out critical information (to understand why what my mother said had such a great impact on me, I first need to take you back ten years to when my sister and I were teenagers); sometimes it means we have failed to render the events in question in as detailed and precise a manner as is needed. The only difference between fiction and nonfiction, in the case of transference (or lack of it), is that with fiction you have the freedom to make things up, whereas with nonfiction you need to stick to facts (or some form of the facts) in order to get your emotional point across. Otherwise, all the things we discuss about transference apply equally to fiction and creative nonfiction.

Making Things Carry More Emotional Weight than They Logically Should

We should always keep in mind what Robert Stone said: to paraphrase, our job as writers is to push the reader out of his space, and occupy it ourselves.

Very aggressive: Push. Occupy. Writing is an aggressive business. "I am going to make you feel what I want you feel." You may never have been lost in the woods and stalked by wolves, but by God I will make you feel as though you have had this experience.

Not necessarily agree with, not necessary enjoy, not necessarily understand completely, but *experience*: yes.

Sometimes we're lucky. The surface events are so wonderful (or so awful) that they carry all the weight we need. But most of the time, we have to tinker. We have to choose. We have to edit, rearrange. Sometimes we exaggerate or lie or make things up; if we do that enough, we call it fiction.

But here's the important part: The surface events can be faked. The underlying subtext cannot. It must ring true emotionally. Of course, anyone who has survived their teens probably has enough material—emotional material, that is—to do this writing thing. Loss. Love. Yearning. Loneliness. Joy. We've all felt that. "Attaching" the right surface details takes skill, ingenuity, even talent. But it's this—subtext—that is the heart of what we try to do.

Writing can fail on either, or both, levels:

- Our readers do not believe the physical events. (That's implausible. Too much of a coincidence, or blatantly untrue; e.g., I know how birds mate, and that's wrong.)
- Our readers are not convinced by the subtext. As we said above, "But this is *true*" misses the point entirely. But it's true, I knew a woman who just suddenly packed her bags and left her husband and five children and moved to Tibet. It's true, there was a guy, without any warning, who killed everyone in his office. That "truth" doesn't matter if the material hasn't been rendered on the page skillfully enough to *convince*.

Here are some examples of writing where emotional subtext has been masterfully linked to concrete details in fiction:

> I began to walk very quickly, then stopped because the light was differ-ent. A green light. I had reached the forest and you cannot mistake the for-est. It is hostile. The path was overgrown but it was possible to follow it. I went on without looking at the tall trees on either side. Once I stepped over a fallen log swarming with white ants. How can one discover truth? I thought and that thought led me nowhere. No one would tell me the truth. Not my father nor Richard Mason, certainly not the girl I had married. I stood still, so sure I was being watched that I looked over my shoulder. Nothing but the trees and the green light under the trees. A track was just visible and I went on, glancing from side to side and sometimes quickly behind me. This was why I stubbed my foot on a stone and nearly fell. The stone I had tripped on was not a boulder but part of the paved road. There had been a paved road through this forest. The track led to a large clear space. Here were the ruins of a stone house and round the ruins rose trees that had grown to an incredible height. At the back of the ruins a wild orange tree covered with fruit, the leaves a dark green. A beautiful place. And calm—so calm that it seemed foolish to think or plan. What had I to think about, and how could I possibly plan?

In this novel *Wide Sargasso Sea* by Jean Rhys, a trip through the forest becomes much more than just a walk through a forest. It becomes some-thing strange, and exotic, an almost druglike experience that induces in the narrator a sense of rootlessness and hopelessness that is quite unlike his usual personality.

> After that, I wanted a drink, so the second work was over, I headed for the bar. But I couldn't step in the door of The Blue and The Gold. It stank. I found myself walking east again until the dirty bodega shone like a star from the corner of Avenue C just like it did that night with Punkette. I

bought a beer and sat on a milk crate in the back drinking it in the store while the Puerto Rican woman on the register watched TV. I don't exactly understand Spanish, but you get used to hearing it and I could tell what was going on because the emotions were so huge. Men and women in fabulous costumes were fretting, threatening, falling passionately in and out of love. The characters yelled and screamed and cried and danced around. They felt everything very deeply. American TV actors just stare at each other and move their mouths. Sitting there watching those people on Channel 47 let it all out, I learned something very personal. I learned that sometimes a person's real feelings are so painful they have to pretend just to get by.

In the back of the store they had three shelves filled with devotional candles covered with drawings of the saints. I bought one for Santa Barbara and lit it right there. The woman didn't blink. People probably made novenas on the spot every day, next to the cans of Goya beans. On the back of the candle was written *O Dios! Aparta de mi lado esos malvados.* Oh God! Keep the wicked away from me.

I had to laugh at myself, going to all the trouble of praying and then only asking for less of something. I didn't want more of anything, not money or love or sex. I was praying to Saint Barbara simply to take some of the pain away.

This passage from the novel *After Delores* by Sarah Schulman is, on one level, just about a walk to a local store and a brief glimpse of a television show. But there's so much longing and yearning infused into this piece, so much sadness and loss that has been inextricably tied to the concrete sensory events in the story.

The sight of cigarettes and nitrites piled up on the glass ashtray made me want to empty it, to clean it, get it to sparkle, get it immaculate—and get a cigarette and light up. I did all that; now the ashtray is as full as it was.

It is getting dark outside; in this room it's getting late. I have cleaned the glasses by the bed, and am about to drink what is left of the tequila. I want the bottle out of the room, away from the bed. This is a small matter, I admit, but I do not like liquor bottles in bedrooms. It is not that I have rules against drinking in bed; on the contrary, I have taken many drinks to bed. But what I take is the drink—the liquor in the glass. To make another drink, I leave the bed; I put on a robe and take the glass to the bottle, in another room. Unless I have cleared some messy evenings from my mind, I can claim truthfully that taking a liquor bottle into a bedroom is something I have never done, and which I, unlike Nicholas, would be incapable of doing.

This passage from the novel *I Look Divine* by Christopher Coe shows how something as simple as a bottle in the bedroom can carry tremendous emotional weight. It's just a bottle, but in this passage it becomes a moral issue: the narrator would never take a bottle to the bedroom—he would take the drink, but not a bottle. The bottle has taken on more weight than it logically should, and that reveals something about this narrator, about his situation.

Transference and Creative Nonfiction

Here are some examples of writing where emotional subtext has been masterfully linked to the underlying concrete details in nonfiction.

> When I returned from the hospital, depressed and exhausted, Luise called me up in her smallest voice: "May I come up for a little while? I want to see you. I had a very bad day."
>
> We walked out in a fine drizzle. She wanted to talk about her three problems: Her acting—should she accept an offer from Hollywood? Odets—should she separate from him definitely? Her health—she is aware that she maltreats her body, eats erratically at any hour, capriciously, whimsically. I listened.
>
> Luise said: "I have something at home I want you to hear."
>
> She drove me to her apartment. There is a curved staircase which leads from the living room to the bedroom. Halfway up there is a large window of quartz which sheds a diamond-splintered light. Luise put a record on the record player, turned off the light, and we sat on the stairs. While we listened to the music the telephone rang several times. Luise did not answer it. She whispered: "It is Odets, and I don't want to see him." It was as if she thought the music and I would help her not to yield again. At one moment in the music we heard a subtle melody interwoven with a loud, pretentious inflated trombone. Luise said: "Odets!" We laughed.
>
> We sat at the top of the stairs, as if to escape from Odets's power, listening to the trombone overwhelming the delicacy of the violin.
>
> The telephone rang four times. Then it stopped. Luise felt she had won a great victory. Every time she yields to him she experiences more pain. It seems like a hopeless relationship.
>
> "When you are too busy," said Luise, "you must not see me. I do not want to be a burden."
>
> "But Luise, we are like sisters. We need each other."
>
> "You always remind me that everything that happens is really a marvelous story. I begin to look at everything that happens as a fascinating drama, a tale happening to someone else."

In this passage from the diaries of Anaïs Nin, written in October 1941, we're privy to witnessing two women sitting on a staircase, listening to music while the phone keeps ringing. On the one hand, it's just that: two women listening to music that is being interrupted by the telephone. But on the other hand, the emotional subtext makes it so much more than that: the two women are feeling alternately exhilarated by the music and oppressed by the phone ringing (a call from Luise's lover, who intrudes himself into this delicate moment). The meaning has been successfully transferred onto the concrete sensory events.

> Francis was reading a book about the life of Genghis Khan, making notes into the recorder, and muttering about Kurtz. The kids and I went to the cheese store. We got some terrific ash Chèvre, a burgundy Cheddar, ripe Camembert, some soft French cheeses I never heard of that were in the case with the Boursin, and some Gruyère. When we got back, Gio picked grape leaves, and we laid the cheeses out on the breadboard among the leaves. We took a picnic, fruit, bread, and cheese, out on the lawn, under the magnolia tree which is in full bloom. Francis opened a good Cabernet Sauvignon; the kids drank it, too.

In this passage from *Notes on the Making of Apocalypse Now* by Eleanor Coppola (a journal entry from June 21, 1976), a spontaneous picnic on the lawn takes on the excitement and good cheer of a celebration; the emotion is transferred successfully onto the concrete sensory details of the lunch: the cheese, the fruit, the wine, and the magnolia tree.

> Wet lunch at the club. Taking a taxi home I ask the driver to leave me off at Hawkes Avenue. He thinks I'm crazy. "Let me take you to where you've paid to go," he says, but I ask him to let me off, and walk home. It is very cold and the cold air seems as stimulating as gin. I pound along the road, dragging the heels of my loafers with pleasure. Why is this? It is the kind of irresolute or sloppy conduct that used to trouble my father. I think I enjoy dragging the heels of my loafers because it was something he asked me not to do, thirty-five years ago.
>
> Mary is resting in bed and, fully dressed, I lie down beside her and take her in my arms. Then I experience a sense—as heady as total drunkenness— of our being fused, of our indivisibility for better or for worse, an exhilarat- ing sense of our oneness. While I hold her she falls asleep—my child, my goddess, the mother of my children. Her breathing is a little harsh, and I am supremely at peace. When she wakes, she asks, "Did I snore?" "Terribly," I say. "It was earsplitting. You sounded like a chain saw." "It was a nice sleep," she said. "It was very nice to have you asleep in my arms," I say. "It was very, very nice."

This passage from *The Journals of John Cheever* shows what happens to a walk home through the cold in the hands of an accomplished writer. It becomes so much more than just a walk home—it's an opportunity to relive a childhood memory/grudge, and to translate that joy into the joy of a (temporarily) happy marital encounter.

Part 2: EXERCISES

Exercise 1: Getting an Image to Spill Its Secrets

      Goal: To illustrate the complexity of the transference we do all the time onto everyday objects.

What to do: 1. Think quickly, without straining, and come up with the first image that comes to mind.

           2. Write down this image (it can be a moving image, hence an event rather than an object) in great detail. Don't try to explain, just get the image down on paper.

           3. Write down all the emotions the image "tells" you.

The following passage was contributed by Jan Ellison:

I had just turned twenty-one, and I'd taken a taxi over to Park Lane from the boarding house in Victoria, where I'd been renting a room.

The building had a doorman. He insisted on carrying my pack up, though I hadn't wanted him to, because then I was afraid I would need to tip him. I did tip him; I pressed a pound coin into his palm and he nodded and left me alone.

The room was more an oversized hotel room than a flat. There was a bathroom, cold white tile, a heavy curtain pulled across the bathtub, gold fixtures, a glass bowl with tiny soaps wrapped in cellophane. There was a kitchenette, stainless steel appliances, gray granite counters. There were a few stiff chairs with floral printed cushions and elaborately carved wooden legs. Chairs I knew I would never sit in.

Across the far wall was a bank of drapes—gold velvet. Luxurious. Oppressive. There was a bed—enormous, with a red and gold spread that looked like a tapestry, pillows stacked against the headboard that would need to be removed before the bed could be used. Before I could sleep there—before Graham and I could lie there together. That was the point of all this—that we would lie there together in the mornings, before work began. And then when we were done we would stay together all day; he would not have to leave me as he had done the first time. He didn't like to leave me, he'd said.

I opened my backpack, put my clothes in the clean empty drawers, stacked my books and notebooks on the bedside table. I went to the window and pulled back the drapes, and there was the city beneath me, the gray buildings, the wide paved roads and the roundabouts. There was London as the last of the day's light drained from the sky and the few white billowing clouds collected it—pink, lavender, then a final flame of orange and it was almost night. I stood and watched as the lights went on, as the sky darkened. What I felt seemed so familiar it was as if I'd predicted it, as if I'd reached for it—a longing for the blue room I'd given up, a feeling that I'd stepped into someone else's life, a whole new kind of loneliness, the kind I imagined might belong to someone much older than I was then.

Emotions suggested by the image: Opulence of a distancing source. Self-doubt. Is this the right step? An optimistic beginning; guilt. Something secretive. Strength in details. Controlling little things to empower larger emotions. Out of placeness in the room. Either an adventure or a sacrifice. This is what it takes to get into this relationship.

Exercise 2: What I Lost

> Goal: To show transference at work (an object taking on more meaning than it logically should).

What to do: 1. Think about a time when you lost something and were inexplicably upset about it. That is, the emotion was out of proportion to the thing lost (the lost object should not be valuable financially or emotionally, but something more mundane, so that the sense of being bereft should be a bit of a mystery).

2. Write down the story, concentrating on concrete details, and immersing the reader in the experience rather than just summarizing it.

The following passage was written by Teresa Heger:

The damn key hangs in the garage on a rusted old nail. It's slyly hidden under a green plastic dustbin that is about forty years old. To get to the key you have to move about thirty ancient brooms, rakes, and hoes, push aside a hundred-foot coil of old greasy rope, and brush away layers of spiderwebs and dust and god knows what else. But when I go back home, they always insist I use that key, the spare key.

Don't lose it! Where's the key? Did you remember to put back the key? Don't go back to California with the key! When I once suggested I make a copy of the key, the idea was met with horror. What if I lost it? What if someone stole it? What if someone broke in because I *lost the key*? Looking around my parents' house, I could only think that a little theft might be a blessing to clear out some of their useless stuff that was—well—everywhere. In fact, I wondered if I should just start giving out copies of the key at garage sales and other events where junk collectors gather. But I gave in. No copy was made and I continued to fight the garage and the brooms and the dustbin and the spiders to get to the damn spare key.

And then one night—the dread event occurred. Alright. I'll admit it. I took the damn key and I had too much to drink. I went to an old high school buddy's house and we drank Pabst Blue Ribbon and watched reruns of *Saturday Night Live* and talked about the good old bad days and so on and so forth. So when I got home around midnight, the backfiring of the old Dodge Dart (as old as the dustbin and the key and the old brooms, etc.) must have announced my arrival to everyone in a twelve-block vicinity. But not my parents—no lights were on in the house.

And that's when it happened. No key. No key in my pockets, my gloves, my purse, my wallet. Frantic searching in the subzero cold under the car produced nothing. No key on the car seat or under the car seat or behind the seat. No key in the ashtray. No key anywhere. I sat in the car and like a naturalized Californian I visualized that key, I imagined its steely coldness in my hand and I willed it to come to me. No luck. No key. Finally I had to pound on the door, our family dog that no longer remembers me barking furiously, and wait until my stepmother came to the door, muttering smugly—happily, really—swearing she knew that I was going to lose that damn key.

The following passage was written by Mary Petrosky:

After I'd asked him the third time if he'd seen the curved blue dish (with the delicate flowers painted on it) I'm sure the painter was convinced I was accusing him of stealing it. I unwrapped all the items I'd removed from the china cabinet before we shimmied it away from the wall—the square crystal candlesticks, the pewter and glass steins, the tiny ceramic bud vases my husband's grandmother had brought over from Germany in the 1920s, the china box with the boater from that Monet painting . . . everything was accounted for except the blue dish.

I searched the garbage cans, the one in the kitchen, the two in the garage, pawing through paper towels sticky with gravy, cat puke, a rotting chicken carcass, the clingy green strings of cucumber peel. But there was no sign of the dish, not a fragment of its pearly sides or the azure that filled its belly.

I asked the painter again if he had seen it. This time he wouldn't answer. He finished up in the next two days and I didn't bother to call him back when I noticed that the baseboards in the dining room were still half white.

Part 3: READING AS A WRITER

Ralph the Duck

FREDERICK BUSCH

I woke up at 5:25 because the dog was vomiting. I carried seventy-five pounds of heaving golden retriever to the door and poured him onto the silver, moonlit snow. "Good boy," I said because he'd done his only trick. Outside he retched, and I went back up, passing the sofa on which Fanny lay. I tiptoed with enough weight on my toes to let her know how considerate I was while she was deserting me. She blinked her eyes. I swear I heard her blink her eyes. Whenever I tell her that I hear her blink her eyes, she tells me I'm lying; but I can hear the damp slap of lash after I have made her weep.

In bed and warm again, noting the red digital numbers (5:29) and certain that I wouldn't sleep, I didn't. I read a book about men who kill each other for pay or for their honor. I forget which, and so did they. It was 5:45, the alarm would buzz at 6:00, and I would make a pot of coffee and start the wood stove; I would call Fanny and pour her coffee into her mug; I would apologize because I always did, and then she would forgive me if I hadn't been too awful—I didn't think I'd been that bad—and we would stagger through the day, exhausted but pretty sure we were all right, and we'd sleep that night, probably after sex, and then we'd awaken in the same bed to the alarm at 6:00, or the dog, if he returned to the frozen deer carcass he'd been eating in the forest on our land. He loved what made him sick. The alarm went off, I got into jeans and woolen socks and a sweatshirt, and I went downstairs to let the dog in. He'd be hungry, of course.

I was the oldest college student in America, I thought. But of course I wasn't. There were always ancient women with their parchment for skin who graduated at seventy-nine from places like Barnard and the University of Georgia. I was only forty-two, and I hardly qualified as a student. I patrolled the college at night in a Bronco with a leaky exhaust system, and I went from room to room in the classroom buildings, kicking out students who were studying or humping in chairs—they'd do it anywhere—and answering emergency calls with my little blue light winking on top of the truck. I didn't carry a gun or a billy, but I had a flashlight that took six batteries and I'd used it twice on some of my overprivileged northeastern-playboy part-time classmates. On Tuesdays and Thursdays I would awaken at 6:00 with my wife, and I'd do my homework, and work around the house, and go to school at 11:30 to sit there for an hour and a half while thirty-five stomachs growled with hunger and boredom, and this guy gave instruction about books. Because I was on the staff, the college let me take a course for nothing every term. I was getting educated, in a kind of slow-motion way—it would have taken me something like fifteen or sixteen years to graduate, and I would no doubt get an F in gym and have to repeat—and there were times when I respected myself for it. Fanny often did, and that was fair incentive.

I am not unintelligent. *You are not an unintelligent writer*, my professor wrote on my paper about Nathaniel Hawthorne. We had to read short stories, I and the other students, and then we had to write little essays about them. I told how I saw Kafka and Hawthorne in similar light, and I was not unintelligent, he said. He ran into me at dusk one time, when I answered a call about a dead battery and found out it was him. I jumped his Buick from the Bronco's battery, and he was looking me over, I could tell, while I clamped onto the terminals and cranked it up. He was a tall, handsome guy who never wore a suit. He wore khakis and sweaters, loafers or sneaks, and he was always talking to the female students with the brightest hair and best builds. But he couldn't get a Buick going on an ice-cold night, and he didn't know enough to look for cells going bad. I told him he was going to need a new battery and he looked me over the way men sometimes do with other men who fix their cars for them.

"Vietnam?"

I said, "Too old."

"Not at the beginning. Not if you were an adviser. So-called. Or one of the Phoenix Project fellas?"

I was wearing a watch cap made of navy wool and an old Marine fatigue jacket. Slick characters like my professor like it if you're a killer or at least a onetime middleweight fighter. I smiled like I knew something. "Take it easy," I said, and I went back to the truck to swing around the cemetery at the top of the campus. They'd been known to screw in down-filled sleeping bags on horizontal stones up there, and the dean of students didn't want anybody dying of frostbite while joined at the hip to a matriculating fellow resident of our northeastern camp for the overindulged.

He blinked his high beams at me as I went. "You are not an unintelligent driver," I said.

Fanny had left me a bowl of something with sausages and sauerkraut and potatoes, and the dog hadn't eaten too much more than his fair share. He watched me eat his leftovers and then make myself a king-sized drink composed of sourmash whiskey and ice. In our back room, which is on the northern end of the house, and cold for sitting in that close to dawn, I sat and watched the texture of the sky change. It was going to snow, and I wanted to see the storm come up the valley. I woke up that way, sitting in the rocker with its loose right arm, holding a watery drink, and thinking right away of the girl I'd convinced to go back inside. She'd been standing outside her dormitory, looking up at a window that was dark in the midst of all those lighted panes—they never turned a light off, and often left the faucets run half the night—crying onto her bathrobe. She was barefoot in shoe-pacs, the brown ones so many of them wore unlaced, and for all I know she was naked under the robe. She was beautiful, I thought, and she was somebody's redheaded daughter, standing in a quadrangle how many miles from home weeping.

"He doesn't love anyone," the kid told me. "He doesn't love his wife— I mean his ex-wife. And he doesn't love the ex-wife before that, or the one before that. And you know what? He doesn't love me. I don't know anyone who *does*!"

"It isn't your fault if he isn't smart enough to love you," I said, steering her toward the truck.

She stopped. She turned. "You know him?"

I couldn't help it. I hugged her hard, and she let me, and then she stepped back, and of course I let her go. "Don't you *touch* me! Is this sexual harassment? Do you know the rules? Isn't this sexual harassment?"

"I'm sorry," I said at the door to the truck. "But I think I have to be able to give you a grade before it counts as harassment."

She got in. I told her we were driving to the dean of students' house. She smelled like marijuana and something very sweet, maybe one of those coffee-with-cream liqueurs you don't buy unless you hate to drink.

As the heat of the truck struck her, she started going kind of clay-gray-green, and I reached across her to open the window.

"You touched my breast!" she said.

"It's the smallest one I've touched all night, I'm afraid."

She leaned out the window and gave her rendition of my dog.

But in my rocker, waking up, at whatever time in the morning in my silent house, I thought of her as someone's child. Which made me think of ours, of course. I went for more ice, and I started on a wet breakfast. At the door of the dean of students' house, she'd turned her chalky face to me and asked, "What grade would you give me, then?"

•   •   •

It was a week composed of two teachers locked out of their offices late at night, a Toyota with a flat and no spare, an attempted rape on a senior girl walking home from the library, a major fight outside a fraternity house (broken wrist and significant concussion), and variations on breaking-and-entering. I was scolded by the director of nonacademic services for embracing a student who was drunk; I told him to keep his job, but he called me back because I was right to hug her, he said, and also wrong, but what the hell, and would I please stay. I thought of the fringe benefits—graduation in only sixteen years—so I went back to work.

My professor assigned a story called "A Rose for Emily," and I wrote him a paper about the mechanics of corpse fucking, and how, since she clearly couldn't screw her dead boyfriend, she was keeping his rotten body in bed because she truly loved him. I called the paper "True Love." He gave me a B and wrote *See me, pls*. In his office after class, his feet up on his desk, he trimmed a cigar with a giant folding knife he kept in his drawer.

"You got to clean the hole out," he said, "or they don't draw."

"I don't smoke," I said.

"Bad habit. Real *habit*, though. I started in smoking 'em in Georgia, in the service. My C.O. smoked 'em. We collaborated on a brothel inspection one time, and we ended up smoking these with a couple of women." He waggled his eyebrows at me, now that his malehood was established.

"Were the women smoking them too?"

He snorted laughter through his nose while the greasy smoke came curling off his thin, dry lips. "They were pretty smoky, I'll tell ya!" Then he propped his feet—he was wearing cowboy boots that day—and he sat forward. "It's a little hard to explain. But—hell. You just don't say *fuck* when you write an essay for a college prof. Okay?" Like a scoutmaster with a kid he'd caught in the outhouse jerking off: "All right? You don't wanna do that."

"Did it shock you?"

"Fuck, no, it didn't shock me. I just told you. It violates certain proprieties."

"But if I'm writing it to you, like a letter—"

"You're writing it for posterity. For some mythical reader someplace, not just me. You're making a *statement*."

"Right. My statement said how hard it must be for a woman to fuck with a corpse."

"And a point worth making. I said so. Here."

"But you said I shouldn't say it."

"No. Listen. Just because you're taking about fucking, you don't have to say *fuck*. Does that make it any clearer?"

"No."

"I wish you'd lied to me just now," he said.

I nodded. I did too.

"Where'd you do your service?" he asked.

"Baltimore. Baltimore, Maryland."

"What's in Baltimore?"

"Railroads. I liaised on freight runs of army matériel. I killed a couple of bums on the rod with my bare hands, though."

He snorted again, but I could see how disappointed he was. He'd been banking on my having been a murderer. Interesting guy in one of my classes, he must have told some terrific woman at an overpriced meal: I just *know* the guy was a rubout specialist in the Nam, he had to have said. I figured I should come to work wearing my fatigue jacket and a red bandana tied around my head. Say "Man" to him a couple of times, hang a fist in the air for grief and solidarity, and look terribly worn, exhausted by experiences he was fairly certain that he envied me. His dungarees were ironed, I noticed.

On Saturday we went back to the campus because Fanny wanted to see a movie called *The Seven Samurai*. I fell asleep, and I'm afraid I snored. She let me sleep until the auditorium was almost empty. Then she kissed me awake. "Who was screaming in my dream?" I asked her.

"Kurosawa," she said.

"Who?"

"Ask your professor friend."

I looked around, but he wasn't there. "Not an un-weird man," I said.

We went home and cleaned up after the dog and put him out. We drank a little Spanish brandy and went upstairs and made love. I was fairly premature, you might say, but one way and another by the time we fell asleep we were glad to be there with each other, and glad that it was Sunday coming up the valley toward us, and nobody with it. The dog was howling at another dog someplace, or at the moon, or maybe just his moon-thrown shadow on the snow. I did not strangle him when I opened the back door and he limped happily past me and stumbled up the stairs. I followed him into our bedroom and groaned for just being satisfied as I got into bed. You'll notice I didn't say fuck.

He stopped me in the hall after class on a Thursday, and asked me How's it goin, just one of the kickers drinking sour beer and eating pickled eggs and watching the tube in a country bar. How's it goin. I nodded. I wanted a grade from the man, and I did want to learn about expressing myself. I nodded and made what I thought was a smile. He'd let his mustache grow out and his hair grow longer. He was starting to wear dark shirts with lighter ties. I thought he looked like someone in *The Godfather*. He still wore those light little loafers or his high-heeled cowboy boots. His corduroy pants looked baggy. I guess he wanted them to look that way. He motioned me to the wall of the hallway, and he looked and said, "How about the Baltimore stuff?"

I said, "Yeah?"

"Was that really true?" He was almost blinking, he wanted so much for me to be a damaged Vietnam vet just looking for a bell tower to climb into and start firing from. The college didn't have a bell tower you could get up into, though I'd once spent an ugly hour chasing a drunken ATO down from the roof of the observatory. "You were just clocking through boxcars in Baltimore?"

I said, "Nah."

"I thought so!" He gave a kind of sigh.

"I killed people," I said.

"You know, I could have sworn you did," he said.

I nodded, and he nodded back. I'd made him so happy.

The assignment was to write something to influence somebody. He called it Rhetoric and Persuasion. We read an essay by George Orwell and "A Modest Proposal" by Jonathan Swift. I liked the Orwell better, but I wasn't comfortable with it. He talked about "niggers," and I felt him saying it two ways.

I wrote "Ralph the Duck."

Once upon a time, there was a duck named Ralph who didn't have any feathers on either wing. So when the cold wind blew, Ralph said, Brr, and shivered and shook.

What's the matter? Ralph's mommy asked.

I'm cold, Ralph said.

Oh, the mommy said. Here. I'll keep you warm.

So she spread her big, feathery wings, and hugged Ralph tight, and when the cold wind blew, Ralph was warm and snuggly, and fell fast asleep.

The next Thursday, he was wearing canvas pants and hiking boots. He mentioned kind of casually to some of the girls in the class how whenever there was a storm he wore his Lake District walking outfit. He had a big, hairy sweater on. I kept waiting for him to make a noise like a mountain goat. But the girls seemed to like it. His boots made a creaky squeak on the linoleum of the hall when he caught up with me after class.

"As I told you," he said, "it isn't unappealing. It's just—not a college theme."

"Right," I said. "Okay. You want me to do it over?"

"No," he said. "Not at all. The D will remain your grade. But I'll read something else if you want to write it."

"This'll be fine," I said.

"Did you understand the assignment?"

"Write something to influence someone—Rhetoric and Persuasion."

We were at his office door and the redheaded kid who had gotten sick in my truck was waiting for him. She looked at me like one of us was in the wrong place, which struck me as accurate enough. He was interested in getting into his office with the redhead, but he remembered to turn around and flash me a grin he seemed to think he was known for.

Instead of going on shift a few hours after class, the way I'm supposed to, I told my supervisor I was sick, and I went home. Fanny was frightened when I came in, because I don't get sick and I don't miss work. She looked at my face and she grew sad. I kissed her hello and went upstairs to change. I always used to change my clothes when I was a kid, as soon as I came home from school. I put on jeans and a flannel shirt and thick wool socks, and I made myself a dark drink of sourmash. Fanny poured herself some wine and came into the cold northern room a few minutes later. I was sitting in the rocker, looking over the valley. The wind was lining up a lot of rows of cloud so that the sky looked like a baked trout when you lift the skin off. "It'll snow," I said to her.

She sat on the old sofa and waited. After a while, she said, "I wonder why they always call it a mackerel sky?"

"Good eating, mackerel," I said.

Fanny said, "Shit! You're never that laconic unless you feel crazy. What's wrong? Who'd you punch out at the playground?"

"We had to write a composition," I said.

"Did he like it?"

"He gave me a D."

"Well, you're familiar enough with D's. I never saw you get this low over a grade."

"I wrote about Ralph the Duck."

She said, "You did?" She said, "Honey." She came over and stood beside the rocker and leaned into me and hugged my head and neck. "Honey," she said. "Honey."

It was the worst of the winter's storms, and one of the worst in years. That afternoon they closed the college, which they almost never do. But the roads were jammed with snow over ice, and now it was freezing rain on top of that, and the only people working at the school that night were the operator who took emergency calls and me. Everyone else had gone home except the students, and most of them were inside. The ones who weren't were drunk, and I kept on sending them in and telling them to act like grown-ups. A number of them said they were, and I really couldn't argue. I had the bright beams on, the defroster set high, the little blue light winking, and a thermos of sourmash and hot coffee that I sipped from every time I had to get out of the truck or every time I realized how cold all that wetness was out there.

About eight o'clock, as the rain was turning back to snow and the cold was worse, the roads impossible, just as I was done helping a country sander on the edge of the campus pull a panel truck out of a snowbank, I got the emergency call from the college operator. We had a student missing. The roommates thought the kid was heading for the quarry. This meant I had to get the Bronco up on a narrow road above the campus, above the old cemetery, into all kinds of woods and rough track that I figured would be choked with ice and snow. Any kid up there would really have to want to be there, and I couldn't go in on foot, because you'd only want to be there on account of drugs, booze, or craziness, and either way I'd be needing blankets and heat, and then a fast ride down to the hospital in town. So I dropped into four-wheel drive to get me up the hill above the campus, bucking snow and sliding on ice, putting all the heater's warmth up onto the windshield because I couldn't see much more than swarming snow. My feet were still cold from the tow job, and it didn't seem to matter that I had on heavy socks and insulated boots I'd coated with waterproofing. I shivered, and I thought of Ralph the Duck.

I had to grind the rest of the way, from the cemetery, in four-wheel low, and in spite of the cold I was smoking my gearbox by the time I was close enough to the quarry—they really did take a lot of rocks for the campus buildings from there—to see I'd have to make my way on foot to where she was. It was a kind of scooped-out shape, maybe four or five stories high, where she stood—well, wobbled is more like it. She was as chalky as she'd been the last time, and her red hair didn't catch the light anymore. It just lay on her like something that had died on top of her head. She was in a white nightgown that was plastered to her body. She had her arms crossed as if she wanted to be warm. She swayed, kind of, in front of the big, dark, scooped-out rock face, where the trees and brush had been cleared for trucks and earthmovers. She looked tiny against all the darkness. From where I stood, I could see the snow driving down in front of the lights I'd left on, but I couldn't see it near her. All it looked like around her was dark. She was shaking with the cold, and she was crying.

I had a blanket with me, and I shoved it down the front of my coat to keep it dry for her, and because I was so cold. I waved. I stood in the lights and I waved. I don't know what she saw—a big shadow, maybe. I surely didn't reassure her, because when she saw me she backed up, until she was near the face of the quarry. She couldn't go any farther.

I called, "Hello! I brought a blanket. Are you cold? I thought you might want a blanket."

Her roommates had told the operator about pills, so I didn't bring her the coffee laced with mash. I figured I didn't have all that much time, anyway, to get her down and pumped out. The booze with whatever pills she'd taken would make her die that much faster.

I hated that word. Die. It made me furious with her. I heard myself seething when I breathed. I pulled my scarf and collar up above my mouth. I didn't want her to see how close I might come to wanting to kill her because she wanted to die.

I called, "Remember me?"

I was closer now. I could see the purple mottling of her skin. I didn't know if I was cold or dying. It probably didn't matter much to distinguish between them right now, I thought. That made me smile. I felt the smile, and I pulled the scarf down so she could look at it. She didn't seem awfully reassured.

"You're the sexual harassment guy," she said. She said it very slowly. Her lips were clumsy. It was like looking at a ventriloquist's dummy.

"I gave you an A," I said.

"When?"

"It's a joke," I said. "You don't want me making jokes. You want me to give you a nice warm blanket, though. And then you want me to take you home."

She leaned against the rock face when I approached. I pulled the blanket out then zipped my jacket back up. The snow had stopped, I realized, and that wasn't really a very good sign. It felt like an arctic cold descending in its place. I held the blanket out to her, but she only looked at it.

"You'll just have to turn me in," I said. "I'm gonna hug you again."

She screamed, "No more! I don't want any more hugs!"

But she kept her arms on her chest, and I wrapped the blanket around her and stuffed a piece into each of her tight, small fists. I didn't know what to do for her feet. Finally, I got down on my haunches in front of her. She crouched down too, protecting herself.

"No," I said. "No. You're fine."

I took off the woolen mittens I'd been wearing. Mittens keep you warmer than gloves because they trap your hand's heat around the fingers and palms at once. Fanny had knitted them for me. I put a mitten as far onto each of her feet as I could. She let me. She was going to collapse, I thought.

"Now, let's go home," I said. "Let's get you better."

With her funny, stiff lips, she said, "I've been very self-indulgent and weird and I'm sorry. But I'd really like to die." She sounded so reasonable that I found myself nodding in agreement as she spoke.

"You can't just die," I said.

"Aren't I dying already? I took all of them," and then she giggled like a child, which of course is what she was. "I borrowed different ones from other people's rooms. See, this isn't some teenage cry for like help. Understand? I'm seriously interested in death and I have to like stay out here a little longer and fall asleep. All right?"

"You can't do that," I said. "You ever hear of Vietnam?"

"I saw that movie," she said. "With the opera in it? *Apocalypse?* Whatever."

"I was there!" I said. "I killed people! I helped to kill them! And when they die, you see their bones later on. You dream about their bones and blood on the ends of the splintered ones, and this kind of mucous stuff coming out of their eyes. You probably heard of guys having dreams like that, didn't you? Whacked-out Vietnam vets? That's me, see? So I'm telling you, I know about dead people and their eyeballs and everything falling out. And people keep dreaming about the dead people they knew, see? You can't make people dream about you like that! It isn't fair!"

"You dream about me?" She was ready to go. She was ready to fall down, and I was going to lift her up and get her to the truck.

"I will," I said. "If you die."

"I want you to," she said. Her lips were hardly moving now. Her eyes were closed. "I want you all to."

I dropped my shoulder and put it into her waist and picked her up and carried her down to the Bronco. She was talking, but not a lot, and her voice leaked down my back. I jammed her into the truck and wrapped the blanket around her better and then put another one down around her feet. I strapped her in with the seat belt. She was shaking, and her eyes were closed and her mouth open. She was breathing. I checked that twice, once when I strapped her in, and then again when I strapped myself in and backed hard into a sapling and took it down. I got us into first gear, held the clutch in, leaned over to listen for breathing, heard it—shallow panting, like a kid asleep on your lap for a nap—and then I put the gear in and howled down the hillside on what I thought might be the road.

We passed the cemetery. I told her that was a good sign. She didn't respond. I found myself panting too, as if we were breathing for each other. It made me dizzy, but I couldn't stop. We passed the highest dorm, and I dropped the truck into four-wheel high. The cab smelled like burnt oil and hot metal. We were past the chapel now, and the observatory, the president's house, then the bookstore. I had the blue light winking and the V-6 roaring, and I drove on the edge of out-of-control, sensing the skids just before I slid into them, and getting back out of them as I needed to. I took a little fender off once, and a bit of the corner of a classroom building, but I worked us back on course, and all I needed to do now was negotiate the sharp left turn around the Administration Building past the library, then floor it for the straight run to the town's main street and then the hospital.

I was panting into the mike, and the operator kept saying, "Say again?"

I made myself slow down some, and I said we'd need stomach pumping, and to get the names of the pills from her friends in the dorm, and I'd be there in less than five or we were crumpled up someplace and dead.

"Roger," the radio said. "Roger all that." My throat tightened and tears came into my eyes. They were helping us, they'd told me: Roger.

I said to the girl, whose head was slumped and whose face looked too blue all through its whiteness, "You know, I had a girl once. My wife, Fanny. She and I had a small girl one time."

I reached over and touched her cheek. It was cold. The truck swerved, and I got my hands on the wheel. I'd made the turn past the Ad Building using just my left. "I can do it in the dark," I sang to no tune I'd ever learned. "I can do it with one hand." I said to her, "We had a girl child, very small. Now, I do *not* want you dying."

I came to the campus gates doing fifty on the ice and snow, smoking the engine, grinding the clutch, and I bounced off a wrought iron fence to give me the curve going left that I needed. On a pool table, it would have been a bank shot worth applause. The town cop picked me up and got out ahead of me and let the street have all the lights and noise I could want. We banged up to the emergency room entrance and I was out and at the other door before the cop on duty, Elmo St. John, could loosen his seat belt. I loosened hers, and I carried her into the lobby of the ER. They had a gurney, and doctors, and they took her away from me. I tried to talk to them, but they made me sit down and do my shaking on a dirty sofa decorated with drawings of little spinning wheels. Somebody brought me hot coffee, I think it was Elmo, but I couldn't hold it.

"They won't," he kept saying to me. "They won't."

"What?"

"You just been sitting there for a minute and a half like St. Vitus dancing, telling me, Don't let her die. Don't let her die."

"Oh."

"You all *right*?"

"How about the kid?"

"They'll tell us soon."

"She better be all right."

"That's right."

"She—somebody's gonna have to tell me plenty if she isn't."

"That's right."

"She better not die this time," I guess I said.

Fanny came downstairs to look for me. I was at the northern windows, looking through the mullions down the valley to the faint red line along the mounds and little peaks of the ridge beyond the valley. The sun was going to come up, and I was looking for it.

Fanny stood behind me. I could hear her. I could smell her hair and the sleep on her. The crimson line widened, and I squinted at it. I heard the dog limp in behind her, catching up. He panted and I knew why his panting sounded familiar. She put her hands on my shoulders and arms. I made muscles to impress her with, and then I let them go, and let my head drop down until my chin was on my chest.

"I didn't think you'd be able to sleep after that," Fanny said.

"I brought enough adrenaline home to run a football team."

"But you hate being a hero, huh? You're hiding in here because somebody's going to call, or come over, and want to talk to you—her parents for shooting sure, sooner or later. Or is that supposed to be part of the service up at the playground? Saving their suicidal daughters. Almost dying to find them in the woods and driving too fast for any weather, much less what we had last night. Getting their babies home. The bastards." She was crying. I knew she would be, sooner or later. I could hear the soft sound of her lashes. She sniffed and I could feel her arm move as she felt for the tissues on the coffee table.

"I have them over here," I said. "On the windowsill."

"Yes." She blew her nose, and the dog thumped his tail. He seemed to think it one of Fanny's finer tricks, and he had wagged for her for thirteen years whenever she'd done it. "Well, you're going to have to talk to them."

"I will," I said. "I will." The sun was in our sky now, climbing. We had built the room so we could watch it climb. "I think that jackass with the smile, my prof? She showed up a lot at his office, the last few weeks. He called her 'my advisee,' you know? The way those guys sound about what they're achieving by getting up and shaving and going to work and saying the same thing every day? Every year? Well, she was his advisee, I bet. He was shoving home the old advice."

"She'll be okay," Fanny said. "Her parents will take her home and love her up and get her some help." She began to cry again, then she stopped. She blew her nose, and the dog's tail thumped. She kept a hand between my shoulder and my neck. "So tell me what you'll tell a waiting world. How'd you talk her out?"

"Well, I didn't, really. I got up close and picked her up and carried her is all."

"You didn't say *any*thing?"

"Sure I did. Kid's standing in the snow outside of a lot of pills, you're gonna say something."

"So what'd you *say*?"

"I told her stories," I said. "I did Rhetoric and Persuasion."

Fanny said, "Then you go in early on Thursday, you go in half an hour early, and you get that guy to jack up your grade."

1. Point out several places where emotion has been successfully "transferred" onto sense-based events in the story. How does the author accomplish this?
2. What are some of the images that work to best effect to establish the mood of the piece?
3. What is this story ultimately about?

The Knife

RICHARD SELZER

One holds the knife as one holds the bow of a cello or a tulip—by the stem. Not palmed nor gripped nor grasped, but lightly, with the tips of the fingers. The knife is not for pressing. It is for drawing across the field of skin. Like a slender fish, it waits, at the ready, then, go! It darts, followed by a fine wake of red. The flesh parts, falling away to yellow globules of fat. Even now, after so many times, I still marvel at its power—cold, gleaming, silent. More, I am still struck with a kind of dread that it is I in whose hand the blade travels, that my hand is its vehicle, that yet again this terrible steel-bellied thing and I have conspired for a most unnatural purpose, the laying open of the body of a human being.

A stillness settles in my heart and is carried to my hand. It is the quietude of resolve layered over fear. And it is this resolve that lowers us, my knife and me, deeper and deeper into the person beneath. It is an entry into the body that is nothing like a caress; still, it is among the gentlest of acts. Then stroke and stroke again, and we are joined by other instruments, hemostats and forceps, until the wound blooms with strange flowers whose looped handles fall to the sides in steely array.

There is sound, the tight click of clamps fixing teeth into severed blood vessels, the snuffle and gargle of the suction machine clearing the field of blood for the next stroke, the litany of monosyllables with which one prays his way down and in: *clamp, sponge, suture, tie, cut.* And there is color. The green of the cloth, the white of the sponges, the red and yellow of the body. Beneath the fat lies the fascia, the tough fibrous sheet encasing the muscles. It must be sliced and the red beef of the muscles separated. Now there are retractors to hold apart the wound. Hands move together, part, weave. We are fully engaged, like children absorbed in a game or the craftsmen of some place like Damascus.

Deeper still. The peritoneum, pink and gleaming and membranous bulges into the wound. It is grasped with forceps, and opened. For the first time we can see into the cavity of the abdomen. Such a primitive place. One expects to find drawings of buffalo on the walls. The sense of trespassing is keener now, heightened by the world's light illuminating the organs, their secret colors revealed—maroon and salmon and yellow. The vista is sweetly vulnerable at this moment, a kind of welcoming. An arc of the liver shines high and on the right, like a dark sun. It laps over the pink sweep of the stomach, from whose lower border the gauzy omentum is draped, and through which veil one sees, sinuous, slow as just-fed snakes, the indolent coils of the intestine.

You turn aside to wash your gloves. It is a ritual cleaning. One enters this temple doubly washed. Here is man as microcosm, representing in all his parts the earth, perhaps the universe.

I must confess that the priestliness of my profession has ever been impressed on me. In the beginning there are vows, taken with all solemnity. Then there is the endless harsh novitiate of training, much fatigue, much sacrifice. At last one emerges as celebrant, standing close to the truth lying curtained in the Ark of the body. Not surplice and cassock but mask and gown are your regalia. You hold no chalice, but a knife. There is no wine, no wafer. There are only the facts of blood and flesh.

And if the surgeon is like a poet, then the scars you have made on countless bodies are like verses into the fashioning of which you have poured your soul. I think that if years later I were to see the trace from an old incision of mine, I should know it at once, as one recognizes his pet expressions.

But mostly you are a traveler in a dangerous country, advancing into the moist and jungly cleft your hands have made. Eyes and ears are shuttered from the land you left behind; mind empties itself of all other thought. You are the root of groping fingers. It is a fine hour for the fingers, their sense of touch so enhanced. The blind must know this feeling. Oh, there is risk everywhere. One goes lightly. The spleen. No! No! Do not touch the spleen that lurks below the left leaf of the diaphragm, a manta ray in a coral cave, its bloody tongue protruding. One poke and it might rupture, exploding with sudden hemorrhage. The filmy omentum must not be torn, the intestine scraped or denuded. The hand finds the liver, palms it, fingers running along its sharp lower edge, admiring. Here are the twin mounds of the kidneys, the apron of the omentum hanging in front of the intestinal coils. One lifts it aside and the fingers dip among the loops, searching, mapping territory, establishing boundaries. Deeper still, and the womb is touched, then held like a small muscular bottle—the womb and its earlike appendages, the ovaries. How they do nestle in the cup of a man's hand, their power all dormant. They are frailty itself.

There is a hush in the room. Speech stops. The hands of the others, assistants and nurses, are still. Only the voice of the patient's respiration remains. It is the rhythm of a quiet sea, the sound of waiting. Then you speak, slowly, the terse entries of a Himalayan climber reporting back.

"The stomach is okay. Greater curvature clean. No sign of ulcer. Pylorus, duodenum fine. Now comes the gall-bladder. No stones. Right kidney, left, all right. Liver . . . uh-oh."

Your speech lowers to a whisper, falters, stops for a long, long moment, then picks up again at the end of a sigh that comes through your mask like a last exhalation.

"Three big hard ones in the left lobe, one on the right. Metastatic deposits. Bad, bad. Where's the primary? Got to be coming from somewhere."

The arm shifts direction and the fingers drop lower and lower into the pelvis—the body impaled now upon the arm of the surgeon to the hilt of the elbow.

"Here it is."

The voice goes flat, all business now.

"Tumor in the sigmoid colon, wrapped all around it, pretty tight. We'll take out a sleeve of the bowel. No colostomy. Not that, anyway. But, God, there's a lot of it down there. Here, you take a feel."

You step back from the table, and lean into a sterile basin of water, resting on stiff arms, while the others locate the cancer.

When I was a small boy, I was taken by my father, a general practitioner in Troy, New York, to St. Mary's Hospital, to wait while he made his rounds. The solarium where I sat was all sunlight and large plants. It smelled of soap and starch and clean linen. In the spring, clouds of lilac billowed from the vases; and in the fall, chrysanthemums crowded the magazine tables. At one end of the great high-ceilinged, glass-walled room was a huge cage where colored finches streaked and sang. Even from the first, I sensed the nearness of that other place, the Operating Room, knew that somewhere on these premises was that secret dreadful enclosure where *surgery* was at that moment happening. I sat among the cut flowers, half drunk on the scent, listening to the robes of the nuns brush the walls of the corridor, and felt the awful presence of *surgery*.

Oh, the pageantry! I longed to go there. I feared to go there. I imagined surgeons bent like storks over the body of the patient, a circle of red painted across the abdomen. Silence and dignity and awe enveloped them, these surgeons; it was the bubble in which they bent and straightened. Ah, it was a place I would never see, a place from whose walls the hung and suffering Christ turned his affliction to highest purpose. It is thirty years since I yearned for that old Surgery. And now I merely break the beam of an electric eye, and double doors swing open to let me enter, and as I enter, always, I feel the surging of a force that I feel in no other place. It is as though I am suddenly stronger and larger, heroic. Yes, that's it!

The operating room is called a theatre. One walks onto a set where the cupboards hold tanks of oxygen and other gases. The cabinets store steel cutlery of unimagined versatility, and the refrigerators are filled with bags of blood. Bodies are stroked and penetrated here, but no love is made. Nor is it ever allowed to grow dark, but must always gleam with a grotesque brightness. For the special congress into which patient and surgeon enter, the one must have his senses deadened, the other his sensibilities restrained. One lies naked, blind, offering; the other stands masked and gloved. One yields; the other does his will.

I said no love is made here, but love happens. I have stood aside with lowered gaze while a priest, wearing the purple scarf of office, administers Last Rites to the man I shall operate upon. I try not to listen to those terrible last questions, the answers, but hear, with scorching clarity, the words that formalize the expectation of death. For a moment my resolve falters before the resignation, the *attentiveness*, of the other two. I am like an executioner who hears the cleric comforting the prisoner. For the moment I am excluded from the centrality of the event, a mere technician standing by. But it is only for the moment.

The priest leaves, and we are ready. Let it begin.

Later, I am repairing the strangulated hernia of an old man. Because of his age and frailty, I am using local anesthesia. He is awake. His name is Abe Kaufman, and he is a Russian Jew. A nurse sits by his head, murmuring to him. She wipes his forehead. I know her very well. Her name is Alexandria, and she is the daughter of Ukrainian peasants. She has a flat steppe of a face and slanting eyes. Nurse and patient are speaking of blintzes, borscht, piroshki—Russian food that they both love. I listen, and think that it may have been her grandfather who raided the shtetl where the old man lived long ago, and in his high boots and his blouse and his fury this grandfather pulled Abe by his side curls to the ground and stomped his face and kicked his groin. Perhaps it was that ancient kick that caused the hernia I am fixing. I listen to them whispering behind the screen at the head of the table. I listen with breath held before the prism of history.

"Tovarich," she says, her head bent close to his.

He smiles up at her, and forgets that his body is being laid open.

"You are an angel," the old man says.

One can count on absurdity. There, in the midst of our solemnities, appears, small and black and crawling, an insect: The Ant of the Absurd. The belly is open; one has seen and felt the catastrophe within. It seems the patient is already vaporizing into angelhood in the heat escaping there from. One could warm one's hands in that fever. All at once that ant is there, emerging from beneath one of the sterile towels that border the operating field. For a moment one does not really see it, or else denies the sight, so impossible it is, marching precisely, heading briskly toward the open wound.

Drawn from its linen lair, where it snuggled in the steam of the great sterilizer, and survived, it comes. Closer and closer, it hurries toward the incision. Ant, art thou in the grip of some fatal *ivresse*? Wouldst hurtle over these scarlet cliffs into the very boil of the guts? Art mad for the reek we handle? Or in some secret act of formication engaged?

The alarm is sounded. An ant! An ant! And we are unnerved. Our fear of defilement is near to frenzy. It is not the mere physical contamination that we loathe. It is the evil of the interloper, that he scurries across our holy place, and filthies our altar. He *is* disease—that for whose destruction we have gathered. Powerless to destroy the sickness before us, we turn to its incarnation with a vengeance, and pluck it from the lip of the incision in the nick of time. Who would have thought an ant could move so fast?

Between thumb and forefinger, the intruder is crushed. It dies as quietly as it lived. Ah, but now there is death in the room. It is a perversion of our purpose. Albert Schweitzer would have spared it, scooped it tenderly into his hand, and lowered it to the ground.

The corpselet is flicked into the specimen basin. The gloves are changed. New towels and sheets are placed where it walked. We are pleased to have done something, if only a small killing. The operation resumes, and we draw upon ourselves once more the sleeves of office and rank. Is our reverence for life in question?

In the room the instruments lie on trays and tables. They are arranged precisely by the scrub nurse, in an order that never changes, so that you can reach blindly for a forceps or hemostat without looking away from the operating field. The instruments lie *thus*! Even at the beginning, when all is clean and tidy and no blood has been spilled, it is the scalpel that dominates. It has a figure the others do not have, the retractors and the scissors. The scalpel is all grace and line, a fierceness. It grins. It is like a cat—to be respected, deferred to, but which returns no amiability. To hold it above a belly is to know the knife's force—as though were you to give it slightest rein, it would pursue an intent of its own, driving into the flesh, a wild energy.

In a story by Borges, a deadly knife fight between two rivals is depicted. It is not, however, the men who are fighting. It is the knives themselves that are settling their own old score. The men who hold the knives are mere adjuncts to the weapons. The unguarded knife is like the unbridled war-horse that not only carries its helpless rider to his death, but tramples all beneath its hooves. The hand of the surgeon must tame this savage thing. He is a rider reining to capture a pace.

So close is the joining of knife and surgeon that they are like the Centaur—the knife, below, all equine energy, the surgeon, above, with his delicate art. One holds the knife back as much as advances it to purpose. One is master of the scissors. One is partner, sometimes rival, to the knife. In a moment it is like the long red fingernail of the Dragon Lady. Thus does the surgeon

curb in order to create, restraining the scalpel, governing it shrewdly, setting the action of the operation into a pattern, giving it form and purpose.

It is the nature of creatures to live within a tight cuirass that is both their
constriction and their protection. The carapace of the turtle is his fortress
and retreat, yet keeps him writhing on his back in the sand. So is the surgeon rendered impotent by his own empathy and compassion. The surgeon cannot weep. When he cuts the flesh, his own must not bleed. Here
it is all work. Like an asthmatic hungering for air, longing to take just one
deep breath, the surgeon struggles not to feel. It is suffocating to press the
feeling out. It would be easier to weep or mourn—for you know that the
lovely precise world of proportion contains, just beneath, *there*, all disaster, all disorder. In a surgical operation, a risk may flash into reality: the
patient dies . . . of *complication*. The patient knows this too, in a more direct
and personal way, and he is afraid.

And what of that *other*, the patient, you, who are brought to the operating
room on a stretcher, having been washed and purged and dressed in a
white gown? Fluid drips from a bottle into your arm, diluting you, leach-
ing your body of its personal brine. As you wait in the corridor, you hear
from behind the closed door the angry clang of steel upon steel, as though
a battle were being waged. There is the odor of antiseptic and ether, and
masked women hurry up and down the halls, in and out of rooms. There
is the watery sound of strange machinery, the tinny beeping that is the
transmitted heartbeat of yet another *human being*. And all the while the
dreadful knowledge that soon you will be taken, laid beneath great lamps
that will reveal the secret linings of your body. In the very act of lying
down, you have made a declaration of surrender. One lies down gladly for
sleep or for love. But to give over one's body and will for surgery, to *lie
down* for it, is a yielding of more than we can bear.

Soon a man will stand over you, gowned and hooded. In time the man
will take up a knife and crack open your flesh like a ripe melon. Fingers
will rummage among your viscera. Parts of you will be cut out. Blood will
run free. Your blood. All the night before you have turned with the presentiment of death upon you. You have attended your funeral, wept with
your mourners. You think, "I should never have had surgery in the spring-
time." It is too cruel. Or on a Thursday. It is an unlucky day.

Now it is time. You are wheeled in and moved to the table. An injection
is given. "Let yourself go," I say. "It's a pleasant sensation," I say. "Give
in," I say.

Let go? Give in? When you know that you are being tricked into the hereafter, that you will end when consciousness ends? As the monstrous silence of anesthesia falls discourteously across your brain, you watch your soul drift off.

Later, in the recovery room, you awaken and gaze through the thickness of drugs at the world returning, and you guess, at first dimly, then surely, that you have not died. In pain and nausea you will know the exultation of death averted, of life restored.

What is it, then, this thing, the knife, whose shape is virtually the same as it was three thousand years ago, but now with its head grown detachable? Before steel, it was bronze. Before bronze, stone—then back into unremembered time. Did man invent it or did the knife precede him here, hidden under ages of vegetation and hoofprints, lying in wait to be discovered, picked up, used?

The scalpel is in two parts, the handle and the blade. Joined, it is six inches from tip to tip. At one end of the handle is a narrow notched prong upon which the blade is slid, then snapped into place. Without the blade, the handle has a blind, decapitated look. It is helpless as a trussed maniac. But slide on the blade, click it home, and the knife springs instantly to life. It is headed now, edgy, leaping to mount the fingers for the gallop to its feast.

Now is the moment from which you have turned aside, from which you have averted your gaze, yet toward which you have been hastened. Now the scalpel sings along the flesh again, its brute run unimpeded by germs or other frictions. It is a slick slide home, a barracuda spurt, a rip of embedded talon. One listens, and almost hears the whine—nasal, high, delivered through that gleaming metallic snout. The flesh splits with its own kind of moan. It is like the penetration of rape.

The breasts of women are cut off, arms and legs sliced to the bone to make ready for the saw, eyes freed from sockets, intestines lopped. The hand of the surgeon rebels. Tension boils through his pores, like sweat. The flesh of the patient retaliates with hemorrhage, and the blood chases the knife wherever it is withdrawn.

Within the belly a tumor squats, toadish, fungoid. A gray mother and her brood. The only thing it does not do is croak. It too is hacked from its bed as the carnivore knife lips the blood, turning in it in a kind of ecstasy of plenty, a gluttony after the long fast. It is just for this that the knife was created, tempered, heated, its violence beaten into paper-thin force.

At last a little thread is passed into the wound and tied. The monstrous booming fury is stilled by a tiny thread. The tempest is silenced. The operation is over. On the table, the knife lies spent, on its side, the bloody meal smear-dried upon its flanks. The knife rests.

And waits.

1. Point out the passages where the writing is most urgent. How does the writer get that effect?
2. Notice how the writer weaves together memories (flashback) with present-day ruminations. How does he do this? What is the effect of this?
3. At one point the narrative goes into second person. What is the reason for that? The effect?

CHAPTER THIRTEEN

Learning to Fail Better

Part 1: ON REVISION

Getting Started

Revision can be one of the most exciting and rewarding aspects of creating fiction and nonfiction. There is nothing some writers like more than taking a raw piece of work and reworking and polishing it to make it shine. Indeed, some people breathe a sigh of relief when the first rough draft is done and they can get to the revision process. The hardest work, that of generating a raw draft, is finished; now they can concentrate on figuring out what the story, novel, or nonfiction piece is really about, and getting it to fulfill its promise.

There's no magic bullet or panacea for revision. Every person's revision process, like his or her writing process, is different. What we will do, in this chapter, is provide you with a flexible model for revision that has worked well for many writing students. But it's not the only way. There are many different paths by which to effectively reimagine or reinvent a piece of creative writing, and this model cannot hope to cover all of them. What this model *does* do is provide an adjunct/alternative to the conventional "workshop" method of helping students with revision that is used in so many writing courses around the country.

In this chapter we'll first review some wise words from established writers on what happens and what it feels like to have completed an early draft. Then we'll talk about the workshop method for giving and receiving criticism on early drafts of stories, novels, and nonfiction pieces, and discuss its benefits as well as its drawbacks. Then we'll go over the various stages of the creative process: although nothing could be more individual than each writer's process for generating creative work, still some things can be said about the general stages that most creative work passes through, and the kind of feedback that is most helpful at each stage.

Finally, we will go over a number of types of exercises that can be useful in what I call the "anti-workshop" method of revision. The main difference between this exercise section and the exercises found in the rest of the book is that these are supposed to teach you how to devise your own exercises so you can continue writing and revising on your own, even after your class or writing workshop has finished.

Advice for Writers from Writers

Perhaps there's no better way to feel relieved and reassured about this thing called creative writing than to read what some of the masters have said about the process. Below you'll find some quotations from some of our most accomplished writers as to what it feels like to have finished an early draft.

> There's not much that I like better than to take a story that I've had around the house for a while and work it over again. It's the same with the poems I write. I'm in no hurry to send something off just after I write it, and I sometimes keep it around the house for months doing this or that to it, taking this out and putting that in. It doesn't take that long to do the first draft of the story, that usually happens in one sitting, but it does take a while to do the various versions of the story. I've done as many as twenty or thirty drafts of a story. Never less than ten or twelve drafts. It's instructive, and heartening both, to look at the early drafts of great writers. I'm thinking of the photographs of galleys belonging to Tolstoy, to name one writer who loved to revise. I mean, I don't know if he loved it or not, but he did a great deal of it. He was always revising, right down to the time of page proofs. He went through and rewrote *War and Peace* eight times and was still making corrections in the galleys. Things like this should hearten every writer whose first drafts are dreadful, like mine are. —Raymond Carver

> What I tend to do is not so much pick at a thing but sit down and rewrite it completely. Both for *A Single Man* and *A Meeting by the River* I wrote three entire drafts. After making notes on one draft I'd sit down and rewrite it again from the beginning. I've found that's much better than patching and amputating things. One has to rethink the thing completely. They say D. H. Lawrence used to write second drafts and never look at the first.
> —Christopher Isherwood

> First drafts are for learning what your novel or story is about. Revision is working with that knowledge to enlarge and enhance an idea, *to reform it.* D. H. Lawrence, for instance, did seven or eight drafts of *The Rainbow.* The

first draft is the most uncertain—where you need the guts, the ability to accept the imperfect until it is better. Revision is one of the true pleasures of writing. "The men and things of today are wont to lie fairer and truer in tomorrow's memory," Thoreau said.   —Bernard Malamud

Progress does seem to come so *very* heavily disguised as chaos.
                                                    —Joyce Grenfell

All of us have failed to match our dream of perfection. I rate us on the basis of our splendid failure to do the impossible. If I could write all my work again, I'm convinced I could do it better. This is the healthiest condition for an artist. That's why he keeps working, trying again: he believes each time that this time he will do it, bring it off. Of course he won't.
                                                    —William Faulkner

Perfection Is Our Enemy

The biggest problem many writers (beginning and otherwise) face is that they are seeking perfection. They want what they write to be smooth and polished and meaningful and affecting from the very first word, and unfortunately that is simply not to be (or not very often). This desire (and it's a strong one) to excel right from the starting gate can have serious consequences. It significantly raises the odds that a writer will freeze and/or go abstract, rather than focusing on the small telling details that will eventually lead to riveting and important material. Anne Lamott discusses this with good humor and grace in "Shitty First Drafts" (pp. 574–78), and the fact is that if you can convince yourself to sit down and write something shitty every day, you'll get a lot more done than if you are determined to write the Great American Novel, or an award-winning essay or short story, in flawless unedited prose.

The Workshop Method

You may be using this book in conjunction with a workshop class. If not, perhaps you have heard about workshops, and wondered how they work. The way workshops are conducted is fairly straightforward: a group of students meets, usually once a week, with an instructor or workshop coordinator. Students provide their colleagues with copies of a piece of work, giving them enough time to read it (hopefully more than once) and comment on the text itself as well as provide a summary report of what they think. Then the class meets together, and everyone discusses the piece in question: what works, what doesn't work, what needs to be further developed, and so on.

The results of a workshop can be magical, or brutal, or extraordinarily helpful, or ludicrously unhelpful, or all of the above. It depends on who is in the class, who is leading the workshop (the experience and personality and skill level of the instructor matters enormously), and the particular story or nonfiction piece being discussed.

In some workshops, the feedback is supposed to be provided along some carefully structured lines: for example, if you are "up" you submit a list of questions to the class, which will be answered within the course of the discussion. In other workshops, what happens is a sort of freeform debate that can range all over the map. In any case, the goal is the same: to provide you (the writer) with sufficient information about your piece so that you can return to it and begin revising it to make it better.

Proponents of the workshop method say that it's the best way to give you a thorough and productive reading of your work. During the most traditional workshops, if you're "up" you are supposed to remain silent throughout the discussion; no matter how misguided or mistaken you think the group is about your piece, you must keep your opinion to yourself until the discussion has been concluded. The idea behind this (and it's a valid one, in many ways) is that, since under most circumstances you wouldn't be there to "defend" or otherwise interpret your work for readers (if the piece were published in a magazine or as part of a book, for example), the more closely the class can replicate a fresh and unbiased reading of the work, the better for you.

And when it works, it works well. You may get valuable information about your work from classmates who respect you and honor your intentions, and you can take the feedback home with you to work productively on the next draft.

However, there are many drawbacks to the workshop method. Problems can occur when there are personality clashes within the workshop, or when certain students are arrogant or disrespectful of one another's work. Some instructors, too, don't do a good job of monitoring and controlling discussion, which can get stalled in unproductive ways. Finally, there's the inclination of the group to want to enforce its aesthetics on the individual. And, as Madison Smartt Bell says in *Narrative Design* about the workshop method, it has no way of rewarding success:

> It sounds almost idyllic: a happy community of cooperating artists. But there are snakes in the garden.
>
> I was aware of the first pitfall before I ever came to Iowa. Fiction workshops are inherently almost incapable of recognizing *success*. The fiction workshop is designed to be a fault-finding mechanism; its purpose is to

diagnose and prescribe. The inert force of this proposition works on all the members, and the teacher too. Whenever I pick up a student manuscript and read a few pages without defect, I start to get very nervous. Because my *job* is to find those flaws. If I *don't* find flaws, I will have *failed*. It takes a wrenching sort of effort to perform the inner *volte-face* that lets me change from a hostile to an enthusiastic critic and start rooting for the story to succeed. [. . .]

At Iowa, I began to recognize some other hazards of the workshop method of which I'd been previously unaware. At Iowa, the students were very diligent about annotating each manuscript and writing an overarching commentary at the end—each student producing a separate version of the instructor's work (and some of them were already teaching undergraduate workshops). When the classroom discussion was finished, these fourteen annotated copies would be handed over to the unfortunate author, along with mine. My heart misgave me every time I watched the student (victim) gather them up, and an inner voice whispered, *Please, when you get home, just burn those things.*

But of course they didn't do that. It would be idiotic if they had. After all, this was the criticism they'd come to receive—they'd paid for it, worked for it, striven for it. I found out through private conversations that many of these students, if not all, would indeed spread out the fifteen different annotated copies and try somehow to incorporate *all* the commentary into a revision of the work.

The results of this kind of revision were often very disheartening. I'd get second drafts that very likely had less obvious flaws than the first, but also a whole lot less interest. These revisions tended to live up to commonly heard, contemptuous descriptions of workshop work being well-tooled, inoffensive, unexceptional, and rather dull.

Jane Smiley, who also teaches MFA workshops, found that a traditional workshop didn't work for her students, who got combative and overly critical of each other's work while eagerly looking for approval from the teacher, rather than learning from the discussion and deciding what *they* thought. In "A Conversation with Jane Smiley," in response to Alexander Neubauer's questions, she talks about her method for conducting workshops these days, which she calls her "fiction writing boot camp":

> Well, the first draft they turn in they're usually pretty proud of, and they think of it as fairly polished. And with the first story always, no matter how hard I've prepared them and no matter how hard they've tried not to, what they're really seeking is praise. They want for the impossible thing to happen, for me and the class to say, "This is great, you don't have to do any more drafts, just send it off now and it'll get published, I guarantee it." In my experience the first drafts are fairly short, fairly polished, and with some

problem in them that seems fairly minimal. Let's say the section that's supposed to be the climax will be confusing. So we'll talk about that and we'll say that the person has to clear up the confusing parts of the climax for next week. But usually that involves all sorts of other things, too, like a more careful defining of the characters, or making the rising action move more slowly and clearly. It ends up requiring a kind of narrative restructuring just to make the climax less confusing.

As soon as they open up this box of the first draft, which is in, what shall we say, a state of *faux* completion, then the whole thing starts to fall apart. And the second draft is often a mess, because they are trying to bring in or explore elements that aren't in balance anymore. They're usually disappointed with the second draft; there's more to it but it's more of a mess, too. The third draft is better but still in a state of "uncontrol." But often by the time we've talked about the third draft we're all saying, "Aha!" and what we're saying "Aha" about is that we as readers feel that we finally understand what the author is getting at, and the author finally understands where *he*'s going, too. Usually then they feel a certain amount of self-confidence about going on to the fourth draft, and it's really much better and more complete but often still unfinished. So they say they want to do a fifth draft, and I say, "No you have to go to the next story."

Other teachers have found individual ways to deal with the pitfalls and problems that the workshop method can have. My personal misgivings about the process are that I feel that the interests of the individual and the group are diametrically opposed. Workshops are great for the students who are critiquing the manuscript in question: they get to sharpen their critical claws and dissect a piece in a way that can be very helpful for their own analytical abilities—they (hopefully) can then take the skills they learn from criticizing their colleagues' work and apply it to their own.

But it's not necessarily a good thing if you're the writer whose work is under discussion. For starters, it can be very discouraging to have each and every flaw pointed out—and not even pointed out, but eagerly discussed and denounced. A teacher meeting with a student on an individual basis wouldn't necessarily redline everything, but would instead focus on a few things—things that student would be able to "hear" without becoming discouraged. All too often, in a workshop the teacher's role becomes one of defending a student against an over-eager throng of well-meaning but ultimately ruthless lynchers.

Then there's the fact that the kind of advice parceled out during workshops isn't always appropriate for the stage that a work is in. You may be trying something new that doesn't work—yet. But a workshop may well decide that a section that isn't working simply needs to be removed. "Take it out!" is a common phrase heard in workshops. Yet the passage in question, when refined, could become a critical part of the story or essay or novel in question. Just because it isn't working now doesn't mean it won't work in the next draft . . . or the next . . . or the next.

Another thing that happens in a workshop is that students, unsure of what to say about a piece, frequently ask for "more." They want more of the mother, of the dog, of the reason that the boy threw away the toy that was so important to him. Sometimes they have a legitimate point: there is a gap in the story or creative nonfiction pieces, and some additional development needs to be done before the piece is complete. But, in my experience, this request for more information can often result in overkill: by asking for more, critics force the writer into tipping the balance between a delicately wrought piece of work and one that has everything spelled out too neatly or obviously.

The net result: after a workshop, you can go home with too many voices in your head, which can pollute the revision process. As Madison Smartt Bell says, all too often the next draft of the piece is tepid, watered down, and has lost its force. People—often with the best intentions—want to remake a story or nonfiction piece in their own image, and it can be difficult to shake the impression that they leave with their comments.

Undue Influence: A Cautionary Tale

Three of the readings at the end of this chapter provide a cautionary tale about the dangers of relying too much on other people while revising your work. These readings have to do with the work of Raymond Carver, especially the work that he generated when working with his longtime friend and editor, Gordon Lish. The article, "The Carver Chronicles" (pp. 578–91), originally published in the *New York Times*, explains how Carver's celebrated minimalism might well have been more Lish's doing than a reflection of Carver's own aesthetic predilections; the two stories that follow show two different treatments of the same material. As you'll see, when given a chance, Carver rewrote one of his stories to reflect a more open, less minimal version of the prose: compare "The Bath" (pp. 591–97) and "A Small, Good Thing" (pp. 597–618) to see how the two versions play out.

This should be a cautionary tale to all of us. Although we might have strong opinions about someone else's work, we must always be respectful of their vision and intentions, and never assume that we have the answer to someone else's creative challenges. I tell my students that they need to approach a workshop critique carrying two equally strong but contradictory thoughts in their heads: to be open to criticism and ready to receive whatever it is they can learn from the discussion, and to retain the option of telling people to go to hell if the advice doesn't make sense.

It takes a lot to hold these two contradictory opinions in one's head at one time. On the one hand, you need to shrug off your pride and tendency to be defensive about your own work, and be genuinely open to what your colleagues tell you; and on the other hand, you have to be resolute about what you believe about your creative impulses and instincts. Unless you can somehow navigate between these two utterly inconsistent ways of thinking about criticism, a workshop will be of little or no use to you—and might even cause some harm.

The Developmental Stages of a Creative Work

It's important to understand that the creative process is not a linear one. You don't move seamlessly from initial concept, to first draft, to revision, to copyediting, to publishing. There are all sorts of reversals, returns, retreats. Sometimes a piece is magically done after just one or two revisions, but more often it takes a lot more than that. Sometimes it's necessary to tear up the latest draft and return to the original source of the material. Sometimes it's necessary to rethink a whole piece even after the twentieth revision.

Still, there *are* some things you can say about the stages of a creative work. Just as Richard Hugo talks about writing one's way from the "triggering" to the "real" subject (p. 65), we can talk in a general way about the various stages that a creative work goes through to get from the initial idea to the final draft.

1. **Initial generating stage**: The piece is being messily generated, as per the "triggering" subject we discussed in Chapter 2. This stage eventually leads to the first (rough) draft, when a piece with a recognizable beginning, middle, and end has begun to take shape. What's the best help that you can provide a colleague with at this stage? Merely an "attaboy" or "attagirl." "Yes, you're writing, and there's something of interest there. Keep going!"

2. **Creative revisioning stage (drafts 1 through 20+)**: Although a first draft has been generated, the piece is still usually under "deep" creative construction that often requires complete rewriting of the point

of view, the setting, the scenes, the characters, the plot, etc. What is happening during this stage is that you (the writer) are gradually working your way from the "triggering" into the "real" subject. What's the best help that can be provided at this stage? Exercise-based revision suggestions (see below).

3. Constructive revisioning stage (drafts 2 through 20+): The piece has solidified, and can now be examined, and critiqued, as a whole piece, rather than as something that is still under primary construction. This is where a traditional workshop is the most helpful, by providing feedback on character development, plot, scene versus narrative—all the things that can be discussed safely once a piece has started to "jell." Prior to this stage, however, a workshop can frequently do more harm than good.

4. Copyediting: The piece is done, and now needs to be examined for wordsmithing, grammar, awkward syntax—anything that detracts from a smooth, polished read.

It's a fact that one of the worst things you can do to a piece is to assume it's more complete than it is. And one of the most critical problems with the workshop method is that a workshop is generally best for critiquing manuscripts that have entered the constructive revisioning stage—which, in other words, are pretty far along. Are the characters believable? Is the plot working? Is the narrative rich and evocative? Do we have the right scenes, dramatized correctly? All these things can be examined once a piece has solidified.

Yet a good many stories are shown to workshops prior to this stage. They are critiqued as though they are more finished than they actually are. And nothing can be more damaging to a piece than to have it "frozen" in place before it is ready. What's critical is that a piece stays "fluid" for as long as necessary to ensure that all the relevant material has been fully explored.

"Hot Spots" and Other Noteworthy Aspects of an Early Draft

So what can we do if a piece is not yet at the constructive revisioning stage? One of the most helpful things we can do when reading an earlier draft by a colleague or student—one that is still in the creative revisioning stage, for example—is to point out what's interesting, or what seem like "hot spots" in the text. You're not assuming that all the scenes are in place, or that the characters or relationships have jelled, or that the plot has solid-ified. Rather, you are merely indicating to the writer the places in the text where you felt a quickening of interest, or, conversely, those places that seem to have the most potential, even though they have yet to be fully developed.

The point is not to help a fellow writer "Band-Aid" together a piece by glossing over defects or superficially mending holes, but to encourage "deep" creative revision by helping the writer question where the heart of a piece really is.

An Exercise-Based Approach to Deep Revision

In addition to pointing out "hot spots," the single most helpful way I've found to help students is what I call the anti-workshop, or an exercise-based approach to deep revision. In it, rather than directly telling a student writer what to do to a piece, I suggest exercises to be done "in the margins." What that means is that the exercises may result in text that never becomes part of the story directly, but somehow informs the writer's understanding of the work.

For example, say that the relationship between two characters—a mother and a daughter—is undeveloped. A workshop would point this out—and probably make recommendations on how it could be fixed. But an exercise-based approach to deep revision doesn't presume to tell you, the writer, what to do (or not to do). Instead, your colleagues would sug-gest exercises that would "explode" open the piece in order to (hopefully) give you a greater understanding of the relationship between the two characters, and help you understand what to do next—even if the actual results of the exercise never make it into the story.

Because, if the relationship between two key characters is undeveloped, it stands to reason that there may be other aspects of the story that are not working—the plot, or the point of view, for example—and an exercise approach to deep revision is a way to help you explore the different aspects of the piece without the critic presuming to know what the right answer might be. (Not incidentally, this approach eliminates the danger that the critic tries to rewrite the story in his or her own image. An exercise-based approach to deep revision enables the writer to go back into the piece and explore and learn for himself or herself.)

For example, one exercise suggestion could be for you to write five vignettes of the last five times the mother and daughter disagreed. Or, conversely, the last five times the mother and daughter *agreed* about something. By writing out these things, you will learn more about the relationship, and more about the situation of the story. You might even learn how to fix the problem of the undeveloped relationship, or at least see your way to the next step. This is what an exercise-based approach to revision is all about: helping you see what can be done next without dictating such "fixes" to you.

The point (again) isn't to put a Band-Aid on the story at a weak spot, but instead to put a metaphorical stick of dynamite there, to explode the piece in a way that teaches you more, and more interesting, things about the piece than you were previously aware of. The goal: to trick yourself into exploding open your material and push it in fresh and surprising directions—by thinking small. (Thinking "big" when attempting revision can cause you to panic and get blocked; it also not uncommonly results in contrived and labored prose.)

There are all sorts of exercises that one can do when working "in the margins." The important thing is to remember that much of what you generate with these types of device may not end up in the story or novel or nonfiction piece itself. But you'll almost certainly learn something about your material, and you might even—if you're lucky—get onto something exciting. And you shouldn't be alarmed if your piece ends up messier and less coherent than when you began. That's usually a good thing: the point of exercise-based revision isn't to copyedit, but to *explore*.

A Word about Constraints

Contrary to what you might think, absolute freedom isn't always beneficial to creativity. Instead, what psychologists and scientists are finding is that *constraints*, or limits in choices, are often more conducive to creativity than the blank page (or empty computer screen).

"The more constraints one imposes, the more one frees oneself of the chains that shackle the spirit," wrote Igor Stravinsky, the composer, talking about this phenomenon. Which, of course, is what we do when we do exercises: we're imposing certain constraints on our ability to write. Instead of being told, "Write about anything," we're being told to write within a very particular context, one with constraints all around it.

OULIPO is an entire movement based on this concept of constraints. Standing for the Ouvroir de Littérature Potentielle, or Workshop of Potential Literature, OULIPO is a group of writers and mathematicians whose members include Raymond Queneau, François Le Lionnais, Claude Berge, Georges Perec, and Italo Calvino. The idea behind OULIPO is to generate new works of literature based on puzzles and formulas—and, yes, constraints. For example, one of the most famous works to come out of the OULIPO movement is a novel by Georges Perec that was written completely without the letter "e." Other OULIPO constraints include writing a piece based on only the letters that make up your name, or by randomly choosing words out of a book. Any method that limits the choices that a writer has involves constraints, and constraints can be very conducive to creativity.

Constraints are important when it comes to exercise-based revision also, because we're not advocating total freedom. We're not saying, "Do anything at this point to open up the text." We're usually giving some very specific instructions (much like the exercises that you've been doing throughout this book). The idea is that the constraints will induce, not inhibit, the creative spark.

Part 2: EXERCISES

As a way to categorize the various types of exercises you can use during the revision process, I have come up with four broad categories of constraint: analytical/mechanical, creative, research-based, and chance-based. Examples of each type are listed below. The goal of this section is to inspire you to build your own exercises, rather than depending on exercises from others. The more adept you are at creating constraint-based writing activities, the closer you are to being able to tackle the revision process on your own.

Analytical/Mechanical Exercises

These kinds of exercise are precisely that: they analyze. These are good to do when your creative juices are running a little low and you want to do something, even if it starts out being mechanical. Because that's what happens with these analytical exercises: they start out slow and methodical, but very often they lead to creative inspiration, which is of course the point. Remember, this is not an exclusive list: there are many mechanical things you can do to a manuscript to jump-start a productive revision session.

- Retype the story (or a section of the story). The idea is that the simple act of going over the piece word by word will spark new ideas.
- Highlight all forms of "to have" and "to be." By replacing them with more active verbs, you can often see where this piece lacks movement or energy.
- Highlight all "-ing" verbs. Then, check each sentence for awkward syntax or unnecessary verbiage. Again, this is usually a sign of a deeper problem, such as imprecise rendering of a key image or action.

- Highlight all abstractions or generalities. Question whether the section has been adequately grounded in concrete sensory detail.
- Examine all imagery (any object, person, or place described using one or more of the senses). Is it *precise* enough? Does it push the reader toward an inevitable (and complex) emotional response? If not, focus and intensify.
- Highlight all metaphors and similes. Make sure they *add something* to the story. Also make sure you're not over-relying on them. Telling us what something is *like* before telling us what it *is* is often a sign you're having difficulty rendering something complex (an emotion or interaction) precisely on the page.
- Read out loud and listen to the rhythm of the language. If you stumble, highlight the sentence.
- Put the damn thing away for six months.

Creative Exercises

Most of the exercises in this book are creative. These are the ones that attempt, through exercises, to get the creative process going, to jump-start ideas and inspiration. There's literally no end to the creative exercises you can come up with: all of them involve constraints of some kind and, as we discussed above, constraints are good for creativity. Some of my favorite creative exercises are list-making ones, such as Things I Was Taught / Things I Was Not Taught (p. 69) and Sins of Commission, Sins of Omission (p. 437). Or generating a handful of "moments" that fulfill a particular requirement, such as "the last five times this character felt rage," or "the last five times she made a mistake." Here are just a few of the creative constraints you can use to open up a piece for revision:

- Change the point of view of the story (or the nonfiction piece) and rewrite. See what you learn.
- Change the tense (from past to present or vice versa). Ditto.
- Introduce a new character who summarizes what happens in his/her own words.
- Write about an event in your character's past without which the current situation couldn't exist.
- Write about the current situation from the point of view of a character looking back from ten years in the future.
- Make a list of the things that *won't* happen to the characters as a result of this scene (situation) being enacted.
- Describe physical aspects of the scene in great detail: the setting, the

characters, the clothes, the food. Do this obsessively. Do not worry about whether it is *interesting*.

- Describe a number of unrelated events occurring nearby as this scene unfolds.
- Describe a number of unrelated events occurring *far away* as this scene unfolds.
- Describe a prediction made in the past that this scene fulfills.
- Change the setting to an unlikely place: e.g., from Paris to Milwaukee. Adjust all details accordingly.
- Describe the scene as each character would describe it in his/her diary, without editing.
- Rewrite the scene as a "family legend" narrated by the child of one of the characters.
- If narrative, rewrite as scene.
- If scene, rewrite as narrative.
- Any sort of "listing" exercise you can think up to learn about a character, place, or dramatic event.

Research-Based Exercises

Another category is of exercises that require the writer to go out into the world and gather additional information. Established writers often use research to help spark creative ideas—for both fiction and nonfiction. Again, this is just a representative sample—this list could go on and on. Anything that you can research at the library or on the Internet is fair game.

- Find out ten facts about the place in which your story or nonfiction piece is set that you didn't know before.
- Interview a person whose profession is being used in the story or nonfiction piece, and find out ten things about what they do that you didn't know before.
- Research five recipes that the people in the story or nonfiction piece were eating (or could have been eating).
- Find out ten things that were happening in the world at the same time as the story or nonfiction piece (they don't necessarily have to be in the story; in fact, it's better if they're not).
- Interview five people about what they would do if one of the events of the piece befell them.
- Research the kind of music that would have been playing on the radio at the time the piece is set.
- Learn ten facts about the religion of one of the characters in your piece.

- Research the type of salary and subsequent budget that your main character has.
- Find out what was in the newspaper the day the events in the piece transpired.

Chance-Based Exercises

Finally, there are chance-based exercises, which are based on events that can't be predicted but are randomly generated or happened upon. Chance-based exercises are exciting and interesting because they open you up to possibilities that would never have occurred to you logically.

- Go to your bookshelf and pick out the third book from the right. Open to the third chapter, write down the first, third, seventh, and ninth words in the chapter, and write several paragraphs for your piece based on that combination of words.
- Take a walk around the block. Make whatever happens (or doesn't happen), or whatever you observe, the basis for a freewrite that you can include in your piece.
- Make a list of all the things that happened to you this week that surprised you. Do a freewrite on one of them that might be relevant to your piece.
- Go out to a café or other place where you can hear people talking. Write down a conversation you hear and then do a freewrite based on it.
- Turn on the radio to a music channel and wait until the fifth song comes on. Do a freewrite based on your associations with the song.
- Roll a die. Whatever number you get, take that many steps outside your door and do a freewrite based on what you immediately see.
- Do a freewrite based on the third phone call you get in a given day (if it's a telemarketer, so be it).
- Turn to page 6 (or page 10, or whatever) of your local newspaper and do a freewrite based on one of the articles you find there.
- Flip a coin. If you get heads, go someplace you wouldn't ordinarily go and do a freewrite based on what happens to you there. If you get tails, go to a familiar place and ditto.

Revision Example

The following texts comprise three versions of the same story, by Jan Ellison, so you can see the extent of a true revision. First is the germ of the story, which is very short, very succinct, less than 1,000 words; following that is the first draft of the "real" story; and then, finally, the finished story as it was published in the *New England Review*. You can see how some scenes are the same, and some descriptions are the same, but by the final draft it's a completely different story, expanded, fully developed. The names of the characters have been changed, and we now have the sense of a narrator with a current life of her own (husband, kids) looking back on her life.

"Germ" of Story (written in response to an exercise)

When I think of Jamie today, I see him in a staggering, energetic drunk, delivering to me the gift of a tall potted plant. He said nothing, only stumbled into my apartment, placed the plant in the center of the room and left without closing the door. He was back in ten minutes with another. Then another, and another, all the time saying nothing, only smiling a wild, hilarious smile. He was stealing the plants from the lobby of the hotel across the street. I laughed and accepted his gifts. Finally he tripped and fell and passed out in the middle of the living room, amidst a modest forest of green. I curled up next to his heavy brown body, my hands in his white-blond hair, and we slept. In the morning he was gone. That was his way. But I knew where to find him. Him and Freddie. Because always, there was Freddie, too.

Jamie and Freddie shared a room the size of a walk-in closet, in a stale, dank apartment in King's Cross, on a street where all the squalor of Sydney collected, where the wasted young whores swayed, in doorways, to and fro, to and fro, where the bars were, where we drank every night. Jamie and Freddie drank martinis and at first I pretended to but I couldn't get to like them so I drank draught beer in pints. We always sat at the bar. They played Bob Dylan on the jukebox and time seemed different, not at all important. Afterward, I slept with Jamie on his mattress on the floor. We rustled and rubbed and sneaked silent orgasms with half our clothes on, and always there was the sound of Freddie's breathing across the room, on the mattress against the other wall, in the room no bigger than a walk-in closet.

When I think of myself at that time I see a picture they took of me—passed out drunk in my black gauze dress, on Jamie's mattress on the floor. My black hair is splayed out behind me on a stained pillow with no case, and they have placed a six-pack of beer next to my head and a pack of cigarettes on my belly. I don't know now what they meant by that; whether it meant they mocked me or loved me. At the time I didn't care; I was one of them; I was a part of it; I belonged.

We were drunk every night and the thing I regret now is not that it went on so long but that it didn't go long or wild enough. I shook off my hangover each morning and left them to go home to my apartment, to shower and change and go off to my typing job, while they slept the morning away, their sweet bodies heavy and still, and woke at noon for a beer. That is what I missed, and what can't be gotten back now, not now with two small children and one on the way and a house—a house about which people say, oh, it's so beautiful, did you pick out all the colors yourself?

My friends, the ones I'd traveled to Australia with, said: "You can't keep doing this. You're getting ugly. You're not yourself. You're drunk every night and you didn't show up for our dinner party." It was something they'd agreed upon, to face me across the coffee table in their pristine living room in their pristine apartment in the complex with a security punchpad at the gate. Their warning worked on me like white noise; mostly I ignored it, but once in awhile it broke through and worked its way into the hilarity of that time, making me pause and wonder. The fun we had felt like happiness, it did, and I was not prepared to give it up. So I kept going out to the bars to find Jamie and Freddie, and when the bars closed I sprinted or stumbled or was carried back to their apartment where I slept on the damp mattress with Jamie, curled into his large sweet body. Always there was Freddie, on the mattress at the other end of the room, breathing.

Only one night it happened that I was there with Freddie, on the other mattress, just sitting, and then we were kissing, this one deep long-remembered kiss, our tongues and our fingers filled up with booze, the memory of that kiss, too, filled up with booze, petrified under half a dozen martinis and ten pints of beer. So it goes on, that kiss, the one that either he or I ended because there was Jamie, on his mattress against the other wall, in the room that was no bigger than a walk-in closet, in a dank apartment in King's Cross, where all the squalor of Sydney gathered for the long, long party, there was Jamie, saying "Hey," at first, laughing, then "Hey," louder, more confused, then "Hey!" a third time, until we stopped. Stopping it was an act of will, an act against nature. I can feel it still, the drag of his lips on mine, the intention of that kiss to go on to its reckless conclusion. Freddie whispered something afterwards, some incoherent words that I remembered then and that I wish I could remember now.

In the morning the kiss was not remembered. At least we never spoke of it. Still, I imagine it to be the moment I lost them, the moment that the trip north, the drunk trip in the rusted green van they bought for a thousand dollars, up through Queensland and the Gold Coast to the hot wastelands around Darwin, before the van gave out, it seemed the moment it was decided that the trip would belong in their memories but not in mine, except as an emptiness.

First draft: working title "Jimmy and Ray"

I met Jimmy on a bus tour on the east coast of New Zealand in a great rain storm. He and his best friend Ray were on a bus tour south, I was on the same tour but headed north, and we ended up in the same tiny bar in the same tiny town in this tremendous storm. I had ridden alone that morning on a rented bicycle three miles along a dirt path to the glacier and on the way back it began to rain. I headed straight into the bar without stopping to fix up my hair and there they were drinking martinis at eleven o'clock in the morning. Jimmy was tall and fair-haired with clear innocent eyes and a lovely face. Ray was smaller and darker and not at all handsome. He had a look of distrust about him, but he shared with Jimmy a Southern drawl that seemed inviting and I went right up behind them and ordered a drink. Jimmy moved over to make a place between them and that was the beginning. We drank for two hours and watched the rain and once in a while my knee would knock up against Jimmy's beneath the bar. Then my bus was going north and theirs was going south and I almost changed directions and went with them but I thought the better of it. What with Jimmy being the one I wanted to knock knees with and Ray being the one I wanted to talk to I thought I better get back on my bus and go north.

It was October when I bumped into them again. I walked into a bar in Sydney, where I'd been living for a few months, and there they were drinking martinis.

"You again," Ray said.

"Have a drink!" Jimmy bellowed out. They were already drunk and in good spirits.

We drank until the bars closed, then Jimmy walked me home and stayed the night on the couch. He was like that, a true Southern gentleman, even after eight straight hours of drinking. My roommates didn't like a guy passed out on the couch so after that we passed out at the flat in King's Cross that he shared with Ray and a half dozen other guys and their backpacks. There was always someone sleeping on the couch there and nobody cared.

It was easy to love Jimmy because he expected nothing and because we were always with Ray and we were always drunk or on our way there. There was no requirement to make conversation or to get to know each other in some essential way, only the necessity of showing up at the bar, where he would be drinking with Ray, and Bob Dylan would be on the jukebox and I could slide in between them and order a beer on their tab. They put everything on one of their father's credit cards and the bills were paid back home.

We got drunk in the bars all over King's Cross and Wooloomooloo and Circular Quay and when it got really hot in December, we celebrated with a case of beer and a ferry ride over to Manly for a long day at the beach. At dusk we played frisbee and watched the sea go from green to indigo to black and then when it was very dark and we were very drunk we went for a last hilarious swim in huge waves that ought to have scared me but that did not. That whole time was like that; I ought to have been afraid, or worried about my health or my safety or my reputation, but I was not. I was safe and drunk and happy and what I regret was not the time we wasted but that it all ended too soon.

We caught the last ferry home and stumbled back to their flat, arms linked with me in the middle, and I slept with Jimmy on his mattress on the floor. We rustled and rubbed and sneaked silent orgasms with half our clothes on, and there was the sound of Ray's breathing a few feet away, on the mattress against the other wall, in the room no bigger than a walk-in closet. Laid end-to-end the two mattresses covered the whole floor. There was a poster of Faye Dunaway and Mickey Rourke in *Barfly* on one wall; there were clothes strewn about and a half a bottle of whiskey and that was all.

Jimmy was a drinker without angst, without remorse, without resolutions. I loved his sweet brown skin and his large lumbering frame and I loved not loving him, not needing to imagine a future with him. I knew almost nothing about him, only that he grew up in the South, in Raleigh, that his parents had a summer house on the beach, that he went to college close to home and joined a fraternity and did lots of drugs. I knew that he was a drinker like me, a drinker who would always say what the hell and have another. Later, it would work that way for me with babies, so that one after another they came, every two years, until my house filled up with little bodies, and still it would seem a good idea to have another, if only to experience one last time that perfectly clean smell, that absolute sense of ownership, that soft head under my chin in the dead of night.

Jimmy was a staggering, energetic drunk. One night, just after we'd met again in Sydney, he stumbled into my apartment and delivered to me the gift of a tall potted plant. He said nothing, only placed the plant in the center of the room and left without closing the door. He was back in ten minutes with another. Then another and another. Sweat broke out on his forehead. He said nothing, only smiled a wild, hilarious smile. He was stealing the plants from the lobby of the hotel across the street. I laughed and accepted his gifts. Finally he tripped and fell and passed out in the middle of the living room amidst the greenery. I curled into his big brown body and we slept. In the morning he was gone, but I knew where to find him.

Jimmy knew something about being kind to women. He held doors open for me; he made me drink a glass of milk before bed to stave off the hangover; he tucked the sheet around me if I passed out first.

Sometimes he was the one to pass out first.

I wanna get drunk, he'd yell, knocking his head against the wall when Ray and I had dragged him home from the bars.

Lay down, I'd say, you're already drunk.

Am I? he'd say with a grin full of straight white teeth.

Then he'd fall down on the bed and close his blue, bloodshot eyes and go to sleep.

I never asked what he studied in college, or what he planned to do when the trip was over, or whether he had ever been in love.

It was Ray I wanted to understand; it was Ray who'd been damaged. Ray was dark and swarthy and all his features seemed bunched up into the middle of his face. He lived right on the edge of ugly but to talk to him was to know something about danger and privilege and heartbreak; to talk to him was to want to heal him or win him. When he was drunk he talked to me about Annalee, Annalee the beauty, with red hair down to her butt riding around in her yellow convertible in the fall. She always drove, he said, Always. Annalee had a cocaine habit; she stole money from him and then left him for her mother's boyfriend. But when he spoke about her it was with reverence; he had not forgiven her but he had not yet given her up. Something about that made me want to make him see other women in the world; it made me want to make him see me.

In March, when the rains began again, Jimmy and Ray made plans for a trip north. They bought a rusted green van with a bed in the back, and though I'd been there with them all through that raucous, timeless summer, in the flat and in the bars and on the beach and on the dirty mattress at the end of that room that was no more than a walk-in closet, with Jimmy and his sweet brown belly and his clear blue eyes and his gentle talk, with Ray at the other end of the room snoring like only a drunk can snore; even though I'd been right in the center of all that, somehow it became clear that I would not be going on the trip north. The bed in the back of the van could only sleep two.

"There's the front seat," I finally said.

Jimmy said, "Ah, c'mon Cath." His voice was soft with apology.

Ray said, "No fuckin' way. It's a guy thing."

I stuck my tongue out at him and he smiled.

The day they left was gray and rainy, like all the days that followed. We stood on the sidewalk while they piled their backpacks and their tent and an arsenal of booze in the van. Jimmy came and stood behind me. His hands were warm on the back of my neck. I was trying to think of something flip to say.

"Well, see ya," I said, and it came out angry. I gave him a hug, but not a kiss and I didn't give Ray a good-bye at all. I walked off before they got in the van so I wouldn't be the girl standing on the wet sidewalk waving good-bye.

I told myself: It was because I was broke and they were tired of buying my drinks. It was because they imagined the women they would meet on the open road, Australian women with darling accents, blond hair, skin still brown from summer. It was because I had played the game badly, had pretended for too long that I didn't want to go on the trip, that I didn't have the money, that I had to work. Right up to that last morning, I expected them to change their minds, to say Ah, c'mon Cath, get your stuff, as if my invitation had simply been overlooked.

But there was also this: There was one deep long-remembered kiss on the wrong side of the room on the wrong dirty threadbare mattress, with Ray.

This is what I remember about the night it happened: Jimmy wears a T-shirt over his big shoulders. The T-shirt is barely hanging on his body and I remember something about that, that we ripped it during the party at the flat that night, not in a rage or a passion but just because there had been a tiny hole, just above his right nipple, and I began to tear and it tore and tore and everyone joined in and then someone poured a beer over our heads. We didn't take offense, nobody did, not ever during all those months. At some point in the night my roommates came by; three lovely girls with bare muscular calves, short skirts, high heels. When they arrived, for some reason I had a paper bag over my head. They stayed only a few minutes, time for one gin and tonic each, then they headed off to a club to go dancing, leaving the boys cheated and me relieved.

Somehow at the end of the night I was sitting cross-legged on Ray's mattress, facing him and that poster of Mickey Rourke. I was watching Mickey for a sign. Then the tips of my fingers were touching the tips of Ray's on both hands, then we were leaning into each other, then we were kissing, this one long boozy necessary kiss. Jimmy said "Hey," at first with laughter in his voice, then "Hey," louder, then "Hey!" a third time, and this time he was standing over us yelling so we stopped. Stopping it was like the pain of coming up out of a deep, dreamless sleep when your baby cries in the night. Ray whispered something to me as we pulled away from each other, some words that I understood and cherished and then forgot and that I can never get back.

In the morning, neither of them remembered. At least it was never mentioned. Still, I imagine it to be the moment I lost them, the moment that the trip north—the drunk trip in the green van they bought for a thousand dollars, up through Queensland and the Gold Coast, all the way up to the hot wastelands around Darwin and then on down along the west coast—it seemed to be the moment that the trip around the whole of Australia in a rusted green van became a thing that would take place without me.

Final story; published in New England Review

The Company of Men

For a few years I had in my possession two rain slickers that smelled of whiskey and cigarettes and aftershave. They were cherry-red and lined with fleece, and I kept them in a cardboard box on a shelf above the toilet in the tiny apartment where I lived alone. Then when I was about to be married and I wanted to be rid of so many failings, so many unhelpful habits and longings, when I believed the past could no longer inform me, I threw the slickers into the Goodwill pile and lost them forever. Now what is left is a single photo I return to now and then, of two young men in bright red coats hitchhiking under a darkened sky.

I met them first on my last full day in New Zealand, after I'd rented a bike and ridden three miles up a dirt path to touch my fingers to a glacier. It began to rain, and by mid-morning when I got back down to the village, I was soaked through to my bra. My bus for Christchurch wasn't leaving until one, and across from the bus depot was a pub. Inside there was a fire in the fireplace and two young men—Jimmy and Ray—standing at the bar in their rain slickers drinking martinis. Ray was stocky and dark, with a sunken torso, small eyes, and a huge, humped nose. His hair was thin and black above a high, smooth forehead, and all his features seemed bunched up in the middle of his face. Jimmy was taller and fair, with square shoulders and fine blue eyes.

His hair curled at his ears and at the nape of his sunburned neck. There was something loopy, almost accidental about the way Jimmy stood in his frame, as if he were blind to the effect his size and good looks might have— the effect they were having—on a wet girl standing in the doorway of a bar seven thousand miles from home.

I'd been traveling alone for a year, since I finished college, through Europe and India and Southeast Asia, and I'd just spent a month at the northern-most tip of the North Island picking tomatoes in the sun for minimum wage, eating cheese sandwiches, and sleeping alone in a pitch-black room of empty bunks. It came to me suddenly as I stood in the doorway of the bar that I was sick of the struggle in it—sick of crouching in the sun, sick of taking it all in, of making notes on yellow legal pads, of stumping across rock and snow in my boots and across sand and kelp and coral and wet grass in my worn-down Tevas. It was not exactly loneliness I wanted to banish as I crossed the bar toward them but a kind of self-imposed austerity, a compulsion to justify the experience, to tear meaning from it, to bring something home. It was the days of weighty, maturing experiences strung together one after another in what seemed to me then a long stretch without a flirtation, a debate, a convergence—a black-out drunk.

Jimmy and Ray had just graduated from the University of North Carolina and they were on a tour of New Zealand and Australia and maybe Bali or Kathmandu. Under their rain slickers, they dressed the way they must have dressed back home, in jeans and leather loafers and button-down shirts, and they drawled when they talked. They addressed me as y'all, which made me feel oddly important, as if I carried with me the authority of a secret entourage. We drank five fast rounds together while the rain beat the window and the mud slid off the hill outside into a great brown puddle. In the distance were the white tips of the glacier rising up out of a black mass of cloud.

While we drank, Jimmy rested his hand against the small of my back and Ray told me about his girl back home—a redhead who'd stolen his money and broken his heart. When it was time for me to go—when the exhaust was shooting from the back of the bus and the faces of passengers began to appear in the windows behind the drenching rain—the wish to stay had hardened into longing. But I had a half-price ticket to Sydney in the morning and my tourist visa was about to expire.

"Y'all need to stay and drink with us," Jimmy said, as I stood and dropped a twenty on the bar. He picked it up and stuck it in the back pocket of my jeans. He downed his martini, put the toothpick between his teeth, and leaned in toward me, so close I could feel his boozy breath in my eyelashes. I slipped off the olive and held it between my teeth, then passed it back to him in an almost-kiss.

"You're still wet," he said. He slipped off his rain slicker.

"Don't give her that, you loser," Ray said.

"Easy boy," Jimmy said. Then he shrugged and slipped the coat back over his own shoulders. I stuck my tongue out at Ray and walked from the bar into the rain and got on the bus.

Everywhere in Sydney I saw people I knew. I'd step out of an underground station into the sun, and there would be a girl from my freshman dorm, sitting at a bus stop, or the married man I'd been with in London the year before, ducking into a cab. My arm would shoot into the air to flag them down, then when they turned toward me, the people I knew vanished into the puzzled faces of strangers. The idea of going home was always with me, but there were good reasons not to. My father had moved out again, before I'd left, and I suspected this time it was for good. "At some point things have to be admitted," was what he'd said, not to my mother but to me. I knew I was making it easy for him, staying away, giving up the cause, but the time and distance had muted my sense of responsibility. It had lulled me into believing my mother might be only heartsick and sad, not despairing, not desperate.

I moved into a flat with three German girls who'd been backpacking around the world together for a year. They hardly spoke English and that made it easy; there was no pretending we would take up as friends. I signed up at a temp agency—one that didn't check work visas and paid in cash every Friday. The agency found me a six-month assignment, typing for an insurance company in the city. The work was dull but the money was good and I buckled into it. In my spare time I renewed my longstanding self-improvement campaign. I quit smoking and stayed out of the bars; I worked on my typing speed; I wrote down words I didn't know on yellow legal pads and looked them up in the dictionary in the library on my way home. From the library I'd walk through the park, past the pub at Woolloomooloo and up over the hill to King's Cross. I'd buy myself a falafel and sit at the fountain in the square, watching the hookers in the doorways, the backpackers and tourists and solitary businessmen moving in and out of the strip joints and clubs, the restaurants and shops and seedy bars.

I was taken up in the change of seasons, the shift from the misty rains of May into the flat gray cold of what was summer back home. Then the holidays approached and the days began to lengthen and grow hot and expectant. On the last day of my typing job, I took the long way home through the park and stopped at the railing overlooking Sydney Harbor. The Opera House glowed white and magnificent in the distance, the water glistened, and a full blue moon floated low in the sky. I was filled up with a vast emptiness, a glorious freedom, and as always I was careful to stay there and treasure it, to take it all in. But what can you do with a feeling like that? It was like other solitary moments during those years of traveling—it was the Himalayas at dusk after a cold day walking alone, it was the deck of a freighter on the Adriatic Sea at sunrise, it was Paris under a velvet snowfall. It was manufactured and overly private and tiresome. The other murkier moments meant more, finally, the dramas that began for the most part in bars, when the swirling motion of the evening would straighten itself and alight on a human form and there was suddenly the possibility not just of desire, and of being desired, but of a story of poverty or addiction or betrayal. There was the promise of some new knowledge—the shape of an ear, the smell of musk—or a shift in one's view of oneself in the world.

I started walking again, fast now through the park, and when I got to the bar at Woolloomooloo I went right in, sat down on an empty stool, and ordered myself a pint. Bob Dylan was on the jukebox. I sang along to "Like a Rolling Stone" and ran my hands over the smooth wood of the bar. I thought I heard my name, but I was done with phantoms and I kept my head steady. I cupped my beer between my hands. Then there was the heat of a body behind me, and sudden hands on my shoulders, and I turned and it was Jimmy.

"Hey, Catherine," he said. He took the seat on one side of me and Ray took the seat on the other. I turned toward Ray. He looked at me deadpan and stuck out his tongue. I stuck out mine and we both laughed, as if this was the way we'd greeted each other every Friday night for a decade. It encouraged me, Ray's laughter, but it unnerved me, too. He was so ugly, so private, until his face was thrown open with that laugh. Then he was all teeth and bright eyes, his forehead wrinkling like linen. What I learned, though, was that he could close down again in an instant and make me wonder what I'd done.

Jimmy opened a tab on Ray's dad's card and ordered us all martinis, and we started drinking hard and fast. Ray began to talk.

"So this girl, Jasmine, back in Raleigh. The reason we're here?" He said it like a question. "Her house was next to mine growing up. Jimmy's was three doors down. She was just punky, a tomboy. Then she lets her hair grow out and she has these green eyes that look like contacts. Junior year in high school, she gets a '67 Mustang convertible for her birthday and we paint it up for her. Yellow like she asked for.

"'Yellow like ladyslipper,' was what she said."

"She was into flowers and shit," Jimmy said.

"Yeah, but only yellow," Ray said. "She planted up her whole front yard with them—roses and tulips and whatever. They even wrote it up in the paper, with her picture and all in a yellow dress. Then she went off to Brown and her mom sold the house and we didn't see her for a while. Until bingo. She turns up last summer on the Cape, and she's still got the car. Jimmy was down in Miami working on a boat so it was just me and Jasmine, staying up all night doing coke, driving around in the Mustang. And in the back seat she's got all these pots she made on a potting wheel in school, like dozens of them, all planted up with yellow flowers."

Ray stared straight ahead as he talked, at the orderly rows of bottles lined up on the bar. He paused and took a swig of his martini.

"So what happened?" I said.

"Well so she transfers to Carolina, right, for senior year? And we spend the whole year pretty much together, and we're talking about moving to New York after graduation. I was dealing, so I knew I could get us an apartment and everything. Then right after finals, she takes five thousand bucks out of the stash in my room and splits. She just drives her car out to California and hooks up with some professor dude—he's ancient, like forty, and he's gotten a job out there—and the way I find out about the whole deal is she sends me a postcard."

"My God, there must have been signs," I said to Ray. "To just take off and leave like that."

"Maybe. But I never had times like that with anybody," Ray said.

"Except me," Jimmy said.

"Even you, Jimmy my boy."

I'd been listening to Ray with my elbows up on the bar and my chin in my hand, with the intensity that can come over you when you've had a lot to drink. His story seemed strange and sad and unforgettable. While Ray talked, Jimmy kept the drinks coming and he let the back of his hand fall against my arm on the bar. He let his thigh rub against my knee beneath it. This seemed to be the arrangement. With the drinks and the roving hands and the sweet eyes and the good looks, Jimmy's role was to draw people to the two of them, and Ray's—with his stories and his mournful eyes—was to keep them there. He would keep us there until finally we could not bear to hear the story again, then Jimmy would rescue us, with a drink or a song or a wild run in the dark through the park.

"Fucking A!" Jimmy said now from the jukebox. He slapped his hands against the glass and dropped in some coins. Neil Young's "Sugar Mountain" came on and he came and sat close beside me and Ray stopped talking while Jimmy and I sang. The song was suddenly something that was ours alone—we both knew every single line—and Ray would not join in. When we pressed him he said, "I don't sing," as if singing were a habit he'd long since outgrown.

Jimmy and I sang it over and over, and after a while Ray and his story seemed to recede until there was only Jimmy and me and those lyrics and the smoky blue glory of the bar. My final memory of that first night is of standing at the jukebox at last call, trying hard to fit a quarter into the slot so we could sing that song one last time. The next morning, I woke up fully dressed under the covers with my shoes placed neatly next to the bed. There was no obvious evidence of intimacy—no chafing or fluids or foreign smells. There wasn't a phone number either, nothing inked on my palm or scribbled on a napkin and tucked into my sock. I spent the day sleeping off my hangover and waking from time to time to wonder how I might track them down— Jimmy and Ray—I didn't know their last names. When I finally got up and showered, it was late afternoon, and the German girls were watching TV. I started a letter to my mother. I wrote things I knew she'd like; I'd saved some money, I was getting along with my roommates, I was enjoying the neighborhood—all the shops, the square, the outdoor cafés. She didn't need to know that it was the seedy heart of the red light district, that the streets were lined with drug dealers and prostitutes and strip joints and bars. I started a letter to my father and crumpled it up and threw it away. It was the first of many letters to him that I started and never finished, or finished and never sent. I was afraid to lose the closeness we'd had, but contact with him seemed duplicitous—an encouragement or even a betrayal.

At six o'clock, Jimmy lumbered in through the open door of the apartment with a tall potted plant held against his chest. The trunk was flung over his shoulder and the branches swept along the carpet behind him. He dropped the plant to the ground, spilling potting soil onto the worn white shag. His eyes were closed to half slits and there was a look of deep concentration on his face. He seemed especially large in the narrow white room and his cheeks were full of color beside the pale German girls, who carefully moved their eyes from the television set to him.

"What are you doing there, sir?" I said.

"'Liverin' you a *gif*," he said, and he walked out the door. I went to the window and watched him. He staggered across the street into the lobby of the old Rex Hotel and emerged again with a plant under each arm. Then he was back in the apartment to deliver them, and still the Germans said nothing. When he left again, they began to murmur amongst themselves, and when he returned with two more plants, they smiled at him and then at me and they actually laughed.

He made a dozen trips, each time pinching a plant or two without anyone seeming to notice and dropping them heavily in the center of our living room floor. Finally he sat down hard on a bare patch of carpet, crossed his legs Indian style, and gave me a triumphant grin made up of perfect white teeth. Then he closed his eyes and his body tipped backward and his head landed on the ground with a thump.

He was too heavy to move. All we could do was straighten his legs and lay his arms over his chest. Later, when the German girls had gone to sleep, I brought out a pillow and blanket and lay down next to him. His shirt was pulled up out of his jeans and I put my palm on his stomach and touched the fuzzy blond hairs around his belly button. His stomach was not exactly fat, but it was not so firm as to suggest vanity or self-discipline, two qualities that at that time I found unpleasant in a man. I ran the back of my hand over his sunburned cheek. He smelled of booze and smoke and the kind of after-shave frat boys wore in college. It was a smell that reminded me of fast, hap-hazard sex.

I curled into him, into the sheer size of his body. There was heat in the places where our bodies touched and the moment seemed simple and absolutely complete. It stayed that way between us. I never knew what he thought about most things, whether he had grave opinions about the econ-omy or the nature of men or the existence of God. The things he knew about—football, sailboats, the business of manufacturing heavy equipment—couldn't power a conversation between us. We were rarely alone and we were almost always drunk, so there was never a requirement to get to know each other in an essential way; there was no imagined future. We were free of the heaviness I had so much of in college and later, when you announce to yourself and the world that you've met someone special and then you must stay the course. You must whisper into the night and you must embrace his terrible flaws—the dandruff at his temples, his tendency to speak rudely to waitresses, his inclination to overdress.

With Jimmy it was simply about putting "Sugar Mountain" on the juke-box and letting our thighs touch under the bar. It was about talking to Ray and drinking and letting time pass without clutching it or measuring it. It wasn't about ideas; it was about the weight and heat of a body against your own. I felt something like it again when I held my firstborn in my arms. The simple physical fact of her moved me—her button chin and the fleshy lobe of ear, her head smooth and blond as sand, her milky breath against my face.

After that first night, the Germans moved the plants onto the balcony of the apartment, and with muted hand gestures and apologetic smiles, made it clear they'd prefer it if Jimmy didn't make a habit of passing out on our living room floor. So we took to passing out at the flat just off the square that Jimmy shared with Ray and a half-dozen other backpackers—mostly Kiwis on summer holidays—who came and went. I was happy in that scrappy flat—the stained green sofa, the tiny kitchenette stocked with beer and tomatoes and sometimes an avocado or a lime, the walk-in closet where Jimmy and Ray slept on bare mattresses that, laid end-to-end, reached the entire length of the room. There was a collection of empty whiskey bottles in one corner, two fishing poles in the other, and their open backpacks in the center, overflowing with clothes. Taped to the wall over Jimmy's bed were photos of their trip so far; Jimmy and Ray in wet underwear beside a lake in the sun, Jimmy and Ray climbing a mountain trail in their loafers, Jimmy and Ray in their rain slickers, hitchhiking under a darkened sky.

We got drunk every night, mostly in the Cross, sometimes down at Wool-loomooloo or The Rocks. We'd sleep until noon and then head out for lunch and start drinking all over again. I had enough money saved that I could have picked up a round or two from time to time, but they never once let me. The drinks were charged to one of their fathers' cards, and the bills were taken care of back home.

Jimmy was a drinker without angst or moderation. He always said yes to the next one, and I was the same. It was not exactly that we set out to get drunk. It was that there was always the idea of that first drink in our minds, and when that one was gone, there was the idea of the next. Later it would work that way for me with babies, so that despite the burdens in it—the chaos and worry, the sleeplessness, the unqualified loss of freedom—when one child was weaned I was ready for the next, for the sweetness of a small hot body against my chest.

Ray was different. He got drunk when he set out to, did not when he did not intend to, and was often sober enough to remember the night and report back in the morning.

"Jesus, you puked on my fucking shoes," he'd say to Jimmy, or "You hit the bartender in the eye with a paper airplane."

"Did I?" Jimmy would ask me, grinning.

"Not that I remember," I'd say, which was most always true.

When I was drunkest, Jimmy would get me onto the mattress, cover me in a blue sheet, and tuck it tight around me. He knew something about being kind to women. He opened doors for me, he held my hair out of my face when I threw up, he made me drink a glass of milk before bed. And when Jimmy was first to get bad at the bars, Ray and I would each take an arm over our shoulders and drag him home. He'd stand on the mattress with his shoulder propped against the wall and yell, "I wanna get drunk."

"Lay down," Ray would order. "You're already drunk."

"Am I?" Jimmy would say. Then he'd sink down and close his bloodshot eyes and sleep for fourteen hours straight. It was a routine they knew by heart, and I sensed that Ray took a deep pleasure in keeping Jimmy safe in the world. I never asked Jimmy what he studied in college, or what he planned to do when the trip was over, or whether he'd ever been in love. It was Ray I wanted to understand. Ray lived right on the edge of ugly but to talk to him was to want to heal him or win him. At the bars, sometimes he ignored me, or coldly put up with me as if I were a wart he might someday burn away. Other times he sat up close and talked to me about Jasmine, telling me the same stories over and over again. For years I carried around a picture in my head of Jasmine driving fast along a coast road in her yellow convertible, her red hair flying out behind her, her back seat filled with flowers. It was a picture that could bring on a tightness in my chest, a vague longing to be an original, a girl who could win love absolutely and then walk away. When Ray spoke of her it was with reverence and regret; he had not forgiven her but he had not given her up either. Something about that made me want to make him see other women in the world; it made me want to make him see me.

On Christmas Day we planned a picnic on the beach. We took the ferry over to Manly early in the morning when the beach was empty and the air was still damp. Ray went off to the boardwalk and came back with three dozen clams in a bucket and a gallon jug of red wine. He opened the clams with his pocketknife and we ate them one after another, washing them down with wine straight from the bottle. By noon the beach was packed and it was so hot you couldn't walk on the sand. Ray went off again and came back with bread and cheese, peaches, pistachios, and a case of Victoria Bitter. Later, the German girls came by, pale and strong in their one-piece suits, and the Kiwis arrived with another case of beer. We assembled for a game of football—gridiron, the Kiwis called it—American style.

I can still feel myself in that day, my stomach flat and brown in an orange bikini, my hair wet down my back, the way I could sense my own ribs under my skin. The sun was hot on my head as I bent for the snap, ready to sprint after the ball. I didn't catch a single pass, and Ray traded me for one of the German girls who caught one and scored. But I didn't care. With every drink I became more beautiful in my own mind and the day grew more perfect. Later I would throw up over the railing of the ferry in the wind. I would pass out on the couch in the flat with a cigarette in my hand and burn a hole in the upholstery, and I would find, in the morning, dark spots of sunburn high on my cheeks that took years of creams and gels to take away. But in the place in my memory where that day lives on, nothing was damaged. Nothing was lost.

By dusk everyone else had gone and I sat between Jimmy and Ray under the changing sky and watched the water go from green to indigo to an oily black. In the half-dark, we staggered into the huge surf. I dove, stayed low to the sand and let the waves beat in my ears and sweep over me. I went through every wave, and I never ran out of breath. I might have been afraid out there in the waves, but I wasn't. That whole time was like that; I might have been worried about my health or my reputation or my safety but I never was. I was protected and drunk and happy, and if there is room for regret it is not for the time we wasted but that it ended too soon. In February, when the Kiwis were leaving Sydney to go back home, Jimmy and Ray threw them a going-away party in the flat. I imagined later that it was the night I lost them, the night that the trip around Australia in the green van—up through Queensland and the Gold Coast to the hot wastelands of Darwin and the white beaches of Perth—became a journey that would take place without me.

What I remember about that night is Jimmy with a threadbare undershirt over his square shoulders and how we ripped it, not in a rage or a passion but because there'd been a tiny hole above the right nipple, and I began to tear and everyone joined in and then someone poured a beer over our heads. At some point in the night the German girls came by—three steady girls with thick calves, short skirts, and high heels. I remember that when they arrived I had a paper bag over my head; someone had cut holes in it so I could see and breathe.

When almost everyone had gone and I was edging toward a blackout, I found myself in the walk-in closet on the wrong side of the room on the wrong mattress—with Ray. We were sitting cross-legged, facing each other, our knees touching, and Ray was holding a fishing pole across his lap. Then he was reaching his fingers out toward me and as I raised mine to meet them, he looked right at me, he leaned in toward me, and we were caught up in a kiss. It was gentle at first, almost a question, then it grew more urgent, until his lips against mine were hard and necessary. Jimmy was suddenly standing over us. *Hey!* he said, laughing at first like it was a joke he might have been in on. Then *hey!* again, then *hey!* a third time, loudly, with his hand pressing the ball of my shoulder away from Ray. So we stopped. Ray whispered something to me as we pulled away from each other, some words that I understood and cherished and then forgot—and that I can never get back.

I woke the next day on the mattress next to Jimmy. The afternoon sun filtered in through the doorway and fell on his face. The circles under his eyes were purple as dusk, and he seemed impossibly dear, the more so because I was afraid I'd lost him. At the same time, there was a small, stubborn part of me that wanted Ray to acknowledge the thing that had happened between us, that wanted him to make it happen again. It was a part of me I had not yet begun to understand—the part in the habit of expecting attention from men under the most extraordinary circumstances. Not just the first glow of desire, of glossy hair and full lips, but the whole messy miracle of love. It was not that I wanted the entrapments that come along with love, or that I would promise to offer it in return. It was that I believed that once a man knew me, he would see how different I was from an everyday girl—how forthright and clever and secretly kind—and he would find me indispensable.

It was a habit that persisted through heartbreak and havoc, through years of evidence to the contrary. Then I was married, and there were glimmers of it sometimes—at the pool where my son takes his swimming lessons, at the grocery store when a bagboy pushed my extra cart to the car—but for the most part I became convinced I'd outgrown it. Then on a hot night in August we threw a dinner party for friends. The kids were at my in-laws for a long-awaited overnight, and afterward, when the wives had kissed me and thanked me and gone home to relieve babysitters, and the other husbands—three men I've known for a decade—had assembled for a game of poker, I sat down in the chair left empty by my husband who had promptly passed out on the couch. One arm was flung across his face and the other hung over the back of the sofa, so that from where I sat I could see his long fingers dangling there, I could see his clean, clipped nails.

The game progressed. There was bluffing and folding. There was whiskey and chain-smoking and there were outrageous bets scribbled onto cocktail napkins. There were forearms—handsome, hairy, manly extremities brushing against mine on the tabletop as we handled the cards. Then all at once there was a knee pressed purposefully against my thigh beneath the table. There were brown eyes intent on my face and breath hot against my ear. And beyond that, where my husband's arm had been, was only the back of the couch. There was no sign of the formidable wrist, the sturdy thumb, the callused, well-loved palm. There was no further sign of my husband in the room at all. I was on my own in the company of men with the makings of a straight in my hand, ace high. Desire was thumping in my chest and the instinct to win, to go forward with abandon, was shooting through me, across the back of my neck and down between my legs.

At the same time—reaching me through the fog of scotch and cards and sex—was the power of my own house. There was the china waiting to be put back in the hutch. There was the cabinet door threatening to come off its hinge and a stack of catalogues to sort and toss. There was the phone, the bulletin board, the family calendar—the command center of our domestic life. Down the hall were my children's rooms, their mattresses and pillows encased in special covers to keep the dust mites at bay. Those rooms where each night I checked breathing and the temperatures of foreheads, where I kissed the gentle dip between cheeks and ears.

The question that persists, that pursues me even now, is whether it was only the card I was dealt—the seven of spades—that saved me. That freed me to shift my legs into open space, to lay my cards down on the table in a fold, and with an unlikely pinch of resolve, take my leave.

Jimmy got a two-week job down at Rushcutter's Bay scraping the underside of a yacht. When he was working that first week, I imagined him there, drinking a Coke in the sun. On Friday, I bought two sandwiches and a six-pack and made my way down to the boat yard. The day was warm and bright and the bay was dotted with sails. Jimmy was there and so was Ray. They were fishing. They weren't sitting close to each other and they weren't talking, but there was something between them, something silent and male, both a history and a future, and I almost turned around and left.

"Hey," Jimmy said, when he saw me. He glanced at Ray.

"I brought beers," I said.

"We never drink when we fish," Ray said. There was a silence. Then he laughed and took two beers. He popped one open for Jimmy and one for himself. "They're biting today. That's damned sure," he said.

I opened myself a beer and sat down on the dock next to Jimmy. The wood was gray and splintered, the water green with moss. We sat in silence for a while and then Ray's line began to move. I stood up as they did, as Ray reeled in his line, a fish slick and panicked at the end of it. Jimmy picked the pliers out of the bait box and worked the hook out, while Ray held the fish and then dropped it in the bucket with three others. There was nothing for me to do but stand and watch.

They finished their beers and began to pack up their fishing gear.

"That Kiwi band's playing at Woolloomooloo a week from Saturday," I said to Ray.

Ray looked at Jimmy then, and something passed between them, something that had already been decided.

"We're gonna be heading north, actually," Jimmy said. "We got a van and all." His face was soft with apology as he said it, and I might imagine now that he touched my cheek or took my hand in his. But he did not. He knocked his elbow against mine and punched me gently in the arm. We were like that together sober—clumsy and halting and overtaken by silences it was Ray's job to fill. But Ray had already turned and was walking up the hill home.

The day they left, the sky came down low and dark. They had their rain slickers on. I was coatless and cold. Ray loaded the arsenal of booze they'd assembled for the trip into the back of the van while Jimmy and I stood on the sidewalk and watched.

"I could sleep in the front seat," I said finally.

"No fucking way," Ray said from the back of the van.

"Ah, c'mon Cath," Jimmy said. He cocked his head to the side and turned his lips down in a pout. Then he took off his slicker and laid it over my shoulders. It had started to rain.

Ray came and stood next to Jimmy. For one long minute, he looked right at me and the lines of his face softened. My nose began to tingle with emotion and I had to look away. He walked toward me, slipped his rain slicker off his shoulders and laid it over me, so that I was wearing both coats, one on top of the other. I didn't know then what he meant by it, and I don't know now, but I hope he meant that I was forgiven—for my secret greed, for wanting to be so universally loved.

When they'd heaved their backpacks into the van and closed the doors and waved and were gone, I stood alone for a moment on the sidewalk in the rain, excessively dry under two rain slickers—cherry-red and lined with fleece. Then I walked up to the flat and let myself in and surveyed the closet that had been their room. They'd left the photos behind and I peeled one off the wall, slipped it into my pocket, and headed out into the rain. I started walking in the opposite direction of home, in and out of weather, into parts of the city I'd never been before, with my hands first in the pockets of one coat, then in the pockets of the other. As I walked, I thought about them hard—Jimmy and Ray—going over each episode in my mind, weighing and measuring, considering cause and effect. Not in an effort to shed the loss but to savor it, to shape it, to give it permanence.

Part 3: READING AS A WRITER

Shitty First Drafts

ANNE LAMOTT

Now, practically even better news than that of short assignments is the idea of shitty first drafts. All good writers write them. This is how they end up with good second drafts and terrific third drafts. People tend to look at successful writers, writers who are getting their books published and maybe even doing well financially, and think that they sit down at their desks every morning feeling like a million dollars, feeling great about who they are and how much talent they have and what a great story they have to tell; that they take in a few deep breaths, push back their sleeves, roll their necks a few times to get all the cricks out, and dive in, typing fully formed passages as fast as a court reporter. But this is just the fantasy of the uninitiated. I know some very great writers, writers you love who write beautifully and have made a great deal of money, and not *one* of them sits down routinely feeling wildly enthusiastic and confident. Not one of them writes elegant first drafts. All right, one of them does, but we do not like her very much. We do not think that she has a rich inner life or that God likes her or can even stand her. (Although when I mentioned this to my priest friend Tom, he said you can safely assume you've created God in your own image when it turns out that God hates all the same people you do.)

Very few writers really know what they are doing until they've done it. Nor do they go about their business feeling dewy and thrilled. They do not type a few stiff warm-up sentences and then find themselves bounding along like huskies across the snow. One writer I know tells me that he sits down every morning and says to himself nicely, "It's not like you don't have a choice, because you do—you can either type or kill yourself." We all often feel like we are pulling teeth, even those writers whose prose ends up being the most natural and fluid. The right words and sentences just do not come pouring out like ticker tape most of the time. Now, Muriel Spark is said to have felt that she was taking dictation from God every morning—sitting there, one supposes, plugged into a Dictaphone, typing away, humming. But this is a very hostile and aggressive position. One might hope for bad things to rain down on a person like this.

For me and most of the other writers I know, writing is not rapturous. In fact, the only way I can get anything written at all is to write really, really shitty first drafts.

The first draft is the child's draft, where you let it all pour out and then let it romp all over the place, knowing that no one is going to see it and that you can shape it later. You just let this childlike part of you channel whatever voices and visions come through and onto the page. If one of the characters wants to say, "Well, so what, Mr. Poopy Pants?" you let her. No one is going to see it. If the kid wants to get into really sentimental, weepy, emotional territory, you let him. Just get it all down on paper, because there may be something great in those six crazy pages that you would never have gotten to by more rational, grown-up means. There may be something in the very last line of the very last paragraph on page six that you just love, that is so beautiful or wild that you now know what you're supposed to be writing about, more or less, or in what direction you might go—but there was no way to get to this without first getting through the first five and a half pages.

I used to write food reviews for *California* magazine before it folded. (My writing food reviews had nothing to do with the magazine folding, although every single review did cause a couple of canceled subscriptions. Some readers took umbrage at my comparing mounds of vegetable puree with various ex-presidents' brains.) These reviews always took two days to write. First I'd go to a restaurant several times with a few opinionated, articulate friends in tow. I'd sit there writing down everything anyone said that was at all interesting or funny. Then on the following Monday I'd sit down at my desk with my notes, and try to write the review. Even after I'd been doing this for years, panic would set in. I'd try to write a lead, but instead I'd write a couple of dreadful sentences, xx them out, try again, xx everything out, and then feel despair and worry settle on my chest like an x-ray apron. It's over, I'd think, calmly. I'm not going to be able to get the magic to work this time. I'm ruined. I'm through. I'm toast. Maybe, I'd think, I can get my old job back as a clerk-typist. But probably not. I'd get up and study my teeth in the mirror for a while. Then I'd stop, remember to breathe, make a few phone calls, hit the kitchen and chow down. Eventually I'd go back and sit down at my desk, and sigh for the next ten minutes. Finally I would pick up my one-inch picture frame, stare into it as if for the answer, and every time the answer would come: all I had to do was to write a really shitty first draft of, say, the opening paragraph. And no one was going to see it.

So I'd start writing without reining myself in. It was almost just typing, just making my fingers move. And the writing would be *terrible*. I'd write a lead paragraph that was a whole page, even though the entire review could only be three pages long, and then I'd start writing up descriptions of the food, one dish at a time, bird by bird, and the critics would be sitting on my shoulders, commenting like cartoon characters. They'd be pretending to snore, or rolling their eyes at my overwrought descriptions, no matter how hard I tried to tone those descriptions down, no matter how conscious I was of what a friend said to me gently in my early days of restaurant reviewing. "Annie," she said, "it is just a piece of *chicken*. It is just a bit of *cake*."

But because by then I had been writing for so long, I would eventually let myself trust the process—sort of, more or less. I'd write a first draft that was maybe twice as long as it should be, with a self-indulgent and boring beginning, stupefying descriptions of the meal, lots of quotes from my black-humored friends that made them sound more like the Manson girls than food lovers, and no ending to speak of. The whole thing would be so long and incoherent and hideous that for the rest of the day I'd obsess about getting creamed by a car before I could write a decent second draft. I'd worry that people would read what I'd written and believe that the accident had really been a suicide, that I had panicked because my talent was waning and my mind was shot.

The next day, though, I'd sit down, go through it all with a colored pen, take out everything I possibly could, find a new lead somewhere on the second page, figure out a kicky place to end it, and then write a second draft. It always turned out fine, sometimes even funny and weird and helpful. I'd go over it one more time and mail it in.

Then, a month later, when it was time for another review, the whole process would start again, complete with the fears that people would find my first draft before I could rewrite it.

Almost all good writing begins with terrible first efforts. You need to start somewhere. Start by getting something—anything—down on paper. A friend of mine says that the first draft is the down draft—you just get it down. The second draft is the up draft—you fix it up. You try to say what you have to say more accurately. And the third draft is the dental draft, where you check every tooth, to see if it's loose or cramped or decayed, or even, God help us, healthy.

What I've learned to do when I sit down to work on a shitty first draft is to quiet the voices in my head. First there's the vinegar-lipped Reader Lady, who says primly, "Well, *that's* not very interesting, is it?" And there's the emaciated German male who writes these Orwellian memos detailing your thought crimes. And there are your parents, agonizing over your lack of loyalty and discretion; and there's William Burroughs, dozing off or shooting up because he finds you as bold and articulate as a house-plant; and so on. And there are also the dogs: let's not forget the dogs, the dogs in their pen who will surely hurtle and snarl their way out if you ever *stop* writing, because writing is, for some of us, the latch that keeps the door of the pen closed, keeps those crazy ravenous dogs contained.

Quieting these voices is at least half the battle I fight daily. But this is better than it used to be. It used to be 87 percent. Left to its own devices, my mind spends much of its time having conversations with people who aren't there. I walk along defending myself to people, or exchanging repartee with them, or rationalizing my behavior, or seducing them with gossip, or pretending I'm on their TV talk show or whatever. I speed or run an aging yellow light or don't come to a full stop, and one nanosecond later am explaining to imaginary cops exactly why I had to do what I did, or insisting that I did not in fact do it.

I happened to mention this to a hypnotist I saw many years ago, and he looked at me very nicely. At first I thought he was feeling around on the floor for the silent alarm button, but then he gave me the following exercise, which I still use to this day.

Close your eyes and get quiet for a minute, until the chatter starts up. Then isolate one of the voices and imagine the person speaking as a mouse. Pick it up by the tail and drop it into a mason jar. Then isolate another voice, pick it up by the tail, drop it in the jar. And so on. Drop in any high-maintenance parental units, drop in any contractors, lawyers, colleagues, children, anyone who is whining in your head. Then put the lid on, and watch all these mouse people clawing at the glass, jabbering away, trying to make you feel like shit because you won't do what they want—won't give them more money, won't be more successful, won't see them more often. Then imagine that there is a volume-control button on the bottle. Turn it all the way up for a minute, and listen to the stream of angry, neglected, guilt-mongering voices. Then turn it all the way down and watch the frantic mice lunge at the glass, trying to get to you. Leave it down, and get back to your shitty first draft.

A writer friend of mine suggests opening the jar and shooting them all in the head. But I think he's a little angry, and I'm sure nothing like this would ever occur to you.

1. What did you think of this essay? Do you agree with it?
2. What happens after you've finished a first draft? Do you feel relieved? Anxious?
3. Do you know what to do after you've finished a first draft? How do you figure out what to do next?

The Carver Chronicles

D. T. MAX

For much of the past twenty years, Gordon Lish, an editor at *Esquire* and then at Alfred A. Knopf who is now retired, has been quietly telling friends that he played a crucial role in the creation of the early short stories of Raymond Carver. The details varied from telling to telling, but the basic idea was that he had changed some of the stories so much that they were more his than Carver's. No one quite knew what to make of his statements. Carver, who died ten years ago this month, never responded in public to them. Basically it was Lish's word against common sense. Lish had written fiction, too: if he was such a great talent, why did so few people care about his own work? As the years passed, Lish became reluctant to discuss the subject. Maybe he was choosing silence over people's doubt. Maybe he had rethought what his contribution had been—or simply moved on.

Seven years ago, Lish arranged for the sale of his papers to the Lilly Library at Indiana University. Since then, only a few Carver scholars have examined the Lish manuscripts thoroughly. When one tried to publish his conclusions, Carver's widow and literary executor, the poet Tess Gallagher, effectively blocked him with copyright cautions and pressure. I'd heard about this scholar's work (and its failure to be published) through a friend. So I decided to visit the archive myself.

What I found there, when I began looking at the manuscripts of stories like "Fat" and "Tell the Women We're Going," were pages full of editorial marks—strikeouts, additions and marginal comments in Lish's sprawling handwriting. It looked as if a temperamental seven-year-old had somehow got hold of the stories. As I was reading, one of the archivists came over. I thought she was going to reprimand me for some violation of the library rules. But that wasn't why she was there. She wanted to talk about Carver. "I started reading the folders," she said, "but then I stopped when I saw what was in there."

It's understandable that Lish's assertions have never been taken seriously. The eccentric editor is up against an American icon. When he died at age fifty from lung cancer, Carver was considered by many to be America's most important short-story writer. His stories were beautiful and moving. At a New York City memorial service, Robert Gottlieb, then the editor of the *New Yorker*, said succinctly, "America has just lost the writer it could least afford to lose." Carver is no longer a writer of the moment, the way David Foster Wallace is today, but many of his stories—"Cathedral," "Will You Please Be Quiet, Please?" and "Errand"—are firmly established in the literary canon. A vanguard figure in the 1980s, Carver has become establishment fiction.

That doesn't capture his claim on us, though. It goes deeper than his work. Born in the rural Northwest, Carver was the child of an alcoholic sawmill worker and a waitress. He first learned to write through a correspondence course. He lived in poverty and suffered multiple bouts of alcoholism throughout his thirties. He struggled in a difficult marriage with his high-school girlfriend, Maryann Burk. Through it all he remained a generous, determined man—fiction's comeback kid. By 1980, he had quit drinking and moved in with Tess Gallagher, with whom he spent the rest of his life. "I know better than anyone a fellow is never out of the woods," he wrote to Lish in one of dozens of letters archived at the Lilly. "But right now it's aces, and I'm enjoying it." Carver's life and work inspired faith, not skepticism.

Still, a quick look through Carver's books would suggest that what Lish claims might have some merit. There is an evident gap between the early style of *Will You Please Be Quiet, Please?* and *What We Talk About When We Talk About Love*, Carver's first two major collections, and his later work in *Cathedral* and *Where I'm Calling From*. In subject matter, the stories share a great deal. They are mostly about the working poor—unemployed salesmen, waitresses, motel managers—in the midst of disheartening lives. But the early collections, which Lish edited, are stripped to the bone. They are minimalist in style with an almost abstract feel. They drop their characters back down where they find them, inarticulate and alone, drunk at noon. The later two collections are fuller, touched by optimism, even sentimentality.

Many critics over the years have noticed this difference and explained it in terms of biography. The Carver of the early stories, it has been said, was in despair. As he grew successful, however, the writer learned about hopefulness and love, and it soaked into his fiction. This redemptive story was burnished through countless retellings by Tess Gallagher. Most critics seemed satisfied by this literal-minded explanation: happy writers write happy stories.

Sitting under the coffered ceiling of the Lilly, I began pulling out folders from the two boxes marked "Carver." Here were the stories from his first two collections as well as from *Cathedral* in versions from manuscript to printer's galleys. I had previously seen some manuscripts in the Carver holdings at Ohio State University, an archive to which Gallagher has said she will ultimately give the Carver papers in her possession. The manuscripts at OSU are clean, almost without editing marks, as if they'd gone straight from author to typesetter. Where there are multiple drafts of a manuscript, the procession is unremarkable: the annotations in Carver's tiny handwriting drive the story confidently from draft to draft until the story achieves its finished form.

The Lilly manuscripts are different. There are countless cuts and additions to the pages; entire paragraphs have been added. Lish's black felt-tip markings sometimes obliterate the original text. In the case of Carver's 1981 collection, *What We Talk About When We Talk About Love*, Lish cut about half the original words and rewrote ten of the thirteen endings. "Carol, story ends here," he would note for the benefit of his typist.

In "Mr. Coffee and Mr. Fixit," for example, Lish cut 70 percent of the original words. With a longer story, "A Small, Good Thing," in which a couple anxiously wait for their child to come out of a coma, Lish cut the text by a third, eliminating most of the description—and all of the introspection. He retitled it "The Bath," altering the story's redemptive tone to one of Beckettian despair. In Lish's version, you no longer know if the child lives or dies.

Lish was constantly on guard against what he saw as Carver's creeping sentimentality. In the original manuscripts, Carver's characters talk about their feelings. They talk about regrets. When they do bad things, they cry. When Lish got hold of Carver, they stopped crying. They stopped feeling. Lish loved deadpan last lines, and he freely wrote them in: "The women, they weren't there when I left, and they wouldn't be there when I got back" ("Night School"). Other times, he cut away whole sections to leave a sentence from inside the story as the end: "There were dogs and there were dogs. Some dogs you just couldn't do anything with" ("Jerry and Molly and Sam"). On occasion, Carver reversed his changes, but in most cases Lish's handwriting became part of Carver's next draft, which became the published story.

"Fat" was one of the first stories Carver gave Lish to edit. It became the lead story in *Will You Please Be Quiet, Please?* In "Fat," a restaurant waitress recounts to her friend Rita a large meal she served to a ravenous but melancholy obese man. The waitress's lover, Rudy, the restaurant cook, feels jealous. When they get home, he insists on having sex with her, but her mind remains with her experiences in the restaurant: the fat man has touched her in some way, made her feel dissatisfied with her life. This was how Carver wrote it, more as an anecdote than a story. It proved excellent material for Lish's talents. Some of what Lish does is technical: he moves the story into the present tense, for example. And he eliminates the waitress's self-reflectiveness, so we seem more involved than she does in what she is feeling. (Critics would later declare such touches to be trademark techniques of Carver.) Most important, Lish picks up on the "long, thick, creamy fingers" Carver gives the fat man, and finds in this the story's core—the connection between longing and sexuality.

"My God, Rita, those were fingers," the waitress tells her girlfriend, who herself has "dainty fingers." At the end, when Rudy gets into bed with her, she observes, "Rudy is a tiny thing and hardly there at all." These lines—and several others—were written by Lish. In Lish's hands, fatness becomes sexual potency, fullness, presence. He finds the resonance Carver missed.

If "Fat" was a successful—if unusually extensive—edit, Lish's efforts on another story, "Tell the Women We're Going," seemed closer to a wholesale rewrite. Written by Carver in the late 1960s or early 70s, the story was unusual for him, one of the few in which the violence implicit in his characters becomes explicit. The story first made an appearance as "Friendship" in *Sou'wester*, a small literary magazine. By the time it appeared in the *What We Talk About* collection, Lish had retitled it—and cut it by 40 percent. The story is set near the town in which Carver grew up, Yakima, Washington. Bill and his tougher friend Jerry take a break from their wives at a barbecue and drive off looking for action. They find two teenage girls bicycling along the road and try to get their attention. Things go awry. After a tense pursuit full of strange pleas and laughs,

Jerry rapes and kills Sharon—a scene that Bill, who has dropped behind, arrives in time to witness. He cries out, asserting in that moment the horror that the reader feels, too.

What's noteworthy about the story is the way Carver makes a boring afternoon build to murder. Lish didn't care about this. He was after more abstract effects. He made cuts on every page. Bill becomes just a passive companion to Jerry. The pursuit is eliminated: the violence now comes out of nowhere and is almost hallucinogenic. "[Bill] never knew what Jerry wanted. But it started and ended with a rock," Lish wrote in. "Jerry used the same rock on both girls, first on the girl called Sharon and then on the one that was supposed to be Bill's." The story ends right there. One wonders how Carver must have felt when he saw that.

As I thumbed through various manuscripts at the Lilly, my face was flushed. I wanted Carver to win, whatever that might mean. He had shown writers the value of measuring your words. He had come along in the early 1970s when the first "postmodern" novelists, writers like John Barth and Donald Barthelme, dominated the literary scene. Their cerebral stories were admirable, but they were hard to love. Carver broke up their racket.

My favorite story had always been the sly "They're Not Your Husband." An unemployed salesman, Earl, goes to the restaurant where his wife, Doreen, is a waitress, and without identifying himself tries to goad the male customers into checking her out. He needs the validation. I particularly loved a description of Doreen's thighs as she bends over to scoop ice cream: "rumpled and gray and a little hairy, [with] veins that spread in a berserk display." The story also has a wonderful ending: "Then she put the unfinished chocolate sundae in front of [Earl] and went to total up his check." Lish didn't edit this story much, I discovered, but it turned out he had written the first sentence and rewritten the second. In Carver's version, the thighs are barely mentioned. In his original ending, Doreen just reaches for a coffeepot.

Overall, Lish's editorial changes generally struck me as for the better. Some of the cuts were brilliant, like the expert cropping of a picture. His additions gave the stories new dimensions, bringing out moments that I was sure Carver must have loved to see. Other changes, like those in "Tell the Women We're Going," struck me as bullying and competitive. Lish was redirecting Carver's vision in the service of his own fictional goals. The act felt parasitic. Lish's techniques also grew tired more quickly than did Carver's. After a while, the endless "I say," "he says" tags Lish placed on so much of the dialogue felt gimmicky. In all cases, however, I had one sustained reaction: for better or worse, Lish was in there.

Back in New York I contacted Lish. Much has changed for "Captain Fiction," as the once dapper Lish was nicknamed during his *Esquire* heyday. Now sixty four, he is a widower, living alone in a spacious apartment on the Upper East Side of Manhattan. He shuffles around in his socks, his long white hair and loose clothes making him look like a vanquished sorcerer.

We sat across from each other at his kitchen table and I asked him what had happened. "I don't like talking about the Carver period," he said, "because of my sustained sense of his betrayal and because it seems bad form to discuss this." I was aware that he had been a radio actor before becoming an editor. Was he playing his reluctance up for me? "This puts me in an absolutely impossible light," he continued. "I can only be despised for my participation."

Lish already has plenty of enemies: by the 1990s, his aggressive editing, controversial private fiction seminars and taste for publicity had cost him many friends. "I said no to the people to whom one doesn't say no," he said. In 1994, after a decade in which the writers he was championing found fewer and fewer readers, Knopf fired him. He now writes fiction full-time. His latest is titled "Self-Imitation of Myself." Reading his stories is like looking at the gears of a clock that's missing a face.

Lish's "sustained sense of betrayal" was, of course, also a strong motivator toward conversation. He was still embittered, he said, by the biting ingratitude of "this mediocrity" he had plucked from obscurity. When Lish is excited, his psoriasis acts up; he pulled a cooking spoon from his shelf and began scratching his back. And he began to tell me his version of the story.

In 1969 he persuaded *Esquire* to hire him as fiction editor. He promised to find new voices, to clear out the cobwebs. It was quite a leap for a part-time literary editor from Palo Alto, California. The pressure was on to produce.

One of his friends was Carver, who was editing educational materials in an office across the street from where Lish had worked. They were drinking pals, Carver tall, handsome, and deliberate, Lish short and wiry. Lish was the more worldly and aggressive. Maryann Burk-Carver recalls them walking down a Palo Alto street with Lish asking every woman they passed to sleep with him; he was trying to prove to Carver that you only had to ask to get what you wanted from life. At this point Carver had a small reputation, but he was not a name. "He was not known, not known at all, to the persons I would be delivering stories to for approval," Lish remembers.

Lish contacted Carver, who quickly sent off several stories to him. Lish reworked and returned them, using as his model the disorienting, unemotive stories of James Purdy, the author of "Why Can't They Tell You Why?" The stories—"Fat," "Neighbors," and "Are You a Doctor?"—wound up as Carver's first national magazine publications. Lish had a genius for beating the drum for his writers. He was friends with important writers like Cynthia Ozick and Harold Brodkey. Critics quickly took notice of the "new" voice in fiction Lish was championing, of its radical compression (many stories were but a few pages long) and stark silences. Much was made of Carver's name—although Lish was the one doing the carving.

In 1976 Carver collected his stories in *Will You Please Be Quiet, Please?* including a version of the title story that Lish had cut. In the *New York Times Book Review,* the novelist Geoffrey Wolff, who would later become a friend of Carver's, hailed the stories, describing them as "carefully shaped" and "shorn of ornamentation," marked by "spells of quiet and tensed apprehension." In fact, Wolff wrote, Carver's prose "carries his mark everywhere: I would like to believe that having read the stories I could identify him on the evidence of a paragraph." The collection was nominated for a National Book Award.

Carver was gaining confidence from his success and writing more ambitiously. And he was finding out the world wasn't so harsh. He had friends now, acolytes even. He separated from Maryann and became involved with Tess Gallagher. He bought a boat and celebrated it in a poem in which he imagined it filled with his friends.

His editor's confidence was also growing. Lish thought of himself as Carver's ventriloquist. "I could not believe no one had stumbled on what was going on," he says. A collision was inevitable.

Initially, Carver had been grateful for Lish's help—or perhaps just compliant or cowed. Carver was in a bad place in his life, beset by drink and poverty. Lish was his way to a readership. Nevertheless, Carver's unease was evident from the beginning. These letters are in the Lish archives. Responding to an edit in December 1969, Carver wrote: "Everything considered, it's a better story now than when I first mailed it your way— which is the important thing, I'm sure." He echoed these sentiments in January 1971. "Took all of yr changes and added a few things here and there," he wrote, taking pains to add that he was "not bothered" by the extent of Lish's edit. Carver had a role in keeping the romance going, too. "You've made a single-handed impression on American letters," he wrote Lish in September 1977. "And, of course, you know, old bean, just what influence you've exercised on my life." He even offered to pay the charges for any work Lish sends out to be retyped.

After *Will You Please Be Quiet, Please?* they began work on a second collection, which Lish would ultimately title *What We Talk About When We Talk About Love*. (Carver had called it "Beginners.") Lish was editing more heavily now. He treated Carver as if he barely had a vote. Meanwhile, Carver was becoming a known literary figure. In 1978 he won a Guggenheim Fellowship. The next year he became a professor of English at Syracuse University.

Carver began to object to Lish's editing, but he wasn't sure what to object to. He wrote a five-page letter in July 1980 telling Lish that he could not allow him to publish *What We Talk About* as Lish had edited it. He wrote, "Maybe if I were alone, by myself, and no one had ever seen these stories, maybe then, knowing that your versions are better than some of the ones I sent, maybe I could get into this and go with it." But he feared being caught. "Tess has seen all of these and gone over them closely. Donald Hall has seen many of the new ones . . . and Richard Ford, Toby Wolff, Geoffrey Wolff, too, some of them. . . . How can I explain to these fellows when I see them, as I will see them, what happened?" He begged to be let out of his contract or at least to delay publication: "Please, Gordon, for God's sake help me in this and try to understand. . . . I've got to pull out of this one. Please hear me. I've been up all night thinking on this. . . . I'll say it again, if I have any standing or reputation or cedibility [sic] in the world, I owe it to you. I owe you this more-or-less pretty interesting life I have [but] I can't take the risk as to what might happen to me." In the same letter, he wrote imploringly, "[M]y very sanity is on the line here. . . . I feel it, that if the book were to be published as it is in its present edited form, I may never write another story."

Lish does not recall being moved. "My sense of it was that there was a letter and that I just went ahead." He knew what was best for Carver— even if Carver didn't see it that way. In the end, *What We Talk About* was published much as Lish wanted.

The book received front-page reviews. Critics praised its minimalist style and announced a new school of fiction. Even so, Carver continued to press for stylistic control over his work. He insisted that if Lish wanted to edit his next collection, he would have to keep his hands off. "I can't undergo [that] kind of surgical amputation and transplantation," he wrote Lish in August 1982. "Please help me with this book as a good editor, the best . . . not as my ghost," he pleaded two months later.

Lish reluctantly complied. "So be it," he wrote in December 1982 after giving the manuscript of *Cathedral* only a light edit—although he wrote some acerbic criticisms in the margins. Even then, Carver feared a sneak attack. "I don't need to tell you that it's critical for me that there not be any messing around with titles or text," he warned Lish. Publicly, Carver also began to make a break. He made a point of telling interviewers that he controlled every aspect of his stories, invoking the adage that he knew a story was finished when he went through it once and put the commas in, then went through again and took the commas out.

Lish was angered by Carver's rebellion. He began asking his friends whether he should make his "surrogate work" public. They advised him to keep quiet. Don DeLillo, for example, warned him against taking Carver on. "I appreciate, and am in sympathy with, everything you say in your letter," he wrote to Lish. "But the fact is: there is no exposing Carver. . . . Even if people knew, from Carver himself, that you are largely responsible for his best work, they would immediately forget it. It is too much to absorb. Too complicated. Makes reading the guy's work an ambiguous thing at best. People wouldn't think less of Carver for having had to lean so heavily on an editor; they'd resent Lish for complicating the reading of the stories.

"In the meantime," he ended, "take good care of your archives."

Once Carver ended his professional relationship with Lish, he never looked back. He didn't need to. *Cathedral* was his most celebrated work yet. Famous writers wanted to meet him; Saul Bellow wrote him an appreciative note. The collection was nominated for both a Pulitzer and a National Book Critics Circle Award. Proudly, Carver wrote a letter to Lish in which he noted that the title story "went straight from the typewriter into the mail."

Indeed, many writers and critics see Carver's later work—stories like "Blackbird Pie" and "Errand"—as his best efforts, his final brilliant flowering. Seen in this light, the Lish period, though responsible for bringing him to national attention, was an apprenticeship to be transcended. Some of Carver's friends certainly saw it that way. The poet Donald Hall read a manuscript copy of "The Bath" before Lish cut it. He asked Carver's permission to publish the original version under its original title, "A Small, Good Thing," in *Ploughshares* magazine. In this more expansive, uplifting form, the story won a 1983 O. Henry Award. "I was hearthurt at what had happened to that story," Hall remembers. "I've wondered in my head why Lish did what he did. Was it unconscious jealousy?"

That is one way to explain the Lish–Carver relationship. The story is complicated by, of all people, Tess Gallagher. The poet, who now lives in Port Angeles, Washington, is generally seen as the heroine of the Carver saga. And with reason. When she met Carver in 1977, he was just turning a corner in his life, trying to control his drinking. She was ready for the job of keeping him sober. "God has given you to me to take care of," she told him. Gallagher made a home for him in which to work. She taught him to say no to Lish and ultimately to free himself from him, winning the long tug of war for Carver's soul. She encouraged him to publish *Where I'm Calling From*, a selection of seven new and thirty old stories, in the form he wanted posterity to read. (Carver never explained, however, that he was, in some cases, reversing Lish's edits.)

So Gallagher helped Carver to find his true voice. Weirdly, though, many of her pronouncements also have the effect of claiming a piece of Carver's work. Although she declined several requests to be interviewed for this article, Gallagher has described in detail her contribution to two of Carver's greatest stories, "Cathedral" and "Errand." Unlike Lish's claims, they cannot be checked against original drafts, because most of Carver's late manuscripts remain in her hands. Besides, the collaboration she describes would be so intimate that no traces were likely to remain.

But in the 1992 PBS documentary *To Write and Keep Kind* and in a series of unpublished interviews, Gallagher emphasized that she had given Carver the original idea for "Cathedral"—or, more accurately, that he had stolen it from her. The story focuses on the discomfort that a husband feels when his wife brings a blind friend into their home. Tess herself had a blind acquaintance whom she talked about with Carver; she said she was planning to write a story about him when Carver "scooped" her. In addition, Gallagher claimed that she had written or helped shape several key lines. She spoke of the story as a joint effort.

Then there's "Errand," Carver's last published story. It tells of Anton Chekhov's early death; the work has a special status among Carver readers because Carver identified with Chekhov and because, although Carver said he did not know he had cancer when he wrote it, it limns his own death. The end of "Errand" takes place in a Badenweiler hotel room in 1904. The point of view of the story gracefully shifts from Chekhov, this man of letters dying of tuberculosis, to a young waiter worrying about a cork that has fallen to the floor in the room. The widow is lost in grief, and he is preoccupied with the cork. The ending is classically Chekhovian in its attention to the waiter and his worries, and it fuses elegantly Carver's death, his life and his work.

As Gallagher explained in *To Write and Keep Kind*, Carver had trouble envisioning the end of the tale: "Ray had written many, many drafts and didn't know how to get out of this story." So she came to his aid. "I was empathizing with his waiter character," she said to the camera, "and I said, that waiter is going to be looking down and you know what he's going to see? He's going to see that cork that popped out of the Champagne. I think the ending is involved with his response to that cork, and that he's going to bend down to get that and we're going to know something from that gesture, that action."

Collaboration between a literary husband and wife is not unusual. Nor is theft: F. Scott Fitzgerald lifted pages from the diaries of his wife, Zelda, for the sanitarium sections of *Tender Is the Night*. Such entanglements still arouse discomfort. In an interview, Gallagher said that she had always kept their collaboration private, because "people's ideas about authorship are perhaps a bit fixed and unimaginative when it comes to what really happens when two writers live together." This has emerged as a theme of hers. Her next book is to be called "Soul Barnacles: On the Literature of a Relationship, Tess Gallagher and Raymond Carver."

Perhaps Gallagher and Lish did make their marks on Carver's fiction. But who needs them? Carver is enough. That's how Carver's friends—Richard Ford, Tobias Wolff, Mona Simpson—feel. "I have absolute confidence that Ray wrote everything in his stories according to my understanding of how writers write what they write," Ford said. He said he feared that any discussion of the archives would "inadvertently diminish Ray." Simpson expressed a lack of surprise. "I think people already assume an editor helps to make the work better. Who would want one who didn't?" Wolff said it reminded him what a good idea it is to destroy your drafts.

I mentioned the competing, and in some cases overlapping, claims of collaboration to Dick Day, Carver's college writing teacher at Humboldt State University. He thought his own influence was negligible. "I know any time I read a sentence by Carver that it's Carver's," he said. "Ray's voice was his own and it's authentic." A top editor at Knopf finds the very idea of co-authorship noxious. "I never met an author so many people claimed a piece of," he says.

How far can one take the question of influence, anyway? When I spoke with Maryann Carver about her ex-husband's work, she cited her impact on the story "Will You Please Be Quiet, Please?" In the story, a husband and wife have an altercation over a past affair. When I pressed for details, she said it would be "crude" to get specific. Then she showed me where her tooth had entered her lip.

DeLillo had pointed out in his letter to Lish how central the idea of authenticity is to our literary culture. We have the text on the printed page. Why complicate our enjoyment of the stories by focusing on how they came to be written? To ask is to transgress. Besides, that writers take the help that is offered is not news. Chekhov, Carver's idol, used to pay friends ten kopecks for an anecdote and twenty for a plot. Carver came out of the 1970s' workshop tradition, in which you showed a story around and took the suggestions you found useful. What's so strange about a smart writer taking smart advice? "I edit my writers a lot or a little," says Gary Fisketjon, the editor-at-large at Knopf who worked with Carver after Lish. "Either way, it's their story."

Academics familiar with the Lish papers see the question of collaboration as more complex. "If you exalt the individual writer as the romantic figure who brings out these things from the depths of his soul," says Carol Polsgrove, a professor at Indiana University who has written about the archives, "then, yes, the awareness of Lish's role diminishes Carver's work somewhat. But if you look at writing and publishing as a social act, which I think it is, the stories are the stories that they are." Her view is becoming more widespread: a new form of literary analysis, "genetic criticism," focuses on the evolution of literary manuscripts from drafts to published form, taking into account the inevitable impact of editors and publishers.

Brian Evenson, a professor of English at Oklahoma State University, is the scholar whose findings Gallagher fought to keep unpublished. (The essay had been under consideration for an upcoming anthology, *Critical Essays on Raymond Carver*, when Gallagher got wind of the submission and issued the publisher a copyright warning.) In Evenson's eyes, "You really have to say that Lish is almost as responsible as Carver for the stories he worked on." He feels the work really has to be admitted to be a "collaboration"—almost like a musical with book and music by different artists. All the characters, the settings and the plots are Carver's. Carver country conceived of as a physical place with a given population is still Carver country. But the minimalist tone, for good or ill, was Lish's. He was more avant-garde than Carver, whose real voice was closer to his plain-spoken poetry. That's how he wrote before he met Lish, and that's how he wrote after. "It's no wonder Carver grew angry when critics called him a minimalist," Evenson says. "That was Lish."

What does one make of literature that is the product of collaboration? Some historical perspective is in order. Consider Ezra Pound's revising of "The Waste Land" in 1922. Pound did for T. S. Eliot something of what Lish did for Carver. He made liberal cuts to the poem, shortening it by half and eliminating the strong element of parody. (The original title had been "He Do the Police in Different Voices.") Pound found a voice—not necessarily the voice Eliot intended—and honed it brilliantly. He helped make him a modernist cause célèbre. Eliot acknowledged the debt obliquely, praising

Pound as *"il miglior fabbro"* ("the greater craftsman") in his dedication. When Eliot outgrew Pound, he moved on. Scholars learned of the extent of this collaboration only with the discovery of the original manuscripts in 1968. This has not hurt Eliot's reputation. Seen in the larger context of his career, the fact that his masterpiece did not read quite like anything else he wrote did not lessen his stature or importance. Somehow it has come to seem natural.

Thomas Wolfe, on the other hand, did not come in for such gentle handling. Wolfe was a brilliant writer, but there was a lot about writing a novel he never understood. He dumped the 330,000-word manuscript of his first novel, *Look Homeward, Angel,* on the desk of his editor, Maxwell Perkins; in long sessions, Perkins cut, revised and made suggestions (always with Wolfe's consent). Wolfe decided to publicize the situation, much to the embarrassment of Perkins, who thought the editing process should be private. By Wolfe's second book, Perkins was mixing and matching batches of manuscripts, connecting the dots with Wolfe as he went along. After Wolfe died in 1938, Edward Aswell, an editor at Harper & Brothers, went even further. He created two more books out of the million words Wolfe left behind, creating composite characters and sometimes adding his own words. As these revelations have become known in the past two decades, Wolfe's reputation has dimmed considerably. "We have been threatened with scholarly publication of Wolfe's original manuscripts, and doubtless the threats will be fulfilled," wrote the critic Harold Bloom in 1987, "but the originals are most unlikely to revive Wolfe's almost-dead reputation."

Between these two examples sits Carver. To be sure, some of the early stories were so transformed by Lish that they should be considered the product of two minds. But what about the later stories Gallagher claims to have influenced? It's hard to say. That Carver's relationship with Gallagher was consensual rather than antagonistic matters, but what's most compelling is that the stories from *Cathedral* feel as if they came from him. They share a common voice, a brightness. If Gallagher helped him, so much the better. To paraphrase Mona Simpson, who would want a wife who didn't? Of course, one day, Gallagher may reveal a deeper level of collaboration. It's one thing to guide the pen; another to hold it. If that day comes, I suspect I will start to feel about Carver the way I do about Wolfe: namely, that he was a writer who never left a clear record of his talents. DeLillo is right: this is a culture in which we want a single name on the front of the book.

But why place so high a price on purity? The stories are what they are, regardless. Perhaps that's why Carver was not inclined to talk openly about the editing process. He was a private man and nonconfrontational. "Ray once said to me, 'Who needs trouble?'" remembers Tobias Wolff. "He wanted everything to be peaceful." When interviewers asked Carver about his relationship with "Captain Fiction," he always acknowledged Lish as a friend, a talented editor, a man who had been there for him at a crucial time. But he carefully avoided talking about the back-and-forth of their editing relationship, why it had ended or what it might reveal for those interested in his work.

In 1982, however, he came close. He was in a discussion with students at the University of Akron and, in response to a student's question, he began talking about the editor–writer relationship. He ticked off all the famous examples of heavy editing: F. Scott Fitzgerald's cutting of Hemingway's *Sun Also Rises*, Perkins and Wolfe, Pound and Eliot. Carver quoted Pound's explanation of the process: "It's immensely important that great poems be written, but it makes not a jot of difference who writes them."

Then he paused. "That's it. That's it exactly," he said.

1. What does this essay say about the danger of depending too much on an editor? Do you think Lish was overstepping the bounds when he influenced Carver's writing to such a degree?
2. What would you do if you had an editor like Lish? Would you push back? Acquiesce?

The Bath

RAYMOND CARVER

Saturday afternoon the mother drove to the bakery in the shopping center. After looking through a loose-leaf binder with photographs of cakes taped onto the pages, she ordered chocolate, the child's favorite. The cake she chose was decorated with a spaceship and a launching pad under a sprinkling of white stars. The name SCOTTY would be iced on in green as if it were the name of the spaceship.

The baker listened thoughtfully when the mother told him Scotty would be eight years old. He was an older man, this baker, and he wore a curious apron, a heavy thing with loops that went under his arms and around his back and then crossed in front again where they were tied in a very thick knot. He kept wiping his hands on the front of the apron as he listened to the woman, his wet eyes examining her lips as she studied the samples and talked.

He let her take her time. He was in no hurry.

The mother decided on the spaceship cake, and then she gave the baker her name and her telephone number. The cake would be ready Monday morning, in plenty of time for the party Monday afternoon. This was all the baker was willing to say. No pleasantries, just this small exchange, the barest information, nothing that was not necessary.

Monday morning, the boy was walking to school. He was in the company of another boy, the two boys passing a bag of potato chips back and forth between them. The birthday boy was trying to trick the other boy into telling what he was going to give in the way of a present.

At an intersection, without looking, the birthday boy stepped off the curb, and was promptly knocked down by a car. He fell on his side, his head in the gutter, his legs in the road moving as if he were climbing a wall.

The other boy stood holding the potato chips. He was wondering if he should finish the rest or continue on to school.

The birthday boy did not cry. But neither did he wish to talk anymore. He would not answer when the other boy asked what it felt like to be hit by a car. The birthday boy got up and turned back for home, at which time the other boy waved good-bye and headed off for school.

The birthday boy told his mother what had happened. They sat together on the sofa. She held his hands in her lap. This is what she was doing when the boy pulled his hands away and lay down on his back.

Of course, the birthday party never happened. The birthday boy was in the hospital instead. The mother sat by the bed. She was waiting for the boy to wake up. The father hurried over from his office. He sat next to the mother. So now the both of them waited for the boy to wake up. They waited for hours, and then the father went home to take a bath.

The man drove home from the hospital. He drove the streets faster than he should. It had been a good life till now. There had been work, fatherhood, family. The man had been lucky and happy. But fear made him want a bath.

He pulled into the driveway. He sat in the car trying to make his legs work. The child had been hit by a car and he was in the hospital, but he was going to be all right. The man got out of the car and went up to the door. The dog was barking and the telephone was ringing. It kept ringing while the man unlocked the door and felt the wall for the light switch.

He picked up the receiver. He said, "I just got in the door!"

"There's a cake that wasn't picked up."

This is what the voice on the other end said.

"What are you saying?" the father said.

"The cake," the voice said. "Sixteen dollars."

The husband held the receiver against his ear, trying to understand. He said, "I don't know anything about it."

"Don't hand me that," the voice said.

The husband hung up the telephone. He went into the kitchen and poured himself some whiskey. He called the hospital.

The child's condition remained the same.

While the water ran into the tub, the man lathered his face and shaved. He was in the tub when he heard the telephone again. He got himself out and hurried through the house, saying, "Stupid, stupid," because he wouldn't be doing this if he'd stayed where he was in the hospital. He picked up the receiver and shouted, "Hello!"

The voice said, "It's ready."

The father got back to the hospital after midnight. The wife was sitting in the chair by the bed. She looked up at the husband and then she looked back at the child. From an apparatus over the bed hung a bottle with a tube running from the bottle to the child.

"What's this?" the father said.

"Glucose," the mother said.

The husband put his hand to the back of the woman's head.

"He's going to wake up," the man said.

"I know," the woman said.

In a little while the man said, "Go home and let me take over."

She shook her head. "No," she said.

"Really," he said. "Go home for a while. You don't have to worry. He's sleeping, is all."

A nurse pushed open the door. She nodded to them as she went to the bed. She took the left arm out from under the covers and put her fingers on the wrist. She put the arm back under the covers and wrote on the clipboard attached to the bed.

"How is he?" the mother said.

"Stable," the nurse said. Then she said, "Doctor will be in again shortly."

"I was saying maybe she'd want to go home and get a little rest," the man said. "After the doctor comes."

"She could do that," the nurse said.

The woman said, "We'll see what the doctor says." She brought her hand up to her eyes and leaned her head forward.

The nurse said, "Of course."

The father gazed at his son, the small chest inflating and deflating under the covers. He felt more fear now. He began shaking his head. He talked to himself like this. The child is fine. Instead of sleeping at home, he's doing it here. Sleep is the same wherever you do it.

The doctor came in. He shook hands with the man. The woman got up from the chair.

"Ann," the doctor said and nodded. The doctor said, "Let's just see how he's doing." He moved to the bed and touched the boy's wrist. He peeled back an eyelid and then the other. He turned back the covers and listened to the heart. He pressed his fingers here and there on the body. He went to the end of the bed and studied the chart. He noted the time, scribbled on the chart, and then he considered the mother and the father.

This doctor was a handsome man. His skin was moist and tan. He wore a three-piece suit, a vivid tie, and on his shirt were cufflinks.

The mother was talking to herself like this. He has just come from somewhere with an audience. They gave him a special medal.

The doctor said, "Nothing to shout about, but nothing to worry about. He should wake up pretty soon." The doctor looked at the boy again. "We'll know more after the tests are in."

"Oh, no," the mother said.

The doctor said, "Sometimes you see this."

The father said, "You wouldn't call this a coma, then?"

The father waited and looked at the doctor.

"No, I don't want to call it that," the doctor said. "He's sleeping. It's restorative. The body is doing what it has to do."

"It's a coma," the mother said. "A kind of coma."

The doctor said, "I wouldn't call it that."

He took the woman's hands and patted them. He shook hands with the husband.

·   ·   ·

The woman put her fingers on the child's forehead and kept them there for a while. "At least he doesn't have a fever," she said. Then she said, "I don't know. Feel his head."

The man put his fingers on the boy's forehead. The man said, "I think he's supposed to feel this way."

The woman stood there awhile longer, working her lip with her teeth. Then she moved to her chair and sat down.

The husband sat in the chair beside her. He wanted to say something else. But there was no saying what it should be. He took her hand and put it in his lap. This made him feel better. It made him feel he was saying something. They sat like that for a while, watching the boy, not talking. From time to time he squeezed her hand until she took it away.

"I've been praying," she said.

"Me too," the father said. "I've been praying too."

A nurse came back in and checked the flow from the bottle.

A doctor came in and said what his name was. This doctor was wearing loafers.

"We're going to take him downstairs for more pictures," he said. "And we want to do a scan."

"A scan?" the mother said. She stood between this new doctor and the bed.

"It's nothing," he said.

"My God," she said.

Two orderlies came in. They wheeled a thing like a bed. They unhooked the boy from the tube and slid him over onto the thing with wheels.

It was after sunup when they brought the birthday boy back out. The mother and father followed the orderlies into the elevator and up to the room. Once more the parents took up their places next to the bed.

They waited all day. The boy did not wake up. The doctor came again and examined the boy again and left after saying the same things again. Nurses came in. Doctors came in. A technician came in and took blood.

"I don't understand this," the mother said to the technician.

"Doctor's orders," the technician said.

The mother went to the window and looked out at the parking lot. Cars with their lights on were driving in and out. She stood at the window with her hands on the sill. She was talking to herself like this. We're into something now, something hard.

She was afraid.

She saw a car stop and a woman in a long coat get into it. She made believe she was that woman. She made believe she was driving away from here to someplace else.

The doctor came in. He looked tanned and healthier than ever. He went to the bed and examined the boy. He said, "His signs are fine. Everything's good."

The mother said, "But he's sleeping."

"Yes," the doctor said.

The husband said, "She's tired. She's starved."

The doctor said, "She should rest. She should eat. Ann," the doctor said.

"Thank you," the husband said.

He shook hands with the doctor and the doctor patted their shoulders and left.

"I suppose one of us should go home and check on things," the man said. "The dog needs to be fed."

"Call the neighbors," the wife said. "Someone will feed him if you ask them to."

She tried to think who. She closed her eyes and tried to think anything at all. After a time she said, "Maybe I'll do it. Maybe if I'm not here watching, he'll wake up. Maybe it's because I'm watching that he won't."

"That could be it," the husband said.

"I'll go home and take a bath and put on something clean," the woman said.

"I think you should do that," the man said.

She picked up her purse. He helped her into her coat. She moved to the door, and looked back. She looked at the child, and then she looked at the father. The husband nodded and smiled.

She went past the nurses' station and down to the end of the corridor, where she turned and saw a little waiting room, a family in there, all sitting in wicker chairs, a man in a khaki shirt, a baseball cap pushed back on his head, a large woman wearing a housedress, slippers, a girl in jeans, hair in dozens of kinky braids, the table littered with flimsy wrappers and styrofoam and coffee sticks and packets of salt and pepper.

"Nelson," the woman said. "Is it about Nelson?"

The woman's eyes widened.

"Tell me now, lady," the woman said. "Is it about Nelson?"

The woman was trying to get up from her chair. But the man had his hand closed over her arm.

"Here, here," the man said.

"I'm sorry," the mother said. "I'm looking for the elevator. My son is in the hospital. I can't find the elevator."

"Elevator is down that way," the man said, and he aimed a finger in the right direction.

"My son was hit by a car," the mother said. "But he's going to be alright. He's in shock now, but it might be some kind of coma too. That's what worries us, the coma part, I'm going out for a little while. Maybe I'll take a bath. But my husband is with him. He's watching. There's a chance everything will change when I'm gone. My name is Ann Weiss."

The man shifted in his chair. He shook his head.

He said, "Our Nelson."

She pulled into the driveway. The dog ran out from behind the house. He ran in circles on the grass. She closed her eyes and leaned her head against the wheel. She listened to the ticking of the engine.

She got out of the car and went to the door. She turned on lights and put on water for tea. She opened a can and fed the dog. She sat down on the sofa with her tea.

The telephone rang.

"Yes!" she said. "Hello!" she said.

"Mrs. Weiss," a man's voice said.

"Yes," she said. "This is Mrs. Weiss. Is it about Scotty?" she said.

"Scotty," the voice said. "It is about Scotty," the voice said. "It has to do with Scotty, yes."

1. Why would this story be considered a "minimalist" story? (Hint: What is kept to a minimum in it?)
2. What are some of the details that are supposed to give us hints to what is going on?
3. Do you miss having more "telling," or narrative, in this story?

A Small, Good Thing

RAYMOND CARVER

Saturday afternoon she drove to the bakery in the shopping center. After looking through a loose-leaf binder with photographs of cakes taped onto the pages, she ordered chocolate, the child's favorite. The cake she chose was decorated with a space ship and launching pad under a sprinkling of white stars, and a planet made of red frosting at the other end. His name, scotty, would be in green letters beneath the planet. The baker, who was an older man with a thick neck, listened without saying anything when she told him the child would be eight years old next Monday. The baker wore a white apron that looked like a smock. Straps cut under his arms, went around in back and then to the front again, where they were secured under his heavy waist. He wiped his hands on his apron as he listened to her. He kept his eyes down on the photographs and let her talk. He let her take her time. He'd just come to work and he'd be there all night, baking, and he was in no real hurry.

She gave the baker her name, Ann Weiss, and her telephone number. The cake would be ready on Monday morning, just out of the oven, in plenty of time for the child's party that afternoon. The baker was not jolly. There were no pleasantries between them, just the minimum exchange of words, the necessary information. He made her feel uncomfortable, and she didn't like that. While he was bent over the counter with the pencil in his hand, she studied his coarse features and wondered if he'd ever done anything else with his life besides be a baker. She was a mother and thirty-three years old, and it seemed to her that everyone, especially someone the baker's age—a man old enough to be her father—must have children who'd gone through this special time of cakes and birthday parties. There must be that between them, she thought. But he was abrupt with her—not rude, just abrupt. She gave up trying to make friends with him. She looked into the back of the bakery and could see a long, heavy wooden table with aluminum pie pans stacked at one end; and beside the table a metal container filled with empty racks. There was an enormous oven. A radio was playing country-Western music.

The baker finished printing the information on the special order card and closed up the binder. He looked at her and said, "Monday morning." She thanked him and drove home.

On Monday morning, the birthday boy was walking to school with another boy. They were passing a bag of potato chips back and forth and the birthday boy was trying to find out what his friend intended to give him for his birthday that afternoon. Without looking, the birthday boy stepped off the curb at an intersection and was immediately knocked down by a car. He fell on his side with his head in the gutter and his legs out in the road. His eyes were closed, but his legs moved back and forth as if he were trying to climb over something. His friend dropped the potato chips and started to cry. The car had gone a hundred feet or so and stopped in the middle of the road. The man in the driver's seat looked back over his shoulder. He waited until the boy got unsteadily to his feet. The boy wobbled a little. He looked dazed, but okay. The driver put the car into gear and drove away.

The birthday boy didn't cry, but he didn't have anything to say about anything either. He wouldn't answer when his friend asked him what it felt like to be hit by a car. He walked home, and his friend went on to school. But after the birthday boy was inside his house and was telling his mother about it—she sitting beside him on the sofa, holding his hands in her lap, saying, "Scotty, honey, are you sure you feel all right, baby?" thinking she would call the doctor anyway—he suddenly lay back on the sofa, closed his eyes, and went limp. When she couldn't wake him up, she hurried to the telephone and called her husband at work. Howard told her to remain calm, remain calm, and then he called an ambulance for the child and left for the hospital himself.

Of course, the birthday party was canceled. The child was in the hospital with a mild concussion and suffering from shock. There'd been vomiting, and his lungs had taken in fluid which needed pumping out that afternoon. Now he simply seemed to be in a very deep sleep—but no coma, Dr. Francis had emphasized, no coma, when he saw the alarm in the parents' eyes. At eleven o'clock that night, when the boy seemed to be resting comfortably enough after the many X-rays and the lab work, and it was just a matter of his waking up and coming around, Howard left the hospital. He and Ann had been at the hospital with the child since that afternoon, and he was going home for a short while to bathe and change clothes. "I'll be back in an hour," he said. She nodded. "It's fine," she said. "I'll be right here." He kissed her on the forehead, and they touched hands. She sat in the chair beside the bed and looked at the child. She was waiting for him to wake up and be all right. Then she could begin to relax.

Howard drove home from the hospital. He took the wet, dark streets very fast, then caught himself and slowed down. Until now, his life had gone smoothly and to his satisfaction—college, marriage, another year of college for the advanced degree in business, a junior partnership in an investment firm. Fatherhood. He was happy and, so far, lucky—he knew that. His parents were still living, his brothers and his sister were established, his friends from college had gone out to take their places in the world. So far, he had kept away from any real harm, from those forces he knew existed and that could cripple or bring down a man if the luck went bad, if things suddenly turned. He pulled into the driveway and parked. His left leg began to tremble. He sat in the car for a minute and tried to deal with the present situation in a rational manner. Scotty had been hit by a car and was in the hospital, but he was going to be all right. Howard closed his eyes and ran his hand over his face. He got out of the car and went up to the front door. The dog was barking inside the house. The telephone rang and rang while he unlocked the door and fumbled for the light switch. He shouldn't have left the hospital, he shouldn't have. "Goddamn it!" he said. He picked up the receiver and said, "I just walked in the door!"

"There's a cake here that wasn't picked up," the voice on the other end of the line said.

"What are you saying?" Howard asked.

"A cake," the voice said. "A sixteen-dollar cake."

Howard held the receiver against his ear, trying to understand. "I don't know anything about a cake," he said. "Jesus, what are you talking about?"

"Don't hand me that," the voice said.

Howard hung up the telephone. He went into the kitchen and poured himself some whiskey. He called the hospital. But the child's condition remained the same; he was still sleeping and nothing had changed there. While water poured into the tub, Howard lathered his face and shaved. He'd just stretched out in the tub and closed his eyes when the telephone rang again. He hauled himself out, grabbed a towel, and hurried through the house, saying, "Stupid, stupid," for having left the hospital. But when he picked up the receiver and shouted, "Hello!" there was no sound at the other end of the line. Then the caller hung up.

He arrived back at the hospital a little after midnight. Ann still sat in the chair beside the bed. She looked up at Howard, and then she looked back at the child. The child's eyes stayed closed, the head was still wrapped in bandages. His breathing was quiet and regular. From an apparatus over the bed hung a bottle of glucose with a tube running from the bottle to the boy's arm.

"How is he?" Howard said. "What's all this?" waving at the glucose and the tube.

"Dr. Francis's orders," she said. "He needs nourishment. He needs to keep up his strength. Why doesn't he wake up, Howard? I don't understand, if he's all right."

Howard put his hand against the back of her head. He ran his fingers through her hair. "He's going to be all right. He'll wake up in a little while. Dr. Francis knows what's what."

After a time, he said, "Maybe you should go home and get some rest. I'll stay here. Just don't put up with this creep who keeps calling. Hang up right away."

"Who's calling?" she asked.

"I don't know who, just somebody with nothing better to do than call up people. You go on now."

She shook her head. "No," she said, "I'm fine."

"Really," he said. "Go home for a while, and then come back and spell me in the morning. It'll be all right. What did Dr. Francis say? He said Scotty's going to be all right. We don't have to worry. He's just sleeping now, that's all."

A nurse pushed the door open. She nodded at them as she went to the bedside. She took the left arm out from under the covers and put her fingers on the wrist, found the pulse, then consulted her watch. In a little while, she put the arm back under the covers and moved to the foot of the bed, where she wrote something on a clipboard attached to the bed.

"How is he?" Ann said. Howard's hand was a weight on her shoulder. She was aware of the pressure from his fingers.

"He's stable," the nurse said. Then she said, "Doctor will be in again shortly. Doctor's back in the hospital. He's making rounds right now."

"I was saying maybe she'd want to go home and get a little rest," Howard said. "After the doctor comes," he said.

"She could do that," the nurse said. "I think you should both feel free to do that, if you wish." The nurse was a big Scandinavian woman with blond hair. There was the trace of an accent in her speech.

"We'll see what the doctor says," Ann said. "I want to talk to the doctor. I don't think he should keep sleeping like this. I don't think that's a good sign." She brought her hand up to her eyes and let her head come forward a little. Howard's grip tightened on her shoulder, and then his hand moved up to her neck, where his fingers began to knead the muscles there.

"Dr. Francis will be here in a few minutes," the nurse said. Then she left the room.

Howard gazed at his son for a time, the small chest quietly rising and falling under the covers. For the first time since the terrible minutes after Ann's telephone call to him at his office, he felt a genuine fear starting in his limbs. He began shaking his head. Scotty was fine, but instead of sleeping at home in his own bed, he was in a hospital bed with bandages around his head and a tube in his arm. But this help was what he needed right now.

Dr. Francis came in and shook hands with Howard, though they'd just seen each other a few hours before. Ann got up from the chair. "Doctor?"

"Ann," he said and nodded. "Let's just first see how he's doing," the doctor said. He moved to the side of the bed and took the boy's pulse. He peeled back one eyelid and then the other. Howard and Ann stood beside the doctor and watched. Then the doctor turned back the covers and listened to the boy's heart and lungs with his stethoscope. He pressed his fingers here and there on the abdomen. When he was finished, he went to the end of the bed and studied the chart. He noted the time, scribbled something on the chart, and then looked at Howard and Ann.

"Doctor, how is he?" Howard said. "What's the matter with him exactly?"

"Why doesn't he wake up?" Ann said.

The doctor was a handsome, big-shouldered man with a tanned face. He wore a three-piece blue suit, a striped tie, and ivory cufflinks. His gray hair was combed along the sides of his head, and he looked as if he had just come from a concert. "He's all right," the doctor said. "Nothing to shout about, he could be better, I think. But he's all right. Still, I wish he'd wake up. He should wake up pretty soon." The doctor looked at the boy again. "We'll know some more in a couple of hours, after the results of a few more tests are in. But he's all right, believe me, except for the hairline fracture of the skull. He does have that."

"Oh, no," Ann said.

"And a bit of a concussion, as I said before. Of course, you know he's in shock," the doctor said. "Sometimes you see this in shock cases. This sleeping."

"But he's out of any real danger?" Howard said. "You said before he's not in a coma. You wouldn't call this a coma, then—would you, doctor?" Howard waited. He looked at the doctor.

"No, I don't want to call it a coma," the doctor said and glanced over at the boy once more. "He's just in a very deep sleep. It's a restorative measure the body is taking on its own. He's out of any real danger, I'd say that for certain, yes. But we'll know more when he wakes up and the other tests are in," the doctor said.

"It's a coma," Ann said. "Of sorts."

"It's not a coma yet, not exactly," the doctor said. "I wouldn't want to call it coma. Not yet, anyway. He's suffered shock. In shock cases, this kind of reaction is common enough; it's a temporary reaction to bodily trauma. Coma. Well, coma is a deep, prolonged unconsciousness, something that could go on for days, or weeks even. Scotty's not in that area, not as far as we can tell. I'm certain his condition will show improvement by morning. I'm betting that it will. We'll know more when he wakes up, which shouldn't be long now. Of course, you may do as you like, stay here or go home for a time. But by all means feel free to leave the hospital for a while if you want. This is not easy, I know." The doctor gazed at the boy again, watching him, and then he turned to Ann and said, "You try not to worry, little mother. Believe me, we're doing all that can be done. It's just a question of a little more time now." He nodded at her, shook hands with Howard again, and then he left the room.

Ann put her hand over the child's forehead. "At least he doesn't have a fever," she said. Then she said, "My God, he feels so cold, though. Howard? Is he supposed to feel like this? Feel his head."

Howard touched the child's temples. His own breathing had slowed. "I think he's supposed to feel this way right now," he said. "He's in shock, remember? That's what the doctors said. The doctor was just in here. He would have said something if Scotty wasn't okay."

Ann stood there a while longer, working her lip with her teeth. Then she moved over to her chair and sat down.

Howard sat in the chair next to her chair. They looked at each other. He wanted to say something else and reassure her, but he was afraid, too. He took her hand and put it in his lap, and this made him feel better, her hand being there. He picked up her hand and squeezed it. Then he just held her hand. They sat like that for a while, watching the boy and not talking. From time to time, he squeezed her hand. Finally, she took her hand away.

"I've been praying," she said.

He nodded.

She said, "I almost thought I'd forgotten how, but it came back to me. All I had to do was close my eyes and say, 'Please God, help us—help Scotty,' and then the rest was easy. The words were right there. Maybe if you prayed, too," she said to him.

"I've already prayed," he said. "I prayed this afternoon—yesterday afternoon, I mean—after you called, while I was driving to the hospital. I've been praying," he said.

"That's good," she said. For the first time, she felt they were together in it, this trouble. She realized with a start that, until now, it had only been happening to her and to Scotty. She hadn't let Howard into it, though he was there and needed all along. She felt glad to be his wife.

The same nurse came in and took the boy's pulse again and checked the flow from the bottle hanging above the bed.

In an hour, another doctor came in. He said his name was Parsons, from Radiology. He had a bushy mustache. He was wearing loafers, a Western shirt, and a pair of jeans.

"We're going to take him downstairs for more pictures," he told them. "We need to do some more pictures, and we want to do a scan."

"What's that?" Ann said. "A scan?" She stood between this new doctor and the bed. "I thought you'd already taken all your X-rays."

"I'm afraid we need some more," he said. "Nothing to be alarmed about. We just need some more pictures, and we want to do a brain scan on him."

"My God," Ann said.

"It's perfectly normal procedure in cases like this," this new doctor said. "We just need to find out for sure why he isn't back awake yet. It's normal medical procedure, and nothing to be alarmed about. We'll be taking him down in a few minutes," this doctor said.

In a little while, two orderlies came into the room with a gurney. They were black-haired, dark-complexioned men in white uniforms, and they said a few words to each other in a foreign tongue as they unhooked the boy from the tube and moved him from his bed to the gurney. Then they wheeled him from the room. Howard and Ann got on the same elevator. Ann gazed at the child. She closed her eyes as the elevator began its descent. The orderlies stood at either end of the gurney without saying anything, though once one of the men made a comment to the other in their own language, and the other man nodded slowly in response.

Later that morning, just as the sun was beginning to lighten the windows in the waiting room outside the X-ray department, they brought the boy out and moved him back up to his room. Howard and Ann rode up on the elevator with him once more, and once more they took up their places beside the bed.

They waited all day, but still the boy did not wake up. Occasionally, one of them would leave the room to go downstairs to the cafeteria to drink coffee and then, as if suddenly remembering and feeling guilty, get up from the table and hurry back to the room. Dr. Francis came again that afternoon and examined the boy once more and then left after telling them he was coming along and could wake up at any minute now. Nurses, different nurses from the night before, came in from time to time. Then a young woman from the lab knocked and entered the room. She wore white slacks and a white blouse and carried a little tray of things which she put on the stand beside the bed. Without a word to them, she took blood from the boy's arm. Howard closed his eyes as the woman found the right place on the boy's arm and pushed the needle in.

"I don't understand this," Ann said to the woman.

"Doctor's orders," the young woman said. "I do what I'm told. They say draw that one, I draw. What's wrong with him, anyway?" she said. "He's a sweetie."

"He was hit by a car," Howard said. "A hit-and-run."

The young woman shook her head and looked again at the boy. Then she took her tray and left the room.

"Why won't he wake up?" Ann said. "Howard? I want some answers from these people."

Howard didn't say anything. He sat down again in the chair and crossed one leg over the other. He rubbed his face. He looked at his son and then he settled back in the chair, closed his eyes, and went to sleep.

Ann walked to the window and looked out at the parking lot. It was night, and cars were driving into and out of the parking lot with their lights on. She stood at the window with her hands gripping the sill, and knew in her heart that they were into something now, something hard. She was afraid, and her teeth began to chatter until she tightened her jaws. She saw a big car stop in front of the hospital and someone, a woman in a long coat, get into the car. She wished she were that woman and somebody, anybody, was driving her away from here to somewhere else, a place where she would find Scotty waiting for her when she stepped out of the car, ready to say *Mom* and let her gather him in her arms.

In a little while, Howard woke up. He looked at the boy again. Then he got up from the chair, stretched, and went over to stand beside her at the window. They both stared out at the parking lot. They didn't say anything. But they seemed to feel each other's insides now, as though the worry had made them transparent in a perfectly natural way.

The door opened and Dr. Francis came in. He was wearing a different suit and tie this time. His gray hair was combed along the sides of his head, and he looked as if he had just shaved. He went straight to the bed and examined the boy. "He ought to have come around by now. There's just no good reason for this," he said. "But I can tell you we're all convinced he's out of any danger. We'll just feel better when he wakes up. There's no reason, absolutely none, why he shouldn't come around. Very soon. Oh, he'll have himself a dilly of a headache when he does, you can count on that. But all of his signs are fine. They're as normal as can be."

"It is a coma, then?" Ann said.

The doctor rubbed his smooth cheek. "We'll call it that for the time being, until he wakes up. But you must be worn out. This is hard. I know this is hard. Feel free to go out for a bite," he said. "It would do you good. I'll put a nurse in here while you're gone if you'll feel better about going. Go and have yourselves something to eat."

"I couldn't eat anything," Ann said.

"Do what you need to do, of course," the doctor said. "Anyway, I wanted to tell you that all the signs are good, the tests are negative, nothing showed up at all, and just as soon as he wakes up he'll be over the hill."

"Thank you, doctor," Howard said. He shook hands with the doctor again. The doctor patted Howard's shoulder and went out.

"I suppose one of us should go home and check on things," Howard said. "Slug needs to be fed, for one thing."

"Call one of the neighbors," Ann said. "Call the Morgans. Anyone will feed a dog if you ask them to."

"All right," Howard said. After a while, he said, "Honey, why don't you do it? Why don't you go home and check on things, and then come back? It'll do you good. I'll be right here with him. Seriously," he said. "We need to keep up our strength on this. We'll want to be here for a while even after he wakes up."

"Why don't *you* go?" she said. "Feed Slug. Feed yourself."

"I already went," he said. "I was gone for exactly an hour and fifteen minutes. You go home for an hour and freshen up. Then come back."

She tried to think about it, but she was too tired. She closed her eyes and tried to think about it again. After a time, she said, "Maybe I will go home for a few minutes. Maybe if I'm not just sitting right here watching him every second, he'll wake up and be all right. You know? Maybe he'll wake up if I'm not here. I'll go home and take a bath and put on clean clothes. I'll feed Slug. Then I'll come back."

"I'll be right here," he said. "You go on home, honey. I'll keep an eye on things here." His eyes were bloodshot and small, as if he'd been drinking for a long time. His clothes were rumpled. His beard had come out again. She touched his face; and then she took her hand back. She understood he wanted to be by himself for a while, not have to talk or share his worry for a time. She picked her purse up from the nightstand, and he helped her into her coat.

"I won't be gone long," she said.

"Just sit and rest for a little while when you get home," he said. "Eat something. Take a bath. After you get out of the bath, just sit for a while and rest. It'll do you a world of good, you'll see. Then come back," he said. "Let's try not to worry. You heard what Dr. Francis said."

She stood in her coat for a minute trying to recall the doctor's exact words, looking for any nuances, any hint of something behind his words other than what he had said. She tried to remember if his expression had changed any when he bent over to examine the child. She remembered the way his features had composed themselves as he rolled back the child's eyelids and then listened to his breathing.

She went to the door, where she turned and looked back. She looked at the child, and then she looked at the father. Howard nodded. She stepped out of the room and pulled the door closed behind her.

She went past the nurses' station and down to the end of the corridor, looking for the elevator. At the end of the corridor, she turned to her right and entered a little waiting room where a Negro family sat in wicker chairs. There was a middle-aged man in a khaki shirt and pants, a baseball cap pushed back on his head. A large woman wearing a housedress and slippers was slumped in one of the chairs. A teenaged girl in jeans, hair done in dozens of little braids, lay stretched out in one of the chairs smoking a cigarette, her legs crossed at the ankles. The family swung their eyes to Ann as she entered the room. The little table was littered with hamburger wrappers and Styrofoam cups.

"Franklin," the large woman said as she roused herself. "Is it about Franklin?" Her eyes widened. "Tell me now, lady," the woman said. "Is it about Franklin?" She was trying to rise from her chair, but the man had closed his hand over her arm.

"Here, here," he said. "Evelyn."

"I'm sorry," Ann said. "I'm looking for the elevator. My son is in the hospital, and now I can't find the elevator."

"Elevator is down that way, turn left," the man said as he aimed a finger.

The girl drew on her cigarette and stared at Ann. Her eyes were narrowed to slits, and her broad lips parted slowly as she let the smoke escape. The Negro woman let her head fall on her shoulder and looked away from Ann, no longer interested.

"My son was hit by a car," Ann said to the man. She seemed to need to explain herself. "He has a concussion and a little skull fracture, but he's going to be all right. He's in shock now, but it might be some kind of coma, too. That's what really worries us, the coma part. I'm going out for a little while, but my husband is with him. Maybe he'll wake up while I'm gone."

"That's too bad," the man said and shifted in the chair. He shook his head. He looked down at the table, and then he looked back at Ann. She was still standing there. He said, "Our Franklin, he's on the operating table. Somebody cut him. Tried to kill him. There was a fight where he was at. At this party. They say he was just standing and watching. Not bothering nobody. But that don't mean nothing these days. Now he's on the operating table. We're just hoping and praying, that's all we can do now." He gazed at her steadily.

Ann looked at the girl again, who was still watching her, and at the older woman, who kept her head down, but whose eyes were now closed. Ann saw the lips moving silently, making words. She had an urge to ask what those words were. She wanted to talk more with these people who were in the same kind of waiting she was in. She was afraid, and they were afraid. They had that in common. She would have liked to have said something else about the accident, told them more about Scotty, that it had happened on the day of his birthday, Monday, and that he was still unconscious. Yet she didn't know how to begin. She stood looking at them without saying anything more.

She went down the corridor the man had indicated and found the elevator. She waited a minute in front of the closed doors, still wondering if she was doing the right thing. Then she put out her finger and touched the button.

She pulled into the driveway and cut the engine. She closed her eyes and leaned her head against the wheel for a minute. She listened to the ticking sounds the engine made as it began to cool. Then she got out of the car. She could hear the dog barking inside the house. She went to the front door, which was unlocked. She went inside and turned on lights and put on a kettle of water for tea. She opened some dogfood and fed Slug on the back porch. The dog ate in hungry little smacks. It kept running into the kitchen to see that she was going to stay. As she sat down on the sofa with her tea, the telephone rang.

"Yes!" she said as she answered. "Hello!"

"Mrs. Weiss," a man's voice said. It was five o'clock in the morning, and she thought she could hear machinery or equipment of some kind in the background.

"Yes, yes! What is it?" she said. "This is Mrs. Weiss. This is she. What is it, please?" She listened to whatever it was in the background. "Is it Scotty, for Christ's sake?"

"Scotty," the man's voice said. "It's about Scotty, yes. It has to do with

Scotty, that problem. Have you forgotten about Scotty?" the man said. Then he hung up.

She dialed the hospital's number and asked for the third floor. She demanded information about her son from the nurse who answered the telephone. Then she asked to speak to her husband. It was, she said, an emergency.

She waited, turning the telephone cord in her fingers. She closed her eyes and felt sick at her stomach. She would have to make herself eat. Slug came in from the back porch and lay down near her feet. He wagged his tail. She pulled at his ear while he licked her fingers. Howard was on the line.

"Somebody just called here," she said. She twisted the telephone cord. "He said it was about Scotty," she cried.

"Scotty's fine," Howard told her. "I mean, he's still sleeping. There's been no change. The nurse has been in twice since you've been gone. A nurse or else a doctor. He's all right."

"This man called. He said it was about Scotty," she told him.

"Honey, you rest for a little while, you need the rest. It must be that same caller I had. Just forget it. Come back down here after you've rested. Then we'll have breakfast or something."

"Breakfast," she said. "I don't want any breakfast."

"You know what I mean," he said. "Juice, something. I don't know. I don't know anything, Ann. Jesus, I'm not hungry, either. Ann, it's hard to talk now. I'm standing here at the desk. Dr. Francis is coming again at eight o'clock this morning. He's going to have something to tell us then, something more definite. That's what one of the nurses said. She didn't know any more than that. Ann? Honey, maybe we'll know something more then. At eight o'clock. Come back here before eight. Meanwhile, I'm right here and Scotty's all right. He's still the same," he added.

"I was drinking a cup of tea," she said, "when the telephone rang. They said it was about Scotty. There was a noise in the background. Was there a noise in the background on that call you had, Howard?"

"I don't remember," he said. "Maybe the driver of the car, maybe he's a psychopath and found out about Scotty somehow. But I'm here with him. Just rest like you were going to do. Take a bath and come back by seven or so, and we'll talk to the doctor together when he gets here. It's going to be all right, honey. I'm here, and there are doctors and nurses around. They say his condition is stable."

"I'm scared to death," she said.

She ran water, undressed, and got into the tub. She washed and dried quickly, not taking the time to wash her hair. She put on clean underwear, wool slacks, and a sweater. She went into the living room, where the dog looked up at her and let its tail thump once against the floor. It was just starting to get light outside when she went out to the car.

She drove into the parking lot of the hospital and found a space close to the front door. She felt she was in some obscure way responsible for what had happened to the child. She let her thoughts move to the Negro family. She remembered the name Franklin and the table that was covered with hamburger papers, and the teenaged girl staring at her as she drew on her cigarette. "Don't have children," she told the girl's image as she entered the front door of the hospital. "For God's sake, don't."

She took the elevator up to the third floor with two nurses who were just going on duty. It was Wednesday morning, a few minutes before seven. There was a page for a Dr. Madison as the elevator doors slid open on the third floor. She got off behind the nurses, who turned in the other direction and continued the conversation she had interrupted when she'd gotten into the elevator. She walked down the corridor to the little alcove where the Negro family had been waiting. They were gone now, but the chairs were scattered in such a way that it looked as if people had just jumped up from them the minute before. The tabletop was cluttered with the same cups and papers, the ashtray was filled with cigarette butts.

She stopped at the nurses' station. A nurse was standing behind the counter, brushing her hair and yawning.

"There was a Negro boy in surgery last night," Ann said. "Franklin was his name. His family was in the waiting room. I'd like to inquire about his condition."

A nurse who was sitting at a desk behind the counter looked up from a chart in front of her. The telephone buzzed and she picked up the receiver, but she kept her eyes on Ann.

"He passed away," said the nurse at the counter. The nurse held the hairbrush and kept looking at her. "Are you a friend of the family or what?"

"I met the family last night," Ann said. "My own son is in the hospital. I guess he's in shock. We don't know for sure what's wrong. I just wondered about Franklin, that's all. Thank you." She moved down the corridor. Elevator doors the same color as the walls slid open and a gaunt, bald man in white pants and white canvas shoes pulled a heavy cart off the elevator. She hadn't noticed these doors last night. The man wheeled the cart out into the corridor and stopped in front of the room nearest the elevator and consulted a clipboard. Then he reached down and slid a tray out of the cart. He rapped lightly on the door and entered the room. She could smell the unpleasant odors of warm food as she passed the cart. She hurried on without looking at any of the nurses and pushed open the door to the child's room.

Howard was standing at the window with his hands behind his back. He turned around as she came in.

"How is he?" she said. She went over to the bed. She dropped her purse on the floor beside the nightstand. It seemed to her she had been gone a long time. She touched the child's face. "Howard?"

"Dr. Francis was here a little while ago," Howard said. She looked at him closely and thought his shoulders were bunched a little.

"I thought he wasn't coming until eight o'clock this morning," she said quickly.

"There was another doctor with him. A neurologist."

"A neurologist," she said.

Howard nodded. His shoulders were bunching, she could see that. "What'd they say, Howard? For Christ's sake, what'd they say? What is it?"

"They said they're going to take him down and run more tests on him, Ann. They think they're going to operate, honey. Honey, they *are* going to operate. They can't figure out why he won't wake up. It's more than just shock or concussion, they know that much now. It's in his skull, the fracture, it has something, something to do with that, they think. So they're going to operate. I tried to call you, but I guess you'd already left the house."

"Oh, God," she said. "Oh, please, Howard, please," she said, taking his arms.

"Look!" Howard said. "Scotty! Look, Ann!" He turned her toward the bed.

The boy had opened his eyes, then closed them. He opened them again now. The eyes stared straight ahead for a minute, then moved slowly in his head until they rested on Howard and Ann, then traveled away again.

"Scotty," his mother said, moving to the bed.

"Hey, Scott," his father said. "Hey, son."

They leaned over the bed. Howard took the child's hand in his hands and began to pat and squeeze the hand. Ann bent over the body and kissed his forehead again and again. She put her hands on either side of his face. "Scotty, honey, it's Mommy and Daddy," she said. "Scotty?"

The boy looked at them, but without any sign of recognition. Then his mouth opened, his eyes scrunched closed, and he howled until he had no more air in his lungs. His face seemed to relax and soften then. His lips parted as his last breath was puffed through his throat and exhaled gently through the clenched teeth.

•   •   •

The doctors called it a hidden occlusion and said it was a one-in-a-million circumstance. Maybe if it could have been detected somehow and surgery undertaken immediately, they could have saved him. But more than likely not. In any case, what would they have been looking for? Nothing had shown up in the tests or in the X-rays.

Dr. Francis was shaken. "I can't tell you how badly I feel. I'm so very sorry, I can't tell you," he said as he led them into the doctors' lounge. There was a doctor sitting in a chair with his legs hooked over the back of another chair, watching an early-morning TV show. He was wearing a green delivery-room outfit, loose green pants and green blouse, and a green cap that covered his hair. He looked at Howard and Ann and then looked at Dr. Francis. He got to his feet and turned off the set and went out of the room. Dr. Francis guided Ann to the sofa, sat down beside her, and began to talk in a low, consoling voice. At one point, he leaned over and embraced her. She could feel his chest rising and falling evenly against her shoulder. She kept her eyes open and let him hold her. Howard went into the bathroom, but he left the door open. After a violent fit of weeping, he ran water and washed his face. Then he came out and sat down at the little table that held a telephone. He looked at the telephone as though deciding what to do first. He made some calls. After a time, Dr. Francis used the telephone.

"Is there anything else I can do for the moment?" he asked them.

Howard shook his head. Ann stared at Dr. Francis as if unable to comprehend his words.

The doctor walked them to the hospital's front door. People were entering and leaving the hospital. It was eleven o'clock in the morning. Ann was aware of how slowly, almost reluctantly, she moved her feet. It seemed to her that Dr. Francis was making them leave when she felt they should stay, when it would be more the right thing to do to stay. She gazed out into the parking lot and then turned around and looked back at the front of the hospital. She began shaking her head. "No, no," she said. "I can't leave him here, no." She heard herself say that and thought how unfair it was that the only words that came out were the sort of words used on TV shows where people were stunned by violent or sudden deaths. She wanted her words to be her own. "No," she said, and for some reason the memory of the Negro woman's head lolling on the woman's shoulder came to her. "No," she said again.

"I'll be talking to you later in the day," the doctor was saying to Howard.

"There are still some things that have to be done, things that have to be cleared up to our satisfaction. Some things that need explaining."

"An autopsy," Howard said.

Dr. Francis nodded.

"I understand," Howard said. Then he said, "Oh, Jesus. No, I don't understand, doctor. I can't, I can't. I just can't."

Dr. Francis put his arm around Howard's shoulders. "I'm sorry. God, how I'm sorry." He let go of Howard's shoulders and held out his hand. Howard looked at the hand, and then he took it. Dr. Francis put his arms around Ann once more. He seemed full of some goodness she didn't understand. She let her head rest on his shoulder, but her eyes stayed open. She kept looking at the hospital. As they drove out of the parking lot, she looked back at the hospital.

At home, she sat on the sofa with her hands in her coat pockets. Howard closed the door to the child's room. He got the coffee-maker going and then he found an empty box. He had thought to pick up some of the child's things that were scattered around the living room. But instead he sat down beside her on the sofa, pushed the box to one side, and leaned forward, arms between his knees. He began to weep. She pulled his head over into her lap and patted his shoulder. "He's gone," she said. She kept patting his shoulder. Over his sobs, she could hear the coffee-maker hissing in the kitchen. "There, there," she said tenderly. "Howard, he's gone. He's gone and now we'll have to get used to that. To being alone."

In a little while, Howard got up and began moving aimlessly around the room with the box, not putting anything into it, but collecting some things together on the floor at one end of the sofa. She continued to sit with her hands in her coat pockets. Howard put the box down and brought coffee into the living room. Later, Ann made calls to relatives. After each call had been placed and the party had answered, Ann would blurt out a few words and cry for a minute. Then she would quietly explain, in a measured voice, what had happened and tell them about arrangements. Howard took the box out to the garage, where he saw the child's bicycle. He dropped the box and sat down on the pavement beside the bicycle. He took hold of the bicycle awkwardly so that it leaned against his chest. He held it, the rubber pedal sticking into his chest. He gave the wheel a turn.

Ann hung up the telephone after talking to her sister. She was looking up another number when the telephone rang. She picked it up on the first ring.

"Hello," she said, and she heard something in the background, a humming noise. "Hello!" she said. "For God's sake," she said. "Who is this? What is it you want?"

"Your Scotty, I got him ready for you," the man's voice said. "Did you forget him?"

"You evil bastard!" she shouted into the receiver. "How can you do this, you evil son of a bitch?"

"Scotty," the man said. "Have you forgotten about Scotty?" Then the man hung up on her.

Howard heard the shouting and came in to find her with her head on her arms over the table, weeping. He picked up the receiver and listened to the dial tone.

Much later, just before midnight, after they had dealt with many things, the telephone rang again.

"You answer it," she said. "Howard, it's him, I know." They were sitting at the kitchen table with coffee in front of them. Howard had a small glass of whiskey beside his cup. He answered on the third ring.

"Hello," he said. "Who is this? Hello! Hello!" The line went dead. "He hung up," Howard said. "Whoever it was."

"It was him," she said. "That bastard. I'd like to kill him," she said. "I'd like to shoot him and watch him kick," she said.

"Ann, my God," he said.

"Could you hear anything?" she said. "In the background? A noise, machinery, something humming?"

"Nothing, really. Nothing like that," he said. "There wasn't much time. I think there was some radio music. Yes, there was a radio going, that's all I could tell. I don't know what in God's name is going on," he said.

She shook her head. "If I could, could get my hands on him." It came to her then. She knew who it was. Scotty, the cake, the telephone number. She pushed the chair away from the table and got up. "Drive me down to the shopping center," she said. "Howard."

"What are you saying?"

"The shopping center. I know who it is who's calling. I know who it is. It's the baker, the son-of-a-bitching baker, Howard. I had him bake a cake for Scotty's birthday. That's who's calling. That's who has the number and keeps calling us. To harass us about that cake. The baker, that bastard."

They drove down to the shopping center. The sky was clear and stars were out. It was cold, and they ran the heater in the car. They parked in front of the bakery. All of the shops and stores were closed, but there were cars at the far end of the lot in front of the movie theater. The bakery windows were dark, but when they looked through the glass they could see a light in the back room and, now and then, a big man in an apron moving in and out of the white, even light. Through the glass, she could see the display cases and some little tables with chairs. She tried the door. She rapped on the glass. But if the baker heard them, he gave no sign. He didn't look in their direction.

They drove around behind the bakery and parked. They got out of the car. There was a lighted window too high up for them to see inside. A sign near the back door said the pantry bakery, special orders. She could hear faintly a radio playing inside and something creak—an oven door as it was pulled down? She knocked on the door and waited. Then she knocked again, louder. The radio was turned down and there was a scraping sound now, the distinct sound of something, a drawer, being pulled open and then closed.

Someone unlocked the door and opened it. The baker stood in the light and peered out at them. "I'm closed for business," he said. "What do you want at this hour? It's midnight. Are you drunk or something?"

She stepped into the light that fell through the open door. He blinked his heavy eyelids as he recognized her. "It's you," he said.

"It's me," she said. "Scotty's mother. This is Scotty's father. We'd like to come in."

The baker said, "I'm busy now. I have work to do."

She had stepped inside the doorway anyway. Howard came in behind her. The baker moved back. "It smells like a bakery in here. Doesn't it smell like a bakery in here, Howard?"

"What do you want?" the baker said. "Maybe you want your cake? That's it, you decided you want your cake. You ordered a cake, didn't you?"

"You're pretty smart for a baker," she said. "Howard, this is the man who's been calling us." She clenched her fists. She stared at him fiercely. There was a deep burning inside her, an anger that made her feel larger than herself, larger than either of these men.

"Just a minute here," the baker said. "You want to pick up your three-day-old cake? That it? I don't want to argue with you, lady. There it sits over there, getting stale. I'll give it to you for half of what I quoted you. No. You want it? You can have it. It's no good to me, no good to anyone now. It cost me time and money to make that cake. If you want it, okay, if you don't, that's okay, too. I have to get back to work." He looked at them and rolled his tongue behind his teeth.

"More cakes," she said. She knew she was in control of it, of what was increasing in her. She was calm.

"Lady, I work sixteen hours a day in this place to earn a living," the baker said. He wiped his hands on his apron. "I work night and day in here, trying to make ends meet." A look crossed Ann's face that made the baker move back and say, "No trouble, now." He reached to the counter and picked up a rolling pin with his right hand and began to tap it against the palm of his other hand. "You want the cake or not? I have to get back to work. Bakers work at night," he said again. His eyes were small, mean-looking, she thought, nearly lost in the bristly flesh around his cheeks. His neck was thick with fat.

"I know bakers work at night," Ann said. "They make phone calls at night, too. You bastard," she said.

The baker continued to tap the rolling pin against his hand. He glanced at Howard. "Careful, careful," he said to Howard.

"My son's dead," she said with a cold, even finality. "He was hit by a car Monday morning. We've been waiting with him until he died. But, of course, you couldn't be expected to know that, could you? Bakers can't know everything—can they, Mr. Baker? But he's dead. He's dead, you bastard!" Just as suddenly as it had welled in her, the anger dwindled, gave way to something else, a dizzy feeling of nausea. She leaned against the wooden table that was sprinkled with flour, put her hands over her face, and began to cry, her shoulders rocking back and forth. "It isn't fair," she said. "It isn't, isn't fair."

Howard put his hand at the small of her back and looked at the baker "Shame on you," Howard said to him. "Shame."

The baker put the rolling pin back on the counter. He undid his apron and threw it on the counter. He looked at them, and then he shook his head slowly. He pulled a chair out from under the card table that held papers and receipts, an adding machine, and a telephone directory. "Please sit down," he said. "Let me get you a chair," he said to Howard. "Sit down now, please." The baker went into the front of the shop and returned with two little wrought-iron chairs. "Please sit down, you people."

Ann wiped her eyes and looked at the baker. "I wanted to kill you," she said. "I wanted you dead."

The baker had cleared a space for them at the table. He shoved the adding machine to one side, along with the stacks of notepaper and receipts. He pushed the telephone directory onto the floor, where it landed with a thud. Howard and Ann sat down and pulled their chairs up to the table. The baker sat down, too.

"Let me say how sorry I am," the baker said, putting his elbows on the table. "God alone knows how sorry. Listen to me. I'm just a baker. I don't claim to be anything else. Maybe once, maybe years ago, I was a different kind of human being. I've forgotten, I don't know for sure. But I'm not any longer, if I ever was. Now I'm just a baker. That don't excuse my doing what I did, I know. But I'm deeply sorry. I'm sorry for your son, and sorry for my part in this," the baker said. He spread his hands out on the table and turned them over to reveal his palms. "I don't have any children myself, so I can only imagine what you must be feeling. All I can say to you now is that I'm sorry. Forgive me, if you can," the baker said. "I'm not an evil man, I don't think. Not evil, like you said on the phone. You got to understand what it comes down to is I don't know how to act anymore, it would seem. Please," the man said, "let me ask you if you can find it in your hearts to forgive me?"

It was warm inside the bakery. Howard stood up from the table and took off his coat. He helped Ann from her coat. The baker looked at them for a minute and then nodded and got up from the table. He went to the oven and turned off some switches. He found cups and poured coffee from an electric coffee-maker. He put a carton of cream on the table, and a bowl of sugar.

"You probably need to eat something," the baker said. "I hope you'll eat some of my hot rolls. You have to eat and keep going. Eating is a small, good thing in a time like this," he said.

He served them warm cinnamon rolls just out of the oven, the icing still runny. He put butter on the table and knives to spread the butter. Then the baker sat down at the table with them. He waited. He waited until they each took a roll from the platter and began to eat. "It's good to eat something," he said, watching them. "There's more. Eat up. Eat all you want. There's all the rolls in the world in here."

They ate rolls and drank coffee. Ann was suddenly hungry, and the rolls were warm and sweet. She ate three of them, which pleased the baker. Then he began to talk. They listened carefully. Although they were tired and in anguish, they listened to what the baker had to say. They nodded when the baker began to speak of loneliness, and of the sense of doubt and limitation that had come to him in his middle years. He told them what it was like to be childless all these years. To repeat the days with the ovens endlessly full and endlessly empty. The party food, the celebrations he'd worked over. Icing knuckle-deep. The tiny wedding couples stuck into cakes. Hundreds of them, no, thousands by now. Birthdays. Just imagine all those candles burning. He had a necessary trade. He was a baker. He was glad he wasn't a florist. It was better to be feeding people. This was a better smell anytime than flowers.

"Smell this," the baker said, breaking open a dark loaf. "It's a heavy bread, but rich." They smelled it, then he had them taste it. It had the taste of molasses and coarse grains. They listened to him. They ate what they could. They swallowed the dark bread. It was like daylight under the fluorescent trays of light. They talked on into the early morning, the high, pale cast of light in the windows, and they did not think of leaving.

1. Point out some of the differences between "The Bath" and this story.
2. What are some of the most effective passages that "tell," or narrate, part of the story?
3. What are some of the more effective descriptions that appear in this story that are missing from "The Bath"?
4. How is the ultimate effect of this story different from that of "The Bath"? What are the emotions that you take away from it, as compared to how you felt about "The Bath"?

CHAPTER FOURTEEN

Getting beyond Facts to Truth

Part 1: SOME FINAL THOUGHTS ON CREATIVE NONFICTION

Getting Started

Since this whole book is devoted to craft, techniques, and processes to be used in creative writing, whether fiction or nonfiction, why an extra chapter on nonfiction? Because it is important to reinforce some of the issues that have been raised, and to highlight a few new ones as well.

More specifically, we've spent a good deal of time going over aspects of creative craft—particularly things traditionally associated with fiction, such as point of view, dialogue, narration, and scene—as well as many of "process" things you can do to "get to" your material. We've discussed how these techniques could (and should) be used to generate and revise nonfiction work as well. Indeed, that is what makes it *creative* nonfiction: the use of fictional techniques brought to factual subject matter.

That seems relatively straightforward. But creative nonfiction is actually a skillful blending of a number of genres. Also known as "literary journalism," "new journalism," and "narrative nonfiction," this genre requires a writer to combine the discipline and integrity of a journalist with a fiction writer's ability to perform complex emotional explorations and character delineations.

Creative nonfiction can focus on birth, death, love, sex to the inner workings of business deals, the machinations of politics, or the intricacies of scientific explorations. And when writing creative nonfiction on these or other topics, inevitably questions arise about the accuracy of the reporting, the subjectivity of the writer, and the ethical considerations involved in revealing what could be sensitive information about an individual or group of individuals.

This chapter is dedicated to examining these points, and providing some additional examples of superb writing to use as models for your own work.

Just the Facts, Ma'am

The most obvious difference between fiction and creative nonfiction is that nonfiction is fact-based. It is based on events that actually occurred. This is a critical distinction: there have been a number of scandals in the mainstream press of so-called nonfiction writers who made things up or exaggerated things in the supposed serving of some higher truth. For example, Janet Cooke, the *Washington Post* reporter who won a Pulitzer Prize for her piece "Jimmy's World," about an eight-year-old heroin addict, eventually admitted to making up Jimmy. He wasn't even a composite character—a character made up from a number of other characters—although that would have been problematic, too. Defending herself, Cooke said that the piece represented a "larger truth." But she was widely viewed as having betrayed her readers and her newspaper, and her career was ruined.

More recently, there was a media maelstrom over a book called *A Million Little Pieces*, by James Frey, a so-called memoir about the rough life and recovery of a drug and alcohol addict. The book, which became a *New York Times* bestseller after Oprah Winfrey chose it as the first nonfiction book for her book club, was exposed as having a large number of embellishments, exaggerations, and outright falsehoods. Indeed, it came out that Frey had initially shopped the book around as fiction; when he didn't have any takers, he changed his tactics, calling it a memoir, and reaping a lucrative publishing contract as a result.

A statement released by Frey's publisher states quite unequivocally the difference between fiction and nonfiction:

> The controversy over James Frey's *A Million Little Pieces* has caused serious concern at Doubleday and Anchor Books. Recent interpretations of our previous statement notwithstanding, it is not the policy or stance of this company that it doesn't matter whether a book sold as nonfiction is true. *A nonfiction book should adhere to the facts as the author knows them* [emphasis mine].

So the number one rule in creative nonfiction is accuracy, and a rigorous adherence to the facts.

This focus on fact means that research is often key. Sometimes this amounts to years of research, including interviews, "shadowing" subjects, poring through relevant books and articles, and using the Internet as a focused research tool. To gauge the amount of painstaking research required to produce a stellar book of creative nonfiction you have only to look at the efforts of writers such as Tom Wolfe, Tracy Kidder, or Mark Kramer. As Kramer himself wrote in *Literary Journalism*:

> Literary journalists hang out with their sources for months or even years. It's a reward—and risk—of the trade, as I've discovered on many projects. I spent one glorious June with a baseball team; I wandered intermittently in backwoods Russia for six years of *perestroika* and the ensuing confused transition. I spent a year in hospital operating rooms and years in the field and corporate offices of America's farms . . . the reporting part of the work is engrossing and tedious. It is not social time. One stays alert for meaningful twists of narrative and character, all the while thinking about how to portray them and about how to sustain one's welcome.

Essential to this process, however, is a strict adherence to facts and to portraying events as they actually occurred. Although the repercussions or meaning of such events can be commented on in a subjective manner (more on this later), the facts must stand on their own.

Recollections and Re-creations

Having said that, there *are* cases in creative nonfiction where the delineations between fact and fiction are less well defined. Sometimes it has to do with making that judgment call: At what point in its development as a compelling narrative has a work of nonfiction crossed the line into fiction?

Some people—especially after the Frey debacle—are purists. They say that once you've begun tweaking things—even slightly—to make a narrative more dramatic or make more emotional sense, you've crossed into fictional territory, and there's no going back. To call something nonfiction that has been embroidered even slightly is to be disingenuous at best and dishonest at worst, or so this line of thinking goes.

Others are more practical-minded. They point out that any time someone sits down to write, certain . . . exaggerations, or distortions, or changes . . . inevitably creep in. They point out that different people's perceptions of an event can differ dramatically: how many times have you personally told an anecdote only to have a family member or friend say, "No, no, it wasn't like that *at all*!"

And you can have artists like Spalding Gray, who talked about his "auto-fiction," which is a blend of fact and fiction:

I start with my memory and begin to play with it and shape it. Memory, for all of us, is our first creative act. Everyone that remembers is creative, is "*remembering*." Everyone that is remembering is always putting something together that is always not the original event. The origin is always lost to us forever. You can't eat the menu, but you can describe more than you can eat. And for me that's often more fun than eating.

I am not anti-fiction. Some of my favorite writers write fiction. I am just more comfortable with the experience of grounding myself in my actual personal history. Staying with the actual is not only a confirmation of my life but through the constant retelling of the story it is often a way into personal insight. I know I have lived when I have told you my story. By referring to the actual I bring it into the imaginary on its own terms . . .

Life is not a story, it's a life. It's a raw and unmediated thing-in-itself. We try to make sense of what happens to us and of who we are in terms of stories. For me, meaning only exists in a story.

As another example of the difficult line between fiction and nonfiction, take the celebrated book *This Boy's Life* by Tobias Wolff. Is this fiction or nonfiction? The author calls it nonfiction, hence the subtitle: *A Memoir*. Yet it reads like a novel. As Wolff said in an interview with Harvey Blume in the *Boston Book Review*, April 1996:

It's a view of memory as a static thing, a tape that gets filed away that will be exactly the same when you pull it out. There's no recognition that memory is something that you do; it is not something that you have. You remember, and when you remember you bring in all the resources of invention, calculation, self-interest and self-protection. Imagination is part of it too. We really have to be a lot more realistic about the limits of memory.

Of course, there's the basic problem for anyone has who has tried to use fictional techniques in a nonfiction piece to re-create something that happened in the past: there's a certain amount of necessary fabrication that goes on. Take scene-building. Even if you were actually present at an event or interaction, how likely is it that you would have a complete record of what was said and done? The best of all possible worlds is that you've got a tape recording of a particular encounter, in which case you do have the actual words at your disposal. But many times when we sit down to write about experiences, we're dealing with notes taken after the fact, or just plain memory (and memory is notoriously unreliable).

In an essay in the *New York Times Book Review*, W. S. DiPiero wrote:

Remembering is an act of imagination. Any account we make of our experience is an exercise in reinventing the self. Even when we think we're accurately reporting past events, persons, objects, places and their sequence, we're theatricalizing the self and its world.

In many of the memoirs published in recent years, I detect a creepy disingenuousness whenever their authors insist on a perfect, untainted recounting of detail. It's no surprise that so many of these memoirs are written in a plain one-foot-in-front-of-the-other style, because this approach works to persuade us that there is no contrivance going on, no performance in progress.

Here's a passage from *In the Belly of the Beast* by Jack Henry Abbott, about a young man brought up in the prison system. How much of this reconstructed memory is accurate? How far can we trust this writer? In this case, and in the case of all good creative nonfiction, it's the details that convince us—the details that bring the scene to life. The fact that it's written in present tense also infuses the text with a lot of urgency, and credibility: we feel as though we're *there*. But the undeniable fact also remains that this is a recollection, a memory, for which there is no objective record, and yet it is presented to us as fact:

> I am about twelve or thirteen years old. It is winter. I am marching in a long double-file of boys. We are marching to the mess hall. There is a guard watching as we march toward him. There is a guard walking behind us as we march.
>
> My testes shrink and the blood is rushing and my eyes burn, ache. My heart is pounding and I am trying hard to breathe slowly, to control myself.
>
> I keep glancing at the guards: in front and behind the lines.
>
> The fields beyond are plowed and covered with an icy blanket of snow. I do not know how far beyond those fields my freedom lies.
>
> Suddenly my confederate at the front of the line whirls and slugs the boy behind him. The front guard, like an attack dog, is on them both—beating them into submission. Seconds later the guard at the back rushes forward, brushing me as he passes.
>
> I break away from the line and run *for my life*. I stretch my legs as far as I can, and as quickly as I can, but the legs of a boy four feet six inches tall cannot stretch very far.
>
> The fields are before me, a still flatland of ice and snow, and the huge clods of frozen, plowed earth are to me formidable obstacles. The sky is baby-blue, almost white. The air is clear.
>
> I haven't covered fifty yards when I hear the pursuit begin. "You! Stop!" I immediately know I will be caught, but I continue to run.

In the following passage from *This Boy's Life*, we see the same thing: how a scene is constructed of gesture, dialogue—and how compelling it is.

Yet how likely is it that Tobias Wolff could have remembered this conversation so accurately? Some reconstitution, at a minimum, was required—which is why the line between fiction and nonfiction can be such a tenuous one at times.

> After a week or so I announced at dinner that I had decided not to go to Paris.
>
> "The hell you aren't," Dwight said. "You're going."
>
> "He gets to choose," Pearl said, on my side for once. "Doesn't he, Rosemary?"
>
> My mother nodded. "That was the deal."
>
> "The books aren't closed on this one,' Dwight said. "Not yet they aren't." He looked at me. "Why do you think you aren't going?"
>
> "I don't want to change my name."
>
> "You don't want to change your name?"
>
> "No, sir."
>
> He put his fork down. His nostrils were flaring. "Why not?"
>
> "I don't know. I just don't."
>
> "Well that's a lot of crap, because you've already changed your name once. Right?"
>
> "Yes sir."
>
> "Then you might as well change the other name too, make a clean sweep."
>
> "But it's my last name."
>
> "Oh, for Christ's sake. You think anybody cares what you call yourself?"
>
> I shrugged.
>
> "Don't badger him," my mother said. "He's already made up his mind."
>
> "We're talking about Paris!" Dwight shouted.
>
> "It was his choice," she said.
>
> Dwight jabbed his finger at me. "You're going."
>
> "Only if he wants to," my mother said.
>
> "You're going," he repeated.

Ethical Considerations

There are always ethical considerations whenever we set pen to paper (or fingers to keyboard, as the case may be). With creative nonfiction, there's a major one: how can we write frankly about the people around us, with the possible invasions of privacy and betrayal that such renderings can cause? At what point do we respect the wishes of those around us not to reveal their secrets? What's allowable in search of artistic inspiration? Sharon Olds calls herself "terribly naive" for actually using the names of her kids in her early autobiographical poems; today when she writes a poem that could be sensitive to her family she holds on to it rather than publishing it straight away, and has special instructions about when certain poems can be released in her will.

One part of the answer, at least, is clear: full disclosure of intentions. It is never right to write about someone secretly, unless they are a true public figure. When performing research—listening to conversations, interviewing subjects, or otherwise observing people as they go about their lives— you must make it clear that you are there as a writer, not as a friend or a family member. This doesn't mean that you have to show what you have written to your subjects, or that you owe them an opportunity to edit what you have written. But you do have to make it clear that they *are* subjects.

What if you are writing about events after the fact? That is, you didn't know at the time that you would be writing about an event, but only in retrospect realize that it would make good material for a personal essay or memoir? That's a trickier subject. In many cases, to avoid potential legal action, writers will get oral or written permission from subjects to write about events. Others will proceed, albeit with caution, on their own, documenting (as much as possible) anything they choose to write about.

It can be a delicate area to write about. Take Mary Karr, author of *The Liar's Club*, who got permission from her family to publish her memoirs, which are about a spectacularly dysfunctional family in Texas. Here's an excerpt:

> That was about the only story I ever heard implying that anybody in Mother's family was inherently Nervous. Oh, she had some outlaws everybody talked about. Her daddy had used his engineering degree to open a garage, which drove his banker daddy nuts. There was her great-uncle Earl who used to dress up like a matador when he got drunk, and her maternal grandfather, who'd been a bootlegger and who used to give her nickels to hear her cuss. I never heard anything more exotic than that. Most of the names block-printed in Grandma's huge family Bible, which sat in a heavy plastic wrapper on her coffee table, meant nothing to me.
>
> The morning Mother decided to go back to Daddy, she and Grandma had a fight about whether her lipstick was too dark. Grandma had brought it up at breakfast and just clamped down on it like a gila monster. Finally, Mother stuffed our new clothes in her dead father's Gladstone bag and piled us in the car in our pajamas again. Again the old woman had crimped her hair. Just before we pulled out, she poked her clamp-studded head in my window. Some curls had sprung loose from the clips so she looked for all the world like the stone head of Medusa that Mother had shown us in her mythology book. The old lady called Leechfield a swamp, a suckhole, and the anus of the planet before Mother cranked up the engine. The too sweet smell of Grandma's hyacinth perfume hung in the car till Mother lit a Salem.

Subjectivity vs. Objectivity

But let's first get one thing out of the way. Just because something sticks to facts doesn't mean it has to be objective. Traditional news stories are supposed to be factual *and* objective (although some would argue that there's no such thing as true objectivity). But creative nonfiction lays no such claims. Indeed, one of the hallmarks of *creative* nonfiction is precisely that: that it infuses a subject with the opinions, emotions, attitudes, and beliefs of the writer.

Look at the difference between the first and second passages below. The first is a straightforward, factual summary of the features of a restaurant. The second, however, qualifies as creative nonfiction.

> The Bright Little Café offers good, wholesome, and—most importantly to anyone on a budget—inexpensive lunches and dinners. The décor is simple chic: plain steel tables and chairs. The house specialty is a pita bread stuffed with fresh grilled tuna and capers. We give it three stars.

> You take the No. 9 bus to Mission Street, and walk three blocks east until you get to Walnut Avenue. A strange atmosphere pervades that section of the city: you have voodoo shops juxtaposed next to occult bookstores next to stripper bars. And then right in the middle of it all, The Bright Little Café shines like a star. It's like seeing Mom waiting for you outside the seedy bus terminal in the worst part of town. When you walk inside, the first thing that strikes you is how *clean* everything is. Everything gleams, from the stainless steel tables and chairs to the burnished black and white tile floor, which, by the way, you'd feel comfortable eating off of. But it's the food that makes going to this restaurant such a sublime experience.

Or, for an example of creative nonfiction that delivers much more than just the facts, read Susan Sontag's essay "Looking at War," which, although it contains carefully researched material, also has a healthy dose of subjective opinion infused into it:

> Who believes today that war can be abolished? No one, not even pacifists. We hope only (so far in vain) to stop genocide and bring to justice those who commit gross violations of the laws of war (for there are laws of war, to which combatants should be held), and to stop specific wars by imposing negotiated alternatives to armed conflict. But protesting against war may not have seemed to futile or naive in the 1930s. In 1924, on the tenth anniversary of the national mobilization in Germany for the First World War, the conscientious objector Ernst Friedrich published *War Against War!* (*Krieg dem Kriege!*), an album of more than 180 photographs that were drawn mainly from German military and medical archives, and almost all of which

were deemed unpublishable by government censors while the war was on. The book starts with pictures of toy soldiers, toy cannons, and other delights of male children everywhere, and concludes with pictures taken in military cemeteries. This is photography as shock therapy. Between the toys and the graves, the reader has an excruciating photo tour of four years of ruin, slaughter, and degradation: wrecked and plundered churches and castles, obliterated villages, ravaged forests, torpedoed passenger steamers, shattered vehicles, hanged conscientious objectors, naked personnel of military brothels, soldiers in death agonies after a poison gas attack, skeletal Armenian children.

Or take this example, the opening from an essay titled "Final Cut" by Atul Gawande, about autopsies. Again, Gawande doesn't pretend to be writing an objective piece about scientific subject matter (although the science is certainly important to the essay). Rather, he is interested in conveying a subjective experience, as rendered using techniques we've traditionally viewed as being in the domain of fiction.

> Your patient is dead; the family is gathered. And there is one last thing that you must ask about: the autopsy. How should you go about it? You could do it offhandedly, as if it were the most ordinary thing in the world: "Shall we do an autopsy, then?" Or you could be firm, use your Sergeant Joe Friday voice: "Unless you have strong objections, we will need to do an autopsy, ma'am." Or you could take yourself out of it: "I am sorry, but they require me to ask, Do you want an autopsy done?"
>
> What you can't be these days is mealy-mouthed about it. I once took care of a woman in her eighties who had given up her driver's license only to get hit by a car—driven by someone even older—while she was walking to a bus stop. She sustained a depressed skull fracture and cerebral bleeding, and despite surgery, she died a few days later. So, on the spring afternoon after the patient took her last breath, I stood beside her and bowed my head with the tearful family. Then, as delicately as I could—not even using the awful word—I said, "If it's all right, we'd like to do an examination to confirm the cause of death."
>
> "An *autopsy*?" a nephew said, horrified. He looked at me as if I were a buzzard circling his aunt's body. "Hasn't she been through enough?"

Thus begins a long, detailed article about autopsies that is full of facts about the medical procedure, but subjectively intertwined with real-life experiences of the author, a medical doctor. Such an article could have included the same type of facts but have been told in a much dryer, more objective way. But it might have lost its immediacy and sense of urgency.

Not incidentally, the piece also leverages other fictional techniques we've discussed in this book. For example, there's the use of second person (see Chapter 7) that draws readers in, pulling them into the experiences so that they almost feel personally implicated in what happens.

Finally, in terms of subjectivity vs. objectivity, take a look at the opening of *Salvador* by Joan Didion. Her goal—to explicate the political, cultural, and economic complexities of El Salvador in the late 1980s—could have been done in a traditional newspaper piece peppered with interviews and facts and objective reporting. But she chose to take a much more subjective viewpoint, filtering her meticulous research through the lens of her own emotional reaction to what she uncovered during her visits to the country:

> The three-year-old El Salvador International Airport is glassy and white and splendidly isolated, conceived during the waning of the Molina "National Transformation" as convenient less to the capital (San Salvador is forty miles away, until recently a drive of several hours) than to a central hallucination of the Molina and Romero regimes, the projected beach resorts, the Hyatt, the Pacific Paradise, tennis, golf, water-skiing, condos, *Costa del Sol*; the visionary invention of a tourist industry in yet another republic where the leading natural cause of death is gastrointestinal infection. In the general absence of tourists these hotels have since been abandoned, ghost resorts on the empty Pacific beaches, and to land at this airport built to service them is to plunge directly into a state in which no ground is solid, no depth of field reliable, no perception so definite that it might not dissolve into its reverse.

The last thing that Didion is here is objective; she wants to push us into an emotional space, carefully prepared through the use of concrete details and facts—based on interviews and research, as all good nonfiction is—but decidedly subjective in nature.

A Trip of Self-Discovery

Frequently, creative nonfiction begins, like fiction does, with the process of self-discovery. One is seeking the truth about something—an event, or a relationship, or a situation—and often that truth becomes a mirror, reflecting back on oneself and one's perceptions of the world. Take this excerpt from Michael Ondaatje's sublime book of family memoir, *Running in the Family*:

> Once a friend had told me that it was only when I was drunk that I seemed to know exactly what I wanted. And so, two months later, in the midst of the farewell party in my growing wildness—dancing, balancing a wine glass on my forehead and falling to the floor twisting round and getting up without letting the glass tip, a trick which seemed only possible when drunk and

relaxed—I knew I was already running . . . I had already planned the journey back. During quiet afternoons I spread maps onto the floor and searched out possible routes to Ceylon. But it was only in the midst of this party, among my closest friends, that I realized I would be traveling back to the family I had grown from—those relations from my parents' generation who stood in my memory like frozen opera. I wanted to touch them into words . . .

In this unusual memoir, Ondaatje, who resides in Canada, is contemplating a trip back to his native Sri Lanka, and realizes he has a special emotional agenda that he wishes to accomplish while he is there, to "touch into words" the lives of his parents' generation. Interestingly enough, at the end of the book Ondaatje thanks a long list of people for their help in constructing the memoir, which consists, among other things, of mini-essays, poems, raw excerpts from notebooks, recorded conversations, and a vivid re-creation of the death of his grandmother—a death that no one, least of all him, could have witnessed. Yet there it is in glorious detail. To any naysayers, Ondaatje writes after the acknowledgments that:

> While all these names may give an air of authenticity, I must confess that the book is not a history but a portrait or "gesture." And if those listed above disapprove of the fictional air I apologize and can only say that in Sri Lanka a well-told lie is worth a thousand facts.

This sort of writing reminds us that one is never so naked as in a personal essay. With fiction, one is exposed in certain ways, but you can always have distance from it; you can say, "No, that isn't really *me*, it's a fictional construct." With the personal essay, you have no such distancing techniques; in fact, it seems sometimes best to embrace the implacable "I" wholeheartedly, as Laura Hillenbrand does in "A Sudden Illness":

> I turned up my radio and wrote as much as I could, mostly equine veterinary medical articles for *Equus*. On breaks, I took brief walks. I bought new shoes—I'd been lying around in socks for years—and discovered that my feet had shrunk two sizes. I had lived for so long in silence and isolation that the world was a sensory explosion. At the grocery store, I dragged my hands along the shelves, touching boxes and bags, smelling oranges and pears and apples. At the hardware store, I'd plunge my arm into the seed bins to feel the pleasing weight of the grain against my skin. I was a toddler again.
>
> After years of seeing people almost exclusively on television, I found their three-dimensionality startling: the light playing off their faces, the complexity of their hands, the strange electric feel of their nearness. One afternoon, I spent fifteen minutes watching a shirtless man clip a hedge, enthralled by the glide of the muscles under his skin.

To Be In or Out of the Story?

It's a critical question that a nonfiction writer faces that a fiction writer doesn't: How far does he or she want to be directly involved in the story? In a sense, this is a point of view choice (see Chapter 7), but it really goes deeper than that: it's a decision about whether to filter the events of the narrative through one's own consciousness, or whether to try and tell the story straight.

Phillip Lopate talks about this in his piece "Writing Personal Essays: On the Necessity of Turning Oneself Into a Character":

> In personal essays, nothing is more commonly met than the letter *I*. I think it a perfectly good word, one no writer should be ashamed to use. Especially is first person legitimate for this form, so drawn to the particulars of character and voice. The problem with "I" is not that it is in bad taste, but that fledgling personal essayists may think they've said or conveyed more than they actually have with that one syllable. In their minds, that "I" is swimming with background and a lush, sticky past, and an almost too fatal specificity, whereas the reader, encountering it for the first time in a new piece, sees only a slender telephone pole standing in the sentence, trying to catch a few signals to send on. In truth, even the barest "I" holds a whisper of promised engagement, and can suggest a caress in the midst of more stolid language. What it doesn't do, however, is give us a clear picture of who is speaking.

In the essay, "Taking Yourself Out of the Story: Narrative Stance and the Upright Pronoun," Phillip Gerard also addresses this issue, although he takes the opposite side of the argument:

> For us, who cut our teeth on the New Journalism of Tom Wolfe and the personal essays of Joan Didion rather than in deadline newsrooms, it seems only natural to participate in the story. And often including ourselves in the story does make it sound more natural, more honest, more real.
>
> But too often these days, I'm afraid we writers of nonfiction fall into the opposite fallacy: We enter the story whether it needs us or not.
>
> For the reader, this can be distracting, even annoying, diverting attention from the real "star" of the piece. The reader perceives us clamoring for attention and rightly resents it. And, as in many of my students' pieces, participation by the author can actually confuse the reader about the literal action of the story.

In the case of *Patrimony*, Philip Roth's memoir of his father's illness and death, it was clear that he belonged in the story:

> So, having arrived at his apartment from my mother's grave, I'd gone into the toilet, where, while eyeing my grandfather's shaving mug, I'd rehearsed

my lines for the fiftieth time; then I'd come back out into the living room and looked at him slumped down in a corner of the sofa waiting for the verdict. Lil waited in the other corner of the sofa. She said to me, "Philip, do you want me to go?"

"Of course not."

"Herman," she said to him, "do you want me to stay?" But he didn't even hear her. And from then on Lil was so silent she might as well not have been there.

"Well," he said slowly, in a very gloomy voice, "what's the sad news?"

I sat in the chair across from him, my heart pounding as though I were the one about to be told something terrible. "You have a serious problem," I began, "but it can be dealt with. You have a tumor in your head. Dr. Meyerson says that given the location, the chances are ninety-five percent that it's benign." I had intended, like Meyerson, to be candid and describe it as large, but I couldn't. That there was a tumor seemed enough for him to take in. Not that he had registered any shock as yet—he sat there emotionless, waiting for me to go on. "It's pressing on the facial nerve, and that's what's caused the paralysis." Meyerson had told me that it was wrapped *around* the facial nerve, but I couldn't say that either. My evasiveness reminded me of his on the night my mother had died. At midnight London time, he had told me that my mother had had a serious heart attack and that I'd better make arrangements to fly home because they didn't know if she was going to survive. "It doesn't look good, Phil," he said; but an hour later, when I phoned back to tell him my flight plans for the next morning, he began to cry and revealed that she had actually died in the restaurant where they had had dinner a few hours earlier.

Here's an example of a writer of creative nonfiction, Honor Moore, who has chosen to remain outside the story, as she writes about her grandmother, the painter Margarett Sargent.

Her line rushes as if attracted to each object in the room: the dark wood bed frame, its tall, ornamental headboard; a small American bedside table—on it, telephone, tumbler, pocket watch; a child's chair at bedside; pictures on the wall; a woman's shoes askew on the floor; the bed itself, linens rumpled, a hat hurled on mussed pillows—all sketched with charcoal. Then, as if composing a variation, she lays in pastel: white-green striates walls, buff paper shows through where light doesn't reach; sky-blue, white-green to model one pillow, heavy cream etching curves of another, bright white for the creases of sheets, all leading the eye to two garments—one rose, the other robin's-egg blue—slung on a bedpost toward the lower right of the drawing. Below, on the slightly tilted floor, the shoes—black with rose insides.

If you enter the room, you see something else: an artist at work, tray of pastels set out beside her, paper on a small easel. This was the bedroom Mar-

garett shared with Shaw, but his bed is not in the picture. In this room, its
walls lined with silk, there were two Venetian beds, one unlike the other;
Margarett has left out her husband's. What you see is a woman's sleeping
room, sunlight falling across the voluptuous shapes of an unmade bed,
sheet, pillow, beautifully made nightclothes.

[from *The White Blackbird* by Honor Moore]

And we should never forget that there can be a hardness, a resiliency to
the facts of a situation, that sometimes weighs in heavily on the side of *not*
fictionalizing things, no matter how tempting that might be. The following excerpt is from the superb essay "The Love of My Life" by Cheryl
Strayed, and it reminds us that some things are just unknowable, and
should remain that way.

If this were fiction, what would happen next is that the woman would
stand up and get into her truck and drive away. It wouldn't matter that the
woman had lost her mother's wedding ring, even though it was gone to her
forever, because the loss would mean something else entirely: that what was
gone now was actually her sorrow and the shackles of grief that had held her
down. And in this loss she would see, and the reader would know, that the
woman had been in error all along. That, indeed, the love she'd had for her
mother was too much love, really; too much love and also too much sorrow.
She would realize this and get on with her life. There would be what happened in the story and also everything it stood for: the river, representing
life's constant changing; the tiny blue flowers, beauty; the spring air, rebirth.
All of these symbols would collide and mean that the woman was actually
lucky to have lost the ring, and not just to have lost it, but to have loved it, to
have ached for it, and to have had it taken from her forever. The story would
end, and you would know that she was the better for it. That she was wiser,
stronger, more interesting, and most of all, finally starting down her path to
glory. I would show you the leaf when it unfurls in a single motion: the end
of one thing, the beginning of another. And you would know the answers to
all the questions without being told. Did she ever write that five-page paper
about the guy who lost his nose? Did she ask Mark to marry her again? Did
she stop sleeping with people who had titles instead of names? Did she
manage to walk 1,638 miles? Did she get to work and become the Incredibly
Talented and Extraordinarily Brilliant and Successful Writer? You'd believe
the answers to all these questions to be yes. I would have given you what
you wanted then: to be a witness to a healing.

But this isn't fiction. Sometimes a story is not about anything except what
it is about. Sometimes you wake up and find that you actually have lost your
nose. Losing my mother's wedding ring in the Tongue River was not OK. I
did not feel better for it. It was not a passage or a release. What happened is

that I lost my mother's wedding ring and I understood that I was not going to get it back, that it would be yet another piece of my mother that I would not have for all the days of my life, and I understood that I could not bear the truth, but that I would have to.

Healing is a small and ordinary and very burnt thing. And it's one thing and one thing only: it's doing what you have to do. It's what I did then and there. I stood up and got into my truck and drove away from a part of my mother. The part of her that had been my lover, my wife, my first love, my true love, the love of my life.

Part 2: READING AS A WRITER

Learning to Drive

KATHA POLLITT

"Over there, the red Jeep. Park!" Ben, my gentle Filipino driving instructor, has suddenly become severe, abrupt, commanding. A slight man, he now looms in his seat; his usually soft voice has acquired a threatening edge. In a scenario that we have repeated dozens of times, and that has kinky overtones I don't even want to think about, he is pretending to be the test examiner, barking out orders as we tool along the streets above Columbia University in the early morning. "Pull out when you are ready!" "Right turn!" "Left turn!" "Straight!" "All right, Ms. Pollitt, pull over." He doesn't even need to say the words. From the rueful look on his once again kindly face, I know that I have failed.

What did I do this time? Did I run a red light, miss a stop sign, fail to notice one of the many bicyclists who sneak up into my blind spot whenever I go into reverse? Each of these mistakes means automatic failure. Or did I fail on points? Five for parallel-parking more than fourteen inches from the curb, ten for rolling when I paused for the woman with the stroller (but at least I saw her! I saw her!), fifteen for hesitating in the intersection so that a driver in a car with New Jersey plates honked and gave me the finger? This time it was points, Ben tells me: in our five-minute practice test, racked up sixty. New York State allows you thirty. "Observation, Kahta, observation! This is your weakness." This truth hangs in the air like mystical advice from a sage in a martial-arts movie. "That and lining up too far away when you go to park." The clock on the dashboard reads 7:47. We will role-play the test repeatedly during my two-hour lesson. I will fail every time.

Observation is my weakness. I did not realize that my mother was a secret drinker. I did not realize that the man I lived with, my soul mate, made for me in Marxist heaven, was a dedicated philanderer, that the drab colleague he insinuated into our social life was his long-standing secret lover, or that the young art critic he mocked as silly and second rate was being groomed as my replacement. I noticed that our apartment was becoming a grunge palace, with papers collecting dust on every surface and kitty litter crunching underfoot. I observed—very good, Kahta!—that I was spending many hours in my study, engaged in arcane e-mail debates with strangers, that I had gained twenty-five pounds in our seven years together and could not fit into many of my clothes. I realized it was not likely that the unfamiliar pink-and-black-striped bikini panties in the clean-clothes basket were the result, as he claimed, of a simple laundry-room mixup. But all this awareness was like the impending danger in one of those slow-motion dreams of paralysis, information that could not be processed. It was like seeing the man with the suitcase step off the curb and driving forward anyway.

I am a fifty-two-year-old woman who has yet to get a driver's license. I'm not the only older woman who can't legally drive—Ben recently had a sixty-five-year-old student, who took the test four times before she passed—but perhaps I am the only fifty-two-year-old feminist writer in this situation. How did this happen to me? For decades, all around me women were laying claim to forbidden manly skills—how to fix the furnace, perform brain surgery, hunt seals, have sex without love. Only I, it seems, stood still, as the machines in my life increased in both number and complexity. When I was growing up, not driving had overtones of New York hipness. There was something beatnik, intellectual, European about being disconnected from the car culture: the rest of America might deliquesce into one big strip mall, but New York City would remain a little outpost of humane civilization, an enclave of ancient modes of transportation—the subway, the bus, the taxi, the bicycle, the foot. Still, my family always had a car—a Buick, a Rambler, some big, lumbering masculine make. My father would sit in it and smoke and listen to the ballgame in the soft summer evening, when he and my mother had had a fight.

"I am trying so hard to help you, Kahta," Ben says. "I feel perhaps I am failing you as your teacher." In a lifetime in and out of academia, I have never before heard a teacher suggest that his student's difficulties might have something to do with him. The truth is, Ben is a natural pedagogue—organized, patient, engaged with his subject, and always looking for new ways to explain some tricky point. Sometimes he illustrates what I should have done by using a pair of toy cars, and I can see the little boy he once was—intent, happy, lost in play. Sometimes he makes up analogies:

"Kahta, how do you know if you've put in enough salt and pepper when you are making beef stew?"

"Um, you taste it?"

"Riiight, you taste it. So what do you do if you've lost track of which way the car is pointing when you parallel-park?"

"I dunno, Ben. You taste it?"

"You just let the car move back a tiny bit and see which way it goes! You taste the direction! Then you—"

"Correct the seasonings?"

"Riiight . . . You adjust!"

Because it takes me a while to focus on the task at hand, Ben and I have fallen into the habit of long lessons—we drive for two hours, sometimes three. We go up to Washington Heights and drive around the winding, hilly roads of Fort Tryon Park and the narrow crooked Tudoresque streets near Castle Village. What a beautiful neighborhood! we exclaim. Look at that Art Deco subway station entrance! Look at those Catholic schoolgirls in front of Mother Cabrini High, in those incredibly cute sexy plaid uniforms! I am careful to stop for the old rabbi, I pause and make eye contact with the mother herding her two little boys. It's like another, secret New York up here, preserved from the forties, in which jogging yuppies in electric-blue spandex look like time travelers from the future among the staid elderly burghers walking their dogs along the leafy sidewalks overlooking the Hudson. In that New York, the one without road-raging New Jersey drivers or sneaky cyclists, in which life is lived at twenty miles an hour, I feel sure I could have got my license with no trouble. I could have been living here all along, coming out of the Art Deco entrance at dusk, with sweet-smelling creamy-pink magnolias all around me.

I spend more time with Ben than with any other man just now. There are days when, except for an exchange of smiles and hellos with Mohammed at the newsstand and my suppertime phone call with a man I am seeing who lives in London, Ben is the only man I talk to. In a way, he's perfect—his use of the double brake is protective without being infantilizing, his corrections are firm but never condescending or judgmental, he spares my feelings but tells the truth if asked. ("Let's say I took the test tomorrow, Ben. What are my chances?" "I'd say maybe fifty-fifty." I must be pretty desperate—those don't seem like such bad odds to me.) He's a big improvement on my former lover, who told a mutual friend that he was leaving me because I didn't have a driver's license, spent too much time on e-mail, and had failed in seven years to read Anton Pannekoek's *Workers' Councils* and other classics of the ultra-left. Ben would never leave me because I don't have a driver's license. Quite the reverse. Sometimes I feel sad to think that these lessons must one day come to an end—will I ever see those little streets again, or drive around Fort Tryon Park in the spring? "Will you still be my teacher, Ben, after I get my license, so I can learn how to drive on the highway?" Ben promises that he will always be there for me, and I believe him.

In at least one way, I am like the other older women learning to drive: I am here because I have lost my man. Most women in my situation are widows or divorcées who spent their lives under Old World rules, in which driving was a male prerogative and being ferried about a female privilege. My lover's mother lived in the wilds of Vermont for years with her Marxist-intellectual husband. With the puritanical zeal for which German Jews are famous, she kept the house spotless, grew all their fruits and vegetables, and raised her son to be a world-class womanizer—while earning a PhD that would enable her to support her husband's life of reading and writing, and, of course, driving. She didn't learn to drive until after his death, when she was over sixty. To hear her tell it now, the whole process took five minutes. When she asked if I'd got my license yet—which she did every time we spoke—she adopted a tone of intense and invasive concern. It was as if she were asking me if the Thorazine had started to work.

Ben is not my first driving teacher. When I was twenty-seven, I took lessons from Mike, a young and rather obnoxious Italian American. "That's OK, I can walk to the curb from here," he would say when I parked too wide. After a month of lessons, I took the test in the Bronx and didn't even notice that I'd hit a stop sign when I parked. Automatic failure. Mike drove me back to Manhattan in hostile silence and didn't call to schedule a lesson again. Ben would never do that.

That was it for driving until four years ago, when I bought a house on the Connecticut shore and signed up for lessons with an instructor I'll call Tom. He was Italian American also, middle-aged, overweight, and rather sweet, but liable to spells of anger and gloom, as if he had raised too many sons like Mike. On bad days, as we drove around the back roads and shopping centers of Clinton and Madison and Guilford, Tom would seethe about the criminal propensities of the black inhabitants of New Haven. On good days, he liked to talk about religion. For example, he believed that Jesus Christ was a space alien, which would explain a lot—the Star of Bethlehem, the walking on water, the Resurrection. Besides, Tom said, "no human being could be that good." He made me memorize his special method of sliding backward into a parking space, failed to impress upon me the existence of blind spots, and, like his predecessor, lost interest in me when I flunked the road test.

I should have taken the test again immediately, but instead I spent several years driving around the shoreline with my lover in the passenger seat, as Connecticut law permits. He had special methods, too—for instance, on tricky maneuvers at an intersection he would urge me to "be one car" with the car in front, which means just do what that car is doing. Ben looked a little puzzled when I told him about that. What if the car in front is doing something really stupid? "Listen to your inner voice," he tells me when I continue going back as I parallel-park, even though I know I am about to go over the curb, which is an automatic failure on the test "You are right, Kahta, you knew! Your inner voice is trying to help you!" You can't listen to your inner voice and be one car, too, is what Ben is getting at.

What was my lover thinking, I wonder, when we cruised Route 1, shuttling between our little house and the bookstore, the movie theater, Al Forno for pizza, the Clam Castle for lobster rolls, Hammonasset Beach to watch the twilight come over that long expanse of shining sand? Was he daydreaming about the young art critic, thinking about how later he would go off on his bicycle and call the drab colleague from the pay phone at the Stop & Shop? Was he thinking what a drag it was to have a girlfriend who couldn't pass a simple road test, even in small-town Connecticut, who did not care about the value-price transformation problem, and who never once woke him up with a blow job, despite being told many times that this was what all men wanted? Perhaps the young art critic is a better girlfriend on these and other scores, and he no longer feels the need for other women. Or perhaps the deception was the exciting part for him, and he will betray her, too, which is, of course, what I hope.

Now as I drive around upper Manhattan with Ben I spend a lot of time ignoring the road and asking myself, "If I had got my driver's license, would my lover have left me?" Perhaps my procrastination about the road test was symbolic to him of other resistances. "In the end," he said as he was leaving, ostensibly to "be alone" but actually, as I soon discovered, to join the young art critic on Fire Island, "our relationship revolves around you." "That's not true!" I wept. He also said, "Every day you wake up happy and cheerful and I'm lonely and miserable." "No, I don't!" I stormed. He continued, "You never read the books I recommend." I protested that I was reading one such book at that very moment—*A World Full of Gods: Pagans, Jews, and Christians in the Roman Empire*, by Keith Hopkins. "I mean serious political books," he said. "Books that are important to me." OK, point taken. Then came the coup de grâce: "I finally saw that you would never change."

What can you say to that? Change what? If I had read Anton Pannekoek's *Workers' Councils*, if I had given up e-mail for blow jobs at dawn, if I had got my license, would we still be together, driving north to buy daylilies at White Flower Farm while learnedly analyzing the Spartacist revolution of 1919? Perhaps, it occurs to me, as a demented cabbie cuts me off on Riverside Drive, it's a lucky thing I didn't get my license. I would still be living with a womanizer, a liar, a cheat, a manipulator, a maniac, a psychopath. Maybe my incompetence protected me.

New York State puts out an official booklet of rules of the road, but there are no textbooks that teach the art of driving itself. The closest is a tattered test result, much passed about by teachers, from the days when examiners filled out a form by hand. "I know his mother!" I exclaim when Ben gives me a copy. The test result happens to belong to a young writer, sometimes written up in gossip columns as a member of an all-boy fast crowd. "You see, Kahta! He failed to anticipate the actions of others. He didn't stop for pedestrians. And he forgot his turn signals, too." Ben shakes his head sorrowfully over the young writer's terrible score—seventy points off! I find this failure oddly cheering.

Mostly, though, driving is a skill transmitted by experience, one to one. In this, it resembles few activities, most of which can be learned from a book, or so we tell ourselves—think how many sex manuals are published every year, not to mention those educational sex videos advertised in high-toned literary publications aimed at people who were fantasizing about Mr. Rochester and Mr. Darcy while their classmates were steaming up the windows of their parents' cars. That was another accusation my lover flung at me the day he left: "You bought *The Joy of Sex*, but you just put it in a drawer!" "Why was it my job to improve our sex life?" I retorted. "You could have opened that book any time." I suppose the truth was that, given his multiple exhausting commitments, he didn't need to.

Sometimes when I am driving I become suddenly bewildered—it is as if I had never turned left or parallel-parked before. How many times have I turned the wheel while angling back into my parking space? I become hot and flushed and totally confused, and for some reason I keep turning the wheel until it's maxed out, and then look frantically at Ben.

"What do I do now, Ben? How far back do I turn it? How do I know when it's where it's supposed to be?"

"Beef stew, Kahta! Remember?"

"You mean I should just let it go back a tiny bit to see where it will go?"

"Riiight. You see, you are learning! Beef-stew it!"

But what if I get my license and I have one of these episodes of befuddlement when I'm alone at the wheel? Ben often has to remind me not to zone out, as I so frequently do even while I'm telling myself to stay focused. For example, I'll be staring at the red light, determined not to let my mind wander, and then I start wondering why red means "stop" and green means "go." Is there some optic science behind this color scheme? Is it arbitrary? Perhaps it derives from an ancient custom, the way the distance between railroad tracks is derived from the distance between the wheels on Roman carts. I think how sad and romantic street lights look when blurred in the rain, and how before electricity no one could experience that exact romantic sadness, because nothing could have looked like that. I savor the odd fact that a street scene that seems so old-fashioned now is actually a product of modernity, and then it hits me that this is the sort of idea my lover was always having, and I wonder if I will ever have my mind back wholly to myself or if I will always feel invaded, abandoned, bereft.

"Kahta," Ben says gently, "the light has been green for some time now. Please, go!"

My lover used to joke that I had missed my chance to rid myself of my former husband forever by failing to run him over while an unlicensed, inexperienced driver. Actually, my ex and I get on very well. He's an excellent father, and when I have a computer problem he helps me over the phone, although he refuses to come and fix the machine himself. Now when I am careering up Riverside Drive I sometimes fantasize that I see my lover and his new girlfriend in the crosswalk. I wave my arms helplessly as the car, taking on a life of its own, homes into them like a magnet smashing into a bar of iron. Sometimes I put the drab colleague in the crosswalk, too, and run all three of them down. No jury would believe it had been an accident, although Ben would surely testify in my favor. I'd go to jail for decades, and the case would be made into a movie for one of those cable channels for women—*Out of Control: The Katha Pollitt Story*. What a disappointing end to my struggle for personal growth! Yet one not without consolations: in jail, after all, I would not need to drive. I could settle into comfy middle age, reorganizing the prison library and becoming a lesbian.

Twelve years ago, I saw a therapist who urged me to learn to drive to set an example for my daughter, who was then a toddler. She pointed out that my mother had never learned to drive, and waited in silence, as they do, for me to see a connection. Well, it's obvious, isn't it? My mother was a kind of professional helpless person. If she was alone in the house and couldn't open a jar, she would take it to the corner bar and ask one of the drunks to open it for her. "Don't be like your mother," my father would say in exasperation when I displayed particular ineptitude in the face of the physical world. And, except for the matter of driving, I'm not. I'm meaner and stronger and I'm not drinking myself to death. I own a special tool for twisting recalcitrant lids. Unlike my mother, I can time a meal so that the rice, the meat, and the vegetables all come out ready together. But it's true that my culinary skills deteriorated precipitously while I was living with my former lover, a fabulous cook who had once prepared dinner for the mayor of Bologna and who took over the kitchen the minute he moved in. gradually, I forgot what I knew and lost the confidence to try new recipes, nor did I ever learn to use any of the numerous appliances he collected: the espresso machine with cappuccino attachment, the Cuisinart mini-prep, or the deep-fat fryer he bought the day after I said I was going on a diet.

My father made my mother sign up with a driving school. In fact, she was taking a lesson at the very moment word came over the car radio that President Kennedy had been shot. She claimed that this event so traumatized her that she could never get back behind the wheel. I didn't believe her—she'd never liked JFK, who had invaded Cuba and brought the world to the brink of nuclear war with the missile crisis. I think she was just afraid, the way I am—afraid of killing myself, afraid of killing someone else. I was fourteen when my mother gave up on her license, the same age that my daughter is now, but I give myself bonus points, because I'm still taking lessons. "You can do it, Mom," my daughter calls to me over her cereal when I dash out the door for my lesson. "Just keep your hands on the wheel." In a weak moment, I mentioned to her that sometimes at a red light I forget and put my hands in my lap—that would earn a warning from the examiner right there. I am trying to set her a good example, as that long-ago therapist urged—the example of a woman who does not fall apart because the man she loved lied to her every single minute of their life together and then left her for a woman young enough to be his daughter. "I'm going to be a little obsessed for a while," I told her. "I'm going to spend a lot of time talking on the phone with my friends and I may cry sometimes, but basically I'm fine. Also, I'm going on a huge diet, and I don't want any teenage anorexia from you."

"Mom!" She gave me the parents-are-weird eye-roll. The truth is though, she's proud of me. When I do something new—figure out what's wrong with the computer without having to call my ex-husband, or retake the big study I vacated for my lover when he moved in, or give away my schlumpy old fat clothes and buy a lot of beautiful velvet pants and tops in deep jewel colors—she pumps her arm and says, *"Mujer de metal!"*

Ben is not just a great driving instructor; he is an interesting conversationalist. On our long lessons, he tells me all about growing up in Manila: the beauty of going to Mass with his mother every day, and how sad it was to lose touch with his sisters when they married and became part of their husbands' families. When he says that he prays for me to pass the driving test, I am so moved—I picture him surrounded by clouds of incense and tropical flowers, dressed in ornate robes, like the Infant of Prague. "Do you think I'm a weird Asian, Kahta?" Ben asks me. "Not at all," I say firmly, although how could I tell? Ben is the only Asian I know. He tells me that Asians repress their anger—which makes me wonder if he is secretly angry at me for making so many mistakes—and that Westerners don't understand their jokes. I tell him that mostly I know about Asians from reading ancient Chinese poetry and the novels of Shusaku Endo. "What about the Kama Sutra?" he asks, and we laugh and insist we've never read it, never even looked at it, and then we laugh some more, because we know we are both lying. "See that pedestrian? He's Bob Marley's son," Ben says, pointing to a handsome young black man with short dreadlocks who's entering Riverside Church. And while I am wondering how Ben would know that—maybe Bob Jr. took lessons from him?—he cracks up: "You believed me!" Ben can be quite a humorist. And yet sometimes I worry about him, going home after a long day to his studio in Floral Park, Long Island. He's forty-four, and it will be years before he can marry his fiancée, who is forty and a schoolteacher back in the Philippines. When he gets home, he has three beers, which seems like a lot to drink alone. ("It used to be two, now three.") If I believed in God, I would pray for him— to get his own driving school, and be able to bring his fiancée over and move with her to a nice apartment in Castle Village, on the side that looks out over the river.

Some mornings, I know I mystify Ben. "Did you notice that hazard, Kahta? That double-parked SUV?" I admit I have no idea what he's talking about. "Always look ahead, Kahta. Look at the big picture, not just what's right in front of you. Observation!" Other days, though, I know I'm making progress. I zip up West End Avenue, enjoying the fresh green of the old plane trees and the early-morning quiet. I perform the physical work of driving, but with a kind of Zen dispersal of attention, so that as I am keeping an even pace and staying in my lane I am also noticing the bakery van signaling a right turn, and the dog walker hesitating on the curb with his cluster of chows and retrievers. A block ahead, I see a school bus stopping in front of the same Italianate apartment building where my daughter, my lover, and I used to wait for the bus when she was in elementary school, and I am already preparing to be careful and cautious, because you never know when a little child might dart out into the street. At that moment, it seems possible that I will pass the driving test, if not this time, then the next. One morning soon, I will put my license in my pocket, I will get into the car, turn the key, and enjoy the rumbly throat-clearing sound of the engine starting up. I will flick the turn signal down, so it makes that satisfying, precise click. I will pull out when I am ready and drive—it doesn't even matter where. I will make eye contact with pedestrians, I will be aware of cyclists coming up behind me; the smooth and confident trajectory of my vehicle will wordlessly convey to cabbies and Jersey drivers that they should keep at least three car lengths away, and more should it be raining. I will listen to my inner voice, I will look ahead to get the big picture, I will observe. I will beef-stew it. I will be *mujer de metal*.

1. This is a deeply personal account that nevertheless tries to make a larger point about being vulnerable, about the perils of being inadequately prepared for life's challenges. How well do you think it works on both these levels?
2. Would this be as effective if it were billed as fiction? Why or why not?
3. What devices does this writer use to retain our interest? What makes it a compelling narrative?

Glossary

ABSTRACT Possessing qualities apart from an object. Referring to intangible attributes, like love, death, happiness, rather than concrete ones, like frog, desk, or chair.

AMBIGUITY Allowing for multiple interpretations.

ANTICLIMAX The "falling action" that takes place after a climax. A sudden drop in tension, often unintentional.

ATMOSPHERE The mood of a piece, related to setting. It can include everything from descriptions of place, to weather, to time of day.

BACKSTORY The history of a character or characters as relevant to the present events of a story.

CHARACTER A made-up person. Considered one of the key ingredients of fiction.

CLICHÉ An overused, familiar phrase, often of figurative language, that has lost its ability to inform due to excessive use.

COMPLICATION Often used as a synonym for "conflict," that aspect of plot that creates tension and sustains the reader's interest, frequently leading to a climax, or epiphany.

CONCRETE DETAIL Particular material objects, rendered with one or more of the five senses. The opposite of ABSTRACT.

CONFLICT Tension arising from opposite forces that is considered necessary by some to sustain a reader's interest. Others feel that this word doesn't adequately describe all the nuanced ways in which a writer can hold the reader's attention.

CONVENTION An accepted means of expression within a particular form. A tried-and-true means of doing something in literature.

643

CREATIVE NONFICTION Fact-based writing that uses fictional techniques to bring the subject to life.

CRISIS Also known as the climax. The point in a narrative where things are at the highest point of tension. The moment after which nothing can ever be the same again.

DEAD METAPHOR a metaphor that has been so overused that it has sunk into our language; the comparison is no longer fresh or surprising. For example, "he ran for office" no longer evokes the image of someone actually running.

DENOUEMENT The falling action, following a climax or crisis, after which things in a narrative are resolved.

DIALOGUE Words spoken between characters in a scene. Specifically, words spoken between two or more characters.

DISTANCE The sense of how close (or far) the narrator is from the characters or the action in a narrative.

EPIPHANY A literary revelation, or lifting of appearances in order to reveal meaning and truth. A moment of realization by a character, or the reader, or both.

EXPOSITION Explanation, usually in narration, of information essential to the story.

FALLING ACTION Denouement, or the wrapping up of loose ends that follows the climax or crisis of a narrative.

FICTION Made-up events presented as if true in a narrative. Can be either a novel, a novella, or a short story.

FIGURATIVE LANGUAGE Expressing one thing in terms of something else. Major figurative language includes metaphor, simile, allegory, symbol, and personification.

FLASHBACK Scene of a prior event juxtaposed against a current scene. Usually triggered by a current event or by a character's memory.

FREEWRITE A kind of writing exercise when you don't think about a specific subject or worry about what comes next, but just write whatever comes into your head.

GENRE A literary form such as novel, short story, poem, or play.

IMAGE Anything that has been rendered by any one (or more) of the five senses. Images are the building blocks of both fiction and creative nonfiction.

IRONY An apparent contradiction or incongruity that dissembles or hides a "truth," not to deceive, but to achieve an effect. *Dramatic irony* is when the reader knows something the character doesn't.

MELODRAMATIC When action dominates over characterization. From the Greek "melo" for song; melodrama originally referred to any drama that was set to music.

METAPHOR Figurative language in which two unlike things are directly compared. "The dog days of August" is a metaphor.

NARRATIVE The events and characters that make up a story.

NARRATOR The intelligence that is telling the story. Can be first person, second person, or third person (see POINT OF VIEW).

NOVEL A work of prose of extended length.

OMNISCIENCE Knowing everything there is to know. An omniscient narrator is a godlike intelligence that knows everything about the universe of the story or novel.

PERSONIFICATION The technique of giving human traits to natural objects.

PLOT That series of events and/or actions that make up the story, arranged in a particular order, and told in a particular way by a narrator.

POINT OF VIEW The vantage point from which the events of the story or novel are narrated. Can be first person, second person, or third person.

RESOLUTION The denouement, or falling action. When the story's elements come together in an emotionally satisfying way.

SCENE Dramatic part of a story, taking place at a specific place at a specific time, between specific characters.

SENTIMENTALITY An excess of sentiment, or feeling, that hasn't been "earned" by a story or novel or nonfiction piece. A clichéd or overly familiar rendering of events or circumstances rather than a rendition that is fresh and surprising.

SETTING The place in which a story or novel takes place. The physical surroundings, as described by a narrator.

SIMILE A comparison of two unlike things, using "like" or "as." "My love is like a red red rose," and "She had a face as round and as innocent as a cabbage" are similes.

STEREOTYPE A clichéd character. A stock character, familiar to the reader through a standard set of traits. The whore with the heart of gold, or the browbeaten husband, are two examples of stock characters that appear in fiction as well as creative nonfiction.

STOCK CHARACTER See STEREOTYPE.

STORY A work of prose with no minimum length and (usually) not exceeding 20,000 words.

STYLE A particular writer's way of expressing himself or herself, dependent on such things as choice of point of view, syntax, or material he/she chooses to explore.

SUBTEXT Meaning that is implied rather than stated. All text has a subtext—the meaning that lies beneath the actual words.

SUSPENSE The state of being uncertain, unresolved. The sense that something of dramatic importance is about to happen.

SYMBOL A concrete object or image (something that can be rendered with the five senses) that stands for something larger than itself. The cross stands for Jesus, Christianity, and all its related tenets; the white whale, in *Moby-Dick*, stands for some forbidden thing that mankind should not attempt to pursue or possess.

TENSION The juxtaposition of two opposing forces.

VOICE The specific way that a writer has of putting his or her thoughts on paper. See STYLE.

Bibliography

Abbott, Jack Henry. *In the Belly of the Beast: Letters from Prison*. New York: Vintage, 1991.

Alvarez, Julia. "The Rudy Elmenhurst Story." In *How the Garcia Girls Lost Their Accents*. Chapel Hill, North Carolina: Algonquin Books, 1991.

Anderson, Sherwood. "Death in the Woods." In *Winesburg, Ohio*. New York: Bantam, 1995.

Anderson, Sherwood. "Hands." In *Winesburg, Ohio*. New York: Bantam, 1995.

Atwood, Margaret. "Significant Moments in the Life of My Mother." In *Bluebeard's Egg*. Toronto: McClelland & Stewart Bantam, 1983.

Austen, Jane. *Pride and Prejudice*. New York: Penguin, 1996.

Baldwin, James. "Sonny's Blues." In *Going to Meet the Man*. New York: Dial Press, 1965.

Barrie, James. *Peter Pan*. New York: Henry Holt & Co., 1987.

Barrie, James. *Peter Pan*. New York: Oxford University Press, Inc., 1995.

Barthelme, Donald. "Not Knowing." In *Not-Knowing: The Essays and Interviews of Donald Barthelme*. New York: Vintage, 1999.

Barthelme, Donald. "The Sandman." In *Sixty Stories*. New York: Penguin, 2003.

Bass, Rick. "An Oilman's Notebook." In *Oil Notes*. Dallas: Southern Methodist University Press, 1995.

Baxter, Charles. "Against Epiphanies." In *Burning Down the House: Essays on Fiction*. St. Paul, Minnesota: Graywolf Press, 1997.

Baxter, Charles. "On Defamiliarization." In *Burning Down the House: Essays on Fiction*. St. Paul, Minnesota: Graywolf Press, 1997.

Beattie, Ann. "The Cinderella Waltz." In *The Burning House*. New York: Vintage, 1995.

Beattie, Ann. "Find and Replace." In *Follies: New Stories*. New York: Scribner, 2005.

Beckett, Samuel. "Krapp's Last Tape." In *Krapp's Last Tape, and Other Dramatic Pieces*. New York: Grove Press, 1957.

Bell, Madison Smartt. *Narrative Design: A Writer's Guide to Structure*. New York: W. W. Norton & Co., 1997.

Berriault, Gina. "Who Is It Can Tell Me Who I Am?" In *Women in Their Beds*. Washington, D.C.: Counterpoint, 1996.

Bishop, Elizabeth. "Letter to NY (for Louise Crane)." In *The Complete Poems: 1927–1979*. New York: Farrar, Straus & Giroux, 1983.

Bowles, Jane. *Two Serious Ladies*. In *My Sister's Hand in Mine: The Collected Works of Jane Bowles*. New York: Farrar, Straus & Giroux, 1966.

Boyle, T. Coraghessan. "Friendly Skies." In *After the Plague and Other Stories*. New York: Viking Penguin, 2001.

Burgess, Anthony. *A Clockwork Orange*. New York: W. W. Norton & Co., 1962.

Busch, Frederick. "Ralph the Duck." In *Absent Friends*. New York: Alfred A. Knopf, 1989.

Carter, Angela, "The Company of Wolves." In *The Bloody Chamber*. New York: Penguin, 1990.

Carver, Raymond. "The Bath." In *What We Talk About When We Talk About Love*. New York: Alfred A. Knopf, 1981.

Carver, Raymond. "Cathedral." In *Cathedral*. New York: Alfred A. Knopf, 1983.

Carver, Raymond. *Fires*. New York: Vintage, 1989.

Carver, Raymond, "A Small, Good Thing." In *Cathedral*. New York: Alfred A. Knopf, 1983.

Cather, Willa. "Paul's Case: A Study in Temperament." In *The Troll Garden*. Edited by James Woodress. Lincoln, Nebraska: University of Nebraska Press, 2000.

Cheever, John. "Interview with John Cheever." In *Paris Review* 67, Fall 1976.

Cheever, John. *The Journals of John Cheever*. Edited by Susan Cheever. New York: Random House, 1995.

Cheever, John. "The Swimmer." In *The Stories of John Cheever*. New York: Alfred A. Knopf, 1978.

Cheever, John. "The Wrysons." In *The Stories of John Cheever*. New York: Alfred A. Knopf, 1978.

Chekhov, Anton. "The Lady with the Little Dog." In *Stories*. Translated by Richard Pevear and Larissa Volokhonsky. New York: Bantam, 2001.

Coe, Christopher. *I Look Divine*. New York: Random House, 1998.

Cooper, Bernard. "Winner Take Nothing." In *The Bill From My Father: A Memoir*. New York: Scribner, 2006.

Coppola, Eleanor. *Notes on the Making of Apocalypse Now*. New York: Simon & Schuster, 1979.

Costello, Mark. "Murphy's Xmas." In *The Murphy Stories*. Champaign, Illinois: Illini Books, 1973.

Crane, Stephen. "The Open Boat." In *The Open Boat and Other Stories*. New York: Doubleday & McClure, 1898.

Davies, Robertson. *Fifth Business*. New York: Penguin, 1977.

DeMarinis, Rick. *The Art and the Craft of the Short Story*. Cincinnati, Ohio: Story Press Books, 2000.

Díaz, Junot. "The Sun, the Moon, the Stars." In *The Best American Short Stories 1999*. Katrina Kenison and Amy Tan, eds. Boston: Houghton Mifflin Co., 1999.

Díaz, Junot. "Ysrael." In *Drown*. New York: Riverhead Books, 1996.

Didion, Joan. "On Keeping a Notebook." In *Slouching Toward Bethlehem*. New York: Farrar, Straus & Giroux, 1961.

Didion, Joan. *Salvador*. New York: Vintage, 1994.

DiPiero, W. S. "In the Flea Market of the Mind." In *New York Times Book Review*, March 8, 1998.

Dixon, Stephen. *Interstate*. New York: Owl Books, 1997.

Drabble, Margaret. *The Waterfall*. New York: Random House, 1969.

Dubus, Andre. "A Father's Story." In *Selected Stories*. Boston: David R. Godine, 1988.

Dybek, Stuart. "Pet Milk." In *Coast of Chicago*. New York: Alfred A. Knopf, 1990.

Dybek, Stuart. "We Didn't." In *I Sailed With Magellan*. New York: Picador, 2003.

Ehrenreich, Barbara. "Welcome to Cancerland." In *Harper's Magazine*, November 2001.

Ellison, Jan. "The Company of Men." In *New England Review*, Vol. 26, No. 4, 2005.

Ellison, Ralph. *Invisible Man*. New York: Random House, 1947.

Ellison, Ralph. "King of the Bingo Game." In *Tomorrow*, November 1944.

Erdrich, Louise. *Four Souls: A Novel*. New York: HarperCollins, 2004.

Eugenides, Jeffrey. *The Virgin Suicides*. New York: Warner Books, 1994.

Faulkner, William. *As I Lay Dying*. New York: Vintage, 1991.

Faulkner, William. "A Rose For Emily." In *The Collected Stories*. New York: Vintage, 1977.

Faulkner, William. *The Sound and the Fury*. New York: Vintage, 1991.

Fitzgerald, F. Scott. *The Great Gatsby*. New York: Scribner, 2003.

Flaubert, Gustave. "A Simple Heart." In *Three Tales*. Translated by Robert Baldick. London: Penguin, 1961.

Forché, Carolyn. "Emergence." In *The Grand Permission: New Writings on Poetics and Motherhood*. Patricia Dienstfrey and Brenda Hillman, eds. Middletown, Connecticut: Wesleyan University Press, 2003.

Ford, Richard. "Rock Springs." In *Rock Springs*. New York: Grove/Atlantic, 1987.

Forster, E. M. *Aspects of the Novel*. Orlando, Florida: Harcourt Inc., 1927.

Forster, E. M. *Howards End*. New York: Alfred A. Knopf, 1921.

Friend, Tad. "Copy Cats." In *The New Yorker*, September 14, 1998.

Gallant, Mavis. "Bernadette." In *My Heart Is Broken*. New York: Random House, 1964.

García Márquez, Gabriel. "The Handsomest Drowned Man in the World." In *Collected Stories*. New York: HarperCollins, 1984.

Gardner, John. *The Art of Fiction*. New York: Alfred A. Knopf, 1984.

Gass, William. "In the Heart of the Heart of the Country." In *In the Heart of the Heart of the Country and Other Stories*. Boston: David R. Godine, 1984.

Gawande, Atul. "Final Cut." In *The New Yorker*, March 19, 2001.

Gerard, Philip. "Taking Yourself Out of the Story: Narrative Stance and the Upright Pronoun." In *Writing Creative Nonfiction: Instruction and Insights from the Teachers of the Associated Writing Programs*. Carolyn Forché and Philip Gerard, eds. Cincinnati, Ohio: Story Press, 2001.

Glaspell, Susan. "A Jury of Her Peers." In *The Best Short Stories of 1917*. Edward J. O'Brien, ed. Boston: Small, Maynard & Co., 1918.

Godshalk, C. S. "The Wizard." In *Agni* 28, 1989.

Grant, Annette. "Interview with John Cheever." In *Paris Review* 67, Fall 1976.

Hanna, Barry. "Testimony of Pilot." In *Airships*. New York: Grove/Atlantic, 1970.

Hansen, Ron. "Nebraska." In *Nebraska: Stories*. New York: Grove/Atlantic, 1989.

Hass, Robert. *20th Century Pleasures*. New York: HarperCollins, 1984.

Hemingway, Ernest. "Hills Like White Elephants." In *Men Without Women*. New York: Scribner, 1927.

Hempel, Amy. "In the Cemetery Where Al Jolson Is Buried." In *Reasons to Live*. New York: Alfred A. Knopf, 1985.

Hillenbrand, Laura. "A Sudden Illness." In *The New Yorker*, July 7, 2003.

Hugo, Richard. *The Triggering Town*. New York: W. W. Norton & Co., 1979.

Isherwood, Christopher. "Goodbye to Berlin." In *Berlin Stories*. New York: New Directions, 1963.

James, Henry. "The Art of Fiction." In *Longman's Magazine* 4 (September 1884). Reprinted in *Partial Portraits*. New York: Macmillan, 1888.

James, Henry. "Four Meetings." In *Complete Stories: 1874–1884*. New York: Literary Classics of the United States, 1999.

Johnson, Denis. "Dirty Wedding." In *Jesus' Son*. New York: Farrar, Straus & Giroux, 1992.

Johnson, Denis. "Emergency." In *Jesus' Son*. New York: Farrar, Straus & Giroux, 1992.

Joyce, James. "Araby." In *Dubliners*. New York: Penguin, 2000.

Kafka, Franz. "The Metamorphosis." In *The Metamorphosis*. Translated and edited by Stanley Corngold. New York: Bantam, 1972.

Karr, Mary. *The Liar's Club: A Memoir*. New York: Penguin, 1998.

Kennedy, William. *Ironweed*. New York: Viking Penguin, 1983.

Kesey, Ken. *One Flew Over the Cuckoo's Nest*. New York: Viking, 1962.

Kincaid, Jamaica. "Girl." In *At the Bottom of the River*. New York: Farrar, Straus & Giroux, 1983.

Kingsolver, Barbara. *Animal Dreams*. New York: HarperCollins, 1990.

Kingston, Maxine Hong. "No Name Woman." In *The Woman Warrior: Memoir of a Girlhood Among Ghosts*. New York: Alfred A. Knopf, 1976.

Kittredge, William. "Redneck Secrets." In *Owning It All*. St. Paul, Minnesota: Graywolf Press, 2002.

Kotzwinkle, William. "Follow the Eagle." In *Elephant Bangs Train*. New York: Equinox, 1974.

Kramer, Mark. *Literary Journalism*. New York: Ballantine Books, 1995.

Lamott, Anne. "Shitty First Drafts." In *Bird by Bird: Some Instructions on Writing and Life*. New York: Pantheon, 1994.

Larkin, Philip. "The Pleasure Principle." In *Required Writing: Miscellaneous Pieces 1955–1982*. Ann Arbor, Michigan: University of Michigan Press, 1999.

Leavitt, David. "Territory." In *Family Dancing*. Boston: Houghton Mifflin Co., 1984.

Le Guin, Ursula K. "The New Atlantis." In *The Blind Geometer / The New Atlantis* (Tor Double Novel, No. 13). Stuttgart, Germany: Tor Books, 1989.

Lessing, Doris. "A Sunrise on the Veld." In *African Stories*. New York: Simon & Schuster, 1951.

Levy, Andrew. "The Anti-Jefferson." In *American Scholar*, Vol. 70, Spring 2001.

Lopate, Phillip. "Portrait of My Body." In *Portrait of My Body*. New York: Doubleday, 1996.

Lopate, Phillip. "Writing Personal Essays: On the Necessity of Turning Oneself Into a Character." In *Writing Creative Nonfiction: Instruction and Insights from the Teachers of the Associated Writing Programs*. Carolyn Forché and Philip Gerard, eds. Cincinnati, Ohio: Story Press, 2001.

Lopez, Barry. *Desert Notes*. New York: HarperCollins, 1990.

Lowry, Beverly. "The Shadow Knows." Originally published as "Patricide." In *Granta 47: Losers*, March 1, 1994.

Macauley, Robie, and George Lanning. *Technique in Fiction*. 2nd ed. New York: St. Martin's Press, 1990.

Madden, David. "No Trace." In *The Shadow Knows*. Baton Rouge, Louisiana: Louisiana State University Press, 1970.

Mamet, David. "The Museum of Science and Industry Story." In *Five Television Plays*. New York: Grove Press, 1990.

Mansfield, Katherine. "Bliss." In *Bliss and Other Stories*. Hertfordshire, Great Britain: Wordsworth, 1998.

Mansfield, Katherine. "Daughters of the Late Colonel." In *The Garden Party, and Other Stories*. New York: Alfred A. Knopf, 1922.

Matthiessen, Peter. *Far Tortuga: A Novel*. New York: Vintage, 1988.

Max, D. T. "The Carver Chronicles." In *New York Times Magazine*, August 9, 1998.

Maxwell, William. "The Thistles in Sweden." In *All the Days and Nights: The Collected Stories of William Maxwell*. New York: Alfred A. Knopf, 1995.

McConkey, James. *Court of Memory*. Boston: Nonpareil Books, 1993.

McInerney, Jay. *Bright Lights, Big City*. New York: Vintage, 1984.

McMurtry, Larry. *Terms of Endearment*. New York: Simon & Schuster, 1975.

Michaels, Leonard. "Journal Entries: 1976–1987." In *Our Private Lives: Journals, Notebooks, and Diaries*. Daniel Halpern, ed. New York: Ecco Press, 1988.

Milosz, Czeslaw. "In a Parish." Translated by Robert Haas. In *New and Collected Poems*. New York: HarperCollins, 2001.

Moore, Honor. *The White Blackbird: A Life of the Painter Margarett Sargent by Her Granddaughter*. New York: Penguin, 1997.

Moore, Lorrie. "How to Be a Writer." In *Self-Help*. New York: Alfred A. Knopf, 1985.

Moore, Lorrie. "People Like That Are the Only People Here: Canonical Babbling in Peed Onk." In *Birds of America*. New York: Alfred A. Knopf, 1998.

Mukherjee, Bharati. "The Management of Grief." In *The Middleman and Other Stories*. New York: Grove Press, 1988.

Mukherjee, Bharati. "The Tenant." In *The Middleman and Other Stories*. New York: Grove Press, 1988.

Munro, Alice. "Wild Swans." In *The Beggar Maid: Stories of Flo and Rose*. New York: Alfred A. Knopf, 1977.

Nabokov, Vladimir. *Lolita*. London: Everyman, 1992.

Nelson, Antonya. "Naked Ladies." In *Family Terrorists*. New York: Scribner, 1996.

Neubauer, Alexander. "A Conversation with Jane Smiley." In *Conversations on Writing Fiction: Interviews with Thirteen Distinguished Teachers of Fiction Writing in America*. New York: Perennial, 1994.

Nin, Anaïs. *The Diary of Anaïs Nin, Volume 3 (1939–1944)*. New York: Harvest/HBJ, 1971.

Oates, Joyce Carol. Introduction to *The Oxford Book of American Short Stories*. New York: Oxford University Press, 1994.

Oates, Joyce Carol. "Where Are You Going, Where Have You Been?" In *Where Are You Going, Where Have You Been? Stories of Young America*. Greenwich, Connecticut: Fawcett, 1974.

O'Brien, Tim. "The Things They Carried." In *The Things They Carried*. Boston: Houghton Mifflin Co., 1990.

O'Connor, Flannery. "Everything That Rises Must Converge." In *Everything That Rises Must Converge*. New York: Farrar, Straus & Giroux, 1965.

O'Connor, Flannery. "Writing Short Stories." In *Mystery and Manners: Occasional Prose*. Edited by Sally and Robert Fitzgerald. New York: Farrar, Straus & Giroux, 1969.

Offutt, Chris. *The Same River Twice: A Memoir*. New York: Simon & Schuster, 1993.

O'Hara, Frank. "Why I Am Not a Painter." In *The Collected Poems of Frank O'Hara*. Edited by Donald Allen. New York: Alfred A. Knopf, 1979.

Olds, Sharon. "Forty-One, Alone, No Gerbil." In *The Wellspring*. New York: Alfred A. Knopf, 1996.

Ondaatje, Michael. *The English Patient*. New York: Alfred A. Knopf, 1992.

Ondaatje, Michael. *Running in the Family*. New York: Vintage, 1993.

Ondaatje, Michael. "7 or 8 Things I Know About Her—A Stolen Biography." In *The Cinnamon Peeler*. New York: Alfred A. Knopf, 1989.

Packer, ZZ. "Brownies." In *Drinking Coffee Elsewhere*. New York: Riverhead Books, 2003.

Paley, Grace. "A Conversation With My Father." In *Enormous Changes at the Last Minute*. New York: Farrar, Straus & Giroux, 1974.

Paley, Grace. "Mother." In *Later the Same Day*. New York: Farrar, Straus & Giroux, 1985.

Pemberton, Gayle. "Do He Have Your Number, Mr. Jeffrey." In *The Hottest Water in Chicago*. London: Faber & Faber, 1992.

Phillips, Jayne Anne. "Souvenir." In *Black Tickets*. New York: Delacorte Press, 1979.

Plath, Sylvia. "Tulips." In *The Collected Poems*. Edited by Ted Hughes. New York: HarperCollins, 1981.

Pollitt, Katha. "Learning to Drive." *The New Yorker*, July 22, 2002.

Prose, Francine. "What Makes a Short Story?" In Tom Bailey, ed., *On Writing Short Stories*. New York: Oxford University Press, 1999.

Proulx, Annie. "Brokeback Mountain." In *Close Range: Wyoming Stories*. New York: Scribner, 2000.

Proulx, E. Annie. *The Shipping News*. New York: Touchstone Books, 1994.

Rhys, Jean. *Wide Sargasso Sea*. New York: W. W. Norton & Co., 1966.

Rich, Adrienne. "Split at the Root: An Essay on Jewish Identity." In *Blood, Bread, and Poetry: Selected Prose 1979–1985*. New York: W. W. Norton & Co., 1994.

Richards, I. M. *Practical Criticism: A Study of Literary Judgment*. Orlando, Florida: Harcourt, Brace, & Co., 1929.

Roth, Philip. *Patrimony: A True Story*. New York: Vintage, 1996.

Russell, Mark. "Spalding Gray: Artist's Notes." In *Out of Character: Rants, Raves, and Monologues from Today's Top Performance Artists*. New York: Bantam, 1996.

Sack, John. "Inside the Bunker." In *Esquire*, February 2001.

Sanders, Scott Russell. "Under the Influence." In *Secrets of the Universe: Scenes from the Journey Home*. New York: Beacon Press, 1992.

Schulman, Sarah. *After Delores*. New York: New American Library, 1989.

Scott, Paul. "Method: The Mystery and the Mechanics." In *On Writing and the Novel*. London: William Morrow & Co., 1987.

Selzer, Richard. "The Knife." In *The Exact Location of the Soul: New and Selected Essays*. New York: Picador, 2001.

Shakespeare, William. *The Complete Sonnets and Poems*. Edited by Colin Burrow. New York: Oxford University Press, 2002.

Shakespeare, William. *Hamlet*. New York: Washington Square Press, 2003.

Sharma, Akhil. "Surrounded by Sleep." In *The New Yorker*, December 13, 2001.

Shelton, Richard. "The Stones." In *Selected Poems 1969–1981*. Pittsburgh, Pennsylvania: University of Pittsburgh Press, 1982.

Shepard, Jim. "I Know Myself Real Well. That's the Problem." In *Bringing the Devil to His Knees: The Craft of Fiction and the Writing Life*. Charles Baxter and Peter Turchi, eds. Ann Arbor, Michigan: University of Michigan Press, 2004.

Smiley, Jane. "A Conversation with Jane Smiley." In Alexander Neubauer, *Conversations on Writing Fiction: Interviews with Thirteen Distinguished Teachers of Fiction Writing in America*. New York: HarperPerennial, 1994.

Smiley, Jane. *A Thousand Acres*. New York: Alfred A. Knopf, 1991.

Sontag, Susan. "Looking at War." In *Regarding the Pain of Others*. New York: Farrar, Straus & Giroux, 2003.

Spark, Muriel. *A Far Cry from Kensington*. New York: New Directions, 2000.

Stone, Robert. "Helping." In *Bear and His Daughter*. Boston: Houghton Mifflin Co., 1997.

Strayed, Cheryl. "The Love of My Life." In *The Sun*, September 2002.

Tan, Amy. *The Joy Luck Club*. New York: Penguin Putnam, 1989.

Tolstoy, Leo. *Anna Karenina*. Translated by Constance Garnett. New York: Random House, 1965.

Weldon, Fay. *Remember Me*. London: Hodder & Stoughton, 1976.

Wideman, John Edgar. *Brothers and Keepers: A Memoir*. Boston: Houghton Mifflin Co., 1984.

Williams, Joy. "Taking Care." In *Taking Care*. New York: Random House, 1982.

Wolff, Tobias. "The Rich Brother." In *Back in the World*. Boston: Houghton Mifflin Co., 1985.

Wolff, Tobias. *This Boy's Life*. New York: Grove/Atlantic, 1989.

Wolff, Tobias. "What Is a Short Short?" In *Sudden Fiction: American Short Short Stories*. Robert Shapard and James Thomas, eds. Layton, Utah: Gibbs M. Smith, 1986.

Wolfson, Penny. "Moonrise." In *Moonrise: One Family, Genetic Identity, and Muscular Dystrophy*. New York: St. Martin's Press, 2003.

Woolf, Virginia. *The Years*. Orlando, Florida: Harcourt, Brace, & Co., 1937.

Wright, C. D. "Scratch Music." In *Steal Away: Selected and New Poems*. Port Townsend, Washington: Copper Canyon Press, 2002.

List of Stories

Permissions

Index